COMPLETE
POEMS & SONGS
of

ROBERT BURNS

COMPLETE
POEMS & SONGS
of

ROBERT
BURNS

HarperCollins*Publishers*

This edition produced for The Book People Ltd, Hall Wood Avenue, Haydock, St Helens, WA11 9UL

HarperCollins*Publishers*
P.O. Box, Glasgow G4 0NB

The James Barke edition of the Poems and Songs of Robert Burns first published 1955. This edition first published 1995.

ISBN 0 00 760489 0
Reprint 10 9 8 7 6 5 4 3 2 1 0

A catalogue record for this book is available from the British Library.

Typeset in Ehrhardt by
Morton Word Processing Ltd,
Douglas House, 4 Belgrave Crescent,
Scarborough YO11 1UB.

Printed in Great Britain by
Omnia Books Limited, Glasgow

INTRODUCTION TO THE 1995 EDITION

by JOHN CAIRNEY

James Barke ended his Introduction to the 1990 reprint of this most popular edition of Burns by paying proper tribute to the collaboration he enjoyed with his wife in the preparation of the original edition in 1955. That this was most fitting no one would gainsay, therefore I feel it might be apt to begin by confessing that the same Mrs Barke once hit me with an umbrella on the steps of an office in St Vincent Place, Glasgow. It was in the late sixties and I was then appearing as Robert Burns in a weekly serial based on his life as well as touring the country in a stage version by Tom Wright called *There Was A Man*. I also had a best-selling L.P. of the show on the market and I think Mrs Barke has the justifiable view that perhaps there was a bit too much of Cairney as Burns; and what was even worse, I should also be making money out of it, especially as her own Jimmy had made so little in comparison. 'And who knows more about him?' she protested. Who indeed?

James Barke (1905-58) was ideally suited to introduce the poems and songs of Robert Burns to a popular audience because his five-book series, *The Immortal Memory* (also published by Collins) and based on Burns's life and loves, was issued to commemorate the 150th anniversary of the printing of the Kilmarnock Edition in 1786. These books probably did more to bring a sense of Burns as a man to ordinary readers than anything written since the poet's own lifetime. Beginning with *The Wind That Shakes the Barley* in 1946 it continued with *The Song in the Green Thorn Tree* (1947), *The Wonder of All the Gay World* (1948), *The Crest of the Broken Wave* (1953) and ended with *The Well of the Silent Harp* in 1954. Each volume was a bestseller in its own right. The biographies served their time as well as their subject and the set joined the Bible in the cupboard of thousands of Scottish homes. My father had his and through them I met Burns for the first time.

How then does Barke serve Burns in the present edition? The immediate answer is that it has been in continuous reprint since it was first published and is still one of the most complete and authoritative collections of Burns's poems and songs in this range. It probably says more about the man than many bulkier tomes given over to exhaustive detail or exhausting hagiography. Since the poet's death in 1796, books on Burns have featured, along with whisky and footballers, as one of Scotland's most consistent growth industries. The supply never seems to dry up. As early as 1828, Thomas Carlyle reassured Lockhart that yet another Burns biography was acceptable because the theme would never become trite. It was the manner of the performance that counted.

That same criterion must now apply to James Barke.

There have been other good editions of the poems and songs — James Kinsley's in 1959 and Alan Bold's in 1993 are two which come at once to mind. There was also David Daiches's 1971 study of *Robert Burns and his World* as well as James Mackay's editions of the *Works* and *Letters* culminating in the comprehensive *Life* in 1992 all of which are illuminating as far as the poems and songs are concerned and succeed as well in throwing fresh light on the man. Nevertheless, as Mackay rightly says, we can be sure they will not be the last word on the subject. Indeed, the final word on Burns may never be written because the man, the life and the work will continue to fascinate and draw speculation, excite interest and incite contradiction. As a result, where two or more Scots are gathered together they are as likely to form a Burns Club as a church, for his star still pulls them powerfully.

He is as much a Scottish hero as William Wallace or Robert Bruce, and has assumed the same mythological perspective in Scottish history and tradition. No other writer in any other country has attained the same supra-literary level in the consciousness of a nation. Burns has gone beyond posthumous fame and through the haze of mere legend to become a continuing dynamic in the contemporary Scottish psyche. Yet he never fought a battle, signed a treaty, invented a machine, discovered a cure or did anything that makes a public figure of a private man.

One book, and a slim volume at that — 'One Volume, Octavo, Price Stitched, Three Shillings' — printed at Kilmarnock on 31 July 1786, was enough to cause an immediate sensation in Ayrshire, then in Edinburgh, then in London and around the globe. One wee book, and it spawned a legion of successive editions, companions, concordances, commentaries and miscellaneous Burnsiana. The same book was enough to lift Robert Burns from rural obscurity in 18th-century Scotland to a giant's status in world literature. It is an incredible metamorphosis. Professor Kinsley makes the point, in the Preface to his 1969 edition, that the canon of Burns's work will never be fully established:

> The core is firm enough; it consists mainly of the Kilmarnock and Edinburgh editions, the signed contributions made to the four volumes of *The Scots Musical Museum* which appeared in his lifetime, and original poems which were unpublished at his death but survive in holograph.'

It has become apparent to Burns scholars, such as Kinsley, Dr David Daiches (perhaps the best commentator on Burns's songs) and Mackay, that not only is Burns holding his ground as a poet of the first rank, he is gaining the same as a songwriter without peer. No less an Englishman than W.E. Henley called Burns 'the most exquisite artist in folk-song the world has ever seen'.

The same Henley, writing in the Preface to his 1896 four-volume edition of *The Poetry of Robert Burns* states:

> 'Genius apart ... he is *ultimus Scotorum*, the last expression of the old Scots world, and therewith the culmination of a school deep-rooted in the past, which by producing such as Dunbar and Scott and Alexander Montgomerie, as Ramsay and Fergusson and the nameless lyricists of the song-books, made it possible for him to be.'

Acknowledging this formidable ancestry, one can consider the poems in the light of their time and place. Everything is here to help the reader understand why Burns has reached the pre-eminence he has as a poet. We can also see for ourselves the extent of the poetic heritage he has left to posterity. What is much less easy to discover is the man behind the legend.

A man who happened out of a remote corner of Scotland in the poorer, northern half of a presumptuous little island broken off from the continent of Europe, and at a time when Scotland itself was having to adjust to becoming North Britain after the scandalous and shameful Union of the Parliament in 1707. It was almost as if this farmer's son from Ayrshire, like some obscure Messiah, had been posted at exactly that point in time to remind the ordinary people of Scotland (who were to read him first) of who they were and what they had been before the then emerging industrial age would convert them into a formless part of the faceless mass. This is what warms a good socialist like Barke to him. Robert Burns could be nothing else than egalitarian because for him nothing in his life was equal to the enormity of his talent.

Artistically, he stood at the watershed in the great tide of change that was sweeping over the new Britain at that time. Revolution was in the air but the ground was thick with entrenched prejudice. The old order was not going to give in easily and Burns himself was unhappily poised with one foot in each camp. Like Janus, he pointed both ways — backwards to the ancient traditions and values, forward towards the Age of the Enlightenment and the beginning of modernity. His work, as well as his personal attitudes, reflect this:

> 'Wha will not sing 'God Save the King'
> Shall hang as high as the steeple;
> But while we sing 'God save the King',
> Let's not forget the people'!

Burns took to writing as a way of life because life itself offered him no favours and he saw poetry first as a way out and up. His first book was ostensibly intended only to raise funds for a flight to the West Indies, but I think that what he really wanted to know was the feel of his own book in his hand, to know that he was a 'poet in print' at last. It is a feeling any writer knows.

> 'That I, for dear, old Scotland's sake,
> Some usefu' plan or book could make,
> Or sing a sang at least ...'

He knew what his destiny was but he also knew he had been born to the wrong parents for such a dream. Lines of demarcation among the classes were very clear between 1759 and 1786, especially in rural Scotland and the son of a failed farmer and the daughter of a smuggler's family did not start with any great advantage. On the contrary, he began with everything against him. There was a fatalism among the labouring classes of the day which deemed God had fashioned the better classes from a finer quality of dust and from the dross he threw together the ever-present poor. The Divine Right that had sustained a line of kings had dwindled to a pre-ordained pecking order that placed the most minor of gentry always a forelock's tug away from the peasantry. Everyone knew their place and Burns was supposed to know his, but the rightful place he knew to be his was not that which was his birthright.

Burns however had been born with an 'independent thought' in his mind which allowed him to aim for a head-high place among equals and he knew his writing was the one weapon he had to break down the barriers that thrust him back among the proletariat. In many ways, he was a snob and an opportunist but one could hardly blame him. It must have been galling for a man of his gifts to have to defer to men of obviously lesser calibre merely because they had been born into privilege just as he had been into penury. Not for young Burns, the true aristocracy of the arts which we know in our own day when talent buys its own place in the market-place and the artist is respected and revered for his skills and flair and rewarded accordingly. Instead of a series of assorted sponsors, what might Burns have done had he had serious sponsorship on the scale we know today?

His strength of personality carried him far into society but his weaknesses brought him down. These were not weaknesses of character nor were they merely the weaknesses of the flesh. The attractive but flawed body cracked, the winning personality was warped by continued frustration and he died prematurely of social fatigue, artistic neglect and doctors' guesses. Yet he was bursting with song at the time and at the very height of his poetic powers.

The demands made by a stringent boyhood had to be met and the price was an early death. His body succumbed to what had been thirty-seven years of slow wastage. Headaches, fevers, colic disorders and poor teeth were recurring symptoms throughout his life and point to the physical strains and possible malnutrition he had endured from his youth. How had he survived? He was saved by his ability to write, by his unashamed joy in arranging words on paper. This facility offered the first escape from animal drudgery and he took it with both hands.

> 'I never thought to turn poet till I got heartily in Love, then Rhyme and Song were, in a manner, the spontaneous language of my heart ...'

He knew that he had no option but to write and he did so everywhere and anywhere — by the side of rig, in the barn, by the burn and even by the light of a tallow candle in the attic room he shared with his stoic brother, Gilbert, and the rats who squeaked from the beams above their heads. The words poured from him and even before he was read by the gentry, his lines were devoured by his fellow-labourers who had them read to them in the field and in the tavern. Burns was already on his way to unbelievable contemporary fame and in these first moves to find a local audience he had taken the first steps towards Parnassus. When he entered Edinburgh for the first time, he could have done so with palm leaves under his feet. He was twenty-six, darkly handsome, articulate and agog.

In his annus mirabilis of 1786 he was carried on its wave to instant fame in his own country and to eventual immortality as a Scottish national icon. It says much for his durability as a poet and song-maker that he has survived all the incoming tides of excessive admiration and the outgoing bore that often carries with it the best of the artist. Reaction and counteraction are concomitants of any posthumous fame. Somehow he has stayed firm in the frame no matter how many gaudy prints and reproductions are thrown on the market in each succeeding generation. The man is in all he wrote and it is there for all to see in the pages of this book. For instance —

P13   *The Twa Dogs* is a brilliant satire on the two Scotlands represented by a
       pair of very different dogs. This is first class character drawing. Both of
       these dogs bite.

P73   *The Auld Farmer's New-Year Morning Salutation to his Auld Mare,*
       Maggie. (The sheer impertinence of the length of title is disarming).
       What underlies it, however, is the same breadth of humanity that in-
       forms *Poor Maillie's Elegy, To a Mouse, To A Louse* and *On Seeing A*
       Wounded Hair Limp by me. Only a true countryman could have penned
       these.

P112   *Epistle to J. Lapraik* is only one of several verse epistles, a genre Burns
       made into an art form. Here was the voice of the man himself talking
       directly across the table although one didn't always have to believe him
       when he says things like—
       'I am nae poet, in a sense;
       But just a rhymer like by chance,
       An' hae to learning nae pretence;
       Yet, what the matter?
       Whene'er my Muse does on me glance,
       I jingle at her.'
       Even if his tongue is in his cheek, the style is easy, fluid and seemingly
       artless. One feels he could go on like this for hours. This he did on oc-
       casions, but in these gentle exercises in philosophical correspondence,
       he was laying the foundations for what would later be his masterpiece,
       Tam O'Shanter (p180).

Written in the wonderful surge of one glorious day at Ellisland it was no
doubt tidied up at leisure and written out again with relish. It has everything
in it; comedy, pathos, colour, suspense and excitement and rolls along with
the seemless inevitability of a work that almost writes itself, so sure is the
hand of the pictures it sees. One can hear the clatter of hooves among the
syllables. This is Robert Burns as virtual playwright, not unexpected from the
author of *Love and Liberty, The Holy Fair* and *The Cotter's Saturday Night*,
which in many ways are plays in themselves. Burns loved to attend the theatre
in Dumfries. After all, he was something of a role-player himself in real life.

> 'He assumed the persona of the peasant poet with a minimum of ar-
> tifice. He found himself on the stage; he did not have to take it from
> the wings. He was part of, and wrote for the rural community which
> made and preserved the old balladry and folk-song, and it is from this
> sympathy in thought and feel as much as from genius and craft, that
> the vigour, precision and immediacy of his poetic language are de-
> rived.'

There may be something of the same histrionic impulse behind his Great
Lover image, his Drunkard façade, his super-Patriot pose, his superficial

aspirations to Country Gentleman. All these postures were extra to his essential reality, prismatic glimpses of a complex and unique man who also happened to be a genius. In the end, that is really all that matters. Everything else is immaterial. At the final count, only the work stands.

The lyrics quoted for the songs — and one can choose one's own favourites among them — represent a genius at work with words and feeling and the best of them deserve their confirmed place in the canon of world song. What is particularly remarkable about them is that they show that Burns was as much a musician as he was a lyricist. He was a genuine singer of his own songs because the man had music in him. It was not that he could literally sing but that he made the words themselves sing. He never technically composed but he knew how to 'take down' a song and, more importantly, what of it to take down.

All his instincts were towards minstrelsy and it was this which embodied his true romanticism. He reached back through the centuries and plucked a fragment from oblivion, breathed on it and sent it out into the air again as a new song. Most of these songs still survive. They are not art songs; they are the genuine product of the people for the people and his skill was in recognising what was lasting in them. By tying imperishable words to ancient airs he made in the fusion, unforgettable songs. In them it may be said that the poet and people are one.

Songmaking for Burns was just another aspect of his life-long love affair with words. Like all great artists, Burns was a realist, a practical worker in the field of words. This was shown in his letters, in his everyday conversation, (his very talk was masterly). He had all the resiliance of his own inner certainty. He knew he was good but he had always to be at pains to prove it because his status as an artist always stretched far beyond his social station. This was a problem to a vigorous, independent individual whose social posture was expected to be the bowed head, if not the bended knee. He found kneeling difficult.

His playing the agricultural oaf to the aristocratic ninnies when required was only another of his several 'performances'. He had sold the literati of his own day the idea that he was no more than a rough, peasant poet visited magically at the plough by the Muses who dictated their verse to his untutored hand.

> 'She bade me sing the rural scenes and the rural pleasures of my natal soil, in my native tongue; I tuned my wild, artless notes, as she inspired.'

This was so much rubbish but it was an image he found hard to live down. No hand could have been less untutored nor was his verse anything other than considered, well-worked and painstakingly revised as any study of the holographs and transcripts will show. They are full of autographed corrections. He was not a born writer but, like Stevenson, he made himself a writer by reading and then copying styles until he had found his own. Then there was no stopping him. He wrote everywhere and anywhere, not only on paper but on window panes, on bank-notes, even on a glass goblet. Burns taught himself to write, doggedly and assiduously from the first day he took a quill in his hand to his last, when it dropped from his fingers.

Single-handedly, he saved a whole body of Scottish song for posterity and in doing so gave the world its accepted anthem, however much it has since been traduced at Arts Balls and New Year parties. Yet who knows much of the young man who wrote *Auld Lang Syne*. Still fewer know what these words mean or what the sense of them is to a Scot. It's more than a question of translation. 'Old Long Since' is meaningless, but a remembering of things past is meaningful to any nationality especially where it touches on family and kin because that is what we really are. Self-memories are more than a manifestation of sentimental nostalgia. They are all part of the celebration of survival and an affirmation of continuity in the physical fact of family and heredity. We are made to realize that none of us is alone. Burns knew this, which is why he goes right to the heart of our common humanity in virtually every line he writes.

Concentrating as he does on the particular of any life situation, he reveals its generality and thus its universality. This is why he is not only Scotland's poet but the world's. His mouse and his louse are international, his bastard wean is a cosmopolitan, Holy Willie Fisher still lives in his hypocrisy and marriages are made for such as John Anderson, even today. His love songs are for all time and speak for anyone who has ever been young. These things are the work of genius — a genius that remains an enigma swathed in myth. An incalculable genetic factor gave him something that is inexplicable, unfathomable and in the end, immaterial. But it gave us Robert Burns. Let us therefore step back from him a bit. His light is too strong for our gaze. We can only diminish him if we try to see him through our own eyes. We must allow genius its size and power — and mystery. Burns is as easily explained as Mozart is, with whom his life had so many parallels. "Genius is not something that comes in the post," as poor old McGonagall used to say. We do not know what makes a Picasso or an Einstein or a Mahler so we have to take them on trust. By their works so shall ye know them ...

What Robert Burns was, is, and always will be, lies somewhere between Pages 1 and 704 of this book and the reader must make his own search and come to his own conclusions. On any page will be found either a smile, a nod of agreement, a stilling thought, a gasp of wonder. It is all there.
One only has to turn the pages.

One of the great Burns admirers, and arguably the greatest Scottish poet since Burns himself, was Hugh MacDiarmid who held that one line from one of Burns's earliest songs, *Mary Morrison*, was worth any other love song. The line was —
'You are na' Mary Morrison ...'

MacDiarmid gives us however, a salutary reminder in his own monumental *A Drunk Man Looks At The Thistle*:

> 'No' wan in fifty kens a wurd Burns wrote
> But misapplied is a 'body's property
> And gin there was his like alive the day
> They'd be the last a kennin' haund to gie.'

Robert Burns is alive and well and living in every reader. What more could any writer ask? And what more could Jimmy Barke deserve than that a lifetime of loving research should culminate not only in his ground-breaking novels but in an elegant volume which reflects not only such scholarship but an understanding of the genius that was Burns. One feels that Mr Barke may have caught something of the divine sickness himself.

Finally, it might be mentioned that the writer and editor, James Barke, was also an amateur actor with the famous Unity Theatre in Glasgow during the Second World War. This link with theatre and our editor prompts the following anecdote:

Sometime in the late sixties, a debate was held in a Working Mens' Club in Bathgate, a mining village between Glasgow and Edinburgh. Shades of the Bachelors' Club in Tarbolton.

The motion presented was —

'That the writer James Barke has contributed more towards an understanding of Robert Burns in our own times through his sequence of novels on the life and loves of Burns than John Cairney, the actor who has played the part of Robert Burns in the theatre and on television'.

The motion was carried.

Mrs Barke would have been delighted.

So too, one feels, would have been our mutual hero.

I commend this volume heartfully.

JOHN CAIRNEY has acted on both stage and screen, probably best known for his solo performance of Robert Burns in Tom Wright's 'There Was A Man' and in his own version of 'The Robert Burns Story'. He is in constant demand as a lecturer and writer on the poet and his own autobiography 'The Man Who Played Robert Burns' (Mainstream Publishing, Edinburgh) was published in 1987. He obtained the degree of M. Litt. from Glasgow University in 1988 and was later awarded a PhD from Victoria University, New Zealand for his thesis on the theatricality of Robert Louis Stevenson.

INTRODUCTION TO THE 1955 EDITION

by JAMES BARKE

ROBERT BURNS was born on 25th January, 1759, at Alloway in Ayrshire, and died on 21st July, 1796, at Dumfries.

His father was a working gardener from south of Stonehaven, in Kincardineshire. He was a hard-working man with high ideals about human worth and conduct. By precept and example, he had much to do with Robert's education and upbringing.

By modern standards, Robert had the sketchiest of education. But at an early age he was proficient in the three Rs and well grounded in the principles of Presbyterian theology. He read what he could lay his hands on and understood what he read.

The only mystery concerning Burns, whether in boyhood or manhood, is that of the quality of his genius.

He belongs to the company of the supremely great—Beethoven, Shakespeare, Rembrandt ...

He could read and write and remember. He was surcharged with emotion, awareness, sensibility. And despite his background and foreground of poverty and hunger and never-ceasing toil, he could laugh. He relished the gift of life as few mortals have. He paid a terrible price for this quality of enjoyment; but he paid it gladly enough. He accepted the penalties imposed by necessity.

Early, too early for his growing, undernourished body, he was at the plough and executing the orra work about a poor, under-capitalised farm. He strained his heart; he became subject to bouts of rheumatic fever or something akin to that baffling ailment.

He laboured on Mount Oliphant. He laboured on Lochlea. When his father died there, prematurely worn out and exhausted (Burns was then twenty-four years of age) he, together with his brother Gilbert, rented the farm of Mossgiel near Mauchline.

Mossgiel was doomed to failure not because Robert or Gilbert were bad farmers, but because they hadn't the necessary minimum of capital to work it economically.

But, brose-and-bannock toil apart, Robert Burns was a genius who expressed himself in poetry. As poet he could not be suppressed. As poet he triumphed. His was by no means an easy triumph—but then few triumphs of the first order are ever easy.

It was the nature of Robert Burns's experience that conditioned his poetry. He knew the nature of man and woman opposed to the bare elements of existence. His experience, if searing, was fundamental and therefore universal.

It is this supreme quality that makes Burns the first world-poet. Burns embraces all humanity. Humanity has, in turn, embraced him. So close (to give a random example) is he to Chinese thought and feeling that the Chinese have suggested that he was of their race. French, Germans, Italians, Austrians, Russians, Americans, have claimed him as their own. The unco guid, the rigidly righteous, the Holy Willies, the Hornbooks, the Cotters, the Man made to Mourn, the Mouse—none of these is exclusive to eighteenth-century Ayrshire. They are universal and timeless.

Burns wrote of them for the most part in the Scottish dialect—a dialect of the great English tongue; and yet a dialect that generations of nobly-gifted Scots have raised to the dignity of a language in its own right.

We remain baffled to know *how* he did what he did. No academic analysis of his poems and songs in relation to their metre or their antecedents tells us anything of other than purely academic interest.

An understanding of his background, his foreground and his times is not without value. But it is mainly in relation to the dominating circumstances of this time, against which Burns and his contemporaries moved, that he can best be understood.

Basically, Burns was a humanitarian. Thus he was a libertarian and equalitarian. Actually, as his *Love and Liberty* shows, he was something more—and the world has yet to catch up on that something more.

Overall, his sympathies were for the poor, the oppressed; and his sympathy extended to the animal kingdom—to the mouse, the auld mare, the wounded hare .... He hated all manner of cruelty, oppression and the arrogance of privilege and mere wealth.

But many other worthy poets have had similar feelings. This in itself is not enough. Burns could look and laugh at a' that. His laughter, however, is as broad as his humanity and there is no bitterness, no malice in his laughter. He laughs with life: never against it.

Burns is universal; but in his universality he is unique. There is no other poet like him. And thus, in a peculiar sense, he isn't a poet at all. He had no predecessors: he has had no disciples; and he is much too gigantic, too overflowing at too many points to be neatly, adequately or illuminatingly categorised, labelled and filed away.

Explain the mystery, the ramifications of human life, love, emotion and intellect and you can explain Robert Burns: not otherwise.

Burns's love for his fellowmen, for humanity, is all-embracing—and this despite the fact that his awareness is such that no other poet has shown such insight into the meanness, the cruelties and the follies of mankind. He is nothing of a sentimentalist.

He also loved women in the particular. He loved many women in his lifetime. Of his fifteen children, nine were born in "lawful wedlock". But in no sense was Burns a libertine. Of no other man is it recorded that he looked upon the children he fathered in or out of wedlock as his, and not the mother's, responsibility. Burns was supremely conscious of the glory of parenthood—legitimacy or illegitimacy were meaningless words to him: he spat the morality that begot them out of his mouth.

The supreme love of his life was Jean Armour, whom he married at the age of twenty-six. It was a supremely happy and altogether fortunate marriage, even if the early years were chequered by circumstances beyond the control of either.

In 1786, while at Mossgiel, and in anticipation of emigrating to the Indies, his first volume of poems and songs was published. It was an immediate success. He was read by high and low alike.

Instead of going to the Indies, he went to Edinburgh and within a few days was acclaimed as one of the wonders of the world.

A new and enlarged edition of his poems resulted. He toured Scotland in triumph—as Caledonia's Bard.

But he endured all this without affectation or illusion. His feet remained firmly on the earth. The pattern of life in Edinburgh or elsewhere in Scotland differed in no essential from the pattern of the small Ayrshire parish. The world of men revolves on the axis of the parish pump.

After Edinburgh, there remained the problem (as ever) of earning a living. He set up as tenant-farmer in Ellisland at Dumfries. Again he was without sufficient capital to see him over the inevitable rainy day.

So he entered the Excise service as a common gauger at £50 a year. In a short space of time he rose to a foot-walk in Dumfries at £70 a year. He was an excellent farmer: he made a good Exciseman.

But he was fundamentally a poet. He could not suppress the poet in him. By having some good friends "in court" he escaped being sent to Botany Bay for treason, sedition and sympathy with the British Reform movement—a by-product of the French Revolution. *Scots Wha hae*, for example, had to be published anonymously. So savage was reaction in the saddle that William Blake observed that to defend the Bible would cost a man his life.

His public work continued, however, and he laboured (unpaid) to supply "words and music" for the collections of James Johnson and George Thomson. In a very real sense Burns was as great a musician as he was a poet.

He dedicated himself to rescuing from oblivion and neglect hundreds of songs without words—or with fragmentary or unsuitable words. He knew that a song without words dies. In supplying words to fit the melodies, he performed a feat unique in the history of art. And the fact that he produced some hundreds of songs in his Dumfries days is a noble tribute to his unflagging energy and dedicated labour.

But the flawed heart from the Mount Oliphant days, and the recurring bouts of rheumatic fever, took their toll. He died at the age of thirty-seven in the direst of poverty and haunted by the threat of a debtors' gaol. On the day of his funeral his widow, in childbed, was literally without a shilling.

He was given a grandiose military funeral with an instrumental band playing the "Dead March in Saul". As a "turn out" it was one of the most extraordinary known to history. Had the military not been present, the "turn out" might have been even more extraordinary.

2

Burns was a genius: a many-sided genius. Despite the fact that he is the most universally-loved poet, he has yet to come into his own. There is no more flaming satire than *Holy Willie's Prayer*. There is no greater tale than *Tam o' Shanter*. If *A Man's a Man for a' that* is the Marseillaise of humanity, *Auld Lang Syne* is the world's "national" anthem. There is no more tender love song than *O, My Luve's like a red, red rose*. There is no finer epistle than *The Epistle to Davie*. There is nothing in world literature to equal the shattering, liberating cosmology of *Love and Liberty* ... The list could be extended.

The poet who laughed the Devil out of Hell (and—more difficult—banished him from Scots Presbyterian theology) and then took pity on him; the poet who asserted that the "light that led astray was light from Heaven", can be measured by no yard-stick known to letters. He is the first poet of common humanity: he is the first poet to transcend poetry.

Just as there can be no greater musician than Beethoven, there can be no greater poet than Burns. Before either can be surpassed, a new race will have to be born—a different and greater species than the *homo sapiens* hitherto known to history.

Should such a "new species" come to redeem the faults and failings of our common clay, Burns will be honoured as one of the greatest to predict such a possibility. For in a world corrupted, bedevilled and bewildered, Burns firmly believed in the perfectibility of the human race.

This may seem a dubious virtue to readers living in the middle of the twentieth century.

For all those who, whatever their faith or lack of faith, respond to the evocations of ordinary mortality, the following pages will give a lifetime of pleasure, inspiration, hope and courage—and the joy of being alive in a world shot through with terror and darkness and fear. It was in such a world that Burns wrote:

"It's coming yet, for a' that, that man to man the world o'er, shall brithers be for a' that." Who are we to say he sang in vain?

Certainly Burns is not for those who mourn, are faint-hearted, lack faith in humanity, or put their trust in legislators; who love without passion and who hate without compassion; who belittle the struggle of man against the Unknown and who blaspheme against the gift of life and put their trust in party politicians. Burns's poems and songs sing of the richness and strangeness and wonder of life. He did not write for those of little faith. Above all, he wrote for those who know that:

"The heart ay's the part ay that makes us right or wrang."

If Shakespeare (for example) be regarded as the poet who scaled the highest peaks of poetic attainment, few will dispute his unique honour and splendour and glory. But mankind cannot dwell on such peaks of rarefied experience: few indeed ever reach the plodding foothills ...

But Burns may be likened to the broad rolling plain of mankind's triumph and travail. For here mankind weep and mourn, sing and rejoice, are born and beget their kind and die. In every stage of the journey from the cradle to the grave, Burns is triumphantly articulate.

3

This edition of Burns owes everything to the work of previous editors of Burns. It does not claim to be definitive or immaculate. What it does do is to give the reader the most complete text of Burns's poems and songs so far presented to the public. Many poems and songs are here collected for the first time. The edition is, therefore, the most complete to date.

An index to the titles and first lines is provided as the easiest method of identification. No attempt has been made here to supply a "critical apparatus" of notes. This would require a volume to itself. What cannot be understood must be skipped. But the bulk of Burns's works needs no elucidation: his general purport is always crystal clear. Nevertheless, a marginal glossary and an alphabetical glossary are included for the convenience of such readers as may care to consult them.

Where possible, the names of the tunes to which Burns wrote his words are given.

Doubtless a few more poems may yet come to light; and building on J. C. Dick, a deeper research into the songs and melodies of the eighteenth and earlier centuries may reveal some hitherto unsuspected songs "mended" by Burns.

But, for the most part, what future research or accident may reveal is not likely to detract from Burns's output: to enhance it in any way is not possible.

A number of items usually included in an edition of Burns have been deleted from this edition where research has conclusively shown that they are not from Burns's pen. Where strong doubt has persisted, it has been thought advisable, at this stage, to give Burns the benefit.

That the question of "literary taste" should have led to the exclusion of several pieces which, in the opinion of the present editor, are without offence, need cause no special heart-burning. Burns would have condoned their exclusion from a popular edition. For though he was justly proud of his bawdry, he held very definite views regarding his own productions in this line, considering them "not quite ladies' reading".

It is regretted that the music to the songs cannot be given here. There is a physical limit to what can be encompassed in one volume. But to be unfamiliar with the music to which Burns wrote his songs is a dire handicap to an adequate awareness of his unique greatness.

4

Finally, I feel that it would be ungrateful to end this introduction without paying tribute to the help and collaboration given by my wife over many years. Indeed, without her arduous labours the accuracy of this edition would not be what it is. But for her steadfast refusal to question my final editorial judgments, I would have insisted on acknowledging her as joint-editor. Such editorial shortcomings as may exist I may fairly claim as my own.

JAMES BARKE.

CHRONOLOGY OF BURNS'S LIFE

NOTE.—By kind permission of Professor DeLancey Ferguson this Chronology is based on that compiled by him for his excellent biography of Burns entitled *Pride and Passion*, first published by the Oxford University Press in 1939. The Chronology has been re-edited by James Barke.

1759   *Jan.* 25. Robert Burns born at Alloway; eldest son of William Burnes (1721-1784) and his wife Agnes Broun (1732-1820). The other children were Gilbert (1760-1832), Agnes (1762-1834), Anabella (1764-1832), William (1767-1790), John 1769-1785), and Isabella (1771-1858).

1765   Robert and Gilbert sent to school to John Murdoch at Alloway.

1766   William Burnes rents Mount Oliphant farm.

1768   Murdoch gives up Alloway school.

1772   Robert and Gilbert attend Dalrymple parish school, week about, during summer quarter.

1773   Robert studies grammar and French with Murdoch for three weeks; writes his first song, 'Handsome Nell,' for Nellie Kilpatrick.

1774   Hard times begin at Mount Oliphant.

1775   Burns attends Hugh Rodger's school at Kirkoswald.

1777   At Whitsun, William Burnes moves from Mount Oliphant to Lochlea.

1779   Burns joins a Tarbolton dancing class 'in absolute defiance' of his father's commands.

1780   The Tarbolton Bachelors' Club organised.

1781   Burns courts Alison Begbie. His father's dispute with David MacLure, his landlord, begins. Burns joins the Freemasons. About midsummer goes to Irvine as a flax-dresser.

1782   *Jan.* 1. The Irvine shop burnt out; soon after, Burns returns to Lochlea.
      Sept. 24. William Burnes's dispute referred to arbiters.

1783   *Jan.* Burns wins a £3 prize for flax-seed.
      April. Burns begins his Commonplace Book.
      May. 17. MacLure gets a writ of sequestration against William Burnes.
      Aug. 18. The 'Oversman' reports in Burnes's favour.
      Aug. 25. Burnes makes first appeal to Court of Session.
      Autumn. Robert and Gilbert secretly arrange to rent Mossgiel.

1784   *Jan.* 27. The Court of Session upholds William Burnes.
      Feb. 13. Death of William Burnes. The family moves to Mossgiel.

1785   *May* 22. Birth of Elizabeth, the poet's daughter by Elizabeth Paton.
      During the Summer Burns meets Jean Armour.
      Sept. Burns attests his marriage to Jean Armour.
      Nov. 1. Burial of John Burns, the poet's youngest brother. During this year Burns began to write his satires, composed 'Love and Liberty', and in October finished his first Commonplace Book.

1786   *Jan.* (?). Burns plans emigration to Jamaica.
      April 3. 'Proposals' for the Kilmarnock *Poems* sent to press.
      c. April 23. James Armour repudiates Burns as a son-in-law.
      Burns "repudiates" Jean Armour.
      May 14. *Sunday.* Farewell and "marriage" to Highland Mary (?).
      July 22. Burns transfers his share in Mossgiel to Gilbert.
      July 29. Burns presides at Freemasons meeting in Mauchline.
      July 30. Burns in hiding from James Armour's writ.

July 31. *Monday*. The Kilmarnock *Poems* published.

August 6. *Sunday*. Burns last penitential appearance in Mauchline Kirk.

c. Sept. 1. First postponement of Jamaica voyage.

Sept. 3. *Sunday*. Jean Armour Burns bears twins, who are christened Robert and Jean.

c. Sept. 27. Second postponement of Jamaica voyage.

Oct. Death of Highland Mary at Greenock and abandonment of Jamaica plans.

Nov. 27. Burns sets out for Edinburgh.

Nov. 29. Burns arrives in Edinburgh.

Dec. 1. Elizabeth Paton accepts Burns's settlement of her claim.

Dec. 9. Henry MacKenzie praises the Kilmarnock *Poems* in *The Lounger*.

Dec. 14. William Creech issues subscription bills for the Edinburgh edition of the *Poems*.

1787   *Jan.* 13. The Grand Lodge of Scotland toasts Burns as 'Caledonia's Bard.'

April 21. Edinburgh *Poems* published.

April 23. Burns sells his copyright to Creech for 100 guineas.

May 5–*June* 1. Burns tours the Borders with Robert Ainslie.

End of May. VOL. I of *Scots Musical Museum* published.

June 2. Burns receives Peggy Cameron's appeal.

June 8. Burns's '*éclatant* return to Mauchline.'

End of June. Burns tours West Highlands as far as Inveraray.

Aug. 2. Burns completes his autobiographical letter to Dr. John Moore.

Aug. 8. Burns returns to Edinburgh.

Aug. 15. Burns freed of Peggy Cameron's writ.

Aug. 25–*Sept.* 16. Highland tour with William Nicol.

*Oct.*4–20. Tour in Stirlingshire.

Oct. Death of poet's daughter, Jean.

Nov. Burns begins active work for the *Scots Musical Museum*.

Dec. 4. Burns meets Mrs. Agnes MacLehose. (Clarinda).

Dec. 7. Burns dislocates his knee.

Dec. 8. The Clarinda correspondence begins.

1788   *Jan.* 4. Burns's first visit to Clarinda.

Feb. 13–14. Peak of the Clarinda correspondence: four letters in two days.

Feb. 18. Burns leaves Edinburgh.

Feb. 23. Burns returns to Mauchline; buys Jean a 'mahogany bed' and sets up house with her, publicly testifying that they are man and wife.

Feb. 27 (?)–*Mar.* 2. Burns visits Ellisland with John Tennant.

Mar. 3. Jean bears twin girls, of whom one dies on March 10 and the other on March 22.

c. Mar. 13. Burns returns to Edinburgh.

Mar. 18. Burns signs lease of Ellisland.

Mar. 24. Burns leaves Edinburgh.

Mar. VOL. II of *Scots Musical Museum* published.

April–May. Burns receives Excise instructions at Mauchline and Tarbolton.

1788   *June* 11. Burns settles at Ellisland.

July 14. Burns's Excise commission issued.

Aug. 5. Rev. William Auld and the Mauchline Kirk Session recognise the authenticity of the marriage of Burns and Jean Armour.

Nov. 5. Centenary of the 'Glorious Revolution'.

Nov. Jenny Clow bears Burns a son.

Dec. Jean joins Burns in borrowed quarters at the Isle.

1789   *Feb.* 16. Burns goes to Edinburgh to close accounts with Creech (*Feb.* 27) and to settle Jenny Clow's suit.

Feb. 28. Burns leaves Edinburgh.

July 14. Fall of the Bastille.

c. July. Burns meets Francis Grose.

Aug. 18. Francis Wallace Burns born.

Sept. Burns begins duty as Excise officer.

Nov. Burns ill with 'malignant squinancy and low fever'.

1790   *Jan.* 27. Burns's name placed on list of those eligible for promotion as Examiners and Supervisors.

Feb. VOL. III of *Scots Musical Museum* published.

July. Burns transferred to Dumfries Third Division.

July 24. Death of William Burns in London.

Dec. 1. MS. of 'Tam o' Shanter' sent to Grose.

1791   *Mar.* 31. Anne Park bears Burns a daughter, Elizabeth.

Apr. 9. William Nicol Burns born.

April. 'Tam o' Shanter' published in Grose's *Antiquities of Scotland* and in the March issue of the *Edinburgh Magazine*.

June 19-22. Burns in Ayrshire to attend Gilbert's wedding.

Aug. 25. Auction of crops at Ellisland.

Sept. 10. Formal renunciation of Ellisland lease signed.

Nov. 11. Burns moves into Dumfries.

Nov. 29-*Dec.* 11. Burns in Edinburgh. Farewell to Mrs. Agnes MacLehose at Lamont's Land.

1792   *Feb.* Burns promoted to Dumfries Port Division.

Feb. 29. Capture of schooner *Rosamond*.

March. Paine's *Rights of Man* (First part) published.

April 10. Burns made honorary member of Royal Company of Archers, Edinburgh.

April 19. Sale of the *Rosamond's* carronades.

May. Paine indicted for treason; escapes to France.

Aug. VOL. IV of *Scots Musical Museum* published.

Sept. Burns begins work for Thomson's *Select Scotish Airs*; William Smellie made freeman of Dumfries; Theatre Royal opened at Dumfries.

Nov. 13. Burns subscribes for Edinburgh *Gazetteer*.

Nov. 21. Birth of Elizabeth Riddell Burns.

Dec. First General Convention of The Friends of the People at Edinburgh.

Mid-Dec. Burns's last visit to Dunlop House.

Dec. 31. Excise inquiry into Burns's loyalty.

1793   *Jan.* 5. Burns defends himself to Graham of Fintry.

Jan. 21. French King (Louis Sixteenth) executed.

Feb. 1. France declares war against Britain.

Feb. 18. Second Edinburgh edition of *Poems* published.

March. Burns asks, and receives, burgess privileges in the Dumfries school. Mrs. MacLehose returns from the West Indies.

May 19. Burns moves to a house in Millbrae Vennel.

June. First number of Thomson's *Select Scotish Airs* published.

c. July 30-*Aug.* 2. First Gallow tour with Syme.

Aug. Thomas Muir arrested at Portpatrick. The Edinburgh "sedition" trials.

c. Aug. 30. 'Scots Wha hae' sent to Thomson.

Dec. 9. Isabella Burns married at Mossgiel.

c. Dec. 31. Beginning of the Riddell quarrel.

1794   *Jan.* 12. Final breach with Maria Riddell.

Feb. 14. Muir, Palmer and their associates sail as convicts from Woolwich to Botany Bay.

April 21. Death of Robert Riddell.

c. May 1. Burns declines a post on the *Morning Chronicle*, London.

c. June 25-28. Second Galloway tour with Syme.

Aug. 12. Birth of James Glencairn Burns.

c. Dec. 22. Burns appointed temporary Acting Supervisor at Dumfries.

1795   *Jan.* 12. Burns posts the letter which estranged Mrs. Dunlop.

Jan. 31. Burns joins in organising the Dumfries Volunteers.

Feb. Reconciliation with Maria Riddell.

April. The Reid miniature painted. Alexander Findlater resumes his duties as Supervisor at Dumfries.

June 24. Death of William Smellie.

Sept. Death of Elizabeth Riddell Burns at Mossgiel.

Dec.-Jan. Burns ill with rheumatic fever.

1796   *Feb.* 11. Muir rescued from Botany Bay by American vessel on order of George Washington.

Mar. 12-14. Food riots in Dumfries.

July 3-16. Burns at the Brow Well.

July 18. Burns writes his last letter.

July 21. Death of Burns.

July 25. Funeral of Burns, and birth of his son Maxwell.

CONTENTS

LOVE AND LIBERTY

A Cantata

RECITATIVO

I

When lyart leaves bestrow the yird,	withered;
Or, wavering like the bauckie-bird,	ground
Bedim cauld Boreas' blast;	
When hailstanes drive wi' bitter skyte,	lash
And infant frosts begin to bite,	
In hoary cranreuch drest;	rime
Ae night at e'en a merry core	One; gang
O' randie, gangrel bodies	lawless; vagrant
In Poosie-Nansie's held the splore,	carousal
To drink their orra duddies:	spare rags
Wi' quaffing and laughing	
They ranted an' they sang,	roistered
Wi' jumping an' thumping	
The vera girdle rang.	very

2

First, niest the fire, in auld red rags	next
Ane sat, weel brac'd wi' mealy bags	
And knapsack a' in order;	
His doxy lay within his arm;	
Wi' usquebae an' blankets warm,	whisky
She blinket on her sodger.	leered
An' ay he gies the tozie drab	flushed with drink
The tither skelpin kiss,	sounding
While she held up her greedy gab	mouth
Just like an aumous dish:	alms-dish
Ilk smack still did crack sull	Each
Like onie cadger's whup;	hawker's
Then, swaggering an' staggering,	
He roar'd this ditty up:—	

SONG

TUNE: *Soldier's Joy*

1

I am a son of Mars, who have been in many wars,
    And show my cuts and scars wherever I come:
This here was for a wench, and that other in a trench,
    When welcoming the French at the sound of the drum.
                        Lal de daudle, *etc.*

2

My prenticeship I past, where my leader breath'd his last,
    When the bloody die was cast on the heights of Abram;
And I servèd out my trade when the gallant game was play'd,
    And the Moro low was laid at the sound of the drum.

3

I lastly was with Curtis among the floating batt'ries,
    And there I left for witness an arm and a limb;
Yet let my country need me, with Eliott to head me
    I'd clatter on my stumps at the sound of the drum.

4

And now, tho' I must beg with a wooden arm and leg,
    And many a tatter'd rag hanging over my bum,
trull   I'm as happy with my wallet, my bottle, and my callet
    As when I us'd in scarlet to follow a drum.

5

What tho' with hoary locks I must stand the winter shocks,
    Beneath the woods and rocks oftentimes for a home?
When the tother bag I sell, and the tother bottle tell,
    I could meet a troop of Hell at the sound of a drum.

RECITATIVO

rafters shook   He ended; and the kebars sheuk
Over   Aboon the chorus roar;
rats   While frighted rattons backward leuk,
inmost hole   An' seek the benmost bore:
tiny: corner   A fairy fiddler frae the neuk,
squeaked   He skirl'd out *Encore*!
dear   But up arose the martial chuck,
               An' laid the loud uproar:—

SONG

TUNE: *Sodger Laddie*

I

I once was a maid, tho' I cannot tell when,
And still my delight is in proper young men.
Some one of a troop of dragoons was my daddie:
No wonder I'm fond of a sodger laddie!

Sing, lal de dal, *etc.*

2

The first of my loves was a swaggering blade:
To rattle the thundering drum was his trade;
His leg was so tight, and his cheek was so ruddy,
Transported I was with my sodger laddie.

3

But the godly old chaplain left him in the lurch;
The sword I forsook for the sake of the church;
He riskèd the soul, and I ventur'd the body:
'Twas then I prov'd false to my sodger laddie.

4

Full soon I grew sick of my sanctified sot;
The regiment at large for a husband I got;
From the gilded spontoon to the fife I was ready
I askèd no more but a sodger laddie.

5

But the Peace it reduc'd me to beg in despair,
Till I met my old boy in a Cunningham Fair;
His rags regimental they flutter'd so gaudy:
My heart it rejoic'd at a sodger laddie.

6

And now I have liv'd—I know not how long!
But still I can join in a cup and a song;
And whilst with both hands I can hold the glass steady,
Here's to thee, my hero, my sodger laddie!

RECITATIVO

Poor Merry-Andrew in the neuk
tinker-wench   Sat guzzling wi' a tinkler-hizzie;
cared not; took   They mind't na wha the chorus teuk,
                          Between themselves they were sae busy.
                          At length, wi' drink an' courting dizzy,
struggled   He stoiter'd up an' made a face;
                          They turn'd an' laid a smack on Grizzie,
Then   Syne tun'd his pipes wi' grave grimace:—

SONG

TUNE: *Auld Sir Symon*

1

drunk   Sir Wisdom's a fool when he's fou;
court   Sir Knave is a fool in a session:
                   He's there but a prentice I trow,
                      But I am a fool by profession.

2

book   My grannie she bought me a beuk,
went off   An' I held awa to the school:
                   I fear I my talent misteuk,
                      But what will ye hae of a fool?

3

                   For drink I wad venture my neck;
                      A hizzie's the half of my craft:
                   But what could ye other expect
cracked   Of ane that's avowedly daft?

4

bullock   I ance was tyed up like a stirk
                      For civilly swearing and quaffing;
rebuked   I ance was abus'd i' the kirk
rumpling; fun   For towsing a lass i' my daffin.

5

                   Poor Andrew that tumbles for sport
                      Let naebody name wi' a jeer:
                   There's even, I'm tauld, i' the Court
                      A tumbler ca'd the Premier.

6

Observ'd ye yon reverend lad
  Mak faces to tickle the mob?
He rails at our mountebank squad—
  It's rivalship just i' the job!

7

And now my conclusion I'll tell,
  For faith! I'm confoundedly dry:
The chiel that's a fool for himsel,   fellow
  Guid Lord! he's far dafter than I.

RECITATIVO

Then niest outspak a raucle carlin,   sturdy beldam
Wha kent fu' weel to cleck the sterlin,
For monie a pursie she had hookèd,
An' had in monie a well been doukèd.   ducked
Her love had been a Highland laddie,
But weary fa' the waefu' woodie!   plague upon
                                                        gallows
Wi' sighs an' sobs she thus began
To wail her braw John Highlandman:—   fine

SONG

TUNE: *O, An' Ye Were Dead, Guidman*

CHORUS

Sing hey my braw John Highlandman!
Sing ho my braw John Highlandman!
There's not a lad in a' the lan'
Was match for my John Highlandman!

1

A Highland lad my love was born,
The lalland laws he held in scorn,   lowland
But he still was faithfu' to his clan,
My gallant, braw John Highlandman.

2

With his philibeg, an' tartan plaid,   kilt
An' guid claymore down by his side,
The ladies' hearts he did trepan,
My gallant, braw John Highlandman.

3

We rangèd a' from Tweed to Spey,
An' liv'd like lords an' ladies gay,
For a lalland face he fearèd none,
My gallant, braw John Highlandman.

4

They banish'd him beyond the sea,
But ere the bud was on the tree,
Adown my cheeks the pearls ran,
Embracing my John Highlandman.

5

But Och! they catch'd him at the last,
And bound him in a dungeon fast.
My curse upon them every one—
They've hang'd my braw John Highlandman!

6

And now a widow I must mourn
The pleasures that will ne'er return;
No comfort but a hearty can
When I think on John Highlandman.

RECITATIVO

I

     A pigmy scraper on a fiddle,
     Wha us'd to trystes an' fairs to driddle,
buxom   Her strappin limb an' gawsie middle
                    (he reach'd nae higher)
blown it   Had hol'd his heartie like a riddle,
               An' blawn't on fire.

2

hip   Wi' hand on hainch and upward e'e,
hummed   He croon'd his gamut, one, two, three,
     Then in an *arioso* key
            The wee Apollo
     Set off wi' *allegretto* glee
            His *giga* solo:—

SONG

TUNE: *Whistle Owre the Lave O't*   rest

CHORUS

I am a fiddler to my trade,
An' a' the tunes that e'er I play'a,
The sweetest still to wife or maid
Was Whistle Owre the Lave O't.

I

Let me ryke up to dight that tear;   reach; wipe
An' go wi' me an' be my dear,
An' then your every care an' fear
    May whistle owre the lave o't.

2

At kirns an' weddins we'se be there,   harvest-homes;
An' O, sae nicely 's we will fare!   we'll
We'll bowse about till Daddie Care
    Sing *Whistle Owre the Lave O't.*

3

Sae merrily the banes we'll pyke,   bones; pick
An' sun oursels about the dyke;   fence
An' at our leisure, when ye like,
    We'll—whistle owre the lave o't!

4

But bless me wi' your heav'n o' charms,
An' while I kittle hair on thairms,   thickle; catgut
Hunger, cauld, an' a' sic harms   such
    May whistle owre the lave o't.

RECITATIVO

1

tinker

Her charms had struck a sturdy caird
   As weel as poor gut-scraper;
He taks the fiddler by the beard,

rusty

   An' draws a roosty rapier;
He swoor by a' was swearing worth

plover

   Te speet him like a pliver,
Unless he would from that time forth
   Relinquish her for ever.

2

Wi' ghastly e'e poor Tweedle-Dee

hams

   Upon his hunkers bended,
An' pray'd for grace wi' ruefu' face,

so

   An' sae the quarrel ended.
But tho' his little heart did grieve
   When round the tinkler prest her,

snigger

He feign'd to snirtle in his sleeve
   When thus the caird address'd her:—

SONG

Patch

TUNE: *Clout the Cauldron*

1

My bonie lass, I work in brass,
   A tinkler is my station;
I've travell'd round all Christian ground
   In this my occupation;
I've taen the gold, an' been enrolled
   In many a noble squadron;
But vain they search'd when off I march'd
   To go an' clout the cauldron.

2

Despise that shrimp, that wither'd imp,
　　With a' his noise an' cap'rin,
An' take a share wi' those that bear
　　The budget and the apron!
And by that stowp, my faith an' houpe!　　　　pot
　　And by that dear Kilbaigie!
If e'er ye want, or meet wi' scant,　　　　short commons
　　May I ne'er weet my craigie!　　　　wet; throat

RECITATIVO

I

The caird prevail'd: th' unblushing fair
　　In his embraces sunk,
Partly wi' love o'ercome sae sair,
　　An' partly she was drunk.
Sir Violino, with an air
　　That show'd a man o' spunk,　　　　spirit
Wish'd unison between the pair,
　　An' made the bottle clunk
　　　　　　To their health that night.

2

But hurchin Cupid shot a shaft,　　　　urchin
　　That play'd a dame a shavie:　　　　trick
The fiddler rak'd her fore and aft
　　Behint the chicken cavie;　　　　hencoop
Her lord, a wight of Homer's craft,
　　Tho' limpin' wi' the spavie,　　　　spavin hobbled;
He hirpl'd up, an lap like daft,　　　　lept like mad
　　An' shor'd them 'Dainty Davie'　　　　offered
　　　　　　O' boot that night.　　　　*Gratis*

3

He was a care-defying blade
  As ever Bacchus listed!
Tho' Fortune sair upon him laid,
  His heart, she ever miss'd it.
He had no wish but—to be glad,
  Nor want but—when he thristed,
He hated nought but—to be sad;
  An' thus the Muse suggested
            His sang that night:—

SONG

TUNE: *For A' That, An' A' That*

CHORUS

For a' that, an' a' that,
  An' twice as muckle's a' that,
I've lost but ane, I've twa behin',
I've wife eneugh for a' that.

much

1

I am a Bard, of no regard
  Wi' gentle folks an' a' that,
But Homer-like the glowrin byke,
  Frae town to town I draw that.

staring crowd

2

I never drank the Muses' stank,
  Castalia's burn, an' a' that;
But there is streams, an' richly reams—
  My Helicon I ca' that.

pond
brook
foams

3

Great love I bear to a' the fair,
  Their humble slave an' a' that;
But lordly will, I hold it still
  A mortal sin to thraw that.

thwart

4

In raptures sweet this hour we meet
  Wi' mutual love an' a' that;
But for how lang the flie may stang,   *fly; sting*
  Let inclination law that!

5

Their tricks an' craft hae put me daft,
  They've taen me in, an' a' that;
But clear your decks, an' here's the Sex!
  I like the jads for a' that.

CHORUS

For a' that, an' a' that,
  An' twice as muckle's a' that,
My dearest bluid, to do them guid,
  They're welcome till't for a' that!   *to it*

RECITATIVO

So sung the Bard, and Nansie's wa's   *walls*
Shook with a thunder of applause,
  Re-echo'd from each mouth!
They toom'd their pocks, they pawn'd their duds, *emptied their*
They scarcely left to coor their fuds,   *bags*
  To quench their lowin drouth.   *cover; tails*
Then owre again the jovial thrang   *company*
  The Poet did request
To lowse his pack, an' wale a sang,   *untie; choose*
  A ballad o' the best:
    He rising, rejoicing
      Between his twa Deborahs,
    Looks round him, an' found them
      Impatient for the chorus:—

SONG

TUNE: *Jolly Mortals, Fill Your Glasses*

CHORUS

A fig for those by law protected!
   Liberty's a glorious feast,
Courts for cowards were erected,
   Churches built to please the priest!

1

See the smoking bowl before us!
   Mark our jovial, ragged ring!
Round and round take up the chorus,
   And in raptures let us sing:

2

What is title, what is treasure,
   What is reputation's care?
If we lead a life of pleasure,
   'Tis no matter how or where!

3

With the ready trick and fable
   Round we wander all the day;
And at night in barn or stable
   Hug our doxies on the hay.

4

Does the train-attended carriage
   Thro' the country lighter rove?
Does the sober bed of marriage
   Witness brighter scenes of love?

5

Life is all a variorum,
   We regard not how it goes;
Let them prate about decorum,
   Who have character to lose.

6

Here's to budgets, bags and wallets!
   Here's to all the wandering train!
Here's our ragged brats and callets!
   One and all, cry out, Amen!

THE TWA DOGS

A Tale

'Twas in that place o' Scotland's isle
That bears the name of auld King Coil,
Upon a bonie day in June,
When wearing thro' the afternoon,
Twa dogs, that were na thrang at hame,   busy
Forgathered ance upon a time.   chance-met

The first I'll name, they ca'd him Caesar,
Was keepit for 'his Honor's pleasure:
His hair, his size, his mouth, his lugs,   ears
Shew'd he was nane o' Scotland's dogs;
But whalpit some place far abroad,
Whare sailors gang to fish for cod.

His lockèd, letter'd, braw brass collar
Shew'd him the gentleman an' scholar;
But tho' he was o' high degree,
The fient a pride, nae pride had he;   fiend
But wad hae spent an hour caressin,
Ev'n wi' a tinkler-gipsy's messin;   mongrel
At kirk or market, mill or smiddie,   smithy
Nae tawted tyke, tho' e'er sae duddie,   matted cur; ragged
But he wad stan't, as glad to see him,   would have stood
An' stroan't on stanes an' hillocks wi' him.   lanted

   The tither was a ploughman's collie,
A rhyming, ranting, raving billie,   rollicking; blade
Wha for his friend an' comrade had him,
And in his freaks had Luath ca'd him,
After some dog in Highland sang,
Was made lang syne—Lord knows how lang.

   He was a gash an' faithfu' tyke,   wise
As ever lap a sheugh or dyke.   ditch; stone

fence
pleasant, white-
streaked
every
shaggy

joyous

buttocks

His honest, sonsie, baws'nt face
Ay gat him friends in ilka place;
His breast was white, his tousie back
Weel clad wi' coat o' glossy black;
His gawsie tail, wi' upward curl,
Hung owre his hurdies wi' a swirl.

glad in

confidential

now

moles; dug

Nae doubt but they were fain o' ither,
And unco pack an' thick thegither;
Wi' social nose whyles snuff'd an' snowkit;
Whyles mice an' moudieworts they howkit;
Whyles scour'd awa' in lang excursion,
An' worry'd ither in diversion;
Till tir'd at last wi' monie a farce,
They sat them down upon their arse,
An' there began a lang disgression
About the 'lords o' the creation.'

CAESAR

I've aften wonder'd, honest Luath,
What sort o' life poor dogs like you have;
An' when the gentry's life I saw,

at all

What way poor bodies liv'd ava.

rents in kind;
dues

Our laird gets in his rackèd rents,
His coals, his kain, an' a' his stents:
He rises when he likes himsel;
His flunkies answer at the bell;
He ca's his coach; he ca's his horse;
He draws a bonie silken purse,

stiches

guinea peeps

As lang's my tail, whare, thro' the steeks,
The yellow letter'd Geordie keeks.

cramming

servants;
stomach

Frae morn to e'en it's nought but toiling,
At baking, roasting, frying, boiling;
An' tho' the gentry first are stechin,
Yet ev'n the ha' folk fill their pechan
Wi' sauce, ragouts, an sic like trashtrie,
That's little short o' downright wastrie:
Our whipper-in, wee, blastit wonner,
Poor, worthless elf, it eats a dinner,
Better than onie tenant-man
His Honor has in a' the lan';

An' what poor cot-folk pit their painch in,   put; paunch
I own it's past my comprehension.

LUATH

Trowth, Cæsar, whyles they're fash't eneugh: sometimes;
A cotter howkin in a sheugh,   bothered
Wi' dirty stanes biggin a dyke,   digging
                                                                                building
Baring a quarry, an' sic like;   clearing
Himsel, a wife, he thus sustains,   litter; brats
A smytrie o' wee duddie weans,
An' nought but his ban' darg to keep   hands' labour
Them right an' tight in thack an' rape.   thatch and rope

An' when they meet wi' sair disasters,
Like loss o' health or want o' masters,
Ye maist wad think, a wee touch langer,   small
An' they maun starve o' cauld and hunger:
But how it comes, I never kend yet,
They're maistly wonderfu' contented;
An' buirdly chiels, an' clever hizzies,   stout lads;
Are bred in sic a way as this is.   young women

CAESAR

But then to see how ye're negleckit,
How huff'd, an' cuff'd, an' disrespeckit!
Lord man, our gentry care as little
For delvers, ditchers, an' sic cattle;
They gang as saucy by poor folk,
As I wad by a stinking brock.   badger

I've notic'd, on our laird's court-day,
(An' monie a time my heart's been wae),   sad
Poor tenant bodies, scant o' cash,
How they maun thole a factor's snash: endure; absue
He'll stamp an threaten, curse an' swear
He'll apprehend them, poind their gear;   seize
While they maun staun', wi' aspect humble,   stand
An' hear it a', an' fear an' tremble!

I see how folk live that hae riches;
But surely poor-folk maun be wretches!

LUATH

      They're nae sae wretched 's ane wad think:
poverty's   Tho' constantly on poortith's brink,
      They're sae accustom'd wi' the sight,
      The view o't gies them little fright.

      Then chance an' fortune are sae guided,
      They're ay in less or mair provided;
      An' tho' fatigu'd wi' close employment,
snatch   A blink o' rest's a sweet enjoyment.

      The dearest comfort o' their lives,
growing   Their grushie weans an' faithfu' wives;
      The prattling things are just their pride,
      That sweeten a' their fire-side.

sometimes   An' whyles twalpennie worth o' nappy
      Can mak the bodies unco happy:
      They lay aside their private cares,
      To mind the Kirk and State affairs;
      They'll talk o' patronage an' priests,
      Wi' kindling fury i' their breasts,
      Or tell what new taxation's comin,
marvel   An' ferlie at the folk in Lon'on.

      As bleak-fac'd Hallowmass returns,
harvest-homes   They got the jovial, ranting kirns,
      When rural life, of ev'ry station,
      Unite in common recreation;
glances   Love blinks, Wit slaps, an' social Mirth
      Forgets there's Care upo' the earth.

      That merry day the year begins,
      They bar the door on frosty win's;
cream   The nappy reeks wi' mantling ream,
      An' sheds a heart-inspiring steam;
smoking; snuff-   The luntin pipe, an' sneeshin mill,
box   Are handed round wi' right guid will;
conversing   The cantie auld folks crackin crouse,
cheerfully
romping   The young anes ranting thro' the house—
      My heart has been sae fain to see them,
      That I for joy hae barkit wi' them.

Still it's owre true that ye hae said
Sic game is now owre aften play'd;   too often
There's monie a creditable stock
O' decent, honest, fawsont folk,   well-doing
Are riven out baith root an' branch,
Some rascal's pridefu' greed to quench,
Wha thinks to knit himsel the faster
In favor wi' some gentle master,
Wha, aiblins thrang a parliamentin',   may be
For Britain's guid his saul indentin'—   indenturing

CAESAR

Haith, lad, ye little ken about it:
For Britain's guid! guid faith! I doubt it.
Say rather, gaun as Premiers lead him: going
An' saying aye or no 's they bid him:
At operas an' plays parading,
Mortgaging, gambling, masquerading:
Or maybe, in a frolic daft,
To Hague or Calais taks a waft,
To mak a tour an' tak a whirl,
To learn *bon ton*, an' see the worl'.

There, at Vienna or Versailles,
He rives his father's auld entails;   splits
Or by Madrid he taks the rout,   road
To thrum guitars an' fecht wi' nowt;   fight; cattle
Or down Italian vista startles,   courses
Whore-hunting amang groves o' myrtles
Then bowses drumlie German-water,   rauddy
To mak himself look fair an' fatter,
An' purge the bitter ga's an' cankers   venereal sores
O' curst Venetian bores an' chancres.

For Britain's guid! for her destruction!
Wi' dissipation, feud an' faction.

LUATH

Hech man! dear sirs! is that the gate   way
They waste sae monie a braw estate!
Are we sae foughten an' harass'd   troubled
For gear ta gang that gate at last?   wealth to go

O would they stay aback frae courts,
An' please themsels wi' countra sports,
It wad for ev'ry ane be better,
The laird, the tenant, an' the cotter!
For thae frank, rantin, ramblin billies,
Fient haet o' them's ill-hearted fellows:
Except for breakin o' their trimmer,
Or speakin lightly o' their limmer,
Or shootin of a hare or moor-cock,
The ne'er-a-bit they're ill to poor folk.

But will ye tell me, master Caesar:
Sure great folk's life's a life o' pleasure?
Nae cauld nor hunger e'er can steer them,
The vera thought o't need na fear them.

CAESAR

Lord, man, were ye but whyles whare I am,
The gentles, ye wad ne'er envý 'em!

It's true, they need na starve or sweat,
Thro' winter's cauld, or simmer's heat;
They've nae sair wark to craze their banes,
An' fill auld-age wi' grips an' granes:
But human bodies are sic fools,
For a' their colleges an' schools,
That when nae real ills perplex them,
They mak enow themsels to vex them;
An' ay the less they hae to sturt them,
In like proportion, less will hurt them.

A countra fellow at the pleugh,
His acre's till'd, he's right eneugh;
A countra girl at her wheel,
Her dizzen's done, she's unco weel;
But gentlemen, an' ladies warst,
Wi' ev'n down want o' wark are curst:
They loiter, lounging, lank an' lazy;
Tho' deil-haet ails them, yet uneasy;
Their days insipid, dull an' tasteless;
Their nights unquiet, lang an' restless.

An' ev'n their sports, their balls an' races,
Their galloping through public places,
There's sic parade, sic pomp an' art,
They joy can scarcely reach the heart.

The men cast out in party-matches,
Then sowther a' in deep debauches;   solder
Ae night they're mad wi' drink an' whoring,   One
Niest day their life is past enduring.   Next

The ladies arm-in-arm in clusters,
As great an' gracious a' as sisters;
But hear their absent thought o' ither,
They're a' run deils an' jads thegither.   downright
Whyles, owre the wee bit cup an' platie,
They sip the scandal-potion pretty;
Or lee-lang nights, wi' crabbit leuks   live-long
Pore owre the devil's pictur'd beuks;   books
Stake on a chance a farmer's stackyard,
An' cheat like onie unhang'd blackguard.

There's some exceptions, man an' woman;
But this is Gentry's life in common.

By this, the sun was out o' sight,
An' darker gloamin brought the night;   twilight
The bum-clock humm'd wi' lazy drone;   beetle
The kye stood rowtin' i' the loan;   cattle; lowing;
                                                       field
When up they gat, an' shook their lugs,   side path
Rejoic'd they were na *men*, but *dogs*;
An' each took aff his several way,
Resolv'd to meet some ither day.

SCOTCH DRINK

Gie him strong drink until he wink,
That's sinking in despair;
An' liquor guid to fire his bluid,
That's prest wi' grief an' care:
There let him bowse, and deep carouse,
Wi' bumpers flowing o'er,
Till he forgets his loves or debts,
An' minds his griefs no more.
SOLOMON'S PROVERBS, xxxi, 6, 7.

I

Let other poets raise a frácas
'Bout veins, an' wines, an' drucken Bacchus,
An' crabbit names an' stories wrack us,
          An' grate our lug:
I sing the juice Scotch bear can mak us,
          In glass or jug.

2

O thou, my Muse! guid auld Scotch drink!
Whether thro' wimplin worms thou jink,
Or, richly brown, ream owre the brink,
          In glorious faem,
Inspire me, till I lisp an' wink,
          To sing thy name!

3

Let husky wheat the haughs adorn,
An' aits set up their awnie horn,
An' pease an' beans, at e'en or morn,
          Perfume the plain:
Leeze me on thee, John Barleycorn,
          Thou king o' grain!

4

On thee aft Scotland chows her cood,
In souple scones, the wale o' food!
Or tumbling in the boiling flood
          Wi' kail an' beef;
But when thou pours thy strong heart's blood,
          There thou shines chief.

Margin glosses:
torment
vex; ear
barley

winding; frisk
cream
foam

hollows
oats; bearded

Blessings on
thee

chews cud
pick

greens

5

Food fills the wame, an' keeps us livin;   belly
Tho' life 's a gift no worth receivin,
When heavy-dragg'd wi' pine an' grievin;
   But oil'd by thee,
The wheels o' life gae down-hill, scrievin,   careering
   Wi' rattlin glee.

6

Thou clears the head o' doited Lear,   muddled
Thou cheers the heart o' drooping Care;   Learning
Thou strings the nerves o' Labour sair,
   At's weary toil;
Thou ev'n brightens dark Despair
   Wi' gloomy smile.

7

Aft, clad in massy siller weed,   dress
Wi' gentles thou erects thy head;
Yet, humbly kind in time o' need,
   The poor man's wine:
His wee drap parritch, or his bread,
   Thou kitchens fine.

8

Thou art the life o' public haunts:
But thee, what were our fairs and rants?   Without;
Ev'n godly meeting o' the saunts,   merry-makings
   By thee inspir'd,
When, gaping, they besiege the tents,
   Are doubly fir'd.

9

That merry night we get the corn in,
O sweetly, then, thou reams the horn in!
Or reekin on a New-Year mornin   smoking
   In cog or bicker,   wooden vessels
An' just a wee drap spiritual burn in,   whisky
   An' gusty sucker!   tasty sugar

10

gear
froth
two-eared cup
the Blacksmith
stroke

When Vulcan gies his bellows breath,
An' ploughmen gather wi' their graith,
O rare! to see thee fizz an' freath
          I' th' lugget caup!
Then Burnewin comes on like death
          At ev'ry chaup.

11

iron
bony, fellow

anvil

Nae mercy, then, for airn or steel:
The brawnie, bainie, ploughman chiel,
Brings hard owrehip, wi' sturdy wheel,
          The strong forehammer,
Till block an' studdie ring an' reel,
          Wi' dinsome clamour

12

squalling babies
babble
cheerfully dolts
Woe befall
midwife
coin

When skirlin weanies see the light,
Thou maks the gossips clatter bright,
How fumbling cuifs their dearies slight;
          Wae worth the name!
Nae howdie gets a social night,
          Or plack frae them.

13

law-case
wild
-brew

When neebors anger at a plea,
An' just as wud as wud can be,
How easy can the barley-brie
          Cement the quarrel!
It's aye the cheapest lawyer's fee,
          To taste the barrel.

14

charge
throat

ask

Alake! that e'er my Muse has reason,
To wyte her countrymen wi' treason!
But monie daily weet their weason
          Wi' liquors nice,
An' hardly, in a winter season,
          E'er spier her price.

15

Wae worth that brandy, burnin trash!
Fell source o' monie a pain an' brash!   illness
Twins monie a poor, doylt, drucken hash,   robs; stupid,
      O' half his days;   drunken oaf
An' sends, beside, auld Scotland's cash
      To her warst faes.   foes

16

Ye Scots, wha wish auld Scotland well!
Ye chief, to you my tale I tell,
Poor, plackless devils like mysel!   penniless
      It sets you ill,   becomes
Wi' bitter, dearthfu' wines to mell,   meddle
      Or forcign gill.

17

May gravels round his blather wrench,   bladder
An' gouts torment him, inch by inch,
Wha twists his gruntle wi' a glunch   phiz; growl
      O' sour disdain,
Out owre a glass o' whisky-punch
      Wi' honest men!

18

O Whisky! soul o' plays an' pranks!
Accept a Bardie's gratefu' thanks!
When wanting thee, what tuneless cranks   creakings
      Are my poor verses!
Thou comes—they rattle i' their ranks
      At ither's arses!

19

Thee, Ferintosh! O sadly lost!
Scotland lament frae coast to coast!
Now colic grips, an' barkin hoast   cough
      May kill us a';
For loyal Forbés' chartered boast
      Is taen awa!

20

Those   Thae curst horse-leeches o' th' Excise,
stills   Wha mak the whisky stells their prize!
Haud up thy han', Deil! ance, twice, thrice!
spies   There, seize the blinkers!
brimstone   An' bake them up in brunstane pies
       For poor damn'd drinkers.

21

Fortune! if thou'll but gie me still
Whole breeches   Hale breeks, a scone, an' whisky gill,
store   An' rowth o' rhyme to rave at will,
       Tak a' the rest,
An' deal't about as thy blind skill
       Directs thee best.

THE AUTHOR'S EARNEST CRY AND PRAYER

TO THE SCOTCH REPRESENTATIVES IN THE HOUSE OF COMMONS

Dearest of distillation! last and best——
——How art thou lost!——
       PARODY ON MILTON

1

Ye Irish lords, ye knights an' squires,
Wha represent our brughs an' shires,
prudently   An' doucely manage our affairs
       In Parliament,
To you a simple Bardie's prayers
       Are humbly sent.

2

hoarse   Alas! my roupet Muse is haerse!
Your Honors' hearts wi' grief 'twad pierce,
To see her sittin on her arse
       Low i' the dust,
And scriechin our prosaic verse,
       An' like to brust!

3

Tell them wha hae the chief direction,
Scotland an' me's in great affliction,
E'er sin' they laid that curst restriction
        On aqua-vitae;
An' rouse them up to strong conviction,
        An' move their pity.

4

Stand forth, an' tell yon Premier youth
The honest, open, naked truth:
Tell him o' mine an' Scotland's drouth,   thirst
        His servants humble:
The muckle deevil blaw you south,
        If ye dissemble!

5

Does onie great man glunch an' gloom?   growl
Speak out, an' never fash your thumb!   care a rap
Let posts an' pensions sink or soom   swim
            Wi' them wha grant 'em:
If honestly they canna come,
        Far better want 'em.

6

In gath'rin votes you were na slack;
Now stand as tightly by your tack:
Ne'er claw your lug, an' fidge your back,   scrath; wriggle
        An' hum an haw;
But raise your arm, an' tell your crack   tale
        Before them a'.

7

Paint Scotland greetin owre her thrissle;   weeping; thistle
Her mutchkin stowp as toom's a whissle;   pint-pot; empty
An' damn'd excisemen in a bustle,
        Seizin a stell,   still
Triumphant, crushin't like a mussel,
        Or lampit shell!   limpet

8

Then, on the tither hand, present her—
A blackguard smuggler right behint her,
cheek-by-jowl;   An' cheek-for-chow, a chuffie vintner
fat-faced   Colleaguing join,
pocket   Pickin her pouch as bare as winter
                Of a' kind coin.

9

Is there, that bears the name o' Scot,
But feels his heart's bluid rising hot,
To see his poor auld mither's pot
broken in pieces   Thus dung in staves,
An' plunder'd o' her hindmost groat,
         By gallows knaves?

10

Alas! I'm but a nameless wight,
Trode i' the mire out o' sight!
But could I like Montgomeries fight,
speak   Or gab like Boswell,
shirt-   There's some sark-necks I wad draw tight,
         An' tie some hose well.

11

God bless your Honors! can ye see't,
jolly matron   The kind, auld, cantie carlin greet,
weep   An' no get warmly to your feet,
make   An' gar them hear it,
An' tell them wi' a patriot-heat,
        Ye winna bear it?

12

Some o' you nicely ken the laws,
To round the period an' pause,
An' with rhetòric clause on clause
         To mak harangues:
Then echo thro' Saint Stephen's wa's
        Auld Scotland's wrangs.

13

Dempster, a true blue Scot I'se warran;
Thee, aith-detesting, chaste Kilkerran;   oath-
An' that glib-gabbet Highland baron,   smooth-tongued
        The Laird o' Graham;
An' ane, a chap that's damn'd auldfarran,   shrewd
        Dundas his name:

14

Erskine, a spunkie Norland billie;   sprightful fellow
True Campbells, Frederick and Ilay;
An' Livistone, the bauld Sir Willie;
        An' monie ithers,
Whom auld Demosthenes or Tully
        Might own for brithers.

15

Thee sodger Hugh, my watchman stented,   assigned
If Bardies e'er are represented;
I ken if that your sword were wanted,
        Ye'd lend your hand;
But when there's ought to say anent it,
        Ye're at a stand.

16

Arouse, my boys! exert your mettle,
To get auld Scotland back her kettle;
Or faith! I'll wad my new pleugh-pettle,   bet: plough-staff
        Ye'll see 't or lang,
She'll teach you, wi' a reekin whittle,   smoking knife
        Anither sang.

17

This while she's been in crankous mood,   fretful
Her lost Militia fir'd her bluid;
(Deil na they never mair do guid,
        Play'd her that pliskie!)   trick
An' now she's like to rin red-wud   stark-mad
        About her whisky.

18

put her to 't   An' Lord! if ance they pit her till't
tuck up   Her tartan petticoat she'll kilt,
                An' durk an' pistol at her belt,
                        She'll tak the streets,
knife   An' rin her whittle to the hilt,
                       I' the first she meets!

19

          For God-sake, sirs! then speak her fair,
stroke; gently   An' straik her cannie wi' the hair,
the Commons   An' to the Muckle House repair,
                     Wi' instant speed,
learning   An' strive, wi' a' your wit an' lear,
redress   To get remead.

20

          Yon ill-tongue'd tinkler, Charlie Fox,
          May taunt you wi' his jeers an' mocks;
hot   But gie him't het, my hearty cocks!
scare the varlet   E'en cowe the cadie!
          An' send him to his dicing box
                  An' sportin lady.

21

          Tell you guid bluid of auld Boconnock's,
mixed-meal   I'll be his debt twa mashlum bonnocks,
bannocks   An' drink his health in auld Nanse Tinnock's
                  Nine times a-week.
windows   If he some scheme, like tea an' winnocks,
                  Wad kindly seek.

22

          Could he some commutation broach,
          I'll pledge my aith in guid braid Scotch,
          He needna fear their foul reproach
                  Nor erudition,
mixed-up   Yon mixtie-maxtie, queer hotch-potch,
                  The Coalition.

23

Auld Scotland has a raucle tongue;   *bitter*
She's just a devil wi' a rung;   *cudgel*
An' if she promise auld or young
     To tak their part,
Tho' by the neck she should be strung,
     She'll no desert.

24

And now, ye chosen Five-and-Forty,
May still your mither's heart support ye;
Then, tho' a minister grow dorty,   *pettish*
     An' kick your place,
Ye'll snap your fingers, poor an' hearty,
     Before his face.

25

God bless your Honors, a' your days,
Wi' sowps o' kail and brats o' claes,   *sups; broth;*
In spite o' a' the hievish kaes,   *scraps; clothes*
     That haunt, St. Jamie's! *jack-daws*
Your humble Bardie sings an' prays,
     While Rab his name is.

POSTSCRIPT

26

Let half-starv'd slaves in warmer skies
See future wines, rich-clust'ring, rise;
Their lot auld Scotland ne'er envies,
     But, blythe and frisky,
She eyes her freeborn, martial boys
     Tak aff their whisky.

27

What tho' their Phœbus kinder warms, *sun*
While fragrance blooms and Beauty charms,
When wretches range, in famish'd swarms,
     The scented groves;
Or, hounded forth, dishonor arms
     In hungry droves!

28

Their gun's a burden on their shouther;
cannot   They downa bide the stink o' powther;
doubt   Their bauldest thought's a hank'ring swither
        To stan' or rin,
crack; pell-mell   Till skelpt—a shot—they're aff, a' throw'ther,
        To save their skin.

29

But bring a Scotsman frae his hill,
Put in his   Clap in his cheek a Highland gill,
mouth   Say, such is royal George's will,
        An' there's the foe!
He has nae thought but how to kill
        Twa at a blow.

30

Nae cauld, faint-hearted doubtings tease him;
Death comes, wi' fearless eye he sees him;
Wi' bluidy han' a welcome gies him;
        An' when he fa's,
His latest draught o' breathin lea'es him
        In faint huzzas.

31

eyes; shut   Sages their solemn een may steek
smoke   An' raise a philosophic reek,
An' physically causes seek
        In clime an' season;
But tell me whisky's name in Greek:
        I'll tell the reason.

32

Scotland, my auld, respected mither!
sometimes   Tho' whiles ye moistify your leather,
heather-tops   Till whare ye sit on craps o' heather
        Ye tine your dam,
Freedom and whisky gang thegither,
        Tak aff your dram!

THE HOLY FAIR

A robe of seeming truth and trust
  Hid crafty observation;
And secret hung, with poison'd crust,
  The dirk of defamation:
A mask that like the gorget show'd,
  Dye-varying on the pigeon;
And for a mantle large and broad,
He wrapt him in Religion.

                    HYPOCRISY À-LA-MODE

I

Upon a simmer Sunday morn,
  When Nature's face is fair,
I walkèd forth to view the corn,
  An' snuff the caller air.   cool
The rising sun, owre Galston Muirs,
  Wi' glorious light was glintin;   glancing
The hares were hirplin down the furs,   hopping furrows
  The lav'rocks they were chantin   larks
          Fu' sweet that day.

2

As lightsomely I glowr'd abroad,   gazed
  To see a scene sae gay,
Three hizzies, early at the road,   young women
  Cam skelpin up the way.
Twa had manteeles o' dolefu' black,   grey
  But ane wi' lyart lining;
The third, that gaed a wee a-back,   walked a bit
  Was in the fashion shining   behind
          Fu' gay that day.

3

The twa appear'd like sisters twin,
  In feature, form, an' claes;   clothes
Their visage wither'd, lang an' thin,
  An' sour as onie slaes:
The third cam up, hap-step-an'-lowp,   hop; jump
  As light as onie lambie,
An' wi' a curchie low did stoop,   curtsey
  As soon as e'er she saw me,
          Fu' kind that day.

4

Wi' bonnet aff, quoth I, 'Sweet lass,
   I think ye seem to ken me;
I'm sure I've seen that bonie face,
   But yet I canna name ye.'
Quo' she, an' laughin as she spak,
   An' taks me by the han's,

bulk   'Ye, for my sake, hae gi'en the feck
   Of a' the Ten Comman's

rip   A screed some day.

5

'My name is Fun—your cronie dear,
   The nearest friend ye hae;
An' this is Superstition here,
   An' that's Hypocrisy.

going   I'm gaun to Mauchline Holy Fair,
larking   To spend an hour in daffin:
wrinkled   Gin ye 'll go there, yon runkl'd pair,
   We will get famous laughin
            At them this day.'

6

Quoth I, 'Wi' a' my heart, I'll do't;
shirt   I'll get my Sunday's sark on,
An' meet you on the holy spot;
we'll   Faith, we'se hae fine remarkin!'
went; porridge-   Then I gaed hame at crowdie-time,
   An' soon I made me ready;
For roads were clad, frae side to side,
Wi' monie a wearie body,
          In droves that day.

7

self-complacent;   Here farmers gash, in ridin graith,
gear
jogging   Gaed hoddin by their cotters;
strapping   There swankies young, in braw braid-claith,
youngsters   Are springin owre the gutters.
padding;   The lasses, skelpin barefit, thrang,
thronging   In silks an' scarlets glitter;
shive   Wi' sweet-milk cheese, in monie a whang,
small cakes   An' farls, bak'd wi' butter,
crisp   Fu' crump that day.

8

When by the plate we set our nose,
  Weel heapèd up wi' ha'pence,
A greedy glowr black-bonnet throws,   the Elder
  An' we maun draw our tippence.
Then in we go to see the show:
  On ev'ry side they're gath'rin;
Some carryin dails, some chairs an' stools,   planks
  An' some are busy bleth'rin   gabbling
      Right loud that day.

9

Here stands a shed to fend the show'rs,   keep off
  An' screen our countra gentry;
There Racer Jess, an' twa-three whores,   two or three
  Are blinkin at the entry.   leering
Here sits a raw o' tittlin jads,   whispering jades
  Wi' heavin breasts an' bare neck;
An' there a batch o' wabster lads,   weaver
  Blackguardin frae Kilmarnock,
      For fun this day.

10

Here some are thinkin on their sins,
  An' some upo' their claes;
Ane curses feet that fyl'd his shins,   soiled
  Anither sighs an' prays:
On this hand sits a chosen swatch,   sample
  Wi' screw'd-up, grace-proud faces;
On that a set o' chaps, at watch,
  Thrang winkin on the lasses   Busy
      To chairs that day.

11

O happy is that man an' blest!
  Nae wonder that it pride him!
Whase ain dear lass, that he likes best,
  Comes clinkin down beside him!
Wi' arm repos'd on the chair back,
  He sweetly does compose him;
Which, by degrees, slips round her neck,
  An's loof upon her bosom,   And his palm
      Unkend that day.

12

Now a' the congregation o'er
  Is silent expectation;

climbs For Moodie speels the holy door,
  Wi' tidings o' damnation:

the Devil Should Hornie, as in ancient days,
  'Mang sons o' God present him;
The vera sight o' Moodie's face

hot To's ain het hame had sent him
      Wi' fright that day.

13

Hear how he clears the points o' Faith
  Wi' rattlin and thumpin!
Now meekly calm, now wild in wrath,
  He's stampin, an' he's jumpin!
His lengthen'd chin, his turn'd-up snout,

unearthly His eldritch squeel an' gestures,
O how they fire the heart devout—
  Like cantharidian plaisters
      On sic a day!

14

But hark! the tent has chang'd its voice;
There's peace an' rest nae langer;
For a' the real judges rise,
  They canna sit for anger:
Smith opens out his cauld harangues,
  On practice and on morals;
An' aff the godly pour in thrangs,
  To gie the jars an' barrels
      A lift that day.

15

What signifies his barren shine,
  Of moral pow'rs an' reason?
His English style, an' gesture fine
  Are a' clean out o' season.
Like Socrates or Antonine,
  Or some auld pagan heathen,
The moral man he does define,
  But ne'er a word o' faith in
      That's right that day.

16

In guid time comes an antidote
  Against sic poison'd nostrum;
For Peebles, frae the water-fit,   river's mouth
  Ascends the holy rostrum;
See, up he's got the word o' God,
  An' meek an' mim has view'd it,
While Common-sense has taen the road,
  An' aff, an' up the Cowgate
            Fast, fast that day.

17

Wee Miller niest, the guard relieves,   next
  An' orthodoxy raibles,   recites by rote
Tho' in his heart he weel believes,
  An' thinks it auld wives' fables:
But faith! the birkie wants a manse: fellow; living
  So, cannilie he hums them;   humbugs
Altho' his carnal wit an' sense
  Like hafflins-wise o'ercomes him   Nearly half
            At times that day.

18

Now butt an' ben the change-house fills,   tavern
  Wi' yill-caup commentators;   ale-cup
Here's crying out for bakes an' gills,   biscuits
  An' there the pint-stowp clatters;
While thick an' thrang, an' loud an' lang,
  Wi' logic an' wi' Scripture,
They raise a din, that in the end
  Is like to breed a rupture
            O' wrath that day

19

Leeze me on drink! it gies us mair   Blessings
  Than either school or college;
It kindles wit, it waukens lear,   learning
  It pangs us fou o' knowledge: crams
Be't whisky-gill or penny wheep,   small beer
  Or onie stronger potion,
It never fails, on drinkin deep,
  To kittle up our notion,   tickle
            By night or day.

20

The lads an' lasses, blythely bent
    To mind baith saul an' body,
Sit round the table, weel content,
    An' steer about the toddy:
On this ane's dress, an' that ane's leuk,
    They're makin observations;
While some are cozie i' the neuk,
    An' formin assignations
            To meet some day.

stir (margin, line 4)

corner (margin, line 7)

21

But now the Lord's ain trumpet touts,
    Till a' the hills are rairin,
And echoes back return the shouts:
    Black Russell is na spairin:
His piercin words, like Highlan' swords,
    Divide the joints an' marrow;
His talk o' Hell, whare devils dwell,
    Our vera 'sauls does harrow'
            Wi' fright that day!

sounds (margin, line 1)

roaring (margin, line 2)

22

A vast, unbottom'd, boundless pit,
    Fill'd fou o' lowin brunstane,
Whase ragin flame, an' scorchin heat,
    Wad melt the hardest whun-stane!
The half-asleep start up wi' fear,
    An' think they hear it roarin;
When presently it does appear,
    'Twas but some neebor snorin
            Asleep that day.

full; flaming (margin, line 2)

23

'Twad be owre lang a tale to tell,
    How monie stories past;
An' how they crouded to the yill,
    When they were a' dismist;
How drink gaed round, in cogs an' caups,
    Amang the furms an' benches;
An' cheese an' bread, frae women's laps,
    Was dealt about in lunches,
            An' dawds that day.

full portions (margin)

lumps (margin)

24

In comes a gawsie, gash guidwife,   jolly
   An' sits down by the fire,
Syne draws her kebbuck an' her knife;   Then; cheese
   The lasses they are shyer:
The auld guidmen, about the grace,
   Frae side to side they bother;
Till some ane by his bonnet lays,
   An' gies them't, like a tether,   rope
      Fu' lang that day.

25

Waesucks! for him that gets nae lass,   Alas!
   Or lasses that hae naething!
Sma' need has he to say a grace,
   Or melvie his braw claithing!   meal dust
O wives, be mindfu', ance yoursel,
   How bonie lads ye wanted;
An' dinna for a kebbuck-heel
   Let lasses be affronted
      On sic a day!

26

Now Clinkumbell, wi' rattlin tow,   the bell-ringer;
   Begins to jow an' croon;   rope
                           swing and toll
Some swagger hame the best they dow,   can
   Some wait the afternoon.
At slaps the billies halt a blink,   openings;
   Till lasses strip their shoon: fellows; bit
                           take off
Wi' faith an hope, an' love an' drink,
   They're a' in famous tune
      For crack that day.   talk

27

How monie hearts this day converts
   O' sinners and o' lasses!
Their hearts o' stane, gin night, are gane   by nightfall;
   As saft as onie flesh is: gone
There's some are fou o' love divine;
   There's some are fou o' brandy;
An' monie jobs that day begin,
   May end in houghmagandie   fornication
      Some ither day.

ADDRESS TO THE DEIL

O Prince! O Chief of many thronèd pow'rs!
That led th' embattl'd seraphim to war.

                                            MILTON

1

O Thou! whatever title suit thee—
Hoofie   Auld Hornie, Satan, Nick, or Clootie—
Wha in yon cavern grim an' sootie,
                    Clos'd under hatches,
Splashes; dish   Spairges about the brunstane cootie,
scald   To scaud poor wretches!

2

Hangman   Hear me, Auld Hangie, for a wee,
An' let poor damnèd bodies be;
I'm sure sma' pleasure it can gie,
                    Ev'n to a deil,
spank; scald   To skelp an' scaud poor dogs like me
                        An' hear us squeel.

3

Great is thy pow'r an' great thy fame;
Far kend an' noted is thy name;
flaming hollow An' tho' yon lowin heugh's thy hame,
                    Thou travels far;
backward   An' faith! thou's neither lag, nor lame,
bashful; afraid   Nor blate, nor scaur.

4

Now   Whyles, ranging like a roarin lion,
For prey, a' holes an' corners trying;
Whyles, on the strong-wing'd tempest flyin,
Stripping   Tirlin the kirks;
Whyles, in the human bosom pryin,
                    Unseen thou lurks.

5

I've heard my rev'rend graunie say,
In lanely glens ye like to stray;
Or, where auld ruin'd castles grey
            Nod to the moon,
Ye fright the nightly wand'rer's way
            Wi' eldritch croon.

6

When twilight did my graunie summon,
To say her pray'rs, douce, honest woman!   sedate
Aft yont the dyke she's heard you bummin,   beyond
            Wi' eerie drone;
Or, rustlin, thro' the boortrees comin,   alders
            Wi' heavy groan.

7

Ae dreary, windy, winter night,
The stars shot down wi' sklentin light,   squinting
Wi' you mysel, I gat a fright:
            Ayont the lough,   pond
Ye, like a rash-buss, stood in sight,   clump of rushes
            Wi' waving sugh.   moan

8

The cudgel in my nieve did shake,   fist
Each bristl'd hair stood like a stake;
When wi' an eldritch, stoor 'quaick, quaick,'   harsh
            Amang the springs,
Awa ye squatter'd like a drake,
            On whistling wings.

9

Let warlocks grim, an' wither'd hags,
Tell how wi' you, on ragweed nags,   ragwort
They skim the muirs an' dizzy crags,
            Wi' wicked speed;
And in kirk-yards renew their leagues,
            Owre howkit dead.   dug-up

10

churn

Thence, countra wives, wi' toil an' pain,
May plunge an' plunge the kirn in vain;
For O! the yellow treasure's taen
           By witching skill;

petted, twelve-
pint cow; gone
dry as; bull

An' dawtit, twal-pint hawkie's gaen
           As yell's the bill.

11

husband;
confident or
cocksure tool
magic

Thence, mystic knots mak great abuse
On young guidmen, fond, keen an' croose;
When the best wark-lume i' the house,
           By cantraip wit,
Is instant made no worth a louse,

nick of time

           Just at the bit.

12

hoard

surface

When thowes dissolve the snawy hoord.
An' float the jinglin icy boord,
Then, water-kelpies haunt the foord,
           By your direction,
An' nighted trav'llers are allur'd
           To their destruction.

13

bog; jack-o'-
lanthorns

And aft your moss-traversing spunkies
Decoy the wight that late an' drunk is:
The bleezin, curst, mischievous monkies
           Delude his eyes,
Till in some miry slough he sunk is,
           Ne'er mair to rise.

14

must

When Masons' mystic word an' grip
In storms an' tempests raise you up,
Some cock or cat your rage maun stop,
           Or, strange to tell!
The youngest brother ye wad whip

straight

           Aff straught to hell.

15

Lang syne in Eden's bonie yard,   garden
When youthfu' lovers first were pair'd,
An' all the soul of love they shar'd,
            The raptur'd hour,
Sweet on the fragrant flow'ry swaird,
            In shady bow'r.

16

Then you, ye auld, snick-drawing dog!   scheming
Ye cam to Paradise incog,
An' play'd on man a cursèd brogue   trick
            (Black be your fa'!),
An' gied the infant warld a shog,   shake
            'Maist ruin'd a'.

17

D'ye mind that day when in a bizz   flurry
Wi' reekit duds, an' reestit gizz,   smoky; scorched
Ye did present your smoutie phiz   wig
            'Mang better folk;   smutty
An' sklented on the man of Uzz
                  Your spitefu' joke?

18

An' how ye gat him i' your thrall,
An' brak him out o' house an' hal',
While scabs an' botches did him gall,   blotches
            Wi' bitter claw;
An' lows'd his ill-tongu'd wicked scaul—   loosed; scold
            Was warst ava?   of all

19

But a' your doings to rehearse,
Your wily snares an' fechtin fierce,   fighting
Sin' that day Michael did you pierce
            Down to this time,
Wad ding a Lallan tongue, or Erse,   beat; Low-land
            In prose or rhyme.

20

Hoofs   An' now, Auld Cloots, I ken ye're thinkin,
rositering   A certain Bardie's rantin, drinkin,
hurrying   Some luckless hour will send him linkin,
                To your black Pit;
dodging   But, faith! he'll turn a corner jinkin,
                An' cheat you yet.

21

But fare-you-weel, Auld Nickie-Ben!
O' wad ye tak a thought an' men'!
perhaps   Ye aiblins might—I dinna ken—
                Still hae a stake:
sad   I'm wae to think upo' yon den,
                Ev'n for your sake!

THE DEATH AND DYING WORDS OF POOR MAILIE

Mollie

THE AUTHOR'S ONLY PET YOWE: AN UNCO MOURNFU' TALE

together   As Mailie, an' lambs thegither
one   Was ae day nibblin on the tether,
hoof; looped   Upon her cloot she coost a hitch,
floundered   An' owre she warsl'd in the ditch:
There, groanin, dying, she did lie,
doddering   When Hughoc he cam doytin by.

staring   Wi' glowrin een, an' lifted han's
Poor Hughoc like a statue stan's;
He saw her days were near-hand ended,
woe   But, wae's my heart! he could na mend it!
He gapèd wide, but naething spak.
At length poor Mailie silence brak:—

'O thou, whase lamentable face
Appears to mourn my woefu' case!
My dying words attentive hear,
An' bear them to my Master dear.

own   'Tell him, if e'er again he keep
much money   As muckle gear as buy a sheep—

O, bid him never tie them mair,
Wi' wicked strings o' hemp or hair!
But ca' them out to park or hill,   drive
An' let them wander at their will:
So may his flock increase, an' grow
To scorcs o' lambs, an' packs o' woo'!

'Tell him, he was a Master kin',
An' ay was guid to me an' mine;
An' now my dying charge I gie him,
My helpless lambs, I trust them wi' him.

'O, bid him save their harmless lives,
Frae dogs, an' tods, an' butchers' knives!   foxes
But gie them guid cow-milk their fill,
Till they be fit to fend themsel;   look after
An' tent them duly, e'en an' morn,   tend
                         small quantities;
Wi' teats o' hay an' ripps o' corn.   handfuls

'An' may they never learn the gaets,   ways
Of ither vile, wanrestfu' pets—   restless
To slink thro' slaps, an' reave an' steal,   breaches
At stacks o' pease, or stocks o' kail!   plants
So may they, like their great forbears,   ancestors
For monie a year come thro' the sheers:
So wives will gie them bits o' bread,
An' bairns greet for them when they're dead.   weep

'My poor toop-lamb, my son an' heir,   tup
O, bid him breed him up wi' care!
An' if he live to be a beast,
To pit some havins in his breast!   conduct
An' warn him—what I winna name—   will not
To stay content wi' yowes at hame;   ewes
An' no to rin an' wear his cloots,
Like other menseless, graceless brutes.   unmannerly

'An' niest, my yowie, silly thing;   ewekins; helpless
Gude keep thee frae a tether string!
O, may thou ne'er forgather up,   make friends
Wi' onie blastit, moorland toop;
But ay keep mind to moop an' mell,   nibble; meddle
Wi' sheep o' credit like thysel!

'And now, my bairns, wi' my last breath,
I lea'e my blessin wi' you baith:
An' when you think upo' your mither,
Mind to be kind to ane anither.

'Now, honest Hughoc, dinna fail,
To tell my master a' my tale;
An' bid him burn this cursèd tether,
bladder   An' for thy pains thou 'se get my blether.'

This said, poor Mailie turn'd her head,
eyes   An' clos'd her een amang the dead!

POOR MAILIE'S ELEGY

1

Lament in rhyme, lament in prose,
Wi' saut tears tricklin down your nose;
Our Bardie's fate is at a close,
remedy   Past a' remead!
The last, sad cape-stane of his woes;
                    Poor Mailie's dead!

2

worldly pelf   It's no the loss of warl's gear,
That could sae bitter draw the tear,
drooping   Or mak our Bardie, dowie, wear
                    The mourning weed:
He's lost a friend an' neebor dear
                    In Mailie dead.

3

farm   Thro' a' the toun she trotted by him;
A lang half-mile she could descry him;
Wi' kindly bleat, when she did spy him,
                    She ran wi' speed:
A friend mair faithfu' ne'er cam nigh him,
                    Than Mailie dead.

4

I wat she was a sheep o' sense,   wot
An' could behave hersel wi' mense: tact
I'll say 't, she never brak a fence,
        Thro' thievish greed.
Our Bardie, lanely, keeps the spence   parlour
        Sin' Mailie's dead.

5

Or, if he wanders up the howe,   glen
Her livin image in her yowe
Comes bleatin till him, owre the knowe,   knoll
        For bits o' bread;
An' down the briny pearls rowe   roll
        For Mailie dead.

6

She was nae get o' moorlan tips,   issue; tups
Wi' tawted ket, an' hairy hips;   matted
                                                                   fleece; rumps
For her forbears were brought in ships,   ancestors
        Frae 'yont the Tweed:
An bonier fleesh ne'er cross'd the clips   fleece; shears
        Than Mailie's dead.

7

Wae worth the man wha first did shape   Woe befall
That vile, wanchancie thing—a rape!   dangerous
It maks guid fellows girn an' gape,   grin
        Wi' chokin dread;
An' Robin's bonnet wave wi' crape
        For Mailie dead.

8

O a' ye bards on bonie Doon!
An' wha an Ayr your chanters tune!   bagpipes
Come, join the melancholious croon
        O' Robin's reed!
His heart will never get aboon!   rejoice
        His Mailie's dead!

EPISTLE TO JAMES SMITH

Friendship, mysterious cement of the soul!
Sweet'ner of Life, and solder of Society!
I owe thee much——

BLAIR

I

artful   Dear Smith, the slee'st, pawkie theif,
plunder   That e'er attempted stealth or rief!
wizard-spell   Ye surely hae some warlock-breef
                                    Owre human hearts;
proof   For ne'er a bosom yet was prief
                                    Against your arts.

2

                    For me, I swear by sun an' moon,
above   And ev'ry star that blinks aboon,
                    Ye've cost me twenty pair o' shoon,
going   Just gaun to see you;
                    And ev'ry ither pair that's done,
taken   Mair taen I'm wi' you.

3

gossip   That auld, capricious carlin, Nature,
stunted   To mak amends for scrimpit stature,
                    She's turn'd you off, a human-creature
                                    On her first plan;
                    And in her freaks, on ev'ry feature
                                    She's wrote the Man.

4

                    Just now I've taen the fit o' rhyme,
                    My barmie noddle 's working prime,
seething brain   My fancy yerkit up sublime,
                                    Wi' hasty summon:
                    Hae ye a leisure-moment's time
                                    To hear what's comin?

5

Some rhyme a neebor's name to lash;
Some rhyme (vain thought!) for needfu' cash;
Some rhyme to court the countra clash,   talk
        An' raise a din;
For me, an aim I never fash;   trouble about
        I rhyme for fun.

6

The star that rules my luckless lot,
Has fated me the russet coat,
An' damn'd my fortune to the groat;
        But, in requit,
Has blest me with a random-shot
        O' countra wit.

7

This while my notion's taen a sklent,   turn
To try my fate in guid, black prent;
But still the mair I'm that way bent,
        Something cries, 'Hoolie!   Softly!
I red you, honest man, tak tent!   heed
        Ye'll shaw your folly:

8

'There's ither poets, much your betters,
Far seen in Greek, deep men o' letters,
Hae thought they had ensur'd their debtors,
        A' future ages;
Now moths deform, in shapeless tatters,
        Their unknown pages.'

9

Then farewell hopes o' laurel-boughs
To garland my poetic brows!
Henceforth I'll rove where busy ploughs
        Are whistling thrang;   at work
An' teach the lanely heights an' howes   hollows
        My rustic sang.

10

careless

I'll wander on, wi' tentless heed
How never-halting moments speed,
Till Fate shall snap the brittle thread;
                    Then, all unknown,
I'll lay me with th' inglorious dead,
                    Forgot and gone!

11

But why o' death begin a tale?
well   Just now we're living sound an' hale;
Then top and maintop crowd the sail,
                    Heave Care o'er-side!
And large, before Enjoyment's gale,
                    Let's tak the tide.

12

This life, sae far's I understand,
Is a' enchanted fairy-land,
Where Pleasure is the magic-wand,
                    That, wielded right,
Maks hours like minutes, hand in hand,
                    Dance by fu' light.

13

The magic-wand then let us wield;
climbed   For, ance that five-an'-forty 's speel'd,
Eld   See, crazy, weary, joyless Eild,
                    Wi' wrinkl'd face,
coughing; Comes hostin, hirplin owre the field,
limping   Wi' creepin pace.

14

twilight   When ance life's day draws near the gloamin,
Then fareweel vacant, careless roamin;
An' fareweel chearfu' tankards foamin,
                    An' social noise:
An' fareweel dear, deluding Woman,
                    The joy of joys!

15

O Life! how pleasant, in thy morning,
Young Fancy's rays the hills adorning!
Cold-pausing Caution's leasson scorning,
            We frisk away,
Like school-boys, at th' expected warning,
                To joy an' play.

16

We wander there, we wander here,
We eye the rose upon the brier,
Unmindful that the thorn is near,
            Among the leaves;
And tho' the puny wound appear,
                Short while it grieves.

17

Some, lucky, find a flow'ry spot,
For which they never toil'd nor swat;   sweated
They drink the sweet and eat the fat,
            But care or pain;   Without
And haply eye the barren hut
                With high disdain.

18

With steady aim, some Fortune chase;
Keen Hope does ev'ry sinew brace;
Thro' fair, thro' foul, they urge the race,
            And seize the prey:
Then cannie, in some cozie place,   quiet; snug
                They close the day.

19

And others like your humble servan',
Poor wights! nae rules nor roads observin,
To right or left eternal swervin,
            They zig-zag on;
Till, curst with age, obscure an' starvin,
                They aften groan.

20

Alas! what bitter toil an' straining—
But truce with peevish, poor complaining!
Is Fortune's fickle *Luna* waning?
          E'en let her gang!
Beneath what light she has remaining,
          Let's sing our sang.

21

My pen I here fling to the door,
And kneel, ye Pow'rs! and warm implore,
'Tho' I should wander *Terra* o'er,
          In all her climes,
Grant me but this, I ask no more,
plenty   Ay rowth o' rhymes.

22

dripping   'Gie dreeping roasts to countra lairds,
Till icicles hing frae their beards;
clothes   Gie fine braw claes to fine life-guards
          And maids of honor;
ale, tinkers   And yill an' whisky gie to cairds,
sicken   Until they sconner.

23

'A title, Dempster merits it;
A garter gie to Willie Pitt;
Gie wealth to some be-ledger'd cit,
          In cent. per cent.;
But give me real, sterling wit,
          And I'm content.

24

'While ye are pleas'd to keep me hale,
meal and water;   I'll sit down o'er my scanty meal,
beefless broth   Be't water-brose or muslin-kail,
          Wi' cheerfu' face,
As lang's the Muses dinna fail
          To say the grace.'

25

An anxious e'e I never throws
Behint my lug, or by my nose;   ear
I jouk beneath Misfortune's blows   duck
    As weel's I may;
Sworn foe to sorrow, care, and prose,
    I rhyme away.

26

O ye douce folk that live by rule,   sedate
Grave, tideless-blooded, calm an' cool,
Compar'd wi' you—O fool! fool! fool!
    How much unlike!
Your hearts are just a standing pool,
    Your lives a dyke!   wall

27

Nae hair-brained, sentimental traces
In your unletter'd, nameless faces!
In *arioso* trills and graces
    Ye never stray;
But *gravissímo*, solemn, basses
    Ye hum away.

28

Ye are sae grave, nae doubt ye 're wise;
Nae ferly tho' ye do despise   marvel
The hairum-scairum, ram-stam boys, headlong
    The rattling squad:
I see ye upwards cast your eyes—
    Ye ken the road!

29

Whilst I—but I shall haud me there, hold
Wi' you I 'll scarce gang onie where—
Then, Jamie, I shall say nae mair,
    But quat my sang.   quit
Content wi' you to mak a pair
    Whare'er I gang.

A DREAM

Thoughts, words, and deeds, the Statute blames with reason;
But surely Dreams were ne'er indicted Treason.

On reading in the public papers, the Laureate's Ode with
the other parade of June 4th, 1786, the Author was no
sooner dropt asleep, than he imagined himself transported to
the Birth-day Levee: and, in his dreaming fancy, made the
following Address:

1

Guid-mornin to your Majesty!
    May Heaven augment your blisses,
On ev'ry new birth-day ye see,
    A humble Poet wishes!
My Bardship here, at your Levee,
    On sic a day as this is,
Is sure an uncouth sight to see,
those   Amang thae birth-day dresses
                    Sae fine this day.

2

busily   I see ye're complimented thrang,
                 By monie a lord an' lady;
             God Save the King 's a cuckoo sang
mighty   That's unco easy said ay:
             The poets, too, a venal gang,
                 Wi' rhymes weel-turn'd an' ready,
make; think Wad gar you trow ye ne'er do wrang,
                 But ay unerring steady,
                         On sic a day.

3

For me! before a Monarch's face,
    Ev'n there I winna flatter;
For neither pension, post, nor place,
    Am I your humble debtor:
So, nae reflection on your Grace,
    Your Kingship to bespatter;
worse   There's monie waur been o' the race,
maybe   And aiblins ane been better
                     Than you this day.

4

'Tis very true my sovereign King,
   My skill may weel be doubted;
But facts are chiels that winna ding,   fellows; be upset
   And downa be disputed:
Your royal nest, beneath your wing,
   Is e'en right reft and clouted,   torn and
And now the third part o' the string,   patched
   An' less, will gang about it
                  Than did ae day.

5

Far be't frae me that I aspire
   To blame your legislation,
Or say, ye wisdom want, or fire
   To rule this mighty nation:
But faith! I muckle doubt, my sire,   greatly
   Ye've trusted ministration
To chaps wha in a barn or byre   cow-shed
   Wad better fill'd their station,   Would have
                  Than courts yon day.

6

And now ye've gien auld Britain peace,
   Her broken shins to plaister;
Your sair taxation does her fleece,
   Till she has scarce a tester: sixpence
For me, thank God, my life's a lease,
   Nae bargain wearin faster,
Or faith! I fear, that, wi' the geese,
   I shortly boost to pasture   behove
                  I' the craft some day.   croft

7

I'm no mistrusting Willie Pitt,
   When taxes he enlarges,
(An' Will's a true guid fallow's get,   breed
   A name not envy spairges),   spatters
That he intends to pay your debt,
   An' lessen a' your charges;
But, God sake! let nae saving fit
   Abridge your bonie barges
                  An' boats this day.

8

sport

Adieu, my Liege! may Freedom geck
  Beneath your high protection;

wring

An' may ye rax Corruption's neck,
  And gie her for dissection!
But since I'm here I'll no neglect,
  In loyal, true affection,
To pay your Queen, wi' due respect,
  My fealty an' subjection
          This great birth-day.

9

Hail, Majesty most Excellent!
  While nobles strive to please ye,
Will ye accept a compliment,
  A simple Bardie gies ye?

brood

Thae bonie bairntime Heav'n has lent,

hoist

  Still higher may they heeze ye
In bliss, till Fate some day is sent,
  For ever to release ye
          Frae care that day.

10

For you, young Potentate' o' Wales,
  I tell your Highness fairly,
Down Pleasure's stream, wi' swelling sails,
  I'm tauld ye're driving rarely;
But some day ye may gnaw your nails,
  An' curse your folly sairly,

broke

That e'er ye brak Diana's pales,
  Or rattl'd dice wi' Charlie
          By night or day.

11

colt
old horse
sedately
gossip

Yet aft a ragged cowte's been known,
  To mak a noble aiver;
So, ye may doucely fill a throne,
  For a' their clish-ma-claver:
There, him at Agincourt wha shone,
  Few better were or braver;
And yet, wi, funny, queer Sir John,
  He was an unco shaver
          For monie a day.

12

For you, right rev'rend Osnaburg,
   Nane sets the lawn-sleeve sweeter,   becomes
Altho' a ribban at your lug   ear
   Wad been a dress completer:
As ye disown yon paughty dog,   haughty
   That bears the keys of Peter,   haste!
Then swith! an' get a wife to hug,
   Or trowth, ye'll stain the mitre
                 Some luckless day!

13

Young, royal Tarry-breeks, I learn,
   Ye're lately come athwart her—
A glorious galley, stem an' stern
   Weel rigg'd for Venus' barter;
But first hang out that she'll discern
   Your hymeneal charter;
Then heave aboard your grapple-airn,   grappling-iron
   An', large upon her quarter,
                Come full that day.

14

Ye, lastly, bonie blossoms a',
   Ye royal lasses dainty,
Heav'n mak you guid as weel as braw,
   An' gie you lads a-plenty!
But sneer na British boys awa!
   For kings are unco scant ay,
An' German gentles are but sma':
   They're better just than want ay
               On onie day.

15

God bless you a'! consider now,
   Ye're unco muckle dautet;   extremely;
                                 petted
But ere the course o' life be through,
   It may be bitter sautet: salted
An' I hae seen their coggie fou,   dish
   That yet hae tarrow't at it;   tarried
But or the day was done, I trow,
   The laggen they hae clautet   bottom; scraped
                Fu' clean that day.

THE VISION

DUAN FIRST

I

The sun had clos'd the winter day,
ceased   The curlers quat their roaring play,
hare   And hunger'd maukin taen her way,
kitchen-gardens   To kail-yards green,
each   While faithless snaws ilk step betray
         Whare she has been.

2

flail   The thresher's weary flingin-tree,
live-long   The lee-lang day had tired me;
     And when the day had clos'd his e'e,
         Far i' the west,
Back; parlour   Ben i' the spence, right pensivelie,
went   I gaed to rest.

3

-side   There, lanely by the ingle-cheek,
voyelling   I sat and ey'd the spewing reek,
cough-; drift   That fill'd, wi hoast-provoking smeek,
structure   The auld clay biggin;
rats   An' heard the restless rattons squeak
rooftree   About the riggin.

4

dusty   All in this mottie, misty clime,
     I backward mus'd on wasted time:
     How I had spent my youthfu' prime,
         An' done naething,
nonsense   But stringing blethers up in rhyme,
         For fools to sing.

5

Had I to guid advice but harkit,
I might, by this, hae led a market,
Or strutted in a bank and clarkit
      My cash-account:
While here, half-mad, half-fed, half-sarkit,   -shirted
      Is a' th' amount.

6

I started, mutt'ring 'Blockhead! coof!'   weakling
An' heav'd on high my waukit loof,   horny palm
To swear by a' yon starry roof,
      Or some rash aith,
That I henceforth would be rhyme-proof
      Till my last breath—

7

When click! the string the snick did draw;   latch
And jee! the door gaed to the wa';
And by my ingle-lowe I saw,   -flame
      Now bleezin bright,
A tight, outlandish hizzie, braw,   young woman
      Come full in sight.

8

Ye need na doubt, I held my whisht;   peace
The infant aith, half-form'd, was crusht;
I glowr'd as eerie's I'd been dusht,   stared; touched
      In some wild glen;
When sweet, like modest Worth, she blusht,
      And steppèd ben.   inside

9

Green, slender, leaf-clad holly-boughs
Were twisted, gracefu', round her brows;
I took her for some Scottish Muse,
      By that same token;
And come to stop those reckless vows,
      Would soon been broken.

10

A 'hair-brain'd, sentimental trace'
Was strongly markèd in her face;
A wildly-witty, rustic grace
          Shone full upon her;
Her eye, ev'n turn'd on empty space,
            Beam'd keen with honor.

11

bright   Down flow'd her robe, a tartan sheen,
barely   Till half a leg was scrimply seen;
And such a leg! my bonie Jean
          Could only peer it;
straight   Sae straught, saw taper, tight an' clean
           Nane else came near it.

12

Her mantle large, of greenish hue,
My gazing wonder chiefly drew;
Deep lights and shades, bold–mingling, threw
          A lustre grand;
And seem'd, to my astonish'd view,
          A well-known land.

13

Here, rivers in the sea were lost;
There, mountains to the skies were toss't;
Here, tumbling billows mark'd the coast
          With surging foam;
There, distant shone Art's lofty boast,
          The lordly dome.

14

Here, Doon pour'd down his far-fetch'd floods;
beats   There, well-fed Irwine stately thuds:
stole   Auld hermit Ayr staw thro' his woods,
          On to the shore;
And many a lesser torrent scuds
          With seeming roar.

15

Low, in a sandy valley spread,
An ancient borough rear'd her head;
Still, as in Scottish story read,
        She boasts a race
To ev'ry nobler virtue bred,
        And polish'd grace.

16

By stately tow'r, or palace fair,
Or ruins pendent in the air,
Bold stems of heroes, here and there,
        I could discern;
Some seem'd to muse, some seem'd to dare
        With feature stern.

17

My heart did glowing transport feel,
To see a race heroic wheel,
And brandish round the deep-dyed steel
        In sturdy blows;
While, back-recoiling, seem'd to reel
        Their suthron foes.

18

His Country's Saviour, mark him well!
Bold Richardton's heroic swell;
The chief, on Sark who glorious fell
        In high command;
And he whom ruthless fates expel
        His native land.

19

There, where a sceptr'd Pictish shade
Stalk'd round his ashes lowly laid,
I mark'd a martial race, pourtray'd
        In colours strong:
Bold, soldier-featur'd, undismay'd,
        They strode along.

20

Thro' many a wild, romantic grove,
Near many a hermit-fancied cove
(Fit haunts for friendship or for love
    In musing mood),
An aged Judge, I saw him rove,
    Dispensing good.

21

With deep-struck, reverential awe,
The learned Sire and Son I saw;
To Nature's God, and Nature's law,
    They gave their lore;
This, all its source and end to draw,
    That, to adore.

22

Brydon's brave ward I well could spy,
Beneath old Scotia's smiling eye;
Who call'd on Fame, low standing by,
    To hand him on,
Where many a patriot-name on high,
    And hero shone.

DUAN SECOND

1

With musing-deep, astonish'd stare,
I view'd the heavenly-seeming Fair;
A whisp'ring throb did witness bear
    Of kindred sweet,
When with an elder sister's air
    She did me greet.

2

'All hail! my own inspirèd Bard!
In me thy native Muse regard!
Nor longer mourn thy fate is hard
    Thus poorly low!
I come to give thee such reward,
    As we bestow.

3

'Know, the great Genius of this land
Has many a light aerial band,
Who, all beneath his high command,
   Harmoniously,
As arts or arms they understand,
    Their labors ply.

4

'They Scotia's race among them share:
Some fire the soldier on to dare;
Some rouse the patriot up to bare
   Corruption's heart;
Some teach the bard—a darling care—
    The tuneful art.

5

' 'Mong swelling floods of reeking gore,
They, ardent, kindling spirits pour;
Or, 'mid the venal Senate's roar,
   They, sightless, stand,
To mend the honest patriot-lore,
    And grace the hand.

6

'And when the bard, or hoary sage,
Charm or instruct the future age,
They bind the wild poetic rage
   In energy;
Or point the inconclusive page
    Full on the eye.

7

'Hence, Fullarton, the brave and young;
Hence, Dempster's zeal-inspirèd tongue;
Hence, sweet, harmonious Beattie sung
   His *Minstrel* lays,
Or tore, with noble ardour stung,
    The sceptic's bays.

8

'To lower orders are assign'd
The humbler ranks of human-kind,
The rustic bard, the laboring hind,
                    The artisan;
All chuse, as various they're inclin'd,
                    The various man.

9

'When yellow waves the heavy grain,
The threat'ning storm some strongly rein,
Some teach to meliorate the plain,
                    With tillage-skill;
And some instruct the shepherd-train,
                    Blythe o'er the hill.

10

'Some hint the lover's harmless wile;
Some grace the maiden's artless smile;
Some soothe the laborer's weary toil
                    For humble gains,
And make his cottage-scenes beguile
                    His cares and pains.

11

'Some, bounded to a district-space,
Explore at large man's infant race,
To mark the embryotic trace
                    Of rustic bard;
And careful note each opening grace,
                    A guide and guard.

12

'Of these am I—Coila my name:
And this district as mine I claim,
Where once the Campbells, chiefs of fame,
                    Held ruling pow'r:
I mark'd thy embryo-tuneful flame,
                    Thy natal hour.

13

'With future hope I oft would gaze,
Fond, on thy little early ways:
Thy rudely caroll'd, chiming phrase,
    In uncouth rhymes;
Fir'd at the simple, artless lays
     Of other times.

14

'I saw thee seek the sounding shore,
Delighted with the dashing roar;
Or when the North his fleecy store
    Drove thro' the sky,
I saw grim Nature's visage hoar
     Struck thy young eye.

15

'Or when the deep green-mantled earth
Warm cherish'd ev'ry flow'ret's birth,
And joy and music pouring forth
    In ev'ry grove;
I saw thee eye the gen'ral mirth
     With boundless love.

16

'When ripen'd fields and azure skies
Call'd forth the reaper's rustling noise,
I saw thee leave their ev'ning joys,
    And lonely stalk,
To vent thy bosom's swelling rise,
     In pensive walk.

17

'When youthful Love, warm-blushing, strong,
Keen-shivering, shot thy nerves along,
Those accents grateful to thy tongue,
    Th' adorèd *Name*,
I taught thee how to pour in song
     To soothe thy flame.

18

'I saw thy pulse's maddening play,
Wild-send thee Pleasure's devious way,
Misled by Fancy's meteor-ray,
          By passion driven;
But yet the light that led astray
          Was light from Heaven.

19

'I taught thy manners-painting strains
The loves, the ways of simple swains,
Till now, o'er all my wide domains
          Thy fame extends;
And some, the pride of Coila's plains,
          Become thy friends.

20

'Thou canst not learn, nor can I show,
To paint with Thomson's landscape glow;
Or wake the bosom-melting throe
          With Shenstone's art;
Or pour, with Gray, the moving flow
          Warm on the heart.

21

'Yet, all beneath th' unrivall'd rose,
The lowly daisy sweetly blows;
Tho' large the forest's monarch throws
          His army-shade,
Yet green the juicy hawthorn grows
          Adown the glade.

22

'Then never murmur nor repine;
Strive in thy humble sphere to shine;
And trust me, not Potosi's mine,
          Nor king's regard,
Can give a biss o'ermatching thine,
          A rustic Bard.

23

'To give my counsels all in one:
Thy tuneful flame still careful fan;
Preserve the dignity of Man,
                    With soul erect;
And trust the Universal Plan
                    Will all protect.

24

'And wear thou *this*'. She solemn said,
And bound the holly round my head:
The polish'd leaves and berries red
                    Did rustling play;
And, like a passing thought, she fled
                    In light away.

HALLOWEEN

Yes! let the rich deride, the proud disdain,
The simple pleasures of the lowly train:
To me more dear, congenial to my heart,
One native charm, than all the gloss of art.

                    GOLDSMITH

1

Upon that night, when fairies light
    On Cassilis Downans dance,
Or owre the lays, in splendid blaze,   partures
    On sprightly coursers prance;
Or for Colean the rout is ta'en,   road
    Beneath the moon's pale beams;
There, up the Cove, to stray and rove,
    Amang the rocks and streams
                    To sport that night:

2

Amang the bonie winding banks,
    Where Doon rins, wimplin, clear;
Where Bruce ance ruled the martial ranks,
    An' shook his Carrick spear;
Some merry, friendly, country-folks
    Together did convene,
To burn their nits, an' pou their stocks,
    An' haud their Hallowe'en
                        Fu' blythe that night.

winding — line 1
nuts; pull; plants — line 7
keep — line 8

3

The lasses feat an' cleanly neat,
    Mair braw than when they're fine;
Their faces blythe fu' sweetly kythe
    Hearts leal, an' warm, an' kin':
The lads sae trig, wi' wooer-babs
    Weel-knotted on their garten:
Some unco blate, an' some wi' gabs
    Gar lasses' hearts gang startin
                        Whyles fast at night.

spruce — line 1
fair — line 2
show — line 3
loyal; kind — line 4
love-knots — line 5
garters — line 6
shy; talk — line 7
make; beating — line 8
Sometimes — line 9

4

Then, first an' foremost, thro' the kail,
    Their stocks maun a' be sought ance;
They steek their een, an' grape an' wale
    For muckle anes, an' straught anes.
Poor hav'rel Will fell aff the drift,
    An' wandered thro' the bow-kail,
An' pow't, for want o' better shift,
    A runt, was like a sow-tail,
                        Sae bow't that night.

shut; eyes;
grope; choose
big; straight
foolish; lost the way
cabbage
pulled; choice
stalk
bent

5

Then, straught or crooked, yird or nane,
    They roar an' cry a' throu'ther;
The vera wee-things, toddlin, rin
    Wi' stocks out-owre their shouther:
An' gif the custock 's sweet or sour,
    Wi' joctelegs they taste them;
Syne coziely, aboon the door,
    Wi' cannie care, they 've plac'd them
                        To lie that night.

mould
pell-mell
children; run
upon
if; pith
pocket-knives
Then; above
prudent

6

The lasses staw frae 'mang them a',   stole
   To pou their stalks o' corn;
But Rab slips out, an' jinks about,   dodges
   Behint the muckle thorn:
He grippet Nelly hard an' fast;
   Loud skirl'd a' the lasses;   squeaked
But her tap-pickle maist was lost,
   Whan kiutlin in the fause-house   cuddling
      Wi' him that night.

7

The auld guid-wife's weel-hoordet nits   well-hoarded
   Are round an' round divided,
An' monie lads' an' lasses' fates
   Are there that night decided:
Some kindle couthie, side by side,   comfortably
   An' burn thegither trimly;
Some start awa wi' saucy pride,
   An' jump out-owre the chimlie   fire-place
      Fu' high that night.

8

Jean slips in twa, wi' tentie e'e;   watchful
   Wha 'twas, she wadna tell;
But this is *Jock*, an' this is *me*,
   She says in to hersel: whispers
He bleez'd owre her, an' she owre him,
   As they wad never mair part;
Till fuff! he started up the lum,   chimney
   And Jean had e'en a sair heart
      To see't that night.

9

Poor Willie, wi' his bow-kail runt,
   Was burnt wi' primsie Mallie;   precise Moll
An' Mary, nae doubt, took the drunt,   huff
   To be compar'd to Willie:
Mall's nit lap out, wi' pridefu' fling,   leaped; start
   An' her ain fit, it burnt it;   foot
While Willie lap, an' swoor by jing,
   'Twas just the way he wanted
      To be that night.

10

Nell had the fause-house in her min',
  She pits hersel an' Rob in;
In loving bleeze they sweetly join,
  ashes   Till white in ase they're sobbin;
Nell's heart was dancin at the view;
  by stealth,   She whisper'd Rob to leuk for't:
  tasted; mouth   Rob, stownlins, prie'd her bonie mou,
  corner   Fu' cozie in the neuk for't,
                                    Unseen that night.

11

  Marian   But Merran sat behint their backs,
                      Her thoughts on Andrew Bell;
  gabbing   She lea'es them gashing at their cracks,
                      An' slips out by hersel:
                    She thro' the yard the nearest taks,
                      An' to the kiln she goes then,
  in the dark;   An' darklins grapit for the bauks,
  cross-beams   And in the blue-clue throws then,
                                    Right fear't that night.

12

  wound; sweated   An' ay she win't, an' ay she swat—
  bet; trifling   I wat she made nae jaukin;
  kiln-pot   Till something held within the pat,
                       Guid Lord! but she was quakin!
                     But whether 'twas the Deil himsel,
  beam-end   Or whether 'twas a bauk-en',
                     Or whether it was Andrew Bell,
                       She did na wait on talkin
  ask   To spier that night.

13

                    Wee Jenny to her graunie says,
                      'Will ye go wi' me, graunie?
                    I'll eat the apple at the glass,
                      I gat frae uncle Johnie':
  puffed smoke   She fuff't her pipe wi' sic a lunt,
                      In wrath she was sae vap'rin,
  cinder burnt   She notic't na an aizle brunt
  worsted   Her braw, new, worset apron
                                    Out thro' that night.

14

'Ye little skelpie-limmer's face!
   I daur ye try sic sportin,
As seek the Foul Thief onie place,   Devil
   For him to spae your fortune: tell
Nae doubt but ye may get a sight!
   Great cause ye hae to fear it;
For monie a ane has gotten a fright,
   An' liv'd an' died deleeret,   mad
                     On sic a night.

15

'Ae hairst afore the Sherra-moor,   harvest;
   I mind't as weel's yestreen—   Sheriffmuir
I was a gilpey then, I'm sure   remember
   I was na past fyfteen: young girl
The simmer had been cauld an' wat,
   An' stuff was unco green;   grain; very
An' ay a rantin kirn we gat,   rollicking
   An' just on Halloween   harvest-home
                     It fell that night.

16

'Our stibble-rig was Rab M'Graen,   chief harvester
   A clever, sturdy fallow;
His sin gat Eppie Sim wi' wean,   son; child
   That lived in Achmachalla:
He gat hemp-seed, I mind it weel,
   An' he made unco light o't;
But monie a day was by himsel,   off his wits
   He was sae sairly frighted
                     That vera night.'

17

Then up gat fechtin Jamie Fleck,   fighting
   An' he swoor by his conscience,
That he could saw hemp-seed a peck;   sow
   For it was a' but nonsense: all merely
The auld guidman raught down the pock,   reached; bag
   An' out a handfu' gied him;
Syne bad him slip frae 'mang the folk,
   Sometime when nae ane see'd him,
                     An' try't that night.

18

staggered

He marches thro' amang the stacks,
    Tho' he was something sturtin;

dungfork
trails; crupper

The graip he for a harrow taks,
    And haurls at his curpin;

sow

And ev'ry now and then, he says,
    'Hemp-seed I saw thee,
An' her that is to be my lass
    Come after me, an' draw thee
              As fast this night'.

19

He whistl'd up *Lord Lenox' March*,
    To keep his courage cheery;
Altho' his hair began to arch,

*scared; awe-
stricken*

    He was sae fley'd an' eerie;
Till presently he hears a squeak,

groan

    An' then a grane an' gruntle;

round; look

He by his shoulder gae a keek,

summersault

    An' tumbl'd wi' a wintle
              Out-owre that night.

20

He roar'd a horrid murder-shout,
    In dreadfu' desperation!
An' young an' auld come rinnin out,
    An' hear the sad narration:

halting

He swoor 'twas hilchin Jean M'Craw,

hunchbacked

    Or crouchie Merran Humphie—
Till stop! she trotted thro' them a';

the pig

    An' wha was it but grumphie

Astir

              Asteer that night?

21

have gone

Meg fain wad to the barn gaen,

winnow;

    To winn three wechts o' naething;

all by herself

But for to meet the Deil her lane,
    She pat but little faith in:

shepherd; few

She gies the herd a pickle nits,
    An' twa red-cheekit apples,
To watch, while for the barn she sets,
    In hopes to see Tam Kipples
              That vera night.

22

She turns they key wi' cannie thraw,   twist
   An' owre the threshold ventures;
But first on Sawnie gies a ca',
   Syne bauldly in she enters:
A ratton rattl'd up the wa',   rat
   An' she cry'd, L—d preserve her!
An' ran thro' midden-hole an' a',
   An' pray'd wi' zeal and fervour
               Fu' fast that night.

23

They hoy't out Will, wi' sair advice;   urged
   They hecht him some fine braw ane;   promised
It chanc'd the stack he faddomt' thrice,
   Was timmer-propt for thrawin: against bending
He taks a swirlie, auld moss-oak   twisted
   For some black gruesome carlin;   beldam
An' loot a winze, an' drew a stroke,   uttered a curse,
   Till skin in blypes cam haurlin   and made a hit
               Aff 's nieves that night.   shreds
                               Off his fists

24

A wanton widow Leezie was,
   As cantie as a kittlin;   lively; kitten
But och! that night, amang the shaws,   woods
   She gat a fearfu' settlin!
She thro' the whins, an' by the cairn,
   An' owre the hill gaed scrievin;   careering
Whare three laird's lands met at a burn,   brook
   To dip her left sark-sleeve in
               Was bent that night.

25

Whyles owre a linn the burnie plays,   Now; fall
   As thro' the glen it wimpl't;
Whyles round a rocky scaur it strays,   cliff
   Whyles in a wiel it dimpl't;   eddy
Whyles glitter'd to the nightly rays,
   Wi' bickerin, dancin dazzle;
Whyles cookit underneath the braes,   hid
   Below the spreading hazel
               Unseen that night.

26

ferns; hillside

young cow in
the open

leaped; sheath

lark-high

foot

ears

Amang the brachens, on the brae,
    Between her an' the moon,
The Deil, or else an outler quey,
    Gat up an' gae a croon:
Poor Leezie's heart maist lap the hool;
    Near lav'rock-height she jumpit;
But mist a fit, an' in the pool
    Out-owre the lugs she plumpit
                    Wi' a plunge that night.

27

1715

empty

In order, on the clean hearth-stane,
    The luggies three are ranged;
And ev'ry time great care is taen
    To see them duly changed:
Auld uncle John, wha wedlock's joys
    Sin Mar's-year did desire,
Because he gat the toom dish thrice,
    He heav'd them on the fire
                    In wrath that night.

28

wot

wondrous

steam

tongues wagging

liquor

Wi' merry sangs, an' friendly cracks,
    I wat they did na weary;
An unco tales, an' funnie jokes—
    Their sports were cheap an' cheery:
Till butter'd sow'ns, wi' fragrant lunt,
    Set a' their gabs a-steerin;
Syne, wi' a social glass o' strunt,
    They parted aff careerin
                    Fu' blythe that night.

THE AULD FARMER'S NEW-YEAR MORNING SALUTATION TO HIS AULD MARE, MAGGIE

ON GIVING HER THE ACCUSTOMED RIPP OF CORN TO HANSEL
IN THE NEW-YEAR

I

A Guid New-Year I wish thee, Maggie!
Hae, there's a ripp to thy auld baggie:
Tho' thou's howe-backit now, an' knaggie,
    I've seen the day
Thou could hae gaen like onie staggie,
     Out-owre the lay.

handful from the sheaf; belly hollow-backed; knobby

gone; colt

lea

2

Tho' now thou's dowie, stiff, an' crazy,
An' thy auld hide as white's a daisie,
I've seen thee dappl't, sleek an' glaizie,
    A bonie gray:
He should been tight that daur't to raize thee,
     Ance in a day.

drooping

shiny

prepared; excite

3

Thou ance was i' the foremost rank,
A filly buirdly, steeve, an' swank:
An' set weel down a shapely shank
    As e'er tread yird;
An' could hae flown out-owre a stank
    Like onie bird.

stately, compact

limber

earth

most

4

It's now some nine-an'-twenty year
Sin' thou was my guid-father's meere;
He gied me thee, o' tocher clear,
    An' fifty mark;
Tho' it was sma', 'twas weel-won gear,
    An' thou was stark.

father-in-law's

wholly as dowry

strong

5

went
mother
sly
mischievous
tractable
good-tempered

When first I gaed to woo my Jenny,
Ye then was trottin wi' your minnie:
Tho' ye was trickie, slee, an' funnie,
                 Ye ne'er was donsie;
But hamely, tawie, quiet, an' cannie,
                 An' unco sonsie.

6

bore

That day, ye pranc'd wi' muckle pride,
When ye bure hame my bonie bride:
An' sweet an' gracefu' she did ride,
                 Wi' maiden air!

have challenged

Kyle-Stewart I could braggèd wide,
                 For sic a pair.

7

can; stumble
stagger
goer
wind
wobble

Tho' now ye dow but hoyte and hobble,
An' wintle like a saumont-coble,
That day, ye was a jinker noble,
                 For heels an' win'!
An' ran them till they a' did wauble,
                 Far, far behin'!

8

skittish
tedious
snort; whinny

aloof

When thou an' I were young and skiegh,
An' stable-meals at fairs were driegh,
How thou wad prance, an' snore, an' skriegh,
                 An' tak the road!
Town's-bodies ran, an' stood abiegh,
                 An' ca't thee mad.

9

wedding-races

When thou was corn't, an' I was mellow,
We took the road ay like a swallow:
At brooses thou had ne'er a fellow,
                 For pith an' speed;
But ev'ry tail thou pay't them hollow,
                 Whare'er thou gaed.

10

The sma, droop-rumpl't, hunter cattle   short-rumped
Might aiblins waur't thee for a brattle;   have beat; spurt
But sax Scotch miles thou try't their mettle,
        An' gar't them whaizle: wheeze
Nae whip nor spur, but just a wattle
        O' saugh or hazle.   willow

11

Thou was a noble fittie-lan',
As e'er in tug or tow was drawn!
Aft thee an' I, in aught hours' gaun,   going
        On guid March-weather,
Hae turn'd sax rood beside our han'   to our own cheek
        For days thegither.

12

Thou never braing't, an' fetch't, an' fliskit;   pulled rashly stopped suddenly; capered
But thy auld tail thou wad hae whiskit,
An' spread abreed thy weel-fill'd brisket,
        Wi' pith an' pow'r;   rooty hillocks would have roared; cracked fallen smoothly over
Till sprittie knowes wad rair't, an' riskit,
        An' slypet owre.

13

When frosts lay lang, an' snaws were deep,
An' threaten'd labour back to keep,
I gied thy cog a wee bit heap   dish
        Aboon the timmer: edge
I ken'd my Maggie wad na sleep
        For that, or simmer.   ere

14

In cart or car thou never reestit;
The steyest brae thou wad hae fac't it;   stiffest incline
Thou never lap, an' sten't, an' breastit,   leaped; sprang
        Then stood to blaw;
But just thy step a wee thing hastit,
        Thou snoov't awa.   jogged along

15

team; issue

more

My pleugh is now thy bairntime a',
Four gallant brutes as e'er did draw;
Forbye sax mae I've sell't awa,
                    That thou hast nurst;
They drew me thretteen pund an' twa.
                    The vera warst.

16

day's work

Monie a sair darg we twa hae wrought,
An' wi' the weary warl' fought!
An' monie an anxious day I thought
                    We wad be beat!
Yet here to crazy age we're brought,
                    Wi' something yet.

17

An' think na, my auld trusty servan',
That now perhaps thou's less deservin,
An' thy auld days may end in starvin;

bushel

quarter-peck

                    For my last fow,
A heapet stimpart, I'll reserve ane
                    Laid by for you.

18

We've worn to crazy years thegither;

totter

change

reserved patch

fill your stomach

We'll toyte about wi' ane anither;
Wi' tentie care I'll flit thy tether
                    To some hain'd rig,
Whare ye may nobly rax your leather
                    Wi' sma' fatigue.

THE COTTER'S SATURDAY NIGHT

INSCRIBED TO R. AIKEN, ESQ.

Let not Ambition mock their useful toil,
Their homely joys, and destiny obscure;
Nor Grandeur hear, with a disdainful smile,
The short and simple annals of the poor.

GRAY

I

My lov'd, my honor'd, much respected friend!
   No mercenary bard his homage pays;
With honest pride, I scorn each selfish end,
   My dearest meed, a friend's esteem and praise:
   To you I sing, in simple Scottish lays,
The lowly train in life's sequester'd scene;
   The native feelings strong, the guileless ways;
What Aiken in a cottage would have been;
Ah! tho' his worth unknown, far happier there I
     ween!

2

November chill blaws loud wi' angry sugh;   *wail*
   The short'ning winter-day is near a close;
The miry beasts retreating frae the pleugh;
   The black'ning trains o' craws to their repose:
   The toil-worn Cotter frae his labor goes—
This night his weekly moil is at an end,
   Collects his spades, his mattocks, and his hoes,
Hoping the morn in ease and rest to spend,
And weary, o'er the moor, his course does
     hameward bend.

3

At length his lonely cot appears in view,
   Beneath the shelter of an aged tree;
Th' expectant wee-things, toddlin, stacher through   *totter*
   To meet their dad, wi' flichterin' noise and glee.   *fluttering*
   His wee bit ingle, blinkin bonilie,
His clean hearth-stane, his thrifty wifie's smile,
   The lisping infant, prattling on his knee,
Does a' his weary carking cares beguile,
And makes him quite forget his labor and his toil.

4

By and bye
follow;

heedful run
quiet

Belyve, the elder bairns come drapping in,
    At service out, amang the farmers roun';
Some ca' the pleugh, some herd, some tentie rin
    A cannie errand to a neebor town:
    Their eldest hope, their Jenny, woman grown,
In youthfu' bloom, love sparkling in her e'e,
    Comes hame; perhaps, to shew a braw new
        gown,

hard-; wages

Or deposite her sair-won penny-fee,
To help her parents dear, if they in hardship be.

5

asks

wonders

Makes; clothes

With joy unfeign'd, brothers and sisters meet,
    And each for other's weelfare kindly spiers:
The social hours, swift-wing'd, unnotic'd fleet;
    Each tells the uncos that he sees or hears.
    The parents partial eye their hopeful years;
Anticipation forward points the view;
    The mother, wi' her needle and her sheers,
Gars auld claes look amaist as weel's the new;
The father mixes a' wi' admonition due.

6

diligent
trifle

Their master's and their mistress's command
    The younkers a' are warned to obey;
And mind their labors wi' an eydent hand,
    And ne'er, tho' out o' sight, to jauk or play:
    'And O! be sure to fear the Lord alway,
And mind your duty, duly, morn and night;
    Lest in temptation's path ye gang astray,
Implore His counsel and assisting might:
They never sought in vain that sought the Lord
        aright.'

7

But hark! a rap comes gently to the door;
    Jenny, wha kens the meaning o' the same,
Tells how a neebor lad came o'er the moor,
    To do some errands, and convey her hame.
    The wily mother sees the conscious flame
Sparkle in Jenny's e'e, and flush her cheek;
    With heart-struck anxious care, enquires his
        name,

While Jenny hafflins is afraid to speak;   half
Weel-pleas'd the mother hears, it's nae wild,
    worthless rake.

8

With kindly welcome, Jenny brings him ben;   inside
  A strappin' youth, he takes the mother's eye;
Blythe Jenny sees the visit's no ill taen;
  The father cracks of horses, pleughs, and kye.   chats; cattle
  The youngster's artless heart o'erflows wi' joy,
But blate and laithfu', scarce can weel behave;   shy: sheepish
  The mother, wi' a woman's wiles, can spy
What makes the youth saw bashfu' and sae grave;
Weel-pleas'd to think her bairn's respected like
    the lave.   rest

9

O happy love! where love like this is found:
  O heart-felt raptures! bliss beyond compare!
I've pacèd much this weary, mortal round,
  And sage experience bids me this declare:—
  'If Heaven a draught of heavenly pleasure spare,
One cordial in this melancholy vale,
  'Tis when a youthful, loving, modest pair,
In other's arms, breathe out the tender tale
Beneath the milk-white thorn that scents the
    ev'ning gale.'

10

Is there, in human form, that bears a heart,
  A wretch! a villain! lost to love and truth!
That can, with studied, sly, ensnaring art,
  Betray sweet Jenny's unsupecting youth?
  Curse on his perjur'd arts! dissembling, smooth!
Are honor, virtue, conscience, all exil'd?
  Is there no pity, no relenting ruth,
Points to the parents fondling o'er their child?
Then paints the ruin'd maid, and their distraction
    wild?

11

But now the supper crowns their simple board,
    The healsome parritch, chief o' Scotia's food;
The soupe their only hawkie does afford,
    That, 'yont the hallan snugly chows her cood;
    The dame brings forth, in complimental mood,
To grace the lad, her weel-hain'd kebbuck, fell;
    And aft he's prest, and aft he ca's it guid;
The frugal wifie, garrulous, will tell,
How 'twas a townmond auld, sin' lint was i' the
             bell.

12

The chearfu' supper done, wi' serious face,
    They, round the ingle, form a circle wide;
The sire turns o'er, wi' patriarchal grace,
    The big ha'-Bible, ance his father's pride.
    His bonnet rev'rently is laid aside,
His lyart haffets wearing thin and bare;
    Those strains that once did sweet in Zion glide,
He wales a portion with judicious care,
And 'Let us worship God!' he says, with solemn
             air.

13

They chant their artless notes in simple guise,
    They tune their hearts, by far the noblest aim;
Perhaps *Dundee's* wild-warbling measures rise,
    Or plaintive *Martyrs*, worthy of the name;
    Or noble *Elgin* beets the heaven-ward flame,
The sweetest far of Scotia's holy lays:
    Compar'd with these, Italian trills are tame;
The tickl'd ears no heart-felt raptures raise;
Nae unison hae they, with our Creator's praise.

14

The priest-like father reads the sacred page,
    How Abram was the friend of God on high;
Or, Moses bade eternal warfare wage
    With Amalek's ungracious progeny;
    Or, how the royal Bard did groaning lie

Beneath the stroke of Heaven's avenging ire;
  Or Job's pathetic plaint, and wailing cry;
Or rapt Isaiah's wild, seraphic fire;
  Or other holy Seers that tune the sacred lyre.

15

Perhaps the Christian volume is the theme:
  How guiltless blood for guilty man was shed;
How He, who bore in Heaven the second name,
  Had not on earth whereon to lay His head;
  How His first followers and servants sped;
The precepts sage they wrote to many a land:
  How he, who lone in Patmos banishèd,
Saw in the sun a mighty angel stand,
And heard great Bab'lon's doom pronounc'd by
    Heaven's command.

16

Then kneeling down to Heaven's Eternal King,
  The saint, the father, and the husband prays:
Hope 'springs exulting on triumphant wing.'
  That thus they all shall meet in future days,
  There, ever bask in uncreated rays,
No more to sigh or shed the bitter tear,
  Together hymning their Creator's praise,
In such society, yet still more dear;
While circling Time moves round in an eternal
    sphere.

17

Compar'd with this, how poor Religion's pride,
  In all the pomp of method, and of art;
When men display to congregations wide
  Devotion's ev'ry grace, except the heart!
  The Power, incens'd, the pageant will desert,
The pompous strain, the sacerdotal stole:
  But haply, in some cottage far apart,
May hear, well-pleas'd, the language of the soul,
And in His Book of Life the inmates poor enroll.

18

Then homeward all take off their sev'ral way;
   The youngling cottagers retire to rest:
The parent-pair their secret homage pay,
   And proffer up to Heaven the warm request,
   That He who stills the raven's clam'rous nest,
And decks the lily fair in flow'ry pride,
   Would, in the way His wisdom sees the best,
For them and for their little ones provide;
But, chiefly, in their hearts with Grace Divine
      preside.

19

From scenes like these, old Scotia's grandeur springs
   That makes her lov'd at home, rever'd abroad:
Princes and lords are but the breath of kings,
   'An honest man's the noble(st) work of God';
   And certes, in fair Virtue's heavenly road,
The cottage leaves the palace far behind;
   What is a lordling's pomp? a cumbrous load,
Disguising oft the wretch of human kind,
Studied in arts of Hell, in wickedness refin'd!

20

O Scotia! my dear, my native soil!
   For whom my warmest wish to Heaven is
      sent!
Long may thy hardy sons of rustic toil
   Be blest with health, and peace, and sweet
      content!
   And O! may Heaven their simple lives prevent
From Luxury's contagion, weak and vile!
   Then, howe'er crowns and coronets be rent,
A virtuous populace may rise the while,
And stand a wall of fire around their much-lov'd
      Isle.

21

O Thou! who pour'd the patriotic tide,
   That stream'd thro' Wallace's undaunted heart,
Who dar'd to, nobly, stem tyrannic pride,
   Or nobly die, the second glorious part:
   (The patriot's God, peculiarly Thou art,

His friend, inspirer, guardian, and reward!)
O never, never Scotia's realm desert;
But still the patriot, and the patriot-bard
In bright succession raise, her ornament and
    guard!

TO A MOUSE

ON TURNING HER UP IN HER NEST WITH THE PLOUGH,
NOVEMBER 1785

1

Wee, sleekit, cowrin, tim'rous beastie,   *sleek*
O, what a panic's in thy breastie!
Thou need na start awa sae hasty
    Wi' bickering brattle!   *hurrying*
                            scamper
I wad be laith to rin an' chase thee,   *loth*
    Wi' murdering pattle!   *plough-staff*

2

I'm truly sorry man's dominion
Has broken Nature's social union,
An' justifies that ill opinion
    Which makes thee startle
At me, thy poor, earth-born companion
    An' fellow mortal!

3

I doubt na, whyles, but thou may thieve;   *sometimes*
What then? poor beastie, thou maun live!   *odd ear;*
A daimen icker in a thrave   *twenty-four*
                          sheaves
    'S a sma' request;
I'll get a blessin wi' the lave,   *what's left*
    An' never miss't!

4

Thy wee-bit housie, too, in ruin!
Its silly wa's the win's are strewin!   *febble; winds*
An' naething, now, to big a new ane,
    O' foggage green!   *coarse grass*
An' bleak December's win's ensuin,
    Baith snell an' keen!   *bitter*

5

Thou saw the fields laid bare an' waste,
An' weary winter comin fast,
An' cozie here, beneath the blast,
                    Thou thought to dwell,
Till crash! the cruel coulter past
                    Out thro' thy cell.

6

stubble

That wee bit heap o' leaves an' stibble,
Has cost thee monie a weary nibble!
Now thou's turned out, for a' thy trouble,

Without;
holding
endure
hoar-frost

                    But house or hald,
To thole the winter's sleety dribble,
                    An' cranreuch cauld!

7

alone

But Mousie, thou art no thy lane,
In proving foresight may be vain:
The best-laid schemes o' mice an' men

askew

                    Gang aft agley,
An' lea'e us nought but grief an' pain,
                    For promis'd joy!

8

Still thou art blest, compared wi' me!
The present only toucheth thee:
But och! I backward cast my e'e,
                    On prospects drear!
An' forward, tho' I canna see,
                    I guess an' fear!

EPISTLE TO DAVIE, A BROTHER POET

1

While winds frae aff Ben-Lomond blaw,
And bar the doors wi' drivin' snaw,
   And hing us owre the ingle,   *fire*
I set me down to pass the time,
And span a verse or twa o' rhyme,
   In hamely, westlin jingle: *westland*
While frosty winds blaw in the drift,   *Right to the*
  Ben to the chimla lug,   *chimney corner*
I grudge a wee the great-folk's gift,
   That live sae bien an' snug: *prosperous*
     I tent less, and want less   *value*
       Their roomy fire-side;
      But hanker, and canker,
         To see their cursed pride.

2

It's hardly in a body's pow'r,
To keep, at times, frae being sour,
   To see how things are shar'd;
How best o' chiels are whyles in want,   *chaps;*
                              sometimes
While coofs on countless thousands rant, *dolts; roister*
  And ken na how to ware't;   *spend*
But Davie, lad, ne'er fash your head,   *trouble*
  Tho' we hae little gear;   *wealth*
We 're fit to win our daily bread,   *whole;*
  As lang 's we're hale and fier;   *sound*
    'Mair spier na, nor fear na',   *ask not*
      Auld age ne'er mind a feg;   *fig*
     The last o't, the warst o't,
       Is only but to beg.

3

To lie in kilns and barns at e'en,
When banes are craz'd, and bluid is thin,
   Is, doubtless, great distress!
Yet then content could make us blest;
Ev'n then, sometimes, we'd snatch a taste
   Of truest happiness.

The honest heart that's free frae a'
  Intended fraud or guile,
However Fortune kick the ba',
  Has ay some cause to smile;
    And mind still, you'll find still,
      A comfort this nae sma';
    Nae mair then, we'll care then,
      Nae farther can we fa'.

4

What tho', like commoners of air,
We wander out, we know not where,
  But either house or hal'?
Yet Nature's charms, the hills and woods,
The sweeping vales, and foaming floods,
  Are free alike to all.
In days when daisies deck the ground,
  And blackbirds whistle clear,
With honest joy our hearts will bound,
  To see the coming year:
    On braes when we please then,
      We'll sit an' sowth a tune;
    Syne rhyme till't we'll time till't,
      An' sing't when we hae done.

Without; holding (gloss for line 2)

hill-sides (gloss)
hum (gloss)
Then (gloss)

5

It's no in titles nor in rank:
It's no in wealth like Lon'on Bank,
  To purchase peace and rest.
It's no in makin muckle, mair;
It's no in books, it's no in lear,
  To make us truly blest:
If happiness hae not her seat
  An' centre in the breast,
We may be wise, or rich, or great,
  But never can be blest!
    Nae treasures nor pleasures
      Could makes us happy lang;
    The heart ay's the part ay
      That makes us right or wrang.

much, more (gloss)
learning (gloss)

6

Think ye, that sic as you and I,
Wha drudge and drive thro' wet and dry,
    Wi' never ceasing toil;
Think ye, are we less blest than they,
Wha scarcely tent us in their way,
    As hardly worth their while?
Alas! how oft, in haughty mood,
    God's creatures they oppress!
Or else, neglecting a' that's guid,
    They riot in excess!
        Baith careless and fearless
            Of either Heaven or Hell;
        Esteeming and deeming
            It a' an idle tale!

7

Then let us chearfu' acquiesce,
Nor make our scanty pleasures less
    By pining at our state:
And, even should misfortunes come,
I here wha sit hae met wi' some,
    An's thankfu' for them yet,   And am
They gie the wit of age to youth;
    They let us ken oursel;
They make us see the naked truth,
    The real guid and ill:
        Tho' losses and crosses
            Be lessons right severe,
        There's wit there, ye 'll get there,
            Ye'll find nae other where.

8

But tent me, Davie, ace o' hearts!   listen to
(To say aught less wad wrang the cartes,   cards
    And flatt'ry I detest)
This life has joys for you and I;
And joys that riches ne'er could buy,
    And joys the very best.

There's a' the pleasures o' the heart,
  The lover an' the frien':
Ye hae your Meg, your dearest part,
  And I my darling Jean!
    I warms me, it charms me
      To mention but her name:
kindles   It heats me, it beets me,
        And sets me a' on flame!

9

O all ye Pow'rs who rule above!
O Thou whose very self art love!
  Thou know'st my words sincere!
The life-blood streaming thro' my heart,
Or my more dear immortal part,
  Is not more fondly dear!
When heart-corroding care and grief
  Deprive my soul of rest,
Her dear idea brings relief
  And solace to my breast.
    Thou Being All-seeing,
      O, hear my fervent pray'r!
    Still take her, and make her
      Thy most peculiar care!

10

All hail! ye tender feelings dear!
The smile of love, the friendly tear,
  The sympathetic glow!
Long since, this world's thorny ways
Had number'd out my weary days,
  Had it not been for you!
Fate still has blest me with a friend
  In every care and ill;
And oft a more endearing band,
  A tie more tender still.
    It lightens, it brightens
      The tenebrific scene,
    To meet with, and greet with
      My Davie or my Jean!

II

O, how that Name inspires my style!
The words come skelpin' rank an' file,   spanking
   Amaist before I ken!
The ready measure rins as fine,
As Phœbus and the famous Nine
   Were glowrin owre my pen.   overlooking
My spaviet Pegasus will limp,   spavined
   Till ance he's fairly het;   hot
And then he'll hilch, an' stilt, an' jimp,   hobble; limp;
   And rin an unco fit;   jump
                      uncommon
     But least then, the beast then   burst
       Should rue this hasty ride,
     I'll light now, and dight now   wipe
       His sweaty, wizen'd hide.

THE LAMENT
TUNE: *Scots Queen*

OCCASIONED BY THE UNFORTUNATE ISSUE OF A FRIEND'S
AMOUR

Alas! how oft does Goodness wound itself,
And sweet Affection prove the spring of Woe!
                          HOME

I

O thou pale Orb that silent shines
   While care-untroubled mortals sleep!
Thou seest a wretch who inly pines,
   And wanders here to wail and weep!
   With Woe I nightly vigils keep,
Beneath thy wan, unwarming beam;
   And mourn, in lamentation deep,
How life and love are all a dream!

2

I joyless view thy rays adorn
  The faintly-markèd, distant hill;
I joyless view thy trembling horn
  Reflected in the gurgling rill:
  My fondly-fluttering heart, be still!
Thou busy pow'r, Remembrance, cease!
  Ah! must the agonizing thrill
For ever bar returning Peace?

3

No idly-feign'd, poetic pains
  My sad, love-lorn lamentings claim:
No shepherd's pipe—Arcadian strains;
  No fabled tortures quaint and tame.
  The plighted faith, the mutual flame,
The oft-attested Pow'rs above,
  The promis'd father's tender name,
These were the pledges of my love!

4

Encircled in her clasping arms,
  How have the raptur'd moments flown!
How have I wished for Fortune's charms,
  For her dear sake, and her's alone!
  And, must I think it! is she gone,
My secret heart's exulting boast?
  And does she heedless hear my groan?
And is she ever, ever lost?

5

O! can she bear so base a heart,
  So lost to honour, lost to truth,
As from the fondest lover part,
  The plighted husband of her youth?
  Alas! Life's path may be unsmooth!
Her way may lie thro' rough distress!
  Then, who her pangs and pains will soothe,
Her sorrows share, and make them less?

6

Ye wingèd Hours that o'er us pass'd,
   Enraptur'd more the more enjoy'd,
Your dear remembrance in my breast
   My fondly treasur'd thoughts employ'd:
   That breast, how dreary now, and void,
For her too scanty once of room!
   Ev'n ev'ry ray of Hope destroy'd,
And not a wish to gild the gloom!

7

The morn, that warns th' approaching day,
   Awakes me up to toil and woe;
I see the hours in long array,
   That I must suffer, lingering slow:
   Full many a pang, and many a throe,
Keen Recollection's direful train,
   Must wring my soul, ere Phœbus, low,
Shall kiss the distant western main.

8

And when my nightly couch I try,
   Sore-harass'd out with care and grief,
My toil-beat nerves and tear-worn eye
   Keep watchings with the nightly thief:
   Or, if I slumber, Fancy, chief,
Reigns, haggard-wild, in sore affright:
   Ev'n day, all-bitter, brings relief
From such a horror-breathing night.

9

O thou bright Queen, who, o'er th' expanse
   Now highest reign'st, with boundless sway!
Oft has thy silent-marking glance
   Observ'd us, fondly-wand'ring, stray!
   The time, unheeded, sped away,
While Love's luxurious pulse beat high,
   Beneath thy silver-gleaming ray,
To mark the mutual-kindling eye.

10

O scenes in strong remembrance set!
  Scenes, never, never to return!
Scenes if in stupor I forget,
  Again I feel, again I burn!
  From ev'ry joy and pleasure torn,
Life's weary vale I wander thro';
  And hopeless, comfortless, I'll mourn
A faithless woman's broken vow!

DESPONDENCY

An Ode

1

Oppress'd with grief, oppress'd with care,
A burden more than I can bear,
  I set me down and sigh;
O Life! thou art a galling load,
Along a rough, a weary road,
  To wretches such as I!
Dim-backward, as I cast my view,
  What sick'ning scenes appear!
What sorrows yet may pierce me thro',
  Too justly I may fear!
    Still caring, despairing,
      Must be my bitter doom;
    My woes here shall close ne'er
      But with the closing tomb!

2

Happy ye sons of busy life,
Who, equal to the bustling strife,
   No other view regard!
Ev'n when the wishèd end's denied,
Yet while the busy means arc plied,
   They bring their own reward:
Whilst I, a hope-abandoned wight,
   Unfitted with an aim,
Meet ev'ry sad returning night
   And joyless morn the same.
      You, bustling and justling,
         Forget each grief and pain;
      I, listless yet restless,
         Find ev'ry prospect vain.

3

How blest the Solitary's lot,
Who, all-forgetting, all-forgot,
   Within his humble cell—
The cavern, wild with tangling roots—
Sits o'er his newly-gather'd fruits,
   Beside his crystal well!
Or haply to his ev'ning thought,
   By unfrequented stream,
The ways of men are distant brought,
   A faint-collected dream;
      While praising, and raising
         His thoughts to Heav'n on high,
      As wand'ring, meand'ring,
         He views the solemn sky.

4

Then I, no lonely hermit plac'd
Where never human footsteps trac'd,
   Less fit to play the part;
The lucky moment to improve,
And just to stop, and just to move,
   With self-respecting art:

But ah! those pleasures, loves, and joys,
　　Which I too keenly taste,
The Solitary can despise—
　　Can want and yet be blest!
He needs not, he heeds not
　　Or human love or hate;
Whilst I here must cry here
　　At perfidy ingrate!

5

O enviable early days,
When dancing thoughtless pleasure's maze,
　　To care, to guilt unknown!
How ill exchang'd for riper times,
To feel the follies or the crimes
　　Of others, or my own!
Ye tiny elves that guiltless sport,
　　Like linnets in the bush,
Ye little know the ills ye court,
　　When manhood is your wish!
　　The losses, the crosses
　　　　That active man engage;
　　The fears all, the tears all
　　　　Of dim declining Age!

MAN WAS MADE TO MOURN

A Dirge
TUNE: *Peggy Bawn*

I

When chill November's surly blast
　　Made fields and forests bare,
One ev'ning, as I wand'red forth
　　Along the banks of Ayr,
I spied a man, whose agèd step
　　Seem'd weary, worn with care,
His face was furrow'd o'er with years,
　　And hoary was his hair.

2

'Young stranger, whither wand'rest thou?'
    Began the rev'rend Sage;
'Does thirst of wealth thy step constrain,
    Or youthful pleasure's rage?
Or haply, prest with cares and woes,
    Too soon thou hast began
To wander forth, with me to mourn
    The miseries of Man.

3

'The sun that overhangs yon moors,
    Out-spreading far and wide,
Where hundreds labour to support
    A haughty lordling's pride:
I've seen you weary winter-sun
    Twice forty times return;
And ev'ry time has added proofs,
    That Man was made to mourn.

4

'O Man! while in thy early years,
    How prodigal of time!
Mis-spending all thy precious hours,
    Thy glorious, youthful prime!
Alternate follies take the sway,
    Licentious passions burn:
Which tenfold force gives Nature's law,
    That Man was made to mourn.

5

'Look not alone on youthful prime,
    Or manhood's active might;
Man then is useful to his kind,
    Supported is his right:
But see him on the edge of life,
    With cares and sorrows worn;
Then Age and Want—O ill-match'd pair!—
    Shew Man was made to mourn.

6

'A few seem favourites of Fate,
   In Pleasure's lap carest;
Yet think not all the rich and great
   Are likewise truly blest:
But oh! what crowds in ev'ry land,
   All wretched and forlorn,
Thro' weary life this lesson learn,
   That Man was made to mourn.

7

'Many and sharp the num'rous ills
   Inwoven with our frame!
More pointed still we make ourselves
   Regret, remorse, and shame!
And Man, whose heav'n-erected face
   The smiles of love adorn,—
Man's inhumanity to man
   Makes countless thousands mourn!

8

'See yonder poor, o'erlabour'd wight,
   So abject, mean, and vile,
Who begs a brother of the earth
   To give him leave to toil;
And see his lordly fellow-worm
   The poor petition spurn,
Unmindful, tho' a weeping wife
   And helpless offspring mourn.

9

'If I'm design'd yon lordling's slave—
   By Nature's law design'd—
Why was an independent wish
   E'er planted in my mind?
If not, why am I subject to
   His cruelty, or scorn?
Or why has Man the will and pow'r
   To make his fellow mourn?

10

'Yet let not this too much, my son,
    Disturb thy youthful breast:
This partial view of human-kind
    Is surely not the last!
The poor, oppressèd, honest man
    Had never, sure, been born,
Had there not been some recompense
    To comfort those that mourn!

11

'O Death! the poor man's dearest friend,
    The kindest and the best!
Welcome the hour my agèd limbs
    Are laid with thee at rest!
The great, the wealthy fear thy blow,
    From pomp and pleasure torn;
But oh! a blest relief to those
    That weary-laden mourn!'

WINTER

A Dirge

TUNE: *MacPherson's Rant*

1

The wintry west extends his blast,
    And hail and rain does blaw;
Or the stormy north sends driving forth
    The blinding sleet and snaw:
Wild-tumbling brown, and burn comes down,
    And roars frae bank to brae:
While bird and beast in covert rest,
    And pass the heartless day.

2

'The sweeping blast, the sky o'ercast,'
   The joyless winter day
Let others fear, to me more dear
   Than all the pride of May:
The tempest's howl, it soothes my soul,
   My griefs it seems to join;
The leafless trees my fancy please,
   Their fate resembles mine!

3

Thou Pow'r Supreme, whose mighty scheme
   These woes of mine fulfil,
Here, firm I rest, they must be best,
   Because they are Thy will!
Then all I want (O, do Thou grant
   This one request of mine!):
Since to enjoy Thou dost deny,
   Assist me to resign.

A PRAYER IN THE PROSPECT OF DEATH

1

O Thou unknown, Almighty Cause
   Of all my hope and fear!
In whose dread presence, ere an hour,
   Perhaps I must appear!

2

If I have wander'd in those paths
   Of life I ought to shun—
As something, loudly, in my breast,
   Remonstrates I have done—

3

Thou know'st that Thou has formèd me
   With passions wild and strong;
And list'ning to their witching voice
   Has often led me wrong.

4

Where human weakness has come short,
    Or frailty stept aside,
Do Thou, All-good—for such Thou art—
    In shades of darkness hide.

5

Where with intention I have err'd,
    No other plea I have,
But, Thou art good; and Goodness still
    Delighteth to forgive.

TO A MOUNTAIN DAISY

ON TURNING ONE DOWN WITH THE PLOUGH IN APRIL 1786

1

Wee, modest, crimson-tippèd flow'r,
Thou's met me in an evil hour;
For I maun crush amang the stoure   dust
            Thy slender stem:
To spare thee now is past my pow'r,
            Thou bonie gem.

2

Alas! it's no thy neebor sweet,
The bonie lark, companion meet,
Bending thee 'mang the dewy weet,   wet
            Wi' spreckl'd breast!
When upward-springing, blythe, to greet
            The purpling east.

3

Cauld blew the bitter-biting north
Upon thy early, humble birth;
Yet cheerfully thou glinted forth   sparkled
            Amid the storm,
Scarce rear'd above the parent-earth
            Thy tender form.

4

The flaunting flow'rs our gardens yield,
High shelt'ring woods and wa's maun shield;
But thou, beneath the random bield
         O' clod or stane,
Adorns the histie stibble-field,
           Unseen, alane.

must

shelter

bare stubble

5

There, in thy scanty mantle clad,
Thy snawie bosom sun-ward spread,
Thou lifts thy unassuming head
         In humble guise;
But now the share uptears thy bed,
         And low thou lies!

6

Such is the fate of artless maid,
Sweet flow'ret of the rural shade!
By love's simplicity betray'd,
         And guileless trust;
Till she, like thee, all soil'd, is laid
         Low i' the dust.

7

Such is the fate of simple Bard,
On Life's rough ocean luckless starr'd!
Unskilful he to note the card
         Of prudent lore,
Till billows rage, and gales blow hard,
         And whelm him o'er.

8

Such fate to suffering Worth is giv'n,
Who long with wants and woes has striv'n,
By human pride or cunning driv'n
         To mis'ry's brink;
Till, wrench'd of ev'ry stay but Heav'n,
         He, ruin'd, sink!

9

Ev'n thou who mourn'st the Daisy's fate,
That fate is thine—no distant date;
Stern Ruin's plough-share drives elate,
                    Full on thy bloom,
Till crush'd beneath the furrow's weight
                    Shall be thy doom!

TO RUIN

1

All hail, inexorable lord!
At whose destruction-breathing word,
    The mightiest empires fall!
Thy cruel, woe-delighted train,
The ministers of grief and pain,
    A sullen welcome, all!
With stern-resolv'd, despairing eye,
    I see each aimèd dart;
For one has cut my dearest tie,
    And quivers in my heart.
        Then low'ring and pouring,
            The storm no more I dread;
        Tho' thick'ning and black'ning
            Round my devoted head.

2

And thou grim Pow'r, by Life abhorr'd,
While Life a pleasure can afford,
    O! hear a wretch's pray'r!
No more I shrink appall'd, afraid;
I court, I beg thy friendly aid,
    To close this scene of care!
When shall my soul, in silent peace,
    Resign Life's joyless day?
My weary heart its throbbings cease,
    Cold-mould'ring in the clay?
        No fear more, no tear more
            To stain my lifeless face,
        Enclaspèd and graspèd
            Within thy cold embrace!

EPISTLE TO A YOUNG FRIEND

1

I lang hae thought, my youthfu' friend,
　　A something to have sent you,
Tho' it should serve nae ither end
　　Than just a kind memento:
But how the subject-theme may gang,
　　Let time and chance determine:
Perhaps it may turn out a sang;
　　Perhaps, turn out a sermon.

2

Ye'll try the world soon, my lad;
　　And, Andrew dear, believe me,
Ye'll find mankind an unco squad,
　　And muckle they may grieve ye:
For care and trouble set your thought,
　　Ev'n when your end's attainèd;
And a' your views may come to nought,
　　Where ev'ry nerve is strainèd.

strange

3

I'll no say, men are villains a':
　　The real, harden'd wicked,
Wha hae nae check but human law,
　　Are to a few restricked;
But, och! mankind are unco weak
　　An' little to be trusted;
If Self the wavering balance shake,
　　It's rarely right adjusted!

mighty

4

Yet they wha fa' in Fortune's strife,
　　Their fate we should na censure;
For still, th' important end of life
　　They equally may answer:
A man may hae an honest heart,
　　Tho' poortith hourly stare him;
A man may tak a neebor's part,
　　Yet hae nae cash to spare him.

poverty

5

Ay free, aff han', your story tell,
   When wi' a bosom cronie;
But still keep something to yoursel
   Ye scarcely tell to onie:
Conceal yoursel as weel's ye can
   Frae critical dissection:
But keek thro' ev'ry other man   pry
   Wi' sharpen'd, sly inspection.

6

The sacred lowe o' weel-plac'd love,   flame
   Luxuriantly indulge it;
But never tempt th' illicit rove,   attempt
   Tho' naething should divulge it:
I waive the quantum o' the sin,
   The hazard of concealing;
But, och! it hardens a' within,
   And petrifies the feeling!

7

To catch Dame Fortune's golden smile,
   Assiduous wait upon her;
And gather gear by ev'ry wile
   That's justify'd by honor:
Not for to hide it in a hedge,
   Nor for a train-attendant;
But for the glorious privilege
   Of being independent.

8

The fear o' Hell's a hangman's whip
   To haud the wretch in order;
But where ye feel your honour grip,
   Let that ay be your border:
It's slightest touches, instant pause—
   Debar a' side-pretences;
And resolutely keep its laws,
   Uncaring consequences.

9

The great Creator to revere
   Must sure become the creature;
But still the preaching cant forbear,
   And ev'n the rigid feature:
Yet ne'er with wits profane to range
   Be complaisance extended;
An atheist-laugh's a poor exchange
   For Deity offended!

10

frolicking

When ranting round in Pleasure's ring,
   Religion may be blinded;
Or if she gie a random sing,
   It may be little minded;
But when on Life we're tempest-driv'n—
   A conscience but a canker—
A correspondence fix'd wi' Heav'n
   Is sure a noble anchor!

11

Adieu, dear, amiable youth!
   Your heart can ne'er be wanting!
May prudence, fortitude, and truth,
   Erect your brow undaunting!
In ploughman phrase, 'God send you speed,'
   Still daily to grow wiser;

heed the counsel

And may ye better reck the rede,
   Than ever did th' adviser!

ON A SCOTCH BARD

GONE TO THE WEST INDIES

1

sups

rhyme

A' ye wha live by sowps o' drink,
A' ye wha live by crambo–clink,
A' ye wha live and never think,
          Come, mourn wi' me!

comrade; given
us all the slip

Our billie 's gien us a' a jink
          An' owre the sea!

2

Lament him a' ye rantin core,   jovial set
Wha dearly like a random-splore;   frolic
Nae mair he'll join the merry roar
          In social key;
For now he's taen anither shore,
          An' owre the sea!

3

The bonie lasses weel may wiss him,   wish
And in their dear petitions place him:
The widows, wives, an' a' may bless him
          Wi' tearfu' e'e,
For weel I wat they'll sairly miss him   wot
          That's owre the sea!

4

O Fortune, they hae room to grumble!
Hadst thou taen aff some drowsy bummle,   drone
Wha can do nought but fyke an' fumble,   fuss
          'Twad been nae plea;
But he was gleg as onie wumble,   nimble; wimble
          That's owre the sea!

5

Auld, cantie Kyle may weepers wear,   cheerful
An' stain them wi' the saut, saut tear:
'Twill mak her poor auld heart, I fear,
          In flinders flee: splinters
He was her Laureat monie a year,
          That's owre the sea!

6

He saw Misfortune's cauld nor-west
Lang-mustering up a bitter blast;
A jillet brak his heart at last,   jilt
          Ill may she be!
So, took a birth afore the mast,   berth
          An' owre the sea.

7

rod

meal and water

To tremble under Fortune's cummock,
On scarce a bellyfu' o' drummock,
Wi' his proud, independent stomach,
        Could ill agree;

rolled; buttocks

So, row't his hurdies in a hammock,
        An' owre the sea.

8

He ne'er was gien to great misguiding,

pockets

Yet coin his pouches wad na bide in;
Wi' him it ne'er was under hiding,
        He dealt it free:
The Muse was a' that he took pride in,
        That's owre the sea.

9

Jamaica bodies, use him weel,

shelter; place

An' hap him in a cozie biel:
Ye'll find him ay a dainty chiel,
        An' fou o' glee:

would not have

He wad na wrang'd the vera Deil,
        That's owre the sea.

10

Fareweel, my rhyme-composing billie!

unkind

Your native soil was right ill-willie;
But may ye flourish like a lily,
        Now bonilie!

last gill

I'll toast you in my hindmost gillie,
        Tho' owre the sea!

A DEDICATION

TO GAVIN HAMILTON, ESQ

wheedling,
flattering

    Expect na, Sir, in this narration,
A fleechin, fleth'rin Dedication,
To roose you up, an' ca' you guid,
An' sprung o' great an' noble bluid,
Because ye're surnam'd like His Grace,
Perhaps related to the race:

Then, when I'm tired—and sae are ye,
Wi' monie a fulsome, sinfu' lie—
Set up a face how I stop short,
For fear your modesty be hurt.

This may do—maun do, Sir, wi' them wha
Maun please the great-folk for a wamefou';   bellyful
For me! saw laigh I need na bow,   low
For, Lord be thankit, I can plough;
And when I downa yoke a naig,   cannot
Then, Lord be thankit, I can beg;
Sae I shall say, an' that's nae flatt'rin,
It's just sic poet an' sic patron.

The Poet, some guid angel help him
Or else, I fear, some ill ane skclp him!   trounce
He may do weel for a' he's done yet,
But only he's no just begun yet.

The Patron (sir, ye maun forgie me;
I winna lie, come what will o' me),
On ev'ry hand it will allow'd be,
He's just—nae better than he should be.

I readily and freely grant,
He downa see a poor man want;
What's no his ain he winna tak it;
What ance he says, he winna break it;
Ought he can lend he'll no refus 't,
Till aft his guidness is abus'd;
And rascals whyles that do him wrang,   sometimes
Ev'n that, he does na mind it lang;
As master, landlord, husband, father,
He does na fail his part in either.

But then, nae thanks to him for a' that;
Nae godly symptom ye can ca' that;
It's naething but a milder feature
Of our poor, sinfu', corrupt nature:
Ye'll get the best o' moral works,
'Mang black Gentoos, and pagan Turks,
Or hunters wild on Ponotaxi,
Wha never heard of orthodoxy.

That he's the poor man's friend in need,
The gentleman in word and deed,
It's no thro' terror of damnation:
It's just a carnal inclination,
And och! that's nae regeneration.

Morality, thou deadly bane,
Thy tens o' thousands thou hast slain!
Vain is his hope, whase stay an' trust is
In moral mercy, truth, and justice!

farthing   No—stretch a point to catch a plack;
Abuse a brother to his back;
window   Steal thro' the winnock frae a whore,
But point the rake that taks the door;
Be to the poor like onie whunstane,
grindstone   And haud their noses to the grunstane;
Ply ev'ry art o' legal thieving;
No matter—stick to sound believing.

Learn three-mile pray'rs, an' half-mile graces,
palms   Wi' weel-spread looves, an' lang, wry faces;
Grunt up a solemn, lengthen'd groan,
And damn a' parties but your own;
I'll warrant then, ye're nae deceiver,
A steady, sturdy, staunch believer.

O ye wha leave the springs o' Calvin,
muddy puddles   For gumlie dubs of your ain delvin!
Ye sons of Heresy and Error,
Ye'll some day squeel in quaking terror,
When Vengeance draws the sword in wrath,
And in the fire throws the sheath;
When Ruin, with his sweeping besom,
Just frets till Heav'n commission gies him;
While o'er the harp pale Misery moans,
And strikes the ever-deep'ning tones,
Still louder shrieks, and heavier groans!

Your pardon, sir, for this digression:
almost   I maist forgat my Dedication;
But when divinity comes 'cross me,
My readers still are sure to lose me.

So, Sir, you see 'twas nae daft vapour;   mad
But I maturely thought it proper,
When a' my works I did review,
To dedicate them, Sir, to you:
Because (ye need na tak' it ill),
I thought them something like yoursel.

Then patronize them wi' your favor
And your petitioner shall ever——
I had amaist said, ever pray,
But that's a word I need na say;
For prayin, I hae little skill o't,   extremely
I'm baith dead-sweer, an' wretched ill o't;   reluctant; bad at
                                                       it
But I'se repeat each poor man's pray'r,   I'll
That kens or hears about you, Sir:——

'May ne'er Misfortune's gowling bark
Howl thro' the dwelling o' the clerk!   lawyer
May ne'er his gen'rous, honest heart,
For that same gen'rous spirit smart!
May Kennedy's far-honor'd name
Lang beet his hymeneal flame,   feed
Till Hamiltons, at least a dizzen,
Are frae their nuptial labors risen:
Five bonie lasses round their table,
And sev'n braw fellows, stout an' able,
To serve their king an' country weel,
By word, or pen, or pointed steel!
May Health and Peace, with mutual rays,
Shine on the ev'ning o' his days;
Till his wee, curlie John's ier-oe,   great-grandchild
When ebbing life nae mair shall flow,
The last, sad, mournful rites bestow!'

I will not wind a lang conclusion,
With complimentary effusion;
But, whilst your wishes and endeavours
Are blest with Fortune's smiles and favours,
I am, dear sir, with zeal most fervent,
Your much indebted, humble servant.

But if (which Pow'rs above prevent)
That iron-hearted carl, Want,
Attended, in his grim advances,

By sad mistakes, and black mischances,
While hopes, and joys, and pleasures fly him,
Make you as poor a dog as I am,
Your 'humble servant' then no more;
For who would humbly serve the poor?
But, by a poor man's hopes in Heav'n!
While recollection's pow'r is giv'n,
If, in the vale of humble life,
The victim sad of Fortune's strife,
I, thro' the tender-gushing tear,
Should recognise my master dear;
If friendless, low, we meet together,
Then, sir, your hand—my FRIEND and BROTHER!

TO A LOUSE

ON SEEING ONE ON A LADY'S BONNET AT CHURCH

1

Ha! whare ye gaun, ye crowlin ferlie?   *crawling*
Your impudence protects you sairly,   *wonder*
I canna say but ye strunt rarely   *swagger*
          Owre gauze and lace,
Tho' faith! I fear ye dine but sparely
          On sic a place.

2

Ye ugly, creepin, blastit wonner,
Detested, shunn'd by saunt an' sinner,
How daur ye set your fit upon her—   *foot*
          Sae fine a lady!
Gae somewhere else and seek your dinner
          On some poor body.

3

Swith! in some beggar's hauffet squattle: *Off! temples*
There ye may creep, and sprawl, and sprattle,   *squat*
Wi' ither kindred, jumping cattle,   *scramble*
          In shoals and nations;
Whare horn nor bane ne'er daur unsettle
          Your thick plantations.

4

Now haud you there! ye're out o' sight,   keep
Below the fatt'rils, snug an' tight;   falderals
Na, faith ye yet! ye'll no be right,
                    Till ye've got on it—
The vera tapmost, tow'ring height
                    O' Miss's bonnet.

5

My sooth! right bauld ye set your nose out,
As plump an' grey as onie grozet: gooseberry
O for some rank, mercurial rozet,   rosin
                    Or fell, red smeddum,   deadly;
                                                          powder
I'd gie ye sic a hearty dose o't,
                    Wad dress your droddum!   breech

6

I wad na been surpris'd to spy   would not have
You on an auld wife's flainen toy;   flannel cap
Or aiblins some bit duddie boy,   maybe; small
                                                          ragged
                    On's wyliecoat;   undervest
But Miss's fine Lunardi! fye!   balloon-bonnet
                    How daur ye do't!

7

O Jenny, dinna toss your head,
An' set your beauties a' abread!   abroad
Ye little ken what cursèd speed
                    The blastie's makin!
Thae winks an' finger-ends, I dread,   Those
                    Are notice takin!

8

O wad some Power the giftie gie us
To see oursels as ithers see us!
It wad frae monie a blunder free us,
                    An' foolish notion:
What airs in dress an' gait wad lea'e us,
                    An' ev'n devotion!

EPISTLE TO J. LAPRAIK

AN OLD SCOTTISH BARD, APRIL 1, 1785

I

partridges
calling
the hare
scudding

While briers an' woodbines budding green,
And paitricks scraichin loud at e'en,
An' morning poussie whiddin seen,
    Inspire my Muse,
This freedom, in an unknown frien'
    I pray excuse.

2

meeting

have a chat

set-to

On Fasten-e'en we had a rockin,
To ca' the crack and weave our stockin;
And there was muckle fun and jokin,
    Ye need na doubt;
At length we had a hearty yokin,
    At 'sang about.'

3

one
Above

thrilled

There was ae sang, amang the rest,
Aboon them a' it pleas'd me best,
That some kind husband had addrest
    To some sweet wife:
It thirl'd the heart-strings thro' the breast,
    A' to the life,

4

chap

I've scarce heard ought describ'd sae weel,
What gen'rous, manly bosoms feel;
Thought I, 'Can this be Pope or Steele,
    Or Beattie's wark?'
They tald me 'twas an odd kind chiel
    About Muirkirk.

5

It pat me fidgin-fain to hear't,   tingling-wild
An' sae about him there I spier't;   asked
Then a' that kent him round declar'd
        He had ingine;   genius
That nane excell'd it, few cam near't,
        It was sae fine:

6

That, set him to a pint of ale,
An' either douce or merry tale,   sober
Or rhymes an' sangs he'd made himsel,
        Or witty catches,
'Tween Inverness an' Teviotdale,
        He had few matches.

7

Then up I gat, an' swoor an aith,   swore
Tho' I should pawn my pleugh an' graith,   harness
Or die a cadger pownie's death,   hawker
        At some dyke-back,   Behind a fence
A pint an' gill I'd gie them baith,
        To hear your crack.   talk

8

But, first an' foremost, I should tell,
Amaist as soon as I could spell,
I to the crambo-jingle fell;   rhyming
        Tho' rude an' rough—
Yet crooning to a body's sel,   humming
        Does weel eneugh.

9

I am nae poet, in a sense;
But just a rhymer like by chance,
An' hae to learning nae pretence;
        Yet, what the matter?
Whene'er my Muse does on me glance,
        I jingle at her.

10

Your critic-folk may cock their nose,
And say, 'How can you e'er propose,
You wha ken hardly verse frae prose,
                    To mak a sang?'
But, by your leaves, my learned foes,
                    Ye're maybe wrang.

11

What's a' your jargon o' your Schools,
Your Latin names for horns an' stools?
If honest Nature made you fools,
serves   What sairs your grammers
Ye'd better taen up spades and shools,
stone-breaking   Or knappin-hammers.

12

dunderheads   A set o'dull, conceited hashes
Confuse their brains in college-classes,
young bullocks They gang in stirks, and come out asses,
                    Plain truth to speak;
then   An' syne they think to climb Parnassus
                    By dint o' Greek!

13

Gie me ae spark o' Nature's fire,
That's a' the learning I desire;
puddle   Then, tho' I drudge thro' dud an' mire
                    At pleugh or cart,
My Muse, tho' hamely in attire,
                    May touch the heart.

14

spark   O for a spunk o' Allan's glee,
sly   Or Fergusson's, the bauld an' slee,
Or bright Lapraik's, my friend to be,
                    If I can hit it!
learning   That would be lear eneugh for me,
                    If I could get it.

15

Now, sir, if ye hae friends enow,
Tho' real friends I b'lieve are few;
Yet, if your catalogue be fow,   full
        I'se no insist: I'll
But, gif ye want ae friend that's true,
        I'm on your list.

16

I winna blaw about mysel,   brag
As ill I like my fauts to tell;
But friends, an' folks that wish me well,
        They sometimes roose me;   praise
Tho', I maun own, as monie still
        As far abuse me.

17

There's ae wee faut they whyles lay to me,   one
I like the lasses—Gude forgie me!   God
For monie a plack they wheedle frae me   coin
        At dance or fair;
Maybe some ither thing they gie me,
        They weel can spare.

18

But Mauchline Race or Mauchline Fair,
I should be proud to meet you there:
We'se gie ae night's discharge to care,   We'll
        If we forgather;
And hae a swap o' rhymin-ware
        Wi' ane anither.

19

The four-gill chap, we'se gar him clatter,   four-gill cup
An' kirsen him wi' reekin water;   we'll make
                          christen;
Syne we'll sit down an' tak our whitter,   steaming
        To cheer our heart;   Then; draught
An' faith, we'se be acquainted better
        Before we part.

20

worldly

manners

the hunt for
coin

Awa ye selfish, warly race,
Wha think that havins, sense, an' grace,
Ev'n love an' friendship should give place
        To Catch-the-Plack!
I dinna like to see your face,
        Nor hear your crack.

21

But ye whom social pleasure charms,
Whose hearts the tide of kindness warms,
Who hold your being on the terms,
        'Each aid the others,'
Come to my bowl, come to my arms,
        My friends, my brothers!

22

tingle

But, to conclude my lang epistle,
As my auld pen's worn to the grissle,
Twa lines frae you wad gar me fissle,
        Who am most fervent,
While I can either sing or whistle,
        Your friend and servant.

SECOND EPISTLE TO J. LAPRAIK

APRIL 21, 1785

1

new-driven; low
smoke; harrow

While new-ca'd kye rowte at the stake
An' pownies reek in pleugh or braik,
This hour on e'enin's edge I take,
        To own I'm debtor
To honest-hearted, auld Lapraik,
        For his kind letter.

2

Forjesket sair, with weary legs,	Jaded
Rattlin the corn out-owre the rigs,	ridges
Or dealing thro' amang the naigs	distributing
Their ten-hours' bite,	
My awkart Muse sair pleads and begs,	
I would na write.	

3

The tapetless, ramfeezl'd hizzie,	feckless,
She's saft at best an' something lazy:	exhausted girl
Quo' she: 'Ye ken we've been sae busy	
This month an' mair,	
That trowth, my head is grown right dizzie,	
An' something sair,"	aching

4

Her dowff excuses pat me mad:	dull
'Conscience', says I, 'ye thowless jad!	lazy
I'll write, an' that a hearty blaud,	
This vera night;	
So dinna ye affront your trade,	do not
But rhyme it right.	

5

'Shall bauld Lapraik, the king o' hearts,	
Tho' mankind were a pack o' cartes,	
Roose you sae weel for your deserts,	Praise
In terms sae friendly;	
Yet ye'll neglect to shaw your parts	
An' thank him kindly?'	

6

Sae I gat paper in a blink,	twinkling
An' down gaed stumpie in the ink:	
Quoth I: 'Before I sleep a wink,	
I vow I'll close it:	
An' if ye winna mak it clink,	rhyme
By Jove, I'll prose it!'	

7

Sae I've begun to scrawl, but whether
In rhyme, or prose, or baith thegither,
Or some hotch-potch that's rightly neither,
     Let time mak proof;
But I shall scribble down some blether   *nonsense*
     Just clean aff-loof.   *off-hand*

8

My worthy friend, ne'er grudge an' carp,
Tho' Fortune use you hard an' sharp;
Come, kittle up your moorland harp   *tickle*
     Wi' gleesome touch!
Ne'er mind how Fortune waft an' warp;   *woof*
     She's but a bitch.

9

She's gien me monie a jirt an' fleg,   *jerk; scare*
Sin' I could striddle owre a rig;   *straddle*
But, by the Lord, tho' I should beg
     Wi' lyart pow,   *grey head*
I'll laugh an' sing, an' shake my leg,   *dance*
     As lang's I dow!   *can*

10

Now come the sax-an-twentieth simmer
I've seen the bud upo' the timmer,   *woods*
Still persecuted by the limmer   *jade*
     Frae year to year;
But yet, despite the kittle kimmer,   *fickle gossip*
     I, Rob, am here.

11

Do ye envý the city gent,
Behint a kist to lie an' sklent;   *counter; cheat*
Or purse-proud, big wi' cent. per cent.
     An' muckle wame,   *stomach*
In some bit brugh to represent   *borough*
     A bailie's name?   *town* / *magistrate's*

12

Or is't the paughty feudal thane,   haughty
Wi' ruffl'd sark an' glancing cane,   shirt; shining
Wha thinks himsel nae sheep-shank bane,
   But lordly stalks;
While caps an' bonnets aff are taen,
   As by he walks?

13

'O Thou wha gies us each guid gift!
Gie me o' wit an' sense a lift,   load
Then turn me, if Thou please, adrift
   Thro' Scotland wide;
Wi' cits nor lairds I wadna shift,
   In a' their pride!'

14

Were this the charter of our state,
'On pain o' hell be rich an' great,'
Damnation then would be our fate,
   Beyond remead;   remedy
But, thanks to heaven, that's no the gate   way
   We learn our creed.

15

For thus the royal mandate ran,
When first the human race began:
'The social, friendly, honest man,
   Whate'er he be,
'Tis he fulfils great Nature's plan,
   And none but he.'

16

O mandate glorious and divine!
The followers o' the ragged Nine—
Poor, thoughtless devils!—yet may shine
   In glorious light;
While sordid sons o' Mammon's line
   Are dark as night!

17

Tho' here they scrape, an' squeeze, an' growl,

fistful   Their worthless neivefu' of a soul
May in some future carcase howl,
The forest's fright;
Or in some day-detesting owl
May shun the light.

18

Then may Lapraik and Burns arise,
To reach their native, kindred skies,
And sing their pleasures, hopes an' joys,
In some mild sphere;
Still closer knit in friendship's ties,
Each passing year!

TO WILLIAM SIMPSON OF OCHILTREE

MAY, 1785

1

I gat your letter, winsome Willie;

handsomely   Wi' gratefu' heart I thank you brawlie;
Tho' I maun say't, I wad be silly

mighty   And unco vain,
fellow   Should I believe, my coaxin billie,
Your flatterin strain.

2

I'll   But I'se believe ye kindly meant it:
sideways   I sud be laith to think ye hinted
squinted   Ironic satire, sidelins sklented,
On my poor Musie;
wheedling   Tho' in sic phraisin terms ye've penn'd it,
I scarce excuse ye.

3

My senses wad be in a creel,
Should I but dare a hope to speel,   climb
Wi' Allan, or wi' Gilbertfield,
    The braes o' fame;
Or Fergusson, the writer-chiel,   lawyer-chap
    A deathless name.

4

(O Fergusson! thy glorious parts
Ill suited law's dry, musty arts!
My curse upon your whunstane hearts,   whinstone
    Ye E'nbrugh gentry!
The tythe o' what ye waste at cartes   Would have
    Wad stow'd his pantry!)   stored

5

Yet when a tale comes i' my head,
Or lasses gie my heart a screed—   rent
As whyles they're like to be my dead,   sometimes;
    (O sad disease!)   death
I kittle up my rustic reed;   tickle
    It gies me ease.

6

Auld Coila, now, may fidge fu' fain,   tingle with
She's gotten bardies o' her ain;   delight
Chiels wha their chanters winna hain,   spare
    But tune their lays,
Till echoes a' resound again
    Her weel-sung praise.

7

Nae Poet thought her worth his while,
To set her name in measur'd style;
She lay like some unkend-of isle
    Beside New Holland,
Or whare wild-meeting oceans boil
    Besouth Magellan.   South of

8

Ramsay an' famous Fergusson
a lift-up   Gied Forth an' Tay a lift aboon;
Yarrow an' Tweed, to monie a tune,
         Owre Scotland rings;
While Irwin, Lugar, Ayr, an' Doon
         Naebody sings.

9

Th' Illissus, Tiber, Thames, an' Seine,
Glide sweet in monie a tunefu' line:
foot   But, Willie, set your fit to mine,
         An' cock your crest!
make; brooklets   We'll gar our streams and burnies shine
         Up wi' the best.

10

We'll sing auld Coila's plains an' fells,
Her moors red-brown wi' heather bells,
hill-sides   Her banks an' braes, her dens an' dells,
         Whare glorious Wallace
bore off the prize   Aft bure the gree, as story tells,
         Frae Suthron billies.

11

At Wallace' name, what Scottish blood
But boils up in a spring-tide flood?
Oft have our fearless fathers strode
         By Wallace' side,
red-wet-shod   Still pressing onward, re-wat-shod,
         Or glorious dy'd!

12

hollows   O, sweet are Coila's haughs an' woods,
linnets   When lintwhites chant amang the buds,
sporting   And jinkin hares, in amorous whids,
gambols   Their loves enjoy;
coos   While thro' the braes the cushat croods
         With wailfu' cry!

13

Ev'n winter bleak has charms to me,
When winds rave thro' the naked tree;
Or frosts on hills of Ochiltree
   Are hoary gray;
Or blinding drifts wild-furious flee,
    Dark'ning the day!

14

O Nature! a' thy shews an' forms
To feeling, pensive hearts hae charms!
Whether the summer kindly warms,
    Wi' life an' light;
Or winter howls, in gusty storms,
    The lang, dark night!

15

The Muse, nae poet ever fand her,   found
Till by himsel he learn'd to wander,
Adown some trottin burn's meander,   brook's
    An' no think lang:
O, sweet to stray, an' pensive ponder
    A heart-felt sang!

16

The warly race may drudge an' drive,   worldly
Hog-shouther, jundie, stretch, an' strive; push; ply the elbows
Let me fair Nature's face descrive,   describe
    And I, wi' pleasure,
Shall let the busy, grumbling hive
    Bum owre their treasure.   Hum

17

Fareweel, my rhyme-composing brither!
We've been owre lang unkend to ither: too long
Now let us lay our heads thegither,
    In love fraternal:
May Envy wallop in a tether,   dangle in a rope
    Black fiend, infernal!

18

While Highlandmen hate tolls an' taxes;
While moorlan' herds like guid, fat braxies;
While Terra Firma, on her axis,
      Diurnal turns;
Count on a friend, in faith an' practice,
      In Robert Burns.

POSTSCRIPT

19

pin

My memory's no worth a preen:
I had amaist forgotten clean,
Ye bade me write you what they mean
      By this New–Light,

shepherds

'Bout which our heads sae aft hae been
      Maist like to fight.

20

striplings

In days when mankind were but callans;
At grammar, logic, an' sic talents,
They took nae pains their speech to balance,
      Or rules to gie;

vernacular

But spak their thoughts in plain, braid Lallans,
      Like you or me.

21

those
shirt
round
Went

In thae auld times, they thought the moon,
Just like a sark, or pair o' shoon,
Wore by degrees, till her last roon
      Gaed past their viewin;
An' shortly after she was done,
      They gat a new ane.

22

fellows

This past for certain, undisputed;
It ne'er cam i' their heads to doubt it,
Till chiels gat up an' wad confute it,
      An' ca'd it wrang;
An' muckle din there was about it,
      Baith loud an' lang.

23

Some herds, weel learn'd upo' the Beuk,
Wad threap auld folk the thing misteuk;   maintain
For 'twas the auld moon turn'd a neuk   corner
       An' out o' sight.
An' backlins-comin to the leuk,   backwards-; look
       She grew mair bright.

24

This wad deny'd, it was affirm'd;
The herds and hissels were alarm'd;   flocks
The rev'rend gray-beards rav'd an' storm'd,
       That breadless laddies
Should think they better were inform'd
       Than their auld daddies.

25

Frae less to mair, it gaed to sticks;
Frae words an' aiths, to clours an' nicks;   bumps; cuts
An' monie a fallow gat his licks,   punishment
       Wi' hearty crunt;   blow
An some, to learn them for their tricks,   teach
       Were hang'd an' brunt.   burned

26

This game was play'd in monie lands,
An' Auld-Light caddies bure sic hands,   varlets; bore
That faith, the youngsters took the sands
       Wi' nimble shanks
Till lairds forbade, by strict commands,
       Sic bluidy pranks.

27

But New-Light herds gat sic a cowe,   down-setting
Folk thought them ruin'd stick-an-stowe;   completely
Till now, amaist on ev'ry knowe   hillock
       Ye'll find ane placed;
An' some, their New-Light fair avow,
       Just quite barefac'd.

28

Nae doubt the Auld-Light flocks are bleatin;
Their zealous herds are vex'd and sweatin;
weeping   Myself, I've even seen them greetin
snarling   Wi' girnin spite,
To hear the moon sae sadly lie'd on
               By word an' write.

29

scare; rascals   But shortly they will cowe the louns!
Some Auld-Light herds in neebor touns
Are mind't, in things they ca' balloons,
             To tak a flight,
An' stay ae month amang the moons
              An' see them right.

30

Guid observation they will gie them;
An' when the auld moon's gaun to lea'e them,
shard   The hindmost shaird, they'll fetch it wi' them,
pockets   Just i' their pouch;
An' when the New-Light billies see them,
              I think they'll crouch!

31

Sae, ye observe that a' this clatter
Is naething but a 'moonshine matter';
But tho' dull prose-folk Latin splatter
squabble   In logic tulzie,
I hope we, Bardies, ken some better
such a brawl   Than mind sic brulzie.

EPISTLE TO JOHN RANKINE

ENCLOSING SOME POEMS

1

O rough, rude, ready-witted Rankine,
The wale o' cocks for fun an' drinkin!   pick
There's monie godly folks are thinkin'
    Your dreams and tricks
Will send you, Korah-like, a-sinkin
    Straught to Auld Nick's.

2

Ye hae sae monie cracks an' cants,   stories
And in your wicked drucken rants,
Ye mak a devil o' the saunts,
    An' fill them fou';
And then their failings, flaws, an' wants
    Are a' seen thro'.

3

Hypocrisy, in mercy spare it!
That holy robe, O, dinna tear it!
Spare't for their sakes, wha aften wear it—
    The lads in black;
But your curst wit, when it comes near it,
    Rives't aff their back.   tears

4

Think, wicked sinner, wha ye're skaithing: injuring
It's just the Blue-gown badge an' claithing
O' saunts; tak that, ye lea'e them naething
    To ken them by
Frae onie unregenerate heathen,
    Like you or I.

5

I've sent you here some rhyming ware
A' that I bargain'd for, an' mair;
Sae, when ye hae an hour to spare,
      I will expect,
send it   Yon sang ye'll sen't, wi' cannie care,
      And no neglect.

6

Tho' faith, sma' heart hae I to sing:
can   My Muse dow scarcely spread her wing!
tune   I've play'd myself a bonie spring,
      An' danc'd my fill!
have gone;   I'd better gaen an' sair't the King
served   At Bunker's Hill.

7

'Twas ae night lately, in my fun,
went   I gaed a rovin wi' the gun,
partridge   An' brought a paitrick to the grun'—
      A bonie hen;
And, as the twilight was begun,
      Thought nane wad ken.

8

The poor, wee thing was little hurt;
stroked; a bit   I straikit it a wee for sport,
worry   Ne'er thinkin they wad fash me for't;
      But, Deil-ma-care!
The Kirk-   Somebody tells the Poacher-Court
Session   The hale affair.
whole

9

Some auld, us'd hands had taen a note,
That sic a hen had got a shot;
I was suspected for the plot;
      I scorn'd to lie;
lost my money   So gat the whissle o' my groat,
      An' pay't the fee.

10

But, by my gun, o' guns the wale,   pick
An' by my pouther an' my hail,   shot
An' by my hen, an' by her tail,
        I vow an' swear!
The game shall pay, owre moor an' dale,
        For this, niest year!   next

11

As soon's the clockin-time is by,   clucking-
An' the wee pouts begun to cry,   chicks
Lord, I'se hae sportin by an' by   I'll
        For my gowd guinea;
Tho' I should herd the buckskin kye
        For't, in Virginia!

12

Trowth, they had muckle for to blame!
'Twas neither broken wing nor limb,
But twa-three chaps about the wame,   knocks; belly
        Scarce thro' the feathers;
An' baith a yellow George to claim   guinea
        An' thole their blether!   endure;
                                      nonsense

13

It pits me ay as mad's a hare;
So I can rhyme nor write nae mair;
But pennyworths again is fair,   tit-for-tat
        When time's expedient:
Meanwhile I am, respected Sir,
        Your most obedient.

THE FAREWELL

TO THE BRETHREN OF ST. JAMES'S LODGE, TARBOLTON

TUNE: *Good-night, and joy be wi' you a'*

1

Adieu! a heart-warm, fond adieu;
  Dear Brothers of the *Mystic Tie*!
Ye favour'd, ye enlighten'd few,
  Companions of my social joy!
  Tho' I to foreign lands must hie,
slippery   Pursuing Fortune's slidd'ry ba';
  With melting heart and brimful eye,
I'll mind you still, tho' far awa.

2

Oft have I met your social band,
  And spent the cheerful, festive night;
Oft, honour'd with supreme command,
  Presided o'er the *Sons of Light*;
  And by that *Hieroglyphic* bright,
Which none but *Craftsmen* ever saw!
  Strong Mem'ry on my heart shall write
Those happy scenes, when far awa.

3

May Freedom, Harmony, and Love,
  Unite you in the *Grand Design*,
Beneath th' Omniscient Eye above—
  The glorious *Architect* Divine—
  That you may keep th' *Unerring Line*,
Still rising by the *Plummet's Law*,
  Till *Order* bright completely shine,
Shall be my pray'r, when far awa.

4

And You farewell! whose merits claim
  Justly that *Highest Badge* to wear:
Heav'n bless your honour'd, noble Name,
  To Masonry and Scotia dear!

A last request permit me here,
When yearly ye assemble a',
    One round, I ask it with a tear,   *health round*
To him, the Bard that's far awa.

DEATH AND DOCTOR HORNBOOK

A True Story

1

Some books are lies frae end to end,
And some great lies were never penn'd:
Ev'n ministers, they hae been kend,
        In holy rapture,
A rousing whid at times to vend,   *fib*
        And nail't wi' Scripture.

2

But this that I am gaun to tell,   *going*
Which lately on a night befel,
Is just as true's the Deil's in hell
        Or Dublin city: *(in effigy)*
That e'er he nearer comes oursel
        'S a muckle pity!

3

The clachan yill had made me canty,   *village ale; jolly*
I was na fou, but just had plenty: *drunk*
I stacher'd whyles, but yet took tent ay   *staggered now and then; care*
        To free the ditches;
An' hillocks, stanes, an' bushes, kend ay   *clear*
        Frae ghaists an' witches.

4

The rising moon began to glowr   *stare*
The distant Cumnock Hills out-owre: *above*
To count her horns, wi' a' my pow'r
        I set mysel;
But whether she had three or four,
        I cou'd na tell.

5

I was come round about the hill,
And todlin down on Willie's mill,
Setting my staff wi' a' my skill

steady
                        To keep my sicker;
at times   Tho' leeward whyles, against my will,
run   I took a bicker.

6

I there wi' *Something* does forgather,

put; ghostly   That pat me in an eerie swither;
dread
across one   An awfu' scythe, out-owre ae shouther,
hung   Clear-dangling, hang;
three-pronged   A three-tae'd leister on the ither
fish-spear   Lay, large an' lang.

7

Its stature seem'd lang Scotch ells twa;
The queerest shape that e'er I saw,

fiend; belly;   For fient a wame it had ava;
at all   And then its shanks,
They were as thin, as sharp an' sma'
                 As cheeks o' branks.

8

'Guid-een,' quo' I; 'Friend! hae ye been mawin,
When ither folk are busy sawin?'

halt   It seem'd to mak a kind o' stan',
                 But naething spak.
where are ye   At length, says I: 'Friend! whare ye gaun?
going
i.e. to the   Will ye go back?'
tavern

9

hollow   It spak right howe: 'My name is Death,
scared   But be na' fley'd.' Quoth I: 'Guid faith,
Ye're may be come to stap my breath;
heed; comrade   But tent me, billie:
advise; damage   I red ye weel, take care o' skaith,
large knife   See, there's a gully!'

10

'Gudeman,' quo' he, 'put up your whittle,   blade
I'm no design'd to try its mettle;
But if I did, I wad be kittle
                    To be mislear'd:
I wad na mind it, no that spittle
                    Out-owre my beard.'

11

'Weel, weel!' says I, 'a bargain be't;
Come, gie's your hand, an' say we're gree't;   give us; agreed
We'll ease our shanks, an' tak a seat:
                    Come, gie's your news:
This while ye hae been monie a gate,   road
                    At monie a house.'

12

'Ay, ay!' quo' he, an' shook his head,
'It's e'en a lang, lang time indeed
Sin' I began to nick the thread   cut
                    An' choke the breath:
Folk maun do something for their bread,
                    An' sae maun Death.

13

'Sax thousand years are near-hand fled   well-high
Sin' I was to the butching bred,   butchering
An' monie a sheme in vain's been laid
                    To stap or scar me;   stop; scare
Till ane Hornbook's ta'en up the trade,
                    And faith! he'll waur me.   worst

14

'Ye ken Jock Hornbook i' the clachan?
Deil mak his king's-hood in a spleuchan!—   scrotum;
He's grown saw weel acquaint wi' *Buchan*   toabacco-pouch
                    And ither chaps,
The weans haud out their fingers laughin,   children
                    An' pouk my hips.   poke; buttocks

15

'See, here's a scythe, an' there's a dart,
They hae pierc'd monie a gallant heart;
But Doctor Hornbook wi' his art
               An' cursèd skill,
Has made them baith no worth a fart,

The devil a one   Damn'd haet they'll kill!

16

gone   ''Twas but yestreen, nae farther gane,
I threw a noble throw at ane;
Wi' less, I'm sure, I've hundreds slain;
               But Deil-ma-care!

went tinkle   It just played dirl on the bane,
               But did nae mair.

17

'Hornbook was by wi' ready art,
An' had sae fortify'd the part,
That when I lookèd to my dart,
               It was sae blunt,
Fient haet o't wad hae pierc'd the heart

cabbage-stalk   Of a kail-runt.

18

'I drew my scythe in sic a fury,

tumbled   I near-hand cowpit wi' my hurry,
But yet the bauld Apothecary
               Withstood the shock:
I might as weel hae try'd a quarry
               O' hard whin-rock.

19

'Ev'n them he canna get attended,
Altho' their face he ne'er had kend it,

cabbage-leaf   Just shite in a kail-blade an' send it,
               As soon's he smells't,
Baith their disease and what will mend it,
               At once he tells't.

20

'And then a' doctor's saws and whittles   knives
Of a' dimensions, shapes, an' mettles,
A' kinds o' boxes, mugs, and bottles,
                              He's sure to hae;
Their Latin names as fast he rattles
                              As A B C.

21

'Calces o' fossils, earth, and trees;
True *sal-marinum* o' the seas;
The *farina* of beans an' pease,
                              He has't in plenty;
Aqua-fontis, what you please,
                              He can content ye.

22

'Forbye some new, uncommon weapons,
Urinus spiritus of capons;
Or mite-horn shavings, filings, scrapings,
                              Distill'd *per se*;
Sal-alkali o' midge-tail-clippings,
                              And monie mae.'   more

23

'Waes me for Johnie Ged's Hole now,'
Quoth I, 'if that thae news be true!   these
His braw calf-ward whare gowans grew   grazing plot;
                                                                daisies
                              Sae white and bonie,
Nae doubt they'll rive it wi' the plew: split
                              They'll ruin Johnie!'

24

The creature grain'd an eldritch laugh   groaned
And says: 'Ye needna yoke the pleugh,
Kirkyards will soon be till'd eneugh,
                              Tak ye nae fear:
They'll a' be trench'd wi' monie a sheugh   ditch
                              In twa-three year.

25

straw, *i.e.* bed

'Whare I kill'd ane, a fair strae death
By loss o' blood or want o' breath,
This night I'm free to tak my aith,
                    That Hornbook's skill

cloth

Has clad a score i' their last claith
                    By drap an' pill.

26

weaver
fists

'An honest wabster to his trade,
Whase wife's twa nieves were scarce weel-bred,
Gat tippence-worth to mend her head,

aching

                    When it was sair;

crept quietly

The wife slade cannie to her bed,
                    But ne'er spak mair.

27

botts
commotion

'A countra laird had taen the batts,
Or some curmurring in his guts,
His only son for Hornbook sets,
                    An' pays him well:

pet-ewes

The lad, for twa guid gimmer-pets,
                    Was laird himsel.

28

'A bonie lass—ye kend her name—

put up; belly

Some ill-brewn drink had hov'd her wame;
She trusts hersel, to hide the shame,
                    In Hornbook's care;
Horn sent her aff to her lang hame
                    To hide it here.

29

sample

'That's just a swatch o' Hornbook's way;
Thus goes he on from day to day,
Thus does he poison, kill, an' slay,
                    An's weel paid for't;
Yet stops me o' my lawfu' prey
                    Wi' his damn'd dirt:

30

'But, hark! I'll tell you of a plot,
Tho' dinna ye be speakin o't:
I'll nail the self-conceited sot,
    As dead's a herrin;
Niest time we meet, I'll wad a groat,   next; wager
    He gets his fairin!'   reward

31

But just as he began to tell,
The auld kirk-hammer strak the bell   small; beyond
Some wee short hour ayont the twal,   twelve
    Which raised us baith: got us to our
I took the way that pleas'd mysel,   legs
    And sae did Death.

THE BRIGS OF AYR

A Poem

INSCRIBED TO JOHN BALLANTINE, ESQ., AYR

Sir, think not with a mercenary view
Some servile Sycophant approaches you.
To you my Muse would sing these simple lays,
To you my heart its grateful homage pays,
I feel the weight of all your kindness past,
But thank you not as wishing it to last;
Scorn'd be the wretch whose earth-born grov'lling soul
Would in his ledger-hopes his Friends enroll.
Tho' I, a lowly, nameless, rustic Bard,
Who ne'er must hope your goodness to reward,
Yet man to man, Sir, let us fairly meet,
And like masonic Level, equal greet.
How poor the balance! ev'n what Monarch's plan,
Between two noble creatures such as Man.
That to your Friendship I am strongly tied
I still shall own it, Sir, with grateful pride,
When haply roaring seas between us tumble wide.

Or if among so many cent'ries waste,
Thro the long vista of dark ages past,
Some much-lov'd honor'd name a radiance cast,
Perhaps some Patriot of distinguish'd worth,
I'll match him if My Lord will please step forth.
Or Gentleman and Citizen combine,
And I shall shew his peer in Ballantine:
Tho' honest men were parcell'd out for sale,
He might be shown a sample for the hale.

The simple Bard, rough at the rustic plough,
Learning his tuneful trade from ev'ry bough
(The chanting linnet, or the mellow thrush,
Hailing the setting sun, sweet, in the green thorn bush;
The soaring lark, the perching red-breast shrill,
Or deep-ton'd plovers grey, wild-whistling o'er the hill):
Shall he—nurst in the peasant's lowly shed,
To hardy independence bravely bred,
By early poverty to hardship steel'd,
And train'd to arms in stern misfortune's field—
Shall he be guilty of their hireling crimes,
The servile, mercenary Swiss of rhymes?
Or labour hard the panegyric close,
With all the venal soul of dedicating prose?
No! though his artless strains he rudely sings,
And throws his hand uncouthly o'er the strings,
He glows with all the spirit of the bard,
Fame, honest fame, his great, his dear reward.
Still, if some patron's gen'rous care he trace,
Skill'd in the secret to bestow with grace;
When Ballantine befriends his humble name,
And hands the rustic stranger up to fame,
With heartfelt throes his grateful bosom swells:
The godlike bliss, to give, alone excels.

wrap
thatch; rope;
crop
heaps; damage

    'Twas when the stacks get on their winter hap,
And thack and rape secure the toil-won crap;
Potatoe-bings are snuggèd up frae skaith
O' coming winter's biting, frosty breath;
The bees, rejoicing o'er their summer toils—
Unnumber'd buds' an' flowers' delicious spoils,
Seal'd up with frugal care in massive waxen piles—

Are doom'd by man, that tyrant o'er the weak,
The death o' devils smoor'd wi' brimstone reek: *smothered; smoke*
The thundering guns are heard on ev'ry side,
The wounded coveys, reeling, scatter wide;
The feather'd field-mates, bound by Nature's tie,
Sires, mothers, children, in one carnage lie:
(What warm, poetic heart but inly bleeds,
And execrates man's savage, ruthless deeds!)
Nae mair the flower in field or meadow springs;
Nae mair the grove with airy concert rings,
Except perhaps the robin's whistling glee,
Proud o' the height o' some bit half-lang tree;   *small half-grown*
The hoary morns precede the sunny days;
Mild, calm, serene, widespreads the noontide blaze,
While thick the gossamour waves wanton in the rays.

　　'Twas in that season, when a simple Bard,
Unknown and poor—simplicity's reward!—
Ae night, within the ancient brugh of Ayr,   *One*
By whim inspir'd, or haply prest wi' care,
He left his bed, and took his wayward route,
And down by Simpson's wheel'd the left about
(Whether impell'd by all-directing Fate,
To witness what I after shall narrate;
Or whether, rapt in meditation high,
He wander'd forth, he knew not where nor why):
The drowsy Dungeon-Clock had number'd two,
And Wallace Tower had sworn the fact was true;
The tide-swoln Firth, with sullen-sounding roar,
Through the still night dash'd hoarse along the shore;
All else was hush'd as Nature's closèd e'e;
The silent moon shone high o'er tower and tree;
The chilly frost, beneath the silver beam,
Crept, gently-crusting, o'er the glittering stream.

　　When, lo! on either hand the list'ning Bard,
The clanging sugh of whistling wings is heard;   *swish*
Two dusky forms dart thro' the midnight air,
Swift as the gos drives on the wheeling hare;
Ane on th' Auld brig his airy shape uprears,
The ither flutters o'er the rising piers:
Our warlock rhymer instantly descried   *wizard*
The Sprites that owre the Brigs of Ayr preside.
(That bards are second-sighted is nae joke,

And ken the lingo of the sp'ritual folk;
Fays, spunkies, kelpies, a', they can explain them,
And ev'n the vera deils they brawly ken them.)
Auld Brig appear'd of ancient Pictish race,
The vera wrinkles Gothic in his face;
He seem'd as he wi' Time had warstl'd lang,
Yet, teughly doure, he bade an unco bang.
New Brig was buskit in a braw new coat,
That he, at Lon'on, frae ane Adams got;
In's hand five taper staves as smooth's a bead,
Wi' virls an' whirlygigums at the head.
The Goth was stalking round with anxious search,
Spying the time-worn flaws in ev'ry arch.
It chanc'd his new-come neebor took his e'e,
And e'en a vex'd and angry heart had he!
Wi' thieveless sneer to see his modish mien,
He, down the water, gies him this guid-een:—

Marginal glosses (left column):
know
jack-o'-lanthorns;
water-demons
known them
well

wrestled

toughly
stubborn

rings; flourishes

forbidding

river

AULD BRIG

'I doubt na, frien', ye'll think ye're nae sheep-shank,
Ance ye were streekit owre frae bank to bank!
But gin ye be a brig as auld as me—
Tho' faith, that date, I doubt, ye'll never see—
There'll be, if that day come, I'll wad a boddle,
Some fewer whigmeleeries in your noddle.'

Marginal glosses (left column):
stretched across

when

wager a farthing
crotchets

NEW BRIG

'Auld Vandal! ye but show your little mense,
Just much about it wi' your scanty sense:
Will your poor, narrow foot-path of a street,
Where twa wheel-barrows tremble when they meet,
Your ruin'd, formless bulk o' stane an' lime,
Compare wi' bonie brigs o' modern time?
There's men of taste would tak the Ducat stream,
Tho' they should cast the vera sark and swim,
E'er they would grate their feelings wi' the view
O' sic an ugly, Gothic hulk as you.'

Marginal glosses (left column):
discretion

AULD BRIG

'Conceited gowk! puff'd up wi' windy pride!   cuckoo
This monie a year I've stood the flood an' tide;
And tho' wi crazy eild I'm sair forfairn,   eld; worn out
I'll be a brig when ye're a shapeless cairn!   pile of stones
As yet ye little ken about the matter,
But twa-three winters will inform ye better.   two or three
When heavy, dark, continued, a'-day rains   day-long
Wi' deepening deluges o'erflow the plains;
When from the hills where springs the brawling Coil,
Or stately Lugar's mossy fountains boil,
Or where the Greenock winds his moorland course,
Or haunted Garpal draws his feeble source,
Arous'd by blustering winds an' spotting thowes, thaws
In monie a torrent down the snaw-broo rowes; snow-brew rolls
While crashing ice, borne on the roaring speat,
Sweeps dams, an' mills, an' brigs, a' to the gate; flood
And from Glenbuck down to the Ratton-Key   the road seaward
Auld Ayr is just one lengthen'd, tumbling sea—
Then down ye'll hurl (deil nor ye never rise!), crash
And dash the gumlie jaups up to the pouring skies! muddy splashes
A lesson sadly teaching, to your cost,
That Architecture's noble art is lost!'

NEW BRIG

'Fine architecture, trowth, I needs must say't o't,
The Lord be thankit that we've tint the gate o't! lost the trick
Gaunt, ghastly, ghaist-alluring edifices,
Hanging with threat'ning jut, like precipices;
O'er-arching, mouldy, gloom-inspiring coves,
Supporting roofs fantastic—stony groves;
Windows and doors in nameless sculptures drest,
With order, symmetry, or taste unblest;
Forms like some bedlam statuary's dream,
The craz'd creations of misguided whim;
Forms might be worshipp'd on the bended knee,
And still the second dread Command be free:
Their likeness is not found on earth, in air, or sea!
Mansions that would disgrace the building taste
Of any mason reptile, bird or beast,
Fit only for a doited monkish race,   muddled
Or frosty maids forsworn the dear embrace,

dolts

Or cuifs of later times, wha held the notion,
That sullen gloom was sterling true devotion:
Francies that our guid brugh denies protection,
And soon may they expire, unblest with resurrection!'

AULD BRIG

coevals
 'O ye, my dear-remember'd, ancient yealings,
Were ye but here to share my wounded feelings!

provosts
Ye worthy proveses, an' monie a bailie,
Wha in the paths o' righteousness did toil ay;

sedate
Ye dainty deacons, an' ye douce conveeners,

causeway-
To whom our moderns are but causey-cleaners;
Ye godly councils, wha hae blest this town;
Ye godly brethren o' the sacred gown,

buttocks
Wha meekly gie your hurdies to the smiters;

Lawyers
And (what would now be strange), ye godly Writers;

sedate; across;
water
A' ye douce folk I've borne aboon the broo,
Were ye but here, what would ye say or do!
How would your spirits groan in deep vexation
To see each melancholy alteration;
And, agonising, curse the time and place
When ye begat the base degen'rate race!
Nae langer rev'rend men, their country's glory,
In plain braid Scots hold forth a plain, braid story;
Nae langer thrify citizens, an' douce,
Meet owre a pint or in the council-house:

half-witted
But staumrel, corky-headed, graceless gentry,

spoliation
The herryment and ruin of the country;
Men three-parts made by tailors and by barbers,
Wha waste your weel-hain'd gear on damn'd New

well-saved
wealth
   Brigs and harbours!'

NEW BRIG

 'Now haud you there! for faith ye've said enough,

make good
And muckle mair than ye can mak to through.

As for your priesthood, I shall say but little,
Corbies and clergy are a shot right kittle: ravens; sort;
But, under favour o' your langer beard,   ticklish
Abuse o' magistrates might weel be spar'd;
To liken them to your auld-warld squad,
I must need say, comparisons are odd.
In Ayr, wag-wits nae mair can hae a handle
To mouth 'a Citizen,' a term o' scandal;
Nae mair the council waddles down the street,
In all the pomp of ignorant conceit;
Men wha grew wise priggin owre hops an' raisins,   haggling
Or gather'd lib'ral views in bonds and seisins;
If haply Knowledge, on a random tramp,
Had shor'd them with a glimmer of his lamp,   menaced
And would to common-sense for once betray'd them,
Plain, dull stupidity stept kindly in to aid them.'

What farther clish-ma-claver might been said,   nonsense
What bloody wars, if Sprites had blood to shed,
No man can tell; but, all before their sight,
A fairy train appear'd in order bright:
Adown the glittering stream they featly danc'd;
Bright to the moon their various dresses glanc'd;
They footed o'er the wat'ry glass so neat,
The infant ice scarce bent beneath their feet;
While arts of minstrelsy among them rung,
And soul-ennobling Bards heroic ditties sung.

O, had M'Lauchlan, thairm-inspiring sage,   (cat-) gut-
Been there to hear this heavenly band engage,
When thro' his dear strathspeys they bore with Highland
rage;
Or when they struck old Scotia's melting airs,
The lover's raptured joys or bleeding cares;
How would his Highland lug been nobler fir'd,   ear
And ev'n his matchless hand with finer touch inspir'd!
No guess could tell what instrument appear'd,
But all the soul of Music's self was heard;
Harmonious concert rung in every part,
While simple melody pour'd moving on the heart.

The Genius of the Stream in front appears,
A venerable chief advanc'd in years;
His hoary head with water-lilies crown'd,
His manly leg with garter-tangle bound.
Next came the loveliest pair in all the ring,
Sweet Female Beauty hand in hand with Spring;
Then, crown'd with flow'ry hay, came Rural Joy,
And Summer, with his fervid-beaming eye:
All-cheering Plenty, with her flowing horn,
Led yellow Autumn wreath'd with nodding corn;
Then Winter's time-bleach'd locks did hoary show,
By Hospitality, with cloudless brow.
Next follow'd Courage, with his martial stride,
From where the Feal wild-woody coverts hide;
Benevolence, with mild, benignant air,
A female form, came from the towers of Stair;
Learning and Worth in equal measures trode
From simple Catrine, their long-lov'd abode;
Last, white-rob'd Peace, crown'd with a hazel wreath,
To rustic Agriculture did bequeath
The broken, iron instruments of death:
At sight of whom our Sprites forgat their kindling wrath.

THE ORDINATION

For sense, they little owe to frugal Heav'n:
To please the mob they hide the little giv'n.

I

weavers; Kilmarnock wabsters, fidge an' claw,
shrug; An' pour your creeshie nations;
scratch An' ye wha leather rax an' draw,
greasy Of a' denominations;
stretch Switch! to the Laigh Kirk, ane an' a',
  An' there tak up your stations;
Then aff to Begbie's in a raw,
  An' pour divine libations
     For joy this day.

2

Curst Common-sense, that imp o' hell,
   Cam in wi' *Maggie Lauder*:
But Oliphant aft made her yell,
   An' Russell sair misca'd her:
This day Mackinlay taks the flail,
   An' he's the boy will blaud her!   slap
He'll clap a shangan on her tail,   cleft stick
   An' set the bairns to daud her   pelt
             Wi' dirt this day.

3

Mak haste an' turn King David owre,
   An' lilt wi' holy clangor;
O' double verse come gie us four,
   An' skirl up the *Bangor*:   shrill
This day the Kirk kicks up a stoure: dust
   Nae mair the knaves shall wrang her,
For Heresy is in her pow'r,
   And gloriously she'll whang her   flog
            Wi' pith this day.

4

Come, let a proper text be read,
   An' touch it aff wi' vigour,
How graceless Ham leugh at his dad,   laughed
   Which made Canàan a nigger;
Or Phineas drove the murdering blade
   Wi' whore-abhorring rigour;
Or Zipporah, the scauldin jad,
   Was like a bluidy tiger
             I' th' inn that day.

5

There, try his mettle on the Creed,
   And bind him down wi' caution,—
That stipend is a carnal weed
   He taks but for the fashion—
And gie him o'er the flock to feed,
   And punish each transgression;
Especial, rams that cross the breed,
   Gie them sufficient threshin:
            Spare them nae day.

6

Now auld Kilmarnock, cock thy tail,
   An' toss thy horns fu' canty; *joyful*
Nae mair thou'lt rowte out-owre the dale, *low*
   Because thy pasture's scanty;
For lapfu's large o' gospel kail
   Shall fill thy crib in plenty,
An' runts o' grace, the pick an' wale, *stalks; choice*
   An gien by way o' dainty,
            But ilka day. *every*

7

Nae mair by Babel's streams we'll weep
   To think upon our Zion;
And hing our fiddles up to sleep,
   Like baby-clouts a-dryin! *cloths*
Come, screw the pegs wi' tunefu' cheep,
   And o'er the thairms be tryin; *strings*
O, rare! to see our elbucks wheep, *elbows jerk*
   And a' like lamb-tails flyin
                Fu' fast this day!

8

Lang, Patronage, wi' rod o' airn, *iron*
   Has shor'd the Kirk's undoin; *theatened*
As lately Fenwick, sair forfairn, *forlorn*
   Has proven to its ruin:
Our patron, honest man! Glencairn,
   He saw mischief was brewin;
An' like a godly, elect bairn,
   He's waled us out a true ane, *chosen*
            And sound this day.

9

Now Robertson harangue nae mair,
   But steek your gab for ever; *shut; mouth*
Or try the wicked town of Ayr,
   For there they'll think you clever;
Or, nae reflection on your lear, *learning*
   Ye may commence a shaver; *set up for a barber*
Or to the Netherton repair,
   An' turn a carpet-weaver
            Aff-hand this day.

10

Mu'trie and you were just a match,
  We never had sic twa drones:
Auld Hornie did the Laigh Kirk watch,   *The Devil*
  Just like a winkin baudrons,   *cat*
And ay he catch'd the tither wretch,
  To fry them in his caudrons;
But now his Honor maun detach,
  Wi' a' his brimstone squadrons,
              Fast, fast this day.

11

See, see auld Orthodoxy's faes   *foes*
  She's swingein thro' the city!
Hark, how the nine-tail'd cat she plays!   *flogging*
  I vow it's unco pretty: *mighty*
There, Learning, with his Greekish face,
  Grunts out some Latin ditty;
And Common-Sense is gaun, she says,
  To mak to Jamie Beattie
             Her plaint this day.

12

But there's Morality himsel,
  Embracing all opinions
Hear, how he gies the tither yell
  Between his twa companions!
See, how she peels the skin an' fell,   *flesh under the*
  As ane were peelin onions!   *skin*
Now there, they're packèd aff to hell,
  An' banish'd our dominions,
             Henceforth this day.

13

O happy day! rejoice, rejoice!
  Come bouse about the porter!
Morality's demure decoys
  Shall here nae mair find quarter:
Mackinlay, Russell, are the boys
  That Heresy can torture;
They'll gie her on a rape a hoyse,   *rope; hosit*
  And cowe her measure shorter   *crop*
           By th' head some day.

14

pint

> Come, bring the tither mutchkin in,
>   And here's—for a conclusion—
> To ev'ry New Light mother's son,
>   From this time forth, confusion!

deafen

> If mair they deave us wi' their din
>   Or patronage intrusion

match

> We'll light a spunk, and ev'ry skin
>   We'll run them aff in fusion,
>   Like oil some day.

THE CALF

To the Rev. James Steven, on his text, MALACHI IV. 2:—
'And ye shall go forth, and grow up as calves of the stall.'

1

> Right, sir! your text I'll prove it true,
>   Tho' heretics may laugh;
> For instance, there's yoursel just now,

uncommon

>   God knows, an unco *calf.*

2

> And should some patron be so kind
>   As bless you wi' a kirk,
> I doubt na, sir, but then we'll find

yearling

>   You're still as great a *stirk.*

3

> But, if the lover's raptur'd hour
>   Shall ever be your lot,
> Forbid it, every heavenly Power,

ox

>   You e'er should be a *stot!*

4

> Tho', when some kind connubial dear
>   Your but-an'-ben adorns,
> The like has been that you may wear
>   A noble head of *horns.*

5

And, in your lug, most reverend James,   ear
    To hear your roar and rowte,   low
Few men o' sense will doubt your claims
    To rank among the *nowte*.   cattle

6

And when ye're number'd wi' the dead
    Below a grassy hillock,
With justice they may mark your head:—
    'Here lies a famous *bullock*!'

ADDRESS TO THE UNCO GUID

OR THE RIGIDLY RIGHTEOUS

My Son, these maxims make a rule,
    An' lump them ay thegither:
The Rigid Righteous is a fool,
    The Rigid Wise anither;
The cleanest corn that e'er was dight   sifted
    May hae some pyles o' caff in;   chaff
So ne'er a fellow-creature slight
    For random fits o' daffin.   larking
SOLOMON (*Eccles.* vii. 16)

I

O ye, wha are sae guid yoursel,
    Sae pious and sae holy,
Ye've nought to do but mark and tell
    Your neebours' fauts and folly;
Whase life is like a weel-gaun mill,   well-going
    Supplied wi' store o' water;
The heapet happer's ebbing still,   hopper
    An' still the clap plays clatter!   clapper

2

company

sober
giddy

put forward

restive

Hear me, ye venerable core,
   As counsel for poor mortals
That frequent pass douce Wisdom's door
   For glaikit Folly's portals:
I for their thoughtless, careless sakes
   Would here propone defence—
Their donsie tricks, their black mistakes,
   Their failings and mischances.

3

exchange

rest

Ye see your state wi' theirs compared,
   And shudder at the niffer;
But cast a moment's fair regard,
   What makes the mighty differ?
Discount what scant occasion gave;
   That purity ye pride in;
And (what's aft mair than a' the lave)
   Your better art o' hidin.

4

Think, when your castigated pulse
   Gies now and then a wallop,
What ragings must his veins convulse,
   That still eternal gallop!
Wi' wind and tide fair i' your tail,
   Right on ye scud your sea-way;
But in the teeth o' baith to sail,

uncommon
   It maks an unco lee-way.

5

See Social-life and Glee sit down
   All joyous and unthinking,
Till, quite transmurgirfy'd, they're grown
   Debauchery and Drinking:
O, would they stay to calculate,
   Th' eternal consequences,
Or—your more dreaded hell to state—
   Damnation of expenses!

6

Ye high, exalted, virtuous dames,
  Tied up in godly laces,
Before ye gie poor Frailty names,
  Suppose a change o' cases:
A dear-lov'd lad, convenience snug,
  A treach'rous inclination—
But, let me whisper i' your lug,   ear
  Ye're aiblins nae temptation.   maybe

7

Then gently scan your brother man,
  Still gentler sister woman;
Tho' they may gang a kennin wrang,
  To step aside is human:
One point must still be greatly dark,
  The moving *why* they do it;
And just as lamely can ye mark
  How far perhaps they rue it.

8

Who made the heart, 'tis He alone
  Decidedly can try us:
He knows each chord, its various tone,
  Each spring, its various bias:
Then at the balance let's be mute,
  We never can adjust it;
What's done we partly may compute,
  But know not what's resisted.

TAM SAMSON'S ELEGY

An honest man's the noblest work of God.
POPE

I

Has auld Kilmarnock seen the Deil?
Or great Mackinlay thrawn his heel?
Or Robertson again grown weel
        To preach an' read?   worse;
'Na, waur than a'!' cries ilka chiel,   everybody
        'Tam Samson's dead!'

2

Kilmarnock lang may grunt an' grane,
weep alone An' sigh, an' sab, an' greet her lane,
clothe, child An' cleed her bairns—man, wife an' wean—
   In mourning weed;
rent in kind To Death she's dearly pay'd the kain:
   Tam Samson's dead!

3

The Brethren o' the mystic level
slope May hing their head in woefu' bevel,
While by their nose the tears will revel,
   Like onie bead;
Death's gien the Lodge an unco devel:
stunning blow   Tam Samson's dead!

4

When Winter muffles up his cloak,
And binds the mire like a rock;
ponds When to the loughs the curlers flock,
   Wi' gleesome speed,
mark Wha will they station at the cock?—
   Tam Samson's dead!

5

company He was the king of a' the core,
To guard, or draw, or wick a bore,
Or up the rink like Jehu roar
   In time o' need;
But now he lags on Death's hog-score:
   Tam Samson's dead!

6

salmon Now safe the stately sawmont sail,
And trouts bedropp'd wi' crimson hail,
And eels, weel-kend for souple tail,
pikes   And geds for greed,
Since, dark in Death's fish-creel, we wail,
   Tam Samson dead!

7

Rejoice, ye birring paitricks a';
Ye cootie moorcocks, crously craw;
Ye maukins, cock your fud fu' braw
   Withouten dread;
Your mortal fae is now awa:
   Tam Samson's dead!

    partridges
    leg-plumed;
    confidently
    hares; tail

8

That woefu' morn be ever mourn'd,
Saw him in shootin graith adorn'd,
While pointers round impatient burn'd,
   Frae couples free'd;
But och! he gaed and ne'er return'd:
   Tam Samson's dead.

    attire

    leashes

9

In vain auld-age his body batters,
In vain the gout his ancles fetters,
In vain the burns cam down like waters,
   An acre braid!
Now ev'ry auld wife, greetin, clatters:
   'Tam Samson's dead!'

    ankles
    brooks; lakes

    weeping

10

Owre monie a weary hag he limpit,
An' ay the tither shot he thumpit,
Till coward Death behint him jumpit,
   Wi' deadly feide;
Now he proclaims wi' tout o' trumpet:
   'Tam Samson's dead!'

    moss

    feud

    blast

11

When at his heart he felt the dagger,
He reel'd his wonted bottle-swagger,
But yet he drew the mortal trigger
   Wi' weel-aim'd heed;
'Lord, five!' he cry'd, an' owre did stagger—
   Tam Samson's dead!

12

Each

Ilk hoary hunter mourn'd a brither;
Ilk sportsman-youth bemoan'd a father;
Yon auld gray stane, amang the heather,
        Marks out his head;

babble

Whare Burns has wrote, in rhyming blether:
        'Tam Samson's dead!'

13

There low he lies in lasting rest;
Perhaps upon his mould'ring breast

builds

Some spitefu' moorfowl bigs her nest,
        To hatch an' breed:
Alas! nae mair he'll them molest:
        Tam Samson's dead!

14

When August winds the heather wave,
And sportsmen wander by yon grave,
Three volleys let his memory crave
        O' pouther an' lead,
Till Echo answers frae her cave:
        'Tam Samson's dead!'

15

'Heav'n rest his saul whare'er he be!'

more

Is th' wish o' monie mae than me:
He had twa fauts, or maybe three,
        Yet what remead?

One

Ae social, honest man want we:
        Tam Samson's dead!

THE EPITAPH

Tam Samson's weel-worn clay here lies:
    Ye canting zealots, spare him!
If honest worth in Heaven rise,
    Ye'll mend or ye win near him.

PER CONTRA

Go, Fame, an' canter like a filly
Thro' a' the streets an neuks o' Killie;
Tell ev'ry social honest billie   fellow
            To cease his grievin;
For, yet unskaith'd by Death's gleg gullie,   guick knife
            Tam Samson's leevin!

A WINTER NIGHT

Pour naked wretches, wheresoe'er you are,
That bide the pelting of this pityless storm!
How shall your houseless heads and unfed sides,
Your loop'd and window'd raggedness, defend you
From seasons such as these?

SHAKESPEARE

I

When biting Boreas, fell and doure,   cruel; hard
Sharp shivers thro' the leafless bow'r;
When Phœbus gies a short-liv'd glow'r,   stare
            Far south the lift,   horizon
Dim-dark'ning thro' the flaky show'r
            Or whirling drift:

2

Ae night the storm the steeples rocked;   One
Poor Labour sweet in sleep was locked;
While burns, wi' snawy wreaths up-choked,   brooks
            Wild-eddying swirl,
Or, thro' the mining outlet bocked,   vomited
            Down headlong hurl:

3

List'ning the doors an' winnocks rattle,   windows
I thought me on the ourie cattle,   shivering
Or silly sheep, wha bide this brattle   helpless
            O' winter war,
And thro' the drift, deep-lairing, sprattle   scramble
            Beneath a scaur.   jutting rock

4

Each

Ilk happing bird—wee, helpless thing!—
That in the merry months o' spring
Delighted me to hear thee sing,
            What comes o' thee?
Whare wilt thou cow'r thy chittering wing,
            An' close thy e'e?

5

Ev'n you, on murd'ring errands toil'd,
Lone from your savage homes exil'd,
The blood-stain'd roost and sheep-cote spoil'd
            My heart forgets,
While pityless the tempest wild
            Sore on your beats!

6

Now Phœbe, in her midnight reign,
Dark-muffl'd, view'd the dreary plain;
Still crowding thoughts, a pensive train.
            Rose in my soul,
When on my ear this plaintive strain,
            Slow-solemn, stole:—

7

'Blow, blow, ye winds, with heavier gust!
And freeze, thou bitter-biting frost!
Descend, ye chilly, smothering snows!
Not all your rage, as now united, shows
    More hard unkindness unrelenting,
    Vengeful malice, unrepenting,
Than heaven-illumin'd Man on brother Man bestows!
    See sterm Oppression's iron grip,
        Or mad Ambition's gory hand,
    Sending, like blood-hounds from the slip,
        Woe, Want, and Murder o'er a land!
    Ev'n in the peaceful rural vale,
    Truth, weeping, tells the mournful tale:

How pamper'd Luxury, Flatt'ry by her side,
  The parasite empoisoning her ear,
  With all the servile wretches in the rear,
Looks o'er proud Property, extended wide;
  And eyes the simple, rustic hind,
  Whose toil upholds the glitt'ring show—
  A creature of another kind,
  Some coarser substance, unrefin'd—
Plac'd for her lordly use, thus far, thus vile, below!
  Where, where is Love's fond, tender throe,
  With lordly Honor's lofty brow,
    The pow'rs you proudly own?
  Is there, beneath Love's noble name,
  Can harbour, dark, the selfish aim,
    To bless himself alone?
  Mark Maiden-Innocence a prey
    To love-pretending snares:
  This boasted Honor turns away,
  Shunning soft Pity's rising sway,
Regardless of the tears and unavailing pray'rs!
  Perhaps this hour, in Misery's squalid nest,
  She strains your infant to her joyless breast,
And with a mother's fears shrinks at the rocking blast!

8

'O ye! who, sunk in beds of down,
  Feel not a want but what yourselves create,
  Think, for a moment, on his wretched fate,
Whom friends and fortune quite disown!
  Ill satisfy'd keen nature's clam'rous call,
  Stretch'd on his straw, he lays himself to sleep;
While through the ragged roof and chinky wall,
  Chill, o'er his slumbers piles the drifty heap!
  Think on the dungeon's grim confine,
  Where Guilt and poor Misfortune pine!
  Guilt, erring man, relenting view!
  But shall thy legal rage pursue
  The wretch, already crushèd low
  By cruel Fortune's undeservèd blow?
Affliction's sons are brothers in distress;
A brother to relieve, how exquisite the bliss!'

9

I heard nae mair, for Chanticleer
    Shook off the pouthery snaw,
And hail'd the morning with a cheer,
    A cottage-rousing craw.

powdery

10

But deep this thruth impress'd my mind:
    Thro' all His works abroad,
The heart benevolent and kind
    The most resembles God.

STANZAS WRITTEN IN PROSPECT OF DEATH

1

Why am I loth to leave this earthly scene?
    Have I so found it full of pleasing charms?
Some drops of joy with draughts of ill between;
    Some gleams of sunshine mid renewing storms.
Is it departing pangs my soul alarms?
    Or death's unlovely, dreary, dark abode?
For guilt, for guilt, my terrors are in arms:
    I tremble to approach an angry God,
And justly smart beneath his sin-avenging rod.

2

Fain would I say: 'Forgive my foul offence,'
    Fain promise never more to disobey.
But should my Author health again dispense,
    Again I might desert fair virtue's way;
Again in folly's path might go astray;
    Again exalt the brute and sink the man:
Then how should I for heavenly mercy pray,
    Who act so counter heavenly mercy's plan?
Who sin so oft have mourn'd, yet to temptation ran?

3

O Thou great Governor of all below!—
  If I may dare a lifted eye to Thee,—
Thy nod can make the tempest cease to blow,
  Or still the tumult of the raging sea:
With that controlling pow'r assit ev'n me
  Those headlong furious passions to confine,
For all unfit I feel my pow'rs to be
  To rule their torrent in th' allowèd line:
O, aid me with Thy help, Omnipotence Divine!

PRAYER: O THOU DREAD POWER

*Lying at a reverend friend's house one night the author
left the following verses in the room where he slept.*

1

O Thou dread Power, who reign'st above,
  I know thou wilt me hear,
When for this scene of peace and love
  I make my prayer sincere.

2

The hoary Sire—the mortal stroke,
  Long, long be peas'd to spare:
To bless his little filial flock,
  And show what good men are.

3

She, who her lovely offspring eyes
  With tender hopes and fears—
O, bless her with a mother's joys,
  But spare a mother's tears!

4

Their hope, their stay, their darling youth,
  In manhood's dawning blush,
Bless him, Thou God of love and truth,
  Up to a parent's wish.

5

The beauteous, seraph sister-band—
   With earnest tears I pray—
Thou know'st the snares on every hand,
   Guide Thou their steps alway.

6

When, soon or late, they reach that coast,
   O'er Life's rough ocean driven,
May they rejoice, no wand'rer lost,
   A family in Heaven!

PARAPHRASE OF THE FIRST PSALM

1

The man, in life wherever plac'd,
   Hath happiness in store,
Who walks not in the wicked's way
   Nor learns their guilty lore;

2

Nor from the seat of scornful pride
   Casts forth his eyes abroad,
But with humility and awe
   Still walks before his God!

3

That man shall flourish like the trees,
   Which by the streamlets grow:
The fruitful top is spread on high,
   And firm the root below.

4

But he, whose blossom buds in guilt,
   Shall to the ground be cast,
And, like the rootless stubble, tost
   Before the sweeping blast.

5

For why? that God the good adore
      Hath giv'n them peace and rest,
But hath decreed that wicked men
      Shall ne'er be truly blest.

PRAYER UNDER THE PRESSURE OF VIOLENT ANGUISH

1

O Thou Great Being! what Thou art
      Surpasses me to know;
Yet sure I am, that known to Thee
      Are all Thy works below.

2

Thy creature here before Thee stands,
      All wretched and distrest;
Yet sure those ills that wring my soul
      Obey Thy high behest.

3

Sure Thou, Almighty, canst not act
      From cruelty or wrath!
O, free my weary eyes from tears,
      Or close them fast in death!

4

But, if I must afflicted be,
      To suit some wide design,
Then man my soul with firm resolves
      To bear and not repine!

THE NINETIETH PSALM VERSIFIED

1

O Thou, the first, the greatest friend
      Of all the human race!
Whose strong right hand has ever been
      Their stay and dwelling place!

2

Before the mountains heav'd their heads
 Beneath Thy forming hand,
Before this ponderous globe itself
 Arose at Thy command:

3

That Power, which rais'd and still upholds
 This universal frame,
From countless, unbeginning time
 Was ever still the same.

4

Those mighty periods of years,
 Which seem to us so vast,
Appear no more before Thy sight
 Than yesterday that's past.

5

Thou giv'st the word: Thy creature, man,
 Is to existence brought;
Again Thou say'st: 'Ye sons of men,
 Return ye into nought!'

6

Thou layest them, with all their cares,
 In everlasting sleep;
As with a flood Thou tak'st them off
 With overwhelming sweep.

7

They flourish like the morning flower
 In beauty's pride array'd,
But long ere night, cut down, it lies
 All wither'd and decay'd.

TO MISS LOGAN

WITH BEATTIE'S POEMS FOR A NEW-YEAR'S GIFT—
JANUARY 1, 1787

I

Again the silent wheels of time
  Their annual round have driv'n,
And you, tho' scarce in maiden prime,
  Are so much nearer Heav'n.

2

No gifts have I from Indian coasts
  The infant year to hail;
I send you more than India boasts
  In Edwin's simple tale.

3

Our sex with guile, and faithless love,
  Is charg'd—perhaps too true;
But may, dear maid, each lover prove
  An Edwin still to you.

ADDRESS TO A HAGGIS

I

Fair fa' your honest, sonsie face,   jolly
Great chieftain o' the puddin-race!
Aboon them a' ye tak your place,   Above
      Painch, tripe, or thairm: Paunch; small guts
Weel are ye wordy of a grace
      As lang's my arm.

2

The groaning trencher there ye fill,
Your hurdies like a distant hill,   buttocks
Your pin wad help to mend a mill   skewer
      In time o' need,
While thro' your pores the dews distil
      Like amber bead.

3

His knife see rustic Labour dight,
wipe
An' cut ye up wi' ready slight,
skill
Trenching your gushing entrails bright,
        Like onie ditch;
And then, O what a glorious sight,
        Warm-reekin, rich!

4

spoon
Then, horn for horn, they stretch an' strive:
Deil tak the hindmost, on they drive,
bellies; by-and-
bye
Till a' their weel-swall'd kytes belyve
        Are bent like drums;
burst
Then auld Guidman, maist like to rive,
        'Bethankit!' hums.

5

Is there that owre his French *ragout*,
Or *olio* that wad staw a sow,
sicken
Or *fricassee* wad mak her spew
disgust
        Wi' perfect sconner,
Looks down wi' sneering, scornfu' view
        On sic a dinner?

6

Poor devil! see him owre his trash,
weak; rush
As feckless as a wither'd rash,
His spindle shank a guid whip-lash,
        His nieve a nit;
Thro' bluidy flood or field to dash,
        O how unfit!

7

But mark the Rustic, haggis-fed,
The trembling earth resounds his tread,
ample
Clap in his walie nieve a blade,
        He'll make it whissle;
crop
An' legs, an' arms, an' heads will sned
        Like taps o' thrissle.

8

Ye Pow'rs, wha mak mankind your care,
And dish them out their bill o' fare,
Auld Scotland wants nae skinking ware,   watery
        That jaups in luggies;   splashes;
But, if ye wish her gratefu' prayer,   porringers
        Gie her a Haggis!

ADDRESS TO EDINBURGH

1

Edina! Scotia's darling seat!
  All hail thy palaces and tow'rs,
Where once, beneath a Monarch's feet,
  Sat Legislation's sov'reign pow'rs:
  From marking wildly-scatt'red flow'rs,
As on the banks of Ayr I stray'd,
  And singing, lone, the ling'ring hours,
I shelter in thy honor'd shade.

2

Here Wealth still swells the golden tide,
  As busy Trade his labours plies;
There Architecture's noble pride
  Bids elegance and splendour rise:
  Here Justice, from her native skies,
High wields her balance and her rod;
  There Learning, with his eagle eyes,
Seeks Science in her coy abode.

3

Thy sons, Edina, social, kind,
  With open arms the stranger hail,
Their views enlarg'd, their lib'ral mind,
  Above the narrow, rural vale;
  Attentive still to Sorrow's wail,
Or modest Merit's silent claim:
  And never may their sources fail!
And never Envy blot their name!

4

Thy daughters bright thy walks adorn,
　Gay as the gilded summer sky,
Sweet as the dewy, milk-white thorn,
　Dear as the raptur'd thrill of joy!
　Fair Burnet strikes th' adoring eye,
Heav'n's beauties on my fancy shine:
　I see the Sire of Love on high,
And own His work indeed divine!

5

There, watching high the least alarms,
　Thy rough, rude fortress gleams afar;
Like some bold vet'ran, grey in arms,
　And mark'd with many a seamy scar:
　The pond'rous wall and massy bar,
Grim-rising o'er the rugged rock,
　Have oft withstood assailing war,
And oft repell'd th' invader's shock.

6

With awe-struck thought and pitying tears,
　I view that noble, stately dome,
Where Scotia's kings of other years,
　Fam'd heroes! had their royal home:
　Alas, how chang'd the times to come!
Their royal name low in the dust!
　Their hapless race wild-wand'ring roam!
Tho' rigid Law cries out: ''Twas just!'

7

Wild beats my heart to trace your steps,
　Whose ancestors, in days of yore,
Thro' hostile ranks and ruin'd gaps
　Old Scotia's bloody lion bore:
　Ev'n I, who sing in rustic lore,
Haply my sires have left their shed,
　And fac'd grim Danger's loudest roar,
Bold-following where your fathers led!

8

Edina! Scotia's darling seat!
    All hail thy palaces and tow'rs;
Where once, beneath a Monarch's feet,
    Sat Legislation's sov'reign pow'rs:
    From marking wildly-scatt'red flow'rs,
As on the banks of Ayr I stray'd,
    And singing, lone, the ling'ring hours,
I shelter in thy honour'd shade.

WRITTEN IN FRIARS CARSE HERMITAGE, ON NITHSIDE

Thou whom chance may hither lead,
Be thou clad in russet weed,
Be thou deckt in silken stole,
Grave these counsels on thy soul.

    Life is but a day at most,
Sprung from night,—in darkness lost:
Hope not sunshine ev'ry hour,
Fear not clouds will always lour.

    As Youth and Love with sprightly dance
Beneath thy morning star advance,
Pleasure with her siren air
May delude the thoughtless pair:
Let Prudence bless Enjoyment's cup,
Then raptur'd sip, and sip it up.

    As thy day grows warm and high,
Life's meridian flaming nigh,
Dost thou sprun the humble vale?
Life's proud summits would'st thou scale?
Check thy climbing step, elate,
Evils lurk in felon wait:
Dangers, eagle-pinioned, bold,
Soar around each cliffy hold;
While cheerful Peace with linnet song
Chants the lowly dells among.

    As the shades of ev'ning close,
Beck'ning thee to long repose;

As life itself becomes disease,
Seek the chimney-nook of ease:
There ruminate with sober thought,
On all thou'st seen, and heard, and wrought;
And teach the sportive younkers round,
Saws of experience, sage and sound:
Say, man's true, genuine estimate,
The grand criterion of his fate,
Is not, Art thou high or low?
Did thy fortune ebb or flow?
Did many talents gild thy span?
Or frugal Nature grudge thee one?
Tell them, and press it on their mind,
As thou thyself must shortly find,
The smile or frown of awful Heav'n
To Virtue or to Vice is giv'n;
Say, to be just, and kind, and wise—
There solid self-enjoyment lies;
That foolish, selfish, faithless ways
Lead to be wretched, vile, and base.

Thus resign'd and quiet, creep
To the bed of lasting sleep:
Sleep, whence thou shall ne'er awake,
Night, where dawn shall never break;
Till future life, future no more,
To light and joy the good restore,
To light and joy unknown before.

Stranger, go! Heav'n be thy guide!
Quod the beadsman of Nithside.

ODE SACRED TO THE MEMORY OF MRS. OSWALD OF AUCHENCRUIVE

Dweller in yon dungeon dark,
Hangman of creation, mark!
Who in widow-weeds appears,
Laden with unhonoured years,
Noosing with care a bursting purse,
Baited with many a deadly curse?

STROPHE

View the wither'd beldam's face:
Can thy keen inspection trace
Aught of Humanity's sweet, melting grace?
Note that eye, 'tis rheum o'erflows—
Pity's flood there never rose.
See those hands, ne'er stretch'd to save,
Hands that took but never gave.
Keeper of Mammon's iron chest,
Lo, there she goes, unpitied and unblest,
She goes, but not to realms of everlasting rest!

ANTISTROPHE

Plunderer of Armies! lift thine eyes
  (A while forbear, ye torturing fiends),
Seest thou whose step, unwilling, hither bends?
No fallen angel, hurl'd from upper skies!
  'Tis thy trusty, quondam Mate,
  Doom'd to share thy fiery fate;
    She, tardy, hell-ward plies.

EPODE

  And are they of no more avail,
Ten thousand glittering pounds a-year?
  In other words can Mammon fail,
    Omnipotent as he is here?
O bitter mockery of the pompous bier!
  While down the wretched vital part is driven,
The cave-lodg'd beggar, with a conscience clear,
  Expires in rags, unknown, and goes to Heaven.

ELEGY ON CAPTAIN MATTHEW HENDERSON

A GENTLEMAN WHO HELD THE PATENT FOR HIS HONOURS
IMMEDIATELY FROM ALMIGHTY GOD!

But now his radiant course is run,
For Matthew's course was bright:
His soul was like the glorious sun
A matchless, Heavenly light.

1

O Death! thou tyrant fell and bloody!
The meikle Devil wi' a woodie
   O'er hurcheon hides,
And like stock-fish come o'er his studdie
   Wi' thy auld sides!

great; halter — The meikle Devil wi' a woodie
Trail; smithy — Haurl thee hame to his black smiddie
hedgehog
anvil

2

He's gane, he's gane! he's frae us torn,
The ae best fellow e'er was born!
Thee, Matthew, Nature's sel shall mourn,
   By wood and wild,
Where, haply, Pity strays forlorn,
   Frae man exil'd.

gone
one

3

Ye hills, near neebors o' the starns,
That proudly cock your cresting cairns!
Ye cliffs, the haunts of sailing yearns,
   Where Echo slumbers!
Come join ye, Nature's sturdiest bairns.
   My wailing numbers!

stars
mounds
eagles

4

Mourn, ilka grove the cushat kens!
Ye hazly, shaws and briery dens!
Ye burnies, wimplin down your glens
   Wi' toddlin din,
Or foaming, strang, wi' hasty stens,
   Frae lin to lin!

every
woods brooklets,
winding
purling
quick leaps

5

Mourn, little harebells o'er the lea;
Ye stately foxgloves, fair to see;
Ye woodbines, hanging bonilie
                    In scented bowers;
Ye roses on your thorny tree,
                    The first o' flowers!

6

At dawn, when every grassy blade
Droops with a diamond at his head;
At ev'n, when beans their fragrance shed
                    I' th' rustling gale;
Ye maukins, whiddin through the glade;   harse, scudding
                    Come join my wail!

7

Mourn, ye wee songsters o' the wood;
Ye grouse that crap the heather bud;
Ye curlews, calling thro' a clud;   cloud
                    Ye whistling plover;
And mourn, ye whirring paitrick brood: partridge
                    He's gane for ever!

8

Mourn, sooty coots, and speckled teals;
Ye fisher herons, watching eels;
Ye duck and drake, wi' airy wheels
                    Circling the lake;
Ye bitterns, till the quagmire reels,
                    Rair for his sake!   Boom

9

Mourn, clam'ring craiks, at close o' day,   corncrakes
'Mang fields o' flow'ring clover gay!
And when you wing your annual way
                    Frae our cauld shore,
Tell thae far warlds wha lies in clay,   those
                    Wham we deplore.

10

owls

haunted

stare

Ye houlets, frae your ivy bower
In some auld tree, or eldritch tower,
What time the moon, wi' silent glowr,
                    Sets up her horn,
Wail thro' the dreary midnight hour

wakeful
                    Till waukrife morn!

11

O rivers, forests, hills, and plains!

cheerful

But tales of
woe?

eyes

Must

Oft have ye heard my canty strains:
But now, what else for me remains
                    But tales of woe?
And frae my een the drapping rains
                    Maun ever flow.

12

Mourn, Spring, thou darling of the year!

catch

Ilk cowslip cup shall kep a tear:
Thou, Simmer, while each corny spear
                    Shoots up its head,
Thy gay, green, flowery tresses shear
                    For him that's dead!

13

Thou, Autumn, wi' thy yellow hair,
In grief thy sallow mantle tear!
Thou, Winter, hurling thro' the air
                    The roaring blast,
Wide o'er the naked world declare
                    The worth we've lost!

14

Mourn him, thou Sun, great source of light!
Mourn, Empress of the silent night!

starlets

And you, ye twinkling starnies bright,
                    My Matthew mourn!
For through your orbs he's taen his flight,
                    Ne'er to return.

15

O Henderson! the man! the brother!
And art thou gone, and gone for ever?
And hast thou crost that unknown river,
                    Life's dreary bound?
Like thee, where shall I find another,
                    The world around?

16

Go to your sculptur'd tombs, ye Great,
In a' the tinsel trash o' state!
But by thy honest turf I'll wait,
                    Thou man of worth!
And weep the ae best fellow's fate
                    E'er lay in earth!

THE EPITAPH

1

Stop, passenger! my story's brief,
    And truth I shall relate, man:
I tell nae common tale o' grief,
    For Matthew was a great man.

2

If thou uncommon merit hast,
    Yet spurn'd at Fortune's door, man;
A look of pity hither cast,
    For Matthew was a poor man.

3

If thou a noble sodger art,
    That passest by this grave, man;
There moulders her a gallant heart,
    For Matthew was a brave man.

4

If thou on men, their works and ways,
    Canst throw uncommon light, man;
Here lies wha weel had won thy praise,
    For Matthew was a bright man.

5

If thou, at Friendship's sacred ca',
   Wad life itself resign, man;
Thy sympathetic tear maun fa',
   For Matthew was a kind man.

6

If thou art staunch, without a stain,
   Like the unchanging blue, man;
This was a kinsman o' thy ain,
   For Matthew was a true man.

7

If thou hast wit, and fun, and fire,
   And ne'er guid wine did fear, man;
brother   This was thy billie, dam, and sire,
   For Matthew was a queer man.

8

whining   If onie whiggish, whingin sot,
   To blame poor Matthew dare, man;
woe   May dool and sorrow be his lot!
   For Matthew was a rare man.

TO ROBERT GRAHAM OF FINTRY, ESQ.

Late crippl'd of an arm, and now a leg;
About to beg a pass for leave to beg;
Dull, listless, teas'd, dejected, and deprest
(Nature is adverse to a cripple's rest);
Will generous Graham list to his Poet's wail
(It soothes poor Misery, hearkening to her tale),
And hear him curse the light he first survey'd,
And doubly curse the luckless rhyming trade?

Thou, Nature! partial Nature! I arraign;
Of thy caprice maternal I complain:
The lion and the bull thy care have found,
One shakes the forests, and one spurns the ground;
Thou giv'st the ass his hide, the snail his shell;
Th' envenom'd wasp, victorious, guards his cell;
Thy minions kings defend, control, devour,
In all th' omnipotence of rule and power.

Foxes and statesmen subtile wiles ensure;
The cit and polecat stink, and are secure;
Toads with their poison, doctors with their drug,
The priest and hedgehog in their robes, are snug;
Ev'n silly woman has her warlike arts,
Her tongue and eyes—her dreaded spear and darts.

But O thou bitter step-mother and hard,
To thy poor, fenceless, naked child—the Bard!
A thing unteachable in world's skill,
And half an idiot too, more helpless still:
No heels to bear him from the op'ning dun,
No claws to dig, his hated sight to shun;
No horns, but those by luckless Hymen worn,
And those, alas! not, Amalthea's horn;
No nerves olfact'ry, Mammon's trusty cur,
Clad in rich Dulness' comfortable fur;
In naked feeling, and in aching pride,
He bears th' unbroken blast from ev'ry side.
Vampyre booksellers drain him to the heart,
And scorpion critics cureless venom dart.

Critics—appall'd, I venture on the name;
Those cut-throat bandits in the paths of fame;
Bloody dissectors, worse than ten Monroes:
He hacks to teach, they mangle to expose.

His heart by causeless wanton malice wrung,
By blockheads' daring into madness stung;
His well-won bays, than life itself more dear,
By miscreants torn, who ne'er one sprig must wear;
Foil'd, bleeding, tortur'd in th' unequal strife,
The hapless Poet flounders on thro' life:
Till, fled each hope that once his bosom fir'd,
And fled each Muse that glorious once inspir'd,
Low sunk in squalid, unprotected age,
Dead even resentment for his injur'd page,
He heeds or feels no more the ruthless critic's rage!
So, by some hedge, the gen'rous steed deceas'd,
For half-starv'd snarling curs a dainty feast,
By toil and famine wore to skin and bone,
Lies, senseless of each tugging bitch's son.

O Dulness! portion of the truly blest!
Calm shelter'd haven of eternal rest!
Thy sons ne'er madden in the fierce extremes
Of Fortune's polar frost, or torrid beams.
If mantling high she fills the golden cup,
With sober, selfish ease they sip it up:
Conscious the bounteous meed they well deserve,
They only wonder 'some folks' do not starve.
The grave, sage hern thus easy picks his frog,
And thinks the mallard a sad, worthless dog.
When Disappointment snaps the clue of hope,
And thro' disastrous night they darkling grope,
With deaf endurance sluggishly they bear,
And just conclude 'that fools are fortune's care.'
So, heavy, passive to the tempest's shocks,
Strong on the sign-post stands the stupid ox.

Not so the idle Muses' mad-cap train;
Not such the workings of their moon-struck brain:
In equanimity they never dwell;
By turns in soaring heav'n, or vaulted hell.

I dread thee, Fate, relentless and severe,
With all a poet's, husband's, father's fear!
Already one strong hold of hope is lost:
Glencairn, the truly noble, lies in dust
(Fled, like the sun eclips'd as noon appears,
And left us darkling in a world of tears).
O, hear my ardent, grateful, selfish pray'r!
Fintry, my other stay, long bless and spare!
Thro' a long life his hopes and wishes crown,
And bright in cloudless skies his sun go down!
May bliss domestic smooth his private path;
Give energy to life; and soothe his latest breath,
With many a filial tear circling the bed of death!

LAMENT FOR JAMES, EARL OF GLENCAIRN

1

The wind blew hollow frae the hills;
   By fits the sun's departing beam
Look'd on the fading yellow woods,
   That wav'd o'er Lugar's winding stream.
Beneath a craigy steep a Bard,   *craggy*
   Laden with years and meikle pain,   *much*
In loud lament bewail'd his lord,
   Whom Death had all untimely taen.

2

He lean'd him to an ancient aik,   *oak*
   Whose trunk was mould'ring down with years;
His locks were bleachèd white with time,
   His hoary cheek was wet wi' tears;
And as he touch'd his trembling harp,
   And as he tun'd his doleful sang,
The winds, lamenting thro' their caves,
   To echo bore the notes alang:—

3

'Ye scatter'd birds that faintly sing,
   The reliques of the vernal quire!
Ye woods that shed on a' the winds
   The honours of the agèd year!
A few short months, and, glad and gay,
   Again ye'll charm the ear and e'e;
But nocht in all revolving time
   Can gladness bring again to me.

4

'I am a bending agèd tree,
   That long has stood the wind and rain;
But now has come a cruel blast
   And my last hold of earth is gane;
Nae leaf o' mine shall greet the spring,
   Nae simmer sun exalt my bloom;
But I maun lie before the storm,
   And ithers plant them in my room.

5

'I've seen sae monie changefu' years,
  On earth I am a stranger grown:
I wander in the ways of men,
  Alike unknowing and unknown:
Unheard, unpitied, unreliev'd,
  I bear alane my lade o' care;
For silent, low, on beds of dust,
  Lie a' that would my sorrows share.

6

'And last (the sum of a' my griefs!)
  My noble master lies in clay;
  His country's pride, his country's stay:
In weary being now I pine,
  For a' the life of life is dead,
And hope has left my agèd ken,
  On forward wing for ever fled.

7

'Awake thy last sad voice, my harp!
  The voice of woe and wild despair!
Awake, resound thy latest lay,
  Then sleep in silence evermair!
And thou, my last, best, only friend,
  That fillest an untimely tomb,
Accept this tribute from the Bard
  Thou brought from Fortune's mirkest gloom.

8

'In Poverty's low barren vale,
  Thick mists obscure involv'd me round;
Though oft I turn'd the wistful eye,
  Nae ray of fame was to be found;
Thou found'st me, like the morning sun
  That melts the fogs in limpid air:
The friendless Bard and rustic song
  Became alike thy fostering care.

9

'O, why has Worth so short a date,
  While villains ripen grey with time!
Must thou, the noble, gen'rous, great,
  Fall in bold manhood's hardy prime?
Why did I live to see that day,
  A day to me so full of woe?
O, had I met the mortal shaft
  Which laid my benefactor low!

10

'The bridegroom may forget the bride
  Was made his wedded wife yestreen;
The monarch may forget the crown
  That on his head an hour has been;
The mother may forget the child
  That smiles sae sweetly on her knee;
But I'll remember thee, Glencairn,
  And a' that thou hast done for me!'

LINES TO SIR JOHN WHITEFOORD,
BART.

SENT WITH THE FOREGOING POEM

Thou, who thy honour as thy God rever'st,
Who, save thy mind's reproach, nought earthly fear'st,
To thee this votive off'ring I impart,
The tearful tribute of a broken heart.
The Friend thou valued'st, I the Patron lov'd;
His worth, his honour, all the world approv'd:
We'll mourn till we too go as he has gone,
And tread the shadowy path to that dark world
  unknown.

TAM O'SHANTER

A Tale

Of Brownyis and Bogillis full is this Buke.
GAWIN DOUGLAS

<table>
<tr><td>pedlar</td><td>When chapman billies leave the street,</td></tr>
<tr><td>thirsty fellows</td><td>And drouthy neebors neebors meet;</td></tr>
<tr><td></td><td>As market-days are wearing late,</td></tr>
<tr><td>road</td><td>An' folk begin to tak the gate;</td></tr>
<tr><td>ale</td><td>While we sit bousing at the nappy,</td></tr>
<tr><td>full; mighty</td><td>An' getting fou and unco happy,</td></tr>
<tr><td>not</td><td>We think na on the lang Scots miles,</td></tr>
<tr><td>bogs; pools</td><td>The mosses, waters, slaps, and styles,</td></tr>
<tr><td>breaches; stiles</td><td>That lie between us and our hame,</td></tr>
<tr><td></td><td>Whare sits our sulky, sullen dame,</td></tr>
<tr><td></td><td>Gathering her brows like gathering storm,</td></tr>
<tr><td></td><td>Nursing her wrath to keep it warm.</td></tr>
</table>

<table>
<tr><td>found</td><td>This truth fand honest Tam o' Shanter,</td></tr>
<tr><td>one</td><td>As he frae Ayr ae night did canter:</td></tr>
<tr><td></td><td>(Auld Ayr, wham ne'er a town surpasses.</td></tr>
<tr><td></td><td>For honest men and bonie lasses.)</td></tr>
</table>

<table>
<tr><td></td><td>O Tam, had'st thou but been sae wise,</td></tr>
<tr><td>to have taken</td><td>As taen thy ain wife Kate's advice!</td></tr>
<tr><td>good-for-
nothing</td><td>She tauld thee weel thou was a skellum,</td></tr>
<tr><td>chattering;
babbler</td><td>A blethering, blustering, drunken blellum;</td></tr>
<tr><td></td><td>That frae November till October,</td></tr>
<tr><td></td><td>Ae market-day thou was nae sober;</td></tr>
<tr><td>meal-grinding</td><td>That ilka melder wi' the miller,</td></tr>
<tr><td>money</td><td>Thou sat as lang as thou had siller;</td></tr>
<tr><td>shod</td><td>That ev'ry naig was ca'd a shoe on,</td></tr>
<tr><td></td><td>The smith and thee gat roaring fou on;</td></tr>
<tr><td></td><td>That at the Lord's house, even on Sunday,</td></tr>
<tr><td></td><td>Thou drank wi' Kirkton Jean till Monday.</td></tr>
<tr><td></td><td>She prophesied, that, late or soon,</td></tr>
<tr><td></td><td>Thou would be found deep drown'd in Doon,</td></tr>
<tr><td>wizards; dark</td><td>Or catch'd wi' warlocks in the mirk</td></tr>
<tr><td></td><td>By Alloway's auld, haunted kirk.</td></tr>
</table>

<table>
<tr><td>makes; weep</td><td>Ah! gentle dames, it gars me greet,</td></tr>
<tr><td></td><td>To think how monie counsels sweet,</td></tr>
</table>

How monie lengthen'd, sage advices
The husband frae the wife despises!

But to our tale:—Ae market-night,
Tam had got planted unco right,   uncommonly
Fast by an ingle, bleezing finely,
Wi' reaming swats, that drank divinely;   foaming new ale
And at his elbow, Souter Johnie,   Cobbler
His ancient, trusty, drouthy cronie:
Tam lo'ed him like a very brither;
They had been fou for weeks thegither.
The night drave on wi' sangs and clatter;
And ay the ale was growing better:
The landlady and Tam grew gracious
Wi' secret favours, sweet and precious:
The Souter tauld his queerest stories;
The landlord's laugh was ready chorus:
The storm without might rair and rustle,   roar
Tam did na mind the storm a whistle.

Care, mad to see a man sae happy,
E'en drown'd himsel amang the nappy.
As bees flee hame wi' lades o' treasure,
The minutes wing'd their way wi' pleasure:
Kings may be blest but Tam was glorious,
O'er a' the ills o' life victorious!

But pleasures are like poppies spread:
You seize the flow'r, its bloom is shed;
Or like the snow falls in the river,
A moment white—then melts for ever;
Or like the Borealis, race,
That flit ere you can point their place;
Or like the rainbow's lovely form
Evanishing amid the storm.
Nae man can tether time or tide;
The hour approaches Tam maun ride: must
That hour, o' night's black arch the key-stane,
That dreary hour Tam mounts his beast in;
And sic a night he taks the road in,
As ne'er poor sinner was abroad in.

The wind blew as 'twad blawn its last;   would have
The rattling showers rose on the blast;

The speedy gleams the darkness swallow'd;
Loud, deep, and lang the thunder bellow'd:
That night, a child might understand,
The Deil had business on his hand.

Weel mounted on his grey meare Meg,
A better never lifted leg,
_{spanked; puddle} Tam skelpit on thro' dub and mire,
Despising wind, and rain, and fire;
_{Now} Whiles holding fast his guid blue bonnet,
_{song} Whiles crooning o'er some auld Scots sonnet,
_{staring} Whiles glow'ring round wi' prudent cares,
_{hobgoblins} Lest bogles catch him unawares:
Kirk-Alloway was drawing nigh,
Whares ghaists and houlets nightly cry.

_{across} By this time he was cross the ford,
_{smothered} Whare in the snaw the chapman smoor'd;
_{birches; big} And past the birks and meikle stane,
Whare drunken Charlie brak's neck-bane;
_{furze; pile of stones} And thro' the whins, and by the cairn,
Whare hunters fand the murder'd bairn;
_{above} And near the thorn, aboon the well,
Whare Mungo's mither hang'd hersel.
Before him Doon pours all his floods;
The doubling storm roars thro' the woods;
The lightnings flash from pole to pole;
Near and more near the thunders roll:
When, glimmering thro' the groaning trees,
Kirk-Alloway seem'd in a bleeze,
_{every chink} Thro' ilka bore the beams were glancing,
And loud resounding mirth and dancing.

Inspiring, bold John Barleycorn!
What dangers thou canst make us scorn!
_{ale} Wi' tippenny, we fear nae evil;
_{whisky} Wi' usquabae, we'll face the Devil!
The swats sae ream'd in Tammie's noddle,
_{not; farthing} Fair play, he car'd na deils a boddle.
But Maggie stood, right sair astonish'd,
Till, by the heel and hand admonish'd,
She ventur'd forward on the light;
_{wondrous} And, wow! Tam saw an unco sight!

Warlocks and witches in a dance;
Nae cotillion, brent new frae France,   brand
But hornpipes, jigs, strathspeys, and reels,
Put life and mettle in their heels.
A winnock-buncker in the east,   window-seat
There sat Auld Nick, in shape o'beast;
A tousie tyke, black, grim, and large,   shaggy dog
To gie them music was his charge;
He screw'd the pipes and gart them skirl,   squeal
Till roof and rafters a' did dirl.   ring
Coffins stood round, like open presses,   cupboards
That shaw'd the dead in their last dresses;
And, by some devilish cantraip sleight,   magic device
Each in its cauld hand held a light;
By which heroic Tam was able
To note upon the haly table,
A murderer's banes, in gibbet-airns;   -irons
Twa span-lang, wee, unchristen'd bairns;
A theif new-cutted frae a rape—
Wi' his last gasp his gab did gape;   mouth
Five tomahawks wi' bluid red-rusted;
Five scymitars wi' murder crusted;
A garter which a babe had strangled;
A knife a father's throat had mangled—
Whom his ain son o' life bereft—
The grey-hairs yet stack to the heft;
Wi' mair of horrible and awefu',
Which even to name wad be unlawfu'.
Three Lawyers' tongues, turned inside out,
Wi' lies seamed like a beggar's clout;
Three Priests' hearts, rotten, black as muck,
Lay stinking, vile, in every neuk.

As Tammie glowr'd, amaz'd, and curious,   stared
The mirth and fun grew fast and furious;
The pipe loud and louder blew,
The dancers quick and quicker flew,
They reel'd, they set, they cross'd, they cleekit,   took hold
Till ilka carlin swat and reekit,   beldam
                                                               sweated and
And coost her duddies to the wark,   steamed
                                                               rags
And linket at it in her sark!   tripped

Now Tam, O Tam! had thae been queans,   these
A' plump and strapping in their teens!

greasy

Their sarks, instead o' creeshie flannen,
Been snaw-white seventeen hunder linen!—

These

Thir breeks o'mine, my only pair,
That ance were plush, o' guid blue hair,

buttocks

I wad hae gi'en them off my hurdies

maidens

For ae blink o' the bonie burdies!

wizened

But wither'd beldams, auld and droll,

wean

Rigwoodie hags wad spean a foal,

leaping; kicking;
cudgel

Louping and flinging on a crummock,
I wonder did na turn thy stomach!

well

But Tam kend what was what fu' brawlie:

comely; choice

There was ae winsome wench and wawlie,

company

That night enlisted in the core,
Lang after kend on Carrick shore
(For monie a beast to dead she shot,
An' perish'd monie a bonie boat,

much; barley

And shook baith meikle corn and bear,
And kept the country-side in fear.)

short shift;
coarse cloth

Her cutty sark, o' Paisley harn,
That while a lassie she had worn,
In longitude tho' sorely scanty,

proud

It was her best, and she was vauntie....
Ah! little kend they reverend grannie,

bought

That sark she coft for her wee Nannie,
Wi' twa pund Scots ('twas a' her riches),

Would have

Wad ever grac'd a dance of witches!

stoop

But here my Muse her wing maun cour,
Sic flights as far beyond her power:

leaped and
kicked

To sing how Nannie lap and flang
(A souple jad she was and strang);
And how Tam stood like ane bewitch'd,
And though his very een enrich'd;

fidgeted; fond

Even Satan glowr'd, and fidg'd fu' fain,

jerked

And hotch'd and blew wi' might and main;

then

Till first ae caper, syne anither,

lost

Tam tint his reason a' thegither,
And roars out: 'Weel done, Cutty-sark!'
And in an instant all was dark;
And scarcely had he Maggie rallied,
When out the hellish legion sallied.

As bees bizz out wi' angry fyke,   fret
When plundering herds assail their byke;   hive
As open pussie's mortal foes,   the hare's
When, pop! she starts before their nose;
As eager runs the market-crowd,
When 'Catch the thief!' resounds aloud:
So Maggie runs, the witches follow,
Wi' monie an eldritch skriech and hollo.   unearthly

Ah, Tam! Ah, Tam! thou'll get thy fairin!
In hell they'll roast thee like a herrin!
In vain thy Kate awaits thy comin!
Kate soon will be a woefu' woman!
Now, do thy speedy utmost, Meg,
And win the key-stane of the brig;
There, at them thou thy tail may toss,
A running stream they dare na cross!
But ere the key-stane she could make,
The fient a tail she had to shake;   devil
For Nannie, far before the rest,
Hard upon noble Maggie prest,
And flew at Tam wi' furious ettle;   aim
But little wist she Maggie's mettle!
Ae spring brought off her master hale,   whole
But left behind her ain grey tail:
The carlin claught her by the rump,   seized
And left poor Maggie scarce a stump.

Now, wha this tale o' truth shall read,
Ilk man, and mother's son, take heed:
Whene'er to drink you are inclin'd,
Or cutty sarks run in your mind,
Think! ye may buy the joys o'er dear:
Remember Tam o' Shanter's meare.

ON SEEING A WOUNDED HARE LIMP
BY ME WHICH A FELLOW HAD JUST
SHOT AT

I

Inhuman man! curse on thy barb'rous art,
  And blasted be thy murder-aiming eye;
  May never pity soothe thee with a sigh,
Nor never pleasure glad thy cruel heart!

2

Go live, poor wanderer of the wood and field,
     The bitter little that of life remains!
     No more the thickening brakes and verdant plains
To thee shall home, or food, or pastime yield.

3

Seek, manglèd wretch, some place of wonted rest,
     No more of rest, but now thy dying bed!
     The sheltering rushes whistling o'er thy head,
The cold earth with thy bloody bosom prest.

4

Oft as by wnding Nith I musing, wait
     The sober eve, or hail the cheerful dawn,
     I'll miss thee sporting o'er the dewy lawn,
And curse the ruffian's aim, and mourn thy hapless fate.

ADDRESS TO THE SHADE OF THOMSON

ON CROWNING HIS BUST AT EDNAM, ROXBURGHSHIRE,
WITH A WREATH OF BAYS

I

While virgin Spring by Eden's flood
     Unfolds her tender mantle green,
Or pranks the sod in frolic mood,
     Or tunes Eolian strains between:

2

While Summer, with a matron grace,
     Retreats to Dryburgh's cooling shade,
Yet oft, delighted, stops to trace
     The progress of the spikey blade:

3

While Autumn, benefactor kind,
     By Tweed erects his aged head,
And sees, with self-approving mind,
     Each creature on his bounty fed:

4

While maniac Winter rages o'er
   The hills whence classic Yarrow flows,
Rousing the turbid torrent's roar,
   Or sweeping, wild, a waste of snows:

5

So long, sweet Poet of the year!
   Shall bloom that wreath thou well has won;
While Scotia, with exulting tear,
   Proclaims that Thomson was her son.

ON THE LATE CAPTAIN GROSE'S PEREGRINATIONS THRO' SCOTLAND

COLLECTING THE ANTIQUITIES OF THAT KINGDOM

1

Hear, Land o' Cakes, and brither Scots
Frae Maidenkirk to Johnie Groat's,
If there's a hole in a' your coats,
         I rede you tent it: *look to*
A chield's amang you takin notes,   *fellow*
         And faith he'll prent it:

2

If in your bounds ye chance to light
Upon a fine, fat, fodgel wight,   *dumpy*
O' stature short but genius bright,
         That's he, mark weel:
And wow! he has an unco sleight   *skill*
         O' cauk and keel.   *In chalk and ruddle*

3

By some auld, houlet-haunted biggin,   *owl-dwelling*
Or kirk deserted by its riggin,   *roof*
It's ten to ane ye'll find him snug in
         Some eldritch part,   *fearsome*
Wi' deils, they say, Lord safe's! colleaguin   *save us*
         At some black art.

4

Each; chamber

Ilk ghaist that haunts auld ha' or chamer,
Ye gipsy-gang that deal in glamour,
And you, deep-read in hell's black grammar,
                    Warlocks and witches:
Ye'll quake at his conjúring hammer,
                    Ye midnight bitches!

5

It's tauld he was a sodger bred,

would have
quitted; pot-
stick
(=sword)

And ane wad rather fa'n than fled;
But now he's quat the spurtle-blade
                    And dog-skin wallet,
And taen the—Antiquarian trade,
                    I think they call it.

6

abundance   He has a fourth o' auld nick-nackets:
iron   Rusty airn caps and jinglin jackets
shoenails   Wad haud the Lothians three in tackets
twelvemonth   A towmont guid;
porridge-pots; And parritch-pats and auld saut-backets
sallt-boxes   Before the Flood.

7

Of Eve's first fire he has a cinder;
Auld Tubalcain's fire-shool and fender;
That which distinguishèd the gender
                    O' Balaam's ass;
A broomstick o' the witch of Endor,
                    Weel shod wi' brass.

8

Besides; smartly   Forbye, he'll shape you aff fu' gleg
kilt   The cut of Adam's philibeg;
slit; throat   The knife that nicket Abel's craig
                                   He'll prove you fully,
Jacques de Liège   It was a faulding jocteleg,
(= a clasp knife)   Or lang-kail gullie.

9

But wad ye see him in his glee—
For meikle glee and fun has he—   much
Then set him down, and twa or three
                Guid fellows wi' him;
And port, O port! shine thou a wee,
                And then ye'll see him!

10

Now, by the Pow'rs o' verse and prose!
Thou art a dainty chield, O Grose!—
Whae'er o' thee shall ill suppose,
                They sair misca' thee;
I'd take the rascal by the nose,
                Wad say, 'Shame fa' thee.'   befall

ON READING IN A NEWSPAPER THE DEATH OF JOHN M'LEOD, ESQ.

BROTHER TO A YOUNG LADY, A PARTICULAR FRIEND OF THE AUTHOR'S

1

Sad thy tale, thou idle page,
   And rueful thy alarms:
Death tears the brother of her love
   From Isabella's arms.

2

Sweetly deckt with pearly dew
   The morning rose may blow;
But cold successive noontide blasts
   May lay its beauties low.

3

Fair on Isabella's morn
   The sun propitious smil'd;
But, long ere noon, succeeding clouds
   Succeeding hopes beguil'd.

4

Fate oft tears the bosom-chords
  That Nature finest strung;
So Isabella's heart was form'd,
  And so that heart was wrung.

5

Dread Omnipotence alone
  Can heal the wound he gave—
Can point the brimful, grief-worn eyes
  To scenes beyond the grave.

6

Virtue's blossoms there shall blow,
  And fear no withering blast;
There Isabella's spotless worth
  Shall happy be at last.

THE HUMBLE PETITION OF BRUAR WATER

TO THE NOBLE DUKE OF ATHOLE

I

My lord, I know, your noble ear
  Woe ne'er assails in vain;
Embolden'd thus, I beg you'll hear
  Your humble slave complain,
How saucy Phœbus' scorching beams,
  In flaming summer-pride,
Dry-withering, waste my foamy streams,
  And drink my crystal tide.

2

The lightly-jumping, glowrin trouts,   staring
    That thro' my waters play,
If, in their random, wanton spouts,
    They near the margin stray;
If, hapless chance! they linger lang,
    I'm scorching up so shallow,
They're left the whitening stanes amang
    In gasping death to wallow.

3

Last day I grat wi' spite and teen,   wept; vexation
    As Poet Burns came by,
That, to a Bard, I should be seen
    Wi' half my channel dry;
A panegyric rhyme, I ween,
    Ev'n as I was, he shor'd me;   offer'd
But had I in my glory been,
    He, kneeling, wad ador'd me.   would have

4

Here, foaming down the skelvy rocks,   shelvy
    In twisting strength I rin;
There high my boiling torrent smokes,
    Wild-roaring o'er a linn: fall
Enjoying large each spring and well,
    As Nature gave them me,
I am, altho' I say't mysel,
    Worth gaun a mile to see.   going

5

Would, then, my noble master please
    To grant my highest wishes,
He'll shade my banks wi' tow'ring trees
    And bonie spreading bushes.
Delighted doubly then, my lord,
    You'll wander on my banks,
And listen monie a grateful bird
    Return you tuneful thanks.

6

lark

The sober laverock, warbling wild,
   Shall to the skies aspire;

goldfinch

The gowdspink, Music's gayest child,
   Shall sweetly join the choir;

linnet

The blackbird strong, the lintwhite clear,
   The mavis mild and mellow,
The robin, pensive Autumn cheer
   In all her locks of yellow.

7

This, too, a covert shall ensure
   To shield them from the storm;

hare

And coward maukin sleep secure,
   Low in her grassy form:
Here shall the shepherd make his seat
   To weave his crown of flow'rs;
Or find a shelt'ring, safe retreat
   From prone-descending show'rs.

8

And here, by sweet, endearing stealth,
   Shall meet the loving pair,
Despising worlds with all their wealth,
   As empty idle care:
The flow'rs shal vie, in all their charms,
   The hour of heav'n to grace;

birches

And birks extend their fragrant arms
   To screen the dear embrace.

9

Here haply too, at vernal dawn,
   Some musing Bard may stray,
And eye the smoking, dewy lawn
   And misty mountain grey;
Or, by the reaper's nightly beam,
   Mild-chequering thro' the trees,
Rave to my darkly dashing stream,
   Hoarse-swelling on the breeze.

10

Let lofty firs and ashes cool
   My lowly banks o'erspread,
And view, deep-bending in the pool,
   Their shadows' wat'ry bed:
Let fragrant birks, in woodbines drest,
   My craggy cliffs adorn,
And, for the little songster's nest,
   The close embow'ring thorn!

11

So may, old Scotia's darling hope,
   Your little angle band
Spring, like their fathers, up to prop
   Their honour'd native land!
So may, thro' Albion's farthest ken,
   To social-flowing glasses,
The grace be: 'Athole's honest men
   And Athole's bonie lasses!'

ON SCARING SOME WATER-FOWL IN LOCH TURIT

A WILD SCENE AMONG THE HILLS OF OUGHTERTYRE

Why, ye tenants of the lake,
For me your wat'ry haunt forsake?
Tell me, fellow creatures, why
At my presence thus you fly?
Why disturb your social joys,
Parent, filial, kindred ties?—

Common friend to you and me,
Nature's gifts to all are free:
Peaceful keep your dimpling wave,
Busy feed, or wanton lave;
Or, beneath the sheltering rock,
Bide the surging billow's shock.

Conscious, blushing for our race,
Soon, too soon, your fears I trace.
Man, your proud, usurping foe,
Would be lord of all below:

Plumes himself in freedom's pride,
Tyrant stern to all beside.

   The eagle, from the cliffy brow
Marking you his prey below,
In his breast no pity dwells,
Strong necessity compels:
But Man, to whom alone is giv'n
A ray direct from pitying Heav'n,
Glories in his heart humane—
And creatures for his pleasure slain!

   In these savage, liquid plains,
Only known to wand'ring swains,
Where the mossy riv'let strays
Far from human haunts and ways,
All on Nature you depend,
And life's poor season peaceful spend.

   Or, if Man's superior might
Dare invade your native right,
On the lofty ether borne,
Man with all his powers you scorn;
Swiftly seek, on clanging wings,
Other lakes, and other springs;
And the foe you cannot brave,
Scorn at least to be his slave.

VERSES WRITTEN WITH A PENCIL

OVER THE CHIMNEY-PIECE, IN THE PARLOUR OF THE INN AT
KENMORE, TAYMOUTH

Admiring Nature in her wildest grace,
These northern scenes with weary feet I trace;
O'er many a winding dale and painful steep,
Th' abodes of covey'd grouse and timid sheep,
My savage journey, curious, I pursue,
Till fam'd Breadalbane opens to my view.
The meeting cliffs each deep-sunk glen divides:
The woods, wild-scatter'd, clothe their ample sides;
Th' outstretching lake, imbosomed 'mong the hills,
The eye with wonder and amazement fills:
The Tay meand'ring sweet in infant pride,
The palace rising on his verdant side,
The lawns wood-fring'd in Nature's native taste,
The hillocks dropt in Nature's careless haste,
The arches striding o'er the new-born stream,
The village glittering in the noontide beam—

*   *   *   *   *

Poetic ardors in my bosom swell,
Lone wand'ring by the hermit's mossy cell;
The sweeping theatre of hanging woods,
Th' incessant roar of headlong tumbling floods—

*   *   *   *   *

Here Poesy might wake her heav'n-taught lyre,
And look through Nature with creative fire;
Here, to the wrongs of Fate half reconcil'd,
Misfortune's lighten'd steps might wander wild;
And Disappointment, in these lonely bounds,
Find balm to soothe her bitter rankling wounds;
Here heart-struck Grief might heav'nward stretch her
scan,
And injur'd Worth forget and pardon man.

*   *   *   *   *

LINES ON THE FALL OF FYERS NEAR LOCH NESS

WRITTEN WITH A PENCIL ON THE SPOT

Among the heathy hills and ragged woods
The roaring Fyers pours his mossy floods;
Till full he dashes on the rocky mounds,
Where, thro' a shapeless breach, his stream resounds.
As high in air the bursting torrents flow,
As deep recoiling surges foam below,
Prone down the rock the whitening sheet descends,
And viewless Echo's ear, astonish'd, rends.
Dim-seen through rising mists and ceaseless show'rs,
The hoary cavern, wide-surrounding, lours:
Still thro' the gap the struggling river toils,
And still, below, the horrid caldron boils—

* * * * *

ON THE BIRTH OF A POSTHUMOUS CHILD

BORN IN PECULIAR CIRCUMSTANCES OF FAMILY DISTRESS

I

much

Sweet flow'ret, pledge o' meikle love,
　And ward o' monie a prayer,
What heart o' stane wad thou na move,
　Sae helpless, sweet, and fair!

2

hobbles

November hirples o'er the lea,
　Chill, on thy lovely form;
And gane, alas! the shelt'ring tree,
　Should shield three frae the storm.

3

May He who gives the rain to pour,
　And wings the blast to blaw,
Protect thee frae the driving show'r,
　The bitter frost and snaw!

4

May He, the friend of Woe and Want,
　Who heals life's various stounds,   shocks
Protect and guard the mother plant,
　And heal her cruel wounds!

5

But late she flourish'd, rooted fast,
　Fair on the summer morn,
Now feebly bends she in the blast,
　Unshelter'd and forlorn.

6

Blest be thy bloom, thou lovely gem,
　Unscath'd by ruffian hand!
And from thee many a parent stem
　Arise to deck our land!

THE TWA HERDS: OR, THE HOLY
TULYIE   squabble

AN UNCO MOURNFU' TALE   mighty

Blockheads with reason wicked wits abhor,
But fool with fool is barbarous civil war.
　　　　　　　　　　　　　　　POPE

I

O a' ye pious godly flocks,
Weel fed on pastures orthodox,
Wha now will keep you frae the fox
　　　　　Or worrying tykes?   dogs
Or wha will tent the waifs an' crocks   tend;
　　　　　About the dykes?   stragglers
                                                    and old ewes
                                                    stone fences

2

west	The twa best herds in a' the wast,
gave	That e'er gae gospel horn a blast
	These five an' twenty simmers past—
sad	O, dool to tell!—
quarrel	Hae had a bitter, black out-cast
Between	Atween themsel.

3

O Moodie, man, an' wordy Russell,
How could you raise so vile a bustle?
Ye'll see how New-Light herds will whistle,
An' think it fine!

such a sprain	The Lord's cause gat na sic a twistle
can remember	Sin' I hae min'.

4

O Sirs! whae'er wad hae expeckit

would have so　　Your duty ye wad sae negleckit?

Ye wha were no by lairds respeckit
To wear the plaid,
But by the brutes themselves eleckit
To be their guide!

5

What flock wi' Moodie's flock could rank,

sound; leg	Sae hale an' hearty every shank?
pond	Nae poison'd, soor Arminian stank
	He let them taste;

But Calvin's fountainhead they drank—
O, sic a feast!

6

polecat, wildcat, badger and fox	The thummart, wilcat, brock, an' tod

Weel kend his voice thro' a' the wood;
He smell'd their ilka hole an' road,
Baith out and in;
An' weel he lik'd to shed their bluid
An' sell their skin.

7

What herd like Russell tell'd his tale?
His voice was heard thro' muir and dale;
He kend the Lord's sheep, ilka tail,   *every*
      O'er a' the height;
An' tell'd gin they were sick or hale   *if*
      At the first sight.

8

He fine a mangy sheep could scrub;   *scabbed*
Or nobly swing the gospel club;
Or New-Light herds could nicely drub
      And pay their skin;
Or hing them o'er the burning dub   *puddle*
      Or heave them in.

9

Sic twa—O, do I live to see't?—
Sic famous twa sud disagree't,   *should have*
An' names like villian, hypocrite,
      Ilk ither gi'en,   *Each other*
While New-Light herds wi' laughin spite
      Say neither's liein!   *lying*

10

A' ye wha tent the gospel fauld,
Thee Duncan deep, an' Peebles shaul',   *shallow*
But chiefly great apostle Auld,
      We trust in thee,
That thou wilt work them hot an' cauld
      Till they agree!

11

Consider, sirs, how we're beset:
There's scarce a new herd that we get
But comes frae 'mang that cursed set
      I winna name: *will not*
I hope frae heav'n to see them yet
      In fiery flame!

12

Dalrymple has been lang our fae,
muchM'Gill has wrought us meikle wae,
An' that curs'd rascal ca'd M'Quhae,
    An' baith the Shaws,
blueThat aft hae made us black an' blae
     Wi' vengefu' paws.

13

Auld Wodrow lang has hatch'd mischíef:
We thought ay death wad bring relief,
But he was gotten to our grief
    Ane to succeed him,
fellow; bangA chield wha'll soundly buff our beef—
     I meikle dread him.

14

moreAn' monie mae that I could tell,
Wha fain would openly rebel,
BesidesForby turn-coats amang oursel:
     There's Smith for ane—
I doubt he's but a greyneck still,
     An' that ye'll fin'!

15

O a' ye flocks o'er a' the hills,
bogs; hill-sidesBy mosses, meadows, moors, an' fells,
Come, join your counsel and your skills
daunt   To cowe the lairds,
An' get the brutes the power themsels
     To chuse their herds!

16

The Orthodoxy yet may prance,
halterAn' Learning in a woody dance,
formidableAn' that fell cur ca'd Common-sense,
     That bites sae sair,
Be banish'd o'er the sea to France—
     Let him bark there!

17

Then Shaw's an' D'rymple's eloquence,
M'Gills close, nervous excellence,
M'Quhae's pathetic, manly sense,
      An' guid M'Math
Wha thro' the heart can brawly glance,
      May a' pack aff!

HOLY WILLIE'S PRAYER

And send the godly in a pet to pray.
        POPE

1

O Thou that in the Heaven does dwell,
Wha, as it pleases best Thysel,
Sends ane to Heaven an' ten to Hell
      A' for Thy glory,
And no for onie guid or ill
      They've done before Thee!

2

I bless and praise Thy matchless might,
When thousands Thou hast left in night,
That I am here before Thy sight,
      For gifts an' grace
A burning and a shining light
      To a' this place.

3

What was I, or my generation,
That I should get sic exaltation?   such
I, wha deserv'd most just damnation
      For broken laws
Sax thousand years ere my creation,   Six
      Thro' Adam's cause!

4

When from my mither's womb I fell,
Thou might hae plung'd me deep in hell
gums   To gnash my gooms, and weep, and wail
       In burning lakes,
Whare damnèd devils roar and yell,
       Chain'd to their stakes.

5

Yet I am here, a chosen sample,
To show Thy grace is great and ample:
I'm here a pillar o' Thy temple,
       Strong as a rock
A guide, a buckler, and example
       To a' Thy flock!

6

But yet, O Lord! confess I must:
irked   At times I'm fash'd wi' fleshly lust;
An' sometimes, too, in warldly trust,
       Vile self gets in;
But Thou remembers we are dust,
       Defiled wi' sin.

7

last night;   O Lord! yestreen, Thou kens, wi' Meg—
knowest   Thy pardon I sincerely beg—
O, may't ne'er be a living plague
       To my dishonour!
An' I'll ne'er lift a lawless leg
       Again upon her.

8

must   Besides, I farther maun avow—
Wi' Leezie's lass, three times, I trow—
drunk   But, Lord, that Friday I was fou,
       When I cam near her,
would; meddle   Or else, Thou kens, Thy servant true
with   Wad never steer her.

9

Maybe Thou lets this fleshly thorn
Buffet Thy servant e'en and morn,
Lest he owre proud and high should turn   *too*
        That he's sae gifted:
If sae, Thy han' maun e'en be borne
        Until Thou lift it.

10

Lord, bless Thy chosen in this place,
For here Thou has a chosen race!
But God confound their stubborn face
        An' blast their name,
Wha bring Thy elders to disgrace
        An' open shame!

11

Lord, mind Gau'n Hamilton's deserts:
He drinks, an' swears, an' plays at cartes,   *cards*
Yet has sae monie takin arts
        Wi' great and sma',
Frae God's ain Priest the people's hearts
        He steals awa.

12

And when we chasten'd him therefore,
Thou kens how he bred sic a splore,   *row*
And set the warld in a roar
        O' laughin at us:
Curse Thou his basket and his store,
        Kail an' potatoes!

13

Lord, hear my earnest cry and pray'r
Against that Presbyt'ry of Ayr!
Thy strong right hand, Lord, mak it bare
        Upo' their heads!
Lord, visit them, an' dinna spare,   *do not*
        For their misdeeds!

14

O Lord, my God! that glib-tongu'd Aiken,
My vera heart and flesh are quakin
To think how we stood sweatin, shakin,
          An' pish'd wi' dread,

sneering

While he, wi' hingin lip an' snakin,
          Held up his head.

15

Lord, in Thy day o' vengeance try him!
Lord, visit him wha did employ him!
And pass not in Thy mercy by them,
          Nor hear their pray'r,
Bur for Thy people's sake destroy them,
          An' dinna spare!

16

But, Lord, remember me and mine
Wi' mercies tempral and divine,

wealth

That I for grace an' gear may shine
          Excell'd by nane;
And a' the glory shall be Thine—
          Amen, Amen!

WELCOME TO A BASTART WEAN

1

little one;
Mishap befall

Thou's welcome, wean! Mishanter fa' me,
If thoughts o' thee or yet thy mammie
Shall ever daunton me or awe me,
          My sweet, wee lady,
Or if I blush when thou shalt ca' me
          Tyta or daddie!

2

What tho' they ca' me fornicator,

country gossip

An' tease my name in kintra clatter?
The mair they talk, I'm kend the better;

tattle

          E'en let them clash!

feeble

An auld wife's tongue's a feckless matter

give one
annoyance

          To gie ane fash.

3

Welcome, my bonie, sweet, wee dochter!
Tho' ye come here a wee unsought for,
And tho' your comin I hae fought for
                    Baith kirk and queir;
Yet, by my faith, ye're no unwrought for—
                    That I shall swear!

4

Sweet fruit o' monie a merry dint,
My funny toil is no a' tint: not all lost
Tho' thou cam to the warl' asklent,   askew
                    Which fools may scoff at,
In my last plack they part's be in't   coin
                    The better half o't.

5

Tho' I should be the waur bestead,   worse provided
Thou's be as braw and bienly clad,   finely;
And thy young years as nicely bred   comfortably
                    Wi' education,
As onie brat o' wedlock's bed
                    In a' thy station.

6

Wee image o' my bonie Betty,
As fatherly I kiss and daut thee,   pet
As dear and near my heart I set thee,
                    Wi' as guid will,
As a' the priests had seen me get thee
                    That's out o' Hell.

7

Gude grant that thou may ay inherit   God
Thy mither's looks an' gracefu' merit,
An' thy poor, worthless daddie's spirit
                    Without his failins!
'Twill please me mair to see thee heir it
                    Than stocket mailins.   farms

8

And if thou be what I wad hae thee,
An' tak the counsel I shall gie thee,
I'll never rue my trouble wi' thee—
                    The cost nor shame o't—
But be a loving father to thee,
                    And brag the name o't.

THE INVENTORY

IN ANSWER TO A MANDATE BY THE SURVEYOR OF TAXES

Sir, as your mandate did request,
I send you here a faithfu' list

chattles   O' guids an' gear an' a' my graith,
To which I'm clear to gie my aith.

Imprimis, then, for carriage cattle:—
I hae four brutes o' gallant mettle

plough-staff   As ever drew before a pettle:
My lan'-afore's a guid auld 'has been',

strong   An' wight an' wilfu' a' his days been.

well-going   My lan'-ahin's a weel-gaun fillie,

Kilmarnock   That aft has borne me hame frae Killie,

Ayr   An' your auld borough monie a time
In days when riding was nae crime.
(But ance, when in my wooing pride

must needs   I, like a blockhead, boost to ride,

distress'd   The wilfu' creature sae I pat to—
Lord, pardon a' my sins, an' that too!—

ill turn   I play'd my fillie sic a shavie,

spavin   She's a' bedevil'd wi' the spavie.)

worthy   My fur-ahin's a wordy beast
As e'er in tug or tow was traced.
The fourth's a Highland Donald hastie,

stark-mad;   A damn'd red-wud Kilburnie blastie!
Kilbirnie
Besides; colt;   Foreby, a cowte, o' cowtes the wale,
pick   As ever ran afore a tail:
If he be spar'd to be a beast,

fetch; £ stg.   He'll draw me fifteen pund at least.

Wheel-carriages I hae but few:
Three carts, an' twa are feckly new;   partly
An auld wheelbarrow—mair for token,
Ae leg an' baith the trams are broken: One; shafts
I made a poker o' the spin'le,   axle
An' my auld mither brunt the trin'le.   wheel

For men, I've three mischievous boys,
Run-deils for fechtin an' for noise: Stark-devils;
                                                       fighting
A gaudsman ane, a thrasher t' other,
Wee Davoc hauds the nowte in fother.   David; cattle;
                                                       fodder
I rule them, as I ought, discreetly,
An' aften labour them completely;   make them work
                                                       their hardest
An' ay on Sundays duly, nightly,
I on the *Questions* tairge them tightly:
Till, faith! wee Davoc's grown sae gleg,   sharp
Tho' scarcely langer than your leg,
He'll screed you aff 'Effectual Calling'   rattle;
As fast as onie in the dwalling.

I've nane in female servan' station
(Lord keep me ay frae a' temptation!):
I hae nae wife—and that my bliss is—
An' ye hae laid nae tax on misses;   mistresses
An' then, if kirk folks dinna clutch me,
I ken the deevils darena touch me.

Wi' weans I'm mair than weel contented: brats
Heav'n sent me ane mair than I wanted!
My sonsie, smirking, dear-bought Bess,   good-natured
She stares the daddie in her face,
Enough of ought ye like but grace:
I've paid enough for her already;
An' gin ye tax her or her mither,   if
By the Lord, ye'se get them a' thegither!

But pray, remember, Mr. Aiken,   ye'll altogether
Nae kind of licence out I'm takin:
Frae this time forth, I do declare
I'se ne'er ride horse nor hizzie mair;   wench
Thro' dirt and dub for life I'll paidle,   mire and slush;
Ere I sae dear pay for a saddle;   wade
I've sturdy stumps, the Lord be thankit,   ways
And a' my gates on foot I'll shank it.

pot
do not

The Kirk and you may tak' you that,
It puts but little in your pat:
Sae dinna put me in your beuk,
Nor for my ten white shillings leuk.

This list, wi' my ain hand I've wrote it,
The day and date as under notit;
Then know all ye whom it concerns,
Subscripsi huic,   ROBERT BURNS.

A MAUCHLINE WEDDING

1

When Eighty-five was seven months auld
    And wearing thro' the aught,
When rolling rains and Boreas bauld
    Gied farmer-folks a faught;
Ae morning quondam Mason W...,
    Now Merchant Master Miller,
Gaed down to meet wi' Nansie B...,
    And her Jamaica siller
                    To wed, that day.

eight

Gave; fight

Went
money

2

The rising sun o'er Blacksideen
    Was just appearing fairly,
When Nell and Bess got up to dress
    Seven lang half-hours o'er early!
Now presses clink, and drawers jink,
    For linens and for laces:
But modest Muses only *think*
    What ladies' underdress is
                    On sic a day!

too

such

3

But we'll suppose the stays are lac'd,
  And bonie bosoms steekit,   *covered*
Tho' thro' the lawn—but guess the rest!
  An angel scarce durst keek it.   *spy*
Then stockins fine o' silken twine
  Wi' cannie care are drawn up;   *prudent*
An' garten'd tight whare mortal wight—   *gartered*

. . . . . .

. . . . . .

4

But now the gown wi' rustling sound
  Its silken pomp displays;
Sure there's nae sin in being vain
  O' siccan bonie claes!   *such very*
Sae jimp the waist, the tail sae vast—
  Trouth, they were bonie birdies!   *maidens*
O Mither Eve, ye wad been grieve
  To see their ample hurdies   *posteriors*
            Sae large that day!

5

The Sandy, wi's red jacket braw,   *with his;*
  Comes whip-jee-woa! about,
And in he gets the bonie twa—
  Lord, send them safely out!
And auld John Trot wi' sober phiz,
  As braid and braw's a Bailie,   *broad; fine as*
His shouthers and his Sunday's jiz   *wig*
  Wi' powther and wi' ulzie   *oil*
            Weel smear'd that day...

ADAM ARMOUR'S PRAYER

1

Gude pity me, because I'm little!   *God*
For though I am an elf o'mettle,   *weaver's*
And can like onie wabster's shuttle   *Dodge*
                                   cabbage-knife
            Jink there or here,
Yet, scarce as lang's a guid kail-whittle, *uncommon*
            I'm unco queer.   *funny*

2

knows | An' now Thou kens our woefu' case:
maid | For Geordie's jurr we're in disgrace,
Because we stang'd her through the place,
An' hurt her spleuchan;
dare not | For whilk we daurna show our face
hamlet | Within the clachan.

3

hid; glens | An' now we're dern'd in dens and hollows,
And hunted, as was William Wallace,
those | Wi' constables—thae blackguard fallows—
An' sodgers baith;
But Gude preserve us frae the gallows,
That shamefu' death!

4

Auld, grim, black-bearded Geordie's sel'—
O, shake him owre the mouth o'Hell!
There let him hing, an' roar, an' yell
Wi' hideous din,
And if he offers to rebel,
Then heave him in!

5

glance | When Death comes in wi' glimmerin blink,
An' tips auld drucken Nanse the wink,
backside | May Sautan gie her doup a clink
gate | Within his yett,
An' fill her up wi' brimstone drink
hot | Red-reekin het.

6

Though Jock an' hav'rel Jean are merry,
Some devil seize them in a hurry,
An' waft them in th' infernal wherry
Straught through the lake,
An' gie their hides a noble curry
oak | Wi' oil of aik!

7

As for the jurr—puir worthless body!—   creature
She's got mischief enough already;
Wi' stanget hips and buttocks bluidy
    She's suffer'd sair;   sorely
But may she wintle in a woody   wriggle in a
    If she whore mair!   rope

EPITHALAMIUM

1

O a' ye hymeneal powers
That rule the essence-mixing hours!
Whether in eastern monarch's bow'rs
    Or Greenland caves,
A nuptial scene in Machlin tow'rs
    Your presence craves.

2

Threescore-fyfteen, a blooming bride,
This night with seventy-four is ty'd;
O mak the bed baith saft an' wide
    Wi' canie toil,
An' lay them gently side by side,
    At least a while.

NATURE'S LAW

HUMBLY INSCRIBED TO GAVIN HAMILTON, ESQUIRE

Great Nature spoke, observant man obeyed.

POPE

I

Let other heroes boast their scars,
    The marks o' sturt and strife,
But other poets sing of wars,
    The plagues o' human life!
Shame fa' the fun: wi' sword and gun
    To slap mankind like lumber!
I sing his name and nobler fame
    Wha multiples our number.

struggle (gloss: The marks o' sturt)
befall (gloss: Shame fa')

2

Great Nature spoke, with air benign:—
    'Go on, ye human race;
This lower world I you resign;
    Be fruitful and increase.
The liquid fire of strong desire,
    I've poured it in each bosom;
Here on this hand does Mankind stand,
    And there, is Beauty's blossom!'

3

The Hero of these artless strains,
    A lowly Bard was he,
Who sung his rhymes in Coila's plains
    With meikle mirth and glee:
Kind Nature's care had given his share
    Large of the flaming current;
And, all devout, he never sought
    To stem the sacred torrent.

much (gloss: With meikle mirth)

4

He felt the powerful, high behest
  Thrill vital thro' and thro;
And sought a correspondent breast
  To give obedience due.
Propitious Powers screen'd the young flow'rs
  From mildews of abortion;
And lo! the Bard—a great reward—
  Has got a double portion!

5

Auld cantie Coil may count the day,	jolly
As annual it returns,	
The third of Libra's equal sway,	September's
That gave another Burns,	

With future rhymes an' other times
  To emulate his sire,
To sing auld Coil in nobler style
  With more poetic fire!

6

Ye Powers of peace and peaceful song,
  Look down with gracious eyes,
And bless auld Coila large and long
  With multiplying joys!
Lang may she stand to prop the land,
  The flow'r of ancient nations,
And Burnses spring her fame to sing
  To endless generations!

LINES ON MEETING WITH LORD DAER

I

This wot ye all whom it concerns:	know
I, Rhymer Rab, *alîas* Burns,	
October twenty-third,	
A ne'er-to-be-forgotten day,	
Sae far I sprachl'd up the brae	clambered hill
I dinner'd wi' a Lord.	

2

Lawyers'
-drunk

I've been at drucken Writers' feasts,
Nay, been bitch-fou 'mang godly Priests—
        Wi' rev'rence be it spoken!—
I've even join'd the honor'd jorum,
When mighty Squireships o' the Quorum

slake

        Their hydra drouth did sloken.

3

But wi' a Lord!—stand out my shin!
A Lord, a Peer, an Earl's son!—
        Up higher yet, my bonnet!

such

An' sic a Lord!—lang Scotch ell twa
Our Peerage he looks o'er them a',
        As I look o'er my sonnet.

4

But O, for Hogarth's magic pow'r

disordered gaze

To show Sir Bardie's willyart glow'r,

looking dazedly
as; an ox's bridle

        An' how he star'd an' stammer'd,
When, goavin's he'd been led wi' branks,
An' stumpin on his ploughman shanks,
        He in the parlour hammer'd!

5

To meet good Stewart little pain is,
Or Scotia's sacred Demosthénes:
        Thinks I: 'They are but men'!

doddered
knocked
went to the
parlour

But 'Burns'!—'My Lord'!—Good God! I doited,
My knees on ane anither knoited
        As faultering I gaed ben.

6

corner
stole

I sidling shelter'd in a neuk,
An' at his Lordship staw a leuk,
        Like some portentous omen:
Except good sense and social glee
An' (what surpris'd me) modesty,
        I markèd nought uncommon.

7

I watch'd the symptoms o' the Great—
The gentle pride, the lordly state,
      The arrogant assuming:
The fient a pride, nae pride had he,   fiend
Nor sauce, nor state, that I could see,
      Mair than an honest ploughman!

8

Then from his Lordship I shall learn
Henceforth to meet with unconcern
      One rank as well's another;
Nae honest, worthy man need care   be perturbed
To meet with noble youthfu' Daer,
      For he but meets a brother.

ADDRESS TO THE TOOTHACHE

1

My curse upon your venom'd stang,   sting
That shoots my tortur'd gooms alang,   gums
An' thro' my lug gies monie a twang   ear
      Wi' gnawing vengeance,
Tearing my nerves wi' bitter pang,
      Like racking engines!

2

A' down my beard the slavers trickle,
I throw the wee stools o'er the mickle,
While round the fire the giglets keckle   cackle
      To see me loup,   jump
An', raving mad, I wish a heckle   heckling-comb
      Were i' their doup!   backside

3

When fevers burn, or ague freezes,
Rheumatics gnaw, or colic squeezes,
Our neebors sympathise to ease us
      Wi' pitying moan;
But thee!—thou hell o' a' diseases,
      They mock our groan!

4

woes
Bad harvests;
mad; crumbling
earth

annoyance
tak'st the prize

Of a' the num'rous human dools—
Ill-hairsts, daft bargains, cutty-stools,
Or worthy frien's laid i' the mools,
      Sad sight to see!
The tricks o' knaves, or fash o' fools—
      Thou bear'st the gree!

5

Whare'er that place be priests ca' Hell,
Whare a' the tones o' misery yell,
An' rankèd plagues their numbers tell
      In dreadfu' raw,
Thou, Toothache, surely bear'st the bell
      Amang them a'!

6

chap

makes

Give
twelve-month's

O thou grim, mischief-making chiel,
That gars the notes o' discord squeel,
Till humankind aft dance a reel
      In gore a shoe-thick,
Gie a' the faes o' Scotland's weal
      A towmond's toothache.

LAMENT FOR THE ABSENCE OF WILLIAM CREECH, PUBLISHER

I

mother-hen

trimmed
at all

Auld chuckie Reekie's sair distrest,
Down droops her ance weel burnish'd crest,
Nae joy her bonie buskit nest
      Can yield ava:
Her darling bird that she lo'es best,
      Willie's awa.

2

in; uncommon
skill
in order
trim; handsome

garb

O, Willie was a witty wight,
And had o' things an unco sleight!
Auld Reekie ay he keepit tight
      And trig an' braw;
But now they'll busk her like a fright—
      Willie's awa!

3

The stiffest o' them a' he bow'd;
The bauldest o' them a' he cow'd;   daunted
They durst nae mair than he allow'd—
      That was a law:
We've lost a birkie weel worth gowd—   blade; gold
      Willie's awa!

4

Now gawkies, tawpies, gowks, and fools
Frae colleges and boarding schools
May sprout like simmer puddock-stools   mushrooms
      In glen or shaw: wood
He wha could brush them down to mools,   dust
      Willie's awa!

5

The brethren o' the Commerce-Chaumer
May mourn their loss wi' doolfu' clamour: woeful
He was a dictionar and grammar
      Amang them a'.
I fear they'll now mak monie a stammer:
      Willie's awa!

6

Nae mair we see his levee door
Philosophers and Poets pour,
And toothy Critics by the score
      In bloody raw:
The adjutant of a' the core,
      Willie's awa!

7

Now worthy Greg'ry's Latin face,
Tytler's and Greenfield's modest grace,
M'Kenzie, Stewart, such a brace
      As Rome ne'er saw,
They a' maun meet some ither place—   must
      Willie's awa!

8

Poor Burns ev'n 'Scotch Drink' canna quicken:
cries He cheeps like some bewilder'd chicken
mother; brood Scar'd frae its minnie and the cleckin
carrion-crow   By hoodie-craw.
Grief's gien his heart an unco kickin—
               Willie's awa!

9

ill-tongued, Now ev'ry sour-mou'd, girnin blellum,
snarling railer And Calvin's folk, are fit to fell him;
kill
Each; scullion Ilk self-conceited critic-skellum
               His quill may draw:
finely repel He wha could brawlie ward their bellum,
assault   Willie's awa!

10

meandering Up wimpling, stately Tweed I've sped,
And Eden scenes on crystal Jed,
And Ettrick banks, now roaring red
               While tempests blaw;
But every joy and pleasure's fled:
               Willie's awa!

11

May I be Slander's common speech,
A text for Infamy to preach,
stretched And, lastly, streekit out to bleach
               In winter snaw,
When I forget thee, Willie Creech,
               Tho' far awa!

12

May never wicked Fortune touzle him,
May never wicked men bamboozle him,
poll; old as Until a pow as auld's Methusalem
cheerfully   He canty claw!
scratch Then to the blessed new Jerusalem
               Fleet-wing awa!

VERSES IN FRIARS CARSE HERMITAGE

Thou whom chance may hither lead,
Be thou clad in russet weed,
Be thou deckt in silken stole,
Grave these maxims on thy soul:—

Life is but a day at most,
Sprung from night in darkness lost;
Hope not sunshine every hour,
Fear not clouds will always lour.
Happiness is but a name,
Make content and ease thy aim.
Ambition is a meteor-gleam;
Fame a restless airy dream;
Pleasures, insects on the wing
Round Peace, th' tend'rest flow'r of spring;
Those that sip the dew alone—
Make the butterflies thy own;
Those that would the bloom devour—
Crush the locusts, save the flower.
For the future be prepar'd:
Guard wherever thou can'st guard;
But, thy utmost duly done,
Welcome what thou can'st not shun.
Follies past give thou to air—
Make their consequence thy care.
Keep the name of Man in mind,
And dishonour not thy kind.
Reverence with lowly heart
Him, whose wondrous work thou art;
Keep His Goodness still in view—
Thy trust, and thy example too.

Stranger, go! Heaven be thy guide!
Quod the Beadsman on Nidside.   Nithside

ELEGY ON THE DEPARTED YEAR 1788

do not   For lords or kings I dinna mourn;
E'en let them die—for that they're born;
But O, progidious to reflect,
Twelve-month   A Towmont, sirs, is gane to wreck!
O Eighty-Eight, in thy sma' space
What dire events hae taken place!
Of what enjoyments thou hast reft us!
In what a pickle thou hast left us!

lost   The Spanish empire's tint a head,
dog   An' my auld teethless Bawtie's dead;
conflict; tough   The tulyie's teugh 'tween Pitt and Fox,
An' our guidwife's wee birdie cocks:
one   The tane is game, a bluidie devil,
mighty   But to the hen-birds unco civil;
stubborn;   The tither's dour—has nae sic breedin,
manners   But better stuff ne'er claw'd a midden.
scratched;
dunghill

parsons; pulpit   Ye ministers, come mount the poupit,
hoarse   An' cry till ye be haerse an' roupet,
For Eighty-Eight, he wished you weel,
gave; money;   An' gied ye a' baith gear an' meal:
coin   E'en monie a plack and monie a peck,
return   Ye ken yoursels, for little feck!

wipe; eyes   Ye bonie lasses, dight your een,
For some o' you hae tint a frien':
In Eighty-Eight, ye ken, was taen
What ye'll ne'er hae to gie again.

cattle   Observe the vera nowte an' sheep,
dull;   How dowff an' dowilie they creep!
droopingly
ground   Nay, even the yirth itsel does cry,
wept   For Embro' wells are grutten dry!

child   O Eighty-Nine, thou's but a bairn,
too   An' no owre auld, I hope, to learn!
Thou beardless boy, I pray tak care,
Thou now has got thy Daddie's chair:

muzzled   Nae hand-cuff'd, mizzl'd, half-shackl'd Regent,
But, like himsel, a full free agent,

Be sure ye follow out the plan
Nae waur than he did, honest man!   worse
As muckle better as ye can.   much

January 1, 1789.

CASTLE GORDON

I

Streams that glide in Orient plains,
Never bound by Winter's chains;
   Glowing here on golden sands,
There immixed with foulest stains
   From tyranny's empurpled hands;
These, their richly gleaming waves,
I leave to tyrants and their slaves:
Give me the stream that sweetly laves
   The banks by Castle Gordon.

2

Spicy forests ever gay,
Shading from the burning ray
   Hapless wretches sold to toil;
Or, the ruthless native's way,
   Bent on slaughter, blood and spoil;
Woods that ever verdant wave,
I leave the tyrant and the slave:
Give me the groves that lofty brave
   The storms of Castle Gordon.

3

Wildly here without control
Nature reigns, and rules the whole;
   In that sober pensive mood,
Dearest to the feeling soul,
   She plants the forest, pours the flood.
Life's poor day I'll, musing, rave,
And find at night a sheltering cave,
Where waters flow and wild woods wave
   By bonie Castle Gordon.

NEW YEAR'S DAY
1791

TO MRS. DUNLOP

This day Time winds th' exhausted chain,
To run the twelvemonth's length again:
I see the old, bald-pated fellow,
With ardent eyes, complexion sallow,
Adjust the unimpair'd machine
To wheel the equal, dull routine.

The absent lover, minor heir,
In vain assail him with their prayer:
Deaf as my friend, he sees them press,
Nor makes the hour one moment less.
Will you (the Major's with the hounds;
The happy tenants share his rounds;
Coila's fair Rachel's care to-day,
And blooming Keith's engaged with Gray)
From housewife care a minute borrow
(That grandchild's cap will do to-morrow),
And join with me a-moralizing?
This day's propitious to be wise in!

First, what did yesternight deliver?
'Another year has gone for ever.'
And what is this day's strong suggestion?
'The passing moment's all we rest on!'
Rest on—for what? what do we here?
Or why regard the passing year?
Will Time, amus'd with proverb'd lore,
Add to our date one minute more?
A few days may—a few years must—
Repose us in the silent dust:
Then, is it wise to damp our bliss?
Yes: all such reasonings are amiss!
The voice of Nature loudly cries,
And many a message from the skies,
That something in us never dies;
That on this frail, uncertain state
Hang matters of eternal weight;

That future life in worlds unknown
Must take its hue from this alone,
Whether as heavenly glory bright
Or dark as Misery's woeful night.

Since, then, my honor'd first of friends,
On this poor being all depends,
Let us th' important Now employ,
And live as those who never die.
Tho' you, with days and honours crown'd,
Witness that filial circle round
(A sight life's sorrows to repulse,
A sight pale Envy to convulse),
Others now claim your chief regard:
Yourself, you wait your bright reward.

FROM ESOPUS TO MARIA

From those drear solitudes and frowsy cells,
Where Infamy with sad Repentance dwells;
Where turnkeys make the jealous portal fast,
And deal from iron hands the spare repast;
Where truant 'prentices, yet young in sin,
Blush at the curious stranger peeping in;
Where strumpets, relics of the drunken roar,
Resolve to drink, nay half—to whore—no more;
Where tiny thieves, not destin'd yet to swing,
Beat hemp for others riper for the string:
From these dire scenes my wretched lines I date,
To tell Maria her Esopus' fate.

'Alas! I feel I am no actor here!'
'Tis real hangmen real scourges bear!
Prepare, Maria, for a horrid tale
Will turn thy very rouge to deadly pale;
Will make thy hair, tho' erst from gipsy poll'd,
By barber woven and by barber sold,
Though twisted smooth with Harry's nicest care,
Like hoary bristles to erect and stare!
The hero of the mimic scene, no more
I start in Hamlet, in Othello roar;
Or, haughty Chieftain, 'mid the din of arms,
In Highland bonnet woo Malvina's charms:

While sans-culottes stoop up the mountain high,
And steal me from Maria's prying eye.
Blest Highland bonnet! once my proudest dress,
Now, prouder still, Maria's temples press!
I see her wave thy towering plumes afar,
And call each coxcomb to the wordy war!
I see her face the first of Ireland's sons,
And even out-Irish his Hibernian bronze!
The crafty Colonel leaves the tartan'd lines
For other wars, where he a hero shines;
The hopeful youth, in Scottish senate bred,
Who owns a Bushby's heart without the head,
Comes 'mid a string of coxcombs to display
That *Veni, vidi, vici*, is his way;
The shrinking Bard adown the alley skulks,
And dreads a meeting worse than Woolwich hulks,
Though there his heresies in Church and State
Might well award him Muir and Palmer's fate:
Still she, undaunted, reels and rattles on,
And dares the public like a noontide sun.
What scandal called Maria's jaunty stagger
The ricket reeling of a crooked swagger?
What slander nam'd her seeming want of art
The flimsy wrapper of a rotten heart—
Whose spleen (e'en worse than Burns's venom, when
He dips in gall unmix'd his eager pen,
And pours his vengeance in the burning line),
Who christen'd thus Maria's lyre-divine,
The idiot strum of Vanity bemus'd,
And even th' abuse of Poesy abus'd?
Who called her verse a Parish Workhouse, made
For motley foundling Fancies, stolen or strayed?

A Workhouse! Ah, that sound awakes my woes,
And pillows on the thorn my rack'd repose!
In durance vile here must I wake and weep,
And all my frowsy couch in sorrow steep:
That straw where many a rogue has lain of yore,
And vermin'd gipsies litter'd heretofore.

Why, Lonsdale, thus thy wrath on vagrants pour?
Must earth no rascal save thyself endure?
Must thou alone in guilt immortal swell,
And make a vast monopoly of Hell?

Thou know'st the Virtues cannot hate thee worse:
The Vices also, must they club their curse?
Or must no tiny sin to others fall,
Because thy guilt's supreme enough for all?

Maria, send me too thy griefs and cares,
In all of thee sure thy Esopus shares:
As thou at all mankind the flag unfurls,
Who on my fair one Satire's vengeance hurls!
Who calls thee, pert, affected, vain coquette,
A wit in folly, and a fool in wit!
Who says that fool alone is not thy due,
And quotes thy treacheries to prove it true!

Our force united on thy foes we'll turn,
And dare the war with all of woman born:
For who can write and speak as thou and I?
My periods that decyphering defy,
And thy still matchless tongue that conquers all reply!

THE HUE AND CRY OF JOHN LEWARS,
A POOR MAN RUINED AND UNDONE
BY ROBBERY AND MURDER

BEING AN AWEFUL WARNING TO THE YOUNG MEN OF THIS
AGE, HOW THEY LOOK WELL TO THEMSELVES IN THIS
DANGEROUS, TERRIBLE WORLD

I

A Thief and a Murderer! stop her who can!
Look well to your lives and your goods!
Good people, ye know not the hazard you run,
'Tis the far-famed and much-noted Woods.

2

While I looked at her eye, for the devil is in it,
In a trice she whipt off my poor heart:
Her brow, cheek and lip—in another sad minute
My peace felt her murderous dart.

3

Her features I'll tell you them over—but hold!
  She deals with your wizards and books;
And to peep in her face, if but once you're so bold,
  There's witchery kills in her looks.

4

But softly—I have it—her hauts are well known,—
  At midnight so slily I'll watch her;
And sleeping, undrest, in the dark, all alone—
  Good lord! the dear Thief how I'll catch her!

TO JOHN RANKINE

IN REPLY TO AN ANNOUNCEMENT

I

I am a keeper of the law
In some sma' points, altho' not a';
Some people tell me, gin I fa'
      Ae way or ither,
The breaking of ae point, tho sma',
      Breaks a' thegither.

2

I hae been in for't ance or twice,
And winna say o'er far for thrice,
Yet never met wi' that surprise
      That broke my rest.
But now a rumour's like to rise—
      A whaup's i' the nest!

if; fall
one; other

the whole

will not; too
surely

curlew

TO JOHN GOLDIE

AUGUST 1785

I

O Goudie, terror o' the Whigs,
Dread o' black coats and rev'rend wigs!
Sour Bigotry on her last legs
               Girns and looks back   snarls
Wishing the ten Egyptian plagues
               May seize you quick.

2

Poor gapin, glowrin Superstition!   staring
Wae's me, she's in a sad condition!
Fye! bring Black Jock, her state physician,
               To see her water!
Alas! there's ground for great suspicion
               She'll ne'er get better.

3

Enthusiasm's past redemption
Gane in a gallopin consumption:
Not a' her quacks wi' a' their gumption
               Can ever mend her;
Her feeble pulse gies strong presumption
               She'll soon surrender.

4

Auld Orthodoxy lang did grapple
For every hole to get a stapple;   stopper
But now she fetches at the thrapple,   gurgles;
               An' fights for breath: windpipe
Haste, gie her name up in the chapel,
               Near unto death!

5

'Tis you an' Taylor are the chief
To blame for a' this black mischíef;
if   But, gin the Lord's ain folk gat leave,
empty   A toom tar barrel
An' twa red peats was bring relief,
            And end the quarrel.

6

For me, my skill's but very sma',
at all   An' skill in prose I've nane ava';
in confidence   But, quietlenswise between us twa,
            Weel may ye speed!
should   And, tho' they sud you sair misca',
bother   Ne'er fash your head!

7

sorely   E'en swinge the dogs, and thresh them sicker!
strike   The mair they squeel ay chap the thicker,
between whiles;   And still 'mang hands a hearty bicker
glass   O' something stout!
makes; author's   It gars an owthor's pulse beat quicker,
            An' helps his wit.

8

liquor   There's naething like the honest nappy:
Whare'll ye e'er see men sae happy,
pleasant   Or women sonsie, saft, and sappy
            'Tween morn and morn,
As them wha like to taste the drappie
            In glass or horn?

9

dazed   I've seen me daez't upon a time,
faintest outline   I scarce could wink or see a styme;
one half-pint   Just ae hauf-mutchkin does me prime
            (Ought less is little);
Then back I rattle on the rhyme
keen; knife   As gleg's a whittle.

TO J. LAPRAIK

(THIRD EPISTLE)

1

Guid speed and furder to you, Johnie,
Guid health, hale han's, an' weather bonie!   whole hands
Now, when ye're nickin down fu' cannie   cutting; expertly
        The staff o' bread,   corn
May ye ne'er want a stoup o' bran'y   cup
        To clear your head!

2

May Boreas never thresh your rigs,   ridges
Nor kick your rickles aff their legs,   ricklets
Sendin the stuff o'er muirs an' haggs   broken bogs
        Like drivin wrack!
But may the tapmost grain that wags
        Come to the sack!

3

I'm bizzie, too, an' skelpin at it;   busy; driving
But bitter, daudin showers hae wat it;   pelting; wetted
Sae my auld stumpie-pen, I gat it,
        Wi' muckle wark,   After long search
An' took my jocteleg, an' whatt it   clasp-knife
        Like onie clark.   whittled

4

It's now twa month that I'm your debtor
For your braw, nameless, dateless letter,   fine
Abusin me for harsh ill-nature
        On holy men,
While deil a hair yoursel ye're better,   devil a bit
        But mair profane!

5

But let the kirk-folk ring their bells!
Let's sing about our noble sel's:
We'll cry nae jads frae heathen hills   call
        To help or roose us,   inspire
But browster wives an' whisky stills—
        They are the Muses!

6

will not give it
up
to
fist

whisky

Your friendship, sir, I winna quat it;
An' if ye mak' objections at it,
Then hand in nieve some day we'll knot it,
        An' witness take;
An', when wi' usquabae we've wat it,
        It winna break.

7

horse and bridle
kine; going;
keeper
grain; rick-yard
thatched
fire-
Some

But if the beast and branks be spar'd
Till kye be gaun without the herd,
And a' the vittel in the yard
        An' theckit right,
I mean your ingle-side to guard
        Ae winter night.

8

enervated

jolly

Then Muse-inspirin aqua-vitæ
Shall mak us baith sae blythe an' witty,
Till ye forget ye're auld an' gatty,
        And be as canty
As ye were nine year less than thretty—
        Sweet ane an' twenty!

9

shocks; tumbled
by
sun peeps; west
must run

leave; song

But stooks are cowpet wi' the blast,
And now the sinn keeks in the wast;
Then I maun rin amang the rest,
        An' quat my chanter;
Sae I subscribe mysel in haste,
        Yours, Rab the Ranter.

Sept. 13, 1785

TO THE REV. JOHN M'MATH

INCLUSING A COPY OF 'HOLY WILLIE'S PRAYER' WHICH HE
HAD REQUESTED, SEPT. 17, 1785

1

While at the stook the shearers cow'r   shock;
To shun the bitter blaudin show'r,   reapers stoop
Or, in gulravage rinnin, scowr: driving
      To pass the time,   horseplay
To you I dedicate the hour   running, scour
      In idle rhyme.

2

My Music, tir'd wi' monie a sonnet
On gown an' ban' an' douse black-bonnet,   sedate;
Is grown right eerie now she's done it,   fearful
      Lest they should blame her,
An' rouse their holy thunder on it,
      And anathém her.

3

I own 'twas rash, an' rather hardy,
That I, a simple, countra Bardie,
Should meddle wi' a pack sae sturdy,
      Wha, if they ken me,
Can easy wi' a single wordie   easily
      Louse Hell upon me.

4

But I gae mad at their grimaces,   furious
Their sighin, cantin, grace-proud faces,
Their three-mile prayers an' hauf-mile graces,
      Their raxin conscience,   elastic
Whase greed, revenge, an' pride disgraces
      Waur nor their nonsense.   Worse than

5

There's Gau'n, misca'd waur than a beast,
Wha has mair honor in his breast
Than monie scores as guid's the priest
                    Wha sea abus't him:
And may a Bard no crack his jest
                    What way they've use't him?

6

See him, the poor man's friend in need,
The gentleman in word an' deed—
An' shall his fame an' honor bleed
railers   By worthless skellums,
An' not a Muse erect her head
daunt; blusterers   To cowe the blellums?

7

O Pope, had I thy satire's darts
To gie the rascals their deserts,
I'd rip their rotten, hollow hearts,
                    An' tell aloud
Their jugglin, hocus-pocus arts
                    To cheat the crowd!

8

God knows, I'm no the thing I should be,
Nor am I even the thing I could be,
But twenty times I rather would be
                    An atheist clean
Than under gospel colors hid be
                    Just for a screen.

9

An honest man may like a glass,
An honest man may like a lass;
false   But mean revenge an' malice fause
                    He'll still disdain
An' then cry zeal for gospel laws
                    Like some we ken.

10

They take Religion in their mouth,
They talk o' Mercy, Grace, an' Truth:
For what? To gie their malice skouth   play
           On some puir wight;
An' hunt him down, o'er right an' ruth,
           To ruin streight.   straight

11

All hail, Religion! Maid divine,
Pardon a Muse sae mean as mine,
Who in her rough imperfect line
           Thus daurs to name thee;
To stigmatise false friends of thine
           Can ne'er defame thee.

12

Tho' blotch't and foul wi' monie a stain
An' far unworthy of thy train,
With trembling voice I tune my strain
           To join with those
Who boldly dare thy cause maintain
           In spite of foes:

13

In spite o' crowds, in spite o' mobs,
In spite of undermining jobs,
In spite o' dark banditti stabs
           At worth an' merit,
By scoundrels, even wi' holy robes
           But hellish spirit!

14

O Ayr! my dear, my native ground,
Within thy presbyterial bound
A candid lib'ral band is found
           Of public teachers,
As men, as Christians too, renown'd,
           An' manly preachers.

15

Sir, in that circle you are nam'd;
Sir, in that circle you are fam'd;
An' some, by whom your doctrine's blam'd
                    (Which gies ye honor),
Even, Sir, by them your heart's esteem'd,
                              An' winning manner.

16

Pardon this freedom I have taen,
An' if impertinent I've been,
Impute it not, good sir, in ane
                    Whase heart ne'er wrang'd ye,
But to his utmost would befriend
was yours   Ought that belang'd ye.

TO DAVIE

SECOND EPISTLE

1

AULD NEEBOR,

          I'm three times doubly o'er your debtor
old-fashioned   For your auld-farrant, frien'ly letter;
must   Tho' I maun say't, I doubt ye flatter,
                   Ye speak sae fair:
babble   For my puir, silly, rhymin clatter
serve   Some less maun sair.

2

Whole   Hale be your heart, hale be your fiddle!
elbow; dance   Lang may your elbuck jink an' diddle
and shake
wriggle   To cheer you thro' the weary widdle
worldly   O' war'ly cares,
grand-children; Till bairns' bairns kindly cuddle
fondle   Your auld grey hairs!

3

But Davíe, lad, I'm red ye're glaikit: afraid; foolish
I'm tauld the Muse ye hae negleckit;
An' gif it's sae, ye sud be lickit   should; whipped
        Until ye fyke;   fidget
Sic han's as you sud ne'er be faiket,   Such hands; let
        Be hain't wha like.   off
                         spared

4

For me, I'm on Parnassus' brink,
Rivin the words to gar them clink;   Tearing; make;
Whyles daez't wi' love, whyles daez't wi' drink   rhyme
        Wi' jads or Masons,   Now dazed
                         Freemasons
An' whyles, but ay owre late I think,   too
        Braw sober lessons.   Fine

5

Of a' the thoughtless sons o' man
Commen' me to the Bardie clan:
Except it be some idle plan
        O' rhymin clink—
The devil-haet that I sud ban!—   -have it
        They never think.

6

Nae thought, nae view, nae scheme o' livin,
Nae cares to gie us joy or grievin,
But just the pouchie put the nieve in,   pocket; fist
        An' while ought's there,
Then, hiltie-skiltie, we gae scrievin,   careering
        An' fash nae mair.   worry

7

Leeze me on rhyme! It's ay a treasure,   Blessings
My chief, amaist my only pleasure;   almost
At hame, a-fiel', at wark or leisure,   a-field
        The Muse, poor hizzie!   girl
Tho' rough an' raploch be her measure,   homespun
        She's seldom lazy.

8

Stick   Haud to the Muse, my dainty Davie:
world; ill-turn   The warl' may play you monie a shavie,
               But for the Muse, she'll never leave ye,
                     Tho' e'er sae puir;
spavin   Na, even tho' limpin wi' the spavie
                     Frae door to door!

LOOK UP AND SEE!

1

Noo, Davie Sillar, that's the plan,
Quo I, last night, when in my han
I gaed your latest screed a scan
            Rebukin me
About your model name-sake man—
            Look up and see!

2

Altho it may be unexpectit,
An' few the facts hae yet detectit,
My Bible hasna been negleckit
            Sin I was wee,
And nae sma lore I hae colleckit,—
            Look up and see!

3

Bad as I am, or hae been ca'd
By jauds that lang hae at me jaw'd
And priests that fain my pash had claw'd,
            I winna lee,
King David's life ye less can laud,—
            Look up and see!

4

Gin I had but a Gowdie's airt
At treating him to his desert,
This saintship after God's ain he'rt,
            As said to be,
I'd prove a villain maist expert—
            Look up and see!

5

Ay, though that Jesus styled Divine
Is shown to be o' David's line
Thro mair than ae poor concubine,
        The pedigree
Has plaguit ither heids than mine,—   plagued
        Look up and see!

6

I'm sure, my frien, ye never heard
That I, although like him a Bard,
Wi' daft, unseemly dancin garr'd
        My shanks to flee,
Till a' the decencies were jarr'd—
        Look up and see!

7

His wife, at least ane o' the lot,
Since by the score he had them got,
For thinkin him a filthy snot—
        Saul's dochter she—
A cruel curse at her he shot—
        Look up and see!

8

And neist his tricks wi' Abigail:
Her man or lang begood to ail
And was as ye may read the tale
        Alloo'd to dee;
Syne David did the widow nail—
        Look up and see!

9

And wha his conduct could defen
When like a coward, as we ken,
He sacrificed sae money men
        Upon the plea
God bann'd the Census Takkers pen?—
        Look up and see!

10

He was a cruel Man o' War
And for his plunder traivell'd far
Defenceless fowk to mash and mar
blood   And spill their bree
In bluidy streams among the glaur—
                    Look up and see!

11

And some for unco little cause
He cut wi' harrows and wi' saws:
Wha likes for that may shout huzzahs,
                    I'll never gie
doings   Sic fiendish deeins my applause—
                    Look up and see!

12

None spared he in his anger wild;
Not age itself, nor yet the child,
Although upon the sword it smiled
                    Or crow'd in glee—
How *can* the texts be reconciled?—
                    Look up and see!

13

For David, as the Scriptures say,
As black a rascal in his day
As ony Tyrant Noo we hae
                    Or e'er may dree
Was God's especial protegé—
                    Look up and see!

14

Can parsons, think ye, close the lid
And keep the awfu' story hid
On hoo the rascal—God forbid
how   We e're sud pree
What he to puir Uriah did—
                    Look up and see!

15

And since the Psalmist, as we learn,
Gat stown Bath-Sheba twice wi' bairn   stolen
He must hae had a hert o' airn   iron
            To shut his e'e
To Nathan's reprimandin stern—
            Look up and see!

16

Fine stock they were we maun alloo!   allow
Himsel—we ken wha he cam through—
And Solomon they'd gar us true
            Bore Wisdom's Key,
But here's my best advice to you—
            Look up and see!

17

Foul-mouth'd auld Davie also was
And mony proofs your Bible has
O' his inspired profaneness as
            Ye maun agree
If 'tis as in my copy 'twas—
            Look up and see!

18

E'en lyin on the bed o' Death
The scoundrel, bent on spreadin scaith,
Kept up his cursin tongue, in faith
            Nc'cr stoppit he
Till Cloutie chokit aff his breath—
            Look up and see!

19

And yet in face o' a' his record,
His lang career sae vilely checker'd,
And hoo his licht sae aften flicker'd,
            In Heaven hie
Nae angel's seat is better siccar'd—
            Look up and see!

20

I've read my Bible, Davie man,
And that's the reason hoo I stan
Opposed to a' the pious ban
   That bow the knee
To saints o' royal David's clan—
   Look up and see!

21

Should a' be true the prophets tell,
If I the lines am fit to spell,
King David mair o' dirt should smell
   Than Deity,
And gin there's sic a place as Hell—
   Look up and see!

TO JOHN KENNEDY, DUMFRIES HOUSE

1

Now, Kennedy, if foot or horse
E'er bring you in by Mauchlin Corss
(Lord, man, there's lasses there wad force
   A hermit's fancy;
And down the gate in faith! they're worse
   An' mair unchancy):

Cross

would

way
dangerous

2

But as I'm sayin, please step to Dow's,
An' taste sic gear as Johnie brews,
Till some bit callan bring me news
   That ye are there;
An' if we dinna hae a bowse,
   I'se ne'er drink mair.

stuff
small boy

I'll

3

It's no I like to sit an' swallow,
Then like a swine to puke an' wallow;
But gie me just a true guid fallow
   Wi' right ingíne,
And spunkie ance to mak us mellow,
   An' then we'll shine!

not that

wit liquor
enough

4

Now if ye're ane o' warl's folk,   the world's
Wha rate the wearer by the cloak,
An' sklent on poverty their joke   squint
            Wi' bitter sneer,
Wi' you nae friendship I will troke,   barter
            Nor cheap nor dear.

5

But if, as I'm informèd weel,
Ye hate as ill's the vera Deil
The flinty heart that canna feel—
            Come, sir, here's tae you!   to
Hae, there's my han', I wiss you weel,   take, wish
            An' Gude be wi' you!

TO GAVIN HAMILTON ESQ., MAUCHLINE

RECOMMENDING A BOY

I hold it, Sir, my bounden duty
To warn you how that Master Tootie,
    Alias Laird M'Gaun,
Was here to hire yon lad away
'Bout whom ye spak the tither day,
    An' wad hae done't aff han';   would; out of
But lest he learn the callan tricks—   hand
    As faith! I muckle doubt him—   youngster
Like scrapin out auld Crummie's nicks,   much
    An' tellin lies about them,
      As lieve then, I'd have then
        Your clerkship he should sair, attorney-ship;
      If sae be ye may be   serve
        Not fitted otherwise.

Altho' I say't, he's gleg enough,   sharp
An' bout a house that's rude an' rough
    The boy might learn to swear;
But then wi' *you* he'll be sae taught,
An' get sic fair example straught,   such
    I hae na onie fear: not

Ye'll catechise him every quirk,
    menace   An' shore him weel wi' 'Hell';
    make   An' gar him follow to the kirk—
    go   Ay when ye gang yoursel!
    must   If ye, then, maun be then
     Frae hame this comin Friday,
    leave   Then please, Sir, to lea'e, Sir,
     The orders wi' your lady.

My word of honour I hae gien,
In Paisley John's that night at e'en
     To meet the 'warld's worm,'
To try to get the twa to gree,
An' name the airles an' the fee
     In legal mode an' form:
I ken he weel a snick can draw,
     When simple bodies let him;
An' if a Devil be at a',
     In faith he's sure to get him.
     To phrase you an' praise you,
      Ye ken, your Laureat scorns:
     The pray'r still you share still
      Of grateful MINSTREL BURNS.

The Whitefoord Arms; miserly (annotation)
reptile (annotation)
handsel (annotation)
latch (annotation)

TO MR. M'ADAM OF CRAIGEN-GILLAN

IN ANSWER TO AN OBLIGING LETTER HE SENT IN THE COMMENCEMENT OF MY POETIC CAREER

I

    drink   Sir, o'er a gill I gat your card,
     I trow it made me proud.
'See wha taks notice o' the Bard!'
    danced   I lap, and cry'd fu' loud.

2

    cuckooing   Now deil-ma-care about their jaw,
     The senseless, gawky million!
    above   I'll cock my nose aboon them a':
    praised   I'm roos'd by Craigen-Gillan!

3

'Twas noble, sir; 'twas like yoursel,
    To grant your high protection:
A great man's smile, ye ken fu' well,
    Is ay a blest infection.

4

Tho', by his banes wha in a tub   *Diogenes*
    Match'd Macedonian Sandy!   *Alexander*
On my ain legs thro' dirt and dub   *Magnus*
    I independent stand ay;   *puddle*

5

And when those legs to guid warm kail   *broth*
    Wi' welcome canna bear me,
A lee dyke-side, a sybow-tail,   *stone fence;*
    An' barley-scone shall cheer me.   *onion-*

6

Heaven spare you lang to kiss the breath
    O' monie flow'ry simmers,
An' bless your bonie lasses baith
    (I'm tauld they're loosome kimmers)!   *lovable girls*

7

An' God bless young Dunaskin's laird,
    The blossom of our gentry,
An' may he wear an auld man's beard,
    A credit to his country!

REPLY TO AN INVITATION

Sir,
    Yours this moment I unseal,
        And faith! I'm gay and hearty.
    To tell the truth and shame the Deil,
        I am as fou as Bartie.   *drunk; the Devil*

But Foorsday, Sir, my promise leal,   *Thursday; true*
    Expect me o' your partie,
If on a beastie I can speel   *climb*
    Or hurl in a cartie.   *trundle*
              Yours,—ROBERT BURNS.

TO DR. MACKENZIE

An Invitation to a Masonic Gathering

    Friday first's the day appointed
    By our Right Worshipful Anointed
      To hold our grand procession,

screed   To get a blaud o' Johnie's morals,
sample   An' taste a swatch o' Manson's barrels
      I' th' way of our profession.
    Our Master and the Brotherhood
      Wad a' be glad to see you.
    For me, I wad be mair than proud
      To share the mercies wi' you.

danger   If Death, then, wi' skaith then
menacing   Some mortal heart is hechtin,
bully   Inform him, an' storm him,
fight   That Saturday ye'll fecht him.

EPISTLE TO DR. JOHN MACKENZIE

I

DEAR THINKER JOHN,
      Your creed I like it past expression,
      I'm sure, o' truth, it's nae transgression
      To say the great Westminster Session,
        Wi a' their clatter,
      In Carraches or large Confession
        Ne'er made a better.

2

      For me, I ken a weel ploughed rigg,
      I ken a handsome hizzie's leg
straight   When, springing taper straught and trig,
        It fires my fancy;
      But *system-Sandy* mills to bigg
        Is nae that chancy.

3

Sma skill in *holy war* I boast,
My wee bit spunk o' *Latin's* lost,
An *Logic* gies me ay the hoast
   An' cuts my win,   wind
So I maun tak the rear-guard post
  Far, far behind.

4

I see the poopet ance a week,   pulpit
An' carefu' every sentence cleek;
Or if frae——a smirking keek   (Jean?)
  Spoil my devotion,
My carnal een I instant steek   eyes
  Wi' double caution.

5

Still, tho' nae staunch polemic head
O lang-win'd Athanasian breed,
I hae a wee-bit cantie *creed*
  Just ae my ain,
An tho' uncouthly it may read,
  It's unco plain.

6

Tho' human-kind be sae at odds,
Poor Waspish, animated clods,
There's just twa patent turnpike roads
  They a maun gang
To dark futurity's abodes—
  The *right* an' *wrang*.

7

If, spite of a' its crooks an' thraws,
The heav'nward road your fancy draws,
If ye *resemble* ought their laws
  An' ways that's there,
Then march awa and never pause:
  Your conduct's fair.

8

But if ye think, within yoursel,
You'll fairly tak your chance o' hell,
An' honestly your notion tell,
   Free, unashamed,
Then faith, I see nae how that well
    Ye can be blam'd.

9

But here the conduct I call evil:
serve   Some at their heart wad sair the devil,
Yet groan, and drone, an' sigh, and snivel,
   An' pray and cant,
An' be to heaven as fair an' civil
saint   As ony saunt.

10

Thae rotten-hearted twa-fac'd wretches,
Wi a' their hypocritic fetches,
I would rejoice in well-splic'd stitches
   O' hempen string
Out owre a tree, the sons o' bitches,
    To see them swing.

11

Ye see my skill's but very sma,
Some folk may think I've nane ava,
But we sall gie our pens a claw
   Some ither time,
An' hae a bout between us twa
    At prose an' rhyme.

12

Farewell, dear death-defying John!
Aft hunt-the-gowke for you he's gone,
But some day he'll come down the loan
stick-like   Wi spurtlin shanks,
make   An' grip ye till he gar you groan,
    By way of Thanks.

13

But first, before that come to pass:
May ye toom many a social glass,   empty
An' bless a dear warm-hearted lass
 That likes you some;
Then after fifty simmers grass
 E'en let him come!

TO JOHN KENNEDY

A Farewell

Farewell, dear friend! may guid luck hit you,
And 'mong her favourites admit you!
If e'er Detraction shore to smit you,   threaten; smite
    May nane believe him!
And onie deil that thinks to get you,
    Good Lord, deceive him!

TO WILLIE CHALMERS' SWEETHEART

1

Wi' braw new branks in mickle pride, fine; bridle
 And eke a braw new brechan,   collar
My Pegasus I'm got astride,
 And up Parnassus pechin: blowing
Whyles owre a bush wi' downward crush
 The doited beastie stammers;   stupid
Then up he gets, and off he sets
 For sake o' Willie Chalmers.

2

I doubt na, lass, that weel kend name
 May cost a pair o' blushes:
I am nae stranger to your fame,
 Nor his warm-urgèd wishes:
Your bonie face, sae mild and sweet,
 His honest heart enamours;
And faith! ye'll no be lost a whit,
 Tho' wair'd on Willie Chalmers.   bestowed

3

Auld Truth hersel might swear ye're fair,
  And Honor safely back her;
And Modesty assume your air,
  And ne'er a ane mistak her;

eyes

And sic twa love-inspiring een
  Might fire even holy palmers:
Nae wonder then they've fatal been
  To honest Willie Chalmers!

4

offer

I doubt na Fortune may you shore

prim-lipped,
powdered
Much

  Some mim-mou'd, pouther'd priestie,
Fu' lifted up wi' Hebrew lore
  And band upon his breastie;
But O, what signifies to you
  His lexicons and grammars?
The feeling heart's the royal blue,
  And that's wi' Willie Chalmers.

5

staring

Some gapin, glowring countra laird

struggle

  May warsle for your favour;

scratch; ear;
stroke
cough

May claw his lug, and straik his beard,
  And hoast up some palaver.

Such; dunces

My bonie maid, before ye wed
  Sic clumsy-witted hammers,

spank

Seek Heaven for help, and barefit skelp
  Awa wi' Willie Chalmers.

6

Forgive the Bard! My fond regard
  For ane that shares my bosom
Inspires my Muse to gie'm his dues,

devil a bit;
flatter
above

  For deil a hair I roose him.
May Powers aboon unite you soon,
  And fructify your ámours,
And every year come in mair dear
  To you and Willie Chalmers!

TO AN OLD SWEETHEART

WRITTEN ON A COPY OF HIS POEMS

1

Once fondly lov'd and still remember'd dear,
   Sweet early object of my youthful vows,
Accept this mark of friendship, warm, sincere—
   (Friendship! 'tis all cold duty now allows);

2

And when you read the simple artless rhymes,
   One friendly sigh for him—he asks no more—
Who, distant, burns in flaming torrid climes,
   Or haply lies beneath th' Atlantic roar.

EXTEMPORE TO GAVIN HAMILTON

STANZAS ON NAETHING

1

To you, Sir, this summons I've sent
   (Pray, whip till the pownie is fraething!);   foaming
But if you demand what I want,
   I honestly answer you—naething.

2

Ne'er scorn a poor Poet like me
   For idly just living and breathing,
While people of every degree
   Are busy employed about—naething.

3

Poor Centum-per-Centum may fast,
   And grumble his hurdies their claithing;   grudge;
He'll find, when the balance is cast,   buttocks;
   He's gane to the Devil for—naething.   clothing

4

The courtier cringes and bows;
    Ambition has likewise its plaything—
A coronet beams on his brows;
    And what is a coronet?—Naething.

5

rail at

vestments

Some quarrel the Presbyter gown,
    Some quarrel Episcopal graithing;
But every good fellow will own
    The quarrel is a' about—naething.

6

little

tricked-out

The lover may sparkle and glow,
    Approaching his bonie bit gay thing;
But marriage will soon let him know
    He's gotten—a buskit-up naething.

7

The Poet may jingle and rhyme
    In hopes of a laureate wreathing,
And when he was wasted his time,
    He's kindly rewarded with—naething.

8

The thundering bully may rage,
    And swagger and swear like a heathen;
But collar him fast, I'll engage,
    You'll find that this courage is—naething.

9

Last night with a feminine Whig—
    A poet she couldna put faith in!
But soon we grew lovingly big,
    I taught her, her terrors were—naething.

10

Her Whigship was wonderful pleased,
    But charmingly tickled wi' ae thing;
Her fingers I lovingly squeezed,
    And kissed her, and promised her—naething.

11

The priest anathèmas may threat—
    Predicament, sir, that we're baith in;
But when Honor's reveillé is beat,
    The holy artillery's—naething.

12

And now I must mount on the wave:
    My voyage perhaps there is death in;
But what is a watery grave?
    The drowning a Poet is—naething.

13

And now, as grim Death's in my thought,
    To you, Sir, I make this bequeathing:
My service as long as ye've ought,
    And my friendship, by God, when ye've—
        naething.

REPLY TO A TRIMMING EPISTLE
RECEIVED FROM A TAILOR

1

What ails ye now, ye lousie bitch,
To thresh my back at sic a pitch?   punish; such
Losh, man, hae mercy wi' your natch!   Lord; notching
                Your bodkin's bauld: weapon
I didna suffer half sae much   needle
                Frae Daddie Auld.

2

What tho' at times, when I grow crouse,   merry
I gie their wames a random pouse,
Is that enough for you to souse
                Your servant sae?
Gae mind your seam, ye prick-the-louse
                An' jag-the-flae!   flea

3

writ

King David o' poetic brief
Wrocht 'mang the lassies sic mischief
As fill'd his after-life with grief

rows

An' bloody rants;
An' yet he's rank'd amang the chief

old-time saints

O' lang-syne saunts.

4

canters
sprees
-Hoofie's
wondrous

And maybe, Tam, for a' my cants,
My wicked rhymes an' drucken rants,
I'll gie auld Cloven-Clootie's haunts
An unco slip yet,
An' snugly sit amang the saunts
At Davie's hip yet!

5

faith; Kirk-
Session; must

making; capsize
the pot
capsize the pot
suffer

midwife

But, fegs! the Session says I maun
Gae fa' upo' anither plan
Than garrin lasses coup the cran,
Clean heels owre body,
An' sairly thole their mither's ban
Afore the howdy.

6

This leads me on to tell for sport
How I did wi' the Session sort:

The Bellman

Auld Clinkum at the inner port
Cried three times:—'Robin!
Come hither lad, and answr for't,
Ye're blam'd for jobbin!'

7

Wi' pinch I put a Sunday's face on,

toddled off

An' snoov'd awa' before the Session:
I made an open, fair confession—
I scorn'd to lie—

then;

An' syne Mess John, beyond expression
Fell foul o' me.

8

A fornicator-loun he call'd me,
An' said my faut frae bliss expell'd me.   fault
I own'd the tale was true he tell'd me,
        'But, what the matter?'
(Quo' I) 'I fear unless ye geld me,
        I'll ne'er be better!'

9

'Geld you!' (quo' he) 'an' what for no?   why not
If that your right hand, leg, or toe
Should ever prove your sp'ritual foe,
        You should remember
To cut it aff; an' what for no
        Your dearest member?'

10

'Na, na' (quo' I), 'I'm no for that,
Gelding's nae better than 'tis ca't;
I'd rather suffer for my faut
        A hearty flewit,   stripe
As sair owre hip as ye can draw't,
        Tho' I should rue it.

11

'Or, gin ye like to end the bother,
To please us a'—I've just ae ither: one other
When next wi' yon lass I forgather,   meet
        Whate'er betide it,
I'll frankly gie her't a' thegither,
        An' let her guide it.'

12

But, Sir, this pleas'd them warst of a',
An' therefore, Tam, when that I saw,
I said 'Guid-night,' an' cam awa,
        An' left the Session:
I saw they were resolvèd a'
        On my oppression.

TO ROBERT AIKEN

1

Assist me, Coila, while I sing
 The virtues o' a crony
That in the blessings friendships bring
 Has ne'er been match'd by mony.
And wha's the man sic land to gain?
 There can be nae mistakin',
As if there could be mair than ane—
  forward Step forrat Robert Aiken!

2

When I had neither poun' nor plack
 To rub on ane anither;
When hope's horizon seemed as black
 As midnicht a'-the-gither:
When chased and challenged by the law
 My he'rt was after quakin',
stood; friend Wha stude my steady fiere for a'?—
 O, wha but Robert Aiken!

3

When he and she baith young and auld
 Were bent on my undoin',
lies; bold And tried by lees and scandals bauld
 To drive me clean to ruin;
Wha never aince withdrew his smile,
gossip Or listened to the claikin'?—
Ah, he's a frien' that's worth the while,
 A man like Robert Aiken!

4

When first I tried my rustic pen
 In little bits o' rhymin'
Wha introduced me but and ben
 And helped me in my climbin'?
Wha advertised abroad my name,
 'A minstrel in the makin','
Wha fairly read me into fame,
 But Lawyer Robert Aiken!

5

And when wi' muckle qualms I socht
  To get my poems printed,
While mony 'frien's' nae copies bocht
  And some, their orders stinted:
Wha by the dizzen and the score
  The names to me was rakin'?—
The king o' a' the buyin' corps
  Was surely Robert Aiken!

6

The time will come when I'll be deemed
  A poet grander, greater,
Than ever prophesied or dreamed
  The loudest, proodest prater.
Then let this fact be published too
  That at the bard's awakin'
The truest, kindest friend he knew
  Was honest Robert Aiken!

TO MAJOR LOGAN

1

Hail, thairm-inspirin, rattlin Willie!	string-
Tho' Fortune's road be rough an' hilly	
To every fiddling, rhyming billie,	brother
We never heed,	
But take it like the unbrack'd filly	unbroken
Proud o' her speed.	

2

When, idly goavin, whyles we saunter,	mooning;
Yirr! Fancy barks, awa we canter,	sometimes
Up hill, down brae, till some mishanter,	mishap
Some black bog-hole,	
Arrests us; then the scathe an' banter	
We're forced to thole.	endure

3

Whole   Hale be your heart! hale be your fiddle!
elbow dance and   Lang may your elbuck jink an' diddle,
shake   To cheer you through the weary widdle
wriggle   O' this vile warl',
                         Until you on a cummock driddle,
old man   A grey-hair'd carl.

4

poverty   Come wealth, come poortith, late or soon,
                         Heaven send your heart-strings ay in tune,
fiddle-pegs   And screw your temper-pins aboon
above   (A fifth or mair)
sorrowful note   The melancholious, sairie croon
crabbed   O' cankrie Care.

5

                         May still your life from day to day,
                         Nae *lente largo* in the play
                         But *allegretto forte* gay,
                                     Harmonious flow,
bold   A sweeping, kindling, bauld strathspey—
                                     Encore! Bravo!

6

                         A' blessings on the cheery gang,
                         Wha dearly like a jig or sang,
                         An' never think o' right an' wrang
                                     By square an' rule,
gadflies; sting   But as the clegs o' feeling stang
                                     Are wise or fool.

7

hand-picked   My hand-wal'd curse keep hard in chase
(*i.e.*choicest)   The harpy, hoodock, purse-proud race,
grasping   Wha count on poortith as disgrace!
                                     Their tuneless hearts,
                         May fireside discords jar a bass
                                     To a' their parts!

8

But come, your hand, my careless brither!
I' th' ither warl', if there's anither— world
An' that there is, I've little swither doubt
      About the matter—
We, cheek for chow, shall job thegither— cheek by jowl; together
      I'se ne'er bid better! I'll; ask

9

We've faults and failins—granted clearly!
We're frail, backsliding mortals merely; blame; wholly
Eve's bonie squad, priests wyte them sheerly
      For our grand fa';
But still, but still—I like them dearly...
      God bless them a'!

10

Ochon for poor Castalian drinkers,
When they fa' foul o' earthly jinkers! gamesters
The witching, curs'd, delicious blinkers oglers
      Hae put me hyte, furious
An' gart me weet my waukrife winkers made; wet; wakeful eyes
      Wi' girnin spite. snarling

11

But by yon moon—and that's high swearin!—
An' every star within my hearin,
An' by her een wha was a dear ane eyes
      I'll ne'er forget,
I hope to gie the jads a clearin jades
      In fair play yet!

12

My loss I mourn, but not repent it;
I'll seek my pursie whare I tint it; lost
Ance to the Indies I were wonted, escaped
      Some cantraip hour witching
By some sweet elf I'll yet be dinted:
      Then *vive l'amour!*

13

Faites mes baissemains respectueusè
To sentimental sister Susie

flatter   And honest Lucky: no to roose you,
         Ye may be proud,
such   That sic a couple Fate allows ye
         To grace your blood.

14

Nae mair at present can I measure,
An' trowth! my rhymin ware's nae treasure;
But when in Ayr, some half-hour's leisure,
         Be't light, be't dark,
Sir Bard will do himself the pleasure
         To call at Park.

TO THE GUIDWIFE OF WAUCHOPE HOUSE

(MRS. SCOTT)

I

GUID WIFE,

remember   I mind it weel, in early date,
bashful   When I was beardless, young, and blate,
         An' first could thresh the barn,
hold; a day's   Or haud a yokin at the pleugh,
work
exhausted   An', tho' forfoughten sair eneugh,
mighty   Yet unco proud to learn;
         When first amang the yellow corn
         A man I reckon'd was,
others each   An' wi the lave ilk merry morn
ridge   Could rank my rig and lass:
reaping   Still shearing, and clearing
row of shocks   The tither stookèd raw,
gossip; nonsense   Wi' clavers an' havers
away   Wearing the day awa.

2

E'en then, a wish (I mind its pow'r),
A wish that to my latest hour
  Shall strongly heave my breast,
That I for poor auld Scotland's sake
Some usefu' plan or book could make,
  Or sing a sang at least.
The rough burr-thistle spreading wide
  Amang the bearded bear,   barley
I turn'd the weeder-clips aside,   -shears
  An' spar'd the symbol dear.
    No nation, no station
      My envy e'er could raise;
    A Scot still, but blot still,   without
      I knew nae higher praise.

3

But still the elements o' sang
In formless jumble, right an' wrang,
  Wild floated in my brain;
Till on that hairst I said before,   harvest;
My partner in the merry core,   mentioned
  She rous'd the forming strain.   band
I see her yet, the sonsie quean   pleasant lass
  That lighted up my jingle,
Her witching smile, her pauky een   artful eyes
  That gart my heart-strings tingle!   made
    I firèd, inspirèd,
      At ev'ry kindling keek,   glance
    But, bashing and dashing,   abashing;
      I fearèd ay to speak.   peacocking

4

Hale to the sex! (ilk guid chiel says):   Health; each;
Wi' merry dance on winter days,   fellow
  An' we to share in common!
The gust o' joy, the balm of woe,
The saul o' life, the heav'n below   soul
  Is rapture-giving Woman.

churls   Ye surly sumphs, who hate the name,
                       Be mindfu' o' your mither:
                She, honest woman, may think shame
                       That ye're connected with her!

sad   Ye're wae men, ye're nae men
                           That slight the lovely dears;
                       To shame ye, disclaim ye,

fellow   Ilk honest birkie swears.

5

not; cowhouse   For you, no bred to barn and byre,
                Wha sweetly tune the Scottish lyre,
                       Thanks to you for your line!
                The marl'd plaid ye kindly spare,

worn   By me should gratefully be ware;

perfection   'Twad please me to the nine.

proud; wrap   I'd be mair vauntie o' my hap,
sedately
hanging;   Douce hingin owre my curple,
crupper   Than onie ermine ever lap,
folded   Or proud imperial purple.

long health   Farewell, then! lang hale, then,

lot   An' plenty be your fa'!
                    May losses and crosses

porch   Ne'er at your hallan ca'!

TO WM. TYTLER, ESQ., OF WOODHOUSELEE

WITH AN IMPRESSION OF THE AUTHOR'S PORTRAIT

1

Reverèd defender of beauteous Stuart,
    Of Stuart!—a name once respected,
A name which to love was once mark of a true heart,
    But now 'tis despis'd and neglected!

2

Tho' something like moisture congloges in my eye—
    Let no one misdeem me disloyal!
A poor friendless wand'rer may well claim a sigh—
    Still more, if that wand'rer were royal.

3

My Fathers that name have rever'd on a throne;
  My Fathers have fallen to right it;
Those Fathers would spurn their degenerate son,
  That name, should be scoffingly slight it.

4

Still in prayers for King George I most heartily join,
  The Queen, and the rest of the gentry;
Be they wise, be they foolish, is nothing of mine:
  Their title's avow'd by my country.

5

But why of that epocha make such a fuss
  That gave us the Hanover stem?
If bringing them over was lucky for us,
  I'm sure 'twas as lucky for them.

6

But loyalty—truce! we're on dangerous ground:
  Who knows how the fashions may alter?
The doctrine, to-day that is loyalty sound,
  To-morrow may bring us a halter!

7

I send you a trifle, a head of a Bard,
  A trifle scarce worthy your care;
But accept it, good Sir, as a mark of regard,
  Sincere as a saint's dying prayer.

8

Now Life's chilly evening dim-shades on your eye,
  And ushers the long dreary night;
But you, like the star that athwart gilds the sky,
  Your course to the latest is bright.

TO MR. RENTON OF LAMERTON

Your billet, Sir, I grant receipt;
Wi' you I'll canter onie gate,
Tho' 'twere a trip to yon blue warl'
Where birkies march on burning marl:
Then, Sir, God willing, I'll attend ye,
And to His goodness I commend ye.

anywhere — *(Wi' you I'll canter onie gate)*
world — *(Tho' 'twere a trip to yon blue warl')*
fellows — *(Where birkies march on burning marl)*

TO MISS ISABELLA MACLEOD

1

The crimson blossom charms the bee,
    The summer sun the swallow:
So dear this tuneful gift to me
    From lovely Isabella.

2

Her portrait fair upon my mind
    Revolving time shall mellow,
And mem'ry's latest effort find
    The lovely Isabella.

3

No Bard nor lover's rapture this
    In fancies vain and shallow!
She is, so come my soul to bliss,
    The Lovely Isabella!

TO MISS FERRIER

1

Nae heathen name shall I prefix
    Frae Pindus or Parnassus;
Auld Reekie dings them a' to sticks
    For rhyme-inspiring lasses.

Edinburgh
knocks

2

Jove's tunefu' dochters three times three
    Made Homer deep their debtor;
But gien the body half an e'e,
    Nine Ferriers wad done better!

daughters

given; fellow
would have

3

Last day my mind was in a bog;   Yesterday
   Down George's Street I stoited;   stumbled
A creeping, cauld, prosaic fog
   My very sense doited;   muddled

4

Do what I dought to set her free,   could
   My saul lay in the mire: soul
Ye turned a neuk, I saw your e'e,   corner
   She took the wing like fire!

5

The mournfu' sang I here enclose,
   In gratitude I send you,
And pray, in rhyme as weel as prose,
   A' guid things may attend you!

SYLVANDER TO CLARINDA

1

When dear Clarinda, matchless fair,
   First struck Sylvander's raptur'd view,
He gaz'd, he listened to despair—
   Alas! 'twas all he dared to do.

2

Love from Clarinda's heavenly eyes
   Transfix'd his bosom thro' and thro',
But still in Friendship's guarded guise—
   For more the demon fear'd to do.

3

That heart, already more than lost,
   The imp beleaguer'd all *perdu*;
For frowning Honor kept his post—
   To meet that frown he shrunk to do.

4

His pangs the Bard refus'd to own,
    Tho' half he wish'd Clarinda knew;
But Anguish wrung the unweeting groan—
    Who blames what frantic Pain must do?

5

That heart, where motley follies blend,
    Was sternly still to Honor true:
To prove Clarinda's fondest friend
    Was what a lover, sure, might do!

6

The Muse his ready quill employ'd;
    No nearer bliss he could pursue;
That bliss Clarinda cold deny'd—
    'Send word by Charles how you do!'

7

The chill behest disarm'd his Muse,
    Till Passion all impatient grew:
He wrote, and hinted for excuse,
    ' 'Twas 'cause he'd nothing else to do.'

8

But by those hopes I have above!
    And by those faults I dearly rue!
The deed, the boldest mark of love,
    For thee that deed I dare to do!

9

O, could the Fates but name the price
    Would bless me with your charms and you,
With frantic joy I'd pay it thrice,
    If human art or power could do!

10

Then take, Clarinda, friendship's hand
    (Friendship, at least, I may avow),
And lay no more your chill command—
    I'll write, whatever I've to do.

TO CLARINDA

(WITH A PRESENT OF A PAIR OF DRINKING GLASSES)

1

Fair Empress of the Poet's soul
    And Queen of poetesses;
Clarinda, take this little boon,
    This humble pair of glasses;

2

And fill them high with generous juice,
    As generous as your mind;
And pledge me in the generous toast:
    'The whole of human kind!'

3

'To those who love us!' second fill;
    But not to those whom *we* love,
Lest we love those who love not us!
    A third:—'To thee and me, love!'

4

'Long may we live! Long may we love!
    And long may we be happy!
And may we never want a glass
    Well charg'd with generous nappy!'

TO MISS CRUIKSHANK
A VERY YOUNG LADY

WRITTEN ON THE BLANK LEAF OF A BOOK, PRESENTED TO
HER BY THE AUTHOR

I

Beauteous Rosebud, young and gay,
Blooming on thy early May,
Never may'st thou, lovely flower,
Chilly shrink in sleety shower!
Never Boreas' hoary path,
Never Eurus' pois'nous breath,
Never baleful stellar lights,
Taint thee with untimely blights!
Never, never reptile thief
Riot on thy virgin leaf!
Nor even Sol too fiercely view
Thy bosom blushing still with dew!

2

May'st thou long, sweet crimson gem,
Richly deck thy native stem;
Till some ev'ning, sober, calm,
Dropping dews and breathing balm,
While all around the woodland rings,
And ev'ry bird thy requiem sings,
Thou, amid the dirgeful sound,
Shed thy dying honours round,
And resign to parent Earth
The loveliest form she e'er gave birth.

TO HUGH PARKER

In this strange land, this uncouth clime,
A land unknown to prose or rhyme;
Where words ne'er cros't the Muse's heckles,   hackles
Nor limpit in poetic shackles:
A land that Prose did never view it,
Except when drunk he stacher't thro' it: staggered
Here, ambush'd by the chimla cheek,   chimney corner
Hid in an atmosphere of reek,   smoke
I hear a wheel thrum i' the neuk,   spin
I hear it—for in vain I leuk:
The red peat gleams, a fiery kernel
Enhuskèd by a fog infernal.
Here, for my wonted rhyming raptures,
I sit and count my sins by chapters;
For life and spunk like ither Christians,   spirit
I'm dwindled down to mere existence;
Wi' nae converse but Gallowa' bodies,   creatures
Wi' nae kend face but Jenny Geddes.
Jenny, my Pegasean pride,
Dowie she saunters down Nithside,   Drooping
And ay a westlin leuk she throws,   westerly look
While tears hap o'er her auld brown nose!   hop
Was it for this wi' cannie care   prudent
Thou bure the Bard through many a shire?   bore
At howes or hillocks never stumbled,   hollows
And late or early never grumbled?
O, had I power like inclination,
I'd heeze thee up a constellation!   hoist
To canter with the Sagitarre,
Or loup the Ecliptic like a bar,   leap
Or turn the Pole like any arrow;
Or, when auld Phœbus bids good-morrow,
Down the Zodíac urge the race,
And cast dirt on his godship's face:
For I could lay my bread and kail   bet; broth
He'd ne'er cast saut upo' thy tail!   salt
Wi' a' this care, and a' this grief,
And sma', sma' prospect of relief,
And nought but peat reek i' my head,
How can I write what ye can read?—
Tarbolton, twenty-fourth o' June,
Ye'll find me in a better tune;

But till we meet and weet our whistle,
Tak this excuse for nae epistle.

TO ALEX. CUNNINGHAM

I

My godlike friend—nay, do not stare:
  You think the praise is odd-like?
But 'God is Love,' the saints declare:
  Then surely thou art god-like!

2

And is thy ardour still the same,
  And kindled still in Anna?
Others may boast a partial flame,
  But thou art a volcano!

3

Even Wedlock asks not love beyond
  Death's tie-dissolving portal;
But thou, omnipotently fond,
  May'st promise love immortal!

4

Thy wounds such healing powers defy,
  Such symptoms dire attend them,
That last great antihectic try—
  Marriage perhaps may mend them.

5

Sweet Anna has an air—a grace,
  Divine, magnetic, touching!
She takes, she charms—but who can trace
  The process of bewitching?

TO ROBERT GRAHAM, ESQ., OF FINTRY

REQUESTING A FAVOUR

When Nature her great master-piece design'd,
And fram'd her last, best work, the human mind,
Her eye intent on all the wondrous plan,
She form'd of various stuff the various Man.
The useful many first, she calls them forth—
Plain plodding Industry and sober Worth:
Thence peasants, farmers, native sons of earth,
And merchandise' whole genus take their birth;
Each prudent cit a warm existence finds,
And all mechanics' many-apron'd kinds.
Some other rarer sorts are wanted yet—
The lead and buoy are needful to the net:
The *caput mortuum* of gross desires
Makes a material for mere knights and squires,
The martial phosphorus is taught to flow;
She kneads the lumpish philosophic dough,
Then marks th' unyielding mass with grave designs—
Law, physic, politics, and deep divines;
Last, she sublimes th' Aurora of the poles,
The flashing elements of female souls.

  The order'd system fair before her stood;
Nature, well pleas'd, pronounc'd it very good;
Yet ere she gave creating labour o'er,
Half-jest, she tried one curious labour more.
Some spumy, fiery, *ignis fatuus* matter,
Such as the slightest breath of air might scatter;
With arch-alacrity and conscious glee
(Nature may have her whim as well as we:
Her Hogarth-art, perhaps she meant to show it),
She forms the thing, and christens it—a Poet:
Creature, tho' oft the prey of care and sorrow,
When blest to-day, unmindful of to-mrrow;
A being form'd t'amuse his graver friends;
Admir'd and prais'd—and there the wages ends;
A mortal quite unfit for Fortune's strife,
Yet oft the sport of all the ills of life;
Prone to enjoy each pleasure riches give,

Yet haply wanting wherewithal to live;
Longing to wipe each tear, to heal each groan,
Yet frequent all unheeded in his own.

But honest Nature is not quite a Turk:
She laugh'd at first, then felt for her poor work.
Viewing the propless climber of mankind,
She cast about a standard tree to find;
In pity for her helpless woodbine state,
She clasp'd his tendrils round the truly great:
A title, and the only one I claim,
To lay strong hold for help on bounteous Graham.

Pity the haples Muses' tuneful train!
Weak, timid landsmen on life's stormy main,
Their hearts no selfish, stern, absorbent stuff,
That never gives—tho' humbly takes—enough:
The little Fate allows, they share as soon,
Unlike sage, proverb'd Wisdom's hard-wrung boon.
The world were blest did bliss on them depend—
Ah, that 'the friendly e'er should want a friend!'
Let Prudence number o'er each sturdy son
Who life and wisdom at one race begun,
Who feel by reason, and who give by rule
(Instinct's a brute, and Sentiment a fool!),
Who make poor 'will do' wait upon 'I should'—
We own they're prudent, but who owns they're good?
Ye wise ones, hence! ye hurt the social eye,
God's image rudely etch'd on base alloy!
But come ye who the godlike pleasure know,
Heaven's attribute distinguish'd—to bestow!
Whose arms of love would grasp all human race:
Come thou who giv'st with all a courtier's grace—
Friend of my life, true patron of my rhymes,
Prop of my dearest hopes for future times!

Why shrinks my soul, half blushing, half afraid,
Backward, abash'd to ask thy friendly aid?
I know my need, I know thy giving hand,
I tax thy friendship at thy kind command.
But there are such who court the tuneful Nine
(Heavens! should the branded character be mine!),
Whose verse in manhood's pride sublimely flows,
Yet vilest reptiles in their begging prose.

Mark, how their lofty independent spirit
Soars on the spurning wing of injur'd merit!
Seek you the proofs in private life to find?
Pity the best of words should be but wind!
So to Heaven's gates the lark's shrill song ascends,
But grovelling on the earth the carol ends.
In all the clam'rous cry of starving want,
They dun Benevolence with shameless front;
Oblige them, patronise their tinsel lays—
They persecute you all your future days!

    Ere my poor soul such deep damnation stain,
My horny fist assume the plough again!
The pie-bald jacket let me patch once more!
On eighteenpence a week I've liv'd before.
Tho', thanks to Heaven, I dare even that last shift,
I trust, meantime, my boon is in thy gift:
That, plac'd by thee upon the wish'd-for height,
With man and nature fairer in her sight,
My Muse may imp her wing for some sublimer flight.

IMPROMPTU TO CAPTAIN RIDDELL

ON RETURNING A NEWSPAPER

I

    Your News and Review, Sir,
      I've read through and through, Sir,
With little admiring or blaming:
      The Papers are barren
      Of home-news or foreign—
No murders or rapes worth the naming.

2

    Our friends, the Reviewers,
      Those chippers and hewers,
Are judges of mortar and stone, Sir;
      But of meet or unmeet
      In a fabric complete
I'll boldly pronounce they are none, Sir.

3

My goose-quill too rude is
To tell all your goodness
Bestow'd on your servant, the Poet;
Would to God I had one
Like a beam of the sun,
And then all the wolrd, Sir, should know it!

REPLY TO A NOTE FROM CAPTAIN RIDDELL

Dear Sir, at onie time or tide
I'd rather sit wi' you than ride,
   Tho' 'twere wi' royal Geordie:
And trowth! your kindess soon and late
makes; sheepish   Aft gars me to mysel look blate—
   The Lord in Heaven reward ye!

TO JAMES TENNANT OF GLENCONNER

Auld comrade dear and brither sinner,
How's a' the folk about Glenconner?
livid; easterly   How do you this blae eastlin wind,
That's like to blaw a body blind?
For me, my faculties are frozen,
torpid   My dearest member nearly dozen'd.
I've sent you here, by Johnie Simson,
Twa sage philosophers to glimpse on:
Smith wi' his sympathetic feeling,
An' Reid to common sense appealing.
Philosophers have fought and wrangled,
much   An' meikle Greek an' Latin mangled,
Till, wi' their logic-jargon tir'd
And in the depth of science mir'd,
To common sense they now appeal—
women; weavers   What wives and wabsters see and feel!
But, hark ye, friend! I charge you strictly,
Peruse them, an' return them quickly:
serious   For now I'm grown sae cursed douse
in the kitchen   I pray and ponder butt the house;
alone   My shins my lane I there sit roastin,
Perusing Bunyan, Brown, an' Boston;

Till by an' by, if I haud on,   hold
I'll grunt a reàl gospel groan.
Already I begin to try it,
To cast me een up like a pyet,   eyes; magpie
When by the gun she tumbles o'er,
Flutt'ring an' gasping in her gore:
Sae shortly you shall see me bright,   So
A burning an' a shining light.

   My heart-warm love to guid auld Glen,
The ace an' wale of honest men: pick
When bending down wi' auld grey hairs
Beneath the load of years and cares,
May He who made him still support him,
An' views beyond the grave comfort him!
His worthy fam'ly far and near,
God bless them a' wi' grace and gear!   wealth

   My auld schoolfellow, preacher Willie,
The manly tar, my Mason-billie,   -brother
And Auchenbay, I wish him joy;
If he's a parent, lass or boy,
May he be dad and Meg the mither
Just five-and-forty years thegither!
And no forgetting wabster Charlie,
I'm tauld he offers very fairly.   promises
An', Lord, remember singing Sannock   Sandie
Wi' hale breeks, saxpence, an' a bannock!   whole
And next, my auld acquaintance, Nancy,
Since she is fitted to her fancy,
An' her kind stars hae airted till her   directed to
A guid chiel wi' a pickle siller!   chap; little
My kindest, best respects, I sen' it,
To cousin Kate, an' sister Janet:
Tell them, frae me, wi' chiels be cautious,   may be;
For, faith! they'll aiblins fin' them fashious;   troublesome
To grant a heart is fairly civil,
But to grant a maidenhead's the devil!
An' lastly, Jamie, for yoursel,
May guardian angels tak a spell,
An' steer you seven miles south o' Hell!
But first, before you see Heaven's glory,
May ye get monie a merry story,
Monie a laugh and monie a drink,

coin

And ay eneugh o' needfu' clink!

Now fare ye weel, an' joy be wi' you!
For my sake, this I beg it o' you:
Assist poor Simson a' ye can;
Ye'll fin' him just an honest man.

leave; song

Sae I conclude, and quat my chanter,
Yours, saint or sinner,

RAB THE RANTER

TO JOHN M'MURDO

WITH SOME OF THE AUTHOR'S POEMS

I

O, could I give thee India's wealth,
    As I this trifle send!
Because thy Joy in both would be
    To share them with a friend!

2

But golden sands did never grace
    The Heliconian stream;
Then take what gold could never buy—
    An honest Bard's esteem.

SONNET TO ROBERT GRAHAM, ESQ., OF FINTRY

ON RECEIVING A FAVOUR, 19TH AUGUST, 1789

I call no Goddess to inspire my strains:
A fabled Muse may suit a Bard that feigns.
Friend of my life! my ardent spirit burns,
And all the tribute of my heart returns,
For boons accorded, goodness ever new,
The gift still dearer, as the giver you.

Thou orb of day! thou other paler light!
And all ye many sparkling stars of night!

If aught that giver from my mind efface,
If I that giver's bounty e'er disgrace,
Then roll to me along your wand'ring spheres
Only to number out a villain's years!

    I lay my hand upon my swelling breast,
And grateful would, but cannot, speak the rest.

EPISTLE TO DR. BLACKLOCK

I

Wow, but your letter made me vauntie!   proud
And are ye hale, and weel, and cantie?   in health; jolly
I kend it still, your wee bit jauntie   little
            Wad bring ye to: excursion
Lord send you ay as weel's I want ye,   set you up
            And then ye'll do!

2

The Ill-Thief blaw the Heron south,   Devil
And never drink be near his drouth!
He tauld mysel by word o' mouth,
            He'd tak my letter:
I lippen'd to the chiel in trowth,   trusted; chap
            And bade nae better.   asked

3

But aiblins honest Master Heron   may be
Had at the time some dainty fair one
To ware his theologic care on   spend
            And holy study,
And, tired o' sauls to waste his lear on,   souls; learning
            E'en tried the body.

4

But what d'ye think, my trusty fier?   companion
I'm turned a gauger—Peace be here!
Parnassian queens, I fear, I fear,
            Ye'll now disdain me,
And then my fifty pounds a year
            Will little gain me!

5

giddy · Ye glaikit, gleesome, dainty damies,
winding · Wha by Castalia's wimplin streamies
Dance · Lowp, sing, and lave your pretty limbies,
     Ye ken, ye ken,
That strang necessity supreme is
    'Mang sons o' men.

6

I hae a wife and twa wee laddies;
must; · They maun hae brose and brats o' duddies:
scraps of clothes · Ye ken yoursels my heart right proud is—
    I need na vaunt—
prune; weave · But I'll sned besoms, thraw saugh woodies,
willow twigs ·   Before they want.

7

Lord help me thro' this warld o' care!
early · I'm weary—sick o't late and air!
Not but I hae a richer share
    Than monie ithers;
one · But why should ae man better fare,
    And a' men brithers?

8

Come, firm Resolve, take thou the van,
male-hemp · Thou stalk o' carl-hemp in man!
remember · And let us mind, faint heart ne'er wan
    A lady fair:
Wha does the utmost that he can
sometimes ·   Will whyles do mair.

9

But to conclude my silly rhyme
(I'm scant o' verse and scant o' time):
To make a happy fireside clime
children ·   To weans and wife,
That's the true pathos and sublime
    Of human life.

10

My compliments to sister Beckie,
And eke the same to honest Lucky;
I wat she is a daintie chuckie   hen
        As e'er tread clay: trod
And gratefully, my guid auld cockie,
        I'm yours for ay.

TO A GENTLEMAN

WHO HAD SENT A NEWSPAPER, AND OFFERED TO CONTINUE IT FREE OF EXPENSE

Kind Sir, I've read your paper through,
And faith, to me 'twas really new!
How guessed ye, Sir, what maist I wanted?
This monie a day I've grain'd and gaunted,   groaned; gaped
To ken what French mischief was brewin;
Or what the drumlie Dutch were doin;   muddy
That vile doup-skelper, Emperor Joseph,   bottom smacker
If Venus yet had got his nose off;
Or how the collieshangie works   squabble
Atween the Russians and the Turks;   Between
Or if the Swede, before he halt,
Would play anither Charles the Twalt;   Twelfth
If Denmark, any body spak o't;   spoke of it
Or Poland, wha had now the tack o't;   lease
How cut-throat Prussian blades were hingin;   hanging
How libbet Italy was singin;   castrated
If Spaniard, Portuguese, or Swiss
Were sayin or takin aught amiss;
Or how our merry lads at hame
In Britain's court kept up the game:
How royal George—the Lord leuk o'er him!—
Was managing St. Stephen's quorum;   assemby
If sleekit Chatham Will was livin,   crafty
Or glaikit Charlie got his nieve in;   giddy; fist
How Daddie Burke the plea was cookin;
If Warren Hastings' neck was yeukin;   itching
How cesses, stents, and fees were rax'd,   assessments;
Or if bare arses yet were tax'd;   dues in kind;
                                   extended
The news o' princes, dukes, and earls,

Pimps, sharpers, bawds, and opera-girls;
mad younker   If that daft buckie, Geordie Wales,
wenches'   Was threshin still at hizzies' tails;
aught sedater   Or if he was grown oughtlins douser,
country stallion   And no a perfect kintra cooser:
A' this and mair I never heard of,
And, but for you, I might despair'd of.
So, gratefu', back your news I send you,
And pray a' guid things may attend you!

TO PETER STUART

Dear Peter, dear Peter,
We poor sons of metre
Are often negleckit, ye ken;
For instance your sheet, man
(Tho' glad I'm to see't, man),
not one   I get it no ae day in ten.

TO JOHN MAXWELL, ESQ. OF TERRAUGHTIE

ON HIS BIRTH-DAY

1

Health to the Maxwells' vet'ran Chief!
Health ay unsour'd by care or grief!
Inspir'd, I turn'd Fate's sibyl leaf
        This natal morn:
stuff of proof   I see thy life is stuff o' prief,
           Scarce quite half-worn.

2

This day thou metes threescore eleven,
And I can tell that bounteous Heaven
(The second-sight, ye ken, is given
every   To ilka Poet)
lease   On thee a tack o' seven times seven,
           Will yet bestow it.

3

If envious buckies view wi' sorrow   younkers
Thy lengthen'd days on thy blest morrow,
May Desolation's lang-teeth'd harrow,
                    Nine miles an' hour
Rake them, like Sodom and Gomorrah,
                    In brunstane stoure!   dust

4

But for thy friends, and they are monie,
Baith honest men and lasses bonie,
May couthie Fortune, kind and cannie   loving; quiet
                    In social glee,
Wi' mornings blythe and e'enings funny
                    Bless them and thee!

5

Fareweel, auld birkie! Lord be near ye,   fellow
And then the Deil, he daurna steer ye!   touch
Your friends ay love, your foes ay fear ye!
                    For me, shame fa' me,   befall
If neist my heart I dinna wear ye,   next; do not
                    While Burns they ca' me!

TO WILLIAM STEWART

I

In honest Bacon's ingle-neuk   chimney-corner
    Here maun I sit and think,   must
Sick o' the warld and warld's folk,
    An' sick, damn'd sick, o' drink!

2

I see, I see there is nae help,
    But still doun I maun sink,   low
Till some day *laigh enough* I yelp:—
    'Wae worth that cursed drink!'   Alas

3

Last night;
drunk
hiccup
sorely

Yestreen, alas! I was sae fu'
   I could but yisk and wink;
And now, this day, sair, sair I rue
   The weary, weary drink.

4

Satan, I fear thy sooty claws,
   I hate thy brunstane stink,
And ay I curse the luckless cause,
sup   The wicked soup o' drink.

5

In vain I would forget my woes
   In idle rhyming clink,
For, past redemption damn'd in Prose,
   I can do nought but drink.

6

To you my trusty, well try'd friend,
smile   May heaven still on you blink,
And may your life flow to the end,
   Sweet as a dry man's drink!

INSCRIPTION TO MISS GRAHAM OF FINTRY

1

Here, where the Scottish Muse immortal lives
   In sacred strains and tuneful numbers join'd,
Accept the gift! Though humble he who gives,
   Rich is the tribute of the grateful mind.

2

So may no ruffian feeling in thy breast,
   Discordant, jar thy bosom-chords among!
But Peace attune thy gentle soul to rest,
   Or Love ecstatic wake his seraph song!

3

Or Pity's notes in luxury of tears,
    As modest Want the tale of woe reveals;
While conscious Virtue all the strain endears,
    And heaven-born Piety her sanction seals!

REMORSEFUL APOLOGY

1

The friend whom, wild from Wisdom's way,
    The fumes of wine infuriate send
(Not moony madness more astray),
    Who but deplores that hapless friend?

2

Mine was th' insensate, frenzied part—
    Ah! why should I such scenes outlive?
Scenes so abhorrent to my heart!
    'Tis thine to pity and forgive.

TO COLLECTOR MITCHELL

1

Friend of the Poet tried and leal,   true
Wha wanting thee might beg or steal;
Alake, alake, the meikle Deil   big
        Wi' a' his witches
Are at it, skelpin jig an' reel   dancing
            In my poor pouches!   pockets

2

I modestly fu' fain wad hint it,   would
That One-pound-one, I sairly want it;
If wi' the hizzie down ye sent it,   maid
        It would be kind;
And while my heart wi' life-blood dunted,   throbbed
            I'd bear't in mind!

3

go

So may the Auld Year gang out moanin
To see the New come laden, groanin

down the road

Wi' double plenty o'er the loanin
     To thee and thine:
Domestic peace and comforts crownin

whole

     The hale design!

POSTSCRIPT

4

beaten
nailed
sleeve-waist coat

Ye've heard this while how I've been licket,
And by fell Death was nearly nicket:
Grim loon! He got me by the fecket,
     And sair me sheuk;

leapt

But by guid luck I lap a wicket,

corner

     And turn'd a neuk.

5

But by that health, I've got a share o't,
And by that life, I'm promis'd mair o't,

health; welfare
more watchful

My hale and weel, I'll tak a care o't
     A tentier way;
Then farewell Folly, hide and hair o't,
     For ance and ay!

TO COLONEL DE PEYSTER

I

My honor'd Colonel, deep I feel
Your interest in the Poet's weal:

climb

Ah! now sma' heart hae I to speel
     The steep Parnassus,
Surrounded thus by bolus pill
     And potion glasses.

2

O, what a canty warld were it,   jolly
Would pain and care and sickness spare it,
And Fortune favor worth and merit
        As they deserve,
And ay a rowth—roast-beef and claret!   plenty
        Syne, wha wad starve?   Then; would

3

Dame Life, tho' fiction out may trick her,
And in paste gems and frippery deck her,
Oh! flickering, feeble, and unsicker   uncertain
        I've found her still:
Ay wavering, like the willow-wicker,
        'Tween good and ill!

4

Then that curst carmagnole, Auld Satan,
Watches, like baudrons by a ratton,   the cat; rat
Our sinfu' saul to get a claut on   soul; clutch
        Wi' felon ire;
Syne, whip! his tail ye'll ne'er cast saut on—
        He's aff like fire.

5

Ah Nick! Ah Nick! it is na fair,
First showing us the tempting ware,
Bright wines and bonie lasses rare,
        To put us daft;   send us wild
Syne weave, unseen, thy spider snare   Then
        O' Hells damned waft!   weft

6

Poor Man, the flie, aft bizzes by,
And aft, as chance he comes thee nigh,
Thy damn'd auld elbow yeuks wi' joy   itches
        And hellish pleasure,
Already in thy fancy's eye
        Thy sicker treasure!   certain

7

topsy-turvy
tongs [for
singeing]
grinning

Soon, heels o'er gowdie, in he gangs,
And, like a sheep-head on a tangs,
Thy girnin laugh enjoys his pangs
                    And murdering wrestle,
As, dangling in the wind, he hangs
                    A gibbet's tassle.

8

But lest you think I am uncivil

tedious

To plague you with this draunting drivel,
Abjuring a' intentions evil,

quit

                    A quat my pen:
The Lord preserve us frae the Devil!
                    Amen! Amen!

TO MISS JESSIE LEWARS

Thine be the volumes, Jessie fair,
And with them take the Poet's prayer:
That Fate may in her fairest page,
With ev'ry kindliest, best presage
Of future bliss enrol thy name;
With native worth, and spotless fame,
And wakeful caution, still aware
Of ill—but chief Man's felon snare!
All blameless joys on earth we find,
And all the treasures of the mind—
These be thy guardian and reward!
So prays thy faithful friend, the Bard.

INSCRIPTION

WRITTEN ON THE BLANK LEAF OF A COPY OF THE LAST
EDITION OF MY POEMS, PRESENTED TO THE LADY WHOM, IN
SO MANY FICTITIOUS REVERIES OF PASSION, BUT WITH THE
MOST ARDENT SENTIMENTS OF REAL FRIENDSHIP, I HAVE
SO OFTEN SUNG UNDER THE NAME OF CHLORIS

1

'Tis Friendship's pledge, my young, fair Friend,
   Nor thou the gift refuse;
Nor with unwilling ear attend
   The moralising Muse.

2

Since thou in all thy youth and charms
   Must bid the world adieu
(A world 'gainst peace in constant arms),
   To join the friendly few;

3

Since, thy gay morn of life o'ercast,
   Chill came the tempest's lour
(And ne'er Misfortune's eastern blast
   Did nip a fairer flower);

4

Since life's gay scenes must charm no more:
   Still much is left behind,
Still nobler wealth hast thou in store—
   The comforts of the mind!

5

Thine is the self-approving glow
   Of conscious honor's part;
And (dearest gift of Heaven below)
   Thine Friendship's truest heart;

6

The joys refin'd of sense and taste,
  With every Muse to rove:
And doubly were the Poet blest,
  These joys could he improve.

PROLOGUE

SPOKEN BY MR. WOODS ON HIS BENEFIT NIGHT, MONDAY,
16TH APRIL, 1787

When by a generous Public's kind acclaim
That dearest need is granted—honest fame;
When here your favour is the actor's lot,
Nor even the man in private life forgot;
What breast so dead to heavenly Virtue's glow
But heaves impassion'd with the grateful throe?

Poor is the task to please a barb'rous throng:
It needs no Siddons's powers in Southern's song.
But here an ancient nation, fam'd afar
For genius, learning high, as great in war.
Hail, Caledonia, name for ever dear!
Before whose sons I'm honor'd to appear!
Where every science, every nobler art,
That can inform the mind or mend the heart,
Is known (as grateful nations oft have found),
Far as the rude barbarian marks the bound!
Philosophy, no idle pedant dream,
Here holds her search by heaven-taught Reason's beam;
Her History paints with elegance and force
The tide of Empire's fluctuating course;
Here *Douglas* forms wild Shakespeare into plan,
And Harley rouses all the God in man.
When well-form'd taste and sparkling wit unite
With manly lore, or female beauty bright
(Beauty, where faultless symmetry and grace
Can only charm us in the second place),
Witness my heart, how oft with panting fear,
As on this night, I've met these judges here!
But still the hope Experience taught to live:
Equal to judge, you're candid to forgive.

No hundred-headed Riot here we meet,
With Decency and Law beneath his feet;
Nor Isolence assumes fair Freedom's name:
Like Caledonians you applaud or blame!

O Thou, dread Power, Whose empire-giving hand
Has oft been stretch'd to shield the honor'd land!
Strong may she glow with all her ancient fire;
May every son be worthy of his sire;
Firm may she rise, with generous disdain
At Tyranny's, or direr Pleasure's chain;
Still self-dependent in her native shore,
Bold may she brave grim Danger's loudest roar,
Till Fate the curtain drop on worlds to be no more!

PROLOGUE SPOKEN AT THE THEATRE OF DUMFRIES

ON NEW YEAR'S DAY EVENING, 1790

No song nor dance I bring from yon great city
That queens it o'er our taste—the more's the pity!
Tho, by the bye, abroad why will you roam?
Good sense and taste are natives here at home.
But not for panegýric I appear:
I come to wish you all a good New Year!
Old Father Time deputes me here before ye,
Not for to preach, but tell his simple story.
The sage, grave Ancient cough'd, and bade me say:
'You're one year older this important day.'
If wiser too—he hinted some suggestion,
But 'twould be rude, you know, to ask the question;
And with a would-be-roguish leer and wink
He bade me on you press this one word—Think!

Ye sprightly youths, quite flush with hope and spirit,
Who think to storm the world by dint of merit,
To you the dotard has a deal to say,
In his sly, dry, sententious, proverb way!
He bids you mind, amid your thoughtless rattle,
That the first blow is ever half the battle;
That, tho' some by the skirt may try to snatch him,

Yet by the forelock is the hold to catch him;
That, whether doing, suffering, or forbearing,
You may do miracles by persevering.

    Last, tho' not least in love, ye youthful fair,
Angelic forms, high Heaven's peculiar care!
To you old Bald-Pate smoothes his wrinkled brow,
And humbly begs you'll mind the important—Now!
To crown your happiness he asks your leave,
And offers bliss to give and to receive.

    For our sincere, the' haply weak endeavours,
With grateful pride we own your many favours;
And howsoe'er our tongues may ill reveal it,
Believe our glowing bosoms truly feel it.

SCOTS PROLOGUE FOR MRS. SUTHERLAND

ON HER BENEFIT-NIGHT AT THE THEATRE, DUMFRIES,
MARCH 3RD, 1790

What needs this din about the town o' Lon'on,
How this new play an' that new song is comin?
much   Why is outlandish stuff sae meikle courted?
Does Nonsense mend like brandy—when imported?
Is there nae poet, burning keen for fame,
Will bauldly try to gie us plays at hame?
For Comedy abroad he need na toil:
A knave and fool are plants of every soil.
Nor need he stray as far as Rome or Greece
To gather matter for a serious piece:
There's themes enow in Caledonian story
Would show the tragic Muse in a' her glory.

    Is there no daring Bard will rise and tell
How glorious Wallace stood, how hapless fell?
Where are the Muses fled that could produce
A drama worthy o' the name o' Bruce?
How here, even here, he first unsheath'd the sword
'Gainst mighty England and her guilty lord,
And after monie a bloody, deathless doing,

Wrench'd his dear country from the jaws of Ruin!
O, for a Shakespeare, or an Otway scene
To paint the lovely, hapless Scottish Queen!
Vain all th' omnipotence of female charms
'Gainst headlong, ruthless, mad Rebellion's arms!
She fell, but fell with spirit truly Roman,
To glut the vengeance of a rival woman:
A woman (tho' the phrase may seem uncivil)
As able—and as cruel—as the Devil!
One Douglas lives in Home's immortal page,
But Douglasses were heroes every age;
And tho' your fathers, prodigal of life,
A Douglas followed to the martial strife,
Perhaps, if bowls row right, and Right succeeds,   roll
Ye yet may follow where a Douglas leads!

    As ye hae generous done, if a' the land
Would take the Muses' servants by the hand;
Not only hear, but patronize, befriend them,
And where ye justly can commend, commend them;
And aiblins, when they winna stand the test,   perhaps; will
Wink hard, and say: 'The folks hae done their best!'   not
Would a' the land do this, then I'll be caition   go bail
Ye'll soon hae Poets o' the Scottish nation
Will gar Fame blaw until her trumpet crack,   make
And warsle Time, an' lay him on his back!   grapple

For us and for our stage, should onie spier:—   ask
'Whase aught thae chiels maks a' this bustle here?'   Who owns
My best leg foremost, I'll set up my brow:—   those fellows
We're your ain bairns, e'en guide us as ye like,
But like good mithers, shore before ye strike;   warn
And gratefu' still, I trust ye'll ever find us
For gen'rous patronage and meikle kindness
We're got frae a' professions, setts an' ranks:
God help us! we're but poor—ye'se get but thanks!   ye'll

THE RIGHTS OF WOMAN

An Occasional Address

SPOKEN BY MISS FONTENELLE ON HER BENEFIT NIGHT,
DUMFRIES, NOVEMBER 26, 1792

While Europe's eye is fix'd on mighty things,
The fate of empires and the fall of kings;
While quacks of State must each produce his plan,
And even children lisp the Rights of Man;
Amid this mighty fuss just let me mention,
The Rights of Woman merit some attention.

First, in the sexes' intermix'd connexion
One sacred Right of Woman is Protection:
The tender flower, that lifts its head elate,
Helpless must fall before the blasts of fate,
Sunk on the earth, defac'd its lovely form,
Unless your shelter ward th' impending storm.

Our second Right—but needless here is caution—
To keep that right inviolate's the fashion:
Each man of sense has it so full before him,
He'd die before he'd wrong it—'tis Decorum!
There was, indeed, in far less polish'd days,
A time, when rough rude Man had naughty ways:
Would swagger, swear, get drunk, kick up a riot,
Nay, even thus invade a lady's quiet!
Now, thank our stars! these Gothic times are fled;
Now, well-bred men—and you are all well-bred—
Most justly think (and we are much the gainers)
Such conduct neither spirit, wit, nor manners.

For Right the third, our last, our best, our dearest:
That right to fluttering female hearts the nearest,
Which even the Rights of Kings, in low prostration,
Most humbly own—'tis dear, dear Admiration!
In that blest sphere alone we live and move;
There taste that life of life—Immortal Love.
Smiles, glances, sighs, tears, fits, flirtations, airs—
'Gainst such an host what flinty savage dares?
When awful Beauty joins with all her charms,
Who is so rash as rise in rebel arms?

But truce with kings, and truce with constitutions,
With bloody armaments and revolutions;
Let Majesty your first attention summon;
Ah! ça ira! the Majesty of Woman!

ADDRESS

SPOKEN BY MISS FONTENELLE ON HER BENEFIT NIGHT,
DECEMBER 4TH, 1793, AT THE THEATRE, DUMFRIES

Still anxious to secure your partial favor,
And not less anxious, sure, this night than ever,
A Prologue, Epilogue, or some such matter,
'Twould vamp my bill, said I, if nothing better:
So sought a Poet roosted near the skies;
Told him I came to feast my curious eyes;
Said, nothing like his works was ever printed;
And last, my prologue-business slily hinted.
'Ma'am, let me tell you,' quoth my man of rhymes,
'I know your bent—these are no laughing times:
Can you—but, Miss, I own I have my fears—
Dissolve in pause, and sentimental tears?
With laden sighs, and solemn-rounded sentence,
Rouse from his sluggish slumbers, fell Repentance?
Paint Vengeance, as he takes his horrid stand,
Waving on high the desolating brand,
Calling the storms to bear him o'er a guilty land?'

I could no more! Askance the creature eyeing:—
'D'ye think,' said I, 'this face was made for crying?
I'll laugh, that's poz—nay more, the world shall know it;
And so, your servant! gloomy Master Poet!'

Firm as my creed, Sirs, 'tis my fix'd belief
That Misery's another word for Grief.
I also think (so may I be a bride!)
That so much laughter, so much life enjoy'd.

Thou man of crazy care and ceaseless sigh,
Still under bleak Misfortune's blasting eye;
Doom'd to that sorest task of man alive—
To make three guineas do the work of five;

Laugh in Misfortune's face—the beldam witch—
Say, you'll be merry, tho' you can't be rich!

Thou other man of care, the wretch in love!
Who long with jiltish arts and airs hast strove;
Who, as the boughs all temptingly project,
Measur'st in desperate thought—a rope—thy neck—
Or, where the beetling cliff o'er hangs the deep,
Peerest to meditate the healing leap:
Would'st thou be cur'd, thou silly, moping elf?
Laugh at her follies, laugh e'en at thyself;
Learn to despise those frowns now so terrific,
And love a kinder: that's your grand specific.

To sum up all: be merry, I advise;
And as we're merry, may we still be wise!

ADDRESS OF BEELZEBUB

To the Right Honorable the Earl of Breadalbane, President of
the Right Honorable the Highland Society, which met on the
23rd of May last, at the *Shakespeare*, Covent Garden, to concert
ways and means to frustrate the designs of five hundred
Highlanders who, as the Society were informed by Mr.
M'Kenzie of Applecross, were so audacious as to attempt an
escape from their lawful lords and masters whose property they
were, by emigrating from the lands of Mr. Macdonald of
Glengary to the wilds of Canada, in search of that fantastic
thing—Liberty.

Long life, my lord, an' health be yours,
Unskaith'd by hunger'd Highland boors! *Unharmed*
Lord grant nae duddie, desperate beggar, *ragged*
Wi' dirk, claymore, or rusty trigger,
May twin auld Scotland o' a life *rob*
She likes—as lambkins like a knife!

Faith! you and Applecross were right
To keep the Highland hounds in sight!
I doubt na! they wad bid nae better *offer*
Than let them ance out owre the water!
Then up amang thae lakes and seas, *those*
They'll mak what rules and laws they please:

Some daring Hancock, or a Franklin,
May set their Highland bluid a-ranklin;
Some Washington again may head them,
Or some Montgomerie, fearless, lead them;
Till (God knows what may be effected
When by such heads and hearts directed)
Poor dunghill sons of dirt an' mire
May to Patrician rights aspire!
Nae sage North now, nor sager Sackville,
To watch and premier owre the pack vile!
An' whare will ye get Howes and Clintons
To bring them to a right repentance?
To cowe the rebel generation,   scare
An' save the honor o' the nation?
They, an' be damn'd! what right hae they
To meat or sleep or light o' day,
Far less to riches, pow'r, or freedom,
But what your lordship likes to gie them?

But hear, my lord! Glengary, hear!
Your hand's owre light on them, I fear: too
Your factors, grieves, trustees, and bailies,
I canna say but they do gaylies: gaily
They lay aside a' tender mercies,   strip; slovens;
An' tirl the hullions to the birses.   bristles;
                                                 distrained;
Yet while they're only poind and herriet,   robbed
They'll keep their stubborn Highland spirit.
But smash them! crush them a' to spails,
An' rot the dyvors i' the jails!   bankrupts
The young dogs, swinge them to the labour:
Let wark an' hunger mak them sober!   girls; at all
The hizzies, if they're aughtlins fawsont,   good-looking
Let them in Drury Lane be lesson'd!
An' if the wives an' dirty brats
Come thiggin at your doors an' yetts,   begging; gates
Flaffin wi' duds an' grey wi' beas',   flapping with
Frightin awa your deuks an' geese,   rags; vermin
Get out a horsewhip or a jowler,   ducks
The langest thong, the fiercest growler,   bull dog
An' gar the tatter'd gypsies pack   make
Wi' a' their bastards on their back!

Go on, my Lord! I lang to meet you,   long
An' in my 'house at hame' to greet you.

shall not

inmost corner;
fireside

weary

Wi' common lords ye shanna mingle;
The benmost neuk beside the ingle,
At my right han' assigned your seat
'Tween Herod's hip an' Polycrate,
Or (if you on your station tarrow)
Between Almagro and Pizarro,
A seat, I'm sure ye're weel deservin't;
An' till ye come—your humble servant,
                                        BEELZEBUB.

              Hell,
1st *June, Anno Mundi* 5790

BIRTHDAY ODE FOR 31ST DECEMBER 1787

Afar the illustrious Exile roams,
    Whom kingdoms on this day should hail,
An inmate in the casual shed,
On transient pity's bounty fed,
    Haunted by busy Memory's bitter tale!
Beasts of the forest have their savage homes,
    But He, who should imperial purple wear,
Owns not the lap of earth where rests his royal head:
    His wretched refuge dark despair,
    While ravening wrongs and woes pursue,
    And distant far the faithful few
    Who would his sorrows share!

False flatterer, Hope, away,
    Nor think to lure us as in days of yore!
We solemnize this sorrowing natal day,
    To prove our loyal truth—we can no more—
And, owning Heaven's mysterious sway,
    Submissive, low, adore.
Ye honor'd, mighty Dead,
    Who nobly perish'd in the glorious cause,
    Your King, your Country, and her laws:
From great Dundee, who smiling Victory led
    And fell a Martyr in her arms
    (What breast of northern ice but warms!),
    To bold Balmerino's undying name,
Whose soul of fire, lighted at Heaven's high flame,
Deserves the proudest wreath departed heroes claim!

Not unrevenged your fate shall lie,
    It only lags, the fatal hour:
Your blood shall with incessant cry
    Awake at last th' unsparing Power.
As from the cliff, with thundering course,
    The snowy ruin smokes along
With doubling speed and gathering force,
Till deep it, crushing, whelms the cottage in the vale,
    So Vengeance' arm, ensanguin'd, strong,
    Shall with resistless might assail,
Usurping Brunswick's pride shall lay,
And Stewart's wrongs and yours with tenfold weight repay.

Perdition, baleful child of night,
Rise and revenge the injured right
    Of Stewart's royal race!
Lead on the unmuzzled hounds of Hell,
Till all the frighted echoes tell
    The blood-notes of the chase!
Full on the quarry point their view,
Full on the base usurping crew,
The tools of faction and the nation's curse!
    Hark how the cry grows on the wind;
    They leave the lagging gale behind;
    Their savage fury, pityless, they pour;
    With murdering eyes already they devour!
    See Brunswick spent, a wretched prey,
    His life one poor despairing day,
Where each avenging hour still ushers in a worse!
    Such Havoc, howling all abroad,
        Their utter ruin bring,
    The base apostates to their God
        Or rebels to their King!

ODE TO THE DEPARTED REGENCY
BILL

Daugther of Chaos' doting years,
Nurse of ten thousand hopes and fears!
Whether thy airy, unsubstantial shade
(The rights of sepulture now duly paid)
Spread abroad its hideous form
On the roaring civil storm,

Deafening din and warring rage
Factions wild with factions wage;
  Or Underground
  Deep-sunk, profound
Among the demons of the earth,
  With groans that make
  The mountains shake
Thou mourn thy ill-starr'd blighted birth;
Or in the uncreated Void,
  Where seeds of future being fight,
With lighten'd step thou wander wide
  To greet thy mother—Ancient Night—
And as each jarring monster-mass is past,
Fond recollect what once thou wast:
In manner due, beneath this sacred oak,
Hear, Spirit, hear! thy presence I invoke!

  By a Monarch's heaven-struck fate;
  By a disunited State;
  By a generous Prince's wrongs;
  By a Senate's war of tongues;
  By a Premier's sullen pride
  Louring on the changing tide;
  By dread Thurlow's powers to awe—
  Rhetoric, blasphemy and law;
  By the turbulent ocean,
  A Nation's commotion;
  By the harlot-caresses
  Of Borough addresses;
  By days few and evil;
  (Thy portion, poor devil!),
  By Power, Wealth, and Show—the Gods by men
    adored;
  By nameless Poverty their Hell abhorred;
  By all they hope, by all they fear,
  Hear! and Appear!

Stare not on me, thou ghostly Power,
Nor, grim with chain'd defiance, lour!
No Babel-structure would I build
  Where, Order exil'd from his native sway,
Confusion might the Regent-sceptre wield,
  While all would rule and none obey,
Go, to the world of Man relate

The story of thy sad, eventful fate;
And call presumptuous Hope to hear
And bid him check his blind career;
And tell the sore prest sons of Care
    Never, never to despair!

Paint Charles's speed on wings of fire,
The object of his fond desire,
Beyond his boldest hopes, at hand.
Paint all the triumph of the Portland Band
(Hark! how they lift the joy-exulting voice,
And how their num'rous creditors rejoice!);
But just as hopes to warm enjoyment rise,
Cry 'Convalescence!' and the vision flies.
Then next pourtray a dark'ning twilight gloom
    Eclipsing sad a gay, rejoicing morn,
While proud Ambition to th' untimely tomb
    By gnashing, grim, despairing fiends is borne!
Paint Ruin, in the shape of high Dundas
    Gaping with giddy terror o'er the brow.
In vain he struggles, the Fates behind him press,
    And clamorous Hell yawns for her prey below!
How fallen That, whose pride late scaled the skies!
And This, like Lucifer, no more to rise!
    Again pronounce the powerful word:
See Day, triumphant from the night, restored!

Then know this truth, ye Sons of Men
    (Thus ends thy moral tale:)
Your darkest terrors may be vain,
    Your brightest hopes may fail!

A NEW PSALM FOR THE CHAPEL OF KILMARNOCK

ON THE THANKSGIVING-DAY FOR HIS MAJESTY'S RECOVERY

I

O, sing a new song to the Lord!
    Make, all and every one,
A joyful noise, ev'n for the King
    His restoration!

2

The sons of Belial in the land
    Did set their heads together.
'Come, let us sweep them off,' said they,
    'Like an o'erflowing river!'

3

They set their heads together, I say,
    They set their heads together:
On right, and left, and every hand,
    We saw none to deliver.

4

Thou madest strong two chosen ones,
    To quell the Wicked's pride:
That Young Man, great in Issachar,
    The burden-bearing tribe;

5

And him, among the Princes, chief
    In our Jerusalem,
The Judge that's mighty in Thy law,
    The man that fears Thy name.

6

Yet they, even they with all their strength,
    Began to faint and fail;
Even as two howling, rav'ning wolves
    To dogs do turn their tail.

7

Th' ungodly o'er the just prevail'd;
    For so Thou hadst appointed,
That Thou might'st greater glory give
    Unto Thine own anointed!

8

And now Thou hast restored our State,
    Pity our Kirk also;
For she by tribulations
    Is now brought very low!

9

Consume that high-place, Patronage,
　　From off Thy holy hill;
And in Thy fury burn the book
　　Even of that man M'Gill!

10

Now hear our prayer, accept our song,
　　And fight Thy chosen's battle!
We seek but little, Lord, from Thee:
　　Thou kens we get as little!

INSCRIBED TO THE RIGHT HON. C. J. FOX

How Wisdom and Folly meet, mix, and unite,
How Virtue and Vice blend their black and their white,
How Genius, th' illustrious father of fiction,
Confounds rule and law, reconciles contradiction,
I sing. If these mortals, the critics, should bustle,
I care not, not I: let the critics go whistle!

　　But now for a Patron, whose name and whose glory
At once may illústrate and honor my story:—

　　Thou first of our orators, first of our wits,
Yet whose parts and acquirements seem mere lucky hits;
With knowledge so vast and with judgment so strong,
No man with the half of 'em e'er could go wrong;
With passions so potent and fancies so bright,
No man with the half of 'em e'er could go right;
A sorry, poor, misbegot son of the Muses,
For using thy name, offers fifty excuses.

　　Good Lord, what is Man! For as simple he looks,
Do but try to develop his hooks and his crooks!
With his depths and his shallows, his good and his evil,
All in all he's a problem must puzzle the Devil.

　　On his one ruling passion Sir Pope hugely labors,
That, like th' old Hebrew walking-switch, eats up its
　　neighbours.
Human Nature's his show-box—your friend, would you
　　know him?

Pull the string, Ruling Passion—the picture will show him.
What pity, in rearing so beauteous a system,
One trifling particular—Truth—should have miss'd him!
For, spite of his fine theoretic positions,
Mankind is a science defies definitions.

Some sort all our qualities each to its tribe,
And think Human Nature they truly describe:
Have you found this, or t'other? There's more in the wind,
As by one drunken fellow his comrades you'll find.
But such is the flaw, or the depth of the plan
In the make of that wonderful creature called Man,
No two virtues, whatever relation they claim,
Nor even two different shades of the same,
Though like as was ever twin brother to brother,
Possessing the one shall imply you've the other.

But truce with abstraction, and truce with a Muse
Whose rhymes you'll perhaps, Sir, ne'er deign to peruse!
Will you leave your justings, your jars, and your quarrels,
Contending with Billy for proud-nodding laurels?
My much-honour'd Patron, believe your poor Poet,
Your courage much more than your prudence, you show it.
In vain with Squire Billy for laurels you struggle:
He'll have them by fair trade—if not, he will smuggle;
Nor cabinets even of kings would conceal 'em,
He'd up the back-stairs, and by God he would steal 'em!
Then feats like Squire Billy's, you ne'er can achieve 'em;
It is not, out-do him—the task is, out-thieve him!

ON GLENRIDDELL'S FOX BREAKING HIS CHAIN

A FRAGMENT, 1791

Thou, Liberty, thou art my theme:
Not such as idle poets dream,
Who trick thee up a heathen goddess
That a fantastic cap and rod has!
Such stale conceits are poor and silly:
I paint thee out a Highland filly,
A sturdy, stubborn, handsome dapple,

As sleek's a mouse, as round's an apple,
That, when thou pleasest, can do wonders,
But when thy luckless rider blunders,
Or if thy fancy should demur there,
Wilt break thy neck ere thou go further.

These things premis'd, I sing a Fox—
Was caught among his native rocks,
And to a dirty kennel chained—
How he his liberty regained.

Glenriddell! a Whig without a stain,
A Whig in principle and grain,
Could'st thou enslave a free-born creature,
A native denizen of Nature?
How could'st thou, with a heart so good
(A better ne'er was sluiced with blood),
Nail a poor devil to a tree,
That ne'er did harm to thine or thee?

The staunchest Whig Glenriddell was,
Quite frantic in his country's cause;
And oft was Reynard's prison passing,
And with his brother-Whigs canvássing
The rights of men, the powers of women,
With all the dignity of Freeman.

Sir Reynard daily heard debates
Of princes', kings', and nations' fates,
With many rueful, bloody stories
Of tyrants, Jacobites, and Tories:
From liberty how angels fell,
That now are galley-slaves in Hell;
How Nimrod first the trade began
Of binding Slavery's chains on man;
How fell Semiramis—God damn her!—
Did first, with sacrilegious hammer
(All ills till then were trivial matters)
For Man dethron'd forge hen-peck fetters;
How Xerxes, that abandoned Tory,
Thought cutting throats was reaping glory,
Until the stubborn Whigs of Sparta
Taught him great Nature's Magna Charta;
How mighty Rome her fiat hurl'd

Resistless o'er a bowing world,
And, kinder than they did desire,
Polish'd mankind with sword and fire:
With much too tedious to relate
Of ancient and of modern date,
But ending still how Billy Pitt
(Unlucky boy!) with wicked wit
Has gagg'd old Britain, drained her coffer,
As butchers bind and bleed a heifer.

Thus wily Reynard, by degrees
In kennel listening at his ease,
Suck'd in a mighty stock of knowledge,
As much as some folks at a college;
Knew Britain's rights and constitution,
Her aggrandisement, diminution;
How Fortune wrought us good from evil:
Let no man, then, despise the Devil,
As who should say: 'I ne'er can need him,'
Since we to scoundrels owe our Freedom.

ON THE COMMEMORATION OF
RODNEY'S VICTORY

KING'S ARMS, DUMFRIES, 12TH APRIL, 1793

Instead of a song, boys, I'll give you a toast:
Here's the Mem'ry of those on the Twelfth what we lost!—
We lost, did I say?—No, by Heav'n, that we found!
For their fame it shall live while the world goes round.
The next in succession I'll give you: the King!
And who would betray him, on high may he swing!
And here's the grand fabric, our Free Constitution
As built on the base of the great Revolution!
And, longer with Politics not to be cramm'd,
Be Anarchy curs'd, and be Tyranny damn'd!
And who would to Liberty e'er prove disloyal,
May his son be a hangman—and he his first trial!

ODE FOR GENERAL WASHINGTON'S BIRTHDAY

No Spartan tube, no Attic shell,
　　No lyre Æolian I awake.
'Tis Liberty's bold note I swell:
　　Thy harp, Columbia, let me take!
See gathering thousands, while I sing,
A broken chain, exulting, bring
　　　　And dash it in a tyrant's face,
　　And dare him to his very beard,
　　And tell him he no more is fear'd,
　　　　No more the despot of Columbia's race!
A tyrant's proudest insults brav'd,
They shout a People freed! They hail an Empire sav'd!
　　Where is man's godlike form?
　　　　Where is that brow erect and bold,
　　　　That eye that can unmov'd behold
　　The wildest rage, the loudest storm
　　That e'er created Fury dared to raise?
　　Avaunt! thou caitiff, servile, base,
　　That tremblest at a despot's nod,
Yet, crouching under the iron rod,
　　　　Canst laud the arm that struck th' insulting blow!
Art thou of man's Imperial line?
Dost boast that countenance divine?
　　Each skulking feature answers: No!
But come, ye sons of Liberty,
Columbia's offspring, brave as free,
In danger's hour still flaming in the van,
Ye know, and dare maintain, The Royalty of Man!

Alfred, on thy starry throne
　　Surrounded by the tuneful choir,
　　The Bards that erst have struck the patriot lyre,
　　And rous'd the freeborn Briton's soul of fire,
No more thy England own!
Dare injured nations form the great design
　　To make detested tyrants bleed?
　　Thy England execrates the glorious deed!
　　Beneath her hostile banners waving,
　　Every pang of honour braving,
England in thunder calls: 'The Tyrant's cause is mine!'
That hour accurst how did the fiends rejoice,

And Hell thro' all her confines raise th' exulting voice!
That hour which saw the generous English name
Link't with such damnèd deeds of everlasting shame!

Thee, Caledonia, thy wild heaths among,
Fam'd for the martial deed, the heaven-taught song,
   To thee I turn with swimming eyes!
Where is that soul of Freedom fled?
Immingled with the mighty dead
   Beneath that hallow'd turf where Wallace lies!
Hear it not, Wallace, in thy bed of death!
   Ye babbling winds, in silence sweep!
   Disturb not ye the hero's sleep,
Nor give the coward secret breath!
Is this the ancient Caledonian form,
Firm as her rock, resistless as her storm?
Show me that eye which shot immortal hate,
   Blasting the Despot's proudest bearing!
Show me that arm which, nerv'd with thundering fate,
   Braved Usurpation's boldest daring!
Dark-quench'd as yonder sinking star,
No more that glance lightens afar,
That palsied arm no more whirls on the waste of war.

ELECTION BALLAD

AT CLOSE OF THE CONTEST FOR REPRESENTING THE DUMFRIES BURGHS, 1790

Addressed to Robert Graham of Fintry

I

Fintry, my stay in worldly strife,
Friend o' my Muse, friend o' my life,
   Are ye as idle's I am?
Come, then! Wi' uncouth kintra fleg
O'er Pegasus I'll fling my leg,
   And ye shall see me try him!

country action

2

But where shall I gae rin or ride,   go run
That I may splatter nane beside!   splash
      I wad na be uncivil: would not
In mankind's various paths and ways
There's ay some doytin body strays,   doddering
      And I ride like a devil.   creature

3

Thus I break aff wi' a' my birr,   force
An' down yon dark, deep alley spur,
      Where Theologics dander: saunter
Alas! curst wi' eternal fogs,
And damn'd in everlasting bogs,
      As sure's the Creed I'll blunder!

4

I'll stain a band, or jaup a gown,   splash
Or rin my reckless, guilty crown
      Against the haly door!
Sair do I rue my luckless fate,   Sore
When, as the Muse an' Deil wad hae't,
      I rade that road before!

5

Suppose I take a spurt, and mix
Amang the wilds o' Politics—
      Electors and elected—
Where dogs at Court (sad sons o' bitches!)
Septennially a madness touches,
      Till all the land's infected?

6

All hail, Drumlanrig's haughty Grace,
Discarded remnant of a race
      Once godlike—great a story!
Thy fathers' virtues all contrasted,
The very name of Douglas blasted,
      Thine that inverted glory!

7

Hate, envy, oft the Douglas bore;
But thou has superadded more,
            And sunk them in contempt!
Follies and crimes have stain'd the name;
But, Queensberry, thine the virgin claim,
            From aught that's good exempt!

8

I'll sing the zeal Drumlanrig bears,
Who left the all-important cares
            Of fiddlers, whores, and hunters,
And, bent on buying Borough Towns,
weaver rascals   Came shaking hands wi' wabster-loons,
harlots   And kissing barefit bunters.

9

Combustion thro' our boroughs rode,
Whistling his roaring pack abroad
            Of mad unmuzzled lions,
As Queensberry buff-and-blue unfurl'd,
And Westerha' and Hopeton hurl'd
            To every Whig defiance.

10

But cautious Queensberry left the war
(Th' unmanner'd dust might soil his star;
            Besides, he hated bleeding),
But left behind him heroes bright,
Heroes in Caesarean fight
            Or Ciceronian pleading.

11

O, for a throat like huge Mons-Meg,
To muster o'er each ardent Whig,
            Beneath Drumlanrig's banner!
Heroes and heroines commix,
All in the field of politics,
            To win immortal honor!

12

M'Murdo and his lovely spouse
(Th' enamour'd laurels kiss her brows!)
   Led on the Loves and Graces:
She won each gaping burgess' heart,
While he, *sub rosa*, played his part
   Among their wives and lasses.

13

Craigdarroch led a light-arm'd core: company
Tropes, metaphores, and figures pour,
   Like Hecla streaming thunder.
Glenriddell, skill'd in rusty coins,
Blew up each Tory's dark designs
   And bared the treason under.

14

In either wing two champions fought:
Redoubted Staig, who set at nought
   The wildest savage Tory;
And Welsh, who ne'er yet flinch'd his ground,
High-wav'd his magnum-bonum round   double-quart
   With Cyclopeian fury.

15

Miller brought up th' artillery ranks,
The many-pounders of the Banks,
   Resistless desolation!
While Maxwelton, that baron bold,
'Mid Lawson's port entrench'd his hold
   And threaten'd worse damnation.

16

To these what Tory hosts oppos'd,
With these what Tory warriors clos'd,
   Surpasses my descriving:
Squadrons, extended long and large,
With furious speed rush to the charge,
   Like furious devils driving.

17

What verse can sing, what prose narrate
The butcher deeds of bloody Fate
         Amid this mighty tulyie?
Grim Horror girn'd, pale Terror roar'd,
As Murther at his thrapple shor'd,
           And Hell mix'd in the brulyie.

tussle
snarled
weasand
threatened
brangle

18

As Highland craigs by thunder cleft,
When lightnings fire the stormy lift,
         Hurl down with crashing rattle,
As flames among a hundred woods,
As headlong foam a hundred floods—
         Such is the rage of Battle!

crags
sky

19

The stubborn Tories dare to die:
As soon the rooted oaks would fly
         Before th' approaching fellers!
The Whigs come on like Ocean's roar,
When all his wintry billows pour
         Against the Buchan Bullers.

20

Lo, from the shades of Death's deep night
Departed Whigs enjoy the fight,
         And think on former daring!
The muffled murtherer of Charles
The Magna Charter flag unfurls,
         All deadly gules its bearing.

21

Nor wanting ghosts of Tory fame:
Bold Scrimgeour follows gallant Graham,
         Auld Covenanters shiver ...
Forgive! forgive! much-wrong'd Montrose!
Now Death and Hell engulph thy foes,
         Thou liv'st on high for ever!

22

Still o'er the field the combat burns;
The Tories, Whigs, give way by turns;
            But Fate the word has spoken;
For woman's wit and strength o' man,
Alas! can do but what they can:
            The Tory ranks are broken.

23

O, that my een were flowing burns!   eyes; brooks
My voice a lioness that mourns
            Her darling cubs' undoing
That I might greet, that I might cry,   weep
While Tories fall, while Tories fly
            From furious Whigs pursuing!

24

What Whig but melts for good Sir James,
Dear to his country by the names,
            Friend, Patron, Benefactor?
Not Pulteney's wealth can Pulteney save;
And Hopeton falls—the generous, brave!—
            And Stewart bold as Hector.

25

Thou, Pitt, shalt rue this overthrow,
And Thurlow growl this curse of woe,
            And Melville melt in wailing!
Now Fox and Sheridan rejoice,
And Burke shall sing:—'O Prince, arise!
            Thy power is all prevailing!'

26

For your poor friend, the Bard, afar
He sees and hears the distant war,
            A cool spectator purely:
So, when the storm the forest rends,
The robin in the hedge descends,
            And, patient, chirps securely.

27

Now, for my friends' and brethren's sakes,
And for my dear-lov'd Land o' Cakes,
　　I pray with holy fire:—
Lord, send a rough-shod troop o' Hell

would

O'er a' wad Scotland buy or sell,
　　　To grind them in the mire!

WHY SHOULD WE IDLY WASTE OUR PRIME

1

Why should we idly waste our prime
　　Repeating our oppressions?
Come rouse to arms! 'Tis now the time
　　To punish past transgressions.
'Tis said that Kings can do no wrong—
　　Their murderous deeds deny it,
And, since from us their power is sprung,
　　We have a right to try it.
Now each true patriot's song shall be:—
'Welcome Death or Libertie!'

2

Proud Priests and Bishops we'll translate
　　And canonize as Martyrs;
The guillotine on Peers shall wait;
　　And Knights shall hang in garters.
Those Despots long have trode us down,
　　And Judges are their engines:
Such wretched minions of a Crown
　　Demand the people's vengeance!
To-day 'tis *theirs*. To-morrow we
Shall don the Cap of Libertie!

3

The Golden Age we'll then revive:
　　Each man will be a brother;
In harmony we all shall live,
　　And share the earth together;
In Virtue train'd, enlighten'd Youth
　　Will love each fellow-creature;
And future years shall prove the truth
　　That Man is good by nature:
Then let us toast with three times three
The reign of Peace and Libertie!

THE TREE OF LIBERTY

1

Heard ye o' the Tree o' France,
　　And wat ye what's the name o't?　　　　wot
Around it a' the patriots dance—
　　Weel Europe kens the fame o't!
It stands where ance the Bastile stood—
　　A prison built by kings, man;
When Superstition's hellish brood
　　Kept France in leading-strings, man.

2

Upo' this tree there grows sic fruit,　　　　such
　　Its virtues a' can tell, man:
It raises man aboon the brute,　　　　　　above
　　It mak's him ken himsel', man!
Gif ance the peasant taste a bit,　　　　　If
　　He's greater than a lord, man,
And wi' the beggar shares a mite
　　O' a' he can afford, man.

3

This fruit is worth a' Afric's wealth:
    To comfort us 'twas sent, man,
To gie the sweetest blush o' health,
    And mak' us a' content, man!
eyes   It clears the een, it cheers the heart,
    Mak's high and low guid friends, man,
And he wha acts the traitor's part,
    It to perdition sends, man.

4

fellow   My blessings ay attend the chiel,
    Wha pitied Gallia's slaves, man,
stole   And staw a branch, spite o' the Deil,
beyond   Frae 'yont the western waves, man!
Fair Virtue water'd it wi' care,
    And now she sees wi' pride, man,
How weel it buds and blossoms there,
    Its branches spreading wide, man.

5

But vicious folk ay hate to see
    The works o' Virtue thrive, man.
The courtly vermin's bann'd the tree,
wept   And grat to see it thrive, man!
King Louis thought to cut it down,
very   When it was unco sma', man;
For this the watchman crack'd his crown,
    Cut aff his head and a', man.

6

then   A wicked crew syne, on a time,
oath   Did tak' a solemn aith, man,
It ne'er should flourish to its prime—
wot   I wat they pledg'd their faith, man!
went   Awa they gaed wi' mock parade,
    Like beagles hunting game, man,
But soon grew weary o' the trade,
    And wish'd they'd been at hame, man.

7

Fair Freedom, standing by the tree,
 Her sons did loudly ca', man.
She sang a sang o' Liberty,
 Which pleas'd them ane and a', man.
By her inspir'd, the new-born race
 Soon drew the avenging steel, man.
The hirelings ran—her foes gied chase,   gave
 And bang'd the despot weel, man.

8

Let Britain boast her hardy oak,
 Her poplar, and her pine, man!
Auld Britain ance could crack her joke,
 And o'er her neighbours shine, man!
But seek the forest round and round,
 And soon 'twill be agreed, man,
That sic a tree can not be found
 'Twixt London and the Tweed, man.

9

Without this tree alake this life
 Is but a vale o' woe, man,
A scene o' sorrow mix'd wi' strife,
 Nae real joys we know, man;
We labour soon, we labour late,
 To feed the titled knave, man,
And a' the comfort we're to get,
 Is that ayont the grave, man.   beyond

10

Wi' plenty o' sic trees, I trow,
 The warld would live in peace, man.
The sword would help to mak' a plough,
 The din o' war wad cease, man.
Like brethren in a common cause,
 We'd on each other smile, man;
And equal rights and equal laws
 Wad gladden every isle, man.

II

woe befall the
fellow

Wae worth the loon wha wadna eat
  Sic halesome, dainty cheer, man!
I'd gie the shoon frae aff my feet,
  To taste the fruit o't here, man!

Then

Syne let us pray, Auld England may
  Sure plant this far-famed tree, man;
And blythe we'll sing, and herald the day
  That gives us liberty, man.

I'LL GO AND BE A SODGER

I

O, why the deuce should I repine,
  And be an ill foreboder?
I'm twenty-three and five feet nine,
  I'll go and be a sodger.

2

wealth; much
together

I gat some gear wi' meikle care,
  I held it weel thegither;
But now it's gane—and something mair:
  I'll go and be a sodger.

APOSTROPHE TO FERGUSSON

INSCRIBED ABOVE AND BELOW HIS PORTRAIT

Curse on ungrateful man, that can be pleas'd
And yet can starve the author of the pleasure!

O thou, my elder brother in misfortune,
By far my elder brother in the Muse,
With tears I pity thy unhappy fate!
Why is the Bard unfitted for the world,
Yet has so keen a relish of its pleasures?

AH, WOE IS ME, MY MOTHER DEAR

Jeremiah, chap. xv. verse 10

1

Ah, woe is me, my Mother dear!
  A man of strife ye've born me:
For sair contention I maun bear;   *must*
  They hate, revile, and scorn me.

2

I ne'er could lend on bill or band,
  That five per cent, might blest me;   *might have blest*
And borrowing, on the tither hand,   *other*
  The deil a ane wad trust me.   *would*

3

Yet I, a coin-denyèd wight,
  By Fortune quite discarded,
Ye see how I am day and night
  By lad and lass blackguarded!

INSCRIBED ON A WORK OF HANNAH MORE'S

PRESENTED TO THE AUTHOR BY A LADY

Thou flatt'ring mark of friendship kind,
Still may thy pages call to mind
  The dear, the beauteous donor!
Tho' sweetly female ev'ry part,
Yet such a head and—more—the heart
  Does both the sexes honor:
She show'd her taste refin'd and just,
  When she selected thee,
Yet deviating, own I must,
  For so approving me:
    But, kind still, I mind still   *remember*
      The giver in the gift;
    I'll bless her, and wiss her   *wish*
      A Friend aboon the lift.   *heavens*

LINES WRITTEN ON A BANK NOTE

Woe befall
Deadly

Wae worth thy power, thou cursed leaf!
Fell source of a' my woe and grief,
For lack o' thee I've lost my lass,
For lack o' thee I scrimp my glass!
I see the children of affliction
Unaided, through thy curs'd restriction.
I've seen the oppressor's cruel smile
Amid his hapless victims' spoil;
And for thy potence vainly wish'd
To crush the villain in the dust.
For lack o' thee I leave this much-lov'd shore,
Never, perhaps, to greet old Scotland more.

THE FAREWELL

The valiant, in himself, what can he suffer?
Or what does he regard his single woes?
But when, alas! he multiples himself,
To dearer selves, to the lov'd tender fair,
To those whose bliss, whose beings hang upon him,
To helpless children,—then, Oh then he feels
The point of misery festering in his heart,
And weakly weeps his fortunes like a coward:
Such, such am I!—undone!

THOMSON'S *Edward and Eleanora*

I

Farewell, old Scotia's bleak domains,
Far dearer than the torrid plains,
   Where rich ananas blow!
Farewell, a mother's blessing dear,
A brother's sigh, a sister's tear,
   My Jean's heart-rending throe!
Farewell, my Bess! Tho' thou'rt bereft
   Of my paternal care,
A faithful brother I have left,
   My part in him thou'lt share!
    Adieu too, to you too,
     My Smith, my bosom frien';
   When kindly you mind me, remember
    O, then befriend my Jean!

2

What bursting anguish tears my heart?
From thee, my Jeany, must I part?
    Thou, weeping, answ'rest: 'No!'
Alas! misfortune stares my face,
And points to ruin and disgrace—
    I for thy sake must go!
Thee, Hamilton, and Aiken dear,
    A grateful, warm adieu:
I with a much-indebted tear
    Shall still remember you!
        All-hail, then, the gale then
            Wafts me from thee, dear shore!
        It rustles, and whistles—
            I'll never see thee more!

ELEGY ON THE DEATH OF ROBERT RUISSEAUX

1

Now Robin lies in his last lair,
He'll gabble rhyme, nor sing nae mair;
Cauld Poverty wi' hungry stare
            Nae mair shall fear him;   terrify
Nor anxious Fear, nor cankert Care,   crabbed
            E'er mair come near him.

2

To tell the truth, they seldom fash'd him,   bothered
Except the moment that they crush'd him;
For sune as Chance or Fate had hush'd 'em,   soon
            Tho' e'er sae short,
Then wi' a rhyme or sang he lash'd 'em,
            And thought it sport.

3

Tho' he was bred to kintra-wark,   country-
And counted was baith wight and stark,   both stout;
Yet that was never Robin's mark   strong
            To mak a man;
But tell him, he was learned and clark,   scholarly
            Ye roos'd him then!   flattered

VERSES INTENDED TO BE WRITTEN BELOW A NOBLE EARL'S PICTURE

1

Whose is that noble, dauntless brow?
   And whose that eye of fire?
And whose that generous princely mien,
   Ev'n rooted foes admire?

2

Stranger! to justly show that brow
   And mark that eye of fire,
Would take His hand, whose vernal tints
   His other works admire!

3

Bright as a cloudless summer sun,
   With stately port he moves;
His guardian Seraph eyes with awe
   The noble Ward he loves.

4

Among the illustrious Scottish sons
   That Chief thou may'st discern:
Mark Scotia's fond-returning eye—
   It dwells upon Glencairn.

ELEGY ON THE DEATH OF SIR JAMES HUNTER BLAIR

1

The lamp of day with ill-presaging glare,
   Dim, cloudy, sank beneath the western wave;
Th' inconstant blast howl'd thro' the darkening air,
   And hollow whistled in the rocky cave.

2

Lone as I wander'd by each cliff and dell,
   Once the lov'd haunts of Scotia's royal train;
Or mus'd where limpid streams, once hallow'd, well,
   Or mould'ring ruins mark the sacred Fane.

bubble up

3

Th' increasing blast roared round the beetling rocks,
  The clouds, swift-wing'd, flew o'er the starry sky,
The groaning trees untimely shed their locks,
  And shooting meteors caught the startled eye.

4

The paly moon rose in the livid east,
  And 'mong the cliffs disclos'd a stately form
In weeds of woe, that frantic beat her breast,
  And mix'd her wailings with the raving storm.

5

Wild to my heart the filial pulses glow:
  'Twas Caledonia's trophied shield I view'd,
Her form majestic droop'd in pensive woe,
  The lightning of her eye in tears imbued;

6

Revers'd that spear redoubtable in war,
  Reclined that banner, erst in fields unfurl'd,
That like a deathful meteor gleam'd afar,
  And brav'd the mighty monarchs of the world.

7

'My patriot son fills an untimely grave!'
  With accents wild and lifted arms, she cried;
'Low lies the hand that oft was stretch'd to save,
  Low lies the heart that swell'd with honor's pride.

8

'A weeping country joins a widow's tear;
  The helpless poor mix with the orphan's cry;
The drooping Arts surround their patron's bier;
  And grateful Science heaves the heart-felt sigh.

9

'I saw my sons resume their ancient fire;
  I saw fair Freedom's blossoms richly blow.
But ah! how hope is born but to expire!
  Relentless fate has laid their guardian low.

10

'My patriot falls, but shall he lie unsung,
    While empty greatness saves a worthless name?
No: every Muse shall join her tuneful tongue,
    And future ages hear his growing fame.

11

'And I will join a mother's tender cares
    Thro' future times to make his virtues last,
That distant years may boast of other Blairs!'—
    She said, and vanish'd with the sweeping blast.

ON THE DEATH OF LORD PRESIDENT DUNDAS

Lone on the bleaky hills, the straying flocks
Shun the fierce storms among the sheltering rocks;
Down foam the rivulets, red with dashing rains;
The gathering floods burst o'er the distant plains;
Beneath the blast the leafless forests groan;
The hollow caves return a hollow moan.
Ye hills, ye plains, ye forests, and ye caves,
Ye howling winds, and wintry swelling waves,
Unheard, unseen, by human ear or eye,
Sad to your sympathetic glooms I fly,
Where to the whistling blast and water's roar
Pale Scotia's recent would I may deplore!
O heavy loss, thy country ill could bear!
A loss these evil days can ne'er repair!
Justice, the high vicegerent of her God,
Her doubtful balance eyed, and sway'd her rod;
Hearing the tidings of the fatal blow,
She sank, abandon'd to the wildest woe.
Wrongs, injuries, from many a darksome den,
Now gay in hope explore the paths of men.
See from his cavern grim Oppression rise,
And throw on Poverty his cruel eyes!
Keen on the helpless victim let him fly,
And stifle, dark, the feebly-bursting cry!
Mark Ruffian Violence, distained with crimes,
Rousing elate in these degenerate times!
View unsuspecting Innocence a prey,
As guileful Fraud points out the erring way;

While subtile Litigation's pliant tongue
The life-blood equal sucks of Right and Wrong!
Hark, injur'd Want recounts th' unlisten'd tale,
And much-wrong'd Mis'ry pours th' unpitied wail!

Ye dark, waste hills, ye brown, unsightly plains,
Congenial scenes, ye soothe my mournful strains.
Ye tempests, rage! ye turbid torrents, roll!
Ye suit the joyless tenor of my soul.
Life's social haunts and pleasures I resign;
Be nameless wilds and lonely wanderings mine,
To mourn the woes my country must endure:
That wound degenerate ages cannot cure.

ELEGY ON WILLIE NICOL'S MARE

TUNE: *Chevy Chase*

I

Peg Nicholson was a good bay mare
   As ever trod on airn;   iron
But now she's floating down the Nith,
   And past the mouth o' Cairn.

2

Peg Nicholson was a good bay mare,
   An' rode thro' thick an' thin;
But now she's floating down the Nith,
   And wanting even the skin.

3

Peg Nicholson was a good bay mare,
   And ance she bore a priest;
But now she's floating down the Nith,
   For Solway fish a feast.

4

Peg Nicholson was a good bay mare,
   An' the priest he rode her sair;   hard
And much oppress'd, and bruis'd she was,
   As priest-rid cattle are.

LINES ON FERGUSSON

1

Ill-fated genius! Heaven-taught Fergusson!
   What heart that feels, and will not yield a tear
To think Life's sun did set, e'er well begun
   To shed its influence on thy bright career!

2

O, why should truest Worth and Genuis pine
   Beneath the iron grasp of Want and Woe,
While titled knaves and idiot-greatness shine
   In all the splendour Fortune can bestow?

ELEGY ON THE LATE MISS BURNET OF MONBODDO

1

Life ne'er exulted in so rich a prize
   As Burnet, lovely from her native skies;
Nor envious Death so triumph'd in a blow
   As that which laid th' accomplish'd Burnet low.

2

Thy form and mind, sweet maid, can I forget?
   In richest ore the brightest jewel set!
In thee high Heaven above was truest shown,
   For by His noblest work the Godhead best is known.

3

In vain ye flaunt in summer's pride, ye groves!
   Thou crystal streamlet with thy flowery shore,
Ye woodland choir that chaunt your idle loves,
   Ye cease to charm: Eliza is no more.

4

Ye heathy wstes immix'd with reedy fens,
   Ye mossy streams with sedge and rushes stor'd,
Ye rugged cliffs o'er hanging dreary glens,
   To you I fly: ye with my soul accord.

5

Princes whose cumb'rous pride was all their worth,
    Shall venal lays their pompous exit hail,
And thou, sweet Excellence! forsake our earth,
    And not a Muse with honest grief bewail?

6

We saw thee shine in youth and beauty's pride
    And Virtue's light, that beams beyond the spheres;
But, like the sun eclips'd at morning tide,
    Thou left us darkling in a world of tears.

7

The parent's heart that nestled fond in thee,
    That heart how sunk, a prey to grief and care!
So deckt the woodbine sweet yon aged tree,
    So, rudely ravish'd, left it bleak and bare.

PEGASUS AT WANLOCKHEAD

1

With Pegasus upon a day
    Apollo, weary flying
(Through frosty hills the journey lay),
    On foot the way was plying.

2

Poor slip-shod, giddy Pegasus
    Was but a sorry walker;
To Vulcan then Apollo goes
    To get a frosty caulker.

3

Obliging Vulcan fell to work,
    Threw by his coat and bonnet,
And did Sol's business in a crack—
    Sol paid him in a sonnet.

4

Ye Vulcan's sons of Wanlockhead,
    Pity my sad disaster!
My Pegasus is poorly shod—
    I'll pay you like my master!

ON SOME COMMEMORATIONS OF THOMSON

1

Dost thou not rise, indignant Shade,
    And smmile wi' spurning scorn,
When they wha wad hae starved thy life
    Thy senseless turf adorn?

2

such

would have
One farthing

They wha about thee mak sic fuss
    Now thou art but a name,
Wad seen thee damn'd ere they had spar'd
    Ae plack to fill thy wame.

3

climb; hill

clutched
hard-

Helpless, alane, thou clamb the brae
    Wi' meikle honest toil,
And claucht th' unfading garland there,
    Thy sair-won, rightful spoil.

4

And wear it there! and call aloud
    This axiom undoubted:—
Would thou hae Nobles' patronage?
    First learn to live without it!

5

those that have

'To whom hae much, more shall be given'
    Is every great man's faith;
But he, the helpless, needful wretch,
    Shall lose the mite he hath.

ON JOHN M'MURDO

Best be M'Murdo to his latest day!
No envious cloud o'ercast his evening ray!
No wrinkle furrow'd by the hand of care,
Nor ever sorrow, add one silver hair!
O may no son the father's honor stain,
Nor ever daughter give the mother pain!

ON HEARING A THRUSH SING IN A MORNING WALK IN JANUARY

Sing on, sweet thrush, upon the leafless bough,
Sing on, sweet bird, I listen to thy strain:
See aged Winter, 'mid his surly reign,
At thy blythe carol clears his furrowed brow.
So in lone Poverty's dominion drear
Sits meek Content with light, unanxious heart,
Welcomes the rapid moments, bids them part,
Nor asks if they bring ought to hope or fear.
I thank Thee, Author of this opening day,
Thou whose bright sun now gilds yon orient skies!
Riches denied, Thy boon was purer joys:
What wealth could never give nor take away!
Yet come, thou child of Poverty and Care,
The mite high Heavn'n bestowed, that mite with thee
    I'll share.

IMPROMPTU ON MRS. RIDDELL'S BIRTHDAY

4TH NOVEMBER, 1793

I

Old Winter, with his frosty beard,
Thus once to Jove his prayer preferred:—
'What have I done of all the year,
To bear this hated doom severe?
My cheerless suns no pleasure know;
Night's horrid car drags dreary slow;
My dismal months no joys are crowning,
But spleeny, English hanging, drowning.

2

Now Jove, for once be mighty civil:
To counterbalance all this evil
Give me, and I've no more to say,
Give me Maria's natal day!
That brilliant gift shall so enrich me,
Spring, Summer, Autumn, cannot match me.'
'Tis done!' says Jove; so ends my story,
And Winter once rejoiced in glory.

SONNET ON THE DEATH OF ROBERT RIDDELL OF GLENRIDDELL

No more, ye warblers of the wood, no more,
Nor pour your descant grating on my soul!
Thou young-eyed Spring, gay in thy verdant stole,
More welcome were to me grim Winter's wildest roar!
How can ye charm, ye flowers, with all your dyes?
Ye blow upon the sod that wraps my friend.
How can I to the tuneful strain attend?
That strain flows round the untimely tomb where Riddell lies.
Yes, pour, ye warblers, pour the notes of woe,
And soothe the Virtues weeping o'er his bier!
The man of worth—and 'hath not left his peer'!—
Is in his 'narrow house' for ever darkly low.
Thee, Spring, again with joy shall others greet;
Me, memory of my loss will only meet.

A SONNET UPON SONNETS

Fourteen, a sonneteer thy praises sings;
What magic myst'ries in that number lie!
Your hen hath fourteen eggs beneath her wings
That fourteen chickens to the roost may fly.
Fourteen full pounds the jockey's stone must be;
His age fourteen—a horse's prime is past.
Fourteen long hours too oft the Bard must fast;
Fourteen bright bumpers—bliss he ne'er must see!
Before fourteen, a dozen yields the strife;
Before fourteen—e'en thirteen's strength is vain.
Fourteen good years—a woman gives us life;
Fourteen good men—we lose that life again.

What lucubrations can be more upon it?
Fourteen good measur'd verses make a sonnet.

TRAGIC FRAGMENT

All villain as I am—a damnèd wretch,
A hardened, stubborn, unrepenting sinner—
Still my heart melts at human wretchedness,
And with sincere, tho' unavailing, sighs
I view the helpless children of distress.
With tears indignant I behold the oppressor
Rejoicing in the honest man's destruction,
Whose unsubmitting heart was all his crime.
Ev'n you, ye hapless crew! I pity you;
Ye, whom the seeming good think sin to pity:
Ye poor, despised, abandoned vagabonds,
Whom Vice, as usual, has turn'd o'er to ruin.
Oh! but for friends and interposing Heaven,
I had been driven forth, like you forlorn,
The most detested, worthless wretch among you!
O injured God! Thy goodness has endow'd me
With talents passing most of my compeers,
Which I in just proportion have abused,
As far surpassing other common villains
As Thou in natural parts has given me more.

REMORSE

Of all the numerous ills that hurt our peace,
That press the soul, or wring the mind with anguish,
Beyond comparison the worst are those
By our own folly, or our guilt brought on:
In ev'ry other circumstance, the mind
Has this to say:—'It was no deed of mine.'
But, when to all the evil of misfortune
This sting is added:—'Blame thy foolish self!'
Or, worser far, the pangs of keen remorse,
The torturing, gnawing consciousness of guilt,
Of guilt, perhaps, where we've involvèd others,
The young, the innocent, who fondly lov'd us;
Nay, more, that very love their cause of ruin!
O burning Hell! in all thy store of torments
There's not a keener lash!

Lives there a man so firm, who, while his heart
Feels all the bitter horrors of his crime,
Can reason down its agonizing throbs,
And, after proper purpose of amendment,
Can firmly force his jarring thoughts to peace?
O happy, happy, enviable man!
O glorious magnanimity of soul!

RUSTICITY'S UNGAINLY FORM

1

Rusticity's ungainly form
   May cloud the highest mind;
But when the heart is nobly warm,
   The good excuse will find.

2

Propriety's cold, cautious rules
   Warm Fervour may o'erlook;
But spare poor Sensibility
   Th' ungentle, harsh rebuke.

ON WILLIAM CREECH

A little upright, pert, tart, tripping wight,
And still his precious self his dear delight;
Who loves his own smart shadow in the streets
Better than e'er the fairest She he meets.
Much specious lore, but little understood
(Veneering oft outshines the solid wood),
His solid sense by inches you must tell,
But mete his subtle cunning by the ell!
A man of fashion, too, he made his tour,
Learn'd 'Vive la bagatelle et vive l'amour':
So travell'd monkies their grimace improve,
Polish their grin—nay, sigh for ladies' love!
His meddling vanity, a busy fiend,
Still making work his selfish craft must mend.

ON WILLIAM SMELLIE

.   .   .   .   .   Crochallan came:
The old cock'd hat, the brown surtout the same;
His grisly beard just bristling in its might
('Twas four long nights and days to shaving-night);
His uncomb'd, hoary locks, wild-staring, thatch'd
A head for thought profound and clear unmatch'd;
Yet, tho' his caustic wit was biting rude,
His heart was warm, benevolent, and good.

SKETCH FOR AN ELEGY

1

Craigdarroch, fam'd for speaking art
And every virtue of the heart,
Stops short, nor can a word impart
       To end his sentence,
When mem'ry strikes him like a dart
        With auld acquaintance.

2

Black James—whase wit was never laith,   *loth*
But, like a sword had tint the sheath,   *which had lost*
Ay ready for the work o' death—
       He turns aside,
And strains wi' suffocating breath
        His grief to hide.

3

Even Philosophic Smellie tries
To choak the stream that floods his eyes: *choke*
So Moses wi' a hazel-rice   *-rod*
       Came o'er the stane;
But, tho' it cost him speaking twice,
        It gush'd amain.

4

vaults

Go to your marble graffs, ye great,
In a' the tinkler-trash of state!
But by thy honest turf I'll wait,
            Thou man of worth,

one

And weep the ae best fallow's fate
            E'er lay in earth!

PASSION'S CRY

Mild zephyrs waft thee to life's farthest shore,
Nor think of me and my distresses more!
Falsehood accurst! No! Still I beg a place,
Still near thy heart some little, little trace!
For that dear trace the world I would resign:
O, let me live, and die, and think it mine!

By all I lov'd, neglected, and forgot,
No friendly face e'er lights my squalid cot.
Shunn'd, hated, wrong'd, unpitied, unredrest
The mock'd quotation of the scorner's jest;
Ev'n the poor support of my wretched life,
Snatched by the violence of legal strife;
Oft grateful for my very daily bread.
To those my family's once large bounty fed;
A welcome inmate at their homely fare,
My griefs, my woes, my sighs, my tears they share:
Their vulgar souls unlike the souls refined,
The fashion'd marble of the polish'd mind.

'I burn, I burn, as when thro' ripen'd corn
By driving winds the crackling fames are borne.'
Now, maddening-wild, I curse that fatal night,
Now bless the hour that charm'd my guilty sight.
In vain the Laws their feeble force oppose:
Chain'd at his feet, they groan Love's vanquish'd foes.
In vain Religion meets my shrinking eye:
I dare not combat, but I turn and fly.
Conscience in vain upbraids th' unhallow'd fire.
Love grasps his scorpions—stifled they expire.
Reason drops headlong from his sacred throne,
Your dear idea reigns, and reigns alone;
Each thought intoxicated homage yields,

And riots wanton in forbidden fields.

By all on high adoring mortals know;
By all the conscious villain fears below;
By what, alas! much more my soul alarms—
My doubtful hopes once more to fill thy arms—
Ev'n shouldst thou, false, forswear the guilty tie,
Thine and thine only I must live and die!

TO CLARINDA

In vain would Prudence with decorous sneer
Point out a cens'ring world, and bid me fear:
Above that world on wings of love I rise.
A know its worst, and can that worst doopine.
Wronged, injured, shunned, unpitied, unredrest.
'The mocked quotation of the scorner's jest,'
Let Prudence' direst bodements on me fall,
Clarinda, rich reward! o'erpays them all.
As low-borne mists before the sun remove,
So shines, so reigns unrivalled mighty LOVE.
In vain the laws their feeble force oppose;
Chained at his feet, they groan Love's vanquished foes;
In vain Religion meets my shrinking eye;
I dare not combat, but I turn and fly:
Conscience in vain upbraids th' unhallowed fire;
Love grasps his scorpions, stifled they expire:
Reason drops headlong from his sacred throne,
Thy dear idea reigns, and reigns alone;
Each thought intoxicated homage yields,
And riots wanton in forbidden fields.

By all on High, adoring mortals know!
By all the conscious villain fears below,
By what, Alas! much more my soul alarms,
My doubtful hopes once more to fill thy arms!
E'en shouldst thou, false, forswear each guilty tie,
Thine, and thine only, I must live and die!

THE CARES O' LOVE

HE

The cares o' Love are sweeter far
   Than onie other pleasure;
And if sae dear its sorrows are,
   Enjoyment, what a treasure!

SHE

I fear to try, I dare na try
   A passion sae ensnaring;
For light's her heart and blythe's her song
   That for nae man is caring.

EPIGRAM ON SAID OCCASION

1

O Death, had'st thou but spar'd his life,
   Whom we this day lament!
We freely wad exchanged the wife,
   An' a' been weel content.

2

grave   Ev'n as he is, cauld in his graff,
exchange   The swap we yet will do't;
   Tak thou the carlin's carcase aff,
into the bargain   Thou'se get the saul o' boot.

ANOTHER

One Queen Artemisa, as old stories tell,
When depriv'd of her husband she lovèd so well,
In respect for the love and affection he'd show'd her,
She reduc'd him to dust and she drank up the powder.
But Queen Netherplace, of a diff'rent complexion,
When call'd on to order the fun'ral direction,
Would have eat her dead lord, on a slender pretence,
Not to show her respect, but—to save the expense!

AT ROSLIN INN

My blessings on ye, honest wife!
  I ne'er was here before;
Ye've wealth o' gear for spoon and knife: stuff
  Heart could not wish for more.
Heav'n keep you clear o' sturt and strife,   worry
  Till far ayont fourscore,   beyond
And by the Lord o' death and life,
  I'll ne'er gae by your door!   go

TO AN ARTIST

DEAR——, I'll gie ye some advice,
  You'll tak it no uncivil:
You shouldna paint at angels, man,
  But try and paint the Devil.
To paint an angel's kittle wark,   delicate
  Wi' Nick there's little danger: Satan
You'll easy draw a lang-kent face,   long-known
  But no sae weel a stranger.

ON ELPHINSTONE'S TRANSLATION OF MARTIAL

O thou whom Poesy abhors,
Whom Prose has turnèd out of doors,
Heard'st thou yon groan?—Proceed no further!   that
'Twas laurel'd Martial calling 'Murther!'

ON JOHNSON'S OPINION OF HAMPDEN

For shame!
Let Folly and Knavery
Freedom oppose:
'Tis suicide, Genius,
To mix with her foes.

UNDER THE PORTRAIT OF MISS BURNS

Cease, ye prudes, your envious railing!
Lovely Burns has charms: confess!
True it is she had ae failing:
Had ae woman ever less?

one

ON MISS AINSLIE IN CHURCH

Fair maid, you need not take the hint,
Nor idle texts pursue;
'Twas guilty sinners that he meant,
Not angels such as you.

AT INVERARAY

1

Whoe'er he be that sojourns here,
I pity much his case,
Unless he come to wait upon
The Lord their God, 'His Grace.'

2

There's naething here but Highland pride
And Highland scab and hunger:
If Providence has sent me here,
'Twas surely in an anger.

AT CARRON IRONWORKS

We cam na here to view your warks
In hopes to be mair wise,
But only, lest we gang to Hell,
It may be nae surprise.
But when we tirl'd at your door
Your porter dought na bear us:
Sae may, should we to Hell's yetts come,
Your billie Satan sair us.

not; works

go

knocked
could not permit
gates
fellow; serve

ON SEEING THE ROYAL PALACE AT STIRLING IN RUINS

Here Stewarts once in glory reign'd,
And laws for Scotland's weal ordain'd;
But now unroof'd their palace stands,
Their sceptre fallen to other hands:
Fallen indeed, and to the earth,
Whence grovelling reptiles take their birth!
The injured Stewart line is gone,
A race outlandish fills their throne:
An idiot race, to honour lost—
Who know them best despire them most.

REPLY TO THE THREAT OF A CENSORIOUS CRITIC

With Æsop's lion, Burns says:—'Sore I feel
Each other blow: but damn that ass's heel!'

A HIGHLAND WELCOME

When Death's dark stream I ferry o'er
    (A time that surely shall come),
In Heaven itself I'll ask no more
    Than just a Highland welcome.

AT WHIGHAM'S INN, SANQUHAR

Envy, if thy jaundiced eye
Through this window chance to spy,
To thy sorrow thou shalt find,
All that's generous, all that's kind.
Friendship, virtue, every grace,
Dwelling in this happy place.

VERSICLES ON SIGN-POSTS

1

He looked
Just as your sign-post Lions do,
With aspect fierce and quite as harmless too.

2

(PATIENT STUPIDITY)

So heavy, passive to the tempest's shocks,
Dull on the sign-post stands the stupid ox.

3

His face with smile eternal drest
Just like the landlord to his guest,
High as they hang with creaking din
To index out the Country Inn.

4

A head, pure, sinless quite of brain and soul,
The very image of a barber's poll:
Just shews a human face, and wears a wig,
And looks, when well friseur'd, amazing big.

ON MISS JEAN SCOTT

O, had each Scot of ancient times
   Been, Jeanie Scott, as thou art,
The bravest heart on English ground
   Had yielded like a coward.

ON CAPTAIN FRANCIS GROSE

The Devil got notice that Grose was a-dying,
So whip! at the summons, old Satan came flying;
But when he approach'd where poor Francis lay moaning,
And saw each bed-post with its burthen a-groaning,
Astonish'd, confounded, cries Satan:—'By God,
I'd want him ere take such a damnable load!'

AN EXTEMPORANEOUS EFFUSION ON BEING APPOINTED TO THE EXCISE

Searching auld wives' barrels,
   Ochon, the day
That clarty barm should stain my laurels;   dirty
   But—what'll ye say?
These movin' things ca'd wives an' weans   children
   Wad move the very hearts o' stanes.

ON MISS DAVIES

Ask why God made the gem so small,
   And why so huge the granite?
Because God meant mankind should set
   That higher value on it.

ON A BEAUTIFUL COUNTRY SEAT

We grant they're thine, those beauties all,
   So lovely in our eye:
Keep them, thou eunuch, Cardoness,
   For others to enjoy.

THE TYRANT WIFE

Curs'd be the man, the poorest wretch in life,
The crouching vassal to the tyrant wife!
Who has no will but by her high permission;
Who has not sixpence but in her possession;
Who must to her his dear friend's secret tell;
Who dreads a curtain lecture worse than hell!
Were such the wife had fallen to my part,
I'd break her spirit, or I'd break her heart:
I'd charm her with the magic of a switch,
I'd kiss her maids, and kick the perverse bitch.

AT JOHN BACON'S BROWNHILL INN

At Brownhill we always get dainty good cheer
And plenty of bacon each day in the year;
every   We've a' thing that's nice, and mostly in season:
But why always bacon?—come, tell me the reason?

THE TOADEATER

Of Lordly acquaintance you boast,
   And the Dukes that you dined with yestreen;
Yet an insect's an insect at most,
   Tho' it crawl on the curl of a Queen!

IN LAMINGTON KIRK

As cauld a wind as ever blew,
A cauld kirk, and in't but few,
As cauld a minister's ever spak—
hot   Ye'se a' be het or I come back!

THE KEEKIN GLASS

Owl-   How daur ye ca' me 'Howlet-face,'
   Ye blear-e'ed, wither'd spectre?
looking-   Ye only spied the keekin-glass,
   An' there ye saw your picture.

AT THE GLOBE TAVERN, DUMFRIES

1

The greybeard, old Wisdom, may boast of his treasures,
   Give me with gay Folly to live!
I grant him his calm-blooded, time-settled pleasures,
   But Folly has raptures to give.

2

My bottle is a holy pool,
sorrow   That heals the wounds o' care an' dool,
And pleasure is a wanton trout—
An ye drink it, ye'll find him out.

3

In politics if thou would'st mix,
    And mean thy fortunes be;
Bear this in mind: Be deaf and blind,
    Let great folks hear and see.

YE TRUE LOYAL NATIVES

Ye true 'Loyal Natives' attend to my song:
In uproar and riot rejoice the night long!
From Envy and Hatred your core is exempt,   corps
But where is your shield from the darts of Contempt?

ON COMMISSARY GOLDIE'S BRAINS

Lord, to account who does Thee call,
    Or e'er dispute Thy pleasure?
Else why within so thick a wall
    Enclose so poor a treasure?

EXTEMPORE:

ON BEING TOLD BY W—— L—— OF THE CUSTOMS, DUBLIN,
THAT COMMISSARY GOLDIE DID NOT SEEM DISPOSED TO
PUSH THE BOTTLE

Friend Commissar, since we are met and happy,
Pray why should we part without having more nappy?
Bring in t'other bottle, for faith I am dry—
Thy drink thou can'st part with and neither can I.

IN A LADY'S POCKET BOOK

Grant me, indulgent Heaven, that I may live
To see the miscreants feel the pains they give!
Deal Freedom's sacred treasures free as air,
Till Slave and Despot be but things that were!

EPIGRAMS ON THE EARL OF GALLOWAY

1

What does thou in that mansion fair?
  Flit, Galloway, and find
Some narrow, dirty, dungeon cave,
  The picture of thy mind.

2

No Stewart art thou, Galloway:
  The Stewarts all were brave.
Besides, the Stewarts were but fools,
  Not one of them a knave.

3

Bright ran thy line, O Galloway,
  Thro' many a far-famed sire!
So ran the far-famed Roman way,
  And ended in a mire.

4

Spare me thy vengeance, Galloway!
  In quiet let me live:
I ask no kindness at thy hand,
  For thou hast none to give.

ON AN OLD ACQUAINTANCE WHO SEEMED TO PASS THE BARD WITHOUT NOTICE

1

Dost hang thy head, Billy, asham'd that thou knowest me?
'Tis paying in kind a just debt that thou owest me.

2

Dost blush, my dear Billy, asham'd of thyself,
  A Fool and a Cuckold together?
The fault is not thine, insignificant elf,
  Thou wast not consulted in either.

EXTEMPORE

ON BEING REQUESTED TO WRITE ON THE BLANK LEAF OF AN ELEGANTLY BOUND BIBLE

Free thro' the leaves ye maggots make your windings;
But for the Owner's sake oh spare the bindings!

EPIGRAM ON JAMES SWAN

(ON HIS BEING ELECTED COUNCILLOR AND BAILLIE, 22ND SEPTEMBER, 1794)

Baillie Swan, Baillie Swan,
Let you do what you can—
God hae mercy on honest Dumfries;
But e'er the year's done,
Good Lord! Provost John
Will find that his *Swans* are but *Geese.*

EPITAPH FOR J—— H——

WRITER IN AYR

Here lies a Scots mile of a chiel,
If he's in heaven, Lord, fill him weel!

ON ALEXANDER FINDLATER, SUPERVISOR, DUMFRIES EXCISE

The Exciseman and the gentleman in one
I point thee Findlater, for thou'st the man

ON EDMUND BURKE BY AN OPPONENT AND A FRIEND TO WARREN HASTINGS

Oft have I wonder'd that on Irish ground
No poisonous Reptile has ever been found:
Revealed stands the secret of great Nature's work:
She preservèd her poison to create a Burke!

ON WEDDING RINGS

She asked why wedding rings are made of gold;
I venture this to instruct her;
Why, madam, love and lightning are the same,
On earth they glance, from Heaven they came.
Love is the soul's electric flame,
And gold its best conductor.

TO A VIOLET

Go, little flower: go bid thy name impart
Each hope, each wish, each beating of my heart;
Go, soothe her sorrows, bid all anguish cease,
Go, be the bearer of thyself—heart's ease.

EPIGRAM

TO —— OF C——DER, ON SOME GENTLEMEN BEING REFUSED
PERMISSION TO TAKE A VIEW OF THE ARCHITECTURE, ETC.,
OF C——DERHOUSE

Why shut your doors and windows thus,
    With such a jealous dread?
We are no children come to eat
    Your works of gingerbread.

EXCHANGE OF EPIGRAMS

BOYD:

Dear Burns, your wit how can you flash
    On such a wretch as this is?

BURNS:

Dear Boyd, how can I let him pass,
    The hangman so remiss is?

ON MR. PITT'S HAIR-POWDER TAX

Pray, Billy Pitt, explain thy rigs,
    This new poll-tax of thine!
'I mean to mark the GUINEA pigs
    From other common SWINE.'

ON THE LAIRD OF LAGGAN

When Morine, deceas'd, to the Devil went down,
'Twas nothing would serve him but Satan's own crown.
'Thy fool's head,' quoth Satan, 'that crown shall wear
        never:
I grant thou'rt as wicked, but not quite so clever.'

ON MARIA RIDDELL

'Praise Woman still,' his lordship roars,
    'Deserv'd or not, no matter!'
But thee whom all my soul adores,
    There Flattery cannot flatter!
Maria, all my thought and dream,
    Inspires my vocal shell:
The more I praise my lovely theme,
    The more the truth I tell.

ON MISS FONTENELLE

Sweet naïveté of feature,
    Simple, wild, enchanting elf,
Not to thee, but thanks to Nature
    Thou art acting but thyself.
Wert thou awkward, stiff, affected,
    Spurning Nature, torturing art,
Loves and Graces all rejected,
    Then indeed thou'dst act a part.

KIRK AND STATE EXCISEMEN

Ye men of wit and wealth, why all this sneering
'Gainst poor Excisemen? Give the cause a hearing.
What are your Landlord's rent-rolls? Taxing ledgers!
What Premiers? What ev'n Monarchs? Mighty Gaugers!
Nay, what are Priests (those seeming godly wisemen)?
What are they, pray, but Spiritual Excisemen!

ON THANKSGIVING FOR A NATIONAL VICTORY

Ye hypocrites! are these your pranks?
To murder men, and give God thanks?
Desist for shame! Proceed no further:
God won't accept your thanks for Murther.

PINNED TO MRS. WALTER RIDDELL'S CARRIAGE

If you rattle along like your mistress's tongue,
    Your speed will out-rival the dart;
But, a fly for your load, you'll break down on the road,
    If your stuff be as rotten's her heart.

TO DR. MAXWELL

ON MISS JESSY STAIG'S RECOVERY

Maxwell, if merit here your crave,
    That merit I deny:
You save fair Jessie from the grave!—
    An Angel could not die!

TO THE BEAUTIFUL MISS ELIZA J——N

ON HER PRINCIPLES OF LIBERTY AND EQUALITY

How, 'Liberty!' Girl, can it be by thee nam'd?
'Equality,' too! Hussey, art not asham'd?
Free and Equal indeed, while mankind thou enchainest,
And over their hearts a proud Despot so reignest.

TO THE HON. WM. R. MAULE OF PANMURE

EXTEMPORE:

ON SEEING THE HON. WM. R. MAULE OF PANMURE DRIVING
AWAY IN HIS FINE AND ELEGANT PHAETON ON THE RACE
GROUND AT TINWALD DOWNS, OCTOBER, 1794

Thou Fool, in thy phaeton towering.
    Art proud when that phaeton's prais'd?
'Tis the pride of a Thief's exhibition
    When higher his pillory's rais'd.

ON SEEING MRS. KEMBLE IN YARICO

Kemble, thou cur'st my unbelief
    Of Moses and his rod:
At Yarico's sweet notes of grief
    The rock with tears had flow'd.

ON DR. BABINGTON'S LOOKS

That there is a falsehood in his looks
    I must and will deny:
They say their Master is a knave,
    And sure they do not lie.

ON ANDREW TURNER

In Se'enteen Hunder'n Forty-Nine
The Deil gat stuff to mak a swine,
    An' coost it in a corner;
But wilily he chang'd his plan,
An' shap'd it something like a man,
    An' ca'd it Andrew Turner.

chucked

THE SOLEMN LEAGUE AND COVENANT

The Solemn League and Covenant
    Now brings a smile, now brings a tear.
But sacred Freedom, too, was theirs:
    If thou'rt a slave, indulge thy sneer.

TO JOHN SYME OF RYEDALE

WITH A PRESENT OF A DOZEN OF PORTER

O had the malt thy strength of mind,
    Or hops the flavour of thy wit,
'Twere drink for first of human kind—
    A gift that e'en for Syme were fit.

ON A GOBLET

There's Death in the cup, so beware!
    Nay, more—there is danger in touching!
But who can avoid the fell snare?
    The man and his wine's so bewitching!

APOLOGY TO JOHN SYME

No more of your guests, be they titled or not,
   And cookery the first in the nation:
Who is proof to thy personal converse and wit
   Is proof to all other temptation.

TO CAPTAIN GORDON

ON BEING ASKED WHY I WAS NOT TO BE OF THE PARTY WITH
HIM AND HIS BROTHER KENMURE AT SYME'S

1

Dost ask, dear Captain, why from Syme
   I have no invitation,
When well he knows he has with him
   My first friends in the nation?

2

Is it because I love to toast,
   And round the bottle hurl?
No! there conjecture wild is lost,
   For Syme, by God, 's no churl!

3

Is't lest with bawdy jests I bore,
   As oft the matter of fact is?
No! Syme the theory can't abhor—
   Who loves so well the practice.

4

Is it a fear I should avow
   Some heresy seditious?
No! Syme (but this is *entre nous*)
   Is quite an old Tiresias.

5

In vain Conjecture thus would flit
   Thro' mental clime and season:
In short, dear Captain, Syme's a Wit—
   Who asks of Wits a reason?

6

Yet must I still the *sort* deplore
  That to my griefs adds one more,
In balking me the social hour
  With you and noble Kenmure.

ON MR. JAMES GRACIE

Gracie, thou art a man of worth,
  O, be thou Dean for ever!
May he be damn'd to Hell henceforth,
challenges Who fauts thy weight or measure!

AT FRIARS CARSE HERMITAGE

To Riddell, much-lamented man,
  This ivied cot was dear:
Wand'rer, dost value matchless worth?
  This ivied cot revere.

FOR AN ALTAR OF INDEPENDENCE

AT KERROUGHTRIE, THE SEAT OF MR. HERON

Thou of an independent mind,
With soul resolv'd, with soul resign'd,
Prepar'd Power's proudest frown to brave,
Who wilt not be, nor have a slave,
Virtue alone who dost revere,
Thy own approach alone dost fear:
Approach this shrine, and worship here.

VERSICLES TO JESSIE LEWARS

THE TOAST

Fill me with the rosy wine;
Call a toast, a toast divine;
Give the Poet's darling flame;
Lovely Jessie be her name:
Then thou mayest freely boast
Thou hast given a peerless toast.

THE MENAGERIE

1

Talk not to me of savages
   From Afric's burning sun!
No savage e'er can rend my heart
   As, Jessie, thou hast done.

2

But Jessie's lovely hand in mine
   A mutual faith to plight—
Not even to view the heavenly choir
   Would be so blest a sight.

JESSIE'S ILLNESS

Say, sages, what's the charm on earth
   Can turn Death's dart aside?
It is not purity and worth
   Else Jessie had not died!

HER RECOVERY

But rarely seen since Nature's birth
   The natives of the sky!
Yet still one seraph's left on earth,
   For Jessie did not die.

ON MARRIAGE

That hackney'd judge of human life,
   The Preacher and the King,
Observes:—'The man that gets a wife
   He gets a noble thing.'
But how capricious are mankind,
   Now loathing, now desirous!
We married men, how oft we find
   The best of things will tire us!

A POET'S GRACE

BEFORE MEAT

O Thou, who kindly dost provide
   For ev'ry creature's want!
We bless the God of Nature wide
   For all Thy goodness lent.
And if it please Thee, heavenly Guide,
   May never worse be sent;
But, whether granted or denied,
   Lord, bless us with content.

AFTER MEAT

O Thou, in whom we live and move,
   Who made the sea and shore,
Thy goodness constantly we prove,
   And, grateful, would adore;
And, if it please Thee, Power above!
   Still grant us with such store
The friend we trust, the fair we love,
   And we desire no more.

AT THE GLOBE TAVERN

BEFORE MEAT

I

O Lord, when hunger pinches sore,
   Do Thou stand us in stead,
And send us from Thy bounteous store
sheep's-head   A tup- or wether-head.

AFTER MEAT

I

Lord Thee we thank, and Thee alone,
   For temporal gifts we little merit!
At present we will ask no more:
   Let William Hislop bring the spirit.

2

O Lord, since we have feated thus,
　　Which we so little merit,
Let Meg now take the flesh away,　　　　　　　meat
　　And Jock bring in the spirit.

3

O Lord, we do Thee humbly thank
　　For that we little merit:
Now Jean may tak the flesh away,
　　And Will bring in the spirit.

EPITAPH ON A HENPECKED SQUIRE

As father Adam first was fool'd,
　　A case that's still too common,
Here lies a man a woman rul'd:
　　The Devil ruled the woman.

ON A CELEBRATED RULING ELDER

Here Souter Hood in death does sleep:　　　Cobbler
　　In hell, if he's gane thither,
Satan, gie him thy gear to keep;　　　　　　money
　　He'll haud it weel thegither.　　　　　　take good care
　　　　　　　　　　　　　　　　　　　　　　of it

ON A NOISY POLEMIC

Below thir stanes lie Jamie's banes:　　　those
　　O Death, it's my opinion,
Thou ne'er took such a bleth'rin bitch　　gabbling
　　Into thy dark dominion.

ON WEE JOHNIE

Hic jacet WEE *Johnie*

Whoe'er thou art, O reader, know,
　　That Death has murder'd Johnie,
An' here his *body* lies fu' low—
　　For *saul* he ne'er had onie.

FOR ROBERT AIKEN, Esq.

Know thou, O stranger to the fame
    Of this much lov'd, much honour'd name!
(For none that knew him need be told),
    A warmer heart Death ne'er made cold.

FOR GAVIN HAMILTON, Esq.

The poor man weeps—here Gavin sleeps,
    Whom canting wretches blam'd;
But with such as he, where'er he be,
    May I be sav'd or damn'd.

ON JAMES GRIEVE, LAIRD OF BOGHEAD, TARBOLTON

Here lies Boghead amang the dead
    In hopes to get salvation;
But if such as he in Heav'n may be,
    Then welcome—hail! damnation.

ON WM. MUIR IN TARBOLTON MILL

An honest man here lies at rest,
As e'er God with His image blest;
The friend of man, the friend of truth,
The friend of age, and guide of youth:
Few hearts like his—with virtue warm'd,
Few heads with knowledge so inform'd:
If there's another world, he lives in bliss;
If there is none, he made the best of this.

ON JOHN RANKINE

One; fellow   Ae day, as Death, that gruesome carl,
other world   Was driving to the tither warl'
                 A mixtie-maxtie, motley squad
                 And monie a guilt-bespotted lad:
preachers and   Black gowns of each denomination,
lawyers   And thieves of every rank and station,
                 From him that wears the star and garter

To him that wintles in a halter: swings
Asham'd himself to see the wretches,
He mutters, glow'ring at the bitches:—
'By God I'll not be seen behint them,
Nor 'mang the sp'ritual core present them,
Without at least ae honest man
To grace this damn'd infernal clan!'
By Adamhill a glance he threw,
'Lord God!' quoth he, 'I have it now,
There's just the man I want, i' faith!'
And quickly stoppit Rankine's breath.

ON TAM THE CHAPMAN

As Tam the chapman on a day
Wi' Death forgather'd by the way,
Weel pleas'd he greets a wight so famous.
And Death was nae less pleas'd wi' Thomas,
Wha cheerfully lays down his pack,
And there blaws up a hearty crack: chat
His social, friendly, honest heart
Sae tickled Death, they could na part;
Sae, after viewing knives and garters.
Death taks him hame to gie him quarters.

ON HOLY WILLIE

I

Here Holy Willie's sair worn clay   sore
    Taks up its last abode;
His saul has taen some other way—   soul
    I fear, the left-hand road.

2

Stop! there he is as sure's a gun!
    Poor, silly body, see him!   creature
Nae wonder he's as black's the grun—   ground
    Observe wha's standing wi' him!

3

brimstone

Your brunstane Devilship, I see,
    Has got him there before ye!
withhold; for a
little

But haud your nine-tail-cat a wee,
    Till ance you've heard my story.

4

Your pity I will not implore,
    For pity ye have nane.
Justice, alas! has gi'en him o'er,
    And mercy's day is gane.

5

But hear me, Sir, Deil as ye are,
    Look something to your credit:
dastard

A cuif like him wad stain your name,
known

If it were kent ye did it!

ON JOHN DOVE, INNKEEPER

1

Here lies Johnie Pigeon:
What was his religion
    Whae'er desires to ken
world

To some other warl'
old fellow

Maun follow the carl,
    For here Johnie Pigeon had nane!

2

Strong ale was ablution;
Small beer, persecution;
    A dram was *memento mori*;
But a full flowing bowl
Was the saving his soul,
    And port was celestial glory!

ON A WAG IN MAUCHLINE

1

Lament him, Mauchline husbands a',
  He aften did assist ye;
For had ye staid hale weeks awa',   whole
  Your wives they ne'er had missed ye!

2

Ye Mauchline bairns, as on ye pass
  To school in bands thegither,   together
O, tread ye lightly on his grass—
  Perhaps he was your father!

ON ROBERT FERGUSSON

ON THE TOMBSTONE IN THE CANONGATE CHURCHYARD
HERE LIES ROBERT FERGUSSON
BORN SEPT. 5TH, 1751
DIED OCT. 16TH, 1774

No sculptur'd Marble here, nor pompous lay,
  No storied Urn nor animated Bust;
This simple stone directs pale Scotia's way
  To pour her sorrow o'er the Poet's dust.

ADDITIONAL STANZAS

NOT INSCRIBED

1

She mourns, sweet tuneful youth, thy hapless fate:
  Tho' all the powers of song thy fancy fir'd,
Yet Luxury and Wealth lay by in State,
  And, thankless, starv'd what they so much admir'd.

2

This humble tribute with a tear he gives,
   A brother Bard—he can no more bestow:
But dear to fame thy Song immortal lives,
   A nobler monument than Art can show.

FOR WILLIAM NICOL

Ye maggots, feed on Nicol's brain,
such   For few six feasts you've gotten;
And fix your claws in Nicol's heart,
      For deil a bit o't's rotten.

FOR WILLIAM CRUIKSHANK, A.M.

Now honest William's gaen to Heaven,
I know not if it   I wat na gin't can mend him:
faults   The fauts he had in Latin lay,
knew   For name in English kent them.

ON ROBERT MUIR

What man could esteem, or what woman could love,
   Was he who lies under this sod:
If such Thou refusest admission above,
   Then whom wilt Thou Favour, Good God?

ON A LAP-DOG

1

In wood and wild, ye warbling throng,
   Your heavy loss deplore:
Now half extinct your powers of song—
   Sweet Echo is no more.

2

Ye jarring, screeching things around,
   Scream your discordant joys:
Now half your din of tuneless sound
   With Echo silent lies.

MONODY

ON A LADY (MARIA RIDDELL) FAMED FOR HER CAPRICE

1

How cold is that bosom which Folly once fired!
　How pale is that cheek where the rouge lately glisten'd!
How silent that tongue which the echoes oft tired!
　How dull is that ear which to flatt'ry so listen'd!

2

If sorrow and anguish their exit await,
　From friendship and dearest affection remov'd,
How doubly severer, Maria, thy fate!
　Thou diedst unwept, as thou livedst unlov'd.

3

Loves, Graces, and Virtues, I call not on you:
　So shy, grave, and distant, ye shed not a tear.
But come, all ye offspring of Folly so true.
　And flowers let us cull for Maria's cold bier!

4

We'll search through the garden for each silly flower,
　We'll roam thro' the forest for each idle weed,
But chiefly the nettle, so typical, shower,
　For none e'er approach'd her but rued the rash deed.

5

We'll sculpture the marble, we'll measure the lay:
　Here Vanity strums on her idiot lyre!
There keen Indignation shall dart on his prey,
　Which spurning Contempt shall redeem from his ire!

THE EPITAPH

Here lies, now a prey to insulting neglect,
　What once was a butterfly, gay in life's beam:
Want only of wisdom denied her respect,
　Want only of goodness denied her esteem.

FOR MR. WALTER RIDDELL

So vile was poor Wat, such a miscreant slave,
That the worms ev'n damn'd him when laid in his grave.
'In his scull there's a famine,' a starved reptile cries;
'And his heart, it is poison,' another replies.

ON A NOTED COXCOMB

(CAPT. WM. RODDICK, OF CORBISTON)

Light lay the earth on Billie's breast,
    His chicken heart's so tender;
But build a castle on his head—
    His scull will prop it under.

ON CAPT. LASCELLES

When Lascelles thought fit from his world to depart,
Some friends warmly spoke of embalming his heart.
A bystander whispers:—'Pray don't make so much o't—
The subject is poison, no reptile will touch it.'

ON A GALLOWAY LAIRD

(DAVID MAXWELL OF CARDONESS)
NOT QUITE SO WISE AS SOLOMON

Bless Jesus Christ, O Cardoness,
    With grateful lifted eyes,
Who taught that not the soul alone
    But body too shall rise!
For had He said:—'The soul alone
    From death I will deliver,'
Alas! alas! O Cardoness,
    Then hadst thou lain for ever!

ON WM. GRAHAM OF MOSSKNOWE

'Stop thief!' Dame Nature call'd to Death,
As Willie drew his latest breath:
'How shall I make a fool again?
My choicest model thou hast taen.'

ON JOHN BUSHBY OF TINWALD DOWNS

Here lies John Bushby—honest man!
Cheat him, Devil—if you can!

ON A SUICIDE

Here lies in earth a root of Hell
Set by the Deil's ain dibble:
This worthless body damn'd himsel
To save the Lord the trouble.

ON A SWEARING COXCOMB

Here cursing, swearing Burton lies,
A buck, a beau, or 'Dem my eyes!'
Who in his life did little good,
And his last words were:—'Dem my blood!'

ON JEAN ARMOUR

O Jeany, thou hast stolen away my soul!
In vain I strive against the lov'd idea:
Thy tender image sallies on my thoughts,
My firm resolves become an easy prey!

IN SOME FUTURE ECCENTRIC PLANET

Where Wit may sparkle all its rays,
    Uncurst with Caution's fears;
And Pleasure, basking in the blaze,
    Rejoice for endless years!

FOR GABRIEL RICHARDSON

Here brewer Gabriel's fire's extinct,
    And empty all his barrels:
He's blest—if as he brew'd, he drink—
    In upright, virtuous morals.

REEKIE'S TOWN

Now, God in heaven bless Reekie's town
    With plenty, joy and peace!
And may her wealth and fair renown
    To latest times increase ! ! !

ON AN INNKEEPER NICKNAMED 'THE MARQUIS'

Here lies a mock Marquis, whose titles were shamm'd.
If ever he rise, it will be to be damn'd.

CORN RIGS ARE BONIE

TUNE: *Corn Rigs*

CHORUS

Corn rigs, an' barley rigs,
An' corn rigs are bonie:
I'll ne'er forget that happy night,
Amang the rigs wi' Annie.

1

It was upon a Lammas night,
  When corn rigs are bonie,   ridges
Beneath the moon's unclouded light,
  I held awa to Annie;
The time flew by, wi' tentless heed;   careless
  Till, 'tween the late and early,   dark and dawn
Wi' sma' persuasion she agreed
  To see me thro' the barley.

2

The sky was blue, the wind was still,
  The moon was shining clearly;
I set her down, wi' right good will,
  Amang the rigs o' barley:
I ken't her heart ws a' my ain;   knew
  I lov'd her most sincerely;
I kiss'd her owre and owre again,
  Amang the rigs o' barley.

3

I lock'd her in my fond embrace;
  Her heart was beating rarely:
My blessings on that happy place,
  Amang the rigs o' barley!
But by the moon and stars so bright,
  That shone that hour so clearly!
She ay shall bless that happy night
  Amang the rigs o' barley.

4

I hae been blythe wi' comrades dear;
   I hae been merry drinking;
money-making   I hae been joyfu' gath'rin gear;
   I hae been happy thinking:
But a' the pleasures e'er I saw,
   Tho' three times doubl'd fairly—
That happy night was worth them a',
   Amang the rigs o' barley.

SONG: COMPOSED IN AUGUST
TUNE: *Port Gordon*

I

western   Now westlin winds and slaught'ring guns
   Bring Autumn's pleasant weather;
moorcock   The gorcock springs on whirring wings
   Amang the blooming heather:
Now waving grain, wide o'er the plain,
   Delights the weary farmer;
The moon shines bright, as I rove by night
   To muse upon my charmer.

2

The paitrick lo'es the fruitfu' fells,
   The plover lo'es the mountains;
The woodcock haunts the lonely dells,
   The soaring hern the fountains;
heron   Thro' lofty groves the cushat roves,
   The path o' man to shun it;
The hazel bush o'erhangs the thrush,
   The spreading thorn the linnet.

3

Thus ev'ry kind their pleasure find,
   The savage and the tender;
Some social join, and leagues combine,
   Some solitary wander:
Avaunt, away, the cruel sway!
   Tyrannic man's dominion!
The sportsman's joy, the murd'ring cry,
   The flutt'ring, gory pinion!

4

But, Peggy dear, the evening's clear,
    Thick flies the skimming swallow,
The sky is blue, the fields in view
    All fading-green and yellow:
Come let us stray our gladsome way,
    And view the charms of Nature;
The rustling corn, the fruited thorn,
    And ilka happy creature.   every

5

We'll gently walk, and sweetly talk,
    While the silent moon shines clearly;
I'll clasp thy waist, and, fondly prest,
    Swear how I lo'e thee dearly:
Not vernal show'rs to budding flow'rs,
    Not Autumn to the farmer,
So dear can be as thou to me,
    My fair, my lovely charmer!

FROM THEE ELIZA

TUNE: *Gilderoy*

1

From thee Eliza, I must go,
    And from my native shore:
The cruel fates between us throw
    A boundless ocean's roar;
But boundless oceans, roaring wide
    Between my Love and me,
They never, never can divide
    My heart and soul from thee.

2

Farewell, farewell, Eliza dear,
  The maid that I adore!
A boding voice is in mine ear,
  We part to meet no more!
But the latest throb that leaves my heart,
  While Death stands victor by,
That throb, Eliza, is thy part,
  And thine that latest sigh!

JOHN BARLEYCORN

A Ballad

TUNE: *Lull Me Beyond Thee*

1

There was three kings into the east,
  Three kings both great and high,
And they hae sworn a solemn oath
  John Barleycorn should die.

2

They took a plough and plough'd him down,
  Put clods upon his head,
And they hae sworn a solemn oath
  John Barleycorn was dead.

3

But the cheerful Spring came kindly on,
  And show'rs began to fall;
John Barleycorn got up again,
  And sore surpris'd them all.

4

The sultry suns of Summer came,
  And he grew thick and strong:
His head weel arm'd wi' pointed spears,
  That no one should him wrong.

5

The sober Autumn enter'd mild,
　　When he grew wan and pale;
His bending joints and drooping head
　　Show'd he began to fail.

6

His colour sicken'd more and more,
　　He faded into age;
And then his enemies began
　　To show their deadly rage.

7

They've taen a weapon long and sharp,
　　And cut him by the knee;
Then ty'd him fast upon a cart,
　　Like a rogue for forgerie.

8

They laid him down upon his back,
　　And cudgell'd him full sore.
They hung him up before the storm,
　　And turn'd him o'er and o'er.

9

They fillèd up a darksome pit
　　With water to the brim,
They heavèd in John Barleycorn—
　　There, let him sink or swim!

10

They laid him out upon the floor,
　　To work him farther woe;
And still, as signs of life appear'd,
　　They toss'd him to and fro.

11

They wasted o'er a scorching flame
　　The marrow of his bones;
But a miller us'd him worst of all,
　　For he crush'd him between two stones.

12

And they hae taen his very heart's blood,
   And drank it round and round;
And still the more and more they drank,
   Their joy did more abound.

13

John Barleycorn was a hero bold,
   Of noble enterprise;
For if you do but taste his blood,
   'Twill make your courage rise.

14

'Twill make a man forget his woe;
   'Twill heighten all his joy:
'Twill make the widow's heart to sing,
   Tho' the tear were in her eye.

15

Then let us toast John Barleycorn,
   Each man a glass in hand;
And may his great posterity
   Ne'er fail in old Scotlànd!

A FRAGMENT: WHEN GUILFORD GOOD

TUNE: *The Black Watch*

1

When Guildford good our pilot stood,
   An' did our hellim thraw, man;   *helm turn*
Ae night, at tea, began a plea,
   Within Americà, man:
Then up they gat the maskin-pat,   *tea-pot*
   And in the sea did jaw, man;   *dash*
An' did nae less, in full Congress,
   Than quite refuse our law, man.

2

Then thro' the lakes Montgomery takes,
    I wat he was na slaw, man;
Down Lowrie's Burn he took a turn,
    And Carleton did ca', man:
But yet, whatreck, he at Quebec   *what matter*
    Montgomery-like did fa', man,
Wi' sword in hand, before his band,
    Amang his en'mies a', man.

3

Poor Tammy Gage within a cage
    Was kept at Boston-ha', man;
Till Willie Howe took o'er the knowe   *hill*
    For Philadelphià, man;
Wi' sword an' gun he thought a sin
    Guid Christian bluid to draw, man;
But at New-York wi' knife an' fork
    Sir-Loin he hackèd sma', man.

4

Burgoyne gaed up, like spur an' whip,
    Till Fraser brave did fa', man;
Then lost his way, ae misty day,
    In Saratoga shaw, man.   *wood*
Cornwallis fought as lang's he dought,   *could*
    An' did the buckskins claw, man;
But Clinton's glaive frae rust to save,
    He hung it to the wa', man.

5

Then Montague, an' Guilford too,
    Began to fear a fa', man;
And Sackville doure, wha stood the stoure   *obstinate; fight*
    The German chief to thraw, man: *thwart*
For Paddy Burke, like onic Turk,
    Nae mercy had at a', man;
An' Charlie Fox threw by the box,
    An' lows'd his tinkler jaw, man.   *let loose*

6

Then Rockingham took up the game,
    Till death did on him ca', man;
When Shelburne meek held up his cheek,
    Conform to gospel law, man:
Saint Stephen's boys, wi' jarring noise,
    They did his measures thraw, man;
For North an' Fox united stocks,
    An' bore him to the wa', man.

7

The clubs an' hearts were Charlie's cartes:
    He swept the stakes awa', man,
Till the diamond's ace, of Indian race,
    Led him a sair *faux pas*, man:
cheers   The Saxon lads, wi' loud placads,
    On Chatham's boy did ca', man;
An' Scotland drew her pipe an' blew:
worst   'Up, Willie, waur them a', man!'

8

Behind the throne then Granville's gone,
    A secret word or twa, man;
sly   While slee Dundas arous'd the class
North of   Be-north the Roman wa', man:
garb   An' Chatham's wraith, in heav'nly graith,
    (Inspirèd bardies saw, man),
Wi' kindling eyes, cry'd: 'Willie, rise!
    Would I hae fear'd them a', man?'

9

But, word an' blow, North, Fox and Co.
golfed   Gowff'd Willie like a ba' man,
rose; cast;   Till Suthron raise an' coost their claise
clothes   Behind him in a raw, man:
bagpipes   An' Caledon threw by the drone,
blade   An' did her whittle draw, man;
An' swoor fu' rude, thro' dirt an' bluid,
    To mak it guid in law, man.

MY NANIE, O

TUNE: *(As Title)*

1

Behind yon hills where Stinchar flows
   'Mang moors an' mosses many, O,
The wintry sun the day has clos'd,
   And I'll awa to Nanie, O.

2

The westlin wind blaws loud an' shill,   western
   The night's baith mirk and rainy, O;   dark
But I'll get my plaid, an' out I'll steal,
   An' owre the hill to Nanie, O.

3

My Nanie's charming, sweet, an' young;
   Nae artfu' wiles to win ye, O;
May ill befa' the flattering tongue
   That wad beguile my Nanie, O!

4

Her face is fair, her heart is true;
   As spotless as she's bonie, O,
The op'ning gowan, wat wi' dew,   daisy
   Nae purer is than Nanie, O.

5

A country lad is my degree,
   An' few there be that ken me, O;
But what care I how few they be?
   I'm welcome ay to Nanie, O.

6

My riches a's my penny-fee,
   An' I maun guide it cannie, O;   manage;
But warl's gear ne'er troubles me,   carefully
   My thoughts are a'—my Nanie, O.

7

kine

    Our auld guidman delights to view
        His sheep an' kye thrive bonie, O;
    But I'm as blythe that hauds his pleugh,
        An' has nae care but Nanie, O.

8

do not care

    Come weel, come woe, I care na by;
        I'll tak what Heav'n will send me, O:
    Nae ither care in life have I,
        But live, an' love my Nanie, O.

GREEN GROW THE RASHES, O

TUNE: *(As Title)*

CHORUS

Green grow the rashes, O;
Green grow the rashes, O;
The sweetest hours that e'er I spend,
Are spent among the lasses, O.

1

    There's nought but care on ev'ry han',
        In every hour that passes, O:
    What signifies the life o' man,
        An' 'twere na for the lasses, O.

2

worldly

    The war'ly race may riches chase,
        An' riches still may fly them, O;
    An' tho' at last they catch them fast,
        Their hearts can ne'er enjoy them, O.

3

quiet

worldly
topsy-turvy

    But gie me a cannie hour at e'en,
        My arms about my dearie, O,
    An' war'ly cares an' war'ly men
        May a' gae tapsalteerie, O!

4

For you sae douce, ye sneer at this;   grave
   Ye're nought but senseless asses, O;
The wisest man the warl' e'er saw,   world
   He dearly lov'd the lasses, O.

5

Auld Nature swears, the lovely dears
   Her noblest work she classes, O:
Her prentice han' she try'd on man,
   An' then she made the lasses, O.

AGAIN REJOICING NATURE

TUNE: *Jockey's Grey Breeks*

CHORUS

And maun I still on Menie doat,
   And bear the scorn that's in her e'e?
For it's jet, jet-black, an' it's like a hawk,
   An' it winna let a body be.

1

Again rejoicing Nature sees
   Her robe assume its vernal hues:
Her leafy locks wave in the breeze,
   All freshly steep'd in morning dews.

2

In vain to me the cowslips blaw,
   In vain to me the vi'lets spring;
In vain to me in glen or shaw,
   The mavis and the lintwhite sing.   linnet

3

The merry ploughboy cheers his team,
   Wi' joy the tentie seedsman stalks;   careful
But life to me's a weary dream,
   A dream of ane that never wauks.   wakes

4

The wanton coot the water skims,
    Amang the reeds the ducklings cry,
The stately swan majestic swims,
    And ev'ry thing is blest but I.

5

shuts; fold-gate

The sheep-herd steeks his faulding slap,
    And o'er the moorlands whistles shill;
Wi' wild, unequal, wand'ring step,
    I meet him on the dewy hill.

6

And when the lark, 'tween light and dark,
    Blythe waukens by the daisy's side,
And mounts and sings on flittering wings,
    A woe-worn ghaist I hameward glide.

7

Come winter, with thine angry howl,
    And raging, bend the naked tree;
Thy gloom will soothe my cheerless soul,
    When nature all is sad like me!

THE GLOOMY NIGHT IS GATHERING FAST

TUNE: *Roslin Castle*

I

The gloomy night is gath'ring fast,
Loud roars the wild inconstant blast;
Yon murky cloud is filled with rain,
I see it driving o'er the plain;
The hunter now has left the moor,
The scatt'red coveys meet secure;
While here I wander, prest with care,
Along the lonely banks of Ayr.

2

The Autumn mourns her rip'ning corn
By early Winter's ravage torn;
Across her placid, azure sky,
She sees the scowling tempest fly;
Chill runs my blood to hear it rave:
I think upon the stormy wave,
Where many a danger I must dare,
Far from the bonie banks of Ayr.

3

'Tis not the surging billows' roar,
'Tis not that fatal, deadly shore;
Tho' death in ev'ry shape appear,
The wretched have no more to fear:
But round my heart the ties are bound,
That heart transpierc'd with many a wound;
These bleed afresh, those ties I tear,
To leave the bonie banks of Ayr.

4

Farewell, old Coila's hills and dales,
Her heathy moors and winding vales;
The scenes where wretched Fancy roves,
Pursuing past unhappy loves!
Farewell my friends! farewell my foes!
My peace with these, my love with those—
The bursting tears my heart declare,
Farewell, my bonie banks of Ayr.

NO CHURCHMAN AM I

TUNE: *Prepare, my dear Brethren*

1

No churchman am I for to rail and to write,
No statesman nor soldier to plot or to fight,
No sly man of business contriving a snare,
For a big-belly'd bottle's the whole of my care.

2

The peer I don't envy, I give him his bow;
I scorn not the peasant, tho' ever so low;
   But a club of good fellows, like those that are
here,
And a bottle like this, are my glory and care.

3

Here passes the squire on his brother—his horse,
There centum per centum, the cit with his purse,
But see you *The Crown*, how it waves in the air?
There a big-belly'd bottle still eases my care.

4

The wife of my bosom, alas! she did die;
For sweet consolation to church I did fly;
I found that old Solomon provèd it fair,
That a big-belly'd bottle's a cure for all care.

5

I once was persuaded a venture to make;
A letter inform'd me that all was to wreck;
But the pursy old landlord just waddlèd up stairs,
With a glorious bottle that ended my cares.

6

'Life's cares they are comforts'—a maxim laid
     down
By the Bard, what d'ye call him? that wore the
     black gown;
And faith I agree with th' old prig to a hair:
For a big-belly'd bottle's a heav'n of a care.

A STANZA ADDED IN A MASON LODGE

The fill up a bumper and make it o'erflow,
And honours Masonic prepare for to throw:
May ev'ry true Brother of the Compass and Square
Have a big-belly'd bottle, when harass'd with care!

LAMENT OF MARY QUEEN OF SCOTS

ON THE APPROACH OF SPRING

TUNE: *Mary Queen of Scots' Lament*

I

Now Nature hangs her mantle green
  On every blooming tree,
And spreads her sheets o' daisies white
  Out o'er the grassy lea;
Now Phœbus cheers the crystal streams,
  And glads the azure skies:
But nought can glad the weary wight
  That fast in durance lies.

2

Now laverocks wake the merry morn,   larks
  Aloft on dewy wing;
The merle, in his noontide bow'r,
  Makes woodland echoes ring;
The mavis wild wi' monie a note
  Sings drowsy day to rest:
In love and freedom they rejoice,
  Wi' care nor thrall opprest.

3

Now blooms the lily by the bank,
  The primrose down the brae;   hill-side
The hawthorn's budding in the glen,
  And milk-white is the slae: sloe
The meanest hind in fair Scotland
  May rove their sweets amang;
But I, the Queen of a' Scotland,
  Maun lie in prison strang.   must

4

I was the Queen o' bonie France,
    Where happy I hae been;
Fu' lightly rase I in the morn,
    As blythe lay down at e'en:
And I'm the sov'reign of Scotland,
    And monie a traitor there;
Yet here I lie in foreign bands
    And never-ending care.

5

But as for thee, thou false woman,
    My sister and my fae,
foe

Grim vengeance yet shall whet a sword
    That thro' thy soul shall gae!
go

The weeping blood in woman's breast
    Was never known to thee;
Nor th' balm that draps on wounds of woe
    Frae woman's pitying e'e.

6

My son! my son! may kinder stars
    Upon thy fortune shine;
And may those pleasures gild thy reign,
    That ne'er wad blink on mine!
glance

God keep thee frae thy mother's faes,
    Or turn their hearts to thee;
And where thou meet'st thy mother's friend,
    Remember him for me!

7

O! soon, to me, may summer suns
    Nae mair light up the morn!
Nae mair to me the autumn winds
    Wave o'er the yellow corn!
And, in the narrow house of death,
    Let winter round me rave;
And the next flow'rs that deck the spring
    Bloom on my peaceful grave.

THE WHISTLE

A Ballad

TUNE: *(As Title)*

1

I sing of a Whistle, a Whistle of worth,
I sing of a Whistle, the pride of the North,
Was brought to the court of our good Scottish King,
And long with this Whistle all Scotland shall ring.

2

Old Loda, still rueing the arm of Fingal,
The God of the Bottle sends down from his hall:
'This Whistle's your challenge, to Scotland get o'er,
And drink them to Hell, Sir! or ne'er see me more!'

3

Old poets have sung, and old chronicles tell,
What champions ventur'd, what champions fell:
The son of great Loda was conqueror still,
And blew on the Whistle their requiem shrill.

4

Till Robert, the lord of the Cairn and the Scaur,
Unmatch'd at the bottle, unconquer'd in war,
He drank his poor god-ship as deep as the sea;
No tide of the Baltic e'er drunker than he.

5

Thus Robert, victorious, the trophy has gain'd;
Which now in his house has for ages remain'd;
Till three noble chieftains, and all of his blood,
The jovial contest again have renew'd.

6

Three joyous good fellows, with hearts clear of flaw;
Craigdarroch, so famous for wit, worth, and law;
And trusty Glenriddel, so skilled in old coins;
And gallant Sir Robert, deep-read in old wines.

7

Craigdarroch began, with a tongue smooth as oil,
Desiring Glenriddel to yield up the spoil;
Or else he would muster the heads of the clan,
And once more, in claret, try which was the man.

8

'By the gods of the ancients!' Glenriddel replies,
'Before I surrender so glorious a prize,
I'll conjure the ghost of the great Rorie More,
And bumper his horn with him twenty times o'er.'

9

Sir Robert, a soldier, no speech would pretend,
But he ne'er turn'd his back on his foe, or his friend;
Said:—'Toss down the Whistle, the prize of the field,'
And, knee-deep in claret, he'd die ere he'd yield.

10

To the board of Glenriddel our heroes repair,
So noted for drowning of sorrow and care;
But for wine and for welcome not more known to fame
Than the sense, wit, and taste, of a sweet lovely dame.

11

A Bard was selected to witness the fray,
And tell future ages the feats of the day;
A Bard who detested all sadness and spleen,
And wish'd that Parnassus a vineyard had been.

12

The dinner being over, the claret they ply,
And ev'ry new cork is a new spring of joy;
In the bands of old friendship and kindred so set,
And the bands grew the tighter the more they were wet.

13

Gay Pleasure ran riot as bumpers ran o'er;
company
Bright Phœbus ne'er witness'd so joyous a core,
And vow'd that to leave them he was quite forlorn,
Till Cynthia hinted he'd see them next morn.

14

Six bottles a-piece had well wore out the night,
When gallant Sir Robert, to finish the fight,
Turn'd o'er in one bumper a bottle of red,
And swore 'twas the way that their ancestor did.

15

Then worthy Glenriddel, so cautious and sage,
No longer the warfare ungodly would wage:
A high Ruling Elder to wallow in wine!
He left the foul business to folks less divine.

16

The gallant Sir Robert fought hard to the end;
But who can with Fate and quart bumpers contend?
Though Fate said, a hero should perish in light;
So uprose bright Phœbus—and down fell the knight.

17

Next uprose our Bard, like a prophet in drink:—
'Craigdarroch thou'lt soar when creation shall sink!
But if thou would flourish immortal in rhyme,
Come—one bottle more—and have at the sublime!

18

'Thy line, that have struggled for freedom with Bruce,
Shall heroes and patriots ever produce:
So thine be the laurel, and mine be the bay;
The field thou hast won, by yon bright God of Day!'

THE KIRK'S ALARM

TUNE: *Come let us prepare*

1

Orthodox! orthodox!—
Wha believe in John Knox—
Let me sound an alarm to your conscience:
A heretic blast
Has been blawn i' the Wast,
That what is not sense must be nonsense—
Orthodox!
That what is not sense must be nonsense.

West

2

Dr. Mac! Dr. Mac!
You should stretch on a rack,
To strike wicked Writers wi' terror:
To join faith and sense,
Upon onie pretence,
Was heretic, damnable error—
Dr. Mac!
'Twas heretic, damnable error.

3

Town of Ayr! Town of Ayr!
It was rash, I declare,
To meddle wi' mischief a-brewing:
Provost John is still deaf
To the church's relief,
And Orator Bob is its ruin—
Town of Ayr!
And Orator Bob is its ruin.

4

D'rymple mild! D'rymple mild!
Tho' your heart's like a child,
An' your life like the new-driven snaw,
Yet that winna save ye:
Auld Satan must have ye,
For preaching that three's ane and twa—
D'rymple mild!
For preaching that three's ane and twa.

will not

5

Calvin's sons! Calvin's sons!
Seize your sp'ritual guns,
Ammunition you never can need:
    Your hearts are the stuff
    Will be powther enough,
And your skulls are store-houses o' lead—
        Calvin's sons!
Your skulls are store-houses o' lead.

6

Rumble John! Rumble John!
Mount the steps with a groan,
Cry:—'The book is wi' heresy cramm'd;
    Then lug out your ladle,
    Deal brimstone like adle,   cow-lant
And roar every note o' the damn'd—
        Rumble John!
And roar every note o' the damn'd.

7

Simper James! Simper James!
Leave the fair Killie dames—   Kilmarnock
There's a holier chase in your view:
    I'll lay on your head
    That the pack ye'll soon lead,
For puppies like you there's but few—
        Simper James!
For puppies like you there's but few.

8

Singet Sawnie! Singet Sawnie!   Shrivelled
Are ye herding the penny,   guarding
Unconscious what evils await!
    Wi' a jump, yell, and howl
    Alarm every soul,
For the Foul Thief is just at your gate—   the Devil
        Singet Sawnie!
The Foul Thief is just at your gate.

9

Daddie Auld! Daddie Auld!
There's a tod in the fauld,
A tod meikle waur than the clerk:
Tho' ye can do little skaith,
Ye'll be in at the death,
And gif ye canna bite, ye may bark—
Daddie Auld!
For gif ye canna bite ye may bark.

fox

much worse;
laywer
damage

if

10

Davie Rant! Davie Rant!
In a face like a saunt
And a heart that would poison a hog,
Raise an impudent roar,
Like a breaker lee-shore,
Or the Kirk will be tint in a bog—
Davie Rant!
Or the Kirk will be tint in a bog.

lost

11

Jamie Goose! Jamie Goose!
Ye hae made but toom roose.
In hunting the wicked lieutenant;
But the Doctor's your mark,
For the Lord's haly ark,
He has cooper'd, and ca'd a wrang pin in't—
Jamie Goose!
He has cooper'd and ca'd a wrang pin in't.

empty
reputation

knocked

12

Poet Willie! Poet Willie!
Gie the Doctor a volley,
Wi' your 'Liberty's chain' and your wit:
O'er Pegasus' side
Ye ne'er laid a stride,
Ye but smelt, man, the place where he shit—
Poet Willie!
Ye smelt but the place where he shit.

13

Andro Gowk! Andro Gowk!   Cuckoo
   Ye may slander the Book,
And the Book not the waur, let me tell ye: worse
   Ye are rich, and look big,
   But lay by hat and wig,
And ye'll hae a calf's head o' sma' value—
      Andro Gowk!
Ye'll hae a calf's head o' sma' value.

14

Barr Steenie! Barr Steenie!
   What mean ye? what mean ye?
If ye'll meddle nae mair wi' the matter,
   Ye may hae some pretence
   To havins and sense   conduct
Wi' people wha ken ye nae better—
      Barr Steenie!
Wi' people wha ken ye nae better.

15

Irvine-side! Irvine-side!
   Wi' your turkey-cock pride,
Of manhood but sma' is your share:
   Ye've the figure, 'tis true,
   Even your faes will allow,   foes
And your friends daurna say ye hae mair—   dare not
      Irvine-side!
Your friends daurna say ye hae mair.

16

Muirland Jock! Muirland Jock!
   Whom the Lord gave a stock
Wad set up a tinkler in brass,
   If ill manners were wit,
   There's no mortal so fit
To prove the poor Doctor an ass—
      Muirland Jock!
To prove the poor Doctor an ass.

17

Holy Will! Holy Will!
There was wit i' your skull,
When ye pilfer'd the alms o' the poor:

material   The timmer is scant,
                 When ye're taen for a saunt
rope   Wha should swing in a rape for an hour—
                   Holy Will!
Ye should swing in a rape for an hour.

18

Poet Burns! Poet Burns!
            Wi' your priest-skelping turns,
-spanking

Why desert ye your auld native shire?
               Your Muse is a gipsy,
               Yet were she ev'n tipsy,
worse   She could ca' us nae waur than we are—
                   Poet Burns!
Ye could ca' us nae waur than we are.

POSTSCRIPTS

I

Afton's Laird! Afton's Laird!
            When your pen can be spared,
A copy of this I bequeath,
strict conditions   On the same sicker scoré
               As I mention'd before,
To that trusty auld worthy, Clackleith—
                 Afton's Laird!
To that trusty auld worthy, Clackleith.

2

Factor John! Factor John!
Whom the Lord made alone,
And ne'er made another thy peer,
Thy poor servant, the Bard,
In respectful regard
He presents thee this token sincere—
Factor John!
He presents thee this token sincere.

ON CAPTAIN GROSE

WRITTEN ON AN ENVELOPE, ENCLOSING A LETTER TO HIM

TUNE: *Sir John Malcolm*

1

Ken ye ought o' Captain Grose?
    Igo and ago
If he's among his friends or foes?
    Iram, coram, dago
Is he south, or is he north?
    Igo and ago
Or drownèd in the River Forth?
    Iram, coram, dago

2

Is he slain by Hielan' bodies?   creatures
    Igo and ago
And eaten like a wether haggis?
    Iram, coram, dago
Is he to Abra'm's bosom gane?
    Igo and ago
Or haudin Sarah by the wame?   holding; belly
    Iram, coram, dago

3

Where'er he be, the Lord be near him!
Igo and ago
As for the Deil, he daur na steer him.
Iram, coram, dago
But please transmit th' enclosèd letter
Igo and ago
Which will oblige your humble debtor
Iram, coram, dago

4

So may ye hae auld stanes in store,
Igo and ago
The very stanes that Adam bore!
Iram, coram, dago
So may ye get in glad possession,
Igo and ago
The coins o' Satan's coronation!
Iram, coram, dago

THE FÊTE CHAMPETRE

TUNE: *Killiecrankie*

1

O, wha will to Saint Stephen's House,
To do our errands there, man?
O, what will to Saint Stephen's House
O' th' merry lads of Ayr, man?
Or will ye send a man o' law?
Or will ye send a sodger?
Or him wha led o'er Scotland a'
The meikle Ursa-Major?

2

Come, will ye court a noble lord,
    Or buy a score o' lairds, man?
For Worth and Honour pawn their word,
    Their vote shall be Glencaird's, man.
Ane gies them coin, ane gies them wine,
    Anither gies them clatter;   talk
Annbank, wha guess'd the ladies' taste,
    He gies a Fête Champetre.

3

When Love and Beauty heard the news
    The gay green-woods amang, man,
Where, gathering flowers and busking bowers,   dressing
    They heard the blackbird's sang, man;
A vow, they seal'd it with a kiss,
    Sir Politics to fetter:
As theirs alone the patent bliss
    To hold a Fête Champetre.

4

Then mounted Mirth on gleesome wing,
    O'er hill and dale she flew, man;
Ilk wimpling burn, ilk crystal spring,   Each winding
    Ilk glen and shaw she knew, man.   wood
She summon'd very social sprite,
    That sports by wood or water,
On th' bonie banks of Ayr to meet
    And keep this Fête Champetre.

5

Cauld Boreas wi' his boisterous crew
    Were bound to stakes like kye, man;   cows
And Cynthia's car, o' silver fu',   full
    Clamb up the starry sky, man: Climbed
Reflected beams dwell in the streams,
    Or down the current shatter;
The western breeze steals through the trees
    To view this Fête Champetre.

6

How many a robe sae gaily floats,
　　What sparkling jewels glance, man,
To Harmony's enchanting notes,
　　As moves the mazy danze, man!
The echoing wood, the winding flood
　　Like Paradise did glitter,

gate

When angels met at Adam's yett
　　To hold their Fête Champetre.

7

When Politics came there to mix

adder-

　　And make his ether-stane, man,
He circled round the magic ground,
　　But entrance found he nane, man:

left

He blush'd for shame, he quat his name,
　　Forswore it every letter,
Wi' humble prayer to join and share
　　This festive Fête Champetre.

THE FIVE CARLINS

TUNE: *Chevy Chase*

I

matrons

There was five carlins in the South:
　　They fell upon a scheme
To send a lad to London Town
　　To bring them tidings hame:

2

Nor only bring them tidings hame,
　　But do their errands there:

maybe gold;
both

And aiblins gowd and honor baith
　　Might be that laddie's share.

3

There was Maggie by the banks o' Nith,
　　A dame wi' pride eneugh;
And Marjorie o' the Monie Lochs,
　　A carlin auld and teugh;

4

And Blinkin Bess of Annandale,   smirking
   That dwelt near Solway-side;
And Brandy Jean, that took her gill
   In Galloway sae wide;

5

And Black Joán, frae Crichton Peel,
   O' gipsy kith an' kin:
Five wighter carlins were na found   more influential
   The South countrie within.

6

To send a lad to London Town
   They met upon a day;
And monie a knight and monie a laird
   This errand fain wad gae.   would go

7

O, monie a knight and monie a laird
   This errand fain wad gae;
But nae ane could their fancy please,
   O, ne'er a ane but tway!   Two

8

The first ane was a belted Knight,
   Bred of a Border band;
And he wad gae to London Town,
   Might nae man him withstand;

9

And he wad do their errands weel,
   And meikle he wad say;   much
And ilka ane at London court   every
   Wad bid to him guid-day.

10

The neist cam in, a Soger boy,   next
   And spak wi' modest grace;
And he wad gae to London Town,
   If sae their pleasure was.

11

promise

He wad na hecht them courtly gifts,
    Nor meikle speech pretend;
But he wad hecht an honest heart
    Wad ne'er desert his friend.

12

those

themselves

Now wham to chuse and wham refuse
    At strife thae carlins fell;
For some had gentle folk to please,
    And some wad please themsel.

13

-mouthed

Then out spak mim-mou'd Meg o' Nith,
    And she spak up wi' pride,
And she wad send the Soger lad,
    Whatever might betide.

14

the King

For the auld Guidman o' London court
    She didna care a pin;
But she wad send the Soger lad
    To greet his eldest son.

15

oath

Then up sprang Bess o' Annandale,
    And swore a deadly aith,
Says:—'I will send the belted Knight,
    Spite of you carlins baith!

16

fond

'For far-aff fowls hae feathers fair,
    And fools o' change are fain;
But I hae tried this Border Knight:
    I'll try him yet again.'

17

gossips

Then Brandy Jean spak owre her drink:—
    'Ye weel ken, kimmers a',
The auld Guidman o' London court,
    His back's been at the wa';

18

'And monie a friend that kiss'd his caup   cup
   Is now a fremit wight;   hostile
But it's ne'er be sae wi' Brandy Jean—
   I'll send the Border Knight.'

19

Says Black Joán frae Crichton Peel,
   A carlin stoor and grim:—   stern
'The auld Guidman or the young Guidman   the Prince
   For me may sink or swim!

20

'For fools will prate o' right or wrang,
   While knaves laugh in their slieve;
But wha blaws best the horn shall win—
   I'll spier nae courtier's leave!'   ask

21

Then slow raise Marjorie o' the Lochs,
   And wrinkled was her brow,
Her ancient weed was russet gray,
   Her auld Scots heart was true:—

22

'There's some great folk set light by me,
   I set as light by them;
But I will send to London Town
   Wham I lo'e best at hame.'

23

Sae how this sturt and strife may end,   turmoil
   There's naebody can tell.
God grant the King and ilka man
   May look weel to themsel!

ELECTION BALLAD FOR WESTERHA'

TUNE: *Up an' waur them a' Willie*

CHORUS

Up and waur them a', Jamie,
Up and waur them a'!
The Johnstones hae the guidin o't:
Ye turncoat Whigs, awa!

I

The Laddies by the banks o' Nith
    Wad trust his Grace wi' a', Jamie;
But he'll sair them as he sair'd the King—
    Turn tail and rin awa, Jamie.

2

The day he stude his country's friend,
    Or gied her faes a claw, Jamie,
Or frae puir man a blessin wan—
    That day the Duke ne'er saw, Jamie.

3

But wha is he, his country's boast?
    Like him there is na twa, Jamie!
There's no a callant tents the kye
    But kens o' Westerha', Jamie.

4

To end the wark, here's Whistlebirk—
    Lang may his whistle blaw, Jamie!—
And Maxwell true, o' sterling blue,
    And we'll be Johnstones a', Jamie.

Marginal glosses:
Would / serve / run
stood / scratch / won
youngster herds; cows

BALLADS ON MR. HERON'S ELECTION, 1795

BALLAD FIRST

TUNE: *For a' that*

I

Wham will we send to London town,
    To Parliament and a' that?
Or wha in a' the country round
    The best desrves to fa' that?   have
        For a' that, and a' that,
        Thro' Galloway and a' that,
      Where is the Laird or belted Knight
        That best deserves to fa' that?

2

Wha sees Kerroughtree's open yett—   gate
    And wha is't never saw that?—
Wha ever wi' Kerroughtree met,
    And has a doubt of a' that?
      For a' that, and a' that,
      Here's Heron yet for a' that!
    The independent patriot,
      The honest man, and a' that!

3

Tho' wit and worth, in either sex,
    Saint Mary's Isle can shaw that,
Wi' Lords and Dukes let Selkirk mix,
    And weel does Selkirk fa' that.   well; suit
      For a' that, and a' that,
      Here's Heron yet for a' that!
    An independent commoner
      Shall be the man for a' that.

4

bend

cuckoo (*i.e.*
dolt)

But why should we to Nobles jeuk,
    And it against the law, that,
And even a Lord may be a gowk,
    Wi' ribban, star, and a' that?
        For a' that, and a' that,
        Here's Heron yet for a' that!
    A Lord may be a lousy loon,
        Wi' ribban, star, and a' that.

5

With his
from among

cattle; nags

A beardless boy comes o'er the hills
    Wi's uncle's purse and a' that;
But we'll hae ane frae 'mang oursels,
    A man we ken, and a' that.
        For a' that, and a' that,
        Here's Heron yet for a' that!
    We are na to be bought and sold,
        Like nowte, and naigs, and a' that.

6

Then let us drink:—'The Stewartry,
    Kerroughtree's laird, and a' that,
Our representative to be':
    For weel he's worthy a' that!
        For a' that, and a' that,
        Here's Heron yet for a' that!
    A House of Commons such as he,
        They wad be blest that saw that.

BALLAD SECOND: THE ELECTION

TUNE: *Fy, Let Us A' to The Bridal*

1

Fy, let us a' to Kirkcudbright,
  For there will be bickerin there;
For Murray's light horse are to muster,
  An' O, how the heroes will swear!
And there will be Murray commander,
  An' Gordon the battle to win:
Like brothers, they'll stan' by each other,
  Sae knit in alliance and kin.

2

An' there'll be black-nebbit Johnie,   -beaked
  The tongue o' the trump to them a':   Jew's-harp
Gin he get na Hell for his haddin,   inheritance
  The Deil gets nae justice ava!   at all
And there'll be Kempleton's birkie,   younker
  A boy no sae black at the bane;   bone
But as to his fine nabob fortune—
  We'll e'en let the subject alane!

3

An' there'll be Wigton's new sheriff—
  Dame Justice fu' brawly has sped: finely
She's gotten the heart of a Bushby,
  But Lord! what's become o' the head?
An' there'll be Cardoness, Esquire,
  Sae mighty in Cardoness' eyes:
A wight that will weather damnation,
  For the Devil the prey would despise.

4

An' there'll be Douglasses doughty,
  New christening towns far and near:
Abjuring their democrat doings
  An' kissing the arse of a peer!
An' there'll be Kenmure sae generous,
  Wha's honor is proof to the storm:
To save them from stark reprobation
  He lent them his name to the firm!

5

will not

creature

money

rope

fellow;
Catechism
to-morrow

But we winna mention Redcastle,
    The body—e'en let him escape!
He'd venture the gallows for siller,
    An' 'twere na the cost o' the rape!
An' whare is our King's Lord Lieutenant,
    Sae fame for his gratefu' return?
The billie is getting his Questions
    To say at St. Stephen's the morn!

6

The Devil a one

An' there'll be lads o' the gospel:
    Muirhead, wha's as guid as he's true;
An' there'll be Buittle's Apostle,
    Wha's mair o' the black than the blue;
An' there'll be folk frae St. Mary's,
    A house o' great merit and note:
The Deil ane but honors them highly,
    The Deil ane will gie them his vote!

7

An' there'll be wealthy young Richard,
    Dame Fortune should hang by the neck:
But for prodigal thriftless bestowing,
    His merit had won him respect.
An' there'll be rich brither nabobs;
    Tho' nabobs, yet men o' the first!
An' there'll be Collieston's whiskers,
    An' Quinton—o' lads no the warst!

8

Take heed

An' there'll be Stamp-Office Johnie:
    Tak tent how ye purchase a dram!
An' there'll be gay Cassencarry,
    An' there'll be Colonel Tam;
An' there'll be trusty Kerroughtree,
    Wha's honour was ever his law:
If the virtues were pack't in a parcel,
    His worth might be sample for a'!

9

An' can we forget the auld Major,
   Wha'll ne'er be forgot in the Greys?   Scots Greys
Our flatt'ry we'll keep for some other:
   Him only it's justice to praise!
An' there'll be maiden Kilkerran,
   An' also Barskimming's guid Knight.
An' there'll be roaring Birtwhistle—
   Yet luckily roars in the right!

10

An' there frae the Niddlesdale border
   Will mingle the Maxwells in droves:
Teuch Johnie, Staunch Geordie, and Wattie   Tough
   That girns for the fishes an' loaves!   gapes
An' there'll be Logan's M'Doual—
   Sculdudd'ry an' he will be there!   Bawdry
An' also the wild Scot o' Galloway,
   Sogering, gunpowther Blair!

11

Then hey the chaste interest of Broughton.
   An' hey for the blessings 'twill bring!
It may send Balmaghie to the Commons—
   In Sodom 'twould mak him a King!
An' hey for the sanctified Murray
   Our land wha wi' chapels has stor'd,
He founder'd his horse among harlots,
   But gie'd the auld naig to the Lord!

BALLAD THIRD: JOHN BUSHBY'S LAMENTATION

TUNE: *The Children in the Wood*

1

'Twas in the Seventeen Hunder year
   O' grace, and Ninety-Five,
That year I was the wae'est man   saddest
   Of onie man alive.

2

In March the three-an-'twentieth morn,
    The sun raise clear an' bright;
But O, I was a waefu' man,
the fall   Ere to-fa' o' the night!

3

Earl   Yerl Galloway lang did rule this land
    Wi' equal right and fame,
Fast knit in chaste and holy bands
    With Broughton's noble name.

4

Yerl Galloway's man o' men was I,
    And chief o' Broughton's host:
So twa blind beggars, on a string,
dog   The faithfu' tyke will trust!

5

But now Yerl Galloway's sceptre's broke,
    And Broughton's wi' the slain,
And I my ancient craft may try,
    Sin' honesty is gane.

6

'Twas by the banks o' bonie Dee,
    Beside Kirkcudbright's towers,
The Stewart and the Murray there
    Did muster a' their powers.

7

Then Murray on the auld grey yaud
    Wi' wingèd spurs did ride:
That auld grey yaud a' Nidsdale rade,
stole   He staw upon Nidside.

8

An' there had na been the Yerl himsel,
    O, there had been nae play!
But Garlies was to London gane,
cattle   And sae the kye might stray.

9

And there was Balmaghie, I ween—
    In front rank he wad shine;
But Balmaghie had better been
    Drinkin' Madeira wine.

10

And frae Glenkens cam to our aid
    A chief o' doughty deed:
In case that worth should wanted be,
    O' Kenmure we had need.

11

And by our banners march'd Muirhead,
    And Buittle was na slack,
Whase haly priesthood nane could stain,
    For wha could dye the black?

12

And there was grave Squire Cardoness,
    Look'd on till a' was done:
Sae in the tower o' Cardoness
    A howlet sits at noon.

13

And there led I the Bushby clan:
    My gamesome billie, Will,
And my son Maitland, wise as brave,
    My footsteps follow'd still.

14

The Douglas and the Heron's name,
    We set nought to their score;
The Douglas and the Heron's name
    Had felt our weight before.

15

But Douglasses o' weight had we:
    The pair o' lusty lairds,
For building cot-houses sae fam'd,
    And christenin kail-yards.   kitchen-gardens

16

And then Redcastle drew his sword
  That ne'er was stain'd wi' gore
Save on a wand'rer lame and blind,
  To drive him frae his door.

17

And last cam creepin Collieston,
  Was mair in fear than wrath;
One   Ae knave was constant in his mind—
harm   To keep that knave frae scaith.

packman
BALLAD FOURTH: THE TROGGER

TUNE: *Buy broom besoms*

CHORUS

fine wares   *Buy braw troggin*
                      Frae the banks o' Dee!
                    Wha wants troggin
                      Let him come to me!

1

Wha will buy my troggin,
  Fine election ware,
Broken trade o' Broughton,
  A' in high repair?

2

There's a noble Earl's
  Fame and high renown,
For an auld sang—it's thought
goods; stolen   The guids were stown.

3

Here's the worth o' Broughton
  In a needle's e'e.
eye   Here's a reputation
lost   Tint by Balmaghie.

4

Here's its stuff and lining,
   Cardoness's head—
Fine for a soger,
   A' the wale o' lead.   *pick*

5

Here's a little wadset—   *mortgage*
   Buittle's scrap o' truth
Pawn'd in a gin-shop,
   Quenching holy drouth.

6

Here's an honest conscience
   Might a prince adorn,
Frae the downs o' Tinwald—   *Bushby's*
   So was never worn!   *residence*

7

Here's armorial bearings
   Frae the manse o' Urr:
The crest, a sour crab-apple
   Rotten at the core.

8

Here is Satan's picture,
   Like a bizzard 'gled   *buzzard hawk*
Pouncing poor Redcastle,
   Sprawlin like a taed.   *toad*

9

Here's the font where Douglas
   Stane and mortar names,
Lately used at Caily
   Christening Murray's crimes.

10

Here's the worth and wisdom
   Collieston can boast:
By a thievish midge
   They had been nearly lost.

11

Here is Murray's fragments
  O' the Ten Commands,
Gifted by Black Jock
  To get them aff his hands.

Bushby

12

Saw ye e'er sic troggin?—
  If to buy ye're slack,
Hornie's turnin chapman:
  He'll buy a' the pack!

such

The Devil

THE DEAN OF THE FACULTY

A New Ballad

TUNE: *The Dragon of Wantley*

1

Dire was the hate at Old Harlaw
  That Scot to Scot did carry;
And dire the discord Langside saw
  For beauteous, hapless Mary.
But Scot to Scot ne'er met so hot,
  Or were more in fury seen, Sir,
Than 'twixt Hal and Bob for the famous job,
  Who should be the Faculty's Dean, Sir.

2

This Hal for genius, wit, and lore
  Among the first was number'd;
But pious Bob, 'mid learning's store
  Commandment the Tenth remember'd.
Yet simple Bob the victory got,
  And won his heart's desire:
Which shows that Heaven can boil the pot,
  Tho' the Deil piss in the fire.

3

Squire Hal, besides, had in this case
   Pretensions rather brassy;
For talents, to deserve a place,
   Are qualifications saucy.
So their worships of the Faculty,
   Quite sick of Merit's rudeness,
Chose one who should owe it all, d'ye see,
   To their gratis grace and goodness.

4

As once on Pisgah purg'd was the sight
   Of a son of Circumcision,
So, may be, on this Pisgah height
   Bob's purblind mental vision.
Nay, Bobby's mouth may be open'd yet,
   Till for eloquence you hail him,
And swear that he has the Angel met
   That met the Ass of Balaam.

5

In your herectic sins may ye live and die,
   Ye heretic Eight-and-Thirty!
But accept, ye sublime majority,
   My congratulations hearty!
With your honors, as with a certain King,
   In your servants this is striking,
The more incapacity they bring
   The more they're to your liking.

THE TARBOLTON LASSES

TUNE: *(Unknown)*

1

If ye gae up to yon hill-tap,
   Ye'll there see bonie Peggy: pretty
She kens her father is a laird,
   And she forsooth's a leddy.   lady

2

There's Sophy tight, a lassie bright,
    Besides a handsome fortune:
Wha canna win her in a night
    Has little art in courtin.

3

Gae down by Faille, and taste the ale,
    And tak a look o' Mysie:

*stubborn;
muddy of
complexion
perhaps*

She's dour and din, a deil within,
    But aiblins she may please ye.

4

If she be shy, her sister try,
    Ye'll maybe fancy Jenny:
If ye'll dispense wi' want o' sense,
    She kens hersel she's bonie.

5

that

As ye gae up by yon hillside,

Call

    Spier in for bonie Bessy:
She'll give ye a beck, and bid ye light,
    And handsomely address ye.

6

There's few sae bonie, nane sae guid
    In a' King George' dominion:
If ye should doubt the truth of this,
    It's Bessy's ain opinion.

THE RONALDS OF THE BENNALS

TUNE: *(Unknown)*

1

In Tarbolton, ye ken, there are proper young men,
    And proper young lasses and a', man:
But ken ye the Ronalds that live in the Bennais?

bear the bell

    They carry the gree frae them a', man.

2

Their father's a laird, and weel he can spare't:
  Braid money to tocher them a', man;
To proper young men, he'll clink in the hand
  Gowd guineas a hunder or twa, man.

Broad; to dower chink

Gold

3

There's ane they ca' Jean, I'll warrant ye've seen
  As bonie a lass or as braw, man;
But for sense and guid taste she'll vie wi' the best,
  And a conduct that beautifies a', man.

well-dressed

4

The charms o' the min', the langer they shine
  The mair admiration they draw, man;
While peaches and cherries, and roses and lilies,
  They fade and they wither awa, man.

5

If ye be for Miss Jean, tak this frae a frien',
  A hint o' a rival or twa, man:
The Laird o' Blackbyre wad gang through the fire,
  If that wad entice her awa, man.

would go

6

The Laird o' Braehead has been on his speed
  For mair than a towmond or twa, man:
The Laird o' the Ford will straught on a board,
  If he canna get her at a', man.

twelvemonth

stretch

7

Then Anna comes in, the pride o' her kin,
  The boast of our bachelors a', man:
Sae sonsy and sweet, sae fully complete,
  She steals our affections awa, man.

pleasant

8

If I should detail the pick and the wale
  O' lasses that live here awa, man,
The faut wad be mine, if they didna shine
  The sweetest and best o' them a', man.

choice

about

fault

9

I lo'e her mysel, but darena weel tell,
 My poverty keeps me in awe, man;
For making o' rhymes, and working at times,
 Does little or naething at a', man.

10

Yet I wadna choose to let her refuse
 Nor hae't in her power to say na, man:
For though I be poor, unnoticed, obscure,
 My stomach's as proud as them a', man.

would not

11

Though I canna ride in well-booted pride,
 And flee o'er the hills like a craw, man,
I can haud up my head wi' the best o' the breed,
 Though fluttering ever so braw, man.

hold
fine

12

My coat and my vest, they are Scotch o' the best;
 O' pairs o' guid breeks I hae twa, man,
And stockings and pumps to put on my stumps,
 And ne'er a wrang steek in them a', man.

trousers

stitch

13

My sarks they are few, but five o' them new—
 Twal' hundred, as white as the snaw, man!
A ten-shillings hat, a Holland cravat—
 There are no monie Poets sae braw, man!

shirts

well-dressed

14

I never had frien's weel stockit in means,
 To leave me a hundred or twa, man;
Nae weel-tocher'd aunts, to wait on their drants
 And wish them in hell for it a', man.

-dowered;
prosings

15

I never was cannie for hoarding o' money,
 Or claughtin't together at a', man;
I've little to spend and naething to lend,
 But devil a shilling I awe, man.

careful
grasping it

owe

THE BELLES OF MAUCHLINE

TUNE: *Bonie Dundee*

1

In Mauchline there dwells six proper young belles,
The pride of the place and its neighbourhood a',
Their carriage and dress, a stranger would guess,
In Lon'on or Paris they'd gotten it a'.

2

Miss Millar is fine, Miss Markland's divine,   handsomely
Miss Smith she has wit, and Miss Betty is braw,   dressed
There's beauty and fortune to get wi' Miss Morton;
But Armour's the jewel for me o' them a'.

ON GENERAL DUMOURIER'S DESERTION

FROM THE FRENCH REPUBLICAN ARMY

TUNE: *Robin Adair*

1

You're welcome to Despots,
          Dumourier!
You're welcome to Despots,
          Dumourier!
How does Dampiere do?
Ay, and Bournonville too?
Why did they not come along with you,
          Dumourier?

2

I will fight France with you,
                    Dumourier,
I will fight France with you,
                    Dumourier;
I will fight France with you,
I will take my chance with you,
By my soul, I'll dance with you,
                    Dumourier!

3

Then let us fight about,
                    Dumourier!
Then let us fight about,
                    Dumourier!
Then let us fight about
Till Freedom's spark be out,
Then we'll be damn'd, no doubt,
                    Dumourier.

EXTEMPORE IN THE COURT OF SESSION

TUNE: *Killiecrankie*

LORD ADVOCATE

He clench'd his pamphlets in his fist,
    He quoted and he hinted,
Till in a declamation-mist
lost   His argument, he tint it:
groped He gapèd for't, he grapèd for't,
found   He fand it was awa, man;
But what his common sense came short,
    He ekèd out wi' law, man.

MR. ERSKINE

Collected, Harry stood awee,   a moment
   Then open'd out his arm, man;
His lordship sat wi' ruefu' e'e,
   And ey'd the gathering storm, man;
Like wind-driv'n hail it did assail,
   Or torrents owre a linn, man;   cascade
The Bench sae wise lift up their eyes,
   Hauf-wauken'd wi' the din, man.

I MURDER HATE BY FIELD OR FLOOD

TUNE: *(Unknown)*

1

I murder hate by field or flood,
   Tho' Glory's name may screen us.
In wars at hame I'll spend my blood—
   Life-giving wars of Venus.
The deities that I adore
   Are Social Peace and Plenty:
I'm better pleas'd to make one more
   Than be the death of twenty.

2

I would not die like Socrates,
   For all the fuss of Plato;
Nor would I with Leonidas,
   Nor yet would I with Cato;
The zealots of the Church and State
   Shall ne'er my mortal foes be;
But let me have bold Zimri's fate
   Within the arms of Cozbi.

ON CHLORIS

REQUESTING ME TO GIVE HER A SPRIG OF BLOSSOMED THORN

TUNE: *(Unknown)*

From the white-blossom'd sloe my dear Chloris requested
  A sprig, her fair breast to adorn:
'No, by Heaven!' I exclaim'd, 'let me perish for ever,
  Ere I plant in that bosom a thorn!'

MY AUNTIE JEAN

TUNE: *John Anderson, my jo*

My auntie Jean held to the shore,
  As Ailsa boats cam' back;
And she has coft a feather bed
  For twenty and a plack;
And in it she wan fifty mark,
  Before a towmond sped;
O! what a noble bargain
  Was auntie Jeanie's bed.

MY GIRL SHE'S AIRY

TUNE: *Black Joke*

My girl she's airy, she's buxom and gay;
Her breath is as sweet as the blossoms in May;
  A touch of her lips it ravishes quite.
She's always good natur'd, good humor'd and free;
She dances, she glances, she smiles upon me;
  I never am happy when out of her sight.
Her slender neck her handsome waist
Her hair well curl'd her stays well lac'd

.   .   .   .   .   .
.   .   .   .   .

And O for the joys of a long winter night.

YOUNG PEGGY

TUNE: *Loch Errochside*

1

Young Peggy blooms our boniest lass:
　Her blush is like the morning,
The rosy dawn the springing grass
　With early gems adorning;
Her eyes outshine the radiant beams
　That gild the passing shower,
And glitter o'er the crystal streams,
　And cheer each fresh'ning flower.

2

Her lips, more than the cherries bright—
　A richer dye has graced them—
They charm the admiring gazer's sight,
　And sweetly tempt to taste them,
Her smile is as the evening mild,
　When feather'd pairs are courting,
And little lambkins wanton wild,
　In playful bands disporting.

3

Were Fortune lovely Peggy's foe,
　Such sweetness would relent her:
As blooming Spring unbends the brow
　Of surly, savage Winter.
Detraction's eye no aim can gain
　Her winning powers to lessen,
And fretful Envy grins in vain
　The poison'd tooth to fasten.

4

Ye Pow'rs of Honour, Love, and Truth,
　From ev'ry ill defend her!
Inspire the highly-favour'd youth
　The destinies intend her!
Still fan the sweet connubial flame
　Responsive in each bosom,
And bless the dear parental name
　With many a filial blossom!

BONIE DUNDEE

TUNE: *Adew Dundee*

1

'O, whar gat ye that hauver-meal bannock?'
do not   'O silly blind body, O, dinna ye see?'
I gat it frae a young, brisk sodger laddie
Perth   Between Saint Johnston and bonie Dundee.
would that   O, gin I saw the laddie that gae me't!
dandled   Aft has he doudl'd me up on his knee:
May Heaven protect my bonie Scots laddie,
        And send him hame to his babie and me!

2

'My blessin's upon thy sweet, wee lippie!
eyebrow   My blessin's upon thy bonie e'e brie!
Thy smiles are sae like my blythe sodger laddie,
Thou art   Thou's ay the dearer and dearer to me!
build   But I'll big a bow'r on yon bonie banks,
meandering   Whare Tay rins wimplin by sae clear;
clothe   And I'll cleed thee in the tartan sae fine,
        And mak thee a man like thy daddie dear.'

TO THE WEAVER'S GIN YE GO

should

TUNE: *(As Title)*

CHORUS

To the weaver's gin ye go, fair maids,
*   To the weaver's gin ye go,*
warn you true;   *I rede you right, gang ne'er at night,*
go   *To the weaver's gin ye go.*

1

My heart was ance as blythe and free
once   As simmer days were lang;
western   But a bonie, westlin weaver lad
made   Has gart me change my sang.

2

My mither sent me to the town,
  To warp a plaiden wab;
But the weary, weary warpin o't
  Has gart me sigh and sab.   *sob*

3

A bonie, westlin weaver lad
  Sat working at his loom;
He took my heart, as wi' a net,
  In every knot and thrum.

4

I sat beside my warpin-wheel,
  And ay I ca'd it roun';   *drove*
And every shot and every knock,
  My heart it gae a stoun.   *ache*

5

The moon was sinking in the west
  Wi' visage pale and wan,
As my bonie, westlin weaver lad
  Convoy'd me thro' the glen.

6

But what was said, or what was done,
  Shame fa' me gin I tell;   *befall; if*
But O! I fear the kintra soon   *country*
  Will ken as weel's mysel!

O, WHISTLE AN' I'LL COME TO YE MY LAD

TUNE: *(As Title)*

CHORUS

O, whistle an' I'll come to ye, my lad!
O, whistle an' I'll come to ye, my lad!
go
Tho' father an' mother an' a' should gae mad,
O, whistle an' I'll come to ye, my lad!

I

spy
But warily tent when ye come to court me,
not; -gate; ajar
And come nae unless the back-yett be a-jee;
Then
Syne up the back-style, and let naebody see,
not
And come as ye were na comin to me,
And come as ye were na comin to me!

2

At kirk, or at market, whene'er ye meet me,
Go; fly
Gang by me as tho' that ye car'd na a flie;
glance
But steal me a blink o' your bonie black e'e,
Yet look as ye were na lookin to me,
Yet look as ye were na lookin to me!

3

sometimes;
Ay vow and protest that ye care na for me,
disparage; little
And whyles ye may lightly my beauty a wee;
But court na anither tho' jokin ye be,
entice
For fear that she wyle your fancy frae me,
For fear that she wyle your fancy frae me!

I'M O'ER YOUNG TO MARRY YET

TUNE: *(As Title)*

CHORUS

I'm o'er young, I'm o'er young,
I'm o'er young to marry yet!
I'm o'er young, 'twad be a sin
  To tak me frae my mammie yet.

1

I am my ammie's ae bairn,   only child
  Wi' unco folk I weary, Sir,   strange
And lying in a man's bed,
  I'm fley'd it make me eerie, Sir.   I fear

2

Hallowmass is come and gane,
  The nights are lang in winter, Sir,
And you an' I in ae bed—   one
  In trowth, I dare na venture, Sir!

3

Fu' loud and shrill the frosty wind
  Blaws thro' the leafless timmer, Sir,   woods
But if ye come this gate again,   way
  I'll aulder be gin simmer, Sir.   older be by

birches

THE BIRKS OF ABERFELDIE

TUNE: *The Birks of Abergeldie*

CHORUS

Bonie lassie, will ye go,
Will ye go, will ye go?
Bonie lassie, will ye go
　　　To the birks of Aberfeldie?

1

shines; slopes

Now simmer blinks on flow'ry braes,
And o'er the crystal streamlets plays,
Come, let us spend the lightsome days
　　　In the birks of Aberfeldie!

2

hang

The little birdies blythely-sing,
While o'er their heads the hazels hing,
Or lightly flit on wanton wing
　　　In the birks of Aberfeldie.

3

woods

The braes ascend like lofty wa's,
The foaming stream, deep-roaring, fa's
O'er hung with fragrant-spreading shaws,
　　　The birks of Aberfeldie.

4

falls; brooklet
wets

The hoary cliffs are crown'd wi' flowers,
White o'er the linns the burnie pours,
And, rising, weets wi' misty showers
　　　The birks of Aberfeldie.

5

Let Fortune's gifts at random flee,
They ne'er shall draw a wish frae me,
Supremely blest wi' love and thee
　　　In the birks of Aberfeldie.

MACPHERSON'S FAREWELL

TUNE: *MacPherson's Rant*

CHORUS

Sae rantingly, sae wantonly,   jovially
 Sae dauntingly gaed he,   went
He play'd a spring, and danc'd it round
 Below the gallows-tree.

1

Farewell, ye dungeons dark and strong,
 The wretch's destinie!
MacPherson's time will not be long
 On yonder gallows-tree.

2

O, what is death but parting breath?
 On many a bloody plain
I've dar'd his face, and in this place
 I scorn him yet again!

3

Untie these bands from off my hands,
 And bring to me my sword,
And there's no a man in all Scotland
 But I'll brave him at a word.

4

I've liv'd a life of sturt and strife;   trouble
 I die by treacherie:
It burns my heart I must depart,
 And not avengèd be.

5

Now farewell light, thou sunshine bright,
 And all beneath the sky!
May coward shame distain his name,
 The wretch that dare not die!

MY HIGHLAND LASSIE, O

TUNE: *MacLauchlin's Scots-Measure*

CHORUS

Within the glen sae bushy, O,
Aboon the plain sae rashy, O,
I set me down wi' right guid will
To sing my Highland lassie, O!

Above; rushy

1

Nae gentle dames, tho' ne'er sae fair,
Shall ever be my Muse's care:
Their titles a' are empty show—
Gie me my Highland lassie, O!

No highborn

Give

2

O, were yon hills and vallies mine,
Yon palace and yon gardens fine,
The world then the love should know
I bear my Highland lassie, O!

3

But fickle Fortune frowns on me,
And I maun cross the raging sea;
But while my crimson currents flow
I'll love my Highland lassie, O.

must

4

Altho' thro' foreign climes I range,
I know her heart will never change;
For her bosom burns with honour's glow,
My faithful Highland lassie, O.

5

For her I'll dare the billows' roar,
For her I'll trace a distant shore,
That Indian wealth may lustre throw
Around my Highland lassie, O.

6

She has my heart, she has my hand,
My secret troth and honour's band!
'Till the mortal stroke shall lay me low,
I'm thine, my Highland lassie, O!

Farewell the glen sae bushy, O!
Farewell the plain sae rashy, O!
To other lands I now must go
To sing my Highland lassie, O.

THO' CRUEL FATE

TUNE: *She Rose and Let Me In*

Tho' cruel fate should bid us part
    Far as the pole and line,
Her dear idea round my heart
    Should tenderly entwine.
Tho' mountains rise, and deserts howl,
    And oceans roar between,
Yet dearer than my deathless soul
    I still would love my Jean.

STAY, MY CHARMER

TUNES: *An gille dubh ciar dubh*—Urbani's *Pit-a-Patty*

1

Feel, oh feel my bosom beating
As the busy moments fleeting,
Pit-a-patty still repeating
        Like the little mallet's blow
        Like the little mallet's blow.

2

Stay, my charmer, can you leave me?
Cruel, cruel to deceive me!
Well you know how much you grieve me:
    Cruel charmer, can you go?
    Cruel charmer, can you go?

3

By my love so ill-requited,
By the faith you fondly plighted,
By the pangs of lovers slighted,
    Do not, do not leave me so!
    Do not, do not leave me so!

STRATHALLAN'S LAMENT

TUNE: *(As Title)*

1

Thickest night, surround my dwelling!
    Howling tempests, o'er me rave!
Turbid torrents wintry-swelling,
    Roaring by my lonely cave!
Crystal streamlets gently flowing,
    Busy haunts of base mankind,
Western breezes softly blowing,
    Suit not my distracted mind.

2

In the cause of Right engagèd,
    Wrongs injurious to redress,
Honour's war we strongly wagèd,
    But the heavens deny'd success.
Ruin's wheel has driven o'er us:
    Not a hope that dare attend,
The wide world is all before us,
    But a world without a friend.

MY HOGGIE   lamb

TUNE: *(As Title)*

I

What will I do gin my hoggie die?   should
   My joy, my pride, my hoggie!
My only beast, I had nae mae,   no more
   And vow but I was vogie!   vain
The lee-lang night we watched the fauld,   live-long; fold
   Me and my faithfu' doggie;
We heard nocht but the roaring linn   waterfall
   Amang the braes sae scroggie.   hill-sides;
                                                         scrubby

2

But the houlet cry'd frae the castle wa',   owl
   The blitter frae the boggie,   snipe
The tod reply'd upon the hill: fox
   I trembled for my hoggie.
When day did daw, and cocks did craw,   dawn
   The morning it was foggie,   strange dog;
An unco tyke lap o'er the dyke,   leaped; stone
                                                          fence
   And maist has kill'd my hoggie!   almost

JUMPIN JOHN

TUNE: *(As Title)*

CHORUS

The lang lad they ca' Jumpin John
   Beguil'd the bonie lassie!
The lang lad they ca' Jumpin John
   Beguil'd the bonie lassie!

I

Her daddie forbad, her minnie forbad;
   Forbidden she wadna be: would not
She wadna trow't, the browst she brew'd   believe it; liquor
   Wad taste sae bitterlie!

2

ewe; half

thirty

dowry; daughter

A cow and a cauf, a yowe and a hauf,
    And thretty guid shillins and three:
A vera guid tocher! a cotter-man's dochter,
    The lass with the bonie black e'e!

UP IN THE MORNING EARLY

TUNE: *(As Title)*

CHORUS

Up in the morning's no for me,
    Up in the morning early!
When a' the hills are covered wi' snaw.
    I'm sure it's winter fairly!

1

sorely

Cauld blaws the wind frae east to west,
    The drift is driving sairly,
Sae loud and shrill's I hear the blast—
    I'm sure it's winter fairly!

2

All

The birds sit chittering in the thorn,
    A' day they fare but sparely;
And lang's the night frae e'en to morn—
    I'm sure it's winter fairly.

THE YOUNG HIGHLAND ROVER

TUNE: *Morag*

1

Loud blaw the frosty breezes,
  The snaws the mountains cover.
Like winter on me seizes,
  Since my young Highland rover
  Far wanders nations over.
Where'er he go, where'er he stray,
  May Heaven be his warden!
Return him safe to fair Strathspey
  And bonie Castle Gordon!

2

The trees, now naked groaning,
  Shall soon wi' leaves be hinging,   hanging
The birdies, dowie moaning,   droopingly
  Shall a' be blythely singing,
  And every flower be springing:
Sae I'll rejoice the lee-lang day,   live-long
  When (by his mighty Warden)
My youth's return'd to fair Strathspey
  And bonie Castle Gordon.

THE DUSTY MILLER

TUNE: *(As Title)*

1

Hey the dusty miller
  And his dusty coat!
He will spend a shilling
  Or he win a groat.   Ere
Dusty was the coat,
  Dusty was the colour,
Dusty was the kiss
  That I gat frae the miller!

2

Hey the dusty miller
    And his dusty sack!
Leeze me on the calling
    Fills the dusty peck!
Fills the dusty peck,
    Brings the dusty siller!
I wad gie my coatie
    For the dusty miller!

I DREAM'D I LAY

TUNE: *(As Title)*

1

I dream'd I lay where flowers were springing
    Gaily in the sunny beam,
List'ning to the wild birds singing,
    By a falling crystal stream;
Straight the sky grew black and daring,
    Thro' the woods the whirlwinds rave,
Threes with agèd arms were warring
turbid   O'er the swelling, drumlie wave.

2

Such was my life's deceitful morning,
    Such the pleasures I enjoy'd!
ere   But lang or noon loud tempests, storming,
All   A' my flowery bliss destroy'd.
Tho' fickle Fortune has deceiv'd me
    (She promis'd fair, and perform'd but ill),
Of monie a joy and hope bereav'd me,
    I bear a heart shall support me still.

DUNCAN DAVISON

TUNE: *Ye'll ay be welcome back again*

1

There was a lass, they ca'd her Meg,
    And she held o'er the moors to spin;
There was a lad that follow'd her,
    They ca'd him Duncan Davison.
The moor was dreigh, and Meg was skeigh,   *dull; skittish*
    Her favour Duncan could na win;
For wi' the rock she wad him knock,   *distaff*
    And ay she shook the temper-pin.

2

As o'er the moor they lightly foor,   *fared*
    A burn was clear, a glen was green;
Upon the banks they eas'd their shanks,
    And ay she set the wheel between:
But Duncan swoor a haly aith,   *holy oath*
    That Meg should be a bride the morn;   *to-morrow*
Then Meg took up her spinnin-graith,   *-instruments*
    And flang them a' out o'er the burn.   *across the brook*

3

We will big a wee, wee house,   *build*
    And we will live like king and queen,
Sae blythe and merry's we will be,
    When ye set by the wheel at e'en!   *aside*
A man may drink, and no be drunk;
    A man may fight, and no be slain;
A man may kiss a bonie lass,
    And ay be welcome back again!

THENIEL MENZIES' BONIE MARY

TUNE: *Ruffian's Rant*

CHORUS

Theniel Menzies' bonie Mary,
Theniel Menzies' bonie Mary,
lost   *Charlie Grigor tint his plaidie,*
Kissin Theniel's bonie Mary!

1

In comin by the brig o' Dye,
while   At Darlet we a blink did tarry;
dawning   As day was dawin in the sky,
We drank a health to bonie Mary.

2

eyes   Her een sae bright, her brow sae white,
side   Her haffet locks as brown's a berry,
And ay they dimpl't wi' a smile.
The rosy cheeks o' bonie Mary.

3

leaped; live-long   We lap an' danc'd the lee-lang day,
sad   Till piper-lads were wae and weary;
tune   But Charlie gat the spring to pay,
For kissin Theniel's bonie Mary.

LADY ONLIE, HONEST LUCKY

TUNE: *Ruffian's Rant*

CHORUS

Lady Onlie, honest lucky,
    Brews guid ale at shore o' Bucky: Buchan
I wish her sale for her guid ale,
    The best on a' the shore o' Bucky!

I

A' the lads o' Thorniebank,
    When they gae to the shore o' Bucky,   go
They'll step in an' tak a pint
    Wi' Lady Onlie, honest lucky.

2

Her house sae bien, her curch sae clean—   smug; kerchief
    I wat she is a dainty chuckie,   old dear
And cheery blinks the ingle-gleede   glances; -blaze
    O' Lady Onlie, honest lucky!

THE BANKS OF THE DEVON

TUNE: *Bhannerach dhon na chrie*

I

How pleasant the banks of the clear winding Devon,
    With green spreading bushes and flow'rs blooming fair!
But the boniest flow'r on the banks of the Devon
    Was once a sweet bud on the braes of the Ayr.   slopes
Mild be the sun on this sweet blushing flower,
    In the gay rosy morn, as it bathes in the dew!
And gentle the fall of the soft vernal shower,
    That steals on the evening each leaf to renew!

2

O, spare the dear blossom, ye orient breezes,
    With chill, hoary wing as ye usher the dawn!
And far be thou distant, thou reptile that seizes
    The verdure and pride of the garden or lawn!
Let Bourbon exult in his gay gilded lilies,
    And Englnad triumphant display her proud rose!
A fairer than either adorns the green vallies,
    Where Devon, sweet Devon, meandering flows.

DUNCAN GRAY

TUNE: *(As Title)*

1

Weary fa' you, Duncan Gray!
    (Ha, ha, the girdin o't!),
Wae gae by you, Duncan Gray!
    (Ha, ha, the girdin o't!).
When a' the lave gae to their play,
Then I maun sit the lee-lang day,
And jeeg the cradle wi' my tae,
    And a' for the girdin o't!

Woe befall — Weary fa'
girthing — girdin
Woe go with — Wae gae by
rest — lave
must; live-long — maun; lee-lang
jog; toe — jeeg; tae

2

Bonie was the Lammas moon
    (Ha, ha, the girdin o't!)
Glowrin a' the hills aboon
    (Ha, ha, the girdin o't!)
The girdin brak, the beast cam down,
I tint my curch and baith my shoon,
And Duncan, ye're an unco loun—
    Wae on the bad girdin o't!

above — aboon
kerchief; shoes — curch; shoon
terrible rogue — unco loun

3

But Duncan, gin ye'll keep your aith   if; oath
  (Ha, ha, the girdin o't!)
I'se bless you wi' my hindmost breath   I'll
  (Ha, ha, the girdin o't!)
Duncan, gin ye'll keep your aith,
The beast again can bear us baith,
And auld Mess John will mend the skaith   damage
  And clout the bad girdin o't.   patch

THE PLOUGHMAN

TUNE: *(As Title)*

CHORUS

Then up wi't a', my ploughman lad,
  And hey, my merry ploughman!
Of a' the trades that I do ken,
  Commend me to the ploughman!

1

The ploughman, he's a bonie lad,
  His mind is ever true, jo!
His garters knit below his knee,
  His bonnet it is blue, jo.

2

I hae been east, I hae been west,
  I hae been at St. Johnston;   Perth
The boniest sight that e'er I saw
  Was the ploughman laddie dancin.

3

Snaw-white stockings on his legs
  And siller buckles glancin,   silver
A guid blue bonnet on his head,
  And O, but he was handsome!

4

stack-
heap
little
dish full

Commend me to the barn-yard
And the corn mou, man!
I never got my coggie fou
Till I met wi' the ploughman.

reckoning

LANDLADY, COUNT THE LAWIN

TUNE: *Hey Tuiti, Taiti*

CHORUS

Hey tutti, taiti,
How tutti, taiti,
Hey tutti, taiti,

drunk

Wha's fou now?

1

Landlady, count the lawin,

dawning

The day is near the dawin;
Ye're a' blind drunk, boys
And I'm but jolly fou.

2

Stoup; full

Cog, an ye were ay fou,
Cog, an ye were ay fou,
I wad sit and sing to you,
If ye were ay fou!

3

all

Weel may ye a' be!
Ill may ye never see!
God bless the king
And the companie!

RAVING WINDS AROUND HER BLOWING

TUNE: *MacGrigor of Rora's Lament*

1

Raving winds around her blowing,
Yellow leaves the woodlands strowing,
By a river hoarsely roaring,
Isabella stray'd deploring:—
'Farewell hours that late did measure
Sunshine days of joy and pleasure!
Hail, thou gloomy night of sorrow—
Cheerless night that knows no morrow!

2

'O'er the Past too fondly wandering,
On the hopeless Future pondering,
Chilly Grief my life-blood freezes,
Fell Despair my fancy seizes.
Life, thou soul of every blessing,
Load to Misery most distressing,
Gladly how would I resign thee,
And to dark Oblivion join thee!'

HOW LANG AND DREARY IS THE NIGHT

TUNE: *A Gaelic Air*

CHORUS

For O, her lanely nights are lang,
And O, her dreams are eerie,   full of fear
And O, her widow'd heart is sair,
That's absent frae her dearie!

1

How lang and dreary is the night,
When I am frae my dearie!
I restless lie frae e'en to morn,
Tho' I were ne'er sae weary.

2

When I think on the lightsome days
  I spent wi' thee, my dearie,
And now what seas between us roar,
  How can I be but eerie?

3

How slow ye move, ye heavy hours!
  The joyless day how dreary!
sparkled   It was na sae ye glinted by,
  When I was wi' my dearie!

MUSING ON THE ROARING OCEAN

TUNE: *Druimionn Dubh*

1

Musing on the roaring ocean,
  Which divides my love and me,
Wearying heav'n in warm devotion
welfare   For his weal where'er he be:

2

Hope and Fear's alternate billow
  Yielding late to Nature's law,
Whispering spirits round my pillow.
  Talk of him that's far awa.

3

Ye whom sorrow never wounded,
  Ye who never shed a tear,
Care-untroubled, joy-surrounded,
  Gaudy day to you is dear!

4

Gentle night, do thou befriend me!
  Downy sleep, the curtain draw!
Spirits kind, again attend me,
  Talk of him that's far awa!

BLYTHE WAS SHE

TUNE: *Andro and his Cutty Gun*

CHORUS

Blythe, blythe and merry was she,
  Blythe was she butt and ben,   in kitchen and
Blythe by the banks of Earn,   parlour
  And blythe in Glenturit glen!

1

By Oughtertyre grows the aik,   oak
  On Yarrow banks the birken shaw;   birch wood
But Phemie was a bonier lass
  Than braes o' Yarrow ever saw.   heights

2

Her looks were like a flow'r in May,
  Her smile was like a simmer morn.
She trippèd by the banks o' Earn
  As light's a bird upon a thorn.   light as

3

Her bonie face it was as meek
  As onie lamb upon a lea.
The evening son was ne'er sae sweet
  As was the blink o' Phemie's e'e.   glance

4

The Highland hills I've wander'd wide,
  As o'er the Lawlands I hae been,
But Phemie was the blythest lass
  That ever trod the dewy green.

conquer

TO DAUNTON ME

TUNE: *(As Title)*

CHORUS

To daunton me, to daunton me,
An auld man shall never daunton me!   } *Bis.*

1

The blude-red rose at Yule may blaw,
The simmer lilies bloom in snaw,
The frost may freeze the deepest sea,
But an auld man shall never daunton me.

2

To daunton me, and me sae young,
Wi' his fause heart and flatt'ring tongue:
That is the thing you ne'er shall see,
For an auld man shall never daunton me.

malt

3

For a' his meal and a' his maut,
For a' his fresh beef and his saut,
For a' his gold and white monie,
An auld man shall never daunton me.

money; kine;
sheep
knolls

4

His gear may buy him kye and yowes,
His gear may buy him glens and knowes;
But me he shall not buy nor fee,
For an auld man shall never daunton me.

hobbles two-
fold; can
mouth; bald
pate

5

He hirples twa-fauld as he dow,
Wi' his teethless gab and his auld beld pow,
And the rain rains down frae his red blear'd e'e—
That auld man shall never daunton me!

O'ER THE WATER TO CHARLIE

TUNE: *Over the Water to Charlie*

CHORUS

We'll o'er the water, we'll o'er the sea,
We'll o'er the water to Charlie!
Come weal, come woe, we'll gather and go,
And live and die wi' Charlie!

I

Come boat me o'er, come row me o'er,
   Come boat me o'er to Charlie!
I'll gie John Ross another bawbee
   To boat me o'er to Charlie.

2

I lo'e weel my Charlie's name,
   Tho' some there be abhor him;
But O, to see Auld Nick gaun hame,   going
   And Charlie's faes before him!

3

I swear and vow by moon and stars
   And sun that shines so early,
If I had twenty thousand lives,
   I'd die as aft for Charlie!

A ROSE-BUD, BY MY EARLY WALK

TUNE: *A Rose-bud*

I

A rose-bud, by my early walk
Adown a corn-inclosèd bawk,   field-path
Sae gently bent its thorny stalk,
   All on a dewy morning.
Ere twice the shades o' dawn are fled,
In a' its crimson glory spread
And drooping rich the dewy head,
   It scents the early morning.

2

Within the bush her covert nest
A little linnet fondly prest,
The dew sat chilly on her breast,
  Sae early in the morning.
She soon shall see her tender brood,
The pride, the pleasure o' the wood,
Amang the fresh green leaves bedew'd,
  Awake the early morning.

3

So thou, dear bird, young Jeany fair,
On trembling string or vocal air
Shall sweetly pay the tender care
guards   That tents thy early morning!
So thou, sweet rose-bud, young and gay,
Shalt beauteous blaze upon the day,
And bless the parent's evening ray
  That watch'd thy early morning!

AND I'LL KISS THEE YET

TUNE: *Braes o' Balquhidder*

CHORUS

And I'll kiss thee yet, yet
 And I'll kiss thee o'er again,
And I'll kiss thee yet, yet,
 My bonie Peggy Alison.

1

When in my arms, wi' a' thy charms,
 I clasp my countless treasure, O,
I seek nae mair o' Heav'n to share
such   Than sic a moment's pleasure, O!

2

eyes And by thy een sae bonie blue
 I swear I'm thine for ever, O!
And on thy lips I seal my vow,
 And break it shall I never, O!

RATTLIN, ROARIN WILLIE

TUNE: *(As Title)*

1

O, rattlin, roarin Willie,
  O, he held to the fair,
An' for to sell his fiddle
  And buy some other ware;
But parting wi' his fiddle,
  The saut tear blin't his e'e—
And, rattlin, roarin Willie,
  Ye're welcome hame to me!

2

'O Willie, come sell your fiddle,
  O, sell your fiddle sae fine!
O Willie, come sell your fiddle
  And buy a pint o' wine!'
'If I should sell my fiddle,
  The warld would think I was mad;
For monie a rantin day   merry
  My fiddle and I hae had.'

3

As I cam by Crochallan,
  I cannily keekit ben,   quietly look in
Rattlin, roarin Willie
  Was sitting at yon boord-en':
Sitting at yon boord-en',
  And amang guid companie!
Rattlin, roarin Willie,
  Ye're welcome hame to me.

WHERE, BRAVING ANGRY WINTER'S STORMS

TUNE: *Lament for Abercairney*

1

Where, braving angry winter's storms,
    The lofty Ochils rise,
Far in their shade my Peggy's charms
    First blest my wondering eyes:
As one who by some savage stream
    A lonely gem surveys,
Astonish'd doubly, marks it beam
    With art's most polish'd blaze.

2

Blest be the wild, sequester'd glade,
    And blest the day and hour,
Where Peggy's charms I first survey'd,
    When first I felt their pow'r!
The tyrant Death with grim control
    May seize my fleeting breath,
But tearing Peggy from my soul
    Must be a stronger death.

O TIBBIE, I HAE SEEN THE DAY

TUNE: *Invercauld's Reel*

CHORUS

would not have

> *O Tibbie, I hae seen the day,*
>   *Ye wadna been sae shy!*

lack of wealth;
scorn
I care not
although you do

> *For laik o' gear ye lightly me,*
>   *But, trowth, I care na by.*

1

Last night

Yestreen I met you on the moor,

spoke not; went;
blowing dust
toss your head
fiend

Ye spak na, but gaed by like stoure!
Ye geck at me because I'm poor—
    But fient a hair care I!

2

When comin hame on Sunday last,
Upon the road as I cam past,
Ye snufft an' gae your head a cast—   gave
    But, trowth, I care't na by!   cared

3

I doubt na, lass, but ye may think,
Because ye hae the name o' clink,   wealth
That ye can please me at a wink,
    Whene'er ye like to try.

4

But sorrow tak him that's sae mean,
Altho' his pouch o' coin were clean,
Wha follows onie saucy quean,
    That looks sae proud and high!

5

Altho' a lad were e'er sae smart,
If that he want the yellow dirt,
Ye'll cast your head anither airt,   direction
    And answer him fu' dry.

6

But if he hae the name o' gear,
Ye'll fasten to him like a brier,
Tho' hardly he for sense or lear   learning
    Be better than the kye.   kine

7

But, Tibbie, lass, tak my advice:
Your daddie's gear maks you sae nice,
The Deil a ane wad spier your price,   ask
    Were ye as poor as I.

8

There lives a lass beside yon park,
I'd rather hae her in her sark   shift
Than you wi' a' your thousand mark,
    That gars you look sae high.   makes

CLARINDA, MISTRESS OF MY SOUL

TUNE: *Clarinda*

1

Clarinda, mistress of my soul,
   The measur'd time is run!
The wretch beneath the dreary pole
   So marks his latest sun.

2

To what dark cave of frozen night
   Shall poor Sylvander hie,
Depriv'd of thee, his life and light,
   The sun of all his joy?

3

We part—but, by these precious drops
   That fill thy lovely eyes,
No other light shall guide my steps
   Till thy bright beams arise!

4

She, the fair sun of all her sex,
   Has blest my glorious day;
And shall a glimmering planet fix
   My worship to its ray?

THE WINTER IT IS PAST

TUNE: *(As Title)*

1

The winter it is past, and the simmer comes at last,
   And the small birds sing on ev'ry tree:
The hearts of these are glad, but mine is very sad,
   For my love is parted from me.

2

The rose upon the brier by the waters running clear
  May have charms for the linnet or the bee:
Their little loves are blest, and their little hearts at rest,
  But my lover is parted from me.

3

My love is like the sun in the firmament does run—
  Forever is constant and true;
But his is like the moon, that wanders up and down,
  And every month it is new.

4

All you that are in love, and cannot it remove,
  I pity the pains you endure,
For experience makes me know that your hearts are full
    of woe,
  A woe that no mortal can cure.

I LOVE MY LOVE IN SECRET

TUNE: *(As Title)*

CHORUS

My Sandy O, my Sandy O,
My bonie, bonie Sandy O!
Tho' the love that I owe
To thee I dare na show,
Yet I love my love in secret,
  My Sandy O!

1

My Sandy gied to me a ring   gave
Was a' beset wi' diamonds fine;
But I gied him a far better thing,
I gied my heart in pledge o' his ring.

2

My Sandy brak a piece o' gowd,   gold
While down his cheeks the saut tears row'd;   salt; rolled
He took a hauf, and gied it to me,   half
And I'll keep it till the hour I die.

SWEET TIBBIE DUNBAR

TUNE: *Johnny MacGill*

I

O, wilt thou go wi' me, sweet Tibbie Dunbar?
O, wilt thou go wi' me, sweet Tibbie Dunbar?
Wilt thou ride on a horse, or be drawn in a car,
Or walk by my side, O Sweet Tibbie Dunbar?

2

I care na thy daddie, his lands and his money;
I car na thy kin, sae high and sae lordly;
But say that thou'lt hae me for better or waur,
And come in thy coatie, sweet Tibbie Dunbar.

FINE FLOWERS IN THE VALLEY

TUNE: *(As Title)*

I

She sat down below a thorn,
    Fine flowers in the valley,
And there she has her sweet babe born
    And the green leaves they grow rarely.

2

Smile na sae sweet, my bonie babe
    Fine flowers in the valley,
And ye smile sae sweet, ye'll smile me dead,
    And the green leaves they grow rarely.

3

She's taen out her little penknife
    Fine flowers in the valley,
And twinn'd the sweet babe o' its life,
    And the green leaves they grow rarely.

4

She's howket a grave by the light o' the moon,   *dug*
    Fine flowers in the valley,
And there she's buried her sweet babe in,
    And the green leaves they grow rarely.

5

    As she was going to the church,
      Fine flowers in the valley,
    She saw a sweet babe in the porch,
      And the green leaves they grow rarely.

6

O sweet babe and thou were mine,
    Fine flowers in the valley,
I wad cleed thee in the silk so fine   *clothe*
    And the green leaves they grow rarely.

7

O mother dear, when I was thine,
    Fine flowers in the valley,
You did na prove to me sae kind,
    And the green leaves the grow rarely.

SONG: ANNA THY CHARMS

TUNE: *Bonny Mary*

1

    Anna thy charms my bosom fire,
      And waste my soul with care;
    But ah! how bootless to admire
      When fated to despair!

2

    Yet in thy presence, lovely Fair,
      To hope may be forgiven:
    For sure 'twere impious to despair
      So much in sight of Heaven.

MY SOGER LADDIE

TUNE: *(As Title)*

CHORUS

My soger laddie, I lang hae lo'ed weel,
Now nearer my heart I tender thee still:
To Country thou'rt loyal, to friendship thou'rt
steady,
My blessin gae wi' thee, my soger laddie.

I

My soger laddie gaed over the sea,
won   And there he wan fame and laurels to me;
And now her embraces thy country has ready
To welcome thee hame, my soger laddie.

AS I WAS A WAND'RING

TUNE: *Rinn m'eudial mo mhealladh*

CHORUS

Weel, since he has left me, may pleasure gae wi' him;
I may be distress'd but I winna complain:
I'll flatter my fancy I may get anither
My heart it shall never be broken for ane.

I

As I was a wand'ring ae midsummer e'enin
The pipers and youngsters were making their
game,
Amang them I spyed my faithless fause luver,
When bled a' the wounds o' my dolour again.

2

I could na get sleepin till dawin, for greetin;
The tears trickl'd down like the hail and the rain:
Had I na got greetin, my heart wad a broken,
For oh, luve forsaken's a tormenting pain!

3

Although he has left me for greed o' the siller,
I dinna envý him the gains he can win:
I rather wad bear a' the lade o' my sorrow,
Than ever hae acted sae faithless to him.

HEY HOW JOHNIE LAD

TUNE: *The Lasses of the Ferry*

1

Hey, how, my Johnie lad, ye're no sae kind's ye sud hae been;   should
Gin your voioo I had na kent, I cou'd na elthly trow my een.
Sae weel's ye might hae touzled me, and sweetly prie'd my
    mou bedeen;
Hey, how, my Johnie lad, ye're no sae kind's ye sud hae been.   mouth
                                                                forthwith

2

My Father he was at the pleugh, my Mither she was at the
    mill,
My Billie he was at the moss, and no ane near our sport to
    spill,   spoil
The feint a Body was therein there was nae fear of being seen,
Hey, how, my Johnie lad, ye're no sae kind's ye sud hae been.

3

Wad only lad who lo'ed her weel, hae left his bonny lass her
    lane,
To sigh and greet ilk langsome hour, and think her sweetest
    minutes gane,
O, had ye been a wooer leal, we shu'd hae met wi' hearts mair
    keen,
Hey, how, my Johnie lad, ye're no sae kind's ye sud hae been.

4

But I maun hae anither joe, whase love gangs never out o'
    mind,
And winna let the moment pass, when to a lass he can be
    kind,
Then gang your wa's to blinken Bess, nae mair for Johnie shall
ways long for   she green,
Hey, how, my Johnie lad, ye're no sae kind's ye sud hae been.

O FARE YE WEEL MY AULD WIFE

TUNE: *(As Title)*

1

O, fare ye weel, my auld wife!
    Sing bum bibery bum,
O fare ye weel my auld wife!
    Sing bum.
O fare ye weel my auld wife!
trouble   The steerer up o' sturt and strife,
The maut's aboon the meal the night
malt   Wi' some.

2

An fare ye weel, my pyke-staff,
    Sing bum bibery bum,
An fare ye weel, my pyke-staff,
    Sing bum.
An fare ye weel, my pyke-staff,
strike   Nae mair wi' you my wife I'll baff,
The maut's aboon the meal the night
        Wi' some.

THE SHEPHERD'S WIFE

TUNE: *(Title not traced)*

I

The shepherd's wife cries o'er the knowe,   hill
  'Will ye come hame, will ye come hame?'
The shepherd's wife cries o'er the knowe,
  'Will ye come hame again e'en jo?'   by even
'O what will ye gie me to my supper,
  Gin I come hame, gin I come hame,
O what will ye gie me to my supper,
  Gin I come hame again e'en jo?'

2

'Ye'se get a panfu' o' plumpin parridge,
  And butter in them, and butter in them,
Ye'se get a panfu' o' plumpin parridge,
  Gin ye'll come hame again e'en, jo?'
'Ha, ha, how! that's naething that dow,
  I winna come hame, I canna come hame;
Ha, ha, how! that's naething that dow,
  I winna come hame gin e'en jo.'

3

The shepherd's wife cries o'er the knowe,
  'Will ye come hame, will ye come hame?'
The shepherd's wife cries o'er the knowe,
  'Will he come hame again e'en jo?'
'O what will ye gie me to my supper,
  Gin I come hame, gin I come hame,
O what will ye gie me to my supper,
  Gin I come hame again e'en jo?'

4

'A reekin fat hen, weel fryth'd i' the pan,
  Gin ye'll come hame, gin ye'll come hame,
A reekin fat hen weel fryth'd i' the pan,
  Gin ye'll come hame again e'en jo.'
'Ha, ha, how! that's naething that dow,
  I winna come hame, I canna come hame;
Ha, ha, how! that's naething that dow,
  I winna come hame gin e'en, jo.'

5

The shepherd's wife cries o'er the knowe,
    'Will ye come hame, will ye come hame?'
The shepherd's wife cries o'er the knowe,
    'Will ye come hame again e'en jo?.
'O what will ye gie me to my supper,
    Gin I come hame, gin I come hame,
O what will ye gie me to my supper,
    Gin I come hame again e'en jo?'

6

'A weel made bed and a pair o' clean sheets,
    Gin ye'll come hame, gin ye'll come hame,
A weel made bed and a pair o' clean sheets,
    Gin ye'll come hame again e'en, jo.'
'Ha, ha, how! that's naething that dow,
    I winna come hame, I canna come hame;
Ha, ha, how! that's naething that dow,
    I winna come hame gin e'en, jo.'

7

The shepherd's wife cries o'er the knowe,
    'Will ye come hame, will ye come hame?'
The shepherd's wife cries o'er the knowe,
    'Will ye come hame again e'en jo?'
'O what will ye gie me to my supper,
    Gin I come hame, gin I come hame,
O what will ye gie me to my supper,
    Gin I come hame again e'en jo?'

8

'A luving wife in lily white linens,
    Gin ye'll come hame, gin ye'll come hame,
A luving wife in lily white linens,
    Gin ye'll come hame again e'en, jo.'
'Ha, ha, how! that's something that dow,
    I will come hame, I will come hame:
Ha, ha, how! that's something that dow,
    I will come hame again e'en, jo.'

MY FIDDLE AND I

TUNE: *Green Sleeves*

1

Green sleeves and tartan ties
  Mark my true love where she lies:
I'll be at her or she rise,
  My fiddle and I thegither.

2

Be it by the crystal burn,
  Be it by the milk-white thorn;
I shall rouse her in the morn,
  My fiddle and I thegither.

I COURTED A LASSIE

TUNE: *(Unknown)*

CHORUS

And e'en let her gang—and e'en let her gang,
And e'en let her gang, say I.

1

I courted a lassie, I courted her lang,
  The lassie she did comply;
But she has proved fickle and broken her vow,
  And e'en let her gang, say I.

NAE BIRDIES SANG THE MIRKY HOUR

TUNE: *Sweet Willy*

1

Nae birdies sang the mirky hour
  Amang the braes o' Yarrow,
But slumber'd on the dewy boughs,
  To wait the wauk'ning morrow.

2

'Where shall I gang, my ain true love,
  Where shall I gang to hide me;
For weel ye ken, i' ye're father's bow'r,
  It wad be death to find me.'

3

'O, go you to yon tavern house,
  An' there count o'er your lawin,
An' if I be a woman true,
  I'll meet you in the dawin.'

4

O, he's gone to yon tavern house,
  An' ay he counted his lawin,
An' ay he drank to her gude health—
  Was to meet him in the dawin.

5

O, he's gone to yon tavern house,
  An' counted owre his lawin,
When in there cam three arméd men
  To meet him in the dawin.

6

'O, woe be unto woman's wit,
  It has beguiléd many!
She promiséd to come hersel,
  But she sent three men to slay me.'

   .   .   .   .   .   .

7

'Get up, get up, now Sister Anne,
  I fear we've wrought you sorrow;
Get up, ye'll find your true love slain
  Among the banks of Yarrow.

8

She sought him east, she sought him west,
  She sought him braid and narrow,
cleft, rock   Till in the clintin of a craig,
  She found him drown'd in Yarrow.

9

She's ta'en three links of her yellow hair
   That hung down long and yellow;
And she's tied it about sweet Willie's waist,
   An' drawn him out of Yarrow.

    .   .   .   .   .   .

10

I made my love a suit of clothes,
   I clad him all in tartan;
But ere the morning sun arose
   He was a' bluid to the gartan.   *garter*

    .   .   .   .   .   .

AS LATE BY A SODGER I CHANCED TO PASS

TUNE: *I'll mak you be fain to follow me*

1

As late by a sodger I chancèd to pass,
I heard him a courtin a bonie young lass,
'My hinny, my life, my dearest,' quo he,
'I'll mak you be fain to follow me.'
'Gin I should follow you a poor sodger lad
Ilk ane o' my cummers wad think I was mad.
For battles I never shall lang to see,
I'll never be fain to follow thee.'

2

'To follow me, I think ye may be glad,
A part o' my supper, a part o' my bed,
A part o' my bed, wherever it be,
I'll mak ye be fain to follow me.
Come try my knapsack on your back,
Alang the king's highgate we'll pack,
Between Saint Johnston and bonie Dundee,
I'll mak you be fain to follow me.'

O DEAR MINNY, WHAT SHALL I DO?

TUNE: *O dear minny*

CHORUS

O dear minny, what shall I do?
O dear minny, what shall I do?
O dear minny, what shall I do?
'Daft thing, doylt thing, do as I do.'

I

If I be black, I canna be lo'ed;
If I be fair I canna be gude;
If I be lordly, the lads will look by me:
O dear minny, what shall I do?

LASSIE, LEND ME YOUR BRAW HEMP HECKLE

TUNE: *The Bob o' Dumblane*

I

Lassie, lend me your braw hemp heckle,
comb   And I'll lend you my thrippling-kame;
My heckle is broken, it canna be gotten,
    And we'll gae dance the Bob o' Dumblane.

2

Twa gaed to the wood, to the wood, to the wood,
    Twa gaed to the wood—three cam hame;
An it be na weel bobbit, weel bobbit, weel bobbit,
    An it be na weel bobbit, we'll bob it again.

O, GALLOWAY TAM CAM HERE TO WOO

TUNE: *Galloway Tam*

I

O, Galloway Tam cam here to woo;
I'd rather we'd gien him the brawnit cow;   red-brown
For our lass Bess may curse and ban
The wanton wit o' Galloway Tam.

2

O, Galloway Tam cam here to shear;
I'd rather we'd gien him the gude gray mare;
He kist the gudewife and strack the gudeman;
And that's the tricks o' Galloway Tam.

THE COLLIER HAS A DOCHTER

TUNE: *The collier's bonie lassie*

I

The Collier has a dochter,
    And O, she's wonder bonie!
A laird he was that sought her,
    Rich baith in lands and money:
She wadna hae a laird,
    Nor wad she be a lady,
But she wad hae a collier
    The color o' her daddie.

SHE PLAY'D THE LOON OR SHE WAS MARRIED

TUNE: *My wife's a wanton wee thing*

CHORUS

My wife's a wanton wee thing,
My wife's a wanton wee thing,
My wife's a wanton wee thing,
She winna be guided by me.

1

strumpet

She play'd the loon or she was married,
She play'd the loon or she was married,
She play'd the loon or she was married,
    She'll do it again or she die.

2

She sell'd her coat and she drank it,
She sell'd her coat and she drank it,
She row'd hersel in a blanket,—
    She winna be guided by me.

3

She mind't na when I forbade her,
She mind't na when I forbade her,
I took a rung and I claw'd her,
    And a braw gude bairn was she.

THERE'S CAULD KAIL IN ABERDEEN

TUNE: *Cauld Kail*

CHORUS

My coggie, Sirs, my coggie, Sirs,   dish
  I cannot want my coggie:
I wadna gie my three-girr'd cap,   -hooped dish
  For e'er a quean on Bogie.

1

There's cauld kail in Aberdeen,
  An castocks in Strathbogie,   cabbage
When ilka lad maun hae his lass,   stalks
  They fye, gie me my coggie.

2

There's Johnie Smith has got a wife
  That scrimps him o' his coggie,
If she were mine, upon my life
  I wad douk her in a bogie.   duck; bog

WHEN WE GAED TO THE BRAES O' MAR

TUNE: *Up, and warn a', Willie*

CHORUS

Up, and warn a', Willie,
Warn, warn a';
To hear my canty Highland sang
Relate the think I saw, Willie.

I

When we gaed to the braes o' Mar,
    And to the weapon–shaw, Willie;
Wi' true design to serve the king
    And banish Whigs awa, Willie.
Up, and warn a', Willie,
    Warn, warn a';
    For lords and lairds came there bedeen,
    And wow! but they were braw, Willie.

-show

2

But when the standard was set up,
    Right fierce the wind did blaw Willie,
The royal nit upon the tap
    Down to the ground did fa', Willie.
Up, and warn a', Willie,
    Warn, warn a';
    Then second-sighted Sandie said
    We'd do nae gude at a', Willie.

nut

3

But when the army join'd at Perth,
    The bravest e'er ye saw, Willie,
We didna doubt the rogues to rout,
    Restore our king an a', Willie.
Up, and warn a', Willie,
    Warn, warn a';
    The pipers play'd frae right to left
    O *whirry Whigs awa*, Willie.

4

But when we march'd to Sherramuir
    And there the rebels saw, Willie;
Brave Argyle attack'd our right,
    Our flank, and front and a', Willie;
Up, and warn a', Willie,
        Warn, warn a';
    Traiter Huntly soon gave way,
        Seaforth, St. Clair and a', Willie.

5

But brave Glengary on our right
    The rebels' left did claw, Willie;
He there the greatest slaughter made
    That ever Donald saw, Willie;
Up, and warn a', Willie,
        Warn, warn a';
    and Whittam fyled his breeks for fear,   soiled
        And fast did rin awa, Willie.

6

For he ca'd us a Highland mob,
    And soon he'd slay us a', Willie;
But we chas'd him back to Stirling brig—
    Dragoons, and foot, and a', Willie.
Up, and warn a', Willie,
        Warn, warn a';
    At length we rallied on a hill,
        And briskly up did draw, Willie.

7

But when Argyle did view our line
    And them in order saw, Willie,
He straight gaed to Dumblane again,
    And back his left did draw, Willie.
Up, and warn a', Willie,
        Warn, warn a';
    Then we to Auchterairder march'd
        To wait a better fa', Willie.

8

Now if ye spier wha wan the day,
　I've tell'd you what I saw, Willie,
We baith did fight, and baith did beat,
　And baith did rin awa, Willie.
Up, and warn a', Willie,
　　Warn, warn a';
For second-sighted Sandie said
　　We'd do nae gude at a', Willie.

SIR JOHN COPE TRODE THE NORTH RIGHT FAR

TUNE: *Johnie Cope*

CHORUS

Hey! Johnie Cope, are ye wauking yet?
Or are ye sleeping I would wit;
O, haste ye get up, for the drums do beat;
　O fye! Cope, rise in the morning.

1

　Sir John Cope trode the north right far,
near　Yet ne'er a rebel he cam naur,
　Until he landed at Dunbar
　　Right early in a morning.

2

　He wrote a challenge from Dunbar,
dare　'Come fight me, Charlie, an ye daur,
　If it be not by the chance of war
　　I'll give you a merry morning.'

3

　When Charlie look'd the letter upon,
　He drew his sword the scabbard from—
　'So Heaven restore to me my own,
　　I'll meet you, Cope, in the morning.'

4

Cope swore, with many a bloody word,
That he would fight them gun and sword,
But he fled frae his next like an ill-scar'd bird,
   And Johnie took wing in the morning.

5

It was upon an afternoon,
Sir Johnie march'd to Preston town,
He says, 'My lads come lean you down,
   And we'll fight the boys in the morning.'

6

But when he saw the Highland lads,
Wi' tartan trews and white cockauds,
Wi' swords, and guns, and rungs, and gauds—
   O Johnie, he took wing in the morning.

7

On the morrow when he did rise,
He looked between him and the skies;
He saw them wi' their naked thighs,
   Which fear'd him in the morning.

8

O, then he flew into Dunbar,
Crying for a man of war;
He thought to have passed for a rustic tar,
   And gotten awa in the morning.

9

Sir Johnie into Berwick rade,
Just as the devil had been his guide;
Gien him the warld he would na stay'd
   To foughten the boys in the morning.   fight

10

Says the Berwickers unto Sir John:
'O what's become of all your men?'
'In faith,' says he, 'I dinna ken—
   I left them a' this morning'.

11

shy

Says Lord Mark Car—'Ye are na blate
To bring us the news o' your ain defeat,
I think you deserve the back o' the gate!
    Get out o' my sight this morning.'

THERE LIV'D A MAN IN YONDER GLEN

TUNE: *Johnie Blunt*

1

There liv'd a man in yonder glen,
    And John Blunt was his name, O;
malt   He maks gude maut, and he brews gude ale,
    And he bears a wondrous fame, O.

2

porch   The wind blew in the hallan ae night,
    Fu' snell out o'er the moor, O;
'Rise up, rise up, auld Luckie' he says,
    'Rise up and bar the door, O;'

3

pact   They made a paction 'tween them twa,
    They made it firm and sure, O,
Whae'er sud speak the foremost word,
    Should rise and bar the door, O.

4

lost; road   Three travellers that had tint their gate,
    As thro' the hills they foor, O;
They airted by the line o' light
    Fu' straight to Johnie Blunt's door, O.

5

dragged   They haurl'd auld Luckie out o' her bed,
    And laid her on the floor, O;
But never a word auld Luckie wad say,
    For barrin o' the door, O.

6

'Ye've eaten my bread, ye hae druken my ale,
  And ye'll mak my auld wife a whore, O.'—
'Aha! Johnie Blunt! ye hae spoke the first word,—
  Get up and bar the door, O.'

UPON THE LOMONDS I LAY, I LAY

TUNE: *The Campbells are comin*

CHORUS

The Campbells are comin, Oho! Oho!
  The Campbells are comin, Oho! Oho!
The Campbells are comin to bonie Lochleven,
  The Campbells are comin, Oho! Oho!

1

Upon the Lomonds I lay, I lay,
  Upon the Lomonds I lay, I lay,
I lookèd down to bonie Lochleven
  And saw three bonie perches play.

2

Great Argyle he goes before;
  He maks his cannons and guns to roar,
Wi' sound o' trumpet, pipe and drum;
  The Campbells are comin, Oho! Oho!

3

The Campbells they are a' in arms,
  Their loyal faith and truth to show,
Wi' banners rattling in the wind,
  The Campbells are comin, Oho! Oho!

TWA BONIE LADS WERE SANDY AND JOCKIE

TUNE: *Jenny's Lamentation*

Twa bonie lads were Sandy and Jockie,
Jockie was lo'ed but Sandy unlucky,
Jockie was laird baith of hills and of vallies,
But Sandy was nought but the king o' gude
    fellows.
Jockie lo'ed Madgie, for Madgie had money,
And Sandy lo'ed Mary for Mary was bonie,
Ane wedded for love, ane wedded for treasure,
So Jockie had siller and Sandy had pleasure.

IT'S UP WI' THE SOUTERS O' SELKIRK

TUNE: *The Souters o' Selkirk*

Cobblers

It's up wi' the Souters o' Selkirk,
    And down wi' the Earl of Hume,
And here is to a' the braw laddies

shoes

    That wear the single-sol'd shoon.
It's up wi' the Souters o' Selkirk,
    For they are baith trusty and leal,
And up wi' the lads o' the Forest,
    And down wi' the Merse to the deil!

OUR LORDS ARE TO THE MOUNTAINS GANE

TUNE: *Druimionn dubh*

I

Ours lords are to the mountains gane,
    A hunting o' the fallow deer;

gripped

And they hae gripit Hughie Graham,
    For stealing o' the bishop's mare.

2

And they hae tied him hand and foot,
    And led him up thro' Stirling town;
The lads and lassies met him there,
    Cried 'Hughie Graham thou art a loun'.

3

'O lowse my right hand free,' he says,   loosen
    'And put my braid sword in the same,
He's no in Stirling town this day,
    Daur tell the tale to Hughie Gramah.'   Dare

4

Up then bespake the brave Whitefoord,
    As he sat by the bishop's knee;
'Five hundred white stots I'll gie you,   cattle
    If ye'll let Hughie Graham gae free.'

5

'O haud your tongue,' the bishop says,
    'And wi' your pleading let me be;
For tho' ten Grahams were in his coat,
    Hughie Graham this day shall die.'

6

Up then bespake the fair Whitefoord,
    As she sat by the bishop's knee,
'Five hundred white pence I'll gie you,
    If ye'll gie Hughie Graham to me.'

7

'O haud your tongue now lady fair,
    And wi' your pleading let it be;
Altho' ten Grahams were in his coat,
    It's for my honor he maun die.'

8

They've taen him to the gallows knowe,
    He lookèd to the gallows tree,
Yet never color left his check,
    Nor ever did he blin' his e'e.

9

At length he lookèd round about,
     To see whatever he could spy,
And there he saw his auld fathèr,
     And he was weeping bitterly.

10

'O haud your tongue, my father dear
     And wi' your weeping let it be;
For tho' they rob me o' my life,
high   They cannot o' the Heaven hie.

11

'And ye may gie my brother John
     My sword that's bent in the middle clear,
And let him come at twelve o'clock,
     And see me pay the bishop's mare.

12

'And ye may gie my brother James
     My sword that's bent in the middle brown,
And bid him come at four o'clock,
     And see his brother Hugh cut down.

13

'Remember me to Maggy, my wife,
next   The niest time ye gang o'er the moor,
stole   Tell her she staw the bishop's mare,
     Tell her she was the bishop's whore.

14

'And ye may tell my kith and kin
     I never did disgrace their blood;
And when they meet the bishop's cloak,
     To make it shorter by the hood.'

AS I CAM DOWN BY YON CASTLE WA'

TUNE: *(As Title)*

1

As I cam down by yon castle wa',
    And in by yon garden green,
O, there I spied a bonie, bonie lass,
    But the flower-borders were us between.

2

A bonie, bonie lassie she was,
    As ever mine eyes did see:
'O, five hundred pounds would I give,
    For to have such a pretty bride as thee.'

3

'To have such a pretty bride as me,   sorely
    Young man ye are sairly mistaen;   mistaken
Tho' ye were king o' fair Scotland,
    I wad disdain to be your queen.'

4

'Talk not so very high, bonie lass,
    O talk not so very, very high:
The man at the fair that wad sell,   would
    He maun learn at the man that wad buy.   must

5

'I trust to climb a far higher tree,
    And herry a far richer nest: rob
Tak this advice o' me bonie lass,
    Humility wad set thee best.'

O, WHERE HAE YE BEEN LORD RONALD, MY SON?

TUNE: *(As Title)*

1

'O, where hae ye been Lord Ronald, my son?
O, where hae ye been Lord Ronald, my son?'
'I hae been wi' my sweetheart, mother, make my bed
    soon,
For I'm weary wi' the hunting, and fain wad lie down.'

2

'What got ye frae your sweetheart, Lord Ronald, my son?
What got ye frae your sweetheart, Lord Ronald, my son?'
'I hae got deadly poison, mother, make my bed soon,
For life is a burden that soon I'll lay down.'

AS I WENT OUT AE MAY MORNING

TUNE: *(As Title)*

1

As I went out ae May morning,
   A May morning it chanc'd to be;
There I was aware of a weel-far'd maid,
   Cam linkin o'er the lea to me.

2

O, but she was a weel-far'd maid,
   The boniest lass that's under the sun;
asked   I spier'd gin she could fancy me,
   But her answer was, 'I am too young.

3

'To be your bride I an too young,
   To be your loun wad shame my kin,
So therefore pray young man begone,
   For you never, never shall my favour win.'

4

But amang yon birks and hawthorns green,
   Where roses blaw and woodbines hing,
O, there I learn'd my bonie lass,
   That she was not a single hour too young.

5

The lassie blush'd, the lassie sigh'd,
   And the tear stood twinklin in her e'e;
'O kind Sir, since ye hae done me this wrang,
   It's pray when will ye marry me.'

6

'It's of that day tak ye nae heed,
   For that's a day ye ne'er shall see;
For ought that passed between us twa,
   Ye had your share as weel as me.'

7

She wrang her hands, she tore her hair,
   She crièd out most bitterlie,
'O, what will I say to my mammie
   When I gae hame wi' a *fause storie.*'   false

8

'O, as ye maut, so maun ye brew,   malt
   And as ye brew, so maun ye tun: cask
But come to my arms, my ae bonie lass,
   For ye never shall rue what ye now hae done.'

THERE WAS A BATTLE IN THE NORTH

TUNE: *A Country Lass*

1

There was a battle in the north,
   And nobles there was many,
And they hae kill'd Sir Charlie Hay,
   And they laid the wyte on Geordie.   blame

2

O, he has written a lang letter—
   He sent it to his lady:—
Ye maun cum up to Enbrugh town
   To see what words o' Geordie.'

3

When first she look'd the letter on,
   She was baith red and rosy;
But she had na read a word but twa,
   Till she wallow't like a lily.

4

'Gar get to me my gude grey steed,
servants   My menzie a' gae wi' me;
For I shall neither eat nor drink
   Till Enbrugh town shall see me.'

5

And she has mountit her gude grey steed,
servants   Her menzie a' gaed wi' her;
And she did neither eat nor drink
   Till Enbrugh town did see her.

6

And first appear'd the fatal block,
axe   And syne the aix to head him,
And Geordie cam down the stair
iron   And bands o' airn upon him.

7

But tho' he was chain'd in fetters strang,
   O' airn and steel sae heavy,
There was na ane in a' the court
   Sae bra' a man as Geordie.

8

O, she's down on her bended knee,
   I wat she's pale and weary;
'O pardon, pardon, noble king
   And gie me back my Dearie!

9

'I hae born seven sons to my Geordie dear
    The seventh ne'er saw his daddie:
O, pardon, pardon, noble king,
    Pity a waefu' lady!'

10

'Gar bid the headin'-man mak haste!'
    Our king reply'd fu' lordly:
'O noble king, tak a' that's mine
    But gie me back my Geordie.'

11

The Gordons cam and the Gordons ran
    And they were stark and steady;
And ay the word amang then a',
    Was, 'Gordons keep you ready.'

12

An aged lord at the king's right hand
    Says: 'Noble king, but hear me:—
Gar her tell down five thousand pound,
    And gie her back her Dearie.'

13

Some gae her marks, some gae her crowns,
    Some gae her dollars many;
And she's tell'd down five thousand pound,
    And she's gotten again her Dearie.

14

She blinkit blythe in her Geordie's face,
    Says: 'Dear I've bought thee, Geordie,
But there sud been bluidy bouks on the green   bodies
    Or I had tint my laddie.'   lost

15

He claspit her by the middle sma',
    And he kist her lips sae rosy,
'The fairest flower o' woman-kind
    Is my sweet bonie Lady.'

O, I FORBID YOU MAIDENS A'

TUNE: *Tam lin*

1

O, I forbid you maidens a',
  That wear gowd on your hair,
To come or gae by Carterhaugh,
  For young Tam Lin in there.

gold

2

There's nane that gaes by Carterhaugh
  But they leave him a wad;
Either their rings, or green mantles,
  Or else their maidenhead.

goes

3

Janet has belted her green kirtle
  A little aboon her knee;
And she has broded her yellow hair
  A little aboon her bree;
And she's awa to Carterhaugh
  As fast as she can hie!

brow

4

But when she cam to Carterhaugh,
  Tam Lin was at the well,
And there she fand his steed standing,
  But away was himsel.

5

She hadna pu'd a double rose,
  A rose but only twae,
Till up then started young Tam Lin
  Says, 'Lady thou's pu' nae mae.

two

6

'Why pu's thou the rose, Janet,
  And why breaks thou the wand!
Or, why comes thou to Carterhaugh
  Withoutten my command?'

7

'Carterhaugh it is my ain;
    My daddie gave it me,
I'll come and gang by Carterhaugh,
    And ask nae leave at thee.'

8

Janet has kilted her green kirtle
    A little aboon her knee,
And she has snooded her yellow hair
    A little aboon her bree,
And she is to her father's ha'
    As fast as she can hie.

9

Four and twenty ladies fair
    Were playing at the ba',
And out then cam the fair Janet
    Ance the flower amang then a'

10

Four and twenty ladies fair
    Were playing at the chess,
And out then cam the fair Janet
    As green as ony glass.

11

Out then spak an auld grey knight
    Lay o'er the castle wa';
And says: 'Alas! fair Janet for thee
    But we'll be blamèd a'.'

12

'Haud your tongue, ye auld fac'd knight,
    Some ill death may ye die,
Father my bairn on whom I will,
    I'll father nane on three.'

13

Out then spak her father dear,
    And he spak meek and mild,
'And ever alas! Sweet Janet, 'he says—
    'I think thou gaes wi' child.'

14

'If that I gae wi' child, father,
    Mysel maun bear the blame,
There's ne'er a laird about your ha',
    Shall get the bairn's name.

15

'If my love were an earthly knight,
    As he's an elfin gray,
I wadna gie my ain true-love
    For nae lord that ye hae.

16

'The steed that my true-love rides on
    Is lighter than the wind;
silver   Wi' siller he is shod before,
gold   Wi' burning gowd behind.'

17

Janet has kilted her green kirtle
    A little aboon her knee;
And she has snooded her yellow hair
    A little aboon her bree;
And she's awa to Carterhaugh
    As fast as she can hie.

18

When she cam to Carterhaugh,
    Tam Lin was at the well;
And there she fand his steed standing,
    But away was himsel.

19

She hadna pu'd a double rose,
    A rose but only twae;
Till up then started young Tam Lin
    Says, 'Lady thou's pu' nae mae.

20

'Why pu's thou the rose, Janet,
    Amang the groves sae green,
And a' to kill the bonie babe
    That we gat us between?'

21

'O, tell me tell me, Tam Lin,' she says,
  'For's sake that died on tree,
If e'er ye was in holy chapel,
  Or Christendom did see.'

22

'Roxbrugh he was my grandfather
  Took me with him to bide,
And ance it fell upon a day,
  That wae did me betide.

23

'And ance it fell upon a day,
  A cauld day and a snell,
When we were frae the hunting come
  That frae my horse I fell.

24

'The Queen o' Fairies she caught me
  In yon green hill to dwell,
And pleasant is the fairy-land:—
  But, an eerie tale to tell!

25

'Ay, at the end o' seven years
  We pay a tiend to hell!
I am sae fair and fu' o' flesh
  I'm fear'd it be mysel.

26

'But the night is Hallowe'en, lady,
  The morn is Hallowday;
Then win me, win me, an ye will,
  For weel I wat ye may.

27

'Just at the mirk and midnight hour
  The fairy folk will ride;
And they that wad their true-love win
  At Milecross they maun bide.'

28

'But how shall I thee ken, Tam Lin,
 Or how my true-love know,
Amang sae mony unco knights
 The like I never saw.'

29

'O first let pass the black, lady,
 And syne let pass the brown;
But quickly run to the milk-white steed,
 Pu' ye his rider down.

30

'For I'll ride on the milk-white steed,
 And ay nearest the town,
Because I was an earthly knight
 They gie me that renown.

31

'My right hand will be glov'd, lady,
 My left hand will be bare,
Cockt up shall my bonnet be
 And kaim'd down shall my hair;
And thae's the tokens I gie thee—
 Nae doubt I will be there:

32

'They'll turn me in your arms, lady,
 Into an esk and adder,
But hold me fast and fear me not—
 I am your bairn's father.

33

'They'll turn me to a bear sae grim,
 And then a lion bold;
But hold me fast and fear me not,
 As ye shall love your child.

34

'Again they'll turn me in your arms
 To a red het gaud of airn;
But hold me fast and fear me not,
 I'll do to you nae harm.

35

'And last they'll turn me in your arms
　　Into the burning lead:
Then throw me into well water;
　　O! throw me in wi' speed.

36

'And then I'll be your ain true love,
　　I'll turn a naked knight;
Then cover me wi' your green mantle,
　　And cover me out o' sight.'

37

Gloomy, gloomy was the night,
　　And eerie was the way,
As fair Jenny in her green mantle,
　　To Milecross she did gae.

38

About the middle o' the night,
　　She heard the bridles ring;
This lady was as glad at that
　　As any earthly thing.

39

First she let the black pass by,
　　And syne she let the brown;
But quickly she ran to the milk-white steed,
　　And pu'd the rider down.

40

Sae weel she minded what he did say
　　And young Tam Lin did win;
Syne cover'd him wi' her green mantle,
　　As blythe's a bird in Spring.

41

Out then spak the queen o' fairies,
　　Out of a bush o' broom;
'Them that has gotten young Tam Lin
　　Has gotten a stately groom.'

42

Out then spak the queen o' fairies,
    And an angry queen was she:
'Shame betide her ill-far'd face,
    And an ill death may she die,
For she's taen awa the boniest knight
    In a' my companie.

43

'But had I kend, Tam Lin,' she says,
    'What now this night I see,
I wad hae taen out thy twa grey een,
    And put in twa een o' tree.'

AFTEN HAE I PLAY'D AT THE CARDS AND THE DICE

TUNE: *The rantin laddie*

I

Aften hae I play'd at the cards and the dice,
    For the love of a bonie rantin laddie;
nook   But now I maun sit in my father's kitchen neuk,
    And balou a bastard babie.

2

For my father he will not me own,
    And my mother she neglects me,
And a' my friends hae lightlied me,
    And their servants they do slight me.

3

But had I a servant at my command—
    As aft times I've had many,
run   That wad rin wi' a letter to bonie Glenswood—
    Wi' a letter to my rantin laddie.

4

'Oh, is he either a laird or a lord,
    Or is he but a cadie,
That ye do him ca' sae aften by name,
    Your bonie, bonie rantin laddie.'

5

'Indeed he is baith a laird and a lord,
    And he never was a cadie,
For he is the Earl o' bonie Aboyne,
    And he is my rantin laddie.'

6

'O ye'se get a servant at your command,
    As aft times ye've had many,
That sall rin wi' a letter to bonie Glenswood—
    A letter to your rantin laddie.'

7

When Lord Aboyne did the letter get,
    O, but he blinket bonie;
But or he had read three lines of it,
    I think his heart was sorry.

8

'O, wha is he daur be sae bauld,   dare; bold
    Sae cruelly to use my lassie?'
(But I'll tak her to bonie Aboyne
    Where oft she did caress me.)

9

'For her father he will not her know,
    And her mother she does slight her;
And a' her friends hae lightlied her,
    And their servants they neglect her.'

10

'Go raise to me my five hundred me,
    Make haste and make them ready;
With a milkwhite steed under every ane
    For to bring hame my lady.'

11

As they came in through Buchan-shire,
    They were a company bonie,
With a gude claymore in every hand
    And O, but they shin'd bonie.

OUR YOUNG LADY'S A-HUNTIN GANE

TUNE: *The rowin't in her apron*

I

Our young lady's a-huntin gane,
Sheets nor blankets has she taen,
But she's born her auld son or she cam hame,

wrapped And she's row'd him in her apron.

2

Her apron was o' the hollan fine,
Laid about wi' laces nine;
She thought it a pity her babie should tyne,
And she's row'd him in her apron.

3

Her apron was o' the hollan sma',
Laid about wi' laces a',
She thought it a pity her babe to let fa';
And she row'd him in her apron.

4

Her father says within the ha',
Among the knights and nobles a':—
call 'I think I hear a babie ca'
In the chamber among our young ladies.'

5

'O father dear! it is a bairn,
I hope it will do you nae harm,
For the laddie I lo'ed, and he'll lo'e me again,
For the rowin't in my apron.'

6

'O, is he a gentleman, or is a clown,
That has brought thy fair body down?
I would not for a' this town
The rowin't in thy apron.'

7

'Young Terreagles is nae clown,
He is the toss of Edinborrow town,
And he'll buy me a braw new gown
    For the rowin't in my apron.'

8

'It's I hae castles, I hae towers,
I hae barns, and I hae bowers;
An' that is mine it shal be thine
    For the rowin't in thy apron.'

'O, FOR MY AIN KING,' QUO' GUDE WALLACE

TUNE: *Gude Wallace*

1

'O, for my ain king,' quo' gude Wallace,
    'The rightfu' king of fair Scotland,
Between me and my sovereign blude,   blood
    I think I see ill seed sawn.'   sown

2

Wallace out over yon river he lap,   leaped
    And he has lighted low down on yon plain,
And he was aware of a gay ladie,
    As she was at the well washing.

3

'What tydins, what tydins, fair lady,' he says,
    'What tydins hast thou to tell unto me—
What tydins, what tydins, fair lady,' he says,
    'What tydins hae ye in the south countrie?'

4

'Low down in yon wee Ostler-house
    There is fyfteen Englishmen,
And they are seekin for gude Wallce;
    It's him to take, a him to hang.'

5

'There's nocht in my purse,' quo' gude Wallace,
    'There's nocht, not even a bare pennie;
But I will down to yon wee Ostler-house
    Thir fyfteen Englishmen to see.'

These

6

And when he cam in to yon wee Ostler-house
    He bad *benedicite* be there;
(The Englishmen at the table sat
    The wine-fac'd captain at him did stare.)

7

crooked

'Where was ye born, auld crookit carl,
    Where was ye born—in what countrie?'
'I am a true Scot born and bred,
    And an auld crookit carl just sic as ye see.'

such

8

'I wad gie fyfteen shillings to onie crookit carl—
    To onie crookit carl just sic as ye,
If ye will get me gude Wallace,
    For he is the man I wad very fain see.'

9

He hit the proud captain alang the chaft blade.
    That never a bit o' meal he ate mair;
And he sticket the rest at the table where they sat,
    And he left them a' lyin sprawlin there.

10

'Get up, get up, gudewife,' he says,
    'And get to me some dinner in haste;
For it will soon be three lang days
    Sin I a bit o' meat did taste.'

since

11

The dinner was na weel readie,
    Nor was it on the table set,
Till other fyfteen Englishmen
    Were a' lighted about the yett.

gate

12

'Come out, come out, now gude Wallace,
   This is the day that thou maun die;'
'I lippen nae sae little to God,' he says,   depend
   'Altho' I be but ill wordie.'

13

The gudewife had an auld gudeman,
   By gude Wallace he stiffly stood;
Till ten o' the fyfteen Englishmen
   Before the door lay in their blude.

14

The other five to the greenwood ran,
   And he hang'd these five upon a grain;   branch
And on the morn wi' his merry men a'
   He sat at dine in Lochmaben town.

NEAR EDINBURGH WAS A YOUNG SON BORN

TUNE: *Hynde Horn*

1

Near Edinburgh was a young son born,—
   Hey lilelu an' a how low lan',
An' his name it was callèd young Hynhorn,
   An' it's hey down down, deedle airo.

2

Seven long years he served the king,—
   Hey lilelu, &c.
And it's a' for the sake of his daughter Jean,—
   An' it's hey down, &c.

3

The king an angry man was he,—
He sent young Hynhorn to the sea.

*   *   *   *   *

4

An' on his finger she put a ring,
(Wi' three shining diamonds set therein.)
When your ring turns pale and wan,
Then I'm in love wi' another man.

*   *   *   *   *

5

Upon a day he look'd at his ring,
It was as pale as any thing.

6

He's left the sea, and he's come to the lan'.
And there he met an auld beggar man.
'What news, what news, my auld beggar man,
What news, what news by sea or by lan'?'

7

'Nae news, nae news,' the auld beggar said,
'But the king's daughter Jean is going to be wed.'
'Cast off, cast off, thy auld beggar weed,
An' I'll gie thee my gude grey steed.'

*   *   *   *   *

8

When he cam to our gude king's yett,
He sought a glass o' wine for young Hynhorn's sake.
He drank out the wine and he put in the ring,
And he bade them carry't to the king's dochter Jean.

*   *   *   *   *

9

'O gat ye't by sea, or gat ye't by lan',
O gat ye't aff a dead man's han'?'
'I gat na't by sea, I gat na't by lan',
But I gat it out of your own fair han'.'

*   *   *   *   *

10

'Go, take away my bridal gown,
And I'll follow him frae town to town.'
'Ye need na leave your bridal gown,
For I'll make ye ladie o' mony a town.'

WHAT MERRIMENT HAS TAEN THE WHIGS

TUNE: *The German lairdie*

CHORUS

Sing heedle liltie, teedle liltie,
  Andum, tandum, tandie,
Sing fal de dal, de dal lal lal,
  Sing howdle liltic dandie.

1

What merriment has taen the Whigs
  I think they be gaen mad, Sir,
Wi' playing up their Whiggish jigs,
  Their dancin may be sad, Sir.

2

The Revolution principles
  Has put their heads in bees, Sir;
They 're a' fa'en out amang themsels—
  Deil tak the first that grees, Sir.

O, THAT I WERE WHERE HELEN LIES

TUNE: *Where Helen lies*

1

O, that I were where Helen lies!
Night and day on me she cries;
O, that I were where Helen lies
  In fair Kirkconnel lee.

2

O Helen fair! beyond compare,
A ringlet of thy flowing hair,
I'll wear it still for evermair
   Until the day I die.

3

Curs'd be the hand that shot the shot,
And curs'd the gun that gave the crack,
leaped   Into my arms bird Helen lap,
   And died for sake o' me.

4

O think na ye but my heart was sair,
My love fell down and spake nae mair,
There did she swoon wi' meikle care
   On fair Kirkconnel lee.

5

I lighted down, my sword did draw,
I cutted him in pieces sma';
I cutted him in pieces sma'
   On fair Kirkconnel lee.

6

O Helen chaste, thou wert modest
If I were with thee I were blest,
Where thou lies low, and takes thy rest
   On fair Kirkconnel lee.

7

I wish my grave was growing green,
eyes   A winding sheet put o'er my een,
And I in Helen's arms lying
   In fair Kirkconnel lee!

8

I wish I were where Helen lies!
Night and day on me she cries;
O, that I were where Helen lies
   On fair Kirkconnel lee.

O HEARD YE OF A SILLY HARPER?

TUNE: *The Lochmaben harper*

1

O, heard ye of a silly harper
   Liv'd long in Lochmaben town?
How he did gang to fair England
   To steal King Henry's wanton brown. } *bis*

2

But first he gaed to his gude-wife
   Wi' a' the speed that he could thole:—
'This wark,' quo' he, 'will never work
   Without a mare that has a foal.' } *bis*

3

Quo' she, 'thou has a gude grey mare
   That'll rin o'er hills baith low and hie;   high
Gae tak the grey mare in thy hand,
   And leave the foal at hame wi' me.' } *bis*

4

'And tak a halter in thy hose,
   And o' thy purpose dinna fail,
But wap it o'er the wanton's nose,   wrap
   And tie her to the grey mare's tail. } *bis*

5

'Syne ca' her out at yon back yeate,
   O'er moss and muir and ilka dale,
For she'll ne'er let the wanton bite,
   Till she come hame to her ain foal.' } *bis*

6

So he is up to England gane,
    Even as fast as he can hie,
Till he came to King Henry's yeate—
    And wha was there but King Henry?   } *bis*

gate

7

'Come in,' quo' he, 'thou silly blind harper,
    And of thy harping let me hear':
'O! by my sooth,' quo' the silly blind harper,
    'I'd rather hae stabling for my mare.'   } *bis*

8

The king looks o'er his left shoulder,
    And says unto his stable groom:—
'Gae tak the silly poor harper's mare,
    And tie her 'side my wanton brown.'   } *bis*

9

And ay he harpèd, and ay he carpit,
    Till a' the lords gaed through the floor;
They thought the music was sae sweet
    That they forgot the stable door.   } *bis*

10

And ay he harpit, and ay he carpit,
    Till a' the nobles were sound asleep;
Then quietly he took aff his shoon
    And saftly down the stair did creep.   } *bis*

11

Syne to the stable door he hies
    Wi' tread as light as light could be,
And when he open'd and gaed in,
    There he fand thirty good steeds and three.} *bis*

found

12

He took the halter frae his hose,
And of his purpose did na fail;
He slipt it o'er the wanton's nose,
And tied it to his grey mare's tail. } *bis*

13

He ca'd her out at yon back yeate
O'er moss and muir and ilka dale;
And she loot ne'er the wanton bite, } *bis*   let
But held her still gaun at her tail.

14

The grey mare was right swift o' fit,
And did na fail to find the way,
For she was at Lochmaben yeate
Fu' lang three hours ere it was day. } *bis*

15

When she came to the harper's door,
There she gae many a nicher and snear;   neigh
'Rise,' quo' the wife, 'thou lazy lass,
Let in thy master and his mare.' } *bis*

16

Then up she raise, pat on her claes,   put; clothes
And lookit out through the lock-hole:
'O! by my sooth, then,' quo' the lass,
'Our mare has gotten a braw big foal.' } *bis*

17

'Come haud thy peace thou foolish lass,
The moon's but glancing in thy e'e;
I'd wad my hail fee 'gainst a groat   whole
It's bigger than e'er our foal will be.' } *bis*

18

The neighbours too that heard the noise
   Cried to the wife to put her in;
'By my sooth, then,' quoth the wife
   'She's better than ever he rade on.'   } *bis*

19

But on the morn at fair daylight,
   When they had ended a' their cheer:
stolen   King Henry's wanton brown was stawn,
   And eke the poor auld harper's mare.   } *bis*

20

'Alace! alace!' says the silly blind harper;
   'Alace! alace! that I came here,
lost   In Scotland I've tint a braw cowte foal,
   In England they've stawn by gude grey   } *bis*
     mare.'

21

'Come haud thy tongue, thou silly blind harper,
   And of thy *alacing* let me be,
For thou shall get a better mare,
   And weel paid shall thy cowte foal be.
For thou shall get a better mare,
   And weel paid shall thy cowte foal be.'

'TWAS PAST ONE O'CLOCK

TUNE: *Cold frosty morning*

1

'Twas past one o'clock in a cauld frosty morning
  When cankert November blaws over the plain,
I heard the kirk-bell repeat the loud warning
  As restless I sought for sweet slumber in vain:
Then up I arose, the silver moon shining bright,
Mountains and vallies appearing all hoary white;
Forth I would go amid the pale, silent night,
  To visit the fair one, the cause of my pain.

2

Sae gently I staw to my lovely maid's chamber,   stole
  And rapp'd at her window, low down on my knee,
Begging that she would awauk from sweet slumber,
  Awauk from sweet slumber and pity me!
For, that a stranger to a' pleasure, peace and rest,
Love into madness had firèd my tortur'd breast,
And that I should be of a' men the maist unblest,
  Unless she would pity my sad miserie!

3

My true love arose and whisperèd to me—
  (The moon lookèd in and envy'd my love's
      charms;—)
'An innocent maiden, ah, would you undo me!'
  I made no reply, but leapt into her arms:
Bright Phoebus peep'd over the hills and found me
      there;
As he has done, now, seven lang years and mair,
A faithfuller, constanter, kinder, more loving pair,
  His sweet chearing beam nor enlightens nor warms.

THE QUEEN O' THE LOTHIANS CAM CRUISIN TO FIFE

TUNE: *(As Title)*

I

The Queen o' the Lothians cam cruisin to Fife,
　Fal de ral, lal de ral, lario,
To see gin a wooer wad tak her for life.
　Sing hey, fal lal de ral, lal de ral, lal de ral,
　Hey, fal lal de ral, lairo.

2

She had na been lang at the brow o' the hill,
Till Jockie cam down to visit Lochnell.

3

nook　　　He took the aunt to the neuk o' the ha',
Whare nobody heard, and whare naebody saw.

4

'Madam,' he says, 'I've thought on your advice,
afraid　　I wad marry your niece, but I'm fley'd she'll be nice.'

5

'Jockie,' she says, 'the wark's done to your hand,
I've spoke to my niece, and she's at your command.'

6

'But troth, Madam, I canna woo,
For aft I hae tried it, and ay I fa' thro'.

7

'But, O dear Madam, and I'se wad begin,
For I'm as fley'd to do it, as it were a sin.'

8

Jenny cam in, and Jockie ran out.
'Madam,' she says, 'what hae ye been about?'

9

'Jenny,' she says, 'I've been workin for you,
For what do you think, Jockie's came here to woo.

10

'Now, Jenny, tak care, and dash na the lad,
For offers like him are na ay to be had.'   not always

11

'Madam, I'll tak the advice o' the wise.
I ken the lad's worth, and I own he's a prize.'

12

Then she cries but the house, 'Jockie, come here,
Ye've naething to do but the question to spier.'

13

The question was spier'd, and the bargain was struck,
The neebors cam in, and wish'd them gude luck.

BROOM BESOMS

TUNE: *Buy broom besoms*

CHORUS

Buy broom besoms! Wha will buy them now?
Fine heather ringers, better never grew.

1

I maun hae a wife, whatsoe'er she be;
An she be a woman, that's eneugh for me.

2

If that she be bony, I shall think her right:
If that she be ugly, where's the odds at night?

3

O, an she be young, how happy shall I be?
If that she be auld, the sooner she will die.

4

If that she be fruitfu', O! what joy is there!
If she should be barren, less will be my care.

5

Be she green or gray; be she black or fair;
Let her be a woman, I shall seek nae mair.

6

If she like a drappie, she and I'll agree;
If she dinna like it, there's the mair for me.

BROOM BESOMS

Second Set

TUNE: *Buy broom besoms*

CHORUS

Buy broom besoms! Wha will buy them now?
Fine heather ringers, better never grew.

1

Young and souple was I, when I lap the dyke;
ditch   Now I'm auld and frail, I douna step a syke.

2

Young and souple was I, when at Lautherslack,
Now I'm auld and frail, and lie at Nansie's back.

3

Had she gien me butter, when she gae me bread,
bolder; bald   I wad looked baulder, wi' my beld head.

EVER TO BE NEAR YE!

TUNE: *The Sutor's Dochter*

1

Ever to be near ye!
Whaur ye bide or whaur ye stray,
　To comfort and to cheer ye!
Be your fortune what it may,
　Hearken noo and hear ye:
I'd be happy nicht and day
　Ever to be near ye;
Happy I'd be nicht and day
　Ever to be near ye!

2

Ever to be near ye!
Neither rocks nor currents rife
　Ever need to fear ye
Frae the stress and frae the strife
　Couthiely I'll steer ye,—
Thro' the stormy sea o' life,
　Ever to be near ye!
Thro' the stormy sea o' life,
　Ever to be near ye!

3

Ever to be near ye!
Good and bonny as ye are,
　Wha could nae revere ye?
In your circle or afar
　Nane there is to peer ye:
O, for better or for waur,
　Ever to be near ye!
O, for better or for waur,
　Ever to be near ye!

TO MR. GOW, VISITING DUMFRIES

TUNE: *Tullochgorum*

1

Thrice welcome, king o' rant and reel!
Whaur is the bard to Scotia leal
such   Wha wadna sing o' sic a chiel
    And sic a glorious fiddle!

2

It's but a weary warl' at best,
Wauf an' weary—aften dreary—
It's but a weary warl' at best,
    A wauf and weary widdle!

3

It's but a weary warl' at best
Gang north, or sooth, or east, or west,
But we will never mak' protest
    When near you and your fiddle.

4

Let prosy parsons pray and preach,
And wise professors try to teach
The secrets far beyond their reach
    As Stradivari's fiddle!

5

We'll leave them to themsel's to read
Things sae vexin'—and preplexin'—
We'll leave them to themsel's to read
    Life's cabalistic riddle!—

6

We'll leave them to themsel's to read
To spin their scheme and mak' their creed;
Come, screw your pins and gie's a screed
    Frae your unrivall'd fiddle!

7

Nae fabled wizard's wand, I trow,
Had e'er the magic airt o' Gow,   art
When wi' a wave he draws his bow
  Across his wondrous fiddle!

8

Sic fays and fairies come and dance—
Lightly tripping—hopping, skipping—
Sic fays and fairies come and dance,
  Their maister in the middle!

9

Sic fays and fairies come and dance,
So gently glide and spryly prance,
And noo retreat and noo advance
  When he strikes up his fiddle!

10

In brisk strathspey or plaintive air
What rival can wi' you compare?
O' wha could think a hank o' hair
  Could thus transform a fiddle?

11

What are the notes o' lyre or lute—
Wizzent, wheezy—slim and sleezy—
What are the notes o' lyre or lute?—
  Inconsequential diddle!

12

What are the notes o' lyre or lute?—
O' pipes, piano, fife, or flute,
Wi' a' that ye can execute,
  On your enchanting fiddle!

13

Wha doesna joy to hear the ring
O' ilka bonny lilt and spring
That ye frae recollection bring
  And wheedle through your fiddle!

14

churl

> The sumph that wadna praises gie
> A soulless clod maun surely be;
> A chiel should never hae to dee
> That half like you can fiddle!

ELIBANKS AND ELIBRAES

TUNE: *Killiecrankie*

1

> O, Elibanks and Elibraes
> It was but aince I saw ye
> But a' my days I'll sing your praise
> Whaever may misca' ye.
> Your trees were in their freshest bloom,
> Your birds were singin' cheery
> When thro' your wavin' yellow broom
> I wander'd wi' my dearie!

2

silver

golden

such

> How sweet the siller mornin' sped
> In cheerful contemplation!
> How fast the gowden gloamin' fled
> In loving conversation!
> Noo doon the bank and up the brae
> How could I ever weary
> In sic a place on sic a day
> Wi' sic a bonnie dearie!

3

> O, Elibanks and Elibraes,
> Aye pleasant be your waters!
> May a' your sons hae winning ways,
> And lovely be your daughters!
> My life to me maun surely be
> Existence dull and dreary
> If I forget the day we met
> When I was wi' my dearie!

HIGHLAND HARRY

TUNE: *Highlander's Lament*

CHORUS

O, for him back again!
O, for him back again!
I wad gie a' Knockhaspie's land
For Highland Harry back again.

1

My Harry was a gallant gay,   strode
    Fu' stately strade he on the plain,
But now he's banish'd far away:
    I'll never see him back again.

2

When a' the lave gae to their bed,   rest; go
    I wander dowie up the glen,   drooping
I set me down, and greet my fill,   weep
    Any ay I wish him back again.

3

O, were some villains hangit high,
    And ilka body had their ain,   every; own
Then I might see the joyfu' sight,
    My Highland Harry back again!

THE TAILOR FELL THRO' THE BED

TUNE: *I rede ye beware o the ripells you man,*

1

The tailor fell thro' the bed, thimble an' a',
The tailor fell thro' the bed, thimble an' a';
The blankets were thin, and the sheets they were
    sma'—
The tailor fell thro' the bed, thimble an' a'!

2

small

The sleepy bit lassie, she dreaded nae ill,
The sleepy bit lassie, she dreaded nae ill;
The weather was cauld, and the lassie lay still:
She thought that a tailor could do her nae ill!

3

gentle

Gie me the groat again, cannie young man!
Gie me the groat again, cannie young man!
The day it is short, and the night it is lang—
The dearest siller that ever I wan!

4

alone

drooping; glad

There's somebody weary wi' lying her lane,
There's somebody weary wi' lying her lane!
There's some that are dowie, I trow wad be fain
To see the bit tailor come skippin again.

awake

AY WAUKIN, O

TUNE: *(As Title)*

CHORUS

Ay waukin, O,
  Waukin still and weary:
Sleep I can get nane
  For thinking on my dearie.

1

Simmer's a pleasant time:
  Flowers of every colour,
crag
The water rins owre the heugh,
  And I long for my true lover.

2

When I sleep I dream,
apprehensive
  When I wauk I'm eerie,
Sleep I can get nane
  For thinkin on my dearie.

3

Lanely night comes on,
   A' the lave are sleepin,   rest
I think on my bonie lad,
   And I bleer my een wi' greetin.   eyes; weeping

BEWARE O' BONIE ANN

TUNE: *Bonie Ann*

I

Ye gallants bright, I rede you right,   warn you
   Beware o' bonie Ann!   true
Her comely face sae fu' o' grace,
   Your heart she will trepan.

2

Her een sae bright like stars by night,   eyes
   Her skin is like the swan.
Sae jimply lac'd her genty waist   trim
   That sweetly ye might span.

3

Youth, Grace, and Love attendant move,
   And Pleasure leads the van:
In a' their charms, and conquering arms,
   They wait on bonie Ann.

4

The captive bands may chain the hands,
   But Love enslaves the man:
Ye gallants braw, I rede you a',   fine
   Beware o' bonie Ann!

LANG HAE WE PARTED BEEN

TUNE: *Laddie, Lie Near Me*

CHORUS

Near me, near me,
Lassie, lie near me!
alone
Lang hast thou lien thy lane,
Lassie, lie near me!

I

Lang hae we parted been,
Lassie, my dearie;
Now we are met again—
Lassie, lie near me!

2

A' that I hae endur'd,
Lassie, my dearie,
Here in thy arms is cur'd—
Lassie, lie near me!

spade
THE GARD'NER WI' HIS PAIDLE

TUNE: *The Gardner's March*

I

When rosy May comes in wi' flowers
To deck her gay, green-speading bowers,
Then busy, busy are his hours,
            The gard'ner wi' his paidle.

2

The crystal waters gently fa',
The merry birds are lovers a',
The scented breezes round him blaw—
            The gard'ner wi' his paidle.

3

When purple morning starts the hare,
To steal upon her early fare,
'Then thro' the dew he maun repair—   must
     The gard'ner wi' his paidle.

4

When Day, expiring in the west,
The curtain draws o' Nature's rest,
He flies to her arms he lo'es best,
     The gard'ner wi' his paidle.

ON A BANK OF FLOWERS

TUNE: *The Bashful Lover*

1

On a bank of flowers in a summer day,
  For summer lightly drest,
The youthful, blooming Nelly lay
  With love and sleep opprest;
When Willie, wand'ring thro' the wood,
Who for her favour oft had sued—
    He gaz'd, he wish'd,
    He fear'd, he blush'd,
And trembled where he stood.

2

Her closèd eyes, like weapons sheath'd,
  Were seal'd in soft repose;
Her lips, still as she fragrant breath'd,
  It richer dyed the rose;
The springing lilies, sweetly prest,
Wild-wanton kiss'd her rival breast:
    He gaz'd, he wish'd,
    He fear'd, he blush'd,
His bosom ill at rest.

3

Her robes, light-waving in the breeze,
　Her tender limbs embrace;
Her lovely form, her native ease,
　All harmony and grace.
Tumultuous tides his pulses roll,
A faltering, ardent kiss he stole:
　　He gaz'd, he wish'd,
　　He fear'd, he blush'd,
And sigh'd his very soul.

4

As flies the partridge from the brake
　On fear-inspirèd wings,
So Nelly starting, half-awake,
　Away affrighted springs.
But Willie follow'd—as he should;
He overtook her in the wood;
　　He vow'd, he pray'd,
　　He found the maid
Forgiving all, and good.

THE DAY RETURNS

TUNE: *Seventh of November*

I

The day returns, my bosom burns,
　The blissful day we twa did meet!
Tho' winter wild in tempest toil'd,
　Ne'er summer sun was half sae sweet.
Than a' the pride that loads the tide,
　And crosses o'er the sultry line,
Than kingly robes, than crowns and globes,
　Heav'n gave me more—it made thee mine!

2

While day and night can bring delight,
   Or Nature aught of pleasure give,
While joys above my mind can move,
   For thee, and thee alone, I live!
When that grim foe of Life below
   Comes in between to make us part,
The iron hand that breaks our band,
   It breaks my bliss, it breaks my heart!

MY LOVE SHE'S BUT A LASSIE YET

TUNE: *(As Title)*

CHORUS

My love, she's but a lassie yet,
My , she's but a lassie yet!
We'll let her stand a year or twa,
She'll no be half sae saucy yet!

1

I rue the day I sought her, O!
I rue the day I sought her, O!
Wha gets her need na say he's woo'd,
   But he may say he has bought her, O.

2

Come draw a drap o' the best o't yet,
Come draw a drap o' the best o't yet!
Gae seek for pleasure whare ye will,   Go
   But here I never missed it yet.

3

We're a' dry wi' drinkin o't,
We're a' dry wi' drinkin o't!
The minister kiss't the fiddler's wife—
   He could na preach for thinkin o't!

JAMIE, COME TRY ME

TUNE: *(As Title)*

CHORUS

Jamie, come try me,
Jamie, come try me!
If thou would win my love,
Jamie, come try me!

1

If thou should ask my love,
   Could I deny thee?
If thou would win my love,
   Jamie, come try me!

2

If thou should kiss me, love,
   Wha could espy thee?
If thou wad be my love,
   Jamie, come try me!

THE SILVER TASSIE

TUNE: *The Secret Kiss*

1

Go, fetch to me a pint o' wine,
   And fill it in a silver tassie,
That I may drink before I go
   A service to my bonie lassie!
The boat rocks at the pier o' Leith,
   Fu' loud the wind blaws frae the Ferry,
The ship rides by the Berwick-Law,
must   And I maun leave my bonie Mary.

2

The trumpets sound, the banners fly,
   The glittering spears are rankèd ready,
The shouts o' war are heard afar,
   The battle closes deep and bloody.
It's not the roar o' sea or shore
   Wad mak me langer wish to tarry,
Nor shouts o' war that's heard afar:
   It's leaving thee, my bonie Mary!

THE LAZY MIST

TUNE: *(As Title)*

1

The lazy mist hangs from the brow of the hill,
Concealing the course of the dark winding rill.
How languid the scenes, late so sprightly, appear,
As Autumn to Winter resigns the pale year!

2

The forests are leafless, the meadows are brown,
And all the gay foppery of summer is flown.
Apart let me wander, apart let me muse,
How quick Time is flying, how keen Fate pursues!

3

How long I have liv'd, but how much liv'd in vain!
How little of life's scanty span may remain!
What aspects old Time in his progress has worn!
What ties cruel Fate in my bosom has torn!

4

How foolish, or worse, till our summit is gain'd!
And downward, how weaken'd, how darken'd, how
   pain'd!
Life is not worth having with all it can give:
For something beyond it poor man, sure, must live.

THE CAPTAIN'S LADY

TUNE: *(As Title)*

CHORUS

O, mount and go,
  Mount and make you ready!
O, mount and go,
  And be the Captain's Lady!

1

When the drums do beat,
  And the cannons rattle,
Thou shalt sit in state,
  And see thy love in battle:

2

When the vanquish'd foe
  Sues for peace and quiet,
To the shades we'll go,
  And in love enjoy it.

directions

OF A' THE AIRTS

TUNE: *Miss Admiral Gordon's Strathspey*

1

Of a' the airts the wind can blaw
  I dearly like the west,
For there the bonie lassie lives,
  The lassie I lo'e best.
roll   There wild woods grow, and rivers row,
  And monie a hill between,
But day and night my fancy's flight
  Is ever wi' my Jean.

2

I see her in the dewy flowers—
  I see her sweet and fair.
I hear her in the tunefu' birds—
  I hear her charm the air.
There's not a bonie flower that springs
  By fountain, shaw, or green,   wood
There's not a bonie bird that sings,
  But minds me o' my Jean.   reminds

CARL, AN THE KING COME   if

TUNE: *(At Title)*

CHORUS

Carl, an the King come,
Carl, an the King come,
Thou shalt dance, and I will sing,
Carl, an the King come!

1

An somebodie were come again,
Then somebodie maun cross the main,   must
And every man shall hae his ain,   own
  Carl, an the King come!

2

I trow we swappèd for the worse: swopped
We gae the boot and better horse,   gave
And that we'll tell them at the Cross,
  Carl, an the King come!

3

Coggie, an the King come,   Stoup
Coggie, an the King come,
I'll be fou, and thou'se be toom,   I'll be full; (i.e.
  Coggie, an the King come!   drunk); thou'lt;
                                                 empty

WHISTLE O'ER THE LAVE O'T

TUNE: *(As Title)*

1

First when Maggie was my care,
Heav'n, I thought, was in her air;
Now we're married, spier nae mair,
    But—whistle o'er the lave o't!
Meg was meek, and Meg was mild,
Sweet and harmless as a child:
Wiser men than me's beguiled—
    Whistle o'er the lave o't!

2

How we live, my Meg and me,
How we love, and how we gree,
I care na by how few may see—
    Whistle o'er the lave o't!
Wha I wish were maggots' meat,
Dish'd up in her winding-sheet,
I could write (but Meg wad see't)—
    Whistle o'er the lave o't!

ask no more (gloss for line 3, stanza 1)
care nothing (gloss for line 3, stanza 2)

O, WERE I ON PARNASSUS HILL

TUNE: *My Love is lost to me*

1

O, were I on Parnassus hill,
Or had o' Helicon my fill,
That I might catch poetic skill
    To sing how dear I love thee!
But Nith maun be my Muses' well,
My Muse maun be thy bonie sel',
On Corsincon I'll glowr and spell,
    And write how dear I love thee.

must (gloss)
gaze (gloss)

2

Then come, sweet Muse, inspire my lay!
For a' the lee-lang simmer's day   live-long
I couldna sing, I couldna say
    How much, how dear I love thee.
I see thee dancing o'er the green,
Thy waist sae jimp, thy limbs sae clean,
Thy tempting lips, thy roguish een—   eyes
    By Heaven and Earth I love thee!

3

By night, by day, a-field, at hame,
The thoughts o' thee my breast inflame,
And ay I muse and sing thy name—
    I only live to love thee.
Tho' I were doom'd to wander on,
Beyond the sea, beyond the sun,
Till my last weary sand was run,
    Till then—and then—I'd love thee!

THERE'S A YOUTH IN THIS CITY

TUNE: *Niel Gow's Lament*

1

There's a youth in this city, it were a great pity
  That he from our lasses should wander awa';
For he's bonie an braw, weel-favor'd witha',   smart
  An' his hair has a natural buckle an' a'.   curl

2

His coat is the hue o' his bonnet sae blue,
  His fecket is white as the new-driven snaw,   waistcoat
His hose they are blae, and his shoon like the slae,   blue; shoe
  And his clear siller buckles, they dazzle us a'.

3

For beauty and fortune the laddie's been courtin;
  Weel-featur'd, weel-tocher'd, weel-mounted, an'
    braw,   -dowered
But chiefly the siller that gars him gang till her—   money;
  The penny's the jewel that beautifies a'!   makes; go to

4

farm; gladly
would have had

There's Meg wi' the mailen, that fain wad a haen him.
  And Susie, wha's daddie was laird of the Ha',

almost

There's lang-tocher'd Nancy maist fetters his fancy;

self

  But the laddie's dear sel he loes dearest of a'.

MY HEART'S IN THE HIGHLANDS

TUNE: *The Musket Salute*

CHORUS

My heart's in the Highlands, my heart is not here,
My heart's in the Highlands a-chasing the deer,
A-chasing the wild deer and following the roe—
My heart's in the Highlands, wherever I go!

1

Farewell to the Highlands, farewell to the North,
The birthplace of valour, the country of worth!
Wherever I wander, wherever I rove,
The hills of the Highlands for ever I love.

2

Farewell to the mountains high cover'd with snow,
Farewell to the straths and green valleys below,
Farewell to the forests and wild-hanging woods,
Farewell to the torrents and loud-pouring floods!

JOHN ANDERSON MY JO

TUNE: *(As Title)*

1

John Anderson my jo, John,
  When we were first acquent,

acquainted

Your locks were like the raven,

straight
bald

  Your bonie brow was brent;
But now your brow is beld, John,
  Your locks are like the snaw,

pate

But blessings on your frosty pow,
  John Anderson my jo!

2

John Anderson my jo, John,
   We clamb the hill thegither,   *climbed;*
And monie a cantie day, John,   *together*
   We've had wi' ane anither;   *jolly*
Now we maun totter down, John,   *must*
   And hand in hand we'll go,
And sleep thegither at the foot,
   John Anderson my jo!

AWA', WHIGS, AWA'

TUNE: *(As Title)*

CHORUS

Awa', Whigs, awa'!
* Awa', Whigs, awa'!*
Ye're but a pack o' traitor louns,
* Ye'll do nae guid at a'.*

1

Our thrissles flourish'd fresh and fair,   *thistles*
   And bonie bloom'd our roses;
But Whigs cam like a frost in June,
   An' wither'd a' our posies.

2

Our ancient crown's fa'n in the dust—   *dust-whirl*
   Deil blin' them wi' the stoure o't,
An' write their names in his black beuk,   *book*
   Wha gae the Whigs the power o't!

3

Our sad decay in church and state
   Surpasses my descriving.   *describing*
The Whigs cam o'er us for a curse,
   And we hae done wi' thriving.

4

awake

> Grim Vengeance lang has taen a nap,
>   But we may see him waukin—
> Gude help the day when Royal heads

hare

>   Are hunted like a maukin!

Drive; ewes
knolls

CA' THE YOWES TO THE KNOWES

TUNE: *Ca' the Yowes*

CHORUS

> *Ca' the yowes to the knowes,*
> *Ca' them whare the heather grows,*

brooklet; rolls

> *Ca' them whare the burnie rowes,*
>   *My bonie dearie!*

1

went

> As I gaed down the water-side,
> There I met my shepherd lad:

wrapped

> He row'd me sweetly in his plaid,

called

>   And he ca'd me his dearie.

2

go

> 'Will ye gang down the water-side,
> And see the waves sae sweetly glide
> Beneath the hazels spreading wide,
>   The moon it shines fu' clearly?'

3

such

> 'I was bred up in nae sic school,
> My shepherd lad, to play the fool,

sorrow

> An' a' the day to sit in dool,
>   An' naebody to see me.'

4

> 'Ye sall get gowns and ribbons meet,

Cauf-

> Cauf-leather shoon upon your feet,
> And in my arms ye'se lie and sleep,
>   An' ye sall be my dearie.'

5

'If ye'll but stand to what ye've said,
I'se gang wi' you, my shepherd lad,   I'll go
And ye may row me in your plaid,
    And I sall be your dearie.'

6

'While waters wimple to the sea,   wind
While day blinks in the lift sae hie,   shines: sky; high
Till clay-cauld death sall blin' my e'e,
    Ye sall be my dearie.'

O, MERRY HAE I BEEN

TUNE: *Lord Breadalbane's March*

1

O, merry hae I been teethin a heckle,   heckling-comb
    An' merry hae I been shapin a spoon!
O, merry hae I been cloutin a kettle,   patching
    An' kissin my Katie when a' was done!
O, a' the lang day I ca' at my hammer,   knock
    An' a' the lang day I whistle an' sing!
O, a' the lang night I cuddle my kimmer,   mistress
    An' a' the lang night as happy's a king!

2

Bitter in dool, I lickit my winnins   sorrow; supped;
    O' marrying Bess, to gie her a slave.   earnings
Blest be the hour she cool'd in her linens,   winding-sheet
    And blythe be the bird that sings on her grave!
Come to my arms, my Katie, my Katie,
    An' come to my arms, and kiss me again!
Drucken or sober, here's to thee, Katie,
    And blest by the day I did it again!

A MOTHER'S LAMENT

TUNE: *Finlayston House*

1

Fate gave the word—the arrow sped,
   And pierc'd my darling's heart,
And with him all the joys are fled
   Life can to me impart.
By cruel hands the sapling drops,
   In dust dishonor'd laid:
So fell the pride of all my hopes,
   My age's future shade.

2

The mother linnet in the brake
   Bewails her ravish'd young:
So I for my lost darling's sake
   Lament the live-day long.
Death, oft I've fear'd thy fatal blow!
   Now fond I bare my breast!
O, do thou kindly lay me low,
   With him I love at rest!

THE WHITE COCKADE

TUNE: *(At Title)*

CHORUS

rollicking

O, he's a ranting, roving lad!
He is a brisk an' a bonie lad!
Betide what may, I will be wed,
And follow the boy wi' the White Cockade!

1

My love was born in Aberdeen,
The boniest lad that e'er was seen;
But now he makes our hearts fu' sad—
He takes the field wi' his White Cockade.

2

I'll sell my rock, my reel, my tow,   distaff; flax
My guid gray mare and hawkit cow,   white-faced
To buy mysel a tartan plaid,
To follow the boy wi' the White Cockade.

THE BRAES O' BALLOCHMYLE   hills

TUNE: *(As Title)*

1

The Catrine woods were yellow seen,
   The flowers decay'd on Catrine lea;
Nae lav'rock sang on hillock green,   lark
   But nature sicken'd on the e'e;   eye
Thro' faded groves Maria sang,
   Hersel in beauty's bloom the while,
And aye the wild-wood echoes rang:—
   'Fareweel the braes o' Ballochmyle!

2

'Low in your wintry beds, ye flowers,
   Again ye'll flourish fresh and fair;
Ye birdies, dumb in with'ring bowers,
   Again ye'll charm the vocal air;
   But here, alas! for me nae mair
Shall birdie charm, or floweret smile:
   Fareweel the bonie banks of Ayr!
Fareweel! fareweel sweet Ballochmyle!'

THE RANTIN DOG, THE DADDIE O'T   rollicking

TUNE: *Whare wad bonie Annie lie?*

1

O, wha my babie-clouts will buy?   -clothes
O, wha will tent me when I cry?   attend to
Wha will kiss me where I lie?—
   The rantin dog, the daddie o't!

2

fault   O, wha will own he did the faut?
midwife's ale   O, what will buy the groanin maut?
name it   O, wha will tell me how to ca't?—
                                   The rantin dog, the daddie o't!

3

                               When I mount the creepie-chair,
                               Wha will sit beside me there?
                               Gie me Rob, I'll seek nae mair—
                                   the rantin dog, the daddie o't!

4

talk; alone   Wha will crack to me my lane?
desirous   Wha will mak me fidgin fain?
                               Wha will kiss me o'er again?—
                                   The rantin dog, the daddie o't!

THOU LINGERING STAR

TUNE: *Captain Cook's Death*

1

Thou ling'ring star with less'ning ray,
   That lov'st to greet the early morn,
Again thou usher'st in the day
   My Mary from my soul was torn.
O Mary, dear departed shade!
   Where is thy place of blissful rest?
See'st thou thy lover lowly laid?
   Hear'st thou the groans that rend his breast?

2

That sacred hour can I forget,
   Can I forget the hallow'd grove,
Where, by the winding Ayr, we met
   To live one day of parting love?
Eternity cannot efface
   Those records dear of transports past,
Thy image at our last embrace—
   Ah! little thought we 'twas our last!

3

Ayr, gurgling, kiss'd his pebbled shore,
   O'erhung with wild woods thickening green;
The fragrant birch and hawthorn hoar
   'Twin'd amorous round the raptur'd scene;
The flowers sprang wanton to be prest,
   The birds sang love on every spray,
Till too, too soon, the glowing west
   Proclaim'd the speed of wingèd day.

4

Still o'er these scenes my mem'ry wakes,
   And fondly broods with miser-care.
Time but th' impression stronger makes,
   As streams their channels deeper wear.
O Mary, dear departed shade!
   Where is thy place of blissful rest?
See'st thou thy lover lowly laid?
   Hear'st thou the groans that rend his breast?

EPPIE ADAIR

TUNE: *(As Title)*

CHORUS

An' O my Eppie,
My jewel, my Eppie!
Wha wadna be happy   wouldn't
Wi' Eppie Adair?

1

By love and by beauty
By law and by duty,
I swear to be true to
   My Eppie Adair!

2

A' pleasure exile me,   All
Dishonour defile me,
If e'er I beguile thee,
   My Eppie Adair!

THE BATTLE OF SHERRAMUIR

TUNE: *Cameronian Rant*

1

'O, can ye here the fight to shun,
   Or herd the sheep wi' me, man?
Or were ye at the Sherra-moor,
   Or did the battle see, man?'

sour and tough   'I saw the battle, sair and teugh,

furrow   And reekin-red ran monie a sheugh;

gave; sigh   My heart for fear gae sough for sough,

clouds   To hear the thuds, and see the cluds

clothes   O' clans frae woods in tartan duds,

grasped   Wha glaum'd at kingdoms three, man.

2

'The red-coat lads wi' black cockauds

not slow   To meet them were na slaw, man:

They rush'd and push'd and bluid outgush'd,

trunk   And monie a bouk did fa', man!

The great Argyle led on his files,

wot; shone   I wat they glanc'd for twenty miles;

hocked; skittles   They hough'd the clans like nine-pin kyles,

They hack'd and hash'd, while braid-swords clash'd,

And thro' they dash'd, and hew'd and smash'd,

fated   Till fey men died awa, man.

3

kilts   'But had ye seen the philibegs

flaring; trousers   And skyrin tartan trews, man,

dared   When in the teeth they daur'd our Whigs

    And Covenant trueblues, man!

In lines extended lang and large,

bayonets   When baig'nets o'erpower'd the targe,

And thousands hasten'd to the charge,

Wi' Highland wrath they frae the sheath

Drew blades o' death, till out o' breath

pigeons   They fled like frighted dows, man!'

4

'O, how Deil! Tam, can that be true?   how the Devil
   The chase gaed frae the north, man!   went
I saw mysel, they did pursue
   The horseman back to Forth, man;
And at Dunblane, in my ain sight,
They took the brig wi' a' their might,   bridge
And straught to Stirling wing'd their flight;
But, cursed lot! the gates were shut,
And monie a huntit poor red-coat,   almost;
   For fear amaist did swarf, man!'   swoon

5

'My sister Kate cam up the gate   road
   Wi' crowdie unto me, man: meal and water
She swoor she saw some rebels run
   To Perth and to Dundee, man!
Their left-hand general had nae skill;
The Angus lads had nae good will
That day their neebors' bluid to spill;
For fear by foes that they should lose
Their cogs o' brose, they scar'd at blows,   mugs of
   And hameward fast did flee, man.   porridge

6

'They've lost some gallant gentlemen,
   Amang the Highland clans, man!
I fear my Lord Panmure is slain,
   Or in his en'mies' hands, man.
Now wad ye sing this double flight,
Some fell for wrang, and some for right,
But monie bade the world guid-night:
Say, pell and mell, wi' muskets' knell
How Tories fell, and Whigs to Hell
   Flew off in frighted bands, man!'

JOCKIE WAS THE BLYTHEST LAD

TUNE: *(As Title)*

1

Young Jockie was the blythest lad,
round about   In a' our town or here awa:
goad   Fu' blythe he whistled at the gaud,
    Fu' lightly danc'd he in the ha'.

2

praised; eyes   He roos'd my een sae bonie blue,
trimly   He roos'd my waist sae genty sma';
mouth   An' ay my heart cam to my mou'
    When ne'er a body heard or saw.

3

My Jockie toils upon the plain
    Thro' wind and weet, thro' frost and snaw;
longingly   And o'er the lea I leuk fu' fain,
oxen; drive   When Jockie's owsen hameward ca'.

4

An' ay the night comes round again,
    When in his arms he taks me a',
An' ay he vows he'll be my ain
    As lang's he has a breath to draw.

wakeful mother   # A WAUKRIFE MINNIE

TUNE: *(As Title)*

1

going   'Whare are you gaun, my bonie lass?
honey   Whare are you gaun, my hinnie?'
    She answer'd me right saucilie:—
    'An errand for my minnie!'

2

'O, whare live ye, my bonie lass?
  O, whare live ye, my hinnie?'
'By yon burnside, gin ye maun ken,   *brookside; if; must*
  In a wee house wi' my minnie!'

3

But I foor up the glen at e'en   *went*
  To see my bonie lassie,
And lang before the grey morn cam
  She was na hauf sae saucy.   *half*

4

O, weary fa' the waukrife cock,   *woe befall; polecat*
  And the foumart lay his crawin!   *stop; crowing woman*
He wauken'd the auld wife frae her sleep
  A wee blink or the dawin.   *bit ere the dawn*

5

An angry wife I wat she raise,   *wot; rose*
  And o'er the bed she brought her,
And wi' a meikle hazel-rung   *big; -cudgel*
  She made her a weel-pay'd dochter.   *well-thrashed*

6

'O, fare-thee-weel, my bonie lass!
  O, fare-thee-weel, my hinnie!
Thou art a gay and a bonie lass,
  But thou has a waukrife minnie!'

THO' WOMEN'S MINDS

TUNE: *For a' that*

CHORUS

For a' that, an' a' that,
much as   *And twice as meikle's a' that,*
The bonie lass that I loe best,
      She'll be my ain for a' that!

1

Tho' women's minds like winter winds
    May shift, and turn, an' a' that,
most   The noblest breast adores them maist—
    A consequence, I draw that.

2

Great love I bear to a' the fair,
    Their humble slave, an' a' that;
But lordly will, I hold it still
contradict   A mortal sin to thraw that.

3

But there is ane aboon the lave,
    Has wit, and sense, and a' that;
A bonie lass, I like her best,
    And wha a crime dare ca' that?

4

In rapture sweet this hour we meet,
    Wi' mutual love an' a' that,
fly; sting   But for how lang the flie may stang,
    Let inclination law that!

5

Their tricks an' craft hae put me daft,
    They've taen me in an' a' that,
But clear your decks, and here's:—'The Sex?'
jades   I like the jads for a' that!

WILLIE BREW'D A PECK O' MAUT   malt

TUNE: *(As Title)*

CHORUS

We are na fou, we're nae that fou,   full (i.e. drunk)
But just a drappie in our e'e!   droplet
The cock may craw, the day may daw,   crow; dawn
And ay we'll taste the barley-bree!   -brew

1

O, Willie brewed a peck o' maut,
  And Rob and Allan cam to prie.
Three blyther hearts that lee-lang night   live-long
  Ye wad na found in Christendie.   would not have;
                                      Christendom

2

Here are we met three merry boys,
  Three merry boys I trow are we;
And monie a night we've merry been,
  And monie mae we hope to be!   more

3

It is the moon, I ken her horn,
  That's blinkin in the lift sae hie: shining; sky;
                                         high
She shines sae bright to wyle us hame,   entice
  But, by my sooth, she'll wait a wee!

4

Wha first shall rise to gang awa,   go
  A cuckold, coward loun is she!   rogue
Wha first beside his chair shall fa',
  He is the King amang us three!

KILLIECRANKIE

TUNE: *An' ye had been where I hae been*

CHORUS

If

would not have;
jolly

heights

An ye had been whare I hae been,
    Ye wad na been sae cantie, O!
An ye had seen what I hae seen
    On the braes o' Killiecrankie, O!

1

fine

spruce

'Whare hae ye been sae braw, lad?
    Whare hae ye been sae brankie, O?
Whare hae ye been sae braw, lad?
    Cam ye by Killiecrankie, O?'

2

'I faught at land, I faught at sea,
    At hame I faught my auntie, O';
But I met the Devil and Dundee
    On the braes o' Killiecrankie, O.

3

furrow

knock

Else; hawk

'The bauld Pitcur fell in a furr,
    An' Clavers gat a clankie, O,
Or I had fed an Athole gled
    On the braes o' Killiecrankie, O!'

THE BLUE-EYED LASSIE

TUNE: *(As Title)*

1

I went a woeful
way last night

eyes

wet

I gaed a waefu' gate yestreen,
    A gate I fear I'll dearly rue:
I gat my death frae twa sweet een,
    Twa lovely een o' bonie blue!
'Twas not her golden ringlets bright,
    Her lips like roses wat wi' dew,
Her heaving bosom lily-white:
    It was her een sae bonie blue.

2

She talk'd, she smil'd, my heart she wyl'd,   snared
 She charm'd my soul I wist na how;
And ay the stound, the deadly wound,   ache
 Cam frae her een sae bonie blue.
But 'spare to speak, and spare to speed'—
 She'll aiblins listen to my vow: may be
Should she refuse, I'll lay my dead   death
 To her twa een sae bonie blue.

THE BANKS OF NITH

TUNE: *Robie donna gorach*

1

The Thames flows proudly to the sea,
 Where royal cities stately stand;
But sweeter flows the Nith to me,
 Where Cummins ance had high command.
 When shall I see that honor'd land,
That winding stream I love so dear?
 Must wayward Fortune's adverse hand
For ever—ever keep me here?

2

How lovely, Nith, thy fruitful vales,
 Where bounding hawthorns gaily bloom,
And sweetly spread thy sloping dales,
 Where lambkins wanton thro' the broom!
 Tho' wandering now must be my doom
Far from the bonie banks and braes,
 May there my latest hours consume
Amand my friends of early days!

TAM GLEN

TUNE: *Mall Roe in the Morning*

1

sister

My heart is a-breaking, dear tittie,
    Some counsel unto me come len',
To anger them a' is a pity,
    But what will I do wi' Tam Glen?

2

such; fine
poverty; shift

I'm thinking, wi' sic a braw fellow
    In poortith I might mak a fen'.
What care I in riches to wallow,

must not

    If I mauna marry Tam Glen?

3

There's Lowrie the laird o' Dumeller:

in

    'Guid day to you,' brute! he comes ben.

money

He brags and he blaws o' his siller,
    But when will he dance like Tam Glen?

4

mother; deafen

My minnie does constantly deave me,
    And bids me beware o' young men.
They flatter, she says, to deceive me—
    But wha can think sae o' Tam Glen?

5

if

My daddie says, gin I'll forsake him,
    He'd gie me guid hunder marks ten.
But if it's ordain'd I maun take him,
    O, wha will I get but Tam Glen?

6

Last night
mouth; spring

Yestreen at the valentines' dealing,
    My heart to my mou gied a sten,
For thrice I drew ane without failing,
    And thrice it was written 'Tam Glen'!

7

The last Halloween I was waukin
   My droukit sark-sleeve, as ye ken—   wetted shift
His likeness came up the house staukin,   stalking
   And the very grey breeks o' Tam Glen!   breeches

8

Come, counsel, dear tittie, don't tarry!
   I'll gie ye my bonie black hen,
Gif ye will advise me to marry   If
   The lad I lo'e dearly, Tam Glen.

CRAIGIEBURN WOOD

TUNE: *(As Title)*

CHORUS

Beyond thee, dearie, beyond thee, dearie,
   And O, to be lying beyond thee!
O, sweetly, soundly, weel may he sleep
   That's laid in the bed beyond thee!

1

Sweet closes the ev'ning on Craigieburn Wood
   And blythely awaukens the morrow;
   But the pride o' the spring in the Craigieburn
Wood
   Can yield me naught but sorrow.

2

I see the spreading leaves and flowers,
   I hear the wild birds singing;
But pleasure they hae nane for me,
   While care my heart is wringing.

3

I can na tell, I maun na tell,   must
   I daur na for your anger;
But secret love will break my heart,
   If I conceal it langer.

4

I see thee gracefu', straight, and tall,
   I see thee sweet and bonie;
But O, what will my torment be,
   If thou refuse thy Johnie!

5

To see thee in another's arms
   In love to lie and languish,
death   'Twad be my dead, that will be seen—
   My heart wad burst wi' anguish!

6

But, Jeanie, say thou wilt be mine,
   Say thou lo'es nane before me,
And a' my days o' life to come
   I'll gratefully adore thee.

FRAE THE FRIENDS AND LAND I LOVE

TUNE: *Carronside*

1

Frae the friends and land I love
relentless   Driv'n by Fortune's felly spite,
Frae my best belov'd I rove,
   Never mair to taste delight!
must   Never mair maun hope to find
   Ease frae toil, relief frae care.
When remembrance wracks the mind,
   Pleasures but unveil despair.

2

gloomy   Brightest climes shall mirk appear,
every   Desert ilka blooming shore,
Till the Fates, nae mair severe,
   Friendship, love, and peace restore;
Till Revenge wi' laurell'd head
   Bring our banish'd hame again,
each   And ilk loyal, bonie lad
   Cross the seas, and win his ain!

JOHN, COME KISS ME NOW

TUNE: *(As Title)*

CHORUS

O John, come kiss me now, now, now!
O John, my love, come kiss me now!
O John, come kiss me by and by,
For weel ye ken the way to woo!

I

O, some will court and compliment,
  And ither some will kiss and daut; others; pet
But I will mak o' my guidman, husband
  My ain guidman—it is nae faut! fault

2

O, some will court and compliment,
  And ither some will prie their mou', taste
And some will hause in ither's arms, cuddle
  And that's the way I like to do!

COCK UP YOUR BEAVER

TUNE: *(As Title)*

I

When first my brave Johnie lad came to this town,
He had a blue bonnet that wanted the crown,
But now he has gotten a hat and a feather—
Hey, brave Johnie lad, cock up your beaver!

2

Cock up your beaver, and cock it fu' sprush! spruce
We'll over the border and gie them a brush:
There's somebody there we'll teach better
  behaviour—
Hey, brave Johnie lad, cock up your beaver!

MY TOCHER'S THE JEWEL

dowry's

TUNE: *The Highway to Edinburgh*

I

much
    O, meikle thinks my luve o' my beauty,
      And meikle thinks my luve o' my kin;
finely
    But little thinks my luve I ken brawlie
      My tocher's the jewel has charms for him.
    It's a' for the apple he'll nourish the tree,
honey
    It's a' for the hiney he'll cherish the bee!
much; money
      My laddie's sae meikle in luve wi' the siller,
    He canna hae luve to spare for me!

2

hansel-
    Your proffer o' luve's an airle-penny,
      My tocher's the bargain ye wad buy;
if
    But an ye be crafty, I am cunnin,
      Sae ye wi' anither your fortune may try.
timber
    Ye're like to the timmer o' yon rotten wood,
      Ye're like to the bark o' yon rotten tree:
    Ye'll slip frae me like a knotless thread,
      An' ye'll crack ye're credit wi' mair nor me!

GUIDWIFE, COUNT THE LAWIN

Hostess;
reckoning

TUNE: *(As Title)*

CHORUS

Then, guidwife, count the lawin,
    The lawin, the lawin!
Then, guidwife, count the lawin,
    And bring a coggie mair!

I

Gone; dark's
    Gane is the day, and mirk's the night,
    But we'll ne'er stray for faut o' light,
    For ale and brandy's stars and moon,
    And blude-red wine's the risin sun.

2

There's wealth and ease for gentlemen,
And semple folk maun fecht and fen';   simple; fight and
But here we're a' in ae accord   defend (i.e. shift
                                              for themselves)
For ilka man that's drunk's a lord.   one
                                              every

3

My coggie is a haly pool,   stoup; holy
That heals the wounds o' care and dool,   sorrow
And Pleasure is a wanton trout:
An ye drink it a', ye'll find him out!   If

THERE'LL NEVER BE PEACE TILL
JAMIE COMES HAME

TUNE: *There are few good fellows when Jamie's awa'*

1

By yon castle wa' at the close of the day,
I heard a man sing, tho' his head it was grey,
And as he was singing, the tears doon came:—
'There'll never be peace till Jamie comes hame!

2

'The Church is in ruins, the State is in jars,
Delusions, oppressions, and murderous wars,
We dare na weel say't, but we ken wha's to blame—
There'll never be peace till Jamie comes hame!

3

'My seven braw sons for Jamie drew sword,   fine
But now I greet round their green beds in the yerd;   weep; earth
It brak the sweet heart o' my faithfu' auld dame—
There'll never be peace till Jamie comes hame!

4

'Now life is a burden that bows me down,
Sin I tint my bairns, and he tint his crown;   since; lost;
But till my last moments my words are the same— children
There'll never be peace till Jamie comes hame!'

WHAT CAN A YOUNG LASSIE

TUNE: *What shall I do with an auld man?*

1

What can a young lassie,
What shall a young lassie,
What can a young lassie
    Do wi' an auld man?
Bad luck on the penny
That tempted my minnie   *mother*
To sell her puir Jenny
    For siller an' lan'!   *money*

2

He's always compleenin
Frae mornin to eenin;
He hoasts and he hirples   *coughs; hobbles*
    The weary day lang;
He's doylt and he 's dozin;   *stupid; torpid*
His blude it is frozen—
O, dreary's the night
    Wi' a crazy auld man!

3

He hums and he hankers,
He frets and he cankers,
I never can please him
    Do a' that I can.
He's peevish an' jealous
Of a' the young fellows—
O, dool on the day   *woe*
    I met wi' an auld man!

4

My auld auntie Katie
Upon me taks pity,
I'll do my endeavour
    To follow her plan:
I'll cross him an' wrack him
Until I heartbreak him,
And then his auld brass
    Will buy me a new pan.

THE BONIE LAD THAT'S FAR AWA

TUNE: *(As Title)*

1

O, how can I be blythe and glad,
   Or how can I gang brisk and braw,   go; fine
When the bonie lad that I lo'e best
   Is o'er the hills and far awa?

2

It's no the frosty winter wind,
   It's no the driving drift and snaw;
But ay the tear comes in my e'e
   To think on him that's far awa.

3

My father pat me frae his door,   put
   My friends they hae disown'd me a';
But I hae ane will tak my part—
   The bonie lad that's far awa.

4

A, pair o' glooves he bought to me,
   And silken snoods he gae me twa,   fillets; gave
And I will wear them for his sake,
   The bonie lad that's far awa.

5

O, weary Winter soon will pass,
   And Spring will cleed the birken shaw,   clothe;
And my sweet babie will be born,   birchwoods
   And he'll be hame that's far awa!

I DO CONFESS THOU ART SAE FAIR

TUNE: *The Cuckoo*

1

I do confess thou art sae fair,
would have; ears   I wad been o'er the lugs in luve,
not   Had I na found the slightest prayer
                    That lips could speak thy heart could muve.
                I do confess thee sweet, but find
                    Thou art so thriftless o' thy sweets,
                Thy favours are the silly wind
every   That kisses ilka thing it meets.

2

                See yonder rosebud rich in dew,
                    Amang its native briers sae coy,
soon; loses   How sune it tines its scent and hue,
pulled   When pu'd and worn a common toy!
Such   Sic fate ere lang shall thee betide,
                    Tho' thou may gaily bloom awhile,
                And sune thou shalt be thrown aside,
                    Like onie common weed, an' vile.

SENSIBILITY HOW CHARMING

TUNE: *Cornwallis's Lament*

1

                Sensibility how charming,
                    Thou, my friend, can'st truly tell!
                But Distress with horrors arming
                    Thou alas! hast known too well!

2

                Fairest flower, behold the lily
                    Blooming in the sunny ray:
                Let the blast sweep o'er the valley,
                    See is prostrate in the clay.

3

Hear the woodlark charm the forest,
   Telling o'er his little joys;
But alas! a prey the surest
   To each pirate of the skies!

4

Dearly bought the hidden treasure
   Finer feelings can bestow:
Chords that vibrate sweetest pleasure
   Thrill the deepest notes of woe.

YON WILD MOSSY MOUNTAINS

TUNE: *Phoebe*

1

Yon wild mossy mountains sae lofty and wide,
That nurse in their bosom the youth o' the Clyde,
Where the grouse lead their coveys thro' the heather to feed,
And the shepherd tents his flock as he pipes on his reed.   tends

2

Not Gowrie's rich valley nor Forth's sunny shores
To me hae the charms o' yon wild, mossy moors;
For there, by a lanely, sequesterèd stream,
Resides a sweet lassie, my thought and my dream.

3

Amang thae wild mountains shall still be my path,   those
Ilk stream foaming down its ain green, narrow strath;   Each
For there wi' my lassie the lang day I rove,
While o'er us unheeded flie the swift hours o' love.

4

She is not the fairest, altho' she is fair;
O' nice education but sma' is her share;
Her parentage humble as humble can be;
But I lo'e the dear lassie because she lo'es me.

5

must

To Beauty what man but maun yield him a prize,
In her armour of glances, and blushes, and sighs?
And when Wit and Refinement hae polish'd her darts,
eyes   They dazzle our een, as they flie to our hearts.

6

But kindness, sweet kindness, in the fond-sparkling e'e
Has lustre outshining the diamond to me,
And the heart beating love as I'm clasp'd in her arms,
O, these are my lassie's all-conquering charms!

I HAE BEEN AT CROOKIEDEN

TUNE: *The Old Highland Laddie*

1

I hae been at Crookieden—
   My bonie laddie, Highland laddie!
William of   Viewing Willie and his men—
Cumberland   My bonie laddie, Highland laddie!
There our foes that burnt and slew—
   My bonie laddie, Highland laddie!
There at last they gat their due—
   My bonie laddie, Highland laddie!

2

corner   Satan sits in his black neuk—
   My bonie laddie, Highland laddie!
Breaking sticks to roast the Duke—
   My bonic laddie, Highland laddie!
The bloody monster gae a yell—
   My bonie laddie, Highland laddie!
And loud the laugh gaed round a' Hell—
   My bonie laddie, Highland laddie!

IT IS NA, JEAN, THY BONIE FACE

TUNE: *The Maid's Complaint*

1

It is na, Jean, thy bonie face   not
   Nor shape that I admire,
Altho' thy beauty and thy grace
   Might weel awauk desire.
Something in ilka part o' thee   every
   To praise, to love, I find;
But, dear as is thy form to me,
   Still dearer is thy mind.

2

Nae mair ungen'rous wish I hae,
   Nor stronger in my breast,
Than, if I canna mak thee sae,   so
   At least to see thee blest:
Content am I, if Heaven shall give
   But happiness to thee,
And, as wi' thee I wish to live,
   For thee I'd bear to dee.

EPPIE MACNAB

TUNE: *(As Title)*

1

O, saw ye my dearie, my Eppie Macnab?
O, saw ye my dearie, my Eppie Macnab?
   'She's down in the yard, she's kissin the laird,
She winna come hame to her ain Jock Rab!'   will not

2

O, come thy ways to me, my Eppie Macnab!
O, come thy ways to me, my Eppie Macnab!
   Whate'er thou has done, be it late, be it soon,
Thou's welcome again to thy Jock Rab.   art

3

What says she, my dearie, my Eppie Macnab?
What says she, my dearie, my Eppie Macnab?
know   'She lets thee to wit that she has thee forgot,
And for ever disowns thee, her ain Jock Rab.'

4

O, had I ne'er seen thee, my Eppie Macnab!
O, had I ne'er seen thee, my Eppie Macnab!
          As light as the air and as fause as thou's fair,
Thou's broken the heart o' thy ain Jock Rab!

WHA IS THAT AT MY BOWER DOOR?

TUNE: *Lass an' I come near thee*

1

'Wha is that at my bower door?'
     'O, wha is it but Findlay!'
go your way, ye   'Then gae your gate, ye'se nae be here.'
shall not   'Indeed maun I!' quo' Findlay.
must   What mak ye, sae like a thief?'
do   'O, come and see!' quo' Findlay.
'Before the morn ye'll work mischíef?'
     'Indeed will I!' quo' Findlay.

2

If   'Gif I rise and let you in'—
               'Let me in!' quo' Findlay—
awake   'Ye'll keep me wauken wi' your din?'
               'Indeed will I!' quo' Findlay.
'In my bower if ye should stay'—
               'Let me stay!' quo' Findlay—
'I fear ye'll bide till break o' day?'
               'Indeed will I!' quo' Findlay.

3

'Here this night if ye remain'—
    'I'll remain!' quo' Findlay—
'I dread ye'll learn the gate again?'
    'Indeed will I!' quo' Findlay.
'What may pass within this bower'
    ('Let it pass!' quo' Findlay!)
'Ye maun conceal till your last hour'—
    'Indeed will I!' quo' Findlay.

BONIE WEE THING

TUNE: *(As Title)*

CHORUS

Bonie wee thing, cannie wee thing,   gentle
    Lovely wee thing, wert thou mine,
I wad wear thee in my bosom
    Lest my jewel it should tine.   lose

I

Wishfully I look and languish
    In that bonie face o' thine,
And my heart it stounds wi' anguish,   aches
    Lest my wee thing be na mine.

2

Wit and Grace and Love and Beauty
    In ae constellation shine!
To adore thee is my duty,
    Goddess o' this soul o' mine!

AE FOND KISS

TUNE: *Rory Dall's Port*

I

Ae fond kiss, and then we sever!
Ae farewell, and then forever!
Deep in heart-wrung tears I'll pledge thee,
Warring sighs and groans I'll wage thee.

2

Who shall say that Fortune grieves him,
While the star of hope she leaves him?
Me, nae cheerfu' twinkle lights me,
Dark despair around benights me.

3

I'll ne'er blame my partial fancy:
Naething could resist my Nancy!
But to see her was to love her,
Love but her, and love for ever.

4

Had we never lov'd sae kindly,
Had we never lov'd sae blindly,
Never met—or never parted—
We had ne'er been broken-hearted.

5

Fare-thee-weel, thou first and fairest!
Fare-thee-weel, thou best and dearest!
every   Thine be ilka joy and treasure,
Peace, Enjoyment, Love and Pleasure!

6

Ae fond kiss, and then we sever!
Ae farewell, alas, for ever!
Deep in heart-wrung tears I'll pledge thee,
Warring sighs and groans I'll wage thee.

LOVELY DAVIES

TUNE: *Miss Muir*

1

O, how shall I, unskilfu', try
  The Poet's occupation?
The tunefu' Powers, in happy hours
  That whisper inspiration,
Even they maun dare an effort mair   must
  Than aught they ever gave us,
Ere they rehearse in equal verse
  The charms o' lovely Davies.

2

Each eye, it cheers, when she appears,
  Like Phœbus in the morning,
When past the shower, and every flower
  The garden is adorning!
As the wretch looks o'er Siberia's shore,
  When winter-bound the wave is,
Sae droops our hearts, when we maun part
  Frae charming, lovely Davies.

3

Her smile's a gift frae 'boon the lift,   above; sky
  That maks us mair than princes.
A sceptred hand, a king's command,
  Is in her darting glances.
The man in arms 'gainst female charms,
  Even he her willing slave is:
He hugs his chain, and owns the reign
  Of conquering lovely Davies.

4

My Muse to dream of such a theme
  Her feeble powers surrenders;
The eagle's gaze alone surveys
  The sun's meridian splendours.
I wad in vain essay the strain—
  That deed too daring brave is!
I'll drap the lyre, and, mute, admire   drop
  The charms o' lovely Davies.

pound; yarn

THE WEARY PUND O' TOW

TUNE: *(As Title)*

CHORUS

The weary pund, the weary pund,
The weary pund o' tow!
I think my wife will end her life
Before she spin her tow.

1

stone; flax

I bought my wife a stane o' lint
 As guid as e'er did grow,
And a' that she has made o' that
one poor
 Is ae puir pund o' tow.

2

hole in the wall

There sat a bottle in a bole
At the back of
the fireplace
other suck
wet the dusty
 Beyont the ingle bow;
And ay she took the tither souk
 To drouk the stourie tow.

3

Quoth I:—'For shame, ye dirty dame,
bunch
 Gae spin your tap o' tow!'
distaff
She took the rock, and wi' a knock
pate
 She brake it o'er my pow.

4

At last her feet—I sang to see't!—
went; hill
 Gaed foremost o'er the knowe,
wed
And or I was anither jad,
kick heels; rope
 I'll wallop in a tow.

I HAE A WIFE O' MY AIN

have

TUNE: *(As Title)*

I

I hae a wife o' my ain,
   I'll partake wi' naebody:
I'll take cuckold frae nane,
   I'll gie cuckold to naebody.

2

I hae a penny to spend,
   There—thanks to naebody!
I hae naething to lend,
   I'll borrow frae naebody.

3

I am naebody's lord,
   I'll be slave to naebody.
I hae a guid braid sword,
   I'll tak dunts frae naebody.

blows

4

I'll be merry and free,
   I'll be sad for naebody,
Naebody cares for me,
   I care for naebody.

WHEN SHE CAM BEN, SHE BOBBED

into the parlour; curtseyed

TUNE: *When she cam ben she bobbit*

I

O, when she cam ben, she bobbéd fu' law!   *low*
O, when she cam ben, she bobbéd fu' law!
And when she cam' ben, she kiss'd Cockpen,
And syne she deny'd she did it at a'!   *then; at all*

2

And was na Cockpen right saucy witha'?
And was na Cockpen right saucy witha',
In leaving the dochter o' a lord,
And kissin a collier lassie an' a'?

3

'O, never look down, my lassie, at a'!
O, never look down, my lassie, at a'!
Thy lips are as sweet, and thy figure complete,
As the finest dame in castle or ha'.

4

fine

'Tho' thou hast nae silk, and holland sae sma',
Tho' thou hast nae silk, and holland sae sma',

shift

Thy coat and thy sark are thy ain handywark,
And Lady Jean was never sae braw.'

One-

O, FOR ANE-AND-TWENTY, TAM

TUNE: *The Moudiewart*

CHORUS

An' O, for ane-and-twenty, Tam!
   And hey, sweet ane-and-twenty, Tan!
I'll learn my kin a rattlin sang

If

   An I saw ane-and-twenty, Tam.

1

snub; sore; keep

They snool me sair, and haud me down,

make; a stupid

   And gar me look like bluntie, Tam;
But three short years will soon wheel roun'—
   And then comes ane-and-twenty, Tam!

2

handful of
money

A gleib o' lan', a claut o' gear
   Was left me by my auntie, Tam.

Of; ask

At kith or kin I needna spier,
   An I saw ane-and-twenty, Tam.

3

They'll hae me wed a wealthy coof,   dolt
   Tho' I mysel hae plenty, Tam;
But hear'st thou, laddie—there's my loof: palm
   I'm thine at ane-and-twenty, Tam!

O, KENMURE'S ON AND AWA, WILLIE

TUNE: *(As Title)*

I

O, Kenmure's on and awa, Willie,
   O, Kenmure's on and awa!
An' Kenmure's lord's the bravest lord
   That ever Galloway saw!

2

Success to Kenmure's band, Willie,
   Success to Kenmure's band!
There's no a heart that fears a Whig
   That rides by Kenmure's hand.

3

Here's Kenmure's health in wine, Willie,
   Here's Kenmure's health in wine!
There ne'er was a coward o' Kenmure's blude,
   Nor yet o' Gordon's line.

4

O, Kenmure's lads are men, Willie,
   O, Kenmure's lads are men!
Their hearts and swords are mental true,
   And that their faes shall ken.   foes

5

They'll live or die wi' fame, Willie,
   They'll live or die wi' fame!
But soon wi' sounding Victorie
   May Kenmure's lord come hame!

6

Here's him that's far awa, Willie,
Here's him that's far awa!
And here's the flower that I lo'e best—
The rose that's like the snaw!

O, LEEZE ME ON MY SPINNIN-WHEEL

TUNE: *Sweet's the lass that loves me*

1

distaff

top to toe;
clothes;
comfortably
wraps; well
place
low

O, leeze me on my spinnin-wheel!
And leeze me on my rock and reel,
Frae tap to tae that cleeds me bien,
And haps me fiel and warm at e'en!
I'll set me down, and sing and spin,
While laigh descends the summer sun,
Blest wi' content, and milk and meal—
O, leeze me on my spinnin-wheel!

2

either; brooklets

thatched

birch

cool

glances; shelter

On ilka hand the burnies trot,
And meet below my theekit cot.
The scented birk and hawthorn white
Across the pool their arms unite,
Alike to screen the birdie's nest
And little fishes' caller rest.
The sun blinks kindly in the biel,
Where blythe I turn my spinnin-wheel.

3

oaks

doleful

linnets; slopes

each other's

corncrake; clover

partridge;
meadow
darting; cottage

On lofty aiks the cushats wail,
And Echo cons the doolfu' tale.
And lintwhites in the hazel braes,
Delighted, rival ither's lays.
The craik amang the claver hay,
The paitrick whirrin o'er the ley,
The swallow jinkin round my shiel,
Amuse me at my spinnin-wheel.

4

Wi' sma to sell and less to buy,   little
Aboon distress, below envý,   Above
O, wha wad leave this humble state
For a' the pride of a' the great?
Amid their flaring, idle toys,
Amid their cumbrous, dinsome joys,   noisy
Can they the peace and pleasure feel
Of Bessy at her spinnin-wheel?

MY COLLIER LADDIE

TUNE: *(As Title)*

I

'O, whare live ye, my bonie lass,
    And tell me how they ca' ye!'   call
'My name,' she says, 'is Mistress Jean,
    And I follow the collier laddie.'

2

'O, see you not yon hills and dales
    The sun shines on sae brawlie?   finely
They a' are mine, and they shall be thine,
    Gin ye'll leave your collier laddie!   if

3

'An' ye shall gang in gay attire,   go
    Weel buskit up sae gaudy,   adorned
And ane to wait on every hand,
    Gin ye'll leave your collier laddie!'

4

'Tho' ye had a' the sun shines on,
    And the earth conceals sae lowly,
I wad turn my back on you and it a',
    And embrace my collier laddie.

5

I can win my five pennies in a day,
  An' spend it at night fu' brawlie,
And make my bed in the collier's neuk
  And lie down wi' my collier laddie.

corner

6

'Loove for loove is the bargain for me,
  Tho' the wee cot-house should haud me,
And the warld before me to win my bread—
  And fair fa' my collier laddie!'

hold

good befall

NITHSDALE'S WELCOME HAME

TUNE: *(As Title)*

1

The noble Maxwells and their powers
  Are coming o'er the border;
And they'll gae big Terreagles' towers,
  And set them a' in order;
And they declare Terreagles fair,
  For their abode they choose it:
There's no a heart in a' the land
  But's lighter at the news o't!

go build

2

Tho' stars in skies may disappear,
  And angry tempests gather,
The happy hour may soon be near
  That brings us pleasant weather;
The weary night o' care and grief
  May hae a joyfu' morrow;
So dawning day has brought relief—
  Fareweel our night o' sorrow!

IN SIMMER, WHEN THE HAY WAS MAWN

TUNE: *The Country Lass*

1

In simmer, when the hay was mawn	
And corn wav'd green in ilka field,	every
While claver blooms white o'er the ley,	clover; pasture
And roses blaw in ilka bield,	sheltered spot
Blythe Bessie in the milking shiel	shed
Says:—'I'll be wed, come o't what will!'	
Out spake a dame in wrinkled eild:—	eld
'O' guid advisement comes nae ill.	

2

'It's ye hae wooers monie ane,	many a one
And lassie, ye're but young, ye ken!	
Then wait a wee, and cannie wale	sensibly choose
A routhie butt, a routhie ben.	well-stocked kitchen; parlour
There Johnie o' the Buskie-Glen,	
Fu' is his barn, fu' is his byre.	Full; cowshed
Tak this frae me, my bonie hen:	
It's plenty beets the luver's fire!'	fans

3

'For Johnie o' the Buskie-Glen	
I dinna care a single flie:	fly
He lo'es sae weel his craps and kye,	crops; kine
He has nae love to spare for me.	
But blythe's the blink o' Robie's e'e,	glance; eye
And weel I wat he lo'es me dear:	wot
Ae blink o' him I wad na gie	One; give
For Buskie-Glen and a' his gear.'	wealth

4

'O thoughtless lassie, life's a faught!
   The canniest gate, the strife is sair.
Buy ay fu'-han't is fechtin best:
   A hungry care's an unco care.
   But some will spend, and some will spare,
An' wilfu' folk maun hae their will.
   Syne as ye brew, my maiden fair,
Keep mind that ye maun drink the yill!'

fight
quietest way
full-handed;
fighting
terrible

must
Then
ale

5

'O, gear will buy me rigs o' land,
   And gear will buy me sheep and kye!
But the tender heart o' leesome loove
   The gowd and siller canna buy!
   We may be poor, Robie and I;
Light is the burden luve lays on;
   Content and loove brings peace and joy:
What mair hae Queens upon a throne?'

ridges

lawful
gold and silver

FAIR ELIZA

TUNE: *A Gaelic air*

1

Turn again, thou fair Eliza!
   Ae kind blink before we part!
Rew on thy despairing lover—
   Canst thou break his faithfu' heart?
Turn again, thou fair Eliza!
   If to love thy heart denies,
For pity hide the cruel sentence
   Under friendship's kind disguise!

One; glance
Take pity

2

Thee, dear maid, hae I offended?
 The offence is loving thee.
Canst thou wreck his peace for ever,
 Wha for thine wad gladly die?
While the life beats in my bosom,
 Thou shalt mix in ilka throe.   every
Turn again, thou lovely maiden,
 Ae sweet smile on me bestow!   One

3

Not the bee upon the blossom
 In the pride o' sinny noon,   sunny
Not the little sporting fairy
 All beneath the simmer moon,
Not the Poet in the moment
 Fancy lightens in his e'e,
Kens the pleasure, feels the rapture,
 That thy presence gies to me.

YE JACOBITES BY NAME

TUNE: *(As Title)*

1

Ye Jacobites by name,
 Give an ear, give an ear!
Ye Jacobites by name,
 Give an ear!
Ye Jacobites by name,
Your fautes I will proclaim,   faults
Your doctrines I maun blame—   must
 You shall hear!

2

What is Right, and what is Wrang,
    By the law, by the law?
What is Right, and what is Wrang
    By the law?
What is Right, and what is Wrang?
A short sword and a lang,
A weak arm and a strang
    For to draw!

3

What makes heroic strife
    Famed afar, famed afar?
What makes heroic strife
    Famed afar?
What makes heroic strife?
To whet th'assassin's knife,
Or hunt a Parent's life
    Wi' bluidy war!

4

Then let your schemes alone,
    In the State, in the State!
Then let your schemes alone.
    In the State!
Then let your schemes alone,
Adore the rising sun,
And leave a man undone
    To his fate!

THE POSIE

TUNE: *(As Title)*

1

O, luve will venture in where it daur na weel be seen!
O, luve will venture in where wisdom ance hath been!
But I will doun yon river rove amang the wood sae green,
pluck   And a' to pu' a posie to my ain dear May!

2

The primrose I will pu', the firstling o' the year,
And I will pu' the pink, the emblem o' my dear,
For she's the pink o' womankind, and blooms without a peer—
    And a' to be a posie to my ain dear May!

3

I'll pu' the budding rose when Phœbus peeps in view,
For it's like a baumy kiss o' her sweet, bonie mou.   *balmy*
The hyacinth's for constancy wi' its unchanging blue—
    And a' to be a posie to my ain dear May!

4

The lily it is pure, and the lily it is fair,
And in her lovely bosom I'll place the lily there.
The daisy's for simplicity and unaffected air
    And a' to be a posie to my ain dear May!

5

The hawthorn I will pu', wi' its locks o' siller gray,
Where, like an agèd man, it stands at break o' day;
But the songster's nest within the bush I winna tak away   *will not*
    And a' to be a posie to my ain dear May!

6

The woodbine I will pu' when the e'ening star is near,
And the diamond draps o' dew shall be her een sae clear!   *eyes*
The violet's for modesty, which weel she fa's to wear—   *claims*
    And a' to be a posie to my ain dear May!

7

I'll tie the posie round wi' the silken band o' luve.
And I'll place it in her breast, and I'll swear by a' above,
That to my latest draught o' life the band shall ne'er remove,
    And this will be a posie to my ain dear May!

THE BANKS O' DOON

TUNE: *Caledonian Hunt's Delight*

1

slopes

Ye banks and braes o' bonie Doon,
    How can ye bloom sae fresh and fair?
How can ye chant, ye little birds,
    And I sae weary fu' o' care!
Thou'll break my heart, thou warbling bird,
    That wantons thro' the flowering thorn!
Thou minds me o' departed joys,
    Departed never to return.

2

Aft hae I rov'd by bonie Doon
    To see the rose and woodbine twine,
every   And ilka bird sang o' its luve,
    And fondly sae did I o' mine.
plucked   Wi' lightsome heart I pu'd a rose,
    Fu' sweet upon its thorny tree!
stole   And my fause luver staw my rose—
    But ah! he left the thorn wi' me.

WILLIE WASTLE

TUNE: *Sic a Wife as Willie had*

1

Willie Wastle dwalt on Tweed,
    The spot they ca'd it Linkumdoddie.
weaver   Willie was a wabster guid
have stolen   Could stown a clue wi' onie bodie.
stubborn; dun   He had a wife was dour and din,
Tinker   O, Tinkler Maidgie was her mither!
Such   Sic a wife as Willie had,
    I wad na gie a button for her.

2

She has an e'e (she has but ane),
    The cat has twa the very colour,
Five rusty teeth, forbye a stump,   besides
    A clapper-tongue wad deave a miller;   deafen
A whiskin beard about her mou,
    Her nose and chin they threaten ither: each other
Sic a wife as Willie had,
    I wad na gie a button for her.

3

She's bow-hough'd, she's hem-shin'd,   bandy
    Ae limpin leg a hand-breed shorter;   one; -breadth
She's twisted right, she's twisted left,
    To balance fair in ilka quarter;   either
She has a hump upon her breast,
    The twin o' that upon her shoulder: shoulder
Sic a wife as Willie had,
    I wad na gie a button for her.

4

Auld baudrans by the ingle sits,   Old pussie
    An' wi' her loof her face a-washin;   palm
But Willie's wife is nae sae trig,   trim
    She dights her grunzie wi' a hushion;   wipes; snout
Her walie nieves like midden-creels,   ample fists
    Her face wad fyle the Logan Water: foul
Sic a wife a Wille had,
    I wad na gie a button for her.

LADY MARY ANN

TUNE: *(At Title)*

1

O, Lady Mary Ann looks o'er the Castle wa',
She saw three bonie boys playing at the ba',
The youngest he was the flower amang them a'—
    My bonie laddie's young, but he's growin yet!

2

'O father, O father, an ye think it fit,
We'll send him a year to the college yet;
We'll sew a green ribbon round about his hat,
    And that will let them ken he's to marry yet!'

3

Lady Mary Ann was a flower in the dew,
Sweet was its smell and bonie was its hue,
And the longer it blossom'd the sweeter it grew,
    For the lily in the bud will be bonier yet.

4

oak   Young Charlie Cochran was the sprout of an aik;
straight   Bonie and bloomin and straucht was its make;
The sun took delight to shine for its sake,
    And it will be the brag o' the forest yet.

5

The simmer is gane when the leaves they were
    green,
And the days are awa that we hae seen;
But far better days I trust will come again,
    For my bonie laddie's young, but he's growin yet.

A PARCEL OF ROGUES IN A NATION

TUNE: *(As Title)*

1

Fareweel to a' our Scottish fame,
    Fareweel our ancient glory!
Fareweel ev'n to the Scottish name,
    Sae famed in martial story!
Now Sark rins over Solway sands,
    An' Tweed rins to the ocean,
To mark where England's province stands—
    Such a parcel of rogues in a nation!

2

What force or guile could not subdue
    Thro' many warlike ages
Is wrought now by a coward few
    For hireling traitor's wages.
The English steel we could disdain,
    Secure in valour's station;
But English gold has beren our bane—
    Such a parcel of rogues in a nation!

3

O, would, or I had seen the day
    That Treason thus could sell us,
My auld grey head had lien in clay
    Wi' Bruce and loyal Wallace!
But pith and power, till my last hour   Even when
    I'll mak this declaration:—   without
'We're bought and sold for English gold'—
    Such a parcel of rogues in a nation!

KELLYBURN BRAES

TUNE: *(As Title)*

1

There livèd a carl in Kellyburn Braes   old man
    (Hey and the rue grows bonie wi' thyme),
And he had a wife was the plague o' his days
    (And the thyme it is wither'd, and rue is prime).

2

Ae day as the carl gaed up the lang glen   One
    (Hey and the rue grows bonie wi' thyme),
He met wi' the Devil, says:—'How do you fen?'   are you getting
    (And the thyme it is wither'd, and rue is in prime).   on

3

'I've got a bad wife, sir, that's a' my complaint
    (Hey and the rue grows bonie wi' thyme),
For, saving your presence, to her ye're a saint,
    (And the thyme it is wither'd, and rue is in prime).

4

steer; young
horse

'It's neither your stot nor your staig I shall crave
    (Hey and the rue grows bonie wi' thyme),
'But gie me your wife, man, for her I must have'
    (And the thyme it is wither'd, and rue is in prime).

5

'O welcome most kindly!' the blythe carl said
    (Hey and the rue grows bonie wi' thyme),

worse

'But if ye can match her ye're waur than ye're ca'd'
    (And the thyme it is wither'd, and rue is in prime).

6

The Devil has got the auld wife on his back
    (Hey and the rue grows bonie wi' thyme),
And like a poor pedlar he's carried his pack
    (And the thyme it is wither'd, and rue is in prime).

7

porch-

He's carried her hame to his ain hallan-door
    (Hey and the rue grows bonie wi' thyme),

Then; go

Syne bade her gae in for a bitch and a whore
    (And the thyme it is wither'd, and rue is in prime).

8

Then straight he makes fifty, the pick o' his band
    (Hey and the rue grows bonie wi' thyme),
Turn out on her guard in the clap o' a hand
    (And the thyme it is wither'd, and rue is in prime).

9

beldam; mad

The carlin gaed thro' them like onie wud bear
    (Hey and the rue grows bonie wi' thyme):
Whae'er she gat hands on cam near her nae mair
    (And the thyme it is wither'd, and rue is in prime).

10

smoky small

A reekit wee deevil looks over the wa
    (Hey and the rue grows bonie wi' thyme):—
'O help, maister, help, or she'll ruin us a'!'
    (And the thyme it is wither'd, and rue is in prime).

11

The Devil he swore by the edge o' his knife
  (Hey and the rue grows bonie wi' thyme),
He pitied the man that was tied to a wife
  (And the thyme it is wither'd, and rue is in prime).

12

The Devil he swore by the kirk and the bell
  (Hey and the rue grows bonie wi' thyme),
He was not in wedlock, thank Heav'n, but in Hell
  (And the thyme it is wither'd, and rue is in prime).

13

Then Satan has travell'd again wi' his pack
  (Hey and the rue grows bonie wi' thyme),
And to her auld husband he's carried her back
  (And the thyme it is wither'd, and rue is in prime).

14

'I hae been a Devil the feck o' my life   most
  (Hey and the rue grows bonie wi' thyme),
But ne'er was in Hell till I met wi' a wife.'
  (And the thyme it is wither'd, and rue is in prime).

THE SLAVE'S LAMENT

TUNE: *(As Title)*

1

It was in sweet Senegal
That my foes did me enthral
  For the lands of Virginia, -ginia, O!
Torn from that lovely shore,
And must never see it more,
  And alas! I am weary, weary, O!

2

All on that charming coast
Is no bitter snow and frost,
　　Like the lands of Virginia, -ginia, O!
There streams for ever flow,
And the flowers for ever blow,
　　And alas! I am weary, weary, O!

3

The burden I must bear,
While the cruel scourge I fear,
　　In the lands of Virginia, -ginia, O!
And I think on friends most dear
With the bitter, bitter tear,
　　And alas! I am weary, weary, O!

THE SONG OF DEATH

TUNE: *Oran an aoig*

1

Farewell, thou fair day, thou green earth, and ye skies,
　　Now gay with the broad setting sun!
Farewell, loves and friendships, ye dear tender ties—
　　Our race of existence is run!
Thou grim King of Terrors! thou Life's gloomy foe,
　　Go, frighten the coward and slave!
Go, teach them to tremble, fell tyrant, but know,
　　No terrors has thou to the brave!

2

Thou strik'st the dull peasant—he sinks in the dark,
　　Nor saves e'en the wreck of a name!
Thou strik'st the young hero—a glorious mark,
　　He falls in the blaze of his fame!
In the field of proud honour, our swords in our hands,
　　Our king and our country to save,
While victory shines on Life's last ebbing sands,
　　O, who would not die with the brave?

SWEET AFTON

TUNE: *Afton Water*

1

Flow gently, sweet Afton, among thy green braes!   slopes
Flow gently, I'll sing thee a song in thy praise!
My Mary's asleep by thy murmuring stream—
Flow gently, sweet Afton, disturb not her dream!

2

Thou stock dove whose echo resounds thro' the glen,
Ye wild whistling blackbirds in yon thorny den
Thou green-crested lapwing, thy screaming forbear—
I charge you, disturb not my slumbering fair!

3

How lofty, sweet Afton, thy neighbouring hills,
Far mark'd with the courses of clear, winding rills!
There daily I wander, as noon rises high,
My flocks and my Mary's sweet cot in my eye.

4

How pleasant thy banks and greens vallies below,
Where wild in the woodlands the primroses blow;
There oft, as mild ev'ning weeps over the lea.
The sweet-scented birk shades my Mary and me.   birch

5

Thy crystal stream, Afton, how lovely it glides,
And winds by the cot where my Mary resides!
How wanton thy waters her snowy feet lave,
As, gathering sweet flowerets, she stems thy clear wave!

6

Flow gently, sweet Afton, among thy green braes!
Flow gently, sweet river, the theme of my lays!
My Mary's asleep by thy murmuring stream—
Flow gently, sweet Afton, disturb not her dream!

BONIE BELL

TUNE: *(As Title)*

1

The smiling Spring comes in rejoicing,
    And surly Winter grimly flies.
Now crystal clear are the falling waters,
    And bonie blue are the sunny skies,
Fresh o'er the mountains breaks forth the morning,
    The ev'ning gilds the ocean's swell:
All creatures joy in the sun's returning,
    And I rejoice in my bonie Bell.

2

The flowery Spring leads sunny Summer,
    The yellow Autumn presses near;
Then in his turn comes gloomy Winter,
    Till smiling Spring again appear.
Thus seasons dancing, life advancing,
    Old Time and Nature their changes tell;
But never ranging, still unchanging,
    I adore my bonie Bell.

THE GALLANT WEAVER

TUNE: *(As Title)*

1

rolling
Where Cart rins rowin to the sea
By monie a flower and spreading tree,
There lives a lad, the lad for me—
    He is a gallant weaver!
O, I had wooers aught or nine,
gave
They gied me rings and ribbons fine,
afraid; be lost
And I was fear'd my heart wad tine,
    And I gied it to the weaver.

2

My daddie sign'd my tocher-band   deed of
To gie the lad that has the land;   settlement
But to my heart I'll add my hand,
   And give it to the weaver.
While birds rejoice in leafy bowers,
While bees delight in opening flowers
While corn grows green in summer showers,
   I love my gallant weaver.

HEY, CA' THRO'   work away

TUNE: *(As Title)*

CHORUS

Hey, ca' thro', ca' thro',
For we hae mickle ado!   much to do
Hey, ca' thro', ca' thro',
For we hae mickle ado!

1

Up wi' the carls of Dysart   old men
   And the lads o' Buckhaven,
And the kimmers o' Largo   gossips
   And the lasses o' Leven!

2

We hae tales to tell,
   And we hae sangs to sing;
We hae pennies to spend
   And we hae pints to bring.

3

We'll live a' our days,
   And them that comes behin',
Let them do the like
   And spend the gear thy win!   wealth

O, CAN YE LABOUR LEA

TUNE: *(As Title)*

CHORUS

O, can ye labour lea, young man,
O, can ye labour lea?
Go; way   *Gae back the gate ye came again—*
Ye shall; despise   *Ye'se never scorn me!*

1

hired   I fee'd a man at Martinmas
hansel-   Wi' airle-pennies three;
                   But a' the faut I had to him
                       He couldna labour lea.

2

stroking   O, clappin's guid in Febarwar,
                       An' kissin's sweet in May;
                   But what signifies a young man's love,
If it do not   An't dinna last for ay?

3

                   O, kissin is the key o' love
                       An' clappin is the lock;
                   An' makin of's the best thing
                       That e'er a young thing got!

THE DEUK'S DANG O'ER MY DADDIE
duck has
knocked

TUNE: *(As Title)*

1

children;   The bairns gat out wi' an unco shout:—
surprising   'The deuk's dang o'er my daddie, O!'
fiend-may-;   'The fien-ma-care,' quo' the feirrie auld wife,
lusty
creature   'He was but a paidlin body, O!
                   He paidles out, and he paidles in,
                       An' he paidles late and early, O!
sapless old   This seven lang years I hae lien by his side,
mannikin   An' he is but a fusionless carlie, O!'

2

'O, haud your tongue, my feirrie auld wife,   hold
     O, haud your tongue, now Nansie, O!
I've seen the day, and sae hae ye,   so have
     Ye wad na been sae donsie, O.   testy
I've seen the day ye butter'd my brose,
     And cuddl'd me late and early, O;
But downa-do's come o'er me now,   cannot-do is
     And och, I find it sairly, O!'   feel it sorely

SHE'S FAIR AND FAUSE   false

TUNE: *The Lads of Leith*

1

She's fair and fause that causes my smart;
     I lo'ed her meikle and lang;   much; long
She's broken her vow, she's broken my heart;
     And I may e'en gae hang.   go
A coof cam in wi' routh o' gear,   ninny; plenty;
And I hae tint my dearest dear;   money
                                                     lost
But Woman is but warld's gear,
     Sae let the bonie lass gang!   go

2

Whae'er ye be that Woman love,
     To this be never blind:
Nae ferlie 'tis, tho' fickle she prove,   No wonder is it
     A woman has't by kind.
O Woman lovely, Woman fair,
An Angel form's faun to thy share,   fallen
'Twad been o'er meikle to gien thee mair!   have given
     I mean an angel mind.

THE DEIL'S AWA WI' TH' EXCISEMAN

TUNE: *The Hemp-dresser*

CHORUS

The Deil's awa, the Deil's awa,
The Deil's awa wi' th' Exciseman!
He's danc'd awa, he's danc'd awa,
He's danc'd awa wi' th' Exciseman!

1

The Deil cam fiddlin thro' the town,
And danc'd awa wi' th' Exciseman,
every   And ilka wife cries:—'Auld Mahoun,
I wish you luck o' the prize, man!

2

malt   'We'll mak our maut, and we'll brew our drink,
We'll laugh, sing, and rejoice, man,
handsome; big   And monie braw thanks to the meikle black Deil,
That danc'd awa wi' th' Exciseman.

3

'There's threesome reels, there's foursome reels,
There's hornpipes and strathspeys, man,
one   But the ae best dance ere cam to the land
Was *The Deil's Awa wi' th' Exciseman!*

THE LOVELY LASS OF INVERNESS

TUNE: *(As Title)*

1

The lovely lass of Inverness,
Nae joy nor pleasure can she see;
For e'en to morn she cries 'Alas!'
salt   And ay the saut tear blin's her e'e:—

2

'Drumossie moor, Drumossie day—
  A waefu' day it was to me!   woeful
For there I lost my father dear,
  My father dear and brethren three.

3

Their winding-sheet the bluidy clay,
  Their graves are growin green to see,
And by them lies the dearest lad
  That ever blest a woman's e'e.

4

Now wae to thee, thou cruel lord,   William of
  A bluidy man I trow thou be,   Cumberland
For monie a heart thou hast made sair   sore
  That ne'er did wrang to thine or thee!'

A RED, RED ROSE

TUNE: *Major Graham*

1

O, my luve's like a red, red rose,
  That's newly sprung in June.
O, my luve's like the melodie,
  That's sweetly play'd in tune.

2

As fair art thou, my bonie lass,
  So deep in luve am I,
And I will luve thee still, my Dear,
  Till a' the seas gang dry.   go

3

Till a' the seas gang dry, my Dear,
  And the rocks melt wi' the sun!
O I will luve thee still, my Dear,
  While the sands o' life shall run.

4

And fare thee weel, my only Luve,
And fare thee weel a while!
And I will come again, my Luve,
Tho' it were ten thousand mile!

AS I STOOD BY YON ROOFLESS TOWER

TUNE: *Cumnock Psalms*

CHORUS

A lassie all alone was making her moan,
Lamenting our lads beyond the sea:—
'In the bluidy wars they fa', and our honor's gane an' a',
must   *And broken-hearted we maun die.'*

I

As I stood by yon roofless tower,
   Where the wa'flow'r scents the dewy air,
owl   Where the houlet mourns in her ivy bower,
   And tells the midnight moon her care:

2

The winds were laid, the air was still,
   The stars they shot along the sky,
fox   The tod was howling on the hill,
   And the distant-echoing glens reply.

3

brook   The burn, adown its hazelly path,
   Was rushing by the ruin'd wa',
Hasting to join the sweeping Nith,
   Whase roarings seem'd to rise and fa'.

4

livid   The cauld blae North was streaming forth
   Her lights, wi' hissing, eerie din:
athwart lost as Athort the lift they start and shift,
soon
as won   Like Fortune's favours, tint as win.

5

Now, looking over firth and fauld,   fold
 Her horn the pale-faced Cynthia rear'd,
When lo! in form of minstrel auld
 A stern and stalwart ghaist appear'd. ghost

6

And frae his harp sic strains did flow, such
 Might rous'd the slumbering Dead to hear, as might have
But O, it was a tale of woe
 As ever met a Briton's ear!

7

He sang wi' joy his former day,
 He, weeping, wail'd his latter times:
But what he said—it was nae play!—
 I winna ventur't in my rhymes. will not

O, AN YE WERE DEAD, GUIDMAN if; husband

TUNE: *(As Title)*

CHORUS

Sing, round about the fire wi' a rung she ran,
An' round about the fire wi' a rung she ran:—
'Your horns shall tie you to the staw, stall
An' I shall bang your hide, guidman!'

1

O, an ye were dead, guidman,
A green turf on your head, guidman!
I wad bestow my widowhood
Upon a rantin Highlandman! roistering

2

There's sax eggs in the pan, guidman, six
There's sax eggs in the pan, guidman:
There's ane to you, and twa to me.
And three to our John Highlandman!

3

A sheep-head's in the pot, guidman,
A sheep-head's in the pot, guidman:

broth

The flesh to him, the broo to me,
An' the horns become your brow, guidman!

AULD LANG SYNE

TUNE: *(As Title)*

CHORUS

And for auld lang syne, my jo,
For auld lang syne,
We'll tak a cup o' kindness yet,
For auld lang syne.

1

Should auld acquaintance be forgot,
And never brought to mind?
Should auld acquaintance be forgot,
And days o' lang syne?

2

pay for

And surely ye'll be your pint-stowp!
And surely I'll be mine!
And we'll tak a cup o' kindness yet,

since

For auld lang syne.

3

We two hae run about the braes
And pu'd the gowans fine;
But we've wander'd many a weary foot
Sin auld lang syne.

4

waded; brook

We twa hae paidl'd i' the burn,

noon

Frae mornin' sun till dine;

broad

But seas between us braid hae roar'd
Sin auld lang syne.

5

And there's a hand, my trusty fiere!   chum
　　And gie's a hand o' thine!   give me
And we'll tak a right gude-willy waught,   good-will drink
　　For auld lang syne.

LOUIS, WHAT RECK I BY THEE

TUNE: *(As Title)*

1

Louis, what reck I by thee,
　　Or Geordie on his ocean?
Dyvor beggar louns to me!   bankrupt;
　　I reign in Jeanie's bosom.   fellows

2

Let her crown my love her law
　　And in her breast enthrone me,
Kings and nations—swith awa!   off away
　　Reif randies, I disown ye.   Thieving rascals

HAD I THE WYTE?   Was I to blame?

TUNE: *Come kiss with me*

1

Had I the wyte? had I the wyte?
　　Had I the wyte? she bade me!
She watch'd me by the hie-gate side,   high
　　And up the loan she shaw'd me;   lane; showed
And when I wadna venture in,   would not
　　A coward loon she ca'd me!   lad
Had Kirk and State been in the gate,   way
　　I'd lighted when she bade me.

2

led me in

Sae craftilie she took me ben

noise

   And bade me mak nae clatter:—

surly; husband

'For our ramgunshoch, glum guidman

beyond

   Is o'er ayont the water.'

Whae'er shall say I wanted grace

fondle

   When I did kiss and dawte her,

Let him be planted in my place,

Then;
transgressor

   Syne say I was the fautor!

3

Could I for shame, could I for shame,

have refused

   Could I for shame refus'd her?

would not;
have been

And wadna manhood been to blame

   Had I unkindly used her?

wool comb

He claw'd her wi' the ripplin-kame,

   And blae and bluidy bruis'd her—

such

When sic a husband was frae hame,

would have

   What wife but wad excus'd her!

4

wiped; eyes

I dighted ay her een sae blue,

cursed;
scoundrel
wot; mouth

   An' bann'd the cruel randy,

And, weel I wat, her willin mou'

   Was sweet as sugarcandie.

sunset

At gloamin-shot, it was, I wot,

   I lighted—on the Monday,

Tuesday's

But I cam thro' the Tyseday's dew

   To wanton Willie's brandy.

COMIN THRO' THE RYE

TUNE: *Miller's Wedding*

CHORUS

O Jenny's a' weet, poor body,   wet; creature
  Jenny's seldom dry:
She draigl't a' her petticoatie,   draggled
  Comin thro' the rye!

1

Comin thro' the rye, poor body,
  Comin thro' the rye,
She draigl't a' her petticoatie,
  Comin thro' the rye!

2

Gin a body meet a body   Should
  Comin thro' the rye,
Gin a body kiss a body,
  Need a body cry?

3

Gin a body meet a body
  Comin thro' the glen,
Gin a body kiss a body,
  Need the warld ken?

4

Gin a body meet a body
  Comin thro' the grain;
Gin a body kiss a body,
  The thing's a body's ain.

YOUNG JAMIE

TUNE: *The carlin o' the glen*

1

Young Jamie, pride of a' the plain,
Sae gallant and sae gay a swain,
Thro' a' our lasses he did rove,
And reign'd resistless King of Love.

2

But now, wi' sighs and starting tears,
briars   He strays amang the woods and breers;
Or in the glens and rocky caves
mournfully   His sad complaining dowie raves:—

3

'I, wha sae late did range and rove,
And chang'd with every moon my love—
I little thought the time was near,
Repentance I should buy sae dear.

4

'The slighted maids my torments see,
suffer   And laugh at a' the pangs I dree;
While she, my cruel, scornful Fair,
Forbids me e'er to see her mair.'

OUT OVER THE FORTH

TUNE: *Charles Graham's welcome hame*

1

Out over the Forth, I look to the north—
    But what is the north, and its Highlands to me?
The south nor the east gie ease to my breast,
    The far foreign land or the wide rolling sea!

2

But I look to the west, when I gae to rest,   go
   That happy my dreams and my slumbers may
     be;
For far in the west lives he I loe best,   love
   The man that is dear to my babie and me.

WANTONNESS FOR EVERMAIR

TUNE: *Wantonness*

Wantonness for evermair,
   Wantonness has been my ruin.
Yet for a' my dool and care
It's wantonness for evermair.
   I hae lo'ed the Black, the Brown;
I hae lo'ed the Fair, the Gowden!   Golden
   A' the colours in the town—
I hae won their wanton favour.

CHARLIE HE'S MY DARLING

TUNE: *(As Title)*

CHORUS

An' Charlie he's my darling,
My darling, my darling,
Charlie he's my darling—
   The Young Chevalier!

I

'Twas on a Monday morning
   Right early in the year,
That Charlie came to our town—
   The Young Chevalier!

2

As he was walking up the street
   The city for to view,
O, there he spied a bonie lass
   The window looking thro'!

3

Sae light's he jimpèd up the stair,
  And tirl'd at the pin;
And wha sae ready as hersel'
  To let the laddie in!

rasped

4

He set his Jenny on his knee,
  All in his Highland dress;
For brawlie weel he kend the way
  To please a bonie lass.

finely well

5

It's up yon heathery mountain
  And down yon scroggy glen,
We daurna gang a-milking
  For Charlie and his men!

scrubby
daren't go

THE LASS O' ECCLEFECHAN

TUNE: *Jack Latin*

I

'Gat ye me, O, gat ye me,
  Gat ye me wi' naething?
Rock an' reel, an' spinning wheel,
  A mickle quarter basin:
Bye attour, my gutcher has
  A heich house and a laich ane,
A' forbye my bonie sel,
  The toss o' Ecclefechan!'

big
Moreover;
goodsire
high; low
All besides

toast

2

'O, haud your tongue now, Lucky Lang,
  O, haud your tongue and jauner!
I held the gate till you I met,
  Syne I began to wander:
I tint my whistle and my sang,
  I tint my peace and pleasure;
But your green graff, now Lucky Lang,
  Wad airt me to my treasure.'

hold
jabber
kept to the strait
path
Then

lost
grave
direct

THE COOPER O' CUDDY

TUNE: *Bab at the bowster*

CHORUS

We'll hide the cooper behint the door,
Behint the door, behint the door,
We'll hide the cooper behint the door
  And cover him under a mawn, O.   basket

1

The Cooper o' Cuddy came here awa,   here about
He ca'd the girrs out o'er us a',   knocked; hoops
An' our guidwife has gotten a ca',   knock
  That's anger'd the silly guidman, O.

2

He sought them out, he sought them in,
Wi 'Deil hae her!' an' 'Deil hae him!'
But the body he was sae doited and blin', creature; stupid
  He wist na where he was gaun, O.   going

3

They cooper'd at e'en, they cooper'd at morn,
Till our guidman has gotten the scorn:
On ilka brow she's planted a horn,   each
  And swears that there they sall stan', O! shall

FOR THE SAKE O' SOMEBODY

TUNE: *(As Title)*

1

My heart is sair—I dare na tell—   sore
  My heart is sair for Somebody:
I could wake a winter night
  For the sake o' Somebody.
   O-hon! for Somebody!
   O-hey! for Somebody!
I could range the world around
  For the sake o' Somebody.

2

Ye Powers that smile on virtuous love,
    O, sweetly smile on Somebody!
each   Frae ilka danger keep him free,
    And send me safe my Somebody!
        O-hon! for Somebody!
        O-hey! for Somebody!
I wad do—what wad I not?—
    For the sake o' Somebody!

THE CARDIN O'T

TUNE: *(As Title)*

CHORUS

The cardin o't, the spinnin o't,
The warpin o't, the winnin o't!
each   *When ilka ell cost me a groat,*
stole *The tailor staw the lynin o't.*

1

bought   I coft a stane o' haslock woo,
web   To mak a wab to Johnie o't,
         For Johnie is my only jo—
             I lo'e him best of onie yet!

2

         For tho' his locks be lyart gray,
bald above   And tho' his brow be beld aboon,
         Yet I hae seen him on a day
             The pride of a' the parishen.

THERE'S THREE TRUE GUID FELLOWS

TUNE: *Three guid fellows ayont the glen*

CHORUS

There's tyree true guid fellows,
There's three true guid fellows,
There's three true guid fellows,
Down ayont yon glen!   beyond

I

It's now the day is dawin,   dawning
But or night do fa' in,   before nightfall
Whase cock's best at crawin,
Willie, thou sall ken!   shall

SAE FLAXEN WERE HER RINGLETS

TUNE: *Oonagh's Waterfall*

I

Sae flaxen were her ringlets,
Her eyebrows of a darker hue,
Bewitchingly o'er-arching
Twa laughing een o' bonie blue.   eyes
Her smiling, sae wyling,   coaxing
Wad make a wretch forget his woe!
What pleasure, what treasure,
Unto those rosy lips to grow!
Such was my Chloris' bonie face,
When first that bonie face I saw,
And ay my Chloris' dearest charm—
She says she lo'es me best of a'!

2

Like harmony her motion,
    Her pretty ankle is a spy
Betraying fair proportion
    Wad make a saint forget the sky!

Would

Sae warming, sae charming,
    Her faultless form and gracefu' air,

Each

Ilk feature—auld Nature

do no more

    Declar'd that she could dae nae mair!
Hers are the willing chains o' love
    By conquering beauty's sovereign law,
And ay my Chloris' dearest charm—
    She says she lo'es me best of a'.

3

Let others love the city,
    And gaudy show a sunny noon!
Gie me the lonely valley,
    The dewy eve, and rising moon,
Fair beaming, and streaming
    Her silver light the boughs amang,
While falling, recalling,
    The amorous thrush concludes his sang!
There, dearest Chloris, wilt thou rove

winding brook;
wood

    By wimpling burn and leafy shaw,
And hear my vows o' truth and love,
    And say thou lo'es me best of a'?

THE LASS THAT MADE THE BED TO ME

TUNE: *(As Title)*

1

When Januar' wind was blawin cauld,
    As to the North I took my way,

darksome

The mirksome night did me enfauld,
    I knew na where to lodge till day.
By my guid luck a maid I met
    Just in the middle o' my care,
And kindly she did me invite
    To walk into a chamber fair.

2

I bow'd fu' low unto this maid,
   And thank'd her for her courtesie;
I bow'd fu' low unto this maid,
   An' bade her mak a bed to me.
She made the bed baith large and wide,
   Wi' twa white hands she spread it down,
She put the cup to her rosy lips,
   And drank:—'Young man, now sleep ye soun'.'

3

She snatch'd the candle in her hand,
   And frae my chamber went wi' speed,
But I call'd her quickly back again
   To lay some mair below my head: *more*
A cod she laid below my head,   *pillow*
   And servèd me with due respeck,
And, to salute her wi' a kiss,
   I put my arms about her neck.

4

'Haud aff your hands, young man,', she said,   *Hold*
   'And dinna sae uncivil be;   *do not*
Gif ye hae onie luve for me,
   O, wrang na my virginitie!'
Her hair was like the links o' gowd,   *gold*
   Her teeth were like the ivorie,
Her cheeks like lilies dipt in wine,
   The lass that made the bed to me!

5

Her bosom was the driven snaw,
   Twa drifted heaps sae fair to see;
Her limbs the polish'd marble stane,
   The lass that made the bed to me!
I kiss'd her o'er and o'er again,
   And ay she wist na what to say.
I laid her 'tween me an' the wa'—   *deemed it not*
   The lassie thocht na lang till day.   *long*

6

rose

Upon the morrow, when we raise,
    I thank'd her for her courtesie,
But ay she blush'd, and ay she sigh'd,
    And said:—'Alas, ye've ruin'd me!'

then
eye

I clasp'd her waist, and kiss'd her syne,
    While the tear stood twinklin in her e'e.
I said:—'My lassie, dinna cry,
    For ye ay shall mak the bed to me.'

7

She took her mither's holland sheets,

shirts

    An' made them a' in sarks to me.
Blythe and merry may she be,
    The lass that made the bed to me!
The bonie lass made the bed to me,

handsome

    The braw lass made the bed to me!
I'll ne'er forget till the day I die,
    The lass that made the bed to me.

SAE FAR AWA

TUNE: *Dalkeith Maiden Bridge*

1

O, sad and heavy should I part
    But for her sake sae for awa,
Unknowing what my way may thwart—
    My native land sae far awa.

2

Thou that of a' things Maker art,
    That formed this Fair sae far awa,

Give

Gie body strength, then I'll ne'er start
    At this my way sae far awa!

3

How true is love to pure desert!
    So mine in her sae far awa,
And nocht can heal my bosom's smart,
    While, O, she is sae far awa!

4

Nane other love, nane other dart
    I feel, but hers sae far awa;
But fairer never touched a heart,
    Than hers, the Fair sae far awa.

THE REEL O' STUMPIE

TUNE: *(As Title)*

1

Wap and rowe, wap and rowe,	wrap; roll
Wap and rowe the feetie o't,	little feet
I thought I was a maiden fair,	
Till I heard the greetie o't!	its little cry

2

My daddie was a fiddler fine,	
My minnie she made mantie, O,	mother
And I myself a thumpin quine,	quean (i.e. lass)
And danc'd the Reel o' Stumpie, O.	

I'LL AY CA' IN BY YON TOWN

TUNE: *I'll gae nae mair to your town*

CHORUS

I'll ay ca' in by yon town	call
An by yon garden green again!	
I'll ay ca' in by yon town,	
And see my bonie Jean again.	

1

There's nane shall ken, there's nane can guess	
What brings me back the gate again,	same way
But she, my fairest faithfu' lass,	
And stow'nlins we sall meet again.	by stealth

2

oaken
meeting

faith

She'll wander by the aiken tree,
 When trystin time draws near again;
And when her lovely form I see,
 O haith! she's doubly dear again.

wot

O, WAT YE WHA'S IN YON TOWN

TUNE: *I'll gae nae mair to your town*

CHORUS

evening

O, wat ye wha's in yon town
 Ye see the e'enin sun upon?
The dearest maid's in yon town
 That e'enin sun is shining on!

1

wood

Now haply down yon gay green shaw
 She wanders by yon spreading tree.
How blest ye flowers that round her blaw!
 Ye catch the glances o' her e'e.

2

How blest ye birds that round her sing,
 And welcome in the blooming year!
And doubly welcome be the Spring,
 The season to my Jeanie dear!

3

glances
heights

The sun blinks blythe in yon town,
 Among the broomy braes sae green;
But my delight in yon town,
 And dearest pleasure, is my Jean.

4

Without my Love, not a' the charms
 O' Paradise could yield me joy;
But gie me Jeanie in my arms,
 And welcome Lapland's dreary sky!

5

My cave wad be a lover's bower,
　Tho' raging Winter rent the air,
And she a lovely little flower,
　That I wad tent and shelter there.　　　　tend

6

O, sweet is she in yon town
　The sinkin sun's gane down upon!
A fairer than's in yon town
　His setting beam ne'er shone upon.

7

If angry Fate be sworn my foe,
　And suff'ring I am doom'd to bear,
I'd careless quit aught else below,
　But spare, O, spare me Jeanie dear!

8

For, while life's dearest blood is warm,
　Ae thought frae her shall ne'er depart,　　　　One
And she, as fairest is her form,
　She has the truest, kindest heart.

O MAY, THY MORN

TUNE: *The Rashes*

I

O May, thy morn was ne'er sae sweet
　As the mirk night o' December!　　　　dark
For sparkling was the rosy wine,
　And private was the chamber,
And dear was she I dare na name,
　But I will ay remember.

2

And here's to them that, like oursel,
    Can push about the jorum!
And here's to them that wish us weel—
    May a' that's guid watch o'er 'em!
And here's to them we dare na tell,
    The dearest o' the quorum!

AS I CAME O'ER THE CAIRNEY MOUNT

TUNE: *The Highland Lassie*

CHORUS

O, my bonie Highland lad!
    My winsome, weel-faur'd Highland laddie!   well-favoured
Wha wad mind the wind and rain
    Sae weel row'd in his tartan plaidie!   wrapped

1

As I came o'er the Cairney mount
    And down among the blooming heather,
Kindly stood the milking-shiel   -shed
    To shelter frae the stormy weather.

2

Now Phœbus blinkit on the bent,   shone; meadow
    And o'er the knowes the lambs were bleating;   knolls
But he wan my heart's consent
    To be his ain at the neist meeting.   next

HIGHLAND LADDIE

TUNE: *The Highland Laddie*

1

The bonniest lad that e'er I saw—
  Bonie laddie, Highland laddie!
Wore a plaid and was fu' braw—   fine
  Bonie Highland laddie!
On his head a bonnet blue—
  Bonie laddie, Highland laddie!
His royal heart was firm and true—
  Bonie Highland laddie!

2

'Trumpets sound and cannons roar,
  Bonie lassie, Lawland lassie!—   Lowland
And a' the hills wi' echoes roar,
  Bonie Lawland lassie!
Glory, Honour, now invite—
  Bonie lassie, Lawland lassie!—
For freedom and my King to fight,
  Bonie Lawland lassie!'

3

'The sun a backward course shall take,
  Bonie laddie, Highland laddie!
Ere aught thy manly courage shake,
  Bonie Highland laddie!
Go, for yoursel' procure renown,
  Bonie laddie, Highland laddie,
And for your lawful King his crown,
  Bonie Highland laddie!'

WILT THOU BE MY DEARIE?

TUNE: *The Sutor's Dochter*

1

Wilt thou be my dearie?
When Sorrow wrings thy gentle heart,
   O, wilt thou let me cheer thee?
By the treasure of my soul—
   That's the love I bear thee—
I swear and vow that only thou
   Shall ever be my dearie!
Only thou, I swear and vow,
   Shall ever be my dearie!

2

Lassie, say thou lo'es me,
Or, if thou wilt na be my ain,
   Say na thou'lt refuse me!
If it winna, canna be,
   Thou for thine may choose me,
Let me, lassie, quickly die,
   Trusting that thou lo'es me!
Lassie, let me quickly die,
   Trusting that thou lo'es me!

(own)
(will not)

LOVELY POLLY STEWART

TUNE: *Ye're welcome Charlie Stewart*

CHORUS

O lovely Polly Stewart,
O charming Polly Stewart,
There's ne'er a flower that blooms in May,
That's half so fair as thou art!

1

The flower it blaws, it fades, it fa's,
   And art can ne'er renew it;
But Worth and Truth eternal youth
   Will gie to Polly stewart!

2

May he whase arms shall fauld thy charms   enfold
 Possess a leal and true heart!   loyal
To him be given to ken the heaven
 He grasps in Polly Stewart!

THE HIGHLAND BALOU

TUNE: *(As Title)*

1

Hee balou, my sweet wee Donald,
Picture o' the great Clanronald!
Brawlie kens our wanton Chief   Finely
Wha gat my young Highland thief.

2

Leeze me on thy bonie craigie!   Blessings; throat
An thou live, thou'll steal a naigie,   horse
Travel the country thro' and thro',
And bring hame a Carlisle cow!

3

Thro' the Lawlands, o'er the Border,
Weel, my babie, may thou furder,   advance
Herry the louns o' the laigh Countrie,   rogues; lowlands
Syne to the Highlands hame to me!   Then

soft cakes;
barley

BANNOCKS O' BEAR MEAL

TUNE: *The Killogie*

CHORUS

Bannocks o' bear meal,
Bannocks o' barley,
Here's to the Highlandman's
Bannocks o' barley!

1

brangle

Wha in a brulyie
   Will first cry 'a parley'?
Never the lads
   Wi' the bannocks o' barley!

2

woeful

Wha, in his wae days,
   Where loyal to Charlie?
Wha but the lads
   Wi' the bannocks o' barley!

WAE IS MY HEART

TUNE: *(At Title)*

1

Wae is my heart, and the tear's in my e'e;
Lang, lang joy's been a stranger to me:
Forsaken and friendless my burden I bear,
And the sweet voice o' pity ne'er sounds in my ear.

2

sorely

Love, thou hast pleasure—and deep hae I lov'd!
Love thou has sorrows—and sair hae I prov'd!
But his bruisèd heart that now bleeds in my breast,
I can feel by its throbbings, will soon be at rest.

3

O, if I were where happy I hae been,
Down by yon stream and yon bonie castle green!
For there he is wand'ring and musing on me,
Wha wad soon dry the tear frae his Phillis' e'e!

HERE'S HIS HEALTH IN WATER

TUNE: *The job of journey work*

1

Altho' my back be at the wa',   wall
  And tho' he be the fautor,   transgressor
Altho' my back be at the wa',
  Yet here's his health in water!
O, wae gae by his wanton sides,   wo go
  Sae brawly's he could flatter!   finely as
Till for his sake I'm slighted sair
  And dree the kintra clatter!   endure the talk of the countryside
But, tho' my back be at the wa',
  Yet here's his health in water!

THE WINTER OF LIFE

TUNE: *East Indian Air*

1

But lately seen in gladsome green,
  The woods rejoiced the day;
Thro' gentle showers the laughing flowers
  In double pride were gay;
But now our joys are fled
  On winter blasts awa,
Yet maiden May in rich array
  Again shall bring them a'.

2

poll; thaw

But my white pow—nae kindly thowe
   Shall melt the snaws of Age!

eld; without
bush and shelter

My trunk of eild, but buss and bield,
   Sinks in Time's wintry rage.
O, Age has weary days
   And nights o' sleepless pain!
Thou golden time o' youthfu' prime,
   Why comes thou not again?

THE TAILOR

TUNE: *The Drummer*

1

The tailor he cam here to sew,
And weel he kend the way to woo,

tasted

For ay he pree'd the lassie's mou',

went from
kitchen to
parlour

   As he gaed but and ben, O,
     For weel he kend the way, O,
     The way, O, the way, O!
     For weel he kend the way, O,
     The lassie's heart to win, O!

2

rose; clothes

The tailor rase and shook his duds,

fleas; clouds

The flaes they flew awa in cluds!
And them that stay'd gat fearfu' thuds—
   The tailor prov'd a man, O!

dusk

     For now it was the gloamin,
     The gloamin, the gloamin!
     For now it was the gloamin,

going

     When a' the rest are gaun, O!

THERE GROWS A BONIE BRIER-BUSH

TUNE: *The Bonie Brier-Bush*

1

kitchen-garden

There grows a bonie brier-bush in our kail-yard,
There grows a bonie brier-bush in our kail-yard;

And below the bonie brier-bush there's a lassie and a lad,
And they're busy, busy courting in our kail-yard.

2

We'll court nae mair below the buss in our kail-yard,   bush
We'll court nae mair below the buss in our kail-yard:
We'll awa to Athole's green, and there we'll no be seen,   not
Where the trees and the branches will be our safeguard.

3

Will ye go to the dancin in Carlyle's ha'?   hall
Will ye go to the dancin in Carlyle's ha',
Where Sandy and Nancy I'm sure will ding them a'?   beat
I winna gang to the dance in Carlyle-ha'!   will not go

4

What will I do for a lad when Sandie gangs awa!
What will I do for a lad when Sandie gangs awa!
I wlll awa to Edinburgh, and win a pennie fee,   earn; hire
And see an onie lad will fancy me.   if

5

He's comin frae the north that's to marry me,
He's comin frae the north that's to marry me,
A feather in his bonnet and ribbon at his knee—
He's a bonie, bonie laddie, an yon be he!   that one

HERE'S TO THY HEALTH

TUNE: *Laggan Burn*

1

Here's to thy health, my bonie lass!
    Guid night and joy be wi' thee!
I'll come nae mair to thy bower-door
    To tell thee that I lo'e thee.
O, dinna think, my pretty pink,
    But I can live without thee: But that
I vow and swear I dinna care   do not
    How lang ye look about ye!

2

desire

friends; every

Thou'rt ay sae free informing me
    Thou hast nae mind to marry,
I'll be as free informing thee
    Nae time hae I to tarry.
I ken thy freens try ilka means
    Frae wedlock to delay thee
(Depending on some higher chance),
    But fortune may betray thee.

3

a little money

I ken they scorn my low estate,
    But that does never grieve me,
For I'm as free as any he—
    Sma' siller will relieve me!
I'll count my health my greatest wealth
    Sae lang as I'll enjoy it.
I'll fear nae scant, I'll bode nae want
    As lang's I get employment.

4

twelve

But far off fowls hae feather's fair,
    And, ay until ye try them,
Tho' they seem fair, still have a care—
    They may prove as bad as I am!
But at twel at night, when the moon shines bright
    My dear, I'll come and see thee,
For the man that loves his mistress weel,
    Nae travel makes him weary.

IT WAS A' FOR OUR RIGHTFU' KING

TUNE: *Mally Stuart*

1

It was a' for our rightfu' king
    We left fair Scotland's strand;
It was a' for our rightfu' king,
    We e'er saw Irish land,
        My dear—
    We e'er saw Irish land.

2

Now a' is done that men can do,
   And a' is done in vain,
My Love and Native Land fareweel,
   For I maun cross the main,   *must*
        My dear—
   For I maun cross the main.

3

He turn'd him right and round about
   Upon the Irish shore,
And gae his bridle reins a shake,   *gave*
   With adieu for evermore,
        My dear—
   And adieu for evermore!

4

The soger frae the wars returns,
   The sailor frae the main,
But I hae parted frae my love
   Never to meet again,
        My dear—
   Never to meet again.

5

When day is gane, and night is come,
   And a' folk bound to sleep,
I think on him that's far awa
   The lee-lang night, and weep,   *live-long*
        My dear—
   The lee-lang night and weep.

THE HIGHLAND WIDOW'S LAMENT

TUNE: *(As Title)*

1

O, I am come to the low countrie—
   Ochon, ochon, ochrie!—
Without a penny in my purse
   To buy a meal to me.

2

not so

It was na sae in the Highland hills—
   Ochon, ochon, ochrie!—
Nae woman in the country wide
   Sae happy was as me.

3

kine

For then I had a score o' kye—
   Ochon, ochon, ochrie!—
Feeding on yon hill sae high
   And giving milk to me.

4

ewes

knolls
wool

And there I had three score o' yowes—
   Ochon, ochon, ochrie!—
Skipping on yon bonie knowes
   And casting woo' to me.

5

sorely
pick of the clan

I was the happiest of a' the clan—
   Sair, sair may I repine!—
For Donald was the brawest man,
   And Donald he was mine.

6

Till Charlie Stewart cam at last
   Sae far to set us free:
My Donald's arm was wanted then
   For Scotland and for me.

7

woeful

Their waefu' fate what need I tell?
   Right to the wrang did yield:
My Donald and his country fell
   Upon Culloden field.

8

Ochon! O Donald, O!
   Ochon, ochon, ochrie!
Nae woman in the warld wide
   Sae wretched now as me!

THOU GLOOMY DECEMBER

TUNE: *Thro' the lang moor*

I

Ance mair I hail thee, thou gloomy December!   Once more
  Ance mair I hail thee wi' sorrow and care!
Sad was the parting thou makes me remember:
  Parting wi' Nancy, O, ne'er to meet mair!

2

Fond lovers' parting is sweet, painful pleasure,
  Hope beaming mild on the soft parting hour;
But the dire feeling, O farewell for ever!
  Anguish unmingled and agony pure!

3

Wild as the winter now tearing the forest,
  Till the last leaf o' the summer is flown—
Such is the tempest has shaken my bosom,
  Till my last hope and last comfort is gone!

4

Still as I hail thee, thou gloomy December,
  Still shall I hail thee wi' sorrow and care;
For sad was the parting thou makes me remember:
  Parting wi' Nancy, O, ne'er to meet mair!

MY PEGGY'S FACE

TUNE: *(As Title)*

I

My Peggy's face, my Peggy's form
The frost of hermit Age might warm.
My Peggy's worth, my Peggy's mind
Might charm the first of human kind.

2

I love my Peggy's angel air,
Her face so truly heavenly fair,
Her native grace so void of art;
But I adore my Peggy's heart.

3

The lily's hue, the rose's dye,
The kindling lustre of an eye—
Who but owns their magic sway?
Who but knows they all decay?

4

The tender thrill, the pitying tear,
The generous purpose nobly dear,
The gentle look that rage disarms—
These are all immortal charms.

STEER HER UP

rouse

TUNE: *(As Title)*

1

O, steer her up, an' haud her gaun—
  Her mither's at the mill, jo,
if; will not An' gin she winna tak a man,
  E'en let her tak her will, jo.
threaten First shore her wi' a gentle kiss,
call for And ca' anither gill, jo,
should she An' gin she tak the thing amiss,
scold E'en let her flyte her fill, jo.

2

not bashful O steer her up, an' be na blate,
  An' gin she tak it ill, jo,
to Then leave the lassie till her fate,
waste And time nae langer spill, jo!
one rebuff Ne'er break your heart for ae rebute,
  But think upon it still, jo,
  That gin the lassie winna do't,
find Ye'll fin' anither will, jo.

WEE WILLIE GRAY

TUNE: *Totum Fogg*

1

Wee Willie Gray an' his leather wallet,
Peel a willow-wand to be him boots and jacket!
The rose upon the brier will be him trouse and
    doublet—
The rose upon the brier will be him trouse and
    doublet!

2

Wee Willie Gray and his leather wallet,
Twice a lily-flower will be him sark and gravat!   shirt; cravat
Feathers of a flie wad feather up his bonnet—   fly
Feathers of a flie wad feather up his bonnet!

WE'RE A' NODDIN

TUNE: *(As Title)*

CHORUS

We're a' noddin,
Nid nid noddin,
We're a' noddin
At our house at hame!

1

'Guid e'en to you, kimmer,   gossip
  And how do ye do?'
'Hiccup!' quo' kimmer,
  'The better that I'm fou!,   drunk

2

Kate sits i' the neuk,   corner
  Suppin hen-broo.   chiken-broth
Deil tak Kate
  An she be na noddin too!

3

How are all

'How's a' wi' you, kimmer?
      And how do you fare?'
'A pint o' the best o't,
      And twa pints mair!'

4

'How's a' wi you, kimmer?
      And how do ye thrive?
How monie bairns hae ye?'
      Quo' kimmer, 'I hae five.'

5

in truth

'Are they a' Johnie's?
      'Eh! atweel na:
Twa o' them were gotten
      When Johnie was awa!'

6

Cats like milk,
      And dogs like broo;
Lads like lasses weel,
      And lasses lads too.

broth

MY WIFE SHE DANG ME

beat

TUNE: *(As Title)*

CHORUS

O, ay my wife she dang me,
An' aft my wife she bang'd me!
If ye gie a woman a' her will,
Guid faith! she'll soon o'er-gang ye.

go beyond
control

I

On peace an' rest my mind was bent,
      And, fool I was! I married;
But never honest man's intent
      Sae cursedly miscarried.

2

Some sairie comfort at the last,   sorry
   When a' thir days are done, man: these
My 'pains o' hell' on earth is past,
   I'm sure o' bliss aboon, man.   above

SCROGGAM

TUNE: *(As Title)*

1

There was a wife wonn'd in Cockpen, Scroggam!   dwelt
She brew'd guid ale for gentlemen:
Sing Auld Cowl, lay you down by me—
Scroggam, my dearie, ruffum!

2

The guidwife's dochter fell in a fever, Scroggam!   daugher
The priest o' the parish fell in anither:
Sing Auld Cowl, lay you down by me—
Scroggam, my dearie, ruffum!

3

They laid the twa i' the bed thegither, Scroggam!   together
That the heat o' the tane might cool the tither;   one; other
Sing Auld Cowl, lay you down by me—
Scroggam, my dearie, ruffum!

O, GUID ALE COMES

TUNE: *The Bottom of the Punch Bowl*

CHORUS

O, guid ale comes, and guid ale goes,
Guid ale gars me sell my hose,   makes
Sell my hose, and pawn my shoon—
Guid ale keeps my heart aboon!   my heart up

1

six oxen

I had sax owsen in a pleugh,
And they drew a' weel eneugh:
I sell'd them a' just ane by ane—
Guid ale keeps the heart aboon!

2

keeps
meddle; girl
censure

Guid ale hauds me bare and busy,
Gars me moop wi' the servant hizzie,
Stand i' the stool when I hae dune—
Guid ale keeps the heart aboon!

reaped; harvest

ROBIN SHURE IN HAIRST

TUNE: *Rob shear'd in hairst*

CHORUS

Fiend; sickle
stuck

Robin shure in hairst,
I shure wi' him:
Fient a heuk had I,
Yet I stack by him.

1

went
web of coarse
woollen
gate

I gaed up to Dunse
   To warp a wab o' plaiden,
At his daddie's yett
   Wha met me but Robin!

2

Wasn't; bold

such
Elder's daugher

Was na Robin bauld,
   Tho' I was a cottar?
Play'd me sic a trick,
   An' me the Eller's dochter!

3

food

Fiend have it
(i.e. Nothing)
Goose-quills;
knife

Robin promis'd me
   A' my winter vittle:
Fient haet he had but three
   Guse feathers and a whittle!

DOES HAUGHTY GAUL INVASION THREAT?

TUNE: *Push about the jorum*

1

Does haughty Gaul invasion threat?
   Then let the loons beware, Sir!   rascals
There's wooden walls upon our seas
   And volunteers on shore, Sir!
The Nith shall run to Corsincon,
   And Criffel sink in Solway,
Ere we permit a foreign foe
   On British ground to rally!

2

O, let us not, like snarling tykes,   dogs
   In wrangling be divided,
Till, slap! come in an unco loun,   foreign
   And wi' a rung decide it!   cudgel
Be Britain still to Britain true,
   Amang oursels united!
For never but by British hands
   Maun British wrangs by righted!   must; wrongs

3

The kettle o' the Kirk and State,
   Perhaps a clout may fail in't;   patch
But Deil a foreign tinkler loon   tinker
   Shall ever ca' a nail in't!   drive
Our fathers' blude the kettle bought,
   And wha wad dare to spoil it,
By Heav'ns! the sacrilegious dog
   Shall fuel be to boil it!

4

The wretch that would a tyrant own,
    And the wretch, his true-sworn brother,
Who would set the mob above the throne,
    May they be damn'd together!
Who will not sing *God save the King*
    Shall hang as high's the steeple;
But while we sing *God save the King*,
    We'll ne'er forget the People!

O, ONCE I LOV'D A BONIE LASS

TUNE: *I am a man unmarried*

1

O, once I lov'd a bonie lass,
    Ay, and I love her still!
And whilst that virtue warms my breast,
    I'll love my handsome Nell.

2

As bonie lasses I hae seen,
    And monie full as braw,
But for a modest gracefu' mien
    The like I never saw.

fine

3

A bonie lass, I will confess,
    Is pleasant to the e'e;
But without some better qualities
    She's no a lass for me.

4

But Nelly's looks are blythe and sweet,
    And, what is best of a',
Her reputation is complete
    And fair without a flaw.

5

She dresses ay sae clean and neat,
    Both decent and genteel;
And then there's something in her gait
    Gars onie dress look weel.   makes

6

A gaudy dress and gentle air
    May slightly touch the heart;
But it's innocence and modesty
    That polishes the dart.

7

'Tis this in Nelly pleases me,
    'Tis this enchants my soul;
For absolutely in my breast
    She reigns without controul.

MY LORD A-HUNTING

TUNE: *My Lady's Gown*

CHORUS

My lady's gown, there's gairs upon't,   gores
And gowden flowers sae rare upon't;   golden
But Jenny's jimps and jirkinet,   stays; bodice
My lord thinks meikle mair upon't!   much more

1

My lord a-hunting he is gane,
But hounds or hawks wi' him are nane;
By Colin's cottage lies his game,
If Colin's Jenny be at hame.

2

My lady's white, my lady's red,
And kith and kin o' Cassillis' blude;
But her ten-pund lands o' tocher guid   dowry
Were a' the charms his lordship lo'ed.

3

bog
moor-
dwells

Out o'er yon muir, out o'er yon moss,
Whare gor-cocks thro' the heather pass,
There wons auld Colin's bonie lass,
A lily in a wilderness.

4

eyes

Sae sweetly move her genty limbs,
Like music notes o' lovers' hymns!
The diamond-dew in her een sae blue,
Where laughing love sae wanton swims!

5

trim

My lady's dink, my lady's drest,
The flower and fancy o' the west;
But the lassie that a man lo'es best,
O, that's the lass to mak him blest!

MEG O' THE MILL

TUNE: *O ken ye what Meg, etc.*

1

got

horse; rat

O, ken ye what Meg o' the Mill has gotten?
An' ken ye what Meg o' the Mill has gotten?
A braw new naig wi' the tail o' a rottan,
And that's what Meg o' the Mill has gotten!

2

liquor

O, ken ye what Meg o' the Mill lo'es dearly?
An, ken ye what Meg o' the Mill lo'es dearly?
A dram o' guid strunt in a morning early,
And that's what Meg o' the Mill lo'es dearly!

3

held up under
the arms

O, ken ye how Meg o' the Mill was married?
An' ken ye how Meg o' the Mill was married?
The priest he was oxter'd, the clark he was carried,
And that's how Meg o' the Mill was married!

4

O, ken ye how Meg o' the Mill was bedded?
An' ken ye how Meg o' the Mill was bedded?
The groom gat sae fu' he fell awald beside it,   bridegroom;
And that's how Meg o' the Mill was bedded!   drunk; backways

JOCKIE'S TA'EN THE PARTING KISS

TUNE: *Bonie lass tak a man*

1

Jockie's ta'en the parting kiss,
    O'er the mountains he is gane,
And with him is a' my bliss—
    Nought but griefs with me remain.

2

Spare my luve, ye winds that blaw,
    Plashy sleets and beating rain!
Spare my luve, thou feathery snaw,
    Drifting o'er the frozen plain!

3

When the shades of evening creep
    O'er the day's fair gladsome e'e,
Sound and safely may he sleep,
    Sweetly blythe his waukening be!   awakening

4

He will think on her he loves,
    Fondly he'll repeat her name;
For where'er he distant roves,
    Jockie's heart is still at hame.

O, LAY THY LOOF IN MINE, LASS

palm

TUNE: *The Cordwarner's March*

CHORUS

O, lay thy loof in mine, lass,
In mine, lass, in mine, lass,
And swear on thy white hand, lass,
That thou wilt be my ain!

own

I

A slave to Love's unbounded sway,
He aft has wrought me meikle wae;
But now he is my deadly fae,
Unless thou be my ain.

foe

2

There's monie a lass has broke my rest,
That for a blink I hae lo'ed best;
But thou art queen within my breast,
But ever to remain.

CAULD IS THE E'ENIN BLAST

TUNE: *Peggy Ramsay*

I

Cauld is the e'enin blast
O' Boreas o'er the pool,
An' dawin, it is dreary,
When birks are bare at Yule.

dawning

birches;
Christmas-tide

2

O, cauld blaws the e'enin blast,
When bitter bites the frost,
And in the mirk and dreary drift
The hills and glens are lost!

dark

3

Ne'er sae murky blew the night
    That drifted o'er the hill,
But bonie Peg-a-Ramsay
    Gat grist to her mill.

THERE WAS A BONIE LASS

TUNE: *A Bonie Lass*

1

There was a bonie lass, and a bonie, bonie lass,
    And she loed her bonie laddie dear,
Till War's loud alarms tore her laddie frae her arms
    Wi' monie a sigh and a tear.

2

Over sea, over shore, where the cannons loudly roar,
    He still was a stranger to fear,
And nocht could him quail, or his bosom assail,   nought
    But the bonie lass he loed sae dear.

THERE'S NEWS, LASSES, NEWS

TUNE: *(As Title)*

CHORUS

The wean wants a cradle,   child
    And the cradle wants a cod,   pillow
An' I'll no gang to my bed   not go
    Until I get a nod.

1

There's news, lasses, news,
    Guid news I've to tell!
There's a boatfu' o' lads
    Come to our town to sell!

2

'Father,' quo' she, 'Mither,' quo' she,
    'Do what you can:
I'll no gang to my bed
    Until I get a man!'

3

croft-ridge   I hae as guid a craft rig
earth   As made o' yird and stane;

woe befall;   And waly fa' the ley-crap
pasture-   For I maun till'd again.
must plough it

O, THAT I HAD NE'ER BEEN MARRIED

TUNE: *Crowdie*

CHORUS

meal and water   *Ance crowdie, twice crowdie,*
                   Three times crowdie in day!
            Gin ye crowdie onie mair,
                   Ye'll crowdie a' my meal away.

1

O, that I had ne'er been married,
    I was never had nae care!
children   Now I've gotten wife an bairns,
           An' they cry 'Crowdie' evermair.

2

scare   Waefu' Want and Hunger fley me,
                  Glowrin by the hallan en';
the end of the   Sair I fecht them at the door,
porch
Hard; fight   But ay I'm eerie they come ben.
frightened; in

MALLY'S MEEK, MALLY'S SWEET   Mollie's

TUNE: *(As Title)*

CHORUS

Mally's meek, Mally's sweet,
Mally's modest and discreet,
Mally's rare, Mally's fair,
Mally's ev'ry way complete.

1

As I was walking up the street,
    A barefit maid I chanc'd to meet;
But O, the road was very hard
    For that fair maiden's tender feet!

2

It were mair meet that those fine feet
    Were weel laced up in silken shoon!
An' 'twere more fit that she should sit
    Within yon chariot grit aboon!   above

3

Her yellow hair, beyond compare,
    Comes tumbling down her swan-white neck,
And her twa eyes, like stars in skies,
    Would keep a sinking ship frae wreck!

WANDERING WILLIE

TUNE: *Here awa, there awa*

1

Here awa, there awa, wandering Willie,
    Here awa, there awa, haud awa hame!   hold
Come to my bosom, my ae only dearie,   one
    And tell me thou bring'st me my Willie the same.

2

Loud tho' the Winter blew cauld at our parting,
   'Twas na the blast brought the tear in my e'e:
Summer   Welcome now Simmer, and welcome my Willie,
   The Simmer to Nature, my Willie to me!

3

Rest, ye wild storms in the cave o' your slumbers—
   How your wild howling a lover alarms!
Awake; roll   Wauken, ye breezes, row gently, ye billows,
   And waft my dear laddie ance mair to my arms.

4

remembers not   But O, if he's faithless, and minds na his Nannie,
   Flow still between us, thou wide-roaring main!
May I never see it, may I never trow it,
   But, dying, believe that my Willie's my ain!

Handsome   # BRAW LADS O' GALLA WATER

TUNE: *The Brave Lads of Galla Water*

1

heights   Braw, braw lads on Yarrow braes,
   They rove amang the blooming heather;
woods   But Yarrow braes nor Ettrick shaws
   Can match the lads o' Galla Water.

2

But there is ane, a secret ane,
Above   Aboon them a' I loe him better;
And I'll be his, and he'll be mine,
   The bonie lad o' Galla Water.

3

Altho' his daddie was nae laird,
much dowry   And tho' I hae nae meikle tocher,
Yet, rich in kindest, truest love,
watch   We'll tent our flocks by Galla Water.

4

It ne'er was wealth, it ne'er was wealth,
   That coft contentment, peace, and pleasure: bought
The bands and bliss o' mutual love,
   O, that's the chiefest warld's treasure!

AULD ROB MORRIS

TUNE: *(As Title)*

1

There's Auld Rob Morris that wons in yon glen,   dwells
He's the king o' guid fellows and wale of auld men: pick
He has gowd in his coffers, he has owsen and kine,   gold
And ae bonie lassie, his dautie and mine.   one; pet

2

She's fresh as the morning the fairest in May,
She's sweet as the ev'ning amang the new hay,
As blythe and as artless as the lambs on the lea,
And dear to my heart as the light to my e'e.

3

But O, she's an heiress, auld Robin's a laird,
And my daddie has nocht but a cot-house and yard!   garden
A wooer like me maunna hope to come speed: mustn't
The wounds I must hide that will soon be my dead.   death

4

The day comes to me, but delight brings me nane;   brings me no
The night comes to me, but my rest it is gane;   delight
I wander my lane like a night-troubled ghaist,   alone, ghost
And I sigh as my heart is wad burst in my breast.

5

O, had she but been of a lower degree,
I then might hae hop'd she wad smil'd upon me!   would have
O, how past descriving had then been my bliss,   describing
As now my distraction no words can express!

OPEN THE DOOR TO ME, O

TUNE: *Open the door softly*

I

O, open the door some pity to shew,
    If love it may na be, O!
Tho' thou hast been false, I'll ever prove true—
    O, open the door to me, O!

2

Cauld is the blast upon my pale cheek,
    But caulder thy love for me, O:
The frost, that freezes the life at my heart,
    Is nought to my pains frae thee, O!

3

The wan moon sets behind the white wave,
    And Time is setting with me, O:
False friends, false love, farewell! for mair
    I'll ne'er trouble them nor thee, O!

4

She has open'd the door, she has open'd it wide,
    She sees the pale corse on the plain, O,
'My true love!' she cried, and sank down by his
      side—
    Never to rise again, O!

WHEN WILD WAR'S DEADLY BLAST

TUNE: *The Mill, Mill O*

I

When wild War's deadly blast was blawn,
    And gentle Peace returning,
Wi' monie a sweet babe fatherless
    And monie a widow mourning,
I left the lines and tented field,
    Where lang I'd been a lodger,
all   My humble knapsack a' my wealth,
    A poor and honest sodger.

2

A leal, light heart was in my breast,   loyal
 My hand unstain'd wi' plunder,
And for fair Scotia, hame again,
 I cheery on did wander:
I thought upon the banks o' Coil,
 I thought upon my Nancy,
And ay I mind't the witching smile   remembered
 That caught my youthful fancy.

3

At length I reach'd the bonie glen,
 Where early life I sported.
I pass'd the mill and trysting thorn,
 Where Nancy aft I courted.
Wha spied I but my ain dear maid,
 Down by her mother's dwelling,
And turn'd me round to hid the flood
 That in my een was swelling!   eyes

4

Wi' alter'd voice, quoth I:—'Sweet lass,
 Sweet as yon hawthorn's blossom,
O, happy, happy may he be,
 That's dearest to thy bosom!
My purse is light, I've far to gang,   go
 And fain wad be thy lodger;
I've serv'd my king and country lang—
 Take pity on a sodger.'

5

Sae wistfully she gaz'd on me,
 And lovelier was then ever.
Quo' she:—'A sodger ance I lo'ed,
 Forget him shall I never.
Our humble cot, and hamely fare,
 Ye freely shall partake it;
That gallant badge—the dear cockade—
 Ye're welcome for the sake o't!'

6

She gaz'd, she redden'd like a rose,
    Syne, pale like onie lily,
She sank within my arms, and cried:—
    'Art thou my ain dear Willie?'
'By Him who made yon sun and sky,
By whom true love's regarded,
I am the man! And thus may still
    True lovers be rewarded!

Then [margin gloss]

7

'The wars are o'er and I'm come hame,
    And find thee still true-hearted.
Tho' poor in gear, we're rich in love,
    And mair, we'se ne'er be parted.'
Quo' she:—'My grandsire left me gowd,
    A mailen plenish'd fairly!
And come, my faithfu' sodger lad,
    Thou'rt welcome to it dearly!'

wealth [margin gloss]
we'll [margin gloss]
gold [margin gloss]
farm [margin gloss]

8

For gold the merchant ploughs the main,
    The farmer ploughs the manor;
But glory is the sodger's prize,
    The sodger's wealth is honor!
The brave poor sodger ne'er despise,
    Nor count him as a stranger:
Remember he's his country's stay
    In day and hour of danger.

DUNCAN GRAY

TUNE: *(As Title)*

1

Duncan Gray cam here to woo
(Ha, ha, the wooing o't!)
On blythe Yule-Night when we were fou   Christmas Eve;
(Ha, ha, the wooing o't!).   drunk
Maggie coost her head fu' high,   cast
Look'd asklent and unco skeigh,   askance; very
Gart poor Duncan stand abeigh—   skittish
    Ha, ha, the wooing o't!   Made; off

2

Duncan fleech'd, and Duncan pray'd   wheedled
(Ha, ha, the wooing o't!),
Meg was deaf as Ailsa Craig
(Ha, ha, the wooing o't!)
Duncan sigh'd baith out and in,   both
Grat his een baith bleer't an' blin',   Wept; eyes
Spak o' lowpin o'er a linn—   leaping; waterfall
    Ha, ha, the wooing o't!

3

Time and Chance are but a tide
(Ha, ha, the wooing o't!):
Slighted love is sair to bide   hard to endure
(Ha, ha, the wooing o't!).
'Shall I like a fool,' quoth he,
'For a haughty hizzie die?   jade
She may gae to—France for me!'—   go
    Ha, ha, the wooing o't!

4

How it comes, let doctors tell
(Ha, ha, the wooing o't!):
Meg grew sick, as he grew hale
(Ha, he, the wooing o't!).
Something in her bosom wrings,
For relief a sigh she brings,
And O! her een they spak sic things!—   eyes; such
    Ha, ha, the wooing o't!

5

Duncan was a lad o' grace
    (Ha, ha, the wooing o't!),
Maggie's was a piteous case
    (Ha, ha, the wooing o't!):
Duncan could na be her death,
smothered   Swelling pity smoor'd his wrath;
proud; jolly   Now they're crouse and canty baith—
    Ha, ha, the wooing o't!

DELUDED SWAIN, THE PLEASURE

TUNE: *The collier's bonie lassie*

1

Deluded swain, the pleasure
    The fickle Fair can give thee
Is but a fairy treasure—
    Thy hopes will soon deceive thee:
The billows on the ocean,
    The breezes idly roaming,
The cloud's uncertain motion,
    They are but types of Woman!

2

O, art thou not ashamèd
    To doat upon a feature?
If Man thou would'st be namèd,
    Despise the silly creature!
Go, find an honest fellow,
    Good claret set before thee,
Hold on till thou art mellow,
    And then to bed in glory!

HERE IS THE GLEN

TUNE: *Banks of Cree*

1

Here is the glen, and here the bower
  All underneath the birchen shade,
The village-bell has toll'd the hour—
  O, what can stay my lovely maid?
'Tis not Maria's whispering call—
  'Tis but the balmy-breathing gale,
Mixed with some warbler's dying fall
  The dewy star of ever to hail!

2

It is Maria's voice I hear!—
  So calls the woodlark in the grove
His little faithful mate to cheer:
  At once 'tis music and 'tis love!
And art thou come? And art thou true?
  O, welcome, dear, to love and me,
And let us all our vows renew
  Along the flowery banks of Cree!

LET NOT WOMEN E'ER COMPLAIN

TUNE: *Duncan Gray*

1

Let not women e'er complain
  Of inconstancy in love!
Let not women e'er complain
  Fickle man is apt to rove!
Look abroad thro' Nature's range,
Nature's mighty law is change:
Ladies, would it not be strange
  Man should then a monster prove?

2

Mark the winds, and mark the skies,
    Ocean's ebb and ocean's flow.
Sun and moon but set to rise.
    Round and round the seasons go.
Why then, ask of silly man
To oppose great Nature's plan?
We'll be constant, while we can—
    You can be no more, you know!

LORD GREGORY

TUNE: *(As Title)*

1

dark

O, mirk, mirk is this midnight hour,
    An loud the tempest's roar!
A waefu' wanderer seeks thy tower—
    Lord Gregory, ope thy door.

2

hall

An exile frae her father's ha',
    And a' for sake o' thee,

show

At least some pity on me shaw,
    If love it may na be.

3

rememb'rest

Lord Gregory mind'st thou not the grove
    By bonie Irwine side,
Where first I own'd that virgin love
    I lang, lang had denied?

4

How aften didst thou pledge and vow,
    Thou wad for ay be mine!
And my fond heart, itsel' sae true,
    It ne'er mistrusted thine.

5

Hard is thy heart, Lord Gregory,
   And flinty is thy breast:
Thou bolt of Heaven that flashest by,
O, wilt thou bring me rest!

6

Ye mustering thunders from above,
   Your willing victim see,
But spare and pardon my fause love
   His wrangs to Heaven and me!

O POORTITH CAULD   cold poverty

TUNE: *Cauld Kail*

CHORUS

O, why should Fate sic pleasure have
   Life's dearest bands untwining?
Or why sae sweet a flower as love
   Depend on Fortune's shining?

1

O Poortith cauld and restless Love,
   Ye wrack my peace between ye!   wreck
Yet poortith a' I could forgive,
   An 'twere na for my Jeanie.   If

2

The warld's wealth when I think on,
   Its pride and a' the lave o't—   rest
My curse on silly coward man,
   That he sould be the slave o't!

3

Her een sae bonie blue betray   eyes
   How she repays my passion;
But prudence is her o'erword ay:
   She talks o' rank and fashion.

4

O, wha can prudence think upon,
    And sic a lassie by him?
O, wha can prudence think upon,
    And sae in love as I am?

5

How blest the wild-wood Indian's fate!
    He woos his artless dearie—
hobgoblins   The silly bogles, Wealth and State,
fearful   Can never make him eerie.

O, STAY, SWEET WARBLING WOOD-LARK

TUNE: *Whare shall our guidman lie*

1

O, stay, sweet warbling wood-lark, stay,
Nor quit for me the trembling spray!
A hapless lover courts thy lay,
    Thy soothing, fond complaining.
Again, again that tender part,
That I may catch thy melting art!
For surely that wad touch her heart,
    Wha kills me wi' disdaining.

2

Say, was thy little mate unkind,
And heard thee as the careless wind?
nothing   O, nocht but love and sorrow join'd
Such; awake   Sic notes o' woe could wauken!
Thou tells o' never-ending care,
O' speechless grief and dark despair—
For pity's sake, sweet bird, nae mair,
    Or my poor heart is broken!

SAW YE BONIE LESLEY

TUNE: *The collier's bonie lassie*

I

O, saw ye bonie Lesley,
   As she gaed o'er the Border?   *went*
She's gane, like Alexander,
   To spread her conquests farther!

2

To see her is to love her,
   And love but her for ever;
For Nature made her what she is,
   And never made anither!

3

Thou art a queen, fair Lesley—
   Thy subjects, we before thee!
Thou art divine, fair Lesley—
   The hearts o' men adore thee.

4

The Deil he could na skaith thee,   *harm*
   Or aught that was belang thee: *belong to*
He'd look into thy bonie face,
   And say:—'I canna wrang thee!'

5

The Powers aboon will tent thee,   *above; guard*
   Misfortune sha'na steer thee: *meddle with*
Thou'rt like themsel' sae lovely,
   That ill they'll ne'er let near thee.

6

Return again, fair Lesley,
   Return to Caledonie!
That we may brag we hae a lass
   There's nane again sae bonie.

SWEET FA'S THE EVE

TUNE: *Craigieburn Wood*

1

Sweet fa's the eve on Craigieburn,
  And blythe awakes the morrow,
But a' the pride o' Spring's return
nothing   Can yield me nocht but sorrow.

2

I see the flowers and spreading trees,
  I hear the wild birds singing;
But what a weary wight can please,
  And Care his bosom is wringing?

3

Fain, fain would I my griefs impart,
  Yet dare na for your anger;
But secret love will break my heart,
  If I conceal it langer.

4

If thou refuse to pity me,
  If thou shalt love another,
When yon green leaves fade frae the tree,
  Around my grave they'll wither.

YOUNG JESSIE

TUNE: *Bonie Dundee*

1

True hearted was he, the sad swain o' the Yarrow,
  And fair are the maids on the banks of the Ayr;
But by the sweet side o' the Nith's winding river
  Are lovers as faithful and maidens as fair;
To equal young Jessie seek Scotia all over—
  To equal young Jessie you seek it in vain!
Grace, beauty, and elegance fetter her lover,
  And maidenly modesty fixes the chain.

2

Fresh is the rose in the gay, dewy morning,
 And sweet is the lily at evening close;
But in the fair presence o' lovely young Jessie
 Unseen is the lily, unheeded the rose.
Love sits in her smile, a wizard ensnaring;
 Enthron'd in her een he delivers his law: eyes
And still to her charms she alone is a stranger;
 Her modest demeanour's the jewel of a'.

ADOWN WINDING NITH

TUNE: *The muckin o' Geordy's byre*

CHORUS

Awa wi' your belles and your beauties—
 They never wi' her can compare!
Whaever hae met wi' my Phillis
 Has met wi' the Queen o' the Fair!

1

Adown winding Nith I did wander
 To mark the sweet flowers as they spring.
Adown winding Nith I did wander
 Of Phillis to muse and to sing.

2

The Daisy amus'd my fond fancy,
 Se artless, so simple, so wild:
'Thou emblem,' said I, 'o' my Phillis'—
 For she is Simplicity's child.

3

The rose-bud's the blush o' my charmer,
 Her sweet balmy lip when 'tis prest.
How fair and how pure is the lily!
 But fairer and purer her breast.

4

Yon knot of gay flowers in the arbour,
   They ne'er wi' my Phillis can vie:
Her breath is the breath of the woodbine,
   Its dew-drop o' diamond her eye.

5

Her voice is the song o' the morning,
   That wakes thro' the green-spreading grove,
When Phebus peeps over the mountains
   On music, and pleasure, and love.

6

But Beauty, how frail and how fleeting!
   The bloom of a fine summer's day!
While Worth in the mind o' my Phillis
   Will flourish without a decay.

A LASS WI' A TOCHER

dowry

TUNE: *Balin a mone*

CHORUS

Then hey for a lass wi' a tocher,
Then hey for a lass wi' a tocher,
Then hey for a lass wi' a tocher,
   The nice yellow guineas for me!

1

Awa wi' your witchcraft o' Beauty's alarms,
The slender bit beauty you grasp in your arms!
O, gie me the lass that has acres o' charms!
O, gie me the lass wi' the weel-stockit farms!

2

Your Beauty's a flower in the morning that blows,
And withers the faster the faster it grows;
knolls
But the rapturous charm o' the bonie green knowes,
ewes
Ilk spring they're new deckit wi' bonie white yowes!

3

And e'en when this Beauty your boson has blest,
The brightest o' Beauty may cloy when possess'd;
But the sweet, yellow darlings wi' Geordie impress'd,
The langer ye hae them, the mair they're carest!

BLYTHE HAE I BEEN ON YON HILL

TUNE: *The Quaker's Wife*

1

Blythe hae I been on yon hill
 As the lambs before me,
Careless ilka thought, and free   *every*
 As the breeze flew o'er me.
Now nae langer sport and play
 Mirth or sang can please me:
Lesley is sae fair and coy,
 Care and anguish seize me.

2

Heavy, heavy is the task,
 Hopeless love declaring!   *can do nothing*
Trembling, I dow nocht but grow'r   *but stare*
 Sighing, dumb despairing!
If she winna ease the thraws   *will not; throes*
 In my bosom swelling,
Underneath the grass-green sod
 Soon maun be my dwelling.   *must*

BY ALLAN STREAM

TUNE: *Allan Water*

1

By Allan stream I chanc'd to rove,
   While Phebus sank beyond Benledi;
The winds were whispering thro' the grove,
   The yellow corn was waving ready;
I listen'd to a lover's sang,
   An' thought on youthfu' pleasures monie,
And ay the wild-wood echoes rang:—
   'O, my love Annie's very bonie!

2

'O, happy be the woodbine bower,
   Nae nightly bogle make it errie!
Nor ever sorrow stain the hour,
   The place and time I met my dearie!
Her head upon my throbbing breast,
   She, sinking, said:—"I'm thine for ever!"
While monie a kiss the seal imprest—
   The sacred vow we ne'er should sever.'

3

The haunt o' Spring's the primrose-brae.
   The Summer joys the flocks to follow.
How cheery thro' her short'ning day
   Is Autumn in her weeds o' yellow!
But can they melt the glowing heart,
   Or chain the soul in speechless pleasure,
Or thro' each nerve the rapture dart,
   Like meeting her, our bosom's treasure?

hobgoblin;
fearful

-bank

CANST THOU LEAVE ME

TUNE: *Ruffian's Rant*

CHORUS

Canst thou leave me thus, my Katie!
  Canst thou leave me thus, my Katie!
Well thou know'st my aching heart,
  And canst thou leave me thus for pity?

I

Is this thy plighted, fond regard:
  Thus cruelly to part, my Katie?
Is this thy faithful swain's reward:
  An aching broken heart, my Katie?

2

Farewell! And ne'er such sorrows tear
  That fickle heart of thine, my Katie!
Thou may'st find those will love thee dear,
  But not a love like mine, my Katie.

COME, LET ME TAKE THEE

TUNE: *Cauld Kail*

I

Come, let me take thee to my breast,
  And pledge we ne'er shall sunder,
And I shall spurn as vilest dust
  The world's wealth and grandeur!
And do I hear my Jeanie own
  That equal transports move her?
I ask for dearest life alone,
  That I may live to love her.

2

Thus in my arms, wi' a' her charms,
   I clasp my countless treasure,
I'll seek nae mair o' Heav'n to share
such   Than sic a moment's pleasure!
eyes   And by thy een sae bonie blue
   I swear I'm thine for ever,
And on thy lips I seal my vow,
   And break it shall I never!

CONTENTED WI' LITTLE

TUNE: *Lumps of Pudding*

1

jolly   Contented wi' little and cantie wi' mair,
         Whene'er I forgather wi' Sorrow and Care,
smack   I gie them a skelp, as they're creepin alang,
new ale Wi' a cog o' guid swats and an auld Scottish sang.

2

sometimes I whyles claw the elbow o' troublesome Thought;
scratch   But Man is a soger, and Life is a faught.
fight   My mirth and guid humour are coin in my pouch,
         And my Freedom's my lairdship nae monarch daur
           touch.

3

twelve-month; A towmond o' trouble, should that be my fa',
lot   A night o' guid fellowship sowthers it a':
solders   When at the blythe end o' our journey at last,
         Wha the Deil ever thinks o' the road he has past?

4

stumble; stagger Blind Chance, let her snapper and stoyte on her way,
go   Be't to me, be't frae me, e'en let the jade gae!
         Come Ease or come Travail, come Pleasure or Pain,
worst   My warst word is:—'Welcome, and welcome again!'

FAREWELL, THOU STREAM

TUNE: *Alace yat I came owr the moor*

1

Farewell, thou stream that winding flows
   Around Eliza's dwelling!
O Mem'ry, spare the cruel throes
   Within my bosom swelling:
Condemn'd to drag a hopeless chain
   And yet in secret languish,
To feel a fire in every vein
   Nor dare disclose my anguish!

2

Love's veriest wretch, unseen, unknown,
   I fain my griefs would cover:
The bursting sigh, th' unweeting groan   unconscious
   Betray the hapless lover
I know thou doom'st me to despair,
   Nor wilt, nor canst relieve me;
But, O Eliza, hear one prayer—
   For pity's sake forgive me!

3

The music of thy voice I heard,
   Nor wist while it enslav'd me!
I saw thine eyes, yet nothing fear'd,
   Till fears no more had sav'd me!
Th' unwary sailor thus, aghast
   The wheeling torrent viewing,
'Mid circling horrors sinks at last
   In overwhelming ruin.

HAD I A CAVE

TUNE: *Robin Adair*

1

Had I a cave
　On some wild distant shore,
Where the winds howl
　To the wave's dashing roar,
　　There would I weep my woes,
　　There seek my lost repose,
　　Till grief my eyes should close,
Ne'er to wake more!

2

Falsest of womankind,
　Can'st thou declare
All thy fond, plighted vows
　Fleeting as air?
　　To thy new lover hie,
　　Laugh o'er thy perjury,
　　Then in thy bosom try
What peace is there!

HERE'S A HEALTH

TUNE: *Here's a health to them that's awa*

CHORUS

Here's a health to ane I loe dear!
Here's a health to ane I loe dear!
Thou art sweet as the smile when fond lovers meet,
And soft as their parting tear,
　　　　　Jessy—
And soft as their parting tear!

1

must

Altho' thou maun never be mine,
　Altho' even hope is denied,
'Tis sweeter for thee despairing
　Than ought in the world beside,
　　　　　Jessy—
Than ought in the world beside!

2

I mourn thro' the gay, gaudy day,
    As hopeless I muse on thy charms;
But welcome the dream o' sweet slumber!
    For then I am lockt in thine arms,
        Jessy—
    For then I am lockt in thine arms!

3

I guess by the dear angel smile
    I guess by the love-rolling e'e;
But why urge the tender confession,
    'Gainst Fortune's fell, cruel decree,
        Jessy—
    'Gainst Fortune's fell, cruel decree.

HOW CRUEL ARE THE PARENTS

TUNE: *John Anderson my jo*

1

How cruel are the parents
    Who riches only prize,
And to the wealthy booby
    Poor Woman sacrifice!
Meanwhile the hapless daughter
    Has but a choice of strife:
To shun a tyrant father's hate
    Become a wretched wife!

2

The ravening hawk pursuing,
    The trembling dove thus flies:
To shun impending ruin
    Awhile her pinion tries,
Till, of escape despairing,
    No shelter or retreat,
She trusts the ruthless falconer,
    And drops beneath his feet.

HUSBAND, HUSBAND, CEASE YOUR STRIFE

TUNE: *My jo, Janet*

1

'Husband, husband, cease your strife,
   Nor longer idly rave, sir!
Tho' I am your wedded wife,
   Yet I am not your slave, sir.'
'One of two must still obey,
   Nancy, Nancy!
Is it Man or Woman, say,
   My spouse Nancy?'

2

'If 'tis still the lordly word,
   Service and obedience,
I'll desert my sov'reign lord,
   And so goodbye, allegiance!'
'Sad will I be so bereft,
   Nancy, Nancy!
Yet I'll try to make a shift,
   My spouse Nancy!'

3

'My poor heart, then break it must,
   My last hour I am near it:
When you lay me in the dust,
   Think, how will you bear it?'
'I will hope and trust in Heaven,
   Nancy, Nancy!
Strength to bear it will be given,
   My spouse Nancy.'

4

'Well, sir, from the silent dead,
  Still I'll try to daunt you:
Ever round your midnight bed
  Horrid sprites shall haunt you!'
'I'll wed another like my dear,
  Nancy, Nancy!
Then all Hell will fly for fear,
  My spouse Nancy!'

IT WAS THE CHARMING MONTH

TUNE: *Dainty Davie*

CHORUS

Lovely was she by the dawn,
  Youthful Chloe, charming Chloe,
Tripping o'er the pearly lawn,
  The youthful, charming Chloe!

1

It was the charming month of May,
When all the flow'rs were fresh and gay,
One morning, by the break of day,
  The youthful, charming Chloe,
From peaceful slumber she arose,
Girt on her mantle and her hose,
And o'er the flow'ry mead she goes—
  The youthful, charming Chloe!

2

The feather'd people you might see
Perch'd all around on every tree!
With notes of sweetest melody
  They hail the charming Chloe,
Till, painting gay the eastern skies,
The glorious sun began to rise,
Outrival'd by the radiant eyes
  Of youthful, charming Chloe.

LAST MAY A BRAW WOOER

fine

TUNE: *The Lothian Lassie*

1

Last May a braw wooer cam down the lang glen,

deafen
   And sair wi' his love he did deave me.

I said there was naething I hated like men:

go
   The deuce gae wi' him to believe me, believe me—
   The deuce gae wi' him to believe me!

2

eyes
He spak o' the darts in my bonie black een,
   And vow'd for my love he was diein.

I said, he might die when he liket for Jean:
   The Lord forgie me for liein, for liein—
   The Lord forgie me for liein!

3

farm; landlord
A weel-stockèt mailen, himsel for the laird,
   And marriage aff-hand were his proffers:

let
I never loot on that I kenn'd it, or car'd,

worse
   But thought I might hae waur offers, waur offers—
   But thought I might hae waur offers.

4

But what wad ye think? In a fortnight or less
   (The Deil tak his taste to gae near her!)

He up the Gate-Slack to my black cousin, Bess!
   Guess ye how, the jad! I could bear her, could bear
      her—
   Guess ye how, the jad! I could bear her.

5

next
But a' the niest week, as I petted wi' care,

cattle-fair
   I gaed to the tryste o' Dalgarnock,

And what but my fine fickle lover was there?

stared
   I glowr'd as I'd seen a warlock, a warlock—
   I glowr'd as I'd seen a warlock.

6

But owre my left shouther I gae him a blink,   *shoulder; glance*
  Lest neebours might say I was saucy.
My wooer he caper'd as he'd been in drink,
  And vow'd I was his dear lassie, dear lassie—
  And vow'd I was his dear lassie!

7

I spier'd for my cousin fu' couthy and sweet: *asked; affable*
  Gin she had recover'd her hearin?   *If*
And how her new shoon fit her auld, shachl'd feet?   *shoes; shapeless*
  But heavens! how he fell a swearin, a swearin—
  But heavens! how he fell a swearin.

8

He beggèd, for gudesake, I wad be his wife,
  Or else I wad kill him wi' sorrow;
So e'en to preserve the poor body in life,
  I think I maun wed him to-morrow, to-morrow—   *must*
  I think I maun wed him to-morrow!

MY NANIE'S AWA

TUNE: *There are few good fellows when Jamie's awa*

1

Now in her green mantle blythe Nature arrays,
And listens the lambkins that bleat o'er the braes,   *heights*
While birds warble welcomes in ilka green shaw,   *every; wood*
But to me it's delightless—my Nanie's awa.

2

The snawdrap and primrose our woodlands adorn,
And violets bathe in the weet o' the morn.   *wet [i.e. dew]*
They pain my sad bosom, sae sweetly they blaw:
They mind me o' Nanie—and Nanie's awa!

3

Thou lav'rock, that springs frae the dews of the lawn
The shepherd to warn o' the grey-breaking dawn,
And thou mellow mavis, that hails the night-fa,
Give over for pity—my Nanie's awa.

4

Come Autumn, sae pensive in yellow and grey,
And soothe me wi' tidings o' Nature's decay!
The dark, dreary Winter and wild-driving snaw
Alane can delight me—now Nanie's awa.

NOW ROSY MAY

TUNE: *Dainty Davie*

CHORUS

knoll

Meet me on the Warlock Knowe,
Dainty Davie, Dainty Davie!
There I'll spend the day wi' you,
own   *My ain dear Dainty Davie.*

1

Now rosy May comes in wi' flowers
To deck her gay, green-spreading bowers;
And now comes in the happy hours
   To wander wi' my Davie.

2

The crystal waters round us fa',
The merry birds are lovers a',
The scented breezes round us blaw,
   A wandering wi' my Davie.

3

When purple morning starts the hare
To steal upon her early fare,
Then thro' the dews I will repair
   To meet my faithfu' Davie.

4

When day, expiring in the west,
The curtain draws o' Nature's rest,
I flee to his arms I loe the best:
   And that's my ain dear Davie!

NOW SPRING HAS CLAD

TUNE: *(Unknown)*

1

Now spring has clad the grove in green,
  And strew'd the lea wi' flowers;
The furrow'd, waving corn is seen
  Rejoice in fostering showers;
While ilka thing in nature join   every
  Their sorrows to forego,
O, why thus all alone are mine
  The weary steps o' woe!

2

The trout within yon wimpling burn   winding
  Glides swift, a silver dart,
And, safe beneath the shady thorn,
  Defies the angler's art:
My life was ance that careless stream,
  That wanton trout was I,
But Love wi' unrelenting beam
  Has scorch'd my fountains dry.

3

The little floweret's peaceful lot,
In yonder cliff that grows,
Which, save the linnet's flight, I wot,   guess
  Nae ruder visit knows,
Was mine, till Love has o'er me past,
  And blighted a' my bloom;
And now beneath the withering blast
  My youth and joy consume.

4

The waken'd lav'rock warbling springs,
  And climbs the early sky,
Winnowing blythe his dewy wings
  In Morning's rosy eye:
As little reck't I Sorrow's power,
  Until the flowery snare
O' witching Love in luckless hour
  Made me the thrall o' care!

5

O, had my fate been Greenland snows
  Or Afric's burning zone,
Wi' Man and Nature leagu'd my foes,
  So Peggy ne'er I'd known!
The wretch, whose doom is 'hope nae mair,'
  What tongue his woes can tell,
Within whose bosom, save Despair,
  Nae kinder spirits dwell!

O, THIS IS NO MY AIN LASSIE

TUNE: *This is no mine ain house*

CHORUS

O, this is no my ain lassie,
  Fair tho' the lassie be:
Weel ken I my ain lassie—
  Kind love is in her e'e.

1

I see a form, I see a face,
Ye weel may wi' the fairest place:
It wants to me the witching grace,
  The kind love that's in her e'e.

2

She's bonie, blooming, straight, and tall,
And lang has had my heart in thrall;
And ay it charms my very saul,
  The kind love that's in her e'e.

3

artful   A thief sae pawkie is my Jean,
glance   To steal a blink by a' unseen!
sharp; eyes   But gleg as light are lover's een,
                When kind love is in the e'e.

4

It may escape the courtly sparks,
It may escape the learned clerks;
But well the watching lover marks
    The kind love that's in here e'e.

O, WAT YE WHA THAT LO'ES ME   wot; who

TUNE: *Morag*

CHORUS

O, that's the lassie o' my heart,
    My lassie ever dearer!
O, that's the queen o' womankind,
    And ne'er a ane to peer her!

I

O, wat ye wha that lo'es me,
    And has my heart a keeping?
O, sweet is she that lo'es me
    As dews o' summer weeping,
    In tears the rosebuds steeping!

2

If thou shalt meet a lassie
    In grace and beauty charming,
That e'en thy chosen lassie,
    Erewhile thy breast sae warming,
    Had ne'er sic powers alarming:—   such

3

If thou hadst heard her talking
    (And thy attention's plighted),
That ilka body talking   every
    But her by thee is slighted,   Except
    And thou art all-delighted:—

4

If thou has met this fair one,
　　When frae her thou hast parted,
If every other fair one
　　But her thou hast deserted,
　　And thou art broken-hearted:—

SCOTS, WHA HAE

TUNE: *Hey, tutti taitie*

1

Scots, wha hae wi' Wallace bled,
Scots, wham Bruce has aften led,
Welcome to your gory bed
　　　　Or to victorie!

2

Now's the day, and now's the hour:
See the front o' battle lour,
See approach proud Edward's power—
　　　　Chains and slaverie!

3

Wha will be a traitor knave?
Wha can fill a coward's grave?
Wha sae base as be a slave?—
　　　　Let him turn, and flee!

4

Wha for Scotland's King and Law
Freedom's sword will strongly draw,
Freeman stand or freeman fa',
　　　　Let him follow me!

5

By Oppression's woes and pains,
By your sons in servile chains,
We will drain our dearest veins
　　　　But they shall be free!

6

Lay the proud usurpers low!
Tyrants fall in every foe!
Liberty's in every blow!
   Let us do, or die!

THEIR GROVES O' SWEET MYRTLE

TUNE: *Humours of Glen*

1

Their groves o' sweet myrtle let foreign lands reckon,
 Where bright-beaming summers exalt the perfume!
Far dearer to me yon lone glen o' green breckan,   ferns
 Wi' the burn stealing under the lang, yellow broom; brook
Far dearer to me are yon humble broom bowers,
 Where the blue-bell and gowan lurk lowly, unseen; wild daisy
For there, lightly tripping among the wild flowers,
 A-list'ning the linnet, aft wanders my Jean.

2

Tho' rich is the breeze in their gay, sunny vallies,
 And cauld Caledonia's blast on the wave,
Their sweet-scented woodlands that skirt the proud
  palace,
 What are they?—The haunt of the tyrant and slave!
The slave's spicy forests and gold-bubbling fountains
 The brave Caledonian views wi' disdain:
He wanders as free as the winds of his mountains,
 Save Love's willing fetters—the chains o' his Jean.

THINE AM I

TUNE: *The Quaker's Wife*

1

Thine am I, my faithful Fair,
  Thine my lovely Nancy!
Ev'ry pulse along my veins,
  Ev'ry roving fancy!
To thy bosom lay my heart
  There to throb and languish.
Tho' despair has wrung its core,
  That would heal its anguish.

2

Take away those rosy lips
  Rich with balmy treasure!
Turn away thine eyes of love,
  Lest I die with pleasure!
What is life when wanting love?
  Night without a morning!
Love the cloudless summer's sun,
  Nature gay adorning.

THOU HAST LEFT ME EVER, JAMIE

TUNE: *Fee him, father, fee him*

1

Thou hast left me ever, Jamie,
  Thou hast left me ever!
Thou hast left me ever, Jamie,
  Thou hast left me ever!
Aften hast thou vow'd that Death
  Only should us sever;
Now thou'st left thy lass for ay—
  I maun see thee never, Jamie,
  I'll see thee never!

must

2

Thou hast me forsaken, Jamie,
  Thou hast me forsaken!
Thou hast me forsaken, Jamie,
  Thou hast me forsaken!
Thou canst love another jo,
  While my heart is breaking;
Soon my weary een I'll close,   eyes
  Never mair to waken, Jamie,   more
  Never mair to waken!

HIGHLAND MARY

TUNE: *Lady Catherine Ogle*

1

Ye banks and braes and streams around
  The castle o' Montgomery,
Green be your woods, and fair your flowers,
  Your waters never drumlie!   turbid
There Summer first unfald her robes,   unfold
  And there the langest tarry!
For there I took the last fareweel
  O' my sweet Highland Mary!

2

How sweetly bloom'd the gay, green birk,
  How rich the hawthorn's blossom,
As underneath their fragrant shade
  I clasp'd her to my bosom!
The golden hours on angel wings
  Flew o'er me and my dearie:
For dear to me as light and life
  Was my sweet Highland Mary.

3

Wi' monie a vow and lock'd embrace
    Our parting was fu' tender;
And, pledging aft to meet again,
    We tore oursels asunder.
But O, fell Death's untimely frost,
    That nipt my flower sae early!
Now green's the sod, and cauld's the clay,
    That wraps my Highland Mary!

4

O, pale, pale now, those rosy lips
    I aft hae kiss'd sae fondly;
And clos'd for ay, the sparkling glance
    That dwalt on me sae kindly;
And mouldering now in silent dust
    That heart that lo'ed me dearly!
But still within my bosom's core
    Shall live my Highland Mary.

MY CHLORIS, MARK

TUNE: *On the Cold Ground*

1

My Chloris, mark how green the groves,
    The primrose banks how fair!
The balmy gales awake the flowers,
    And wave thy flaxen hair

2

lark

The lav'rock shuns the palace gay,
    The o'er the cottage sings:
For Nature smiles as sweet, I ween,
    To shepherds as to kings.

3

Let minstrels sweep the skilfu' string
hall   In lordly, lighted ha':
The shepherd stops his simple reed,
birch wood   Blythe in the birken shaw.

4

The princely revel may survey
 Our rustic dance wi' scorn;
But are their hearts as light as ours
 Beneath the milk-white thorn?

5

The shepherd in the flowery glen
 In shepherd's phrase will woo:
The courtier tells a finer tale—
 But is his heart as true?

6

Here wild-wood flowers I've pu'd, to deck
 That spotless breast o' thine:
The courtier's gems may witness love—
 But 'tis na love like mine!

FAIREST MAID ON DEVON BANKS

TUNE: *Rothiemurchie's Rant*

CHORUS

Fairest maid on Devon banks,
 Crystal Devon, winding Devon,
Wilt thou lay that frown aside,
 And smile as thou wert wont to do?

1

Full well thou know'st I love thee dear—
Couldst thou to malice lend an ear!
O, did not Love exclaim:—'Forbear,
 Nor use a faithful lover so!'

2

Then come, thou fairest of the fair,
Those wonted smiles, O, let me share,
And by thy beauteous self I swear
 No love but thine my heart shall know!

LASSIE WI' THE LINT-WHITE LOCKS

TUNE: *Rothiemurchie's Rant*

CHORUS

Lassie wi' the lint-white locks,
Bonie lassie, artless lassie,
tend   *Wilt thou wi' me tent the flocks—*
Wilt thou be my dearie, O?

I

clothes   Now Nature cleeds the flowery lea,
And a' is young and sweet like thee,
O, wilt thou share it's joys wi' me,
    And say thou'lt be my dearie, O?

2

meandering   The primrose bank, the wimpling burn,
The cuckoo on the milk-white thorn,
The wanton lambs at early morn
    Shall welcome thee, my dearie, O.

3

And when the welcome simmer shower
each   Has cheer'd ilk drooping little flower,
We'll to the breathing woodbine-bower
    At sultry noon, my dearie, O.

4

When Cynthia lights wi' silver ray
reaper's   The weary shearer's hameward way,
Thro' yellow waving fields we'll stray,
    And talk o' love, my dearie, O.

5

And when the howling wintry blast
Disturbs my lassie's midnight rest,
Enclaspèd to my faithfu' breast,
    I'll comfort thee, my dearie, O.

LONG, LONG THE NIGHT

TUNE: *Ay, waukin, O*

CHORUS

Long, long the night,
  Heavy comes the morrow,
While my soul's delight
  Is on her bed of sorrow.

1

Can I cease to care,
  Can I cease to languish,
While my darling fair
  Is on the couch of anguish!

2

Ev'ry hope is fled,
  Ev'ry fear is terror:
Slumber ev'n I dread,
  Ev'ry dream is horror.

3

Here me, Powers Divine:
  O, in pity, hear me!
Take aught else of mine,
  But my Chloris spare me!

LOGAN WATER

TUNE: *(As Title)*

1

O Logan, sweetly didst thou glide
That day I was my Willie's bride,
And years sin syne hae o'er us run   since then have
Like Logan to the simmer sun.
But now thy flowery banks appear
Like drumlie winter, dark and drear,   dull
While my dear lad maun face his faes   must
Far, far frae me and Logan braes.   slopes

2

Again the merry month of May
Has made our hills and vallies gay;
The birds rejoice in leafy bowers,
The bees hum round the breathing flowers;
Blythe Morning lifts his rosy eye,
And Evening's tears are tears o' joy:
My soul delightless a' surveys,
While Willie's far frae Logan braes.

3

Within yon milk-white hawthorn bush,
Amang her nestlings sits the thrush:
Her faithfu' mate will share her toil,
Or wi' his song her cares beguile.
But I wi' my sweet nurslings here,
Nae mate to help, nae mate to cheer,
Pass widow'd nights and joyless days,
While Willie's far frae Logan braes.

4

O, wae upon you, Men o' State,
That brethren rouse in deadly hate!
As ye make monie a fond heart mourn,
Sae may it on your head return!
remember not   Ye mindna 'mid your cruel joys
The widow's tears, the orphan's cries;
But soon may peace bring happy days,
And Willie hame to Logan braes!

YON ROSY BRIER

TUNE: *I wish my love were in a mire*

1

yonder   O, bonie was yon rosy brier
 That blooms sae far frae haunt o' man,
And bonie she—and ah, how dear!—
 It shaded frae the e'enin sun!

2

Yon rosebuds in the morning dew,
   How pure among the leaves sae green!
But purer was the lover's vow
   They witnessed in their shade yestreen.   *last night*

3

All in its rude and prickly bower,
   That crimson rose how sweet and fair!
But love is far a sweeter flower
   Amid life's thorny path o' care.

4

The pathless wild and wimpling burn,   *winding*
   Wi' Chloris in my arms, be mine,
And I the warld nor wish nor scorn—
   Its joys and griefs alike resign!

WHERE ARE THE JOYS

TUNE: *Saw ye my father?*

1

Where are the joys I hae met in the morning,
   That danc'd to the lark's early sang?
Where is the peace that awaited my wand'ring
   At e'ening the wild-woods amang?

2

Nae mair a-winding the course o' yon river
   And marking sweet flowerets sae fair,
Nae mair I trace the light footsteps o' Pleasure,
   But Sorrow and sad-sighing Care.

3

Is is that Summer's forsaken our vallies,
   And grim, surly Winter is near?
No, no, the bees humming round the gay roses
   Proclaim it the pride o' the year.

4

Fain wad I hide what I fear to discover,
　　Yet lang, lang, too well hae I known:
A' that has causèd the wreck in my bosom
　　Is Jenny, fair Jenny alone!

5

Time cannot aid me, my griefs are immortal,
　　Not Hope dare a comfort bestow.
Come then, enamor'd and fond of my anguish,
　　Enjoyment I'll seek in my woe!

BEHOLD THE HOUR

TUNE: *Oran gaoil*

1

Behold the hour, the boat arrive!
　　Thou goest, the darling of my heart!
Sever'd from thee, can I survive?
　　But Fate has will'd and we must part.
I'll often greet the surging swell,
　　Yon distant isle will often hail:—
'E'en here I took the last farewell;
　　There, latest mark'd her vanish'd sail.'

2

Along the solitary shore,
　　While flitting sea-fowl round me cry,
Across the rolling, dashing roar,
　　I'll westward turn my wistful eye:—
'Happy, thou Indian grove,' I'll say,
　　'Where now my Nancy's path may be!
While thro' thy sweets she loves to stray,
　　O, tell me, does she muse on me?'

FORLORN MY LOVE

TUNE: *Let me in this ae night*

CHORUS

O, wert thou, love, but near me,
But near, near, near me,
How kindly thou would cheer me,
And mingle sighs with mine, love!

I

Forlorn my love, no comfort near,
Far, far from thee I wander here;
Far, far from thee, the fate severe,
At which I most repine, love.

2

Around me scowls a wintry sky,
Blasting each bud of hope and joy,
And shelter, shade, nor home have I
Save in these arms of thine, love.

3

Cold, alter'd friendship's cruel part,
To poison Fortune's ruthless dart!
Let me not break thy faithful heart,
And say that fate is mine, love!

4

But, dreary tho' the moments fleet,
O, let me think we yet shall meet!
That only ray of solace sweet
Can on thy Chloris shine, love!

Drive; ewes;
knolls

CA' THE YOWES TO THE KNOWES

TUNE: *Ca' the Yowes*

Second Set

CHORUS

Ca' the yowes to the knowes,
Ca' them where the heather grows,

brooklet runs

Ca' them where the burnie rowes,
My bonie dearie.

1

Hark, the mavis' e'ening sang
Sounding Clouden's woods amang,

go

Then a-faulding let us gang,
My bonie dearie.

2

We'll gae down by Clouden side,
Thro' the hazels, spreading wide
O'er the waves that sweetly glide
To the moon sae clearly.

3

Yonder Clouden's silent towers,
Where, at moonshine's midnight hours,
O'er the dewy bending flowers
Fairies dance sae cheery.

4

hobgoblin

Ghaist nor bogle shalt thou fear—
Thou'rt to Love and Heav'n sae dear
Nocht of ill may come thee near,
My bonie dearie.

5

Fair and lovely as thou art,

stolen

Thou hast stown my very heart;
I can die—but canna part,
My bonie dearie.

HOW CAN MY POOR HEART

TUNE: *O'er the hills and far away*

I

How can my poor heart be glad
When absent from my sailor lad?
How can I the thought forego—
He's on the seas to meet the foe?
Let me wander, let me rove,
Still my heart is with my love.
Nightly dreams and thoughts by day
Are with him that's far away.
  On the seas and far away,
  On stormy seas and far away—
  Nightly dreams and thoughts by day,
  Are ay with him that's far away.

2

When in summer noon I faint,
As weary flocks around me pant,
Haply in this scorching sun
My sailor's thund'ring at his gun.
Bullets, spare my only joy!
Bullets, spare my darling boy!
Fate, do with me what you may,
Spare but him that's far away!
  On the seas and far away,
  On stormy seas and far away—
  Fate, do with me what you may,
  Spare but him that's far away!

3

At the starless, midnight hour
When Winter rules with boundless power,

As the storms the forests tear,
And thunders rend the howling air,
Listening to the doubling roar
Surging on the rocky shore,
All I can—I weep and pray
For his weal that's far away.
  On the seas and far away,
  On stormy seas and far away,
  All I can—I weep and pray
  For his weal that's far away.

4

Peace, thy olive wand extend
And bid wild War his ravage end;
Man with brother man to meet,
And as brother kindly greet!
Then may Heaven with prosperous gales
Fill my sailor's welcome sails,
To my arms their charge convey,
My dear lad that's far away!
  On the seas and far away,
  On stormy seas and far away,
  To my arms their charge convey,
  My dear lad that's far away!

IS THERE FOR HONEST POVERTY

TUNE: *For a' that*

1

Is there for honest poverty
  That hings his head, an' a' that?
The coward slave, we pass him by—
  We dare be poor for a' that!
For a' that, an' a' that,
  Our toils obscure, an' a' that,
The rank is but the guinea's stamp,
  The man's the gowd for a' that.

hings — hangs

gowd — gold

2

What though on hamely fare we dine,
 Wear hoddin grey, an' a' that?   coarse grey
Gie fools their silks, and knaves their wine woollen
 A man's a man for a' that.
For a' that, an' a' that,
 Their tinsel show, an' a' that.
The honest man, tho' e'er sae poor,
 Is king o' men for a' that.

3

Ye see yon birkie ca'd 'a lord,'   fellow; called
 Wha struts, an' states, an' a' that?
Tho' hundreds worship at his word,
 He's but a cuif for a' that.   dolt
For a' that, an' a' that,
 His ribband, star, an' a' that,
The man o' independent mind,
 He looks an' laughs at a' that.

4

A prince can mak a belted knight,
 A marquis, duke, an' a' that!
But an honest man's aboon his might— above
 Guid faith, he mauna fa' that!   must not
For a' that, an' a' that,
 Their dignities, an' a' that,
The pith o' sense an' pride o' worth
 Are higher rank that a' that.

5

Then let us pray that come it may
 (As come it will for a' that)
That Sense and Worth o'er a' the earth
 Shall bear the gree an' a' that! have the first
For a' that, an' a' that,   place
 It's comin yet for a' that,
That man to man the world o'er
 Shall brithers be for a' that.

MARK YONDER POMP

TUNE: *Deil tak the wars*

1

Mark yonder pomp of costly fashion
  Round the wealthy, titled bride!
But, when compar'd with real passion,
  Poor is all that princely pride.

2

  What are the showy treasures?
  What are the noisy pleasures?
The gay, gaudy glare of vanity and art!
  The polish'd jewel's blaze
  May draw the wond'ring gaze,
  And courtly grandeur bright
  The fancy may delight,
But never, never can come near the heart!

3

But did you see my dearest Chloris
  In simplicity's array,
Lovely as yonder sweet opening flower is,
  Shrinking from the gaze of day:

4

  O, then, the heart alarming
  And all resistless charming,
In love's delightful fetters she chains the willing
    soul!
  Ambition would disown
  The world's imperial crown!
  Ev'n Avarice would deny
  His worshipp'd deity,
And feel thro' every vein love's raptures roll!

O, LET ME IN THIS AE NIGHT   one

TUNE: *Will ye lend me your loom, lass?*

CHORUS

O, let me in this ae night,
This ae, ae, ae night!
O, let me in this ae night,
And rise, and let me in!

1

O lassie, are ye sleepin yet,
Or are ye waukin, I wad wit?   awake; know
For Love has bound me hand an' fit,   foot
    And I would fain be in, jo.

2

Thou hear'st the winter wind an' weet: wet
Nae star blinks thro' the driving sleet!   shines
Tak pity on my weary feet,
    And shield me frae the rain, jo.

3

The bitter blast that round me blaws,
Unheeded howls, unheeded fa's:
The cauldness o' thy heart's the cause
    Of a' my care and pine, jo.

HER ANSWER

CHORUS

I tell you now this ae night,
This ae, ae, ae night,
And ance for a' this ae night,
I winna let ye in, jo.   will not

1

O, tell me na o' wind an' rain,   not
Upbraid na me wi' cauld disdain,
Gae back the gate ye cam gain,   way
    I winna let ye in, jo!

2

keenest; darkest

The snellest blast at mirkest hours,
That round the pathless wand'rer pours
nothing
Is nocht to what poor she endures,
  That's trusted faithless man, jo.

3

The sweetest flower that deck'd the mead,
Now trodden like the vilest weed—
Let simple maid the lesson read!
fate; own
  The weird may be her ain, jo.

4

The bird that charm'd his summer day,
And now the cruel fowler's prey,
Let that to witless woman say:—
  'The gratefu' heart of man,' jo.

O PHILLY, HAPPY BE THAT DAY

TUNE: *The Sow's Tail to Geordie*

CHORUS

gold
HE AND SHE. *For a' the joys that gowd can gie,*
do not
I dinna care a single flie!
The $\left\{ \begin{array}{l} lad \\ lass \end{array} \right\}$ I love's the $\left\{ \begin{array}{l} lad \\ lass \end{array} \right\}$ for me,
And that's my ain dear $\left\{ \begin{array}{l} Willy \\ Philly \end{array} \right\}$

I

HE. O Philly, happy be that day
   When, roving thro' the gather'd hay,
stolen
   My youthfu' heart was stown away,
     And by thy charms, my Philly!
SHE. O Willy, ay I bless the grove
   Where first I own'd my maiden love,
   Whilst thou did pledge the Powers above
     To be my ain dear Willy.

2

HE. As songsters of the early year
     Are ilka day mair sweet to hear,   *each succeeding*
     So ilka day to me mair dear
       And charming is my Philly.

SHE. As on the brier the budding rose
     Still richer breathes, and fairer blows,
     So in my tender bosom grows
       The love I bear my Willy.

3

HE. The milder sun and bluer sky,
     That crown my harvest cares wi' joy,
     Were ne'er sae welcome to my eye
       As is a sight o' Philly.

SHE. The little swallow's wanton wing,
     Tho' wafting o'er the flowery spring,
     Did ne'er to me sic tidings bring   *such*
       As meeting o' my Willy.

4

HE. The bee, that thro' the sunny hour
     Sips nectar in the op'ning flower,
     Compar'd wi' my delight is poor
       Upon the lips o' Philly.

SHE. The woodbine in the dewy weet,   *wet*
     When ev'ning shades in silence meet,
     Is nocht sae fragrant or sea sweet   *nothing*
       As is a kiss o' Willy.

5

HE. Let Fortune's wheel at random rin,
     And fools may tyne, and knaves may win!   *lose*
     My thoughts are a' bound up on ane,
       And that's my ain dear Philly.

SHE. What's a' the joys that gowd can gie?
     I dinna care a single flie!
     The lad I love's the lad for me,
       And that's my ain dear Willy.

O, WERE MY LOVE

TUNE: *Gin my love were yon red rose*

I

O, were my love yon lilac fair
   Wi' purple blossoms to the spring,
And I a bird to shelter there,
   When wearied on my little wing,
How I wad mourn when it was torn
   By Autumn wild and Winter rude!
But I wad sing on wanton wing,
   When youthfu' May its bloom renew'd.

2

if

O, gin my love were yon red rose,
   That grows upon the castle wa',
And I myself a drap o' dew
   Into her bonie breast to fa',
O, there, beyond expression blest,
   I'd feast on beauty a' the night,
-soft; folds   Seal'd on her silk-saft faulds to rest,
scared   Till fley'd awa by Phœbus' light!

SLEEP'ST THOU

TUNE: *Deil tak the wars*

I

Sleep'st thou, or wauk'st thou, fairest creature?
   Rosy Morn now lifts his eye,
Numbering ilka bud, which Nature
   Waters wi' the tears o' joy.
   Now to the streaming fountain
   Or up the heathy mountain
The hart, hind, and roe, freely, wildly-wanton stray;
   In twining hazel bowers
   His lay the linnet pours;
   The laverock to the sky
   Ascends wi' sangs o' joy,
While the sun and thou arise to bless the day!

2

Phœbus, gilding the brow of morning,
  Banishes ilka darksome shade,
Nature gladdening and adorning:
  Such to me my lovely maid!
  When frae my Chloris parted,
  Sad, cheerless, broken-hearted,
The night's gloomy shades, cloudy, dark, o'ercast my
    sky;
  But when she charms my sight
  In pride of Beauty's light,
  When thro' my very heart
  Her beaming glories dart,
'Tis then—'tis then I wake to life and joy!

THERE WAS A LASS

TUNE: *(Unknown)*

1

There was a lass, and she was fair!
  At kirk and market to be seen
When a' our fairest maids were met,
  The fairest maid was bonie Jean.

2

And ay she wrought her country wark,
  And ay she sang sae merrilie:
The blythest bird upon the bush
  Had ne'er a lighter heart than she!

3

But hawks will rob the tender joys,
  That bless the little lintwhite's nest,   *linnet's*
And frost will blight the fairest flowers,
  And love will break the soundest rest.

4

Young Robie was the brawest lad,   *handsomest*
  The flower and pride of a' the glen,
And he had owsen, sheep, and kye,   *oxen; kine*
  And wanton naigies nine or ten.   *horses*

5

went

> He gaed wi' Jeanie to the tryste,
>   He danc'd wi' Jeanie on the down,
> And, lang ere witless Jeanie wist,

lost; stolen

>   Her heart was tint, her peace was stown!

6

> As in the bosom of the stream
>   The moon-beam dwells at dewy e'en,
> So, trembling pure, was tender love
>   Within the breast of bonie Jean.

7

> And now she works her country's wark,
>   And ay she sighs wi' care and pain,

knew not;
complaint
well

> Yet wist na what her ail might be,
>   Or what wad make her weel again.

8

not; leap

> But did na Jeanie's heart loup light,

glance

>   And did na joy blink in her e'e,
> As Robie tauld a tale o' love

One

>   Ae e'enin on the lily lea?

9

> While monie a bird sang sweet o' love,
>   And monie a flower blooms o'er the dale,
> His cheek to hers he aft did lay,
>   And whisper'd thus his tender tale:—

10

> 'O Jeanie fair, I lo'e thee dear.
>   O, canst thou think to fancy me?
> Or wilt thou leave they mammie's cot,

tend

>   And learn to tent the farms wi' me?

11

cowhouse

> 'At barn or byre thou shalt na drudge,
>   Or naething else to trouble thee,
> But stray amang the heather-bells,
>   And tent the waving corn wi' me.'

12

Now what could artless Jeanie do?
 She had nae will to say him na!
At length she blush'd a sweet consent,
 And love was ay between then twa.

THE LEA-RIG

meadow-ridge

TUNE: *My ain kind dearie, O*

I

When o'er the hill the eastern star
 Tells bughtin time is near, my jo,   folding
And owsen frae the furrow'd field
 Return sae dowf and weary, O,   dull
Down by the burn, where scented birks
 Wi' dew are hanging clear, my jo,
I'll meet thee on the lea-rig,
 My ain kind dearie, O.

2

At midnight hour in mirkest glen
 I'd rove, and ne'er be eerie, O,   frightened
If thro' that glen I gaed to thee,   went
 My ain kind dearie, O!
Altho' the night were ne'er sae wild,
 And I were ne'er sae weary, O,
I'll meet thee on the lea-rig,
 My ain kind dearie, O.

3

The hunter lo'es the morning sun
 To rouse the mountain deer, my jo;
At noon the fisher takes the glen
 Adown the burn to steer, my jo:
Gie me the hour o' gloamin grey—   twilight
 It maks my heart sae cheery, O,
To meet thee on the lea-rig,
 My ain kind dearie, O!

MY WIFE'S A WINSOME WEE THING

TUNE: *My wife's a wanton wee thing*

CHORUS

She is a winsome wee thing,
She is a handsome wee thing,
She is a lo'esome wee thing,
This sweet wee wife o' mine!

1

I never saw a fairer,
I never lo'ed a dearer,
And neist my heart I'll wear her,
For fear my jewel tine.

next
be lost

2

The warld's wrack, we share o't;
The warstle and the care o't,
Wi' her I'll blythely bear it,
And think my lot divine.

MARY MORISON

TUNE: *Duncan Davison*

1

O Mary, at thy window be!
It is the wish'd, the trysted hour.
Those smiles and glances let me see,
That make the miser's treasure poor.
How blythely was I bide the stoure,
A weary slave frae sun to sun,
Could I the rich reward secure—
The lovely Mary Morison!

bear the struggle

2

Yestreen, who to the trembling string   Last night
    The dance gaed thro' the lighted ha',   went
To thee my fancy took its wing,
    I sat, but neither heard or saw:
    Tho' this was fair, and that was braw,   fine
And yon the toast of a' the town,   the other
    I sigh'd and said amang them a':—
    'Ye are na Mary Morison!'

3

O Mary, canst thou wreck his peace
    Wha for thy sake wad gladly die?
Or canst thou break that heart of his
    Whase only faut is loving thee?   fault
    If love for love thou wilt na gie,   give
At least be pity to me shown:
    A thought ungentle canna be   cannot
The thought o' Mary Morison.

A RUINED FARMER

TUNE: *Go from my window, love, do*

1

The sun he is sunk in the west,
All creatures retirèd to rest,
While here I sit, all sore beset
        With sorrow, grief, and woe:
And it's O fickle Fortune, O!

2

The prosperous man is asleep,
Nor hears how the whirlwinds sweep;
But Misery and I must watch
        The surly tempests blow:
And it's O fickle Fortune, O!

3

There lies the dear Partner of my breast,
Her cares for a moment at rest!
Must I see thee, my youthful pride,
　　　　Thus brought so very low?—
And it's O fickle Fortune, O!

4

There lie my sweet babies in her arms:
No anxious fear their little hearts alarms;
But for their sake my heart does ache,
　　　　With many a bitter throe:
And it's O fickle Fortune, O!

5

I once was by Fortune carest,
I once could relieve the distrest;
Now life's poor support, hardly earn'd,
　　　　My fate will scarce bestow:
And it's O fickle Fortune, O!

6

No comfort, no comfort I have!
How welcome to me were the grave!
But then my wife and children dear—
　　　　O, whither would they go?
And it's O fickle Fortune, O!

7

O, whither, O, whither shall I turn,
All friendless, forsaken, forlorn?
For in this world Rest or Peace
　　　　I never more shall know:
And it's O fickle Fortune, O!

MONTGOMERIE'S PEGGY

TUNE: *Galla Water*

1

Altho' my bed were in yon muir,   yonder
  Amang the heather, in my plaidie,
Yet happy, happy would I be,
  Had I my dear Montgomerie's Peggy.

2

When o'er the hill beat surly storms,
  And winter nights were dark and rainy,
I'd seek some dell, and in my arms
  I'd shelter dear Montgomerie's Peggy.

3

Were I a Baron proud and high,
  And horse and servants waiting ready,
Then a' 'twad gie o' joy to me—   'twould give
  The sharin't with Montgomerie's Peggy.   sharing it

THE LASS OF CESSNOCK BANKS

TUNE: *The Butcher Boy*

1

On Cessnock banks a lassie dwells,
  Could I describe her shape and mien;
Our lasses a' she far excels—
  An' she has twa sparkling, rogueish een!   eyes

2

She's sweeter than the morning dawn,
  When rising Phœbus first is seen,
And dew-drops twinkle o'er the lawn—
  An' she has twa sparkling, rogueish een!

3

yonder

slopes

She's stately like yon youthful ash,
  That grows the cowslip braes between,
And drinks the stream with vigour fresh—
  An' she has twa sparkling, rogueish een!

4

She's spotless like the flow'ring thorn
  With flow'rs so white and leaves so green,
When purest in the dewy morn—
  An' she has twa sparkling, rogueish een!

5

Her looks are like the vernal May,
  When ev'ning Phœbus shines serene,
While birds rejoice on every spray—
  An' she has twa sparkling, rogueish een!

6

Her hair is like the curling mist,
  That climbs the mountain-sides at e'en,
When flow'r-reviving rains are past—
  An' she has twa sparkling, rogueish een!

7

Her forehead's like the show'ry bow,
  When gleaming sunbeams intervene,
And gild the distant mountain's brow—
  An' she has twa sparkling, rogueish een!

8

Her cheeks are like yon crimson gem,
  The pride of all the flowery scene,
Just opening on its thorny stem—
  An' she has twa sparkling, rogueish een!

9

Her teeth are like the nightly snow,
  When pale the morning rises keen,
While hid the murm'ring streamlets flow—
  An' she has twa sparkling, rogueish een!

10

Her lips are like yon cherries ripe,
   That sunny walls from Boreas screen:
They tempt the taste and charm the sight—
   An' she has twa sparkling, rogueish een!

11

Her breath is like the fragrant breeze,
   That gently stirs the blossom'd bean,
When Phœbus sinks behind the seas—
   An' she has twa sparkling, rogueish een!

12

Her voice is like the ev'ning thrush,
   That sings on Cessnock banks unseen,
While his mate sits nestling in the bush—
   An' she has twa sparkling, rogueish een!

13

But it's not her air, her form, her face,
   Tho' matching Beauty's fabled Queen:
'Tis the mind that shines in ev'ry grace—
   An' chiefly in her rogueish een!

THO' FICKLE FORTUNE

TUNE: *I dream'd I lay*

1

Tho' fickle Fortune has deceived me
   (She promis'd fair, and perform'd but ill),
Of mistress, friends, and wealth bereaved me,
   Yet I bear a heart shall support me still.

2

I'll act with prudence as far as I'm able;
   But if success I must never find,
Then come, Misfortune, I bid thee welcome—
   I'll meet thee with an undaunted mind!

RAGING FORTUNE

TUNE: *(Unknown)*

1

O, raging Fortune's withering blast
    Has laid my leaf full low!
O, raging Fortune's withering blast
    Has laid my leaf full low!

2

My stem was fair, my bud was green,
    My blossom sweet did blow;
The dew fell fresh, the sun rose mild,
    And made my branches grow.

3

But luckless Fortune's northern storms
    Laid a' my blossoms low!
But luckless Fortune's northern storms
    Laid a' my blossoms low!

MY FATHER WAS A FARMER

TUNE: *The Weaver and his Shuttle*

1

My father was a farmer upon the Carrick border, O,
And carefully he bred me in decency and order, O.
He bade me act a manly part, though I had ne'er a
    farthing, O,
For without an honest, manly heart no man was
    worth regarding, O.

2

Then out into the world my course I did determine, O:
Tho' to be rich was not my wish, yet to be great was
    charming, O.
My talents they were not the worst, nor yet my
    education, O—
Resolv'd was I least least to try to mend my situation, O.

3

In many a way and vain essay I courted Fortune's
favour, O:
Some cause unseen still slept between to frustrate
each endeavour, O.
Sometimes by foes I was o'erpower'd, sometimes by
friends forsaken, O,
And when my hope was at the top, I still was worst
mistaken, O.

4

Then sore harass'd, and tir'd at last with Fortune's vain
delusion, O,
I dropt my schemes like idle dreams, and came to this
conclusion, O:—
The past was bad, and the future hid; its good or ill
untrièd, O,
But the present hour was in my pow'r, and so I would
enjoy it, O.

5

No help, nor hope, nor view had I, nor person to
befriend me, O;
So I must toil, and sweat, and broil, and labour to
sustain me, O!
To plough and sow, to reap and mow, my father bred
me early, O:
For one, he said, to labour bred was a match for
Fortune fairly, O.

6

Thus all obscure, unknown, and poor, thro' life I'm
doom'd to wander, O,
Till down my weary bones I lay in everlasting slumber,
O.
No view nor care, but shun whate'er might breed me
pain or sorrow, O,
I live to-day as well's I may, regardless of to-morrow,
O!

7

But, cheerful still, I am as well as a monarch in a
    palace, O,
Tho' Fortune's frown still hunts me down, with all
    her wonted malice, O:
I make indeed my daily bread, but ne'er can make
    it farther, O,
But, as daily bread is all I need, I do not much regard
    her, O.

8

When sometimes by my labour I earn a little money,
    O,
Some unforseen misfortune comes gen'rally upon me,
    O:
Mischance, mistake, or by neglect, or my good-
    natur'd folly, O—
But, come what will, I've sworn it still, I'll ne'er be
    melancholy, O.

9

All you who follow wealth and power with unremitting
    ardour, O,
The more in this you look for bliss, you leave your
    view the farther, O.
Had you the wealth Potosi boasts, or nations to adore
    you, O,
A cheerful, honest-hearted clown I will prefer before
    you, O!

O, LEAVE NOVÉLS

TUNE: *Donald Blue*

I

O, leave novéls, ye Mauchline belles—
    Ye're safer at your spinning-wheel!
Such witching books are baited hooks
    For rakish rooks like Rob Mossgiel.

2

Your fine *Tom Jones* and *Grandisons*
　They make your youthful fancies reel!
They heat your brains, and fire your veins,
　And then you're prey for Rob Mossgiel.

3

Beware a tongue that's smoothly hung,
　A heart that warmly seems to feel!
That feeling heart but acts a part—
　'Tis rakish art in Rob Mossgiel.

4

The frank address, the soft caress
　Are worse than poisoned darts of steel:
The frank address and politesse
　Are all finesse in Rob Mossgiel.

THE MAUCHLINE LADY

TUNE: *I had a horse, and I had nae mair*

I

When first I came to Stewart Kyle,
　My mind it was na steady:
Where'er I gaed, where'er I rade,   went; rode
　A mistress still I had ay.

2

But when I came roun' by Mauchline toun,
　Not dreadin anybody,
My heart was caught, before I thought,
　And by a Mauchline lady.

ONE NIGHT AS I DID WANDER

TUNE: *John Anderson my jo*

One night as I did wander,
  When corn begins to shoot,
I sat me down to ponder
  Upon an auld tree-root:
Auld Ayr ran by before me,
    And bicker'd to the seas;
A cushat crooded o'er me,
  That echoed through the trees.

past
hastened
cooed

THERE WAS A LAD

TUNE: *Dainty Davie*

CHORUS

roystering

Robin was a rovin boy,
  Rantin, rovin, rantin, rovin,
Robin was a rovin boy,
  Rantin, rovin Robin!

I

what

There was a lad was born in Kyle,
But whatna day o' whatna style,
I doubt it's hardly worth the while
  To be sae nice wi' Robin.

2

one

January wind

Our monarch's hindmost year but ane
Was five-and-twenty days begun,
'Twas than a blast o' Janwar' win'
  Blew hansel in on Robin.

3

glanced; palm
Quoth she
thumping; dolt

The gossip keekit in his loof,
Quo' scho:—'Wha lives will see the proof,
This waly boy will be nae coof:
  I think we'll ca' him Robin.

4

'He'll hae misfortunes great an' sma',
But ay a heart aboon them a'.　　　　　　*above*
He'll be a credit till us a':　　　　　　*to*
　　We'll a' be proud o' Robin!

5

'But sure as three times three mak nine,
I see by ilka score and line,　　　　　　*every*
This chap will dearly like our kin',　　　*kind*
　　So leeze me on thee, Robin!　　　　*Commend me to*

6

'Guid faith,' quo' scho, 'I doubt you gar　*make*
The bonie lasses lie aspar;　　　　　　　*aspread*
But twenty fauts ye may hae war—　　　*faults; worse*
　　So blessins on thee, Robin!'

WILL YE GO TO THE INDIES, MY MARY

TUNE: *Ewe-bughts Marion*

1

Will ye go to the Indies, my Mary,
　　And leave auld Scotia's shore?
Will ye go to the Indies, my Mary,
　　Across th' Atlantic roar?

2

O, sweet grows the lime and the orange,
　　And the apple on the pine;
But a' the charms o' the Indies
　　Can never equal thine.

3

I hae sworn by the Heavens to my Mary,
　I hae sworn by the Heavens to be true,
And sae may the Heavens forget me,
　　When I forget my vow!

4

O, plight me your faith, my Mary,
　And plight me your lily-white hand!
O, plight me your faith, my Mary,
　Before I leave Scotia's strand!

5

We hae plighted our troth, my Mary,
　In mutual affection to join;
And curst be the cause that shall part us!
　The hour and the moment o' time!

HER FLOWING LOCKS

TUNE: *(Unknown)*

1

　　　　Her flowing locks, the raven's wing,
hang　　　Adown her neckand bosom hing.
　　　　How sweet unto that breast to cling,
　　　　　And round that neck entwine her!

2

　　　　Her lips are roses wat wi' dew—
wet　　　O, what a feast, her bonie mou!
　　　　Her cheeks a mair celestial hue,
　　　　　A crimson still diviner!

THE LASS O' BALLOCHMYLE

TUNE: *Ettrick Banks*

1

　　　　'Twas even: the dewy fields were green,
　　　　　On every blade the pearls hang,
hung　　The zephyr wanton'd round the bean,
　　　　　And bore its fragrant sweets alang,
　　　　　In ev'ry glen the mavis sang,
　　　　All Nature list'ning seem'd the while,
　　　　　Except where greenwood echoes rang
heights　Amang the braes o' Ballochmyle.

2

With careless step I onward stray'd,
  My heart rejoic'd in Nature's joy,
When, musing in a lonely glade,
  A maiden fair I chanc'd to spy.
  Her look was like the Morning's eye,
Her air like Nature's vernal smile.
  Perfection whisper'd, passing by:—
'Behold the lass o' Ballochmyle!'

3

Fair is the morn in flowery May,
  And sweet is night in autumn mild,
When roving thro' the garden gay,
  Or wand'ring in the lonely wild;
  But woman, Nature's darling child—
There all her charms she does compile!
  Even there her other works are foil'd
By the bonie lass o' Ballochmyle.

4

O, had she been a country maid,
  And I the happy country swain,
Tho' shelter'd in the lowest shed
  That ever rose on Scotia's plain,
  Thro' weary winter's wind and rain
With joy, with rapture, I would toil,
  And nightly to my bosom strain
The bonie lass o' Ballochmyle!

5

Then Pride might climb the slipp'ry steep,
  Where fame and honours lofty shine,
And thirst of gold might tempt the deep,
  Or downward seek the Indian mine!
  Give me the cot below the pine,
To tend the flocks or till the soil,
  And ev'ry day have joys divine
With the bonie lass o' Ballochmyle.

THE NIGHT WAS STILL

TUNE: *(Unknown)*

1

The night was still, and o'er the hill
   The moon shone on the castle wa',
The mavis sang, while dew-drops hang
   Around her on the castle wa';

hung

2

Sae merrily they danc'd the ring
   Frae eenin' till the cock did craw,
And ay the o'erword o' the spring
   Was:—'Irvine's bairns are bonie a'!'

evening; crow
refrain; tune

MASONIC SONG

TUNE: *Over the water to Charlie*

1

Ye sons of old Killie, assembled by Willie
   To follow the noble vocation,
Your thrifty old mother has scarce such another
   To sit in that honorèd station!
I've little to say, but only to pray
   (As praying's the *ton* of your fashion).
A prayer from the Muse you well may excuse
   ('Tis seldom her favourite passion):—

2

'Ye Powers who preside o'er the wind and the tide,
   Who markèd each element's border,
Who formèd this frame with beneficent aim,
   Whose sovereign statute is order,
Within this dear mansion may wayward Contention
   Or witherèd Envy ne'er enter!
May Secrecy round be the mystical bound,
   And brotherly Love by the centre!'

THE BONIE MOOR-HEN

TUNE: *The Tailor's March*

CHORUS

I rede you, beware at the hunting, young men!   advise
I rede you, beware at the hunting, young men!
Take some on the wing, and some as they spring,
But cannily steal on a bonie moor-hen.   cautiously

1

The heather was blooming, the meadows were mawn,   mown
Our lads gaed a-hunting ae day at the dawn,   went; one
O'er moors and o'er mosses and monie a glen:
At length they discovered a bonie moor-hen.

2

Sweet bruohing the dew fiom the brown heather bells,
Her colours betray'd her on yon mossy fells!
Her plumage outlustred the pride o' the spring,
And O, as she wanton'd sae gay on the wing.

3

Auld Phœbus himsel', as he peep'd o'er the hill,
In spite at her plumage he tryèd his skill:
He level'd his rays where she bask'd on the brae—   height
His rays were outshone, and mark'd where she lay!

4

They hunted the valley, they hunted the hill,
The best of our lads wi' the best o' their skill;
But still as the fairest she sat in their sight,
Then, whirr! she was over, a mile at a flight.

5

But by cam a retret ohon and alas!   reaver
A slee cunning loun wi' a firelock o' brass.
The brass sae did glitter, it dazzled her eyes,
And now in his budget he boats o' the prize.

HERE'S A BOTTLE

There's nane that's blest of human kind
But the cheerful and the gay, man.

TUNE: *(Unknown)*

1

Here's a bottle and an honest friend!
    What wad ye wish for mair, man?
more Wha kens, before his life may end,
    What his share may be o' care, man?

2

Then catch the moments as they fly,
    And use them as ye ought, man!
Believe me, Happiness is shy,
    And comes not ay when sought, man!

THE BONIE LASS OF ALBANIE

TUNE: *Mary's Dream*

1

sad; extremely My heart is wae, and unco wae,
    To think upon the raging sea,
That roars between her gardens green
    An' the bonie lass of Albanie.

2

This noble maid's of royal blood,
    That rulèd Albion's kingdoms three;
But O, alas for her bonie face!
    They hae wranged the lass of Albanie.

3

In the rolling tide of spreading Clyde
    There sits an isle of high degree,
And a town of fame, whose princely name
    Should grace the lass of Albanie.

4

But there is a youth, a witless youth,
   That fills the place where she should be;
We'll send him o'er to his native shore,
   And bring our ain sweet Albanie!

5

Alas the day, and woe the day!
   A false usurper wan the gree,   *gained the prize*
Who now commands the towers and lands,
   The royal right of Albanie.

6

We'll daily pray, we'll nightly pray,
   On bended knees most fervently,
That the time may come, with pipe and drum
   We'll welcome hame fair Albanie.

AMANG THE TREES

TUNE: *The king o' France he rade a race*

1

Amang the trees, where humming bees
   At buds and flowers were hinging, O,   *hanging*
Auld Caledon drew out her drone,
   And to her pipe was singing, O.
'Twas Pibroch, Sang, Strathspeys and Reels—
   She dirl'd them aff fu' clearly, O,   *rang*
When there cam' a yell o' foreign squeels,
   That dang her tapsalteerie, O!   *knocked; head over heels*

2

Their capon craws an' queer 'ha, ha's,'
   They made our lugs grow ecric, O.   *ears; frightened*
The hungry bike did scrape and fyke,   *swarm; smake ado*
   Till we were wae and weary, O.   *disgusted*
But a royal ghaist, wha ance was cas'd   *ghost*
   A prisoner aughteen year awa,   *eighteen*
He fir'd a Fiddler in the North,
   That dang them tapsalteerie, O!

THE CHEVALIER'S LAMENT

TUNE: *Captain O'Kane*

I

The small birds rejoice in the green leaves returning,
　The murmuring streamlet winds clear thro' the vale,
The primroses blow in the dews of the morning,
　And wild scatter'd cowslips bedeck the green dale:
　　But what can give pleasure, or what can seem fair,
　　When the lingering moments are number'd by care?
　　　No flow'rs gaily springing,
　　　Nor birds sweetly singing
　Can soothe the sad bosom of joyless despair!

2

The deed that I dar'd, could it merit their malice,
　A king and a father to place on his throne?
His right are these hills, and his right are those valleys,
　Where the wild beasts find shelter, tho' I can find none!
　　But 'tis not my suff'rings thus wretched, forlorn—
　　My brave gallant friends, 'tis your ruin I mourn!
　　　Your faith prov'd so loyal
　　　In hot bloody trial,
　Alas! can I make it no better return?

YESTREEN I HAD A PINT O' WINE

Last night

TUNE: *Banks of Banna*

I

Yestreen I had a pint o' wine,
　　A place where body saw na;
Yestreen lay on this breast o' mine
　　The gowden locks of Anna.

nobody saw

2

The hungry Jew in wilderness
　　Rejoicing o'er his manna
Was naething to my hiney bliss
　　Upon the lips of Anna.

honey

3

Ye monarchs take the East and West
    Frae Indus to Savannah:
Gie me within my straining grasp   Give
    The melting form of Anna!

4

There I'll despise Imperial charms,
    An Empress or Sultana,
While dying raptures in her arms
    I give and take wi' Anna!

5

Awa, thou flaunting God of Day!
    Awa, thou pale Diana!
Ilk Star, gae hide thy twinkling ray,   Each; go
    When I'm to meet my Anna!

6

Come, in thy raven plumage, Night
    (Sun, Moon, and Stars, with drawn a'),
And bring an Angel-pen to write
    My transports with my Anna!

POSTSCRIPT

1

The Kirk an' State may join, and tell
    To do sic things I maunna: such; mustn't
The Kirk an' State may gae to Hell,
    And I'll gae to my Anna.

2

She is the sunshine o' my e'e,
    To live but her I canna: without
Had I on earth but wishes three,
    The first should be my Anna.

SWEET ARE THE BANKS

TUNE: *Cambdelmore*

1

Sweet are the banks, the banks o' Doon,
    The spreading flowers are fair,
And everything is blythe and glad,
    But I am fu' o' care.
Thou'll break my heart, thou bonie bird,
    That sings upon the bough!
Thou minds me o' the happy days
    When my fause Luve was true.
Thou'll break my heart, thou bonie bird,
    That sings beside thy mate,
For sae I sat, and sae I sang,
    And wist na o' my fate!

reminds — *Thou minds me*

2

Aft hae I rov'd by bonie Doon,
    To see the woodbine twine,
And ilka bird sang o' its luve,
    And sae did I o' mine.
Wi' lightsome heart I pu'd a rose
    Upon its thorny tree,
But my fause luver staw my rose,
    And left the thorn wi' me.
Wi' lightsome heart I pu'd a rose
    Upon a morn in June,
And sae I flourish'd on the morn,
    And sae was pu'd or noon.

each — *ilka*
plucked — *pu'd*
stole — *staw*
before — *or*

YE FLOWERY BANKS

TUNE: *Cambdelmore*

1

Ye flowery banks o' bonie Doon,
    How can ye blume sae fair?
How can ye chant, ye little birds,
    And I sae fu' o' care?

2

Thou'll break my heart, thou bonie bird,
    That sings upon the bough:
Thou minds me o' the happy days   reminds
    When my fause Luve was true!

3

Thou'll break my heart, thou bonie bird,
    That sings beside thy mate:
For sae I sat, and sae I sang,
    And wist na o' my fate!

4

Aft hae I rov'd by bonie Doon
    To see the woodbine twine,
And ilka bird sang o' its luve,   each
    And sae did I o' mine.

5

Wi' lightsome heart I pu'd a rose
    Frae aff its thorny tree,   From off
An my fause luver staw my rose,   stole
    But left the thorn wi' me.

CALEDONIA

TUNE: *Caledonian Hunt's Delight*

1

There was on a time, but old Time was then young,
    That brave Caledonia, the chief of her line,
From some of your northern deities sprung
    (Who knows not that brave Caledonia's divine?).
From Tweed to the Orcades was her domain,
    To hunt, or to pasture, or do what she would.
Her heav'nly relations there fixed her reign,
    And pledged her their godheads to warrant it good.

2

A lambkin in peace but a lion in war,
  The pride of her kindred the heroine grew.
Her grandsire, old Odin, triumphantly swore:—
  'Whoe'er shall provoke thee, th' encounter shall rue!'
With tillage or pasture at times she would sport,
  To feed her fair flocks by her green rustling corn;
But chiefly the woods were her fav'rite resort,
  Her darling amusement the hounds and the horn.

3

Long quiet she reign'd, till thitherward steers
  A flight of bold eagles from Adria's strand.
Repeated, successive, for many long years,
  They darken'd the air, and they plunder'd the land.
Their pounces were murder, and horror their cry;
  They'd conquer'd and ravag'd a world beside.
She took to her hills, and her arrows let fly—
  The daring invaders, they fled or they died!

4

The Camelon savage disturb'd her repose,
  With tumult, disquiet, rebellion, and strife.
Provok'd beyond bearing, at last she arose,
  And robbed him at once of his hopes and his life.
The Anglian Lion, the terror of France,
  Oft, prowling, ensanguin'd the Tweed's silver flood,
But, taught by the bright Caledonian lance,
  He learnèd to fear in his own native wood.

5

The fell Harpy-Raven took wing from the north,
  The scourge of the seas, and the dread of the shore;
The wild Scandinavian Boar issued forth
  To wanton in carnage and wallow in gore;
O'er countries and kingdoms their fury prevail'd,
  No arts could appease them, no arms could repel;
But brave Caledonia in vain they assail'd,
  As Largs well can witness, and Loncartie tell.

6

Thus bold, independent, unconquer'd, and free,
    Her bright course of glory for ever shall run,
For brave Caledonia immortal must be,
    I'll prove it from Euclid as clear as the sun:—
Rectangle-triangle, the figure we'll chuse;
    The upright is Chance, and old Time is the base,
But brave Caledonia's the hypothenuse;
        Then, *ergo*, she'll match them, and match them
always!

YOU'RE WELCOME, WILLIE STEWART

TUNE: *Ye're welcome, Charlie Stewart*

CHORUS

You're welcome, Willie Stewart!
    You're welcome, Willie Stewart!
There's ne'er a flower that blooms in May,
    That's half sae welcome's thou art!

1

Come, bumpers high! express your joy!
    The bowl we maun renew it—   must
The tappet hen, gae bring her ben,   go
    To welcome Willie Stewart!

2

May foes be strong, and friends be slack!
    Ilk action, may he rue it!   Each
May woman on him turn her back,
    That wrangs thee, Willie Stewart!   wrongs

WHEN FIRST I SAW

TUNE: *Maggy Lauder*

CHORUS

She's aye, aye sae blithe, sae gay,
　She's aye sae blithe and cheerie,
She's aye sae bonie, blithe and gay,
　O, gin I were her dearie!

1

When first I saw fair Jeanie's face,
　I couldna tell what ail'd me:
My heart went fluttering pit-a-pat,
　My een they almost fail'd me.
She's aye sae neat, sae trim, sae tight,
　All grace does round her hover!
Ae look depriv'd me o' my heart,
　And I became her lover.

2

Had I Dundas's whole estate,
　Or Hopetoun's wealth to shine in;
Did warlike laurels crown my brow,
　Or humbler bays entwining;
I'd lay them a' at Jeanie's feet,
　Could I but hope to move her,
And, prouder than a belted knight,
　I'd be my Jeanie's lover.

3

But sair I fear some happier swain,
　Has gain'd sweet Jeanie's favour,
If so, my every bliss be hers,
　Though I maun never have her!
But gang she east, or gang she west,
　'Twixt Forth and Tweed all over,
While men have eyes, or ears, or taste,
　She'll always find a lover.

must

go

BEHOLD THE HOUR

First Set

TUNE: *Oran gaoil*

1

Behold the hour, the boat, arrive!
  My dearest Nancy, O, farewell!
Sever'd the frae thee, can I survive,
  Frae thee whom I hae lov'd sae well?

2

Endless and deep shall be my grief,
  Nae ray of confort shall I see,
But this most precious, dear belief,
  That thou wilt still remember me.

3

Along the solitary shore,
  Where flitting sea-fowl round me cry,
Across the rolling, dashing roar,
  I'll westward turn my wistful eye.

4

'Happy thou Indian grove,' I'll say,
  'Where now my Nancy's path shall be!
While thro' your sweets she holds her way,
  O, tell me, does she muse on me?'

HERE'S A HEALTH TO THEM THAT'S AWA

TUNE: *(As Title)*

1

Here's a health to them that's awa,
    Here's a health to them that's awa!
And wha winna wish guid luck to our cause,
    May never guid luck be their fa'!
It's guid to be merry and wise,
    It's guid to be honest and true,
It's guid to support Caledonia's cause
    And bide by the buff and the blue.

will not
lot

stand

2

Here's a health to them that's awa,
    Here's a health to them that's awa!
Here's a health to Charlie, the chief o' the clan,
    Altho' that his band be sma'!
May Liberty meet wi' success,
    May Prudence protect her frae evil!
May tyrants and Tyranny tine i' the mist
    And wander their way to the Devil!

be lost

3

Here's a health to them that's awa,
    Here's a health to them that's awa!
Here's a health to Tammie, the Norlan' laddie,
    That lives at the lug o' the Law!
Here's freedom to them that wad read,
    Here's freedom to them that would write!
There's nane ever fear'd that the truth should be heard
    But they whom the truth would indite!

indict

4

Here's a health to them that's awa,
    An' here's to them that's awa!
  Here's to Maitland and Wycombe! Let wha does na
like 'em
    Be built in a hole in the wa'!
Here's timmer that's red at the heart,   timber
    Here's fruit that is sound at the core,
And may he that wad turn the buff and blue coat
    But turn'd to the back o' the door!

5

Here's a health to them that's awa,
    Here's a health to them that's awa!
Here's Chieftain M'Leod, a chieftain worth gowd,   gold
    Tho' bred amang mountains o' snaw!
Here's friends on baith sides o' the Firth,
    And friends on baith sides o' the Tweed,
And wha wad betray old Albion's right,
    May they never cat of her bread!

AH, CHLORIS

TUNE: *Major Graham*

1

Ah, Chloris, since it may not be
    That thou of love wilt hear,
If from the lover thou maun flee,   must
    Yet let the friend be dear!

2

Altho' I love my Chloris mair
    Than ever tongue could tell,
My passion I will ne'er declare—
    I'll say, I wish thee well.

3

Tho' a' my daily care thou art,
    And a' my nightly dream,
I'll hide the struggle in my heart,
    And say it is esteem.

PRETTY PEG

TUNE: *(Unknown)*

1

went; yonder
road-

As I gaed up by yon gate-end,
  When day was waxin weary,
Wha did I meet come down the street
  But pretty Peg, my dearie?

2

Her air so sweet, her shape complete,
  Wi' nae proportion wanting—
The Queen of Love could never move
  Wi' motion mair enchanting!

3

With linkèd hands we took the sands
  Down by yon winding river;
And O! that hour, and shady bow'r,
  Can I forget it? Never!

MEG O' THE MILL

Second Set

TUNE: *O bonie lass, will ye lie in a barrack?*

1

got

dolt; hoard of
money

O, ken ye what Meg o' the mill has gotten?
An' ken ye what Meg o' the mill has gotten?
She's gotten a coof wi' a claute o' siller,
And broken the heart o' the barley miller!

2

gallows-worthy;
dwarf

The miller was strappin, the miller was ruddy,
A heart like a lord, and a hue like a lady.
The laird was a widdifu', bleerit knurl—
She's left the guid fellow, and taen the churl!

3

The miller, he hecht her a heart leal and loving.   offered
The laird did address her wi' matter more moving:
A fine pacing-horse wi' a clear, chainèd bridle,   bright
A whip by her side, and a bonie side saddle!

4

O, wae on the siller—it is sae prevailing!   woe; potent
And wae on the love that is fixed on a mailen!   farm
A tocher's nae word in a true lover's parl,   dowry; speech
But gie me my love and a fig for the warl!   world

PHILLIS THE FAIR

TUNE: *Aileen a roon*

1

While larks with little wing
    Fann'd the pure air,
Viewing the breathing Spring,
    Forth I did fare.
Gay, the sun's golden eye
Peep'd o'er the mountains high;
'Such thy bloom, did I cry—
        'Phillis the fair!'

2

In each bird's careless song,
    Glad, I did share;
While yon wild flowers among,
    Chance led me there.
Sweet to the opening day,
Rosebuds bent the dewy spray;
'Such thy bloom,' did I say—
        'Phillis the fair!'

3

Down in a shady walk
  Doves cooing were;
I mark'd the cruel hawk
  Caught in a snare.
So kind may Fortune be!
Such make his destiny,
He who would injure thee,
  Phillis the fair!

O SAW YE MY DEAR, MY PHILLY

TUNE: *When she cam ben she bobbit*

1

O, saw ye my Dear, my Philly?
O, saw ye my Dear, my Philly?
She's down i' the grove, she's wi' a new love,
will not   She winna come hame to her Willy.

2

What says she my Dear, my Philly?
What says she my Dear, my Philly?
know   She lets thee to wit she has thee forgot,
  And for ever disowns thee, her Willy.

3

O, had I ne'er seen thee, my Philly!
O, had I ne'er seen thee, my Philly!
As light as the air, and fause as thou's fair,
  Thou's broken the the heart o' thy Willy.

'TWAS NA HER BONIE BLUE E'E

TUNE: *Laddie, lie near me*

1

'Twas na her bonie blue e'e was my ruin:
Fair tho' she be, that was ne'er my undoin.
'Twas the dear smile when naebody did mind us.
stolen   'Twas the bewitching, sweet, stoun glance o' kindness!

2

Sair do I fear that to hope is denied me,   Sore
Sair do I fear that despair maun abide me;   must
But tho' fell Fortune should fate us to sever,
Queen shall she be in my bosom for ever.

3

Chloris, I'm thine wi' a passion sincerest,
And thou hast plighted me love o' the dearest,
And thou'rt the angel that never can alter—
Sooner the sun in his motion would falter!

WHY, WHY TELL THY LOVER

TUNE: *Caledonian Hunt's Delight*

1

Why, why tell thy lover
Bliss he never must enjoy?
Why, why undeceive him.
And give all his hopes the lie?

2

O, why, while Fancy, raptur'd, slumbers,
'Chloris, Chloris,' all the theme,
Why, why wouldst thou, cruel,
Wake thy lover from his dream?

THE PRIMROSE

TUNE: *Todlin Hame*

1

Dost ask me, why I send thee here
The firstling of the infant year:
This lovely native of the vale,
That hangs so pensive and so pale?

2

Look on its bending stalk, so weak,
That, each way yielding, doth not break,
And see how aptly it reveals
The doubts and fears a lover feels.

3

Look on its leaves of yellow hue
Bepearl'd thus with morning dew,
And these will whisper in thine ears:—
'The sweets of loves are wash'd with tears.'

O, WERT THOU IN THE CAULD BLAST

TUNE: *Lenox love to Blantyre*

1

O, wert thou in the cauld blast
  On yonder lea, on yonder lea,
quarter   My plaidie to the angry airt,
  I'd shelter thee, I'd shelter thee.
Or did Misfortune's bitter storms
  Around thee blaw, around thee blaw,
shelter   Thy bield should be my bosom,
  To share it a', to share it a'.

2

Or were I in the wildest waste,
  Sae black and bare, sae black and bare,
The desert were a Paradise,
  If thou wert there, if thou wert there.
Or were I monarch of the globe,
  Wi' thee to reign, wi' thee to reign,
The brightest jewel in my crown
  Wad be my queen, wad be my queen.

YOUR FRIENDSHIP

TUNE: *Banks of Spey*

1

Your friendship much can make me blest—
  O, why that bliss destroy?
Why urge the only, one request
  You know I will deny?

2

Your thought, if Love must harbour there,
  Conceal it in that thought,
Nor cause me from by bosom tear
  The very friend I sought.

FOR THEE IS LAUGHING NATURE

TUNE: *Scots Queen*

1

For thee is laughing Nature gay,
For thee she pours the vernal day:
For me in vain is Nature drest,
While Joy's a stranger to my breast.

NO COLD APPROACH

TUNE: *Ianthy the lovely*

No cold approach, no alter'd mien,
  Just what would make suspicion start,
No pause the dire extremes between:
  He made me blest—and broke my heart.

LET LOOVE SPARKLE

TUNE: *Jockey fou and Jenny fain*

Ithers seek they kenna what,
Features, carriage and a' that;
Gie me loove in her I court—
Loove to loove maks a' the sport.

Let loove sparkle in her e'e,
Let her lo'e nae man but me:
dower   That's the tocher guid I prize,
There the luver's treasure lies.

brook

AS DOWN THE BURN

TUNE: *Down the burn, Davie*

As down the burn they took their way,
    And thro the flowery dale;
His cheek to hers he aft did lay,
    And love was ay the tale,
With:—'Mary, when shall we return,
such   Sic pleasure to renew?'
Quoth Mary:—'Love, I like the burn,
    And ay shall follow you.'

SKETCH

I

HAIL, Poesie! thou nymph reserv'd!
In chase o' thee, what crowds hae swerv'd
Frae Common Sense, or sunk ennerv'd
nonsense   'Mang heaps o' clavers;
And Och! o'er aft thy joes hae starv'd
sweethearts   'Mid a' thy favors!

2

Say, Lassie, why thy train amang,
While loud the trump's heroic clang,
And Sock and buskin skelp alang   spank
            To death or marriage;
Scarce ane has tried the Shepherd-sang   one
            But wi' miscarriage?

3

In Homer's craft Jock Milton thrives;
Esch'ylus' pen Will Shakespeare drives;
Wee Pope, the knurlin, 'till him rives   dwarf; tugs
            Horatian fame;
In thy sweet sang, Barbauld, survives
            E'en Sappho's flame.

4

But thee, Theocritus, wha matches?
They're no' Herd's ballats, Maro's catches;
Squire Pope but busks his skinklin patches   small
            O' Heathen tatters:
I pass by hunders, nameless wretches,   hundreds
            That ape their betters.

5

In this braw age o' wit and lear,   fine; learning
Will nane the Shepherd's whistle mair
Blaw sweetly in its native air
            And rural grace;
And wi' the far-fam'd Grecian share
            A rival place?

6

Yes! there is ane:—a Scottish callan!   youth
There's ane: come forrit, honest Alan!   forward
Thou need na jouk behint the hallan,   cower; porch
            A chiel sae clever,   fellow
The teeth o' Time may gnaw Tantallan,
            But thou's for ever.

7

perfection

Thou paints auld Nature to the nines,
In thy sweet Caledonian lines;

golden

Nae gowden stream thro' myrtles twines
        Where Philomel,
While midnight gales rustle clustering vines,
          Her griefs will tell!

8

Thy rural loves are Nature's sel';

floods

Nae bombast spates o' nonsense swell;

smart

Nae snap conceits, but that sweet spell
         O' witchin loove,
That charm that can the strongest quell,
          The sternest move.

9

daisied; brooklet

In gowany glens thy burnie stray

clothes

Where bonie lasses bleach their claes;

woods; slopes

Or trots by hazelly shaws and braes
         Wi' hawthorns gray,
Where blackbirds join the shepherd's lays
         At close o' day.

FOR THE AUTHOR'S FATHER

O ye whose cheek the tear of pity stains,
    Draw near with pious rev'rence, and attend!
Here lie the loving husband's dear remains,
    The tender father, and the gen'rous friend.

The pitying heart that felt for human woe,
    The dauntless heart that fear'd no human pride,
The friend of man—to vice alone a foe;
    For 'ev'n his failings lean'd to virtue's side'.

A BARD'S EPITAPH

1

Is there a whim-inspirèd fool,
Owre fast for thought, owre hot for rule,   *too*
Owre blate to seek, owre proud to snool?—   *modest; cringe*
      Let him draw near;
And owre this grassy heap sing dool,   *woe*
      And drap a tear.

2

Is there a Bard of rusic song,
Who, noteless, steals the crowds among,
That weekly this aréa throng?—
      O, pass not by!
But with a frater-feeling strong,
      Here, heave a sigh.

3

Is there a man, whose judgment clear
Can others teach the course to steer,
Yet runs, himself, life's mad career
      Wild as the wave?—
Here pause—and, thro' the starting tear,
      Survey this grave.

4

The poor inhabitant below
Was quick to learn and wise to know,
And keenly felt the friendly glow
      And softer flame;
But thoughtless follies laid him low,
      And stain'd his name.

5

Reader, attend! whether thy soul
Soars Fancy's flights beyond the pole,
Or darkling grubs this earthly hole
      In low pursuit;
Know, prudent, cautious, self-control
      Is wisdom's root.

ON THE AUTHOR

He who of Rankine sang, lies stiff and deid,
And a green, grassy hillock hides his heid:
Alas! alas! a devilish change indeed!

GLOSSARY

A, *sometimes used for he, she, or it.*
A', *all; every one, with the sense of each.*
ABEIGH, *at a distance, aloof.*
ABLINS, v. AIBLINS.
ABOON, *above, overhead, upstairs.*
ABREAD, *abroad.*
ABREED, *in breadth.*
ADLE, *cow lant, putrid water.*
ADO, *to do.*
ADVISEMENT, *advice, counsel.*
AE, *one.*
AFF, *off.*
AFF-HAND, *at once.*
AFF-LOOF, *off-hand, extempore.*
A-FIEL *a-field.*
AFORE, *before.*
AFT, *oft.*
AFTEN, *often.*
AGLEY, *askew.*
AHIN, *behind.*
AIBLINS, *perhaps, possibly.*
AIK, AIKEN, *oak, oaken.*
AIL, *to be ill, to complain.*
AILSA CRAIG, *an island rock in the Firth of Clyde.*
AIN, *own.*
AIR, *early.*
AIRLE-PENNY, AIRLES *earnest-money.*
AIRN, AIRNS, *iron, fetters.*
AIRT, *to direct; a direction, point of the compass.*
AITH, *oath.*
AITS, *oats.*
AIVER *an old horse.*
AIZLE, *a cinder.*
AJEE, *ajar; twisted; sulky, cross.*
ALAKE *alas.*
ALANE, *alone.*
ALANG, *along.*

AMAIST, *almost.*
AMANG, *among.*
AN, *if.*
AN', *and.*
ANCE, *once.*
ANDRO, *Andrew.*
ANE one, *an.*
ANEATH, *beneath.*
ANES, *ones.*
ANEUGH, ANEUCH, *enough.*
ANITHER *another.*
AQUA-FONTIS, *spring-water.*
AQUA-VITAE, *whisky.*
ARLE v. AIRLE-PENNY.
A'S, *all is.*
ASE, *ashes.*
ASKLENT, *awry, off the plumb.*
ASPAR, *spread out.*
A'THEGITHER, *altogether.*
ATHORT, ATHWORT, *athwart, across, over.*
ATTOUR, *moreover, beyond, beside.*
ATWEEL, *truly, indeed, assuredly, of course.*
ATWEEN, *between.*
AUGHT, *to own, to possess; possession; eight.*
AUGHTEEN, *eighteen.*
AUGHTLINS, *at all, in any way.*
AULD, *old.*
AULD REEKIE, *Edinburgh.*
AULD SHOON, *old shoes; a discarded lover.*
AULD-WARLD, *old-world.*
AUMOUS, *alms.*
AUMOUS-DISH, *a beggar's collecting dish, the poor-box.*
AVA, *at all.*
AWA, *away.*

AWALD, *folded or doubled up. A sheep is* AWALD *when it is on its back and cannot rise. Applied to a drunken person having fallen.*

AWAUK, *to awake.*

AWE, *owe.*

A-WEE, *a short time.*

AWKART, *awkward.*

AWNIE, *bearded.*

AY, AYE, *always, assent;* "AY, BUT"=*qualified assent.*

AYONT, *beyond, later than, farther.*

BA', *a ball.*

BABIE-CLOUTS, *baby clothes.*

BACKET, *bucket or box.*

BACKIT, *backed.*

BACKLINS-COMIN, *coming back, returning.*

BACK-YETT, *gate at the back.*

BADE, *did bid; endured.*

BAGGIE, *the belly, the stomach.*

BAIG'NETS, *bayonets.*

BAILLIE, *magistrate of a Scots burgh.*

BAINIE, *bony, big-boned.*

BAIRN, *a child.*

BAIRNTIME, *brood, issue.*

BAITH, *both.*

BAKES, *biscuits.*

BALLATS, *ballads.*

BALOO, BALOW *hush! a lullaby.*

BAMBOOZLE, *to trick by mystifying.*

BAN, *to curse.*

BAN' *a bond; an agreement.*

BANE, *bone.*

BANG, *an effort, a blow, a large number.* UNCO BANG, *great or prolonged effort.*

BANG, *to thump.*

BANIE *v.* BAINIE.

BANN'D, *cursed, sworn.*

BANNET, *bonnet.*

BANNOCK, BONNOCK, *a thick cake baked on a flat pan of iron.*

BARDIE, *dim. of bard.*

BAREFIT, *barefoot.*

BARKET, *barked.*

BARLEY-BREE, *malt liquor, whisky or ale.*

BARM, *yeast.*

BARMIE, *yeasty.*

BARN-YARD, *stackyard.*

BARTIE, *the Devil.*

BASHING, *abashing.*

BASIN, *a dish for holding oatmeal.*

BATCH, *a number, a company.*

BATTS, *the botts (applied to horses), the colic.*

BAUCKIE-BIRD, *a bat.*

BAUDRONS, *a cat.*

BAUK, *a cross-beam.*

BAUK, *v.* BAWK.

BAUK-EN', *beam-end.*

BAULD, *bold.*

BAUMY, *balmy.*

BAWBEE, *a halfpenny.*

BAWDRONS, *v.* BAUDRONS.

BAWK, *a pathway through growing crops.*

BAWSINT, *white-faced.*

BAWTIE, *pet name for a dog.*

BE, BY, *as denoting the cause; let be, let alone.*

BEAR, *barley.*

BEAS', *beast, vermin (*i.e. *lice).*

BEASTIE, *dim. of beast.*

BECK, *a curtsy; to make obeisance.*

BEET, *to kindle, to mend (the fire).*

BEFA', *befall.*

BEHINT, *behind.*

BEILD, *v.* BIELD.

BELANG, *belong.*

BELD, *bald.*

BELLUM, *assault.*

BELLYS, *bellows.*

BELYVE, *by-and-by.*

BEN, *within; the inner room or parlour.*

BENMOST BORE, *the farthest crevice, chink or hole.*

BE-NORTH, *to the northward of.*

BENT, *moorland grass; the open field.*

BE-SOUTH, *to the southward of.*

BEUK, *a book.*

BEYONT, *beyond.*

BICKER, *a beaker, an ale-pot; to flow, to dispute.*

BICKER, *a short run.*

BICKER'D, *flowed, rippled, disputed.*

BICKERIN, *rippling; disputing, wrangling.*

BID, *to ask, to wish, to offer.*

BIDE, *to wait, to stay, to remain.*

BIELD, *a shelter, refuge.*

BIEN, *thriving, comfortable, cosy, snug.*

BIG, *to build; large, swollen.*

BIGGIN, *building.*

BIKE, *v.* BYKE.

BILL, *the bull.*

BILLIE, *fellow, comrade, brother.*

BING, *a heap.*

BIRK, *a birch.*

BIRKEN-SHAW, *a birch-wood.*

BIRKIE, *a smart or conceited person.*

BIRLE, *to drink in company, to carouse.*
   BIRLE THE BAWBEE, *to spend money in social drinking.*

BIRR, *force, vigour.*

BIRRING, *whirring.*

BIRSES, *bristles.*

BIT, *a morsel, a piece; a short time.*

BITCH-FOU, *completely drunk.*

BIZZ, *a flurry.*

BIZZ, *to buzz.*

BIZZARD-GLED, *the buzzard-hawk; a coward.*

BIZZIE, *busy.*

BLACK-BONNET, *the kirk elder.*

BLACK-NEBBIT, *black-beaked.*

BLAE, *blue, the colour of the pollen on the sloe.*

BLASTET, BLASTIT, *blasted.*

BLASTIE, *a blasted (i.e. damned) creature.*

BLATE, *shy, bashful, timid.*

BLATHER, *bladder.*

BLAUD, *a large quantity, a screed.*

BLAUD, *to slap.*

BLAUDIN, *driving, pelting.*

BLAW, *to boast, to exaggerate.*

BLAW, *to blow.*

BLAWING, *blowing.*

BLAWN, *blown.*

BLEER, *to obscure the vision, to deceive.*

BLEERIE, *red about the eyes.*

BLEER'T, BLEERIT, *dimmed, obscured (with weeping).*

BLEEZ'D, *blazed.*

BLEEZE, *a blaze.*

BLEEZIN, *blazing.*

BLELLUM, *a babbler.*

BLETHER, *blethers, nonsense.*

BLETHER, *to talk nonsense.*

BLETHERIN', *talking nonsense.*

BLIN' *blind.*

BLINK, *a glance, an amorous look; a short space of time.*

BLINKERS, *spies, oglers.*

BLINKIN, *blinking, shining.*

BLINKIN, *smirking, leering.*

BLIN'T, *blinded.*

BLITTER, *the common snipe.*

BLUE-BELL, *the harebell, campanula montanis.*

BLUE-GOWN, *the livery of the licensed beggar.*

BLUID, BLUDE, *blood.*

BLUME, *bloom; to bloom.*

BLUNTIE, *having a sheepish look; a stupid or simple person.*

BLYPES, *shreds.*

BLYTH, *cheerful, gay, merry.*

BOBBIT, *to curtsy; up and down motion.*

BOCKED, *vomited.*

BODDLE, *a farthing (properly two pennies Scots, or one-third of an English penny).*

BODE, *a bid, a price offered; to bid.*

BODIE, *a person.*

BODKIN, *tailor's needle.*

BOGGIE, *dim. of bog.*

BOGLE, *a hobgoblin, a spectre.*

BOLE, *a hole or cupboard in the wall.*

BONIE, *beautiful, handsome, pretty, plump; pleasant to see.*

BONNOCK, *v.* BANNOCK.

'BOON, *v.* ABOON.

BOORD, *board, surface.*

BOORD-EN', *board-end.*

BOORTREES, *the shrub—elder.*

BOOST, *behove, must needs.*

BOOT, *payment to the bargain.*

BORE, *a chink, a small hole, an opening.*

BOTCH, *an angry tumour.*

BOUK, BOWK, *bulk; the whole body.*

BOUNTITH, *bounty, reward, bonus.*

BOW-HOUGHED, *bow-thighed.*

BOW-KAIL, *cabbage.*

BOW'T, *bent.*

BRACHENS, *ferns.*

BRACKEN, *the common fern, pteris aquilina.*

BRAE, *a steep bank, the slope of a hill, the broken bank of a river.*

BRAG, *to boast.*

BRAID, *broad.*

BRAID-CLAITH, *broad-cloth.*

BRAIK, *a harrow.*

BRAING'T, *pulled rashly.*

BRAK, *broke, broken.*

BRANKIE, *gaudy, lively, prancing, showy.*

BRANKS, *a (wooden) horse-bridle.*

BRASH, *short illness.*

BRATS, *small pieces, rags.*

BRATS, *small children.*

BRATTLE, *a spurt, a scamper.*

BRATTLE, *noisy onset.*

BRAW, *brave, well-dressed, handsome; very, extremely.*

BRAWLIE, *in good health and cheerful.*

BRAWNIT, *of a mixed red and brown colour, applied to cattle.*

BRAXIES, *sheep that have died.*

BREASTIE, *dim. of breast.*

BREASTIT, *sprang forward.*

BRECHAN, *a horse-collar.*

BRECKAN, *a horse-collar, ferns.*

BREEDIN, *breeding.*

BREEKS, *breeches.*

BREER, *briar.*

BRENT, *smooth, unwrinkled, high.*

BRENT, *brand.*

BRIE, *the brow.*

BRIEF, *writ.*

BRIER, *the briar; to sprout.*

BRIERY, *briary.*

BRIG, *a bridge.*

BRISKET, *breast.*

BRITHER, *brother.*

BROCK, *a badger.*

BROGUE, *a trick.*

BROO, *broth, juice, liquor.*

BROOSES, *wedding races from the church to the home of the bride.*

BROSE, *raw oatmeal mixed with water.*

BROWST, *a brew; the consequence of one's own action.*

BROWSTER WIVES, *ale wives.*

BRUGH, *a burgh, a borough.*

BRULZIE, BRULYIE, *a brawl.*

BRUNSTANE, *brimstone.*

BRUNT, *burned.*

BRUST, *burst.*

BRUYLIE, *a broil, a quarrel.*

BUCKIE, *dim. of buck.*

BUCKLE, *a curl.*

BUCKSKIN, *Virginian.*

BUDGET, *tinker's bag of tools.*

BUFF, *to bang, to thump.*

BUFFET-STOOL, *a low wooden stool set on a frame.*

BUGHT, *a sheepfold.*

BUGHTIN TIME, *the time when cattle are housed for the night.*

BUIRDLY, *stout, stalwart.*

BUM *the buttocks; to hum.*

BUM-CLOCK, *the beetle.*

BUMMLE, *a drone, a useless fellow.*

BUNKER, *a seat.*

BUNTERS, *harlots.*

BURDIES, *dim. of bird or burd.*

BURE, *bore.*

BURN, *a small stream, a rivulet.*

BURNEWIN, *the blacksmith.*

BURNIE, *dim. of burn*

BURR-THISTLE, *spear-thistle.*

BUSK, *to dress, to garb.*

BUSKING, *v.* BUSK.

BUSKIT, *v.* BUSK.

BUSKIT, *adorned, dressed.*

BUSS, *a bush.*

BUSSLE, *bustle.*

BUT, *except, unless, as well as.*

BUT, *the kitchen.*

BUT AND BEN, *the kitchen and parlour; backwards and forwards.*

BY, *relating to, towards, beside, past, aside.*

BYE ATTOUR, *besides, into the bargain.*

BYKE, *a beehive, a swarm, a crowd.*

BYRE, *a cow-house.*

CA', *to call, to knock, to drive.*

CA', *a call, a whistle, a summons.*

CA'D, CA'T, *called.*

CA'D, CA'T, *knocked, driven.*

CADDIE, CADIE, *a servant lad, a varlet.*

CADGER, *a hawker.*

CAFF, *chaff.*

CAIRD, *a tinker.*

CAIRN, *a loose heap of stones.*

CALF-WARD, *grazing plot for calves* (i.e. *churchyard*).

CALLAN, CALLANT, *a stripling.*

CALLER, *fresh, bracing, healthy.*

CALLET, *a drab, a dirty woman, trull.*

CAM, *came, did come.*

CAN, *a tin vessel, a dish of liquor.*

CANKERS, *to be querulous, to grumble.*

CANKERT, *bad-tempered, soured.*

CANKRIE, *crabbed.*

CANNA, *cannot.*

CANNIE, CANNY, *pleasant, cautious, knowing, skilful.*

CANNIEST, *quietest.*

CANNILY, CANNILIE, *softly, gently.*

CANTIE, CANTY, *cheerful, merry.*

CANTRAIP, *magic.*

CANTS, *merry stories; canters or sprees or merry doings.*

CAP, CAUP, *a small wooden dish with a handle; a quaich.*

CAPE-STANE, *cope-stone.*

CAPON, *a castrated cock.*

CAPON-CRAWS, *crowing like a capon (the capon was taken for an emblem of stupidity).*

CARDIN, *combing (wool, flax, etc.).*

CARE NA BY, *do not care.*

CARL, CARLE, *a churl, a fellow, an old man, a peasant, a clown.*

CARLIE, *dim. of carl.*

CARLIN, CARLINE, *an old wrinkled woman, a shrew.*

CARMAGNOLE, *a violent Jacobin.*

CAR'T NA BY, *cared not at all.*

CARTES, *playing cards.*

CARTIE, *dim. of cart.*

CASTOCKS, *stem and pith of the cabbage or colewort.*

CATCH-THE-PLACK, *the hunt for coin.*

CAUDRON, *a caldron.*

CAUF, *a calf, a silly and ridiculous person.*

CAUK, *chalk.*

CAULD, *a cold, the cold shivers.*

CAUSEY-CLEANERS, *causeway-cleaners.*

CAVIE, *a hen-coop.*

CESS, *to tax; the land-tax.*

CHAMER, CHAUMER, *chamber.*

CHANGE-HOUSE, *tavern.*

CHANTER, *bagpipes, the part of the bagpipes which produces the melody.*

CHAP, *a person, a lover; to rap.*

CHAPMAN, *a pedlar.*

CHAPPIN, *a quart pot; calling (the landlord).*

CHAUMER, *v.* CHAMER.

CHAUP (or CHAP), *a stroke, a blow.*

CHEAP, CHEEP, *to chirp, to peep.*

CHEAR, *cheer, to cheer.*

CHEARFU', *cheerful.*

CHEARLESS, *cheerless.*

CHEARY, *cheery.*

CHEEK-FOR-CHOW, *cheek-by-jowl.*

CHIEL, CHIELD, *a young fellow.*

CHIMLA, *chimney.*

CHITTERING, *shivering.*

CHOW, *v.* CHEEK-FOR-CHOW.

CHOWS, *chews.*

CHUCK, *a hen, a chicken; a dear.*

CHUCKIE, *dim. of chuck, but usually signifies mother-hen, an old dear.*

CHUFFIE, *fat-faced.*

CHUSE, *to choose.*

CIT, *the civet.*

CIT, *a citizen, a merchant.*

CLACHAN, *a small village about a church, a hamlet.*

CLAEDING, *clothing.*

CLAES, *clothes.*

CLAITH, CLAITHING, *cloth, clothing.*

CLAIVERS, *v.* CLAVERS.

CLAMB, *climbed.*

CLANKIE, *a striking noise, a sounding blow.*

CLAP, *the clapper of a mill.*

CLAPPIN, *patting gently.*

CLARK, *clerkly, scholarly.*

CLARK, *a clerk.*

CLARKIT, *clerked, wrote.*

CLARTY, *dirty.*

CLASH, *an idle tale, the story of a day.*

CLASH, *to tattle.*

CLATTER, *noise; disputation.*

CLAUGHT, *clutched.*

CLAUGHTIN, *clutching, grasping.*

CLAUT, *to clutch, to hold, to scrape.*

CLAUTET, *scraped.*

CLAVER, *clover; to talk nonsense.*

CLAVERS, *idle talk.*

CLAW, *to scratch, to thrash.*

CLAY-CAULD, *clay-cold.*

CLAYMORE, *a two-handed sword.*

CLECKIN, *a brood.*

CLEED, *to clothe, to cover.*

CLEG, *gadfly.*

CLEEK, *to seize, to snatch.*

CLEEKIT, *hooked, seized.*

CLEEKS, *cramp in the legs.*

CLINK, *money; to jingle, to rhyme.*

CLINKIN, *a bell-like sound; abrupt motion.*

CLINKUM, CLINKUMBELL, *the beadle, the bellman.*

CLIPS, *shears.*

CLISH-MA-CLAVER, *gossip, tale-telling; nonsense.*

CLOCKIN-TIME, *clucking—(=hatching-) time.*

CLOOT, *a hoof; Auld Clootie, the Devil.*

CLOOTIE, CLOOTS, *hoofie, hoofs (a nickname of the Devil).*

CLOUR, *a bump or swelling after a blow.*

CLOUT, *a patch; to patch, to repair.*

CLOUTIN, *patching, repairing.*

CLOUTS, *ragged clothes.*

CLUDS, *clouds.*

CLUE, *a ball of worsted, cotton, etc.*

CLUNK, *the hollow sound produced by emptying a bottle hastily.*

COATIE, *dim. of coat.*

COBLE, *a broad and flat boat.*

COCK, *the mark (in curling).*

COCKETS, *ornamental head-gear.*

COCKIE, *dim. of cock (applied to an old man).*

COCKS, *fellows, good fellows.*

COD, *a pillow, a cushion.*

COFT, *to buy.*

COG, COGGIE, *a small wooden dish without handles.*

COIL, COILA, *Kyle (one of the ancient districts of Ayrshire).*

COLLIE, *a general, and sometimmes a particular, name for country curs; a* sheep-dog.

COLLIESHANGIE, *a squabble.*

COMPLEENIN, *complaining.*

COOD, *cud.*

COOF, CUIF, *a blockhead, a dolt.*

COOKIN, *cooking.*

COOKIT, *hid.*

COOL'D IN HER LINENS, *laid in her shroud.*

COOR, *to cover, to duck down.*

COOSER, *a courser, a stallion.*

COOST, *to cast, to throw.*

COOT, *the water-hen.*

COOTIE, *rough-legged; a small dish.*

COOTS, *hoofs.*

CORBIES, *ravens, crows.*

CORE, *a chorus, a convivial company.*

CORN-MOU', *a stack of corn; where the corn is stacked.*

CORN'T, *fed with corn.*

CORSE, *a corpse.*

CORSS, *cross.*

COU'DNA, COULDNA, *couldn't.*

COUNTRA, *country.*

COUP, *to capsize; head over heels.*

COUR, *to crouch, to duck down.*

COUTHIE, COUTHY, *kind, pleasant, affectionate.*

COWE, *to scare, to daunt.*

COWE, *to crop.*

COWTE, *a colt.*

CRACK, *conversation; to converse.*

CRACKIN, *conversing.*

CRACKS, *stories; conversation.*

CRAFT, *croft.*

CRAFT-RIG, *a croft—ridge; used equiv.*

CRAIBIT, CRABBIT, *crabbed, fretful.*

CRAIG, *a crag, a rock; the neck.*

CRAIG, *the throat.*

CRAIGIE, *the throat, the gullet; craggy.*

CRAIK, *the landrail; to croak.*

CRAMBO-CLINK, *rhyme.*

CRAMBO-JINGLE, *rhyming.*

CRAN, *the support for a pot or kettle.*

CRANKOUS, *fretful.*

CRANKS, *creakings.*

CRANREUCH, *hoar-frost.*

CRAP, *a crop; the top.*

CRAPS, *growing crops.*

CRAW, *crow.*

CREEL, *an osier basket, a hamper; perplexity, confusion of mind.*

CREEPIE-CHAIR, *the stool of repentance in the kirk.*

CREESHIE, *greasy.*

CROCKS, *old ewes.*

CRONIE, *an intimate, a companion.*

CROODED, CROODL'D, *cooed, murmured.*

CROODS, *coos.*

CROOKS, *curvature of the neck or spine.*

CROON, *moan, a low.*

CROON, *to toll.*

CROON'D, *hummed.*

CROONING, *humming.*

CROUCHIE, *hunchbacked.*

CROUSE, *elated; courageous, bold.*

CROUSE, *cheerfully.*

CROUSELY, *confidently.*

CROWDIE, *oatmeal gruel made with water; breakfast-time.*

CROWLIN, *crawling.*

CRUMMIE, *a horned cow.*

CRUMMOCK, CUMMOCK, *a cudgel, a crooked staff.*

CRUMP, *crisp.*

CRUNT, *a blow.*

CUDDLE, *to caress, to embrace; to lie close.*

CUDDLE, *to fondle.*

CUDDL'D, *fondled.*

CUIF, COOF, *a dolt, a ninny, a weakling, a dastard.*

CUMMER *(Fr. commere), a gossip; a midwife, a godmother, a hag.*

CUMMOCK, *v.* CRUMMOCK.

CURCH, *a kerchief; a woman's head-cover.*

CURCHIE, *a curtsy; a head-dress.*

CURLER, *one who plays at curling (a game on the ice)*.

CURMURRING, *commotion*.

CURPIN, *the crupper of a horse*.

CURPLE, *the crupper* (i.e. *buttocks*).

CUSHAT, *the wild pigeon*.

CUSTOCK, *the pith of the colewort*.

CUTES, *feet (properly of an animal), ankles*.

CUTTY, *short, bob-tailed*.

CUTTY-STOOL, *a low stool, v.* CREEPIE-CHAIR.

DADDY, *father, an old person*.

DAEZ'T, *dazed*.

DAFFIN, *folly, pastime, matrimonial intercourse*.

DAFT, *merry, giddy*.

DAFT, *mad, foolish*.

DAIDLIN, *waddling; inactive or tardy*.

DAILS, *planks*.

DAIMEN ICKER, *an odd ear of corn*.

DAINTIE, *pleasant, good-humoured, agreeable*.

DAM, *pent up water, urine*.

DAMIE, *dim. of dame*.

DANG, *knocked over; pushed about, surpassed*.

DANTON, *v.* DAUNTON.

DARENA, *dare not*.

DARG, *labour, task, a day's labour*.

DARKLINS, *in the dark*.

DAUD, *to pelt*.

DAUNTON, *to intimidate, to terrify, to depress*.

DAUNTON, *to daunt*.

DAUR, *to dare*.

DAURNA, *dare not*.

DAUR'T, *dared*.

DAUT, DAWTE, *to caress, to pet, to fondle*.

DAUTIE, *a pet; term of affection*.

DAUTIT, *fondled, caressed, petted*.

DAW, *dawn*.

DAWDS, *lumps, large portions*.

DAWIN, *the dawning*.

DEAD, *death*.

DEARIE, *dim. of dear*.

DEAVE, *to deafen, to stun with noise*.

DEEVIL, *v.* DEIL.

DEIL, *the devil*.

DEIL-HAET, *nothing; Devil have my soul*.

DEIL MA CARE, *do not care a straw*.

DELEERET, *delirious, mad*.

DELVE, *to dig*.

DERN'D, *hid*.

DESCRIVE, *to describe*.

DESCRIVING, *describing*.

DEUK, *a duck*.

DEVEL, *a stunning blow*.

DIDDLE, *to move quickly (of fiddling)*.

DIEIN, *dying*.

DIGHT, DIGHTED, *to wipe, wiped; to clean corn from chaff*.

DIN, *noise; to make a noise*.

DIN, *dun, of complexion*.

DING, *to overcome, to surpass*.

DINK, *neatly, dainty; precise, proper*.

DINMONT, *a two-year-old male sheep*.

DINNA, *do not*.

DIRL'D, *thrilled, vibrated*.

DIRT, *a contemptuous term for money*.

DIZ'N, DIZEN, *dozen*.

DOCHTER, *daughter*.

DOGGIE, *dim. of dog*.

DOITED, *stupid, as in frail old age*.

DONSIE, *self-important, restive*.

DOO, *a dove; term of endearment*.

DOOL, *sorrow; to lament, to mourn*.

DOOLFU', *doleful*.

DORTY, *pettish*.

DOUCE, DOUSE, *steady, grave, gentle, sedate*.

DOUCE, DOUCELY, *dousely, sedately*.

DOUDL'T, *dandled*.

DOUGHT, *pret. of* DOW, *to be able, to possess strength*.

DOUK, DOUKIT, *to duck, ducked*.

DOUN, *down*.

DOUP, *the bottom.*

DOUP-SKELPER, *bottom-smacker.*

DOUR, *obstinate, sullen, mentally strong.*

DOURE, *stubborn, obstinate.*

DOUSE, *v.* DOUCE.

DOUSER, *sedater.*

DOW, *a dove, a pigeon.*

DOW, DOWE, *am able.*

DOWF, DOWFF, *pithless, wanting force, sad, dismal.*

DOWIE, *dull, sorrowful.*

DOWILIE, *drooping.*

DOWN, *low-lying land.*

DOWNA, *cannot; not able.*

DOWNA-DO'S, *listless, fatigued, unable.*

DOXY, *a paramour.*

DOYLT, *stupid, crazed, hebetated.*

DOYEN, *shrivelled, dried up.*

DOYTIN, *doddering.*

DOZEN'D, *torpid.*

DOZIN, *torpid.*

DRAIGL'T, *soaked with mud or water.*

DRAM, *a portion of whisky.*

DRANTS, *tedious talk, long whining prayers.*

DRAP, DRAPPIE, *a drop; a small portion of liquor.*

DRAUNTING, *tedious.*

DREE, *to dread, to suffer, to endure.*

DREIGH, *long and uninteresting, long-winded.*

DRIBBLE, *drizzle.*

DRIDDLE, *to move slowly; more action than motion.*

DRIEGH, *tedious, dull.*

DRODDUM, *the breech.*

DRONE, *the monotonous pipe of the bag-pipe; a prosy person.*

DROOP-RUMPL'T, *short-rumped.*

DROUK, *to wet, to soak.*

DROUKIT, *soaked, wet through.*

DROUTH, *drought.*

DROUTHIE, *very thirsty; always thirsty.*

DRUKEN, DRUCKEN, *drunken.*

DRUMLIE, *drumly, muddy, discoloured.*

DRUMMOCK, *raw meal and cold water.*

DRUNT, *the huff.*

DRY, *thirsty.*

DUB, *puddle, slush.*

DUB, *a puddle.*

DUDDIE, *ragged.*

DUDS, DUDDIES, *ragged clothes.*

DUN, *to stun with a great noise; a brown colour.*

DUNE, *done.*

DUNG, *knocked or pushed about.*

DUNTED, *throbbed.*

DUNTS, *blows; wounds caused by a blow.*

DURK, *dirk.*

DUSHT, *touch'd.*

DWALLING, *dwelling.*

DWALT, *dwelt.*

DYKE, *a wall of undressed stones without mortar.*

DYKE-BACK, *the back of a fence.*

DYKE-SIDE, *side of a fence.*

DYVOR, *a bankrupt, a rascal, a ne'er-do-well.*

EAR', *early.*

EASTLIN, *eastern.*

E'EBRIE, *eyebrow.*

E'E, *eye.*

EEN, *eyes.*

E'EN, *even, even so, just so.*

E'EN, E'ENIN, *evening, the eve of a feast.*

E'ER, *ever.*

EERIE, *sad, weird, ghostly; in fear of future misfortune, feeling superstitious fear.*

EILD, *old age.*

EKE, *also.*

ELBUCK, *elbow.*

ELDRITCH, *unearthly.*

ELEKIT, *elected.*

ELL *(Scots), thirty-seven inches.*

ELLER, *an elder of the kirk.*

EN', *end.*

ENEUGH, *enough.*

ENFAULD, *infold, to encompass.*

ENOW, *enough.*

ERSE, *Gaelic.*

ETHER-STANE, *the adder-stone; an amulet.*

ETTLE, *aim.*

EVERMAIR, *evermore.*

EV'NDOWN, *downright, positive.*

EXPECKIT, *expected.*

EYDENT, *diligent.*

FA', *a fall, autumn; to fall.*

FA', *portion, lot.*

FAEN, FAUN, *fell, has fallen.*

FADDOM'D, *fathomed.*

FAEM, *foam.*

FAIKET, *let off, excused.*

FAIN, *fond, desirous.*

FAINNESS, *fondness.*

FALLOW, *fellow.*

FA'N, *fallen.*

FAIR-FA', *good luck, welcome.*

FAND, *found.*

FAR-AFF, *far-off.*

FARLS, *small, thin oat-cakes.*

FASH, *annoyance.*

FASH, *to trouble, worry.*

FASH'D, FASH'T, *bothered.*

FASHIOUS *troublesome.*

FASTEN-E'EN, *Fasten's Even (the evening before Lent).*

FAUGHT, *worry, fight, trouble.*

FAULD, *a fold; to fold.*

FAULDING, *folding; a sheepfold or farm enclosure.*

FAUN, *fallen.*

FAUSE, *false.*

FAUSE-HOUSE, *hole in a cornstack.*

FAUT, *a fault.*

FAUTLESS, *faultless.*

FAUTOR, *a defaulter, a transgressor.*

FAWSONT, *seemly, well-doing, good-looking.*

FEAT, *spruce.*

FECHT, *a fight.*

FECHT, *to fight.*

FECHTIN, *fighting.*

FECK, *the most or greater part.*

FECKET, *a sleeved waistcoat.*

FECKLESS, *feeble, wanting resource.*

FECKLY, *partly, or mostly.*

FEG, *a fig.*

FEGS, *faith.*

FEIDE, *feud.*

FEINT, *v.* FIENT.

FEIRRIE, *lusty.*

FELL, *keen, biting, fierce, cruel, relentless.*

FELL, *a tableland mountain.*

FELLY, *relentless.*

FEN, *a shift; to get along.*

FEN', *fend, to look after, to care for.*

FENCELESS, *defenceless.*

FERLIE, FERLY, *wonder, marvel, surprise.*

FERLIE, *to marvel.*

FETCHES, *catches, gurgles.*

FETCH'T, *stopped suddenly.*

FEY, *fated, doomed, predestined.*

FIDGE, *to be restless, to be uneasy.*

FIDGIN-FAIN, *to be restless with eagerness.*

FIEL, *comfortable, cosy, clean, meat.*

FIENT, *fiend, a petty oath.*

FIENT A, *not a.*

FIENT A HAIR, *not in the least.*

FIENT HAET, *nothing.*

FIENT HAET O', *not one of.*

FIENT-MA-CARE, *no matter.*

FIER, *sound, healthy.*

FIERE, FEIRE, *friend, companion, comrade.*

FIERIE, FEIRIE, *clever, active, nimble, vigorous, mettlesome.*

FILLABEG, *the short kilt worn by the Highlanders.*

FIN', *to find.*

FISH-CREEL, *v.* CREEL.

FISSLE, *tingle, fidget with delight (it is also used of the agitation caused by frying).*

FIT, *the foot.*

FITTIE-LAN', *the near horse of the hind-most pair in the plough.*

FLAE, *a flea.*

FLAFFIN, *flapping.*

FLAININ, FLANNEN, *flannel.*

FLANG, *flung.*

FLEE, *to fly.*

FLEECH'D, *coaxed, cajoled, wheedled.*

FLEECHIN, *wheedling.*

FLEESH, *fleece.*

FLEG, *either a scare or a blow; action, movement.*

FLETH'RIN, *flattering.*

FLEWIT, *a sharp lash.*

FLEY, FLEY'D, *to frighten; frightened, scared.*

FLICHTERIN, *fluttering.*

FLIE, *a fly; to fly.*

FLINDERS, *shreds, broken pieces.*

FLINGING, *kicking out in dancing, capering.*

FLINGIN-TREE, *a piece of timber hung by way of partition between two horses in a stable; a flail.*

FLISKIT, *fretted, capered.*

FLIT, *to shift.*

FLITTERING, *fluttering.*

FLYTE, *to scold.*

FODGEL, *dumpy.*

FOCK, *folk.*

FOOR, *went, fared.*

FOORSDAY, *Thursday.*

FORBEARS, *forebears.*

FORBY, *besides.*

FORFAIRN, *worn out, forlorn.*

FORFOUGHTEN, *exhausted* (i.e. *by labour or conflict*).

FORGATHER, *to meet, to assemble accidentally.*

FORGIE, *to forgive.*

FORJESKET, *jaded with fatigue.*

FORRIT, *forward.*

FOTHER, *fodder.*

FOU, FOW, *full; not sober, drunk.*

FOUGHTEN, *troubled* (i.e. *by conflict with difficulties*).

FOUMART, *the polecat.*

FOURSOME, *a quartette.*

FOUTH, *abundance, plenty; numerous.*

FOW, *v.* FOU.

FOW, *a bushel.*

FRAE, *from.*

FREATH, *to froth.*

FREMIT, *strange, foreign, unrelated.*

FREWCH, *brittle.*

FRIEN, *a friend.*

FU', *full.*

FU'-HAN'T, *full-handed.*

FUD, *a short tail; the buttocks.*

FUFF'T, *puffed.*

FUR-AHIN, *the hindmost plough-horse in the furrow.*

FURDER, *further.*

FURDER, *to succeed.*

FURM, *a wooden form.*

FUR, FURR, *a furrow.*

FUSHIONLESS, *tasteless, sapless, insipid.*

FYKE, *to fidget, to be restless.*

FYLE, FYLED, *to dirty, to soil; soiled.*

GAB, *the mouth, insolence.*

GABS, *talk.*

GAE (GANG); GAEN, GANE; GAED; GAUN, *to go; gone; went, going.*

GAETS, *ways, manners.*

GAIRS, *ornamental slashes in a lady's dress.*

GAIT, *way, manner, practice, deportment.*

GANE, *gone.*

GANG, *to go.*

GANGREL, *a vagrant.*

GAPIN, *gaping, looking foolish or idiotic.*

GAR, *to make, to cause, to compel.*

GAR'T, *compelled, caused, forced.*

GARTEN, *garter.*

GARTEN'D, *gartered.*

GASH, *wise, sagacious; pert or insolent*

speech.

GASHING, *talking, gabbing.*

GAT, *got.*

GATE, *a way, path, road.*

GAUCIE, GAUSIE, *plump, portly, well-conditioned.*

GAUD, *a good.*

GAU'N, *Gavin.*

GAUN, *going.*

GAUNTED, *gaped, yawned.*

GAWKY, *awkward, ungainly.*

GAWSIE, *buxom, buxom and jolly; big and joyous.*

GAYLIES, *gaily.*

GEAR, *goods, property, wealth, money, harness, tools, tackle, etc.*

GECK, *to toss the head, to sport.*

GED, *a pike.*

GENTLE, *well-born.*

GENTY, *courteous, having good manners.*

GEORDIE, *dim. of George; a guinea.*

GET, *issue, offspring, breed.*

GHAIST, *a ghost.*

GIE, GAE; GIED; GIEN; *to give; gave; given.*

GIF, *if, whether.*

GIFTIE, *dim. of gift.*

GIGLETS, *giggling youngsters or maids.*

GILL, *a half-pint glass; a quarter-pint glass of whisky.* A HAWICK GILL=*two gills.*

GILLIE, *dim. of gill.*

GILPEY, *young girl.*

GIMMER, *a young female sheep, a ewe that has not borne young.*

GIN, *before, until, unless, if, whether, should.*

GIRDLE, *a circular iron plate for baking cakes.*

GIRN, GIRNIN, *to grin, grinning; peevish, complaining.*

GIRR, *a hoop.*

GIZZ, *wig.*

GLAIKIT, *foolish, thoughtless, giddy.*

GLAIKS, TO GET THE, *to be deceived, deluded, cheated, jilted.*

GLAIVE, *a sword, a broadsword.*

GLAIZIE, *glossy, shiny.*

GLAUM'D, *grasped, clutched, snatched.*

GLED, *the common kite, a hawk.*

GLEEDE, *a spark, ember, red-hot coal.*

GLEG, *clear-sighted, sharp, eager.*

GLEIB, *a piece, a portion; the land belonging to the clergy benefice.*

GLENTURIT, *a small lateral valley to the Earn in Perthshire.*

GLIBBER, *smoothly.*

GLIB-GABBET, *smooth-tongued.*

GLINTED, *flashed.*

GLINTIN, *sparkling.*

GLOAMIN, *twilight, dusk, evening.*

GLOAMIN-SHOT, *sunset; a twilight interview.*

GLOOVES, *gloves.*

GLOW'R, *a frown; to stare, to scowl.*

GLOWRIN, *threatening (weather); staring, stormy.*

GLUNCH, *a frown, a growl.*

GLUNCH, *to frown, to growl.*

GOAVIN, *looking dazedly; mooning.*

GOR-COCK, *the moorcock.*

GOTTEN, *got.*

GOWAN, *a generic name for the daisy.*

GOWANY, *covered with wild daisies.*

GOWD, *gold, money.*

GOWDEN, *golden.*

GOWDIE, *the head.*

GOWFF'D, *struck; hit as in the game of golf.*

GOWK, *a blockhead, simpleton, an awkward fellow; the cuckoo.*

GOWLING, *lamenting (as a dog in grief).*

GRAFF, *a grave.*

GRAIN, *a branch; the fork of a tree or the junction of its branches.*

GRAIN'D, *groaned.*

GRAIP, *to grope; a dung-fork.*

GRAITH, *tools, harness, equipment of any*

kind.

GRAITHING, *gearing, vestments.*

GRANE, *a groan; to groan.*

GRANNIE, GRAUNIE, *grandmother.*

GRAPE, *a dung fork.*

GRAT, *wept.*

GRAUNIE, *v.* GRANNIE.

GREE, *to agree; the first place, the highest honours.*

GREET; GRAT; GREETIN, *to cry, to weep; wept; weeping.*

GRIPPIT, *arrested, clasped.*

GRIST, *the corn sent to the mill; used equiv.*

GROANIN-MAUT, *the lying-in drink for the midwife and friends.*

GROZET, *a gooseberry.*

GRUMPHIE, *the pig.*

GRUNTLE, *the face, the phiz.*

GRUNTLE, *dim. of grunt.*

GRUNZIE, *the snout, mouth, face, visage.*

GRUPE, *caught hold, seized.*

GRUSHIE, *growing.*

GRUTTEN, *wept.*

GUDE, GUID, *God, good.*

GUIDE'EN, *good evening, a salutation.*

GUID-FATHER, *father-in-law.*

GUID-WIFE, (*also* GUDE-WIFE), *the mistress of the house, the landlady.*

GUID-WILLY, *hospitable, kindly, generous, good-will.*

GUDEMAN, GUIDMAN, *the master of the house, a husband, a tenant farmer.*

GUDESAKE, *God sake!*

GULLIE, GULLY, *a large knife.*

GUMLIE, *muddy.*

GUMPTION, *wisdom, skill.*

GUSE, *a goose.*

GUSTY, *tasty.*

GUTCHER, *grandfather, grandsire.*

GUT-SCRAPER, *a fiddler.*

HA', *the hall.*

HADDEN, HADDIN, *holding, inheritance.*

HAE, HAEN, *to have; had, been having.*

HAET, *an atom, a very small quantity.*

HAFFETS, *the temples, the side locks.*

HAFFINS, *half, partly.*

HAG, *a moss, a broken bog.*

HAGGIS, *a dish generally consisting of the lungs, heart, and liver of a sheep minced with suet, onions etc., and cooked in a sheep's maw.*

HAIRST, HAR'ST, *harvest.*

HAITH, "*in faith!*" *an exclamation.*

HAILL, *whole, well, healthful.*

HAIN, HAIN'D, *to spare, to save; saved.*

HAIVERS, *v.* HAVERS.

HAL', HALD, *holding, possession; 'house an' hal'(d)'=house and possession.*

HALE, HAIL, *the whole.*

HALE, HAIL, *whole, healthy.*

HALESOME, *wholesome.*

HALLAN, *a porch, a dwelling, a house.*

HALLAN-EN', *the end of the porch or partition-wall between the door and the fire.*

HALLOWEEN, *All Saints' Eve (31st October).*

HALLOWMAS, *All Saints' Day (1st November).*

HALS, *the neck, the throat.*

HALY, *holy.*

HAME, *home.*

HAMMER, *a clumsy, noisy person.*

HAN', *the hand.*

HAN-DARG (*or* DAURK), *v.* DARG.

HAND-BREED, *a handbreadth.*

HAND-WAL'D, *hand-picked* (i.e *choicest*).

HANGIE, *hangman (nickname of the Devil).*

HANKERS, *desires, covets.*

HANSEL, *to use a thing for the first time; the first gift, the first buyer; earnest-money.*

HANSELLING, *the first use or celebration.*

HAP, *to cover for warmth, to wrap, to tuck in; a covering, a wrap.*

HAPPER, *hopper (of a mill).*

HAPPING, *hopping (as a bird).*

HAP-STEP-AN'-LOWP, *hop-step-and-jump.*

HARKIT, *hearkened.*

HARN, *coarse cloth.*

HARRY, HERRY, *to rob, to plunder, to ravage.*

HARST, *v.* HAIRST.

HASH, *an oaf, a dunderhead.*

HASLOCK, *v.* HALS.

HASLOCK-WOO', *the finest wool on the hals or throat of a sheep.*

HAUD, *to hold.*

HAUF, *the half; to halve.*

HAUGHS, *low-lying rich lands, valleys.*

HAUN, *v.* HAN'.

HAURL, HAURL'D, *to drag, dragged.*

HAUSE, *to embrace, to hug, v.* HALS.

HAUVER-MEAL, *oatmeal.*

HAVERIL, HAV'RD, *one who talks nonsense, a half-witted person.*

HAVERS, *nonsense.*

HAVINS, *sense, manners, behaviour.*

HAWKIE, *a white-faced cow, a cow.*

HAWKIT, *a white face, applied to kine.*

HEADIN-MAN, *a headsman, an executioner.*

HEAL, *v.* HALE.

HEALSOME, *v.* HALESOME.

HECHT, *a promise, an offer; to promise, to engage.*

HECKLE, *a flax-comb; to cross-examine.*

HEE, *a call.*

HEELS-O'ER-GOWDIE, *v.* GOWDIE.

HEEZE, *to hoist, to exalt, to raise.*

HEICH, HEIGH, *high.*

HELLIM, *a helm.*

HEM-SHIN'D, *bow-legged, like the shape of the half of a horse-collar.*

HERE AWA, *here about.*

HERN, *the heron.*

HERRYMENT, *spoliation.*

HERSEL, *herself.*

HET, *hot.*

HETTEST, *hottest.*

HEUGH, *a crag, a pit, a hollow.*

HEUK, *a hook, reaping-hook.*

HIE-GATE, *a thoroughfare through a town.*

HILCH, *to hobble, to halt.*

HILLOCK, *dim. of hill, a mound.*

HILTIE-SKILTIE, *helter-skelter.*

HIMSEL, *himself.*

HINEY, HINNY *honey; a term of endearment.*

HING, *to hang.*

HIRPLE, *to hobble, to limp, to walk lamely.*

HISSELS, *so many cattle as one person can attend.*

HISTIE, *bare.*

HIZZIE, *a huzzy; a wench.*

HOAST, *a cough; to cough.*

HODDEN, HODDIN, *homespun cloth made of natural-coloured wool.*

HODDEN-GREY, *a grey homespun.*

HODDIN, *the motion of a sage countryman riding on a cart horse.*

HOG, HOGGIE, *a first-year-old sheep before shearing, v.* DINMONT *and* GIMMER.

HOG-SCORE, *a term in curling.*

HOG-SHOUTHER, *a kind of horseplay by justling with the shoulder, to justle.*

HOLLAN, HOLLAND, *linen imported from there.*

HOODIE, *the hooded and common crow.*

HOODOCK, *grasping, vulturish.*

HOOKED, *caught.*

HOOL, *the outer case, the sheath.*

HOOLIE, *softly.*

HOORD, *hoard.*

HOORDET, *hoarded.*

HORN, *a horn spoon; a toothed comb of horn.*

HORNIE, *the Devil.*

HOST, *v.* HOAST.

HOTCH'D, *jerked.*

HOUGHMAGANDIE, *fornication.*

HOULET, *v.* HOWLET.

HOUPE, *hope.*

HOWDIE, HOWDY, *a midwife.*

HOWE, *a hollow, a dell.*

HOWE, *hollow.*

HOWKET, *digged, dug, unearthed.*

HOWLET, *the owl.*

HOYSE, *a hoist.*

HOY'T, *urged.*

HOYTE, *to amble crazily.*

HUGHOC, *dim. of Hugh.*

HULLIONS, *slovens.*

HUNDER, *a hundred.*

HUNKERS, *bent knees, pleading, in a squatting position, with the haunches, knees, and ankles acutely bent.*

HURCHEON, *the hedgehog.*

HURCHIN, *an urchin.*

HURDIES, *the lions, the crupper* (i.e. *the buttocks*).

HURL, *to trundle.*

HUSHION, *a footless stocking.*

HYTE, *furious.*

I', *in.*

ICKER, *an ear of corn.*

IER-OE, *a great-grandchild.*

ILK, ILKA, *the same, each, every.*

ILL O'T, *bad at it.*

ILL-TAEN, *ill-taken.*

ILL-THIEF, *the Devil.*

ILL-WILLIE, *ill-natured, malicious, niggardly.*

INDENTIN, *indenturing.*

INGINE, *genius, ingenuity, wit.*

INGLE, *the fireplace, a chimney-corner.*

INGLE-GLEEDE, *a blazing fireside.*

INGLE-LOWE, INGLE LOW, *the flame or light of the fire.*

IN-KNEE'D, *knock-kneed.*

IS, *often used for the plural are.*

I'SE, *I shall or will.*

ITHER, *other.*

ITSEL', *itself.*

JAD, *an old worn-out horse; a scurvy woman.*

JANWAR, *January.*

JAUK, *to trifle, to dally.*

JAUNER, *to talk at random, to jabber.*

JAUNTIE, *dim. of jaunt.*

JAUP, *to splash.*

JAW, *impudent talk; to pour, to dash, to splash.*

JAWPISH, *frolicsome, mischievous, tricky.*

JEE'D, *stirred, rocked, jogged.*

JEEG, *to jerk.*

JILLET, *a jilt.*

JIMP, JIMPY or JIMPLY, *neatly, elegantly.*

JIMPS, *easy stays open in front.*

JINK, *to frisk, to sport, to dodge, move out and in.*

JINKER, *'a jinker noble'=a noble goer, dodger, gamester* (i.e. *coquette*).

JINKIN, *dodging, moving quickly.*

JINKS, *tricks, dodges.*

JIRKINET, *a woman's outside jacket.*

JIRT, *a jerk.*

JIZ, *a wig.*

JO, *a sweetheart.*

JO, *joy, an expression of good will, friendly address.*

JOCTELEG, *a clasp-knife.*

JORUM, *a large drinking jug or bowl.*

JOUK, *to cower, to bend, to stoop.*

JOW, *to jow, a verb which includes both the swinging motion and pealing sound of a large bell.*

JUMPET, JUMPIT, *jumped.*

JUNDIE, *to justle.*

JURR, *a servant wench.*

KAE, *a jackdaw.*

KAIL, *colewort, cabbage; broth made from greens.*

KAIL-BLADE, *of leaf of the colewort.*

KAIL-GULLIE, *a cabbage-knife; v.*

GULLIE.

KAIL-RUNT, *the stem of the colewort.*

KAIL-WHITTLE, *a cabbage-knife.*

KAIL-YARD, *a kitchen-garden.*

KAIN, KANE, *rents in kind.*

KAME, KAIM'D, *to comb, combed.*

KEBARS, *beams, rafters.*

KEBBUCK, *a large cheese uncut.*

KECKLE, *to cackle, to giggle loudly (as a girl).*

KEEK, *a look, a glance.*

KEEK, *to look, to peep, to glance.*

KEEKIN-GLASS, *a looking-glass.*

KEEKIT, *pryed, peered, gazed.*

KEEL, *v.* CAUK.

KEEPIT, *kept.*

KELPIES, *river-demons.*

KEN, KEND, KEN'T, *to know; known.*

KENNA, *know not.*

KENNIN, *a very little.*

KENT, *v.* KEND.

KEP, *to catch.*

KET, *the fleece on a sheep's body.*

KEY, *quay.*

KEY-STANE, *key-stone.*

KIAUGH, *cark.*

KILBAIGIE, *a favourite brand of whisky manufactured at Kilbaigie, Clackmannan, one of the earliest distilleries after the abolition of the Ferintosh monopoly.*

KILLOGIE, *a vacuity before the fireplace in a kiln.*

KILT, *a short dress; to tuck up the skirts.*

KIMMER, *v.* CUMMER.

KIN, *blood relations.*

KIN', *kind.*

KING'S-HOOD, *the second stomach in a ruminant (equivocal for the scrotum).*

KINTRA, *country, neighbours.*

KIRK, *a church.*

KIRN, *a churn.*

KIRN, *harvest-home.*

KIRSEN, *to christen.*

KIRTLE, *a woman's short skirt or outer petticoat.*

KIST, *kissed; a chest.*

KITCHEN, *to relish (to add relish to).*

KITH, *acquaintance, those not related by blood.*

KITTLE, *difficult; to tickle.* TO KITTLE HAIR ON THAIRMS=*to play the fiddle.*

KITTLE, *difficult; ticklish, delicate, fickle.*

KITTLE, *to tickle.*

KITTLIN, *a kitten.*

KIUTLIN, *cuddling.*

KNAGGIE, *knobby.*

KNAGGS, *knobs, protuberances.*

KNAPPIN-HAMMERS, *hammers for breaking stones.*

KNOWE, *a knoll, a hillock.*

KNURL, *a dwarf, a hunchback; stunted.*

KYE, *cattle.*

KYLES, *nine-pins (form of skittles).*

KYTES, *bellies.*

KYTHE, *to show.*

LABOUR LEA, *to plough grass land.*

LADDIE, *dim. of lad.*

LADE, *a load.*

LAG, *backward.*

LAGGEN, *the bottom of a wooden dish.*

LAIGH, *low.*

LAIK, *lack, want.*

LAIRD, *a landowner; an abbey laird=one who took refuge from his creditors in Holyrood Abbey.*

LAIRING, *sticking or sinking in moss or mud.*

LAITH, *loath.*

LAITHFU', *loathful, sheepish.*

LALLAN, LALLAND, *lowland.*

LALLANS, *Scots Lowland vernacular.*

LAMMIE, *dim. of lamb.*

LAN', *land.*

LAN'-AFORE, *the foremost horse on the unploughed land side.*

LAN'-AHIN, *the hindmost horse on the un-*

ploughed land side.

LANE, *alone, solitary, lonely.*

LANG, *long.*

LANG-NECKIT, *long-necked.*

LANG-SYNE, *long since.*

LAP, *leaped.*

LAPWING, *the plover.*

LASS, *a girl, a young woman, a sweetheart, the complement of lad.*

LAVE, *flowing freely; the rest or remainder.*

LAVEROCK, *the lark.*

LAW, *low; a round-capped mountain which ascends by stages.*

LAWIN, *the expense, the cost, the bill.*

LEA, *grass, untilled land (also used in an equivocal sense).*

LEAL, *loyal, true, trusty.*

LEAR, LAIR, *learning, knowledge, education.*

LEA-RIG, *a ridge in a field left unploughed between ridges bearing grain.*

LEARN, *to teach.*

LEDDY, *lady, the wife of a landlord.*

LEE, *the slope of a hill; warm, sheltered; (in phrase) an intensive meaning of loneliness.*

LEE-LANG, *livelong.*

LEESOME, *lawful, pleasant.*

LEEZE ME, *an expression of pleasure=dear is to me.*

LEISTER, *a fish-spear.*

LEN', *to lend.*

LET BE, *to let alone, to cease from.*

LEUGH, *laughed.*

LEUK, *looked.*

LEY-CRAP, *the first crop after the ploughing of grass or fallow land.*

LIBBET, *castrated.*

LICKIT MY WINNINS=*dissipated my means or money.*

LICKS, *a beating, punishment.*

LIEIN, *lying, equivocating.*

LIEN, *lain.*

LIFT, *the sky, the heavens; to collect, to steal.*

LIFT, *a load.*

LIGHTLY, *to disparage, to scorn.*

LILT, LILTING, *a song; merry singing.*

LIMMER, *a jade, a mistress.*

LIMPET, LIMPIT, *limped.*

LIMPIN, *limping, hobbling.*

LIN, *v.* LINN.

LINENS, *underclothing; death-clothes.*

LINGLES, *shoemaker's thread.*

LINK, *to trip or dance with the utmost possible activity; to hurry.*

LINKIN, *tripping, dancing, hurrying.*

LINN, *a waterfall.*

LINT, *flax.*

LINTWHITE, LINTIE, *the linnet.*

LINT-WHITE, *flaxen-coloured.*

LIPPEN, *to trust, to believe.*

LIPPIE, *dim. of lip.*

LOAN, LOANING, *a lane, a farm road.*

LO'E, LOO, LO'ED, *to love; loved.*

LOGIE, *v.* KILLOGIE.

LON'ON, *London.*

LOOF, *the palm of the hand, the open hand.*

LOON, LOUN, LOWN, *a rascal, a fellow, a servant, a varlet.*

LOOT, *did let.*

LOOVE, *love.*

LOOVES, *v.* LOOF.

LOSH, *a minced oath (a mild form of Lord).*

LOUGH, *a pond, a lake.*

LOUP, LOWP, *to leap.*

LOUR, *lowering, impending.*

LOWE, *a flame; to flame.*

LOWIN, *lowing, flaming, burning.*

LOWN, *v.* LOON.

LOWPIN, *leaping, jumping.*

LOWRY, *Lawrence; a crafty person.*

LOWSE, *to loose, to untie.*

LUCKIE, LUCKY, *an elderly woman, an alewife, a familiar address.*

LUG, *the ear, a handle.*

LUGGET, *having ears.*

LUGGIE, *a small wooden vessel with a handle.*

LUM, *the chimney.*

LUME, *a loom.*

LUNARDI, *a balloon-bonnet (named after Lunardi, a famous balloonist).*

LUNCHES, *full portions.*

LUNT, *a column of smoke or steam.*

LUNTIN, *smoking.*

LUVE, *love.*

LUNZIE-BANES, *the loin bones.*

LYART, *grey, of a mixed colour.*

LYE, *to lie down.*

LYMMAR *or* LIMMER, *a knave, a jade.*

LYNIN, *lining.*

MAE, *more.*

MAILEN, MAILIN, *a farm, holding, rent; the outfit for a bride.*

MAILIE, *Molly.*

MAIR, *more.*

MAIST, *most, almost.*

MAK, *to make.*

MAK O', MAKE O', *to pet, to fondle.*

MALL, MALLY, *Moll, Molly, (Mary).*

MALVOSIE, *Malmsey wine.*

MANTEELE, *a mantle.*

MANTIE, *a mantle, a lady's cloak.*

MARK, *or* MERK, *an old Scots coin (13⅓d. sterling).*

MASHLUM, *of mixed meal.*

MASKIN-PAT, *a tea-pot, a still.*

MAUKIN, *a hare; a slattern, a term of abuse.*

MAUN, *must.*

MAUNNA, *must not.*

MAUT, *malt, liquor.*

MAVIS, *the thrush.*

MAWIN, *mowing.*

MAWN, *a basket or hamper; mown.*

MAY, *a maid.*

MEAR, MEARE, *a mare.*

MEIKLE, MICKLE, MUCKLE, *much, great, large.*

MELDER, *the quantity of corn sent to be ground.*

MELL, *to mix, to mingle, to have intercourse with.*

MELVIE, *to meal-dust.*

MEN', *to mend.*

MENSE, *tact, discretion.*

MENSELESS, *unmannerly.*

MENZIE, *retainers, followers, men.*

MERLE, *a blackbird.*

MERRAN, *Marian.*

MESS JOHN, *Mass John (the parish priest, the minister).*

MESSIN, *a cur, a mongrel.*

MIDDEN, *a dunghill.*

MIDDEN-CREELS, manure baskets carried on the back.

MIDDEN DUB, *midden puddle.*

MIDDEN-HOLE, *a gutter at the bottom of the dunghill.*

MILKIN-SHIEL, *the milking-shed.*

MIM, *prim, affectedly meek.*

MIM-MOU'D, *said of one who speaks affectedly.*

MIN', *mind, remembrance; to recollect.*

MIND, *to remember, to bear in mind.*

MINDNA, *to mind not, to forget.*

MINNIE, MINNY, *mother.*

MIRK, *gloomy, dark; darkness.*

MIRKEST, *gloomiest, darkest.*

MISCA', *to miscall, to abuse.*

MISHANTER, *mishap.*

MISLEAR'D, *mischievous, unmannerly.*

MISS'T, MIST, *missed.*

MISTAK, *mistake.*

MISTEUK, *mistook.*

MITHER, *mother.*

MITTEN'D, *covered, gloved.*

MONIE, MONY, *many.*

MOOLS, *crumbling earth, dust.*

MOOP, *to mump, to nibble as a sheep.*

MORN, *the next day, to-morrow.*

MOTTIE, *dusty*.

MOU', *the mouth*.

MOUDIEWART, MOUDIEWORTS, *the mole; moles*.

MUCK, *manure*.

MUCKIN, *cleansing the stable or cow-house*.

MUCKLE, *v.* MEIKLE.

MUIR, *moorland, a fell*.

MULTURE *or* MOUTER, *the portion retained by the miller for grinding the corn*.

MUSLIN-KAIL, *beefless broth*.

MYSIE, *Mary*.

MUTCHKIN, *an English pint*.

MYSEL, *myself*.

NA, NAE, *no, not, but, than*.

NAEBODY, *nobody, no one*.

NAETHING, NAITHING, *nothing*.

NAIG, *a nag*.

NAIGIE, *a small riding-horse*.

NANE, *none*.

NAPPY, *ale, liquor*.

NATCH, *a notching implement*.

NAUR, *near to, close to*.

NEB, *the nose, a beak*.

NEBBIT, *shaped like a bird's bill*.

NEEDNA, *needn't*.

NEGLECKIT, *neglected*.

NEIBOR, *a neighbour*.

NEIST, NIEST, *next, nearest*.

NEIVES, NIEVES, *the fists, the closed hands*.

NEUK, NEWK, *a nook, a corner*.

NEW-CA'D, *newly-driven*.

NICHER, *to neigh; the call of a mare to her foal*.

NICK (AULD), NICKIE-BEN, *a name of the Devil*.

NICK, *to sever, to slit, to nail, to seize away*.

NICKIE-BEN, *v.* NICK (AULD).

NICK-NACKETS, *curiosities*.

NICKS, *cuts, the rings on a cow's horns*.

NIEST, *next*.

NIEVE, *the fist*.

NIEVE-FU', *fistful*.

NIFFER, *exchange*.

NIGHT-FA', *nightfall, twilight*.

NIPT, *pinched, shrivelled*.

NIT, *a nut*.

NO, *not*.

NOCHT, *nothing, no more*.

NORLAND, *northland*.

NOWT, NOWTE, *cattle, nolt*.

O', *of*.

OCHILS, *the mountain range dividing Perthshire from Clackmannan*.

O'ERLAY, *a blouse, a smock*.

O'ERWORD, *a refrain, a chorus*.

ONIE, ONY, *any*.

OR, *ere, before*.

ORRA, *extra, superfluous*.

O'S, *of his, of us*.

O'T, *of it*.

OUGHT, *aught*.

OUGHTLINS, AUGHTLINS, *aught in the least, at all*.

OURIE, *shivering, drooping*.

OURSEL, OURSELS, *ourselves*.

OUTLER, *unhoused, in the open fields*.

OUTSKIN'D, *shin-bones turned outwards*.

OUTWITTENS, *without the knowledge of*.

OWRE, *over*.

OWSEN, *oxen*.

OXTER, *the armpit*.

OXTER'D, *held up under the arms*.

PACK AN' THICK, *confidential*.

PACTION, *an agreement, an arrangement*.

PAIDLE, *to paddle*.

PAINCH, *the paunch*.

PAITRICK, *a partridge*.

PANG, *to cram*.

PARISHEN, *the parish*.

PARLE, *speech*.

PARLEY, *a truce, a conference.*

PARRITCH, *porridge.*

PARRITCH-PATS, *porridge-pots.*

PAT, *a pot; did put, ejected.*

PATTLE, PETTLE, *a plough-staff.*

PAUGHTY, *haughty.*

PAUKIE, PAWKIE, *sly, artful, knowing.*

PEAT-CREEL, *a basket for carrying dried bog turf for fuel.*

PECHAN, *the stomach.*

PECHIN, *out of breath, panting.*

PENDLES, *earrings.*

PENNY-FEE, *wages, income.*

PEENY-WHEEP, *small beer.*

PETTLE, *v.* PATTLE.

PHEMIE, *Euphemia.*

PHILIBEG, *the kilt, or Highlander's short dress.*

PHRAISIN, *flattering, wheedling.*

PHRASE, *to flatter, to wheedle.*

PICKLE, *a few, a small quantity.*

PIN, *a wooden bar or door-latch.*

PINE, *pain, care.*

PINK, *to glimmer, to contract the eye in looking; a woman who glimmers.*

PINT *(Scots), two English quarts.*

PINT-STOUP, *a pint-vessel containing two English quarts.*

PIT, *to put.*

PLACADS, *shouts.*

PLACK, *four pennies Scots.*

PLACKLESS, *penniless.*

PLAIDEN, *coarse woollen cloth.*

PLAIDEN-WAB, *homespun tweeled woollen.*

PLAIDIE *or* PLAID, *a broad unformed piece of cloth for wrapping about the shoulders and body.*

PLAISTER, *plaster.*

PLASHY, *applied to a body of water driven violently.*

PLENISH'D, *stocked.*

PLEUGH, *a plough; to plough.*

PLEUGH-PETTLE, *v.* PATTLE.

PLISKIE, *a trick.*

PLIVER, *the plover.*

POCKS, *pockets, bags.*

POIND, *to seize (originally in war, or as prey), to distrain, to impound.*

POIND, *distrained.*

POORTITH, *poverty.*

POU, PU', *to pull.*

POUCH, *a pocket.*

POUK, *to poke.*

POUPIT, *pulpit.*

POUSE, *a push.*

POUSSIE, *a hare (also a cat).*

POUTHERED, *powdered; sanctified.*

POUTS, *chicks.*

POW, *the poll, the head.*

POWNIE, *a pony.*

POW'T, *pulled.*

PREE'D, *tasted.*

PREEN, *a pin; to pin.*

PRENT, *print.*

PRIE, PREE, *to prove, to taste, to try.*

PRIEF, *proof.*

PRIESTIE, *a priest; used derisively.*

PRIGGIN, *haggling.*

PRIMSIE, *dim. of prim, precise.*

PROVESES, *provosts.*

PU', *to pull.*

PUDDOCK-STOOLS, *toad-stools.*

PUIR, *pure, poor.*

PUMPS, *light shoes.*

PUN', PUND, *a pound.*

PURSIE, *a small purse.*

PUSSIE, *a hare.*

PYET, *a magpie.*

PYKE, *to pick.*

PYLES, *grains.*

QUAT, *quit, did quit.*

QUEAN, QUINE, *a young attractive woman.*

QUEY, *a cow that has not calved.*

QUIRE, *choir.*

QUO', QUOD., *quoth.*

RAB, *Rob (dim. of Robert).*

RADE, *rode.*

RAEP, *a rope.*

RAGWEED, *ragwort, benweed.*

RAIBLES, *recites by rote.*

RAIR, *to roar.*

RAIRIN, *roaring.*

RAIR'T, *roared.*

RAISE, *rase, rose.*

RAIZE, *to excite.*

RAMFEEZL'D, *exhausted.*

RAMGUNSHOCH, *surly, cross-grained.*

RAM-STAM, *headlong.*

RANDIE, *randy, a sturdy, abusive or threatening beggar.*

RANT, *to rollick, to roister.*

RANTS, *merry meetings, sprees, rows.*

RANTIN, *boisterous, rollicking.*

RAPE, *v.* RAEP.

RAPLOCH, homespun.

RASH, *a rash.*

RASH-BUSS, *a clump of rushes.*

RASHY, *rushy.*

RATTON, RATTAN, *a rat.*

RATTON-KEY, *the Rat-Quay.*

RAUCLE, RAUCKLE, *stout, clever, rash, fearless.*

RAUGHT, *reached.*

RAW, *a row.*

RAX, *to stretch, to extend.*

REAM, *cream, foam.*

REAVE, *to rob.*

REBUTE, *a rebuff; to rebuke.*

RECK, *to take heed.*

RED, *advised, afraid.*

RED, REDE, *to advise, to counsel.*

REDE, *counsel; to counsel, to advise.*

REEK, *smoke.*

REEKIE, REEKY, *smoky.*

REEKIT, *smoked, dingy.*

REEL, *a dance probably indigenous to Britain (but known in Scandinavia), performed by one or two couples. The chief feature is a circular movement,* the dancers standing face to face and describing rapidly a series of figures of 8 with a gliding motion.

REESTIT, *refused to go.*

REESTIT, *scorched.*

REIF, *to reave, to thieve.*

REMEAD, *remedy.*

REW, *to rue.*

RICKLES, *ricklets (smalls tacks of corn in the fields).*

RIEF, *plunder.*

RIG, *a ridge.*

RIGGIN, *the roof-tree.*

RIGWOODIE, *ancient, lean.*

RIN, *to run.*

RINGLE-EY'D, *with much white in the eye.*

RIPP, *a handful of corn from the sheaf.*

RIPPLES, RIPELLS, *shooting pains in the back and reins.*

RIPPLIN-KAME, *a comb for separating the bolls of flax from the stem; used equiv.*

RISKIT, *cracked.*

RITHER, *a rudder.*

RIVE, *to split, to tear, to tug, to burst.*

ROCK, *a distaff.*

ROOD, *a crucifix, a cross.*

ROON, *round.*

ROOSE, *reputation.*

ROOS'D, *praised, flattered.*

ROOSE, *to praise, to commend.*

ROOSTY, *rusty, disused.*

ROTTAN, ROTTIN, *the rat.*

ROUN', *round.*

ROUPET, *exhausted in voice.*

ROUTH, *plenty, good store.*

ROUTHIE, *well-stocked, of comfortable means.*

ROW'D, *rolled, wrapt.*

ROWE, *to roll, to wrap; to flow.*

ROWIN, *rolling, wrapping.*

ROWTE, *to low, to bellow.*

ROWTH, *plenty, a store.*

ROZET, *rozin.*

RUMPLE-BANE, *the rump-bone.*

RUN-DEILS, *downright devils.*

RUNG, *a stout stick, a cudgel.*

RUNKL'D, *wrinkled.*

RUNT, *a cabbage, or colewort-stalk.*

RYKE, *to reach up.*

SAB, *to sob.*

SAE, *so.*

SAFT, *soft.*

SAIR, SAIR'D, *to serve, served.*

SAIRIE, *sorrowful.*

SALL, *shall.*

SARK, *a shirt, a smock.*

SASSENACH, SASUNNACH, *the Gaelic for Saxon.*

SAUL, *soul.*

SAUMONT, SAWMONT, *the salmon.*

SAUNT, *saint.*

SAUT, *salt.*

SAUT-BACKETS, *v.* BACKET.

SAW, *to sow.*

SAWNEY, SANDIE, *Alexander.*

SAX, *six.*

SCAITH, SKAITH, *damage, hurt, injury.*

SCANT, *devoid, little or few.*

SCAR, *to scare.*

SCAUD, *to scald.*

SCAUL, *scold.*

SCAULD, *to scold, a scold.*

SCAUR, *afraid, apt to be scared.*

SCAUR, *a jutting cliff or bank of earth.*

SCHO, *she.*

SCONE, *a soft cake.*

SCONNER, *disgust.*

SCONNER, *sicken (with disgust).*

SCRAICHIN, *calling hoarsely.*

SCREED, *a rip, a rent.*

SCREED, *to repeat rapidly, to rattle.*

SCRIECHIN, *screeching.*

SCRIEVIN, *careering.*

SCRIMP, *to save, to deal sparingly.*

SCROGGY, *applied to hill slopes covered with brushwood.*

SCUDS, *brisk beer, foaming ale.*

SCULDUDD'RY, *fornication, bawdry.*

SEE'D, *saw (pret. of see).*

SEISINS, *freehold possessions.*

SEL', *self.*

SELL'D, SELL'T, *sold.*

SEMPLE, *simple, low-born.*

SEN', *send.*

SET, *to set off, to start.*

SET, *sat.*

SETS, *becomes.*

SHACHL'D, *twisted, bent, shapeless.*

SHAIRD, *shred, shard.*

SHANGAN, *a cleft stick.*

SHANKS, *the legs.*

SHANNA, *shall not.*

SHAUL, *shallow.*

SHAVER, *a funny fellow.*

SHAVIE, *a prank.*

SHAW, *a wood; to show.*

SHEARER, *a reaper.*

SHEEP-SHANK, *a sheep's trotter.*

SHEERLY, *wholly.*

SHEERS, *scissors.*

SHELLIN-HILL, *the hill or eminence where grain was dried and husked by the wind.*

SHERRA-MOOR, *Sheriffmuir.*

SHEUGH, *a ditch, a trench; the seed-furrow.*

SHEUK, *shook, did shake.*

SHIEL, *a shelter, a hut.*

SHILL, *shrill.*

SHOG, *a shake.*

SHOOL, *a shovel; to shovel.*

SHOOLING, *shovelling.*

SHOON, *shoes.*

SHORE, SHOR'D, *to offer; to threaten; offered.*

SHORT SYNE, *a little time ago.*

SHOULDNA, *should not.*

SHOUTHER, *the shoulder.*

SHURE, *sheared, did shear.*

SHUTE, *to shoot.*

SIC, *such.*

SICCAN, *such kind of.*

SICKER, *steady.*

SIDELINS, *sideways.*

SILLER, *silver, money, wealth.*

SILLY, *frail, in delicate health; harmless.*

SIMMER, *summer.*

SIN', *since.*

SINDRY, *sundry.*

SINGET, *singed, shrivelled.*

SINN, *the sun.*

SINNY, *sunny.*

SINSYNE, *since then.*

SKAIL, *to spill, to pour.*

SKAITH, *damage.*

SKAITH, *to harm, to injure.*

SKEIGH, *skittish, mettlesome.*

SKELLUM, *a good-for-nothing, a scullion.*

SKELP, SKELPIN, *to slap, to smack, to trounce; a smack, smacking.*

SKELPIE-LIMMER'S-FACE, *a technical term in female scolding.*

SKELPIT, *trounced; hastened, ran quickly.*

SKELVY, *shelvy.*

SKIEGH, *v.* SKEIGH.

SKINKING, *watery.*

SKINKLIN, *small.*

SKIRL, *a piercing sound; to shriek.*

SKLENT, *a slanting devious course.*

SKOUTH, *play (freedom).*

SKRIECH, *a scream.*

SKRIEGH, *to scream, to whinny.*

SKYRIN, *flaring.*

SKYTE, *to squirt, to glide, to skate.*

SLADE, *slid.*

SLAE, *the sloe.*

SLAP, *a field gate; a broken fence.*

SLAW, *slow.*

SLEE, *sly.*

SLEEKIT, *sleek, crafty.*

SLIDD'RY, *slippery.*

SLOKEN, *to slake.*

SLYPET, *slipped.*

SMA', *small.*

SMACK, *a sounding kiss: to slap.*

SMEDDUM, *a powder.*

SMEEK, *smoke.*

SMIDDY, *smithy.*

SMOOR, SMOOR'D, *to smother; smothered.*

SMOUTIE, *smutty.*

SMYTRIE, *a small collection, a litter.*

SNAKIN, *sneering.*

SNAPPER, *to stumble; to fail in moral conduct.*

SNASH, *abuse.*

SNAW, *snow.*

SNAW-BROO, *snow-brew (melted snow).*

SNAWDRAP, *the snowdrop.*

SNED, *to crop, to prune.*

SNEESHIN MILL, *a snuff-box.*

SNELL, *keen, sharp, biting.*

SNICK, *a latch.*

SNIRTLE, *to snigger.*

SNOOD, *a ribbon or fillets round the head, worn by maidens.*

SNOODED, *of hair in ribbons.*

SNOOL, *to snub.*

SNOOVE, *to go slowly.*

SNOWKIT, *pried with the nose.*

SNUFF'T, *snuffed, repressed, extinguished.*

SOJER, SODGER, SOGER, *a soldier.*

SONSIE, SONSY *(from sons, plenty), pleasant, comfortable, comely.*

SOOM, *to swim.*

SOOR, *sour.*

SORN, *to take bed and board without payment.*

SOUDIE, SOWDY, *a gross heavy person.*

SOUGH, *south, a sigh; to hum or whistle softly; the sighing noise of wind or water.*

SOUK, *to suck; a draught (of liquor).*

SOUN', *sound.*

SOUPE, *sup, liquid.*

SOUPLE, *supple.*

SOUTER, *cobbler.*

SOUTER or SOWTER, *a shoemaker.*

SOWPS, *sups.*

SOWTH, *to hum or whistle in a low tone.*

SOWTHER, *to solder, to cement.*

SPAE, *to foretell.*

SPAILS, *chips.*

SPAIRGE, *to splash, to spatter.*

SPAK, *spoke, did speak.*

SPATES, *floods.*

SPAVIE, *the spavin.*

SPAVIT, *spavined.*

SPEAN, *to wean.*

SPEAT, *a flood.*

SPEEL, *to climb.*

SPEER, *v.* SPIER.

SPEET, *to spit, to impale.*

SPELL, *to narrate, to discourse.*

SPENCE, *the parlour.*

SPIER, *to ask, to inquire.*

SPLEUCHAN, *tobacco-pouch made of some sort of peltry.*

SPLORE, *to boast; a ramble; a revel, partaking of horse-play.*

SPONTOON, *a half pike or halberd discarded in the British Army in 1787.*

SPRACHL'D, *clambered.*

SPRATTLE, *scramble.*

SPRECKLED, *speckled.*

SPRING, *a quick and cheerful tune, a dance.*

SPRITTIE, *full of roots of sprits (a kind of rush).*

SPRUSH, *spruce, dressed up.*

SPULZIE, *plunder; to despoil or rob.*

SPUNK, *spirit, fire, energy; a splint of wood tipped with sulphur.*

SPUNKIE, *spirited.*

SPUNKIES, *jack-o'-lanthorns.*

SPURTLE-BLADE, *the pot-stick.*

SQUATTLE, *to squat, to settle.*

STACHER, *to totter, to stagger.*

STACK, *stuck; remainder.*

STAGGIE, *dim. of staig (a young horse).*

STAIG, *a young horse under three years.*

STAMMER, *to stutter.*

STAN', *stand.*

STANCED, *stationed.*

STANE, *stone.*

STAN'T, *stood.*

STANG, *stung; a sting.* RIDING THE STANG: *a man who beat his wife or who was an impotent bridegroom was set astride a long pole and carried shoulder-high through the town by his fellows as a mark of infamy.*

STANK, *a pool of standing water.*

STAP, *to stop.*

STAPPLE, *a stopper.*

STARK, *strong.*

STARNIES, *dim. of starn or star.*

STARNS, *stars.*

STARTLE, *to course.*

STAUKIN, *stalking, marching.*

STAUMREL, *half-witted.*

STAW, *a stall; did steal; surfeited.*

STECHIN, *cramming.*

STEEK, *a stitch, to stitch; to shut, to close.*

STEER, *to stir, to rouse, to remove.*

STEEVE, *compact.*

STELL, *a still.*

STEN, *a spring, a leap, to rear as a horse.*

STEN'T, *sprang.*

STENTED, *erected, set on high.*

STENTS, *assessments, dues.*

STEYEST, *steepest.*

STIBBLE, *stubble.*

STIBBLE-RIG, *chief harvester.*

STICK-AN-STOWE, *completely.*

STICKIT, *stuck, stopped.*

STILT, *limp.*

STIMPART, *a quarter peck.*

STIRK, *a heifer or bullock between one and two years old.*

STOCK, *a plant of cabbage or colewort.*

STOITED, *stumbled.*

STOITER'D, *staggered, staggering in walk.*

STOOR, STOURE, *flying dust, used fig.*

STOT, *a bull, or ox three years old.*

STOUN, *a sudden pang.*

STOUP, *a vessel for holding liquid.*

STOURIE, *dusty.*

STOWN, *stolen.*

STOWNLINS, *by stealth, clandestinely.*

STOYT, *to stagger.*

STRAE DEATH, *death in bed* (i.e. *on straw*).

STRAIK, *a stroke; to stroke.*

STRAK, *struck, did strike.*

STRANG, *strong.*

STRAPPIN, *tall and handsome.*

STRATHSPEY, *a reel (which see) deriving its name from the valley of the Spey. The music with the title first appears in a collection, c.1780. It is danced slower than the reel, but the motion is more jerky. The music is a series of alternate dotted quavers and semiquavers, whilst a* REEL *usually consists of equal notes.*

STRAUGHT, *straight; stretched.*

STEEKIT, *stretched.*

STRIDDLE, *to straddle.*

STROAN'T, *lanted.*

STRUNT, *strong drink; to swagger.*

STUDDIE, *an anvil.*

STUMPIE, *curtailed, mutilated.*

STUMPS, *legs and feet.*

STURT, *trouble, strife; to molest.*

STURTIN, *frighted, staggered.*

STYME, *the faintest outline.*

SUCKER, *sugar.*

SUD, *should.*

SUGH, SOUGH, *sigh, wail, swish.*

SUMPH, *a churl.*

SUNE, *soon.*

SUTHRON, *Southern.*

SWAIRD, *the sward.*

SWALL'D, *swelled.*

SWANK, *limber.*

SWANKIES, *strapping fellows.*

SWAPPED, *exchanged.*

SWARF, *to swoon.*

SWAT, *sweated.*

SWATCH, *a sample.*

SWATS, *new light foaming ale.*

SWEER, *lazy unwilling.*

SWIRL, *a curl.*

SWIRLIE, *twisted, knaggy.*

SWITH, *get away!*

SWITHER, *doubt, hesitation.*

SWOOM, *swim.*

SWOOR, *swore.*

SYBOW, *a young onion.*

SYNE, *since, then, ago, afterwards, late as opposed to soon.*

TACK, *possession, lease.*

TACKET, *shoe-nail.*

TAE, *the toe.*

TAE'D, *having toes or forks.*

TAED, *the toad.*

TAEN, *taken.*

TAK, *to take.*

TAIRGE, *to target (with importunities).*

TALD, *told.*

TANE, *the one.*

TANGS, *tongs.*

TAP, *top.*

TAPETLESS, *pithless.*

TAPMOST, *topmost.*

TAP-PICKLE, *the grain at the top of the stalk.*

TAPPIT-HEN, *a large round bottle for holding whisky.*

TAPSALTEERIE, *topsy-turvy.*

TARROW, *to tarry.*

TASSIE, *a glass, a goblet.*

TAUK, *talk.*

TAULD, *told.*

TAWIE, *tractable.*

TAWPIE, *a foolish woman.*

TAWTED, *matted.*

TEATS, *small quantities.*

TEEN, *vexation.*

TEETHIN, *teething.*

TELL'D, *told.*

TEMPER-PIN, *the wooden pin for regula-*

ting the motion of a spinning-wheel.

TENT, to take heed or care for.

TENTIE, careful, attentive.

TENTIER, more watchful.

TENTLESS, careless, heedless.

TESTER, an old Scots silver coin about sixpence in value.

TEUGH, tough.

TEUK, took.

THACK, thatch.

THAE, those.

THAIRMS, catgut fiddle-strings.

THEEKIT, thatched, covered.

THEMSEL, THEMSELS, themselves.

THICK, v. PACK AN' THICK.

THIEVELESS, forbidding, spiteful.

THIGGIN, begging.

THIR, these.

THIRL'D, thrilled, vibrated; enslaved.

THOLE, to endure.

THOU'SE, thou shalt.

THOWE, a thaw; to thaw.

THOWLESS, lazy, useless.

THRANG, busy, thronging in crowds, at work.

THRANG, a throng, a crowd.

THRAPPLE, the windpipe.

THRAVE, twenty-four sheaves of corn.

THRAW, to oppose, to resist.

THRAWIN-BROW, cross-grained, perverse.

THRAWS, death-pangs, last agonies.

THREAP, maintain (with asseverations).

THREESOME, a trio.

THRETTEEN, thirteen.

THRETTY, thirty.

THRIPPLIN-KAME, v. RIPPLIN-KAME.

THRISTED, thirsted.

THROU'THER (through other), pell-mell.

THRUMS, the sound of a spinning-wheel in motion; ends of threads.

THUDS, blows, sounding knocks.

THUMMART, polecat.

THY LANE, alone.

TIBBIE, Elizabeth.

TIGHT, girt, prepared.

TILL, until.

TILL'T, unto it; tilled.

TIMMER, timber; a timmer-tun'd person is one devoid of musical perception, or who sings out of tune.

TINE, TYNE, to lose.

TINKLER, a tinker.

TINT, lost.

TIPPENCE, twopence.

TIPPENNY, two-penny ale.

TIRL, TIRL'D, to knock, to rattle, rattled; tirl'd at the pin, rattled the door-latch.

TITHER, the other.

TITTLIN, whispering.

TOCHER, marriage portion; to endow.

TOCHER-BAND, the marriage contract.

TOD, a fox.

TO-FA', the fall of the year; a lean-to building against a house; a refuge.

TOOM, TOOM'D, empty, to empty; emptied.

TOOP, tup, a ram.

TOSS, a toast, a fashionable beauty.

TOUN, a farm enclosure.

TOURS, turf.

TOUSIE, rough, shaggy.

TOW, flax; a rope.

TOWMOND, twelve months.

TOWSING, teasing, romping, ruffling.

TOYTE, to totter.

TOZIE, flushed with liquor; crapulous.

TRAMS, shafts (of a barrow or cart).

TRASHTRIE, small trash.

TREWS, trousers, breeches.

TRIG, neat, spruce.

TRINKLIN, TRINKLING, dropping.

TRIN'LE, the wheel of a barrow.

TROGGIN, small wares, a pedlar's stock-in-trade.

TROKE, to barter.

TROWSE, trousers.

TROW'T, believed.

TROWTH, in truth.

TRYSTE, *an engagement to meet at a particular place; an appointment; a cattle-market.*

TRYSTED, *trusted, engaged to meet.*

TRYSTING, *meeting.*

TULYIE, TULZIE, *a squabble, a tussle.*

TWA, TWAE, *two.*

'TWAD, *it would.*

TWA-FAULD, *twofold; bent in double.*

TWAL, *twelve.*

TWAL-HUNDRED, *linen of* 1200 *divisions, not so fine as that of* 1700.

TWALPENNIE WORTH=*a penny worth (sterling).*

TWANG, *a twinge.*

TWA-THREE, *two or three.*

TWAY, *two.*

TWIN, *also* TWINE, *to rob.*

TWISTLE, *a twist, a sprain.*

TYESDAY, *Tuesday.*

TYKE, *a mongrel dog; a rough uncultured person.*

TYNE, *to tine.*

TYSDAY, *Tuesday.*

ULZIE, *oil.*

UNCHANCY, *dangerous.*

UNCO, *strange, not allied, alien.*

UNCOS, *news, strange things, wonders.*

UNFAULD, *to unfold.*

UNKEND, *unknown.*

UNSICKER, *uncertain.*

UNSKAITHED, *unhurt.*

USQUE *or* USGIE, *Celt. for water=whisky; usquebah=water of life or whisky.*

VAUNTIE, *proud.*

VERA, *very.*

VIRLS, *rings.*

VITTLE, *victuals, food.*

VOGIE, *vain, proud.*

WA', *a wall; at the wa', in desperate circumstances.*

WAB, *a web.*

WABSTER, *a weaver.*

WAD, *to wed.*

WAD, *would, would have.*

WAD'A, *would have.*

WADNA, *would not.*

WADSET, *a pledge, a mortgage.*

WAEFU', *woeful.*

WAESUCKS, *alas!*

WAE WORTH, *woe befall.*

WAIR'D, *worn.*

WALE, *the choice; to choose, to select.*

WALIE, *ample, large.*

WALLOP, *to dangle, to move quickly.*

WALY, *an interjection of distress.*

WAME, *the belly.*

WAMEFOU, *bellyful.*

WAN, *won; pale, dark-coloured.*

WANCHANCIE, *dangerous.*

WANRESTFU', *restless.*

WAP, *to wrap, to envelop, to cover.*

WARE, WAIR, *to spend, bestow.*

WARE, *worn.*

WARK, *work.*

WARK-LUME, *v.* LUME.

WARL', WARLD, *world.*

WARLOCK, *a wizard, one familiar with the Devil.*

WARLOCK-KNOWE, *a knoll reputed to be haunted.*

WARLY, *worldly.*

WARPIN-WHEEL, *a part of the spinnig-wheel.*

WARRAN, *warrant.*

WARSE, *worse.*

WARSLE, WARSTLE, *wrestle.*

WAST, *west.*

WASTRIE, *waste.*

WAT, *wet; to wot.*

WATER-FIT, *water-foot (the river's mouth).*

WATER-KELPIES, *v.* KELPIES.

WAUBLE, *to wobble.*

WAUGHT, *a long drink.*

WAUK, *to wake.*

WAUKENS, *wakens.*

WAUKRIFE, *sleepless, in a light sleep.*

WAUR, *worse.*

WAUR'T, *worsted, beat (in running).*

WEAN, *a child.*

WEANIES, *babies.*

WEAPON-SHAW, *an exhibition of arms;* (lit.) *showing the weapons.*

WEASON, *weasand.*

WECHT, *a measure for corn.*

WEE, *small, little; a short time.*

WEE THINGS, *children.*

WEEL, *well.*

WEEL-FAURED, *well-favoured.*

WEEL-GAUN, *well-going.*

WEEL-HAIN'D, *well-saved.*

WEEL-STOCKIT, *well-stocked.*

WEEPERS, *mournings (on the sleeve, or hat).*

WEET, *wet.*

WERENA, *were not.*

WE'SE, *we shall.*

WESTLIN, *westerly.*

WHA, *who.*

WHA'S, *who is.*

WHAIZLE, *wheeze.*

WHALPET, *whelped.*

WHAM, *whom.*

WHAN, *when.*

WHANG, *a shive, a large slice.*

WHANG, *flog.*

WHAR, WHARE, WHAUR, *where.*

WHASE, *whose.*

WHAT FOR, *whatfore, wherefore: 'what for no?'=why not?*

WHATNA, *what (partly in contempt).*

WHAT RECK, *what matter.*

WHATT, *whittled.*

WHAUP, *a curlew.*

WHEEP, *jerk.*

WHID, *a fib.*

WHIDDIN, *scudding.*

WHIDS, *gambols.*

WHIGMELEERIES, *crotchets.*

WHILES, *sometimes.*

WHINGIN, *whining.*

WHINS, *furze.*

WHIRLYGIGUMS, *flourishes.*

WHIRRIN, *the sound produced by the wings of a flying bird.*

WHISHT, *silence.*

WHISKIN, *sweeping, lashing.*

WHISSLE, *whistle.*

WHITTER, *a draught.*

WHITTLE, *a knife; to cut.*

WI', *with.*

WI'S, *with his.*

WIDDIFU', *peevish, angry; worthy of the gallows.*

WIDDLE, *wriggle.*

WIEL, *eddy.*

WIGHT, *a sturdy person.*

WIGHTER, *stronger.*

WIL'D, WYL'D, *enticed, artfully captured.*

WILLCAT, *wild cat.*

WILLYART, *disordered.*

WIMPLE, *to meander.*

WIMPLE, *a winding or folding.*

WIMPLING, *winding, meandering (of a course).*

WI'M, *with him.*

WIN, *won.*

WINN, *to winnow.*

WINNA, *will not.*

WINNIN, *winding.*

WINNINS, *means, earnings.*

WINNOCK, *window.*

WI'T, *with it.*

WIN'T, *did wind.*

WINTLE, *a somersault.*

WINTLE, *to stagger, to swing, to wriggle.*

WINZE, *a curse.*

WISS, *wish.*

WITHA', *with all.*

WON, *to win, to dwell; dry by exposure to the air.*

WONNER, *a wonder, a marvel.*

WONS, *dwells, lives.*

WOO', *wool.*

WOODIE, *dim. of wind.*

WOODIES, *twigs, withes.*

WOOER-BABS, *love-knots.*

WORDY, *worthy.*

WORSET, *worsted.*

WORTH, *v.* WAE WORTH.

WRACK, *to vex, to trouble, to contradict.*

WRANG, *wrong.*

WUD, *a wood; mad, distracted, outrageous.*

WUMBLE, *wimble.*

WYLIECOAT, *undervest.*

WYLIN, *enticing, wheedling, beguiling.*

WYTE, *the blame; to blame.*

YARD, *a garden, a stackyard.*

YAUD, *an old mare.*

YEALINGS, *coevals.*

YELL, *dry (milkless).*

YERD, *a yard, an enclosure.*

YERKIT, *jerked.*

YERL, *an earl.*

YE'SE, *ye shall.*

YESTREEN, *last evening or night.*

YETT, *a gate.*

YEUKS, *the itch; a kind of eczema.*

YILL, *ale.*

YILL-CAUP, *ale-stoup.*

YIRD, *earth, the soil.*

YOKIN, YOKING, *a spell, a day's work, a set-to.*

YON, YONDER, *over there; used equiv.*

'YONT, *beyond.*

YOWE, *a ewe.*

YOWIE, *dim. of ewe; a pet ewe.*

INDEX OF TITLES AND FIRST LINES

BIBLIOGRAPHY

WORKS

Poems, Chiefly in the Scottish Dialect ('The Kilmarnock Edition') (1786)
Poems, Chiefly in the Scottish Dialect The Edinburgh Edition') (1787)
James Johnson (ed) *The Scots Musical Museum* 6 Vols, 1787-1803; 1853, 1991)
James C Dick (ed) *The Songs of Robert Burns* 1903, 1962)
Robert D Thornton (ed) *The Tuneful Flame: Songs of Robert Burns As He Sang Them* (1957)
Bawdy Verse and Folksongs 1965, 1982)
John Ashmead and John Davison (eds) *Songs of Robert Burns* 1988)
Alan Bold (ed) *Rhymer Rab Anthology of Poems and Prose* (1993)
Carol McGuirk (ed) *Robert Burns: Selected Poems* (1993)

COLLECTED WORKS

The Complete Illustrated Poems, Songs and Ballads of Robert Burns 1905, 1990)
James Kinsley (ed) *The Poems and Songs of Robert Burns* 1968)
James A Mackay (ed) *The Complete Works of Robert Burns* (1986)
James A Mackay (ed) *The Complete Letters of Robert Burns* (1987)
Donald A Low (ed) *The Songs of Robert Burns* 1993)

BIOGRAPHICAL AND CRITICAL

Robert Chambers (ed, rev William Wallace) *The Life and Works of Robert Burns* (1896)
William A Craigie *A Primer of Burns* (1896)
Henry C Shelley *The Ayrshire Homes and Haunts of Burns* (1897)
Alexander Keith *Burns and Folk)song* (1922, 1976)
John D Ross *Who's Who in Burns* (1927)
Catherine Carswell *The Life of Robert Burns* (1930, 1990)
Franklyn Bliss Snyder *The Life of Robert Burns* 1932, 1968)
J C Ewing and D Cook (eds) *Robert Burns's Commonplace Book, 1783-85* 1938, 1965)
DeLancey Ferguson *Pride and Passion: Robert Burns 1759-1796* 1939, 1964)
Robert T Fitzhugh *Robert Burns: His Associates and Contemporaries, with the Journal of the Border Tour, edited by DeLancey Ferguson* 1943)
Hilton Brown *There was a Lad: an Essay on Robert Burns* (1949)
David Daiches *Robert Burns: the Poet* 1950, rev 1966; 1994)
Hans Hecht *Robert Burns: the Man and His Work* (translated by Jane Lymburn, 2nd rev ed, 1950)
Maurice Lindsay *Robert Burns: the Man, His Work, the Legend* 1954, rev 1979; 1994)

Catalogue of Robert Burns Collection in the Mitchell Library, Glasgow (1959)

Elsie S Rae *Poet's Pilgrimage: the Story of the Life and Times of Robert Burns* (1960)

Thomas Crawford *Burns: a Study of the Poems and Songs* 1960)

J W Egerer *A Bibliography of Robert Burns* 1964)

Raymond Lamont Brown *Robert Burns's Tour of the Borders 5 May-1 June 1787* 1972)

Raymond Lamont Brown *Robert Burns's Tours of the Highlands and Stirling-shire 1787* 1973)

Donald Low (ed) *Robert Burns: the Critical Heritage* 1974)

Catarina Ericson)Roos *The Songs of Robert Burns: a Study of the Unity of Poetry and Music* (1977)

Maurice Lindsay *The Burns Encyclopaedia* (3rd ed, 1980)

Eileen Dunlop and Antony Kamm (eds) *In the Land o' Burns* illustrations by David Octavius Hill (1981)

R D S Jack and Andrew Noble (eds) *The Art of Robert Burns* (1982)

Mary Ellen Brown *Burns and Tradition* 1984)

Carol McGuirk *Robert Burns and the Sentimental Era* (1985)

G Ross Roy and J DeLancey Ferguson *The Letters of Robert Burns* 1985)

Donald A Low *Robert Burns* 1986)

Raymond Bentman *Robert Burns* (1987)

Richard Hindle Fowler *Robert Burns* 1988)

James Mackay *Burns: a Biography of Robert Burns* 1992)

Kenneth Simpson (ed) *Burns Now* (1994)